Administrative Law in Hong Kong

This new text provides the most comprehensive and up-to-date coverage of administrative law in Hong Kong. It includes original commentary on judicial review, administrative tribunals, the Ombudsman, the Legislative Council Redress System, Commissions of Inquiry, the Independent Commission Against Corruption, the Equal Opportunities Commission, the Privacy Commissioner for Personal Data, the Audit Commission, subsidiary legislation and more. Drawing on law, policy and practice, it offers detailed analysis while maintaining accessibility, charting developments as Hong Kong continues to evolve as a Special Administrative Region of the People's Republic of China. *Administrative Law in Hong Kong* is essential reading for judges, practitioners, policymakers, academics, students and commentators with an interest in public law, governance and administration.

Stephen Thomson is an associate professor of law at City University of Hong Kong. He is a legal adviser to the Ombudsman of Hong Kong, a member of the Constitutional Affairs and Human Rights Committee of the Law Society of Hong Kong and an examiner on the Overseas Lawyers Qualification Examination. His work on administrative law has appeared in a number of leading law journals. Dr Thomson has also written the first and only text on the *nobile officium*, the extraordinary equitable jurisdiction of the Supreme Courts of Scotland, cited with approval by the Inner House of the Court of Session and the Scottish Land Court. He also advised the Scottish judiciary on reform of civil procedure, his report being appended to a proposal for legislative reform.

Administrative Law
in Hong Kong

STEPHEN THOMSON
Associate Professor, School of Law,
City University of Hong Kong

CAMBRIDGE
UNIVERSITY PRESS

CAMBRIDGE
UNIVERSITY PRESS

University Printing House, Cambridge CB2 8BS, United Kingdom

One Liberty Plaza, 20th Floor, New York, NY 10006, USA

477 Williamstown Road, Port Melbourne, VIC 3207, Australia

314–321, 3rd Floor, Plot 3, Splendor Forum, Jasola District Centre, New Delhi – 110025, India

79 Anson Road, #06-04/06, Singapore 079906

Cambridge University Press is part of the University of Cambridge.

It furthers the University's mission by disseminating knowledge in the pursuit of education, learning, and research at the highest international levels of excellence.

www.cambridge.org
Information on this title: www.cambridge.org/9781108400329
DOI: 10.1017/9781108227773

© Cambridge University Press 2018

This publication is in copyright. Subject to statutory exception and to the provisions of relevant collective licensing agreements, no reproduction of any part may take place without the written permission of Cambridge University Press.

First published 2018

Printed in Singapore by Markono Print Media Pte Ltd

A catalogue record for this publication is available from the British Library.

Library of Congress Cataloging-in-Publication Data
Names: Thomson, Stephen (Lawyer), author.
Title: Administrative law in Hong Kong / Stephen Thomson.
Description: Cambridge [UK] ; New York, NY : Cambridge University Press, 2018.
Identifiers: LCCN 2018008155 | ISBN 9781108400329 (paperback)
Subjects: LCSH: Administrative law–China–Hong Kong. | BISAC: LAW / Constitutional.
Classification: LCC KNQ9353.3 .T46 2018 | DDC 342.5125/06–dc23 LC record available at https://lccn.loc.gov/2018008155

ISBN 978-1-108-40032-9 Paperback

Cambridge University Press has no responsibility for the persistence or accuracy of URLs for external or third-party internet websites referred to in this publication and does not guarantee that any content on such websites is, or will remain, accurate or appropriate.

To Eugenie

**and to my grandparents,
for many years of support**

Contents

Foreword	page xii
Preface	xv
List of Abbreviations	xvii
Table of Legislation	xviii
Table of Constitutional Documents	xxiii
Table of International Treaties and Instruments	xxiv
Table of Cases	xxv

1	**Introduction**	1
	PART I THE CONSTITUTIONAL AND ADMINISTRATIVE CONTEXT	5
2	**Governance and Administration in Hong Kong**	7
	Central Government	7
	Local Government	12
	Mainland Affairs in Hong Kong	15
	Hong Kong Affairs in the Mainland	17
	Licensing, Permits and Certification	18
	Public Procurement and Tendering	22
3	**The Constitutional Foundation of Judicial Review in Hong Kong**	24
	Constitutional Foundation under UK Sovereignty	24
	Constitutional Foundation under PRC Sovereignty	26
	Constitutional Review, Administrative Review and Human Rights	32
	PART II JUDICIAL REVIEW: THE LEAVE STAGE	35
4	**The Leave Stage: Principles and Procedure**	37

5	**Delay**	42
	Promptness	45
	Reasons Justifying Extension of Time	45
6	**Standing**	52
	Personal Standing	56
	Representative Standing	58
7	**Judicial Review and the Public/Private Divide**	64
	Requirement for a Sufficient Public Element	64
	Collateral Challenge	68
	Consent of the Parties	74
	Definitional Problems: The Concept of Publicness	75
8	**Statutory Exclusion of Review, Non-Justiciability and Variable Intensity of Review**	87
	Statutory Exclusion of Review	87
	Statutory Limitation of Review	93
	Non-Justiciability	97
	Variable Intensity of Review	101
9	**Arguability and Qualitative Filtering**	109
	Threshold	110
	Issues Raised by Arguability Threshold	114
	PART III THE GROUNDS OF JUDICIAL REVIEW	119
10	**Overview of the Grounds of Judicial Review**	121
11	**Excess of Power, the Limits of Discretionary Power and Non-Compliance with Statute**	125
	Authority and Agency	125
	Ancillary and Implied Powers	129
	Effect of Non-Compliance with Statutory Requirements	133
	Estoppel, Acquiescence, Waiver and Consent	137
	Res judicata: Cause of Action Estoppel	140
	Ambiguity and Uncertainty as a Ground of Judicial Review	142

Contents

12	**Improper Purposes, Improper Motives and Abuse of Power**	144
	Multiple Purposes or Motives	146
	Abuse of Power and Misuse of Power	150
13	**Relevance of Considerations**	154
	Insufficiently Relevant Considerations	155
	Relevant Considerations	158
14	**Insufficient Retention of Discretion: Unlawful Delegation, Divestiture and Relinquishment**	163
	Unlawful Delegation	165
	Divestiture and Relinquishment	171
15	**Fettering of Discretion**	175
	Obligation to Decide	175
	Obligation to Decide with a Sufficiently Open Mind	176
	Fettering Discretion through Contract	183
16	**Error of Fact and Error of Law**	190
	Error of Fact	190
	Error of Law	198
	Distinction between Error of Fact and Error of Law	202
17	**Legitimate Expectations**	204
	Representation Made by a Public Body	207
	Knowledge and Reliance	209
	Legitimacy of Expectation	212
	Body Failed to Take into Account Legitimate Expectation as a Relevant Consideration	214
	Overriding Policy Considerations	215
	Judicial Protection of Legitimate Expectations	217
	Ultra vires Representations and Legitimate Expectations	221
	Legitimate Expectations and Other Grounds of Review	223
18	**Unreasonableness and Irrationality**	225
	Standard of Review: *Wednesbury* Unreasonableness	227
	Substantive Review	229

	Procedural Review	230
	Intensity of Review	235
	Unreasonableness vs. Irrationality	242
	Role of Reasons	245
19	**Procedural Fairness, Procedural Impropriety and Natural Justice**	247
	Right to a Fair Hearing	248
	Right to Be Legally Represented	253
	Duty of Disclosure	256
	Duty to Give Adequate Reasons	257
	Bias and Insufficient Impartiality	264

PART IV JUDICIAL REMEDIES, NON-JUDICIAL REMEDIES AND SUBSIDIARY LEGISLATION 273

20	**Remedies in Judicial Review**	275
	Certiorari	280
	Prohibition	281
	Mandamus	282
	Declaration	283
	Injunction	290
	Damages, Restitution and Recovery of a Sum Due	292
	Discretionary Nature of Remedies	293
	Judicial Review Proceedings Continued as Though Begun by Writ	301
21	**Administrative Tribunals and Administrative Complaints**	304
	Administrative Tribunals	304
	Ombudsman	319
	Legislative Council Redress System	330
22	**Other Remedial Mechanisms**	332
	Commissions of Inquiry	332
	Independent Commission Against Corruption	336
	Equal Opportunities Commission	339
	Privacy Commissioner for Personal Data	343
	Audit Commission	349

23 Subsidiary Legislation 352
Scrutiny of Subsidiary Legislation by the Legislative Council 355
Judicial Review of Subsidiary Legislation 358
Administrative Rules 360
Departmental Circulars and Memoranda 363

Index 365

Foreword

In the last fifty years, Hong Kong has undergone the most momentous changes. We have been reunified with the People's Republic of China and established as a Special Administrative Region of China under the principle of "one country, two systems" governed by the Basic Law. Hong Kong has a thriving economy and is an international financial centre. We are an open, vibrant and pluralistic society and are recognised to be Asia's world city.

The governance of Hong Kong as a modern metropolis is complex and challenging. Over the last half century, public administration has had to adapt and expand to cope with the rapid developments in our society. Inevitably, many areas of activities have to be subjected to regulation in the public interest. Since the 1970s, the statute book has grown substantially with an increasing range of powers conferred on public officials. At the same time, citizens have higher expectations of public institutions and officials. They are more conscious of their rights and freedoms and are more prepared to invoke the law in seeking to protect them.

In the last fifty years, administrative law has been transformed in response to this phenomenal expansion in public administration. It will continue to develop in the future. Broadly, this is the body of law that relates to the exercise of public powers. Its purpose is to ensure that public powers are exercised within legal bounds and that citizens are protected against abuse of power. The principles laid down are directed to maintaining the proper conduct of public administration. Looking back, this transformation had to take place. The common law has to evolve to deal with changing times and circumstances. Here, we see the common law at its finest: judges developing principles gradually over time in a pragmatic way in the light of experience.

In the last twenty years since reunification, constitutional law involving the Basic Law has been the focus of attention of many authors. This is understandable as the new order of "one country, two systems" is a novel and exciting one. Relatively speaking, administrative law, which is interlinked with constitutional law, has received less attention.

This is an appropriate time for a major work on administrative law to be published. Professor Stephen Thomson has produced an impressive book on this vital subject.

The book is a thorough and comprehensive work. It begins by setting out the constitutional and administrative context. It deals with the procedure for judicial review for which the leave of the court is necessary. A substantial part of the work considers the grounds of judicial review as developed by the courts. The vast jurisprudence, including the extensive case law in Hong Kong, is analysed in a masterful way with the principles clearly distilled from them. The judicial remedies are examined. There is also a survey of the non-judicial remedies through a range of tribunals and commissions. Further, the subject of subordinate legislation is considered.

The scholarship displayed in this work is of the highest quality. It is an authoritative text on administrative law in Hong Kong and makes a most important contribution to the learning in this field. It will provide invaluable guidance and assistance to judges, lawyers, public administrators, academics and students. This work will be a leading text and deserves to be widely read and used both in and outside Hong Kong.

Andrew Kwok Nang Li
First Chief Justice of the Hong Kong Special Administrative Region of the People's Republic of China (1997–2010)

Preface

Administrative law deserves more attention and study than it currently receives in Hong Kong. It is, however, a subject of great magnitude. An attempt has been made to give as comprehensive an account of administrative law in Hong Kong as possible within the practical constraints of scope and space in this volume. Any chapter could easily have doubled in size. It has for the same reason been necessary to exclude various topics from detailed consideration in this book. Notable among them is constitutional law which, though intertwined with administrative law, is itself a vast topic. A substantive discussion of constitutional law has not been possible due to these constraints. Nor has it been possible to explore human rights in detail, though this is a worthy subject in its own right.

The main focus of the book is instead judicial review, a vital component of administrative law particularly in the common law tradition. Other important forms of administrative control are also discussed, namely, administrative tribunals, the Ombudsman, the Legislative Council Redress System, Commissions of Inquiry, the Independent Commission Against Corruption, the Equal Opportunities Commission, the Privacy Commissioner for Personal Data and the Audit Commission. A chapter has also been included on subsidiary legislation. The book, intended for as general an audience as possible, is hoped to be of use to judges, practitioners, policymakers, public administrators, commentators, scholars and students, and also to anyone with an interest in administrative law both in Hong Kong and elsewhere. Its aim is to inform, assist, generate discussion and make its own small contribution to the advancement of the rule of law. The law is stated as of December 2017, and it will of course be necessary for the reader to chart the developments which will inevitably follow the publication of this book.

I am grateful to Joe Ng and the editorial staff at Cambridge University Press for their outstanding support and assistance throughout this project. I gratefully acknowledge the support made available to me by The Chinese University of Hong Kong, in particular the award of a Lee Hysan Foundation Research Grant and an Endowment Fund Research Grant. I have benefitted from helpful discussions on several topics in the book with various people to whom I express my thanks, in particular Denis Edwards and Eric C. Ip. For their helpful research assistance, I thank Rachel Chiu, Eugene Kwan, Jessica Chu and Icarus Chan. Above all, special gratitude is reserved for my wife Eugenie, who has given unwavering support, encouragement and patience throughout.

Abbreviations

ADR	alternative dispute resolution
CAD	Civil Aviation Department
CEIC	Chief Executive-in-Council
COMAC	Office of the Commissioner for Administrative Complaints
CSSA	Comprehensive Social Security Assistance
DDO	Disability Discrimination Ordinance
EIA	environmental impact assessment
FHAN	Fire Hazard Abatement Notice
FSDO	Family Status Discrimination Ordinance
HKSAR	Hong Kong Special Administrative Region
ICAC	Independent Commission Against Corruption
ICCPR	International Covenant on Civil and Political Rights
ICESCR	International Covenant on Economic, Social and Cultural Rights
LegCo	Legislative Council
LLB	Liquor Licensing Board
MSAB	Municipal Services Appeals Board
NPC	National People's Congress
NPCSC	National People's Congress Standing Committee
OMELCO	Office of Members of the Executive and Legislative Councils
OZP	Outline Zoning Plan
PAC	Public Accounts Committee
PLA	People's Liberation Army
PRC	People's Republic of China
RDO	Race Discrimination Ordinance
SDO	Sex Discrimination Ordinance
UK	United Kingdom
UMELCO	Office of the Unofficial Members of the Executive and Legislative Councils
UNHCR	United Nations High Commissioner for Refugees
VFM	Value For Money

Table of Legislation

Accreditation of Academic and Vocational Qualifications Ordinance, 254n39, 315n64, 315n67, 354n8
Acquisition of Land (Authorisation Procedure) Act 1946, 93n31, 94n32
Administrative Appeals Board Ordinance, 306nn5–6, 311n38, 314n51, 315n60
Aerial Ropeways (Safety) Ordinance, 258n70
Air Navigation (Hong Kong) Order, 20n102, 360n59, 361, 361n62
Air Pollution Control Ordinance, 19n86, 258n67, 314n56
Air Pollution Control (Ocean Going Vessels) (Fuel at Berth) Regulation, 19n88
Air Pollution Control (Open Burning) Regulation, 19n87
Air Pollution Control (Specified Processes) Regulations, 19n86
Air Transport (Licensing of Air Services) Regulations, 19n101, 222
Airport Authority Ordinance, 87n3, 357n33
Amendment Ordinance 1937, 358
Amusement Games Centres Ordinance, 131, 131n30
Amusement Rides (Safety) Ordinance, 313n50
Animals and Plants (Protection of Endangered Species) Ordinance, 18n79
Antiquities and Monuments Ordinance, 59, 88n4
Anti-Money Laundering and Counter-Terrorist Financing (Financial Institutions) Ordinance, 21n126
Audit Ordinance, 350n156, 350n161, 350n164, 351nn168–169
Bahamas Nationality Act 1973, 90n14
Banking Ordinance, 88n4, 316n69
Bathing Beaches Regulation, 21n132
Bedspace Apartments Ordinance, 20n120, 21n134, 316n75
Bill of Rights Ordinance, 32–3, 78n62, 95
Boilers and Pressure Vessels Ordinance, 362n71
Boundary and Election Commission (Electoral Procedure) (Geographical Constituencies) Regulations, 95n37
British Nationality Act 1981, 25n7
Buildings Energy Efficiency Ordinance, 311n39
Business Registration Ordinance, 20n122
Business Registration Regulations, 20n122
Carriage by Air Ordinance, 357nn30–31
Chemical Weapons (Convention) Ordinance, 96n39
Chief Executive Election Ordinance, 87n2
Child Care Services Ordinance, 163n1, 306n5
Civil Procedure Rules, 64n3, 275n2

Civil Service Regulations, 11, 12
Clubs (Safety of Premises) Ordinance, 20n118
Commercial Bathhouses Regulation, 20n115
Commissions of Inquiry Ordinance, 332n1, 334n7, 335n10, 335n21, 335nn17–19, 336, 336n28
Companies Ordinance, 359, 359n45
Competition Ordinance, 337n30
Construction Workers Registration Ordinance, 354n8
Control of Obscene and Indecent Articles Ordinance, 132n32, 259n72, 305nn2–3
Co-operative Societies Ordinance, 87n3
Country Parks Ordinance, 316, 316n78
Crimes Ordinance, 284
Criminal Jurisdiction Ordinance, 357n36
Dangerous Drugs Ordinance, 19n85, 250
Dangerous Drugs Regulations, 250
Disability Discrimination Ordinance, 339n57, 343
Disability Discrimination (Formal Investigations) Rules, 340n68, 341n78
Disability Discrimination (Investigation and Conciliation) Rules, 342nn85–86
District Councils Ordinance, 12nn35–36, 13n41, 14n54
Dumping at Sea Ordinance, 19n91
Dutiable Commodities (Liquor) Regulations, 20n111
Dutiable Commodities Ordinance, 20n111
Dutiable Commodities Regulations, 20n111
Education University of Hong Kong Ordinance (The), 358n38
Elections (Corrupt and Illegal Conduct) Ordinance, 338
Electoral Procedure (Chief Executive Election) Regulation, 87n3
Electoral Provisions Ordinance, 95n37
Emergency Regulations Ordinance, 359, 359n46
Environmental Impact Assessment Ordinance, 19n89, 315n58
Family Status Discrimination Ordinance, 339n56, 343
Family Status Discrimination (Formal Investigations) Rules, 340n68, 341n78
Family Status Discrimination (Investigation and Conciliation) Rules, 342nn85–86
Fire Services Ordinance, 130
Food Business Regulation, 20n108
Foreign Compensation Act 1950, 90, 90n10
Funeral Parlours Regulation, 21n130
Gambling Ordinance, 21n127, 67
Genetically Modified Organisms (Control of Release) Ordinance, 306n6
Government Rent (Assessment and Collection) Ordinance, 88n4
Hawker Regulation, 20, 20n110
Hazardous Chemicals Control Ordinance, 19n95
Heung Yee Kuk Ordinance, 14nn56–57
Highways Act 1959, 94n32
High Court Ordinance, 37n2, 37n6, 38nn11–12, 39n18, 43, 43n5, 50, 51, 53, 61, 65n3, 67, 67nn11–12, 275, 275nn2–3, 279n28, 280, 280n31, 285, 285n57, 290n86, 291, 291nn90–91, 292nn94–96, 296, 297n118, 315n59, 353n3
Hong Kong Academy of Medicine Ordinance, 357n29
Hong Kong Science and Technology Parks Corporation Ordinance, 163n1

Hong Kong Special Administrative Region Passports (Appeal Board) Regulation, 310n34
Hotel and Guesthouse Accommodation Ordinance, 20n119
Housing Act 1957, 68n18
Housing Act 1974, 198
Housing (Homeless Persons) Act 1977, 66
Housing Ordinance, 87n3, 88n4, 91n16, 91n18, 163n1
Human Rights Act 1998, 213n47, 241, 241n88
Immigration Ordinance, 164n6, 206, 315n62
Immigration (Refugee Status Review Boards) (Procedure) Regulations, 91n19
Import and Export (Carriage of Articles) Regulations, 18n82
Import and Export (General) Regulations, 18n77, 20n123
Import and Export Ordinance, 18n77, 357n38
Import and Export (Strategic Commodities) Regulations, 18n83
Imported Game, Meat, Poultry and Eggs Regulations, 18n78
Import (Radiation) (Prohibition) Regulations, 19n84
Independent Commission Against Corruption Ordinance, 337n33, 337n35, 337n37, 338, 338n48, 339
Industrial Relations Act 1967, 91n15
Inland Revenue Ordinance, 46, 135n49, 288n69, 305, 307, 311, 313
Interpretation and General Clauses Ordinance, 91n20, 97, 125n2, 129, 130, 163n2, 163n4, 317nn83–84, 318nn99–100, 352nn1–2, 354n5, 354n9, 355, 358n41, 358n43
Interpretation Ordinance 1911, 358
Interpretation Ordinance 1950, 358
Judicial Officers Recommendation Commission Ordinance, 312n41
Karaoke Establishments (Licensing) Regulation, 20n113
Karaoke Establishments Ordinance, 20n113
Land Survey Ordinance, 357n38
Land Drainage Ordinance, 316n70
Landlord and Tenant Ordinance 1947, 138
Legislation Publication Ordinance, 354n8
Legislative Council Ordinance, 87n2
Legal Aid Ordinance, 57, 358, 359n44
Lifts and Escalators Ordinance, 21n131
Matrimonial Proceedings and Property Ordinance, 137
Medical Clinics Ordinance, 251
Medical Practitioners (Registration and Disciplinary Procedure) Regulations, 132n37
Mental Health Ordinance, 312n42, 314n57
Merchant Shipping (Local Vessels) (Certification and Licensing) Regulation, 19n100
Merchant Shipping (Local Vessels) Ordinance, 19n100
Milk Regulation, 20n109
Miscellaneous Licences Ordinance, 20n117
Misdemeanours Punishment Ordinance 1898, 337n32
Municipal Services Appeals Board Ordinance, 314n52
National Health Service (General Medical and Pharmaceutical Services) Regulations 1974, 73n37
Noise Control Ordinance, 19n90
Nurses Registration Ordinance, 88n4

Oaths and Declarations Ordinance, 61
Offensive Trades Regulation, 21n128
Official Secrets Ordinance, 12n34
Ombudsman Ordinance, 319, 319n108, 320, 322n114, 323n123, 323nn117–118, 325n137, 327n141, 327n144, 328n147, 330n152
Parliamentary Commissioner (Ombudsman) Act 1962, 319
Parliamentary Commissioner Act 1967, 319
Patents Ordinance, 358n38
Payment Systems and Stored Value Facilities Ordinance, 357nn37–38
Pension Benefits (Judicial Officers) Ordinance, 357n36
Pension Benefits Ordinance, 355, 355n19, 357n36
Pensions Ordinance, 357n36
Personal Data (Privacy) Ordinance, 160, 344n92, 345n101, 346n125
Pharmacy and Poisons Ordinance, 316n73
Places of Public Entertainment (Amendment) Ordinance 1970, 336n22
Pleasure Grounds Regulation, 21n133
Police (Discipline) Regulations, 317n80
Prevention of Bribery Ordinance, 338, 338nn48–49, 339
Prevention and Control of Disease Regulation, 18n80
Professional Accountants Ordinance, 357n32
Protection of Endangered Species of Animals and Plants Ordinance, 18n79
Protection of the Harbour Ordinance, 198, 241n89
Protection of Wages on Insolvency Ordinance, 88n3
Public Bodies Act 2011, 309n28
Public Finance Ordinance, 22n143, 317n80
Public Health and Municipal Services Ordinance, 20n114, 21n129, 253n38, 316nn72–73
Public Service Commission Ordinance, 11n23
Public Service (Disciplinary) Regulation, 11, 363
Rabies Ordinance, 310n33, 311n40
Race Discrimination Ordinance, 339n56, 343
Race Discrimination (Formal Investigations) Rules, 340n68, 341n78
Race Discrimination (Investigation and Conciliation) Rules, 342nn85–86
Race Relations Act 1976, 152
Registered Designs Ordinance, 358n38
Residential Care Homes (Elderly Persons) Ordinance, 20n121, 21n135
Road Traffic (Driving Licences) Regulations, 19n96
Road Traffic Ordinance, 354n8, 357n37
Road Traffic (Public Service Vehicles) Regulations, 19nn97–98
Road Traffic (Registration and Licensing of Vehicles) Regulations, 19n98, 231n35
Road Traffic (Traffic Control) Regulations, 142
Rules of the High Court, 38, 38n16, 65
Rules of the Supreme Court, 64n3
Rural Representative Election Ordinance, 14n48
Rural Representative (Election Petition) Rules, 14n53
Sand Ordinance, 18n81
Securities and Futures Commission Ordinance, 258n68
Securities and Futures Ordinance, 315n59, 316n71, 361, 361n64
Senior Courts Act 1981, 64n3
Sex Discrimination Ordinance, 59n29, 339, 339nn56–57, 343, 359

Sex Discrimination (Formal Investigations) Rules, 340n68, 341n78
Sex Discrimination (Investigation and Conciliation) Rules, 342nn85–86
Stores and Procurement Regulations, 22, 22n144
Sunday Entertainments Act 1932, 227
Supplementary Medical Professions Ordinance, 88n4
Supreme Court Act 1981, 64n3, 67n13
Supreme Court Ordinance (No 3 of 1873), 25n6
Surveyors Registration Ordinance, 258n69
Swimming Pools Regulation, 20n116
Tai Lam Tunnel and Yuen Long Approach Road Ordinance, 357n28
Telecommunications Ordinance, 20n125, 288
Terrorism Act 2000, 150
Town and Country Planning Act 1971, 72n34
Town Planning Ordinance, 21n136, 249n9, 316n74
Trade Boards Ordinance, 59
Trade Marks Ordinance, 358n38
Tribunals, Courts and Enforcement Act 2007, 309, 309n29
Tribunals and Inquiries Act 1958, 264n110, 316n68
Tung Chung Cable Car Ordinance, 357n34
United Nations Sanctions Ordinance, 355, 355n20, 356, 356n22, 356n24
Urban Renewal Authority Ordinance, 21n136
Village Representative Election Ordinance, 233
Vocational Training Council Ordinance, 357n38
Volunteer and Naval Volunteer Pensions Ordinance, 357n38
Waste Disposal Ordinance, 19n92
Water Pollution Control Ordinance, 19n94
Western Harbour Crossing Ordinance, 357n27

Table of Constitutional Documents

Basic Law of the Hong Kong Special Administrative Region, 7, 8n8, 9, 10n21, 11n26, 16, 25, 28n16, 33n42, 98n47, 166n14, 308n20, 317n86, 337n34, 359n47, 363n75
Constitution of the People's Republic of China, 26, 27, 98n46
Letters Patent, Hong Kong, 24, 25
Royal Instructions, Hong Kong, 25

Table of International Treaties and Instruments

Convention Against Torture and Other Cruel, Inhuman or Degrading Treatment or Punishment, 1987, 47n22, 179, 241
Convention for the Extension of Hong Kong, 1898, 24n3
Convention for the Protection of Human Rights and Fundamental Freedoms (European Convention on Human Rights), 1950, 241
Convention of Peking, 1860, 24, 24n2
Convention for the Unification of Certain Rules for International Carriage by Air (28 May 1999) (Montreal Convention), 357n30
Free Trade Agreement between Hong Kong, China and Chile (HKC/CL FTA), 22n141
Hong Kong, China–New Zealand Closer Economic Partnership Agreement (HKC/NZ CEPA), 22n140
International Covenant on Civil and Political Rights (ICCPR), 1976, 33
International Covenant on Economic, Social and Cultural Rights (ICESCR), 1976, 33n48, 33n59
Joint Declaration of the Government of the United Kingdom of Great Britain and Northern Ireland and the Government of the People's Republic of China on the Question of Hong Kong (19 December 1984), 26n11, 27
Treaty of Nanking, 1842, 24, 24n1, 100

Table of Cases

A Solicitor *v* Law Society of Hong Kong [2004] HKEC 219, 256n53
AA *v* Securities and Futures Commission [2016] HKEC 1718, 39n20
ABC Containerline NV *v* New Zealand Wool Board [1980] 1 NZLR 372, 186n63
Aguilar Joenalyn Elmedorial *v* Director of Immigration [2014] HKEC 225, 236n57, 236n59
Airedale NHS Trust *v* Bland [1993] AC 789, 279n25
Aita Bahadur Limbu *v* Director of Immigration [1999] HKEC 788, 178n17, 237n62, 239n74
Akram *v* Secretary for Security [2000] 1 HKLRD 164, 253n32, 263n105
Ala *v* General Medical Council (2000) WL 1720374, 230n32
al-Fayed *v* Commissioners of Inland Revenue, 2004 SC 745, 223n88
American Cyanamid *v* Ethicon Ltd [1975] AC 396, 291n88
Amoy Properties Ltd *v* Committee for Takeovers and Mergers [1989] HKCU 367, 270n149
Anderson Asphalt Ltd *v* Secretary for Justice [2009] 3 HKLRD 215, 43n6, 78, 79n64, 80n66, 81n69, 81n72, 82n77, 153n42, 161n30, 261n88
Anderson Asphalt Ltd *v* Town Planning Board [2007] 3 HKLRD 18, 53n4, 54n10, 56n14, 157n17, 161n30
Anglo Starlite Insurance Co Ltd *v* Insurance Authority [1992] 2 HKLR 31, 132n35, 281n34
Anisminic Ltd *v* Foreign Compensation Commission [1969] 2 AC 147, 90, 90n9, 90n11, 198n35, 200
Ansett Transport Industries (Operations) Pty Ltd *v* Commonwealth of Australia (1977) 139 CLR 54, 183n46, 184n47, 188n72
Asia Television Ltd *v* Chief Executive in Council [2012] 3 HKLRD 1, 114n34
Asia Television Ltd *v* Communications Authority (No 2) [2013] 3 HKLRD 618, 257n63
Associated Provincial Picture Houses Ltd *v* Wednesbury Corporation [1948] 1 KB 223, 124n11, 154n1, 225, 225n1, 226n13, 228n15, 232n40
Association of Expatriate Civil Servants of Hong Kong *v* Chief Executive of HKSAR [1998] 1 HKLRD 615, 53n3, 58n25, 363nn78–79
Association of Expatriate Civil Servants of Hong Kong *v* Secretary for the Civil Service [1998] HKCFI 316, 364n87
AT *v* Director of Immigration [2017] HKEC 136, 114n33
Attorney General *v* Chan Foo [1990] HKCU 393, 358n43
Attorney General *v* Chino Industries (In Voluntary Liquidation) [1997] HKLRD 833, 200n47

Attorney General v Chiu Tat-Cheong [1992] 2 HKLR 84, 25n5, 168n26
Attorney General v Lindegren (1819) 6 Price 287, 188n72
Attorney General v Tsang Kwok-kuen [1971] HKLR 266, 359n50
Attorney General v Yau Kwok-Lam, Johnny [1988] 2 HKLR 394, 85n93, 364n85
Attorney-General for the State of New South Wales v Quin (1989–90) 170 CLR 1, 223n89
Attorney-General of Hong Kong v Ng Yuen Shiu [1983] 2 AC 629, 204n1, 205n3, 212n46, 213n51
Attorney-General of Hong Kong v Ng Yuen Shiu [1983] 2 WLR 735, 210n28
Attorney-General v Ng Kee [1978] HKLR 52, 129n20
Attorney-General v Nissan [1970] AC 179, 98nn50–51
Attorney-General v Ryan [1980] AC 718, 90n14
Au Wing Lun v Solicitors Disciplinary Tribunal [2002] HKEC 1141, 173n56
Auckland Casino Ltd v Casino Control Authority [1995] 1 NZLR 142, 269n135
AW v Secretary for Security [2015] HKEC 134, 47n29
Ayr Harbour Trustees v Oswald (1883) 8 App Cas 623, 184, 184n48

B v Torture Claims Appeal Board [2015] 1 HKLRD 681, 306n7
Bahamas District of the Methodist Church in the Caribbean and the Americas v Symonette [2000] ULPC 31, 279n24
Barnard v National Dock Labour Board [1953] 2 QB 18, 170n34, 170n41
Baynham Paul v Liquor Licensing Board [2010] HKEC 1329, 180n32
Benbecula Ltd v Attorney General [1994] 3 HKC 238, 56n15, 78n63, 205n4, 271n151, 278n16, 280n30
BH v Director of Immigration [2015] 4 HKC 107, 155n7, 161n28
Bhupendra Pun v Director of Immigration [2002] HKLRD (Yrbk) 460, 236n56
BI v Director of Immigration [2014] HKEC 64, 47n25
BI v Director of Immigration [2016] 2 HKLRD 520, 38n14, 45n13, 160n25, 160n28, 161nn28–29, 162n34, 183n45, 236n56
Birkdale District Electric Supply Co Ltd v Corporation of Southport [1926] AC 355, 186, 186n59
Blackburn v Attorney-General [1971] 1 WLR 1037, 100n58
Board of Education v Rice [1911] AC 179, 256n56
Board of Trade v Temperley Steam Shipping Co Ltd (1927) 27 Ll L Rep 230, 184n53
Boddington v British Transport Police [1999] 2 AC 143, 71n24, 71n27, 122n2, 122n4, 124n11, 199n42
Bonanza Creek Gold Mining Co Ltd v The King [1916] 1 AC 566, 125n2
British Broadcasting Corporation v Sugar [2007] 1 WLR 2583, 193n7
British Columbia (Attorney General) v Canada (Attorney General), Re An Act Respecting the Vancouver Island Railway [1994] 2 SCR 41, 134n44
British Oxygen Co Ltd v Board of Trade [1971] AC 610, 180nn30–31
Bugg v Director of Public Prosecutions [1993] QB 473, 71n24
Building Authority v Appeal Tribunal (Buildings) [2005] HKEC 1963, 195n18, 196n22
Building Authority v Appeal Tribunal (Buildings) [2013] 1 HKLRD 101, 161n30
Building Authority v Appeal Tribunal (Buildings) (2015) 18 HKCFAR 317, 154nn3–4

Table of Cases

Building Authority *v* Appeal Tribunal (Buildings) [2016] HKEC 334, 306n7
Bunney *v* Burns Anderson plc [2007] EWHC 1240, 68n19
Burmah Oil Co (Burma Trading) Ltd *v* Lord Advocate, 1964 SC (HL) 117, 101n61
Bushell *v* Secretary of State for the Environment [1981] AC 75, 168n22
Buttes Gas & Oil Co *v* Hammer (No 3) [1982] AC 888, 98n49

C *v* Director of Immigration [2013] 16 HKCFAR 280, 30n30, 126n3, 145n5, 151n31, 154n3, 159n22, 177n12, 260n78, 262n98
Calvin *v* Carr [1980] AC 574, 253n33
Canada (Attorney-General) *v* Canada (Commissioner of the Inquiry on the Blood System) (1997) 142 DLR (4th) 237, 336n22
Canadian Overseas Development Co Ltd *v* Attorney General [1991] 1 HKC 288, 78n63, 81n69
Capital Rich Development Ltd *v* Town Planning Board [2007] 2 HKLRD 155, 56n14, 154n1, 155, 155n11, 156n13, 157n16, 157n18, 158n19, 258n65, 261n91, 261n93, 262nn101–102, 264n110
Carltona Ltd *v* Commissioners of Works [1943] 2 All ER 560, 165, 165n9, 166n11
Cathay Pacific Airways Flight Attendants Union *v* Director-General of Civil Aviation [2005] HKEC 1337, 361n60
Cathay Pacific Airways Ltd *v* Administrative Appeals Board [2008] 5 HKLRD 539, 198n33, 306n7
Catholic Diocese of Hong Kong *v* Secretary for Justice [2010] HKEC 163, 46n21
CH *v* Director of Immigration [2011] HKEC 1595, 158n20
Chan Chi Shing *v* Symon Wong [2011] HKEC 591, 195, 195n17, 293n103
Chan Chin Yuen *v* Securities and Futures Commission [2008] HKEC 2196, 296n116
Chan Chiu Kwok Charles *v* Hong Kong Institute of Surveyors [2011] HKEC 1279, 296n116
Chan Ka Man *v* Commissioner of Correctional Services [2009] HKEC 1800, 48n40
Chan Kai Wah *v* HKSAR [2011] HKEC 412, 54n6, 59n34, 151n30
Chan Kam Nga *v* Director of Immigration (1999) 2 HKCFAR 82, 206n6
Chan Kar Yiu *v* Civil Service Bureau [2004–2005] HKCLRT 24, 297n123
Chan Kong *v* Chief Executive of the HKSAR [2008] 1 HKLRD 694, 46n19
Chan Mei Yee *v* Director of Immigration [2000] HKEC 788, 248n4
Chan Mei Yu Paddy *v* Secretary for Justice (No 3) [2008] 2 HKLRD 154, 46nn20–21
Chan Ming Yan *v* Hong Kong Housing Authority [2000] HKEC 798, 181n36
Chan Noi Heung *v* Chief Executive in Council [2007] HKEC 885, 126n6, 176n6
Chan Tak Shing *v* Chief Executive of the HKSAR [1999] 2 HKLRD 389, 256n55, 257n58
Chan To Foon *v* Director of Immigration [2001] 3 HKLRD 109, 208n20, 209n21
Chan Wah *v* Hang Hau Rural Committee [2000] 1 HKLRD 411, 284n49
Chan Wai Keung *v* Commissioner of Police [2010] HKEC 1624, 50n49

Chan Yik Tung v Hong Kong Housing Authority [1989] 2 HKC 394, 87n1, 87n3, 91n16, 91n18, 92n22, 93nn29–30, 200n45
Charles v Judicial and Legal Service Commission [2002] UKPC 34, 136n54
Chau Siu Woon v Cheung Shek Kong [2010] 3 HKLRD 49, 266n121, 267n126
Chau Tam Yuet Ching v Director of Lands [2013] 3 HKLRD 169, 82n77
Cheng Chui Ping v Chief Executive of HKSAR [2002] HKEC 26, 270n144
Cheng Chun Ngai Daniel v Hospital Authority, HCAL 202/2002, 82n77
Cheng Chun-Ngai Daniel v Hospital Authority [2004] HKCU 1315, 77n56
Cheng Ho Kee v Secretary for Justice [2004] HKCFI 114, 364n81
Cheng Ho Kee v Secretary for Justice (2006) 9 HKCFAR 705, 364n81
Cheng Sing Sze v Director of Lands [2007] 1 HKLRD 141, 50, 50n50
Cheung Koon Kit v Commissioner of Correctional Services [2004] HKEC 948, 257n60
Cheung Kwok-hung v Liquor Licensing Board [1995] 2 HKLR 456, 282n41, 283n45
Cheung Man Wai v Director of Social Welfare [2000] 3 HKLRD 255, 284n51
Cheung Mei Yin v Postmaster General [2007] HKEC 1214, 49n40
Cheung Shing Ki v Housing Appeal Panel [2001] HKEC 216, 215n65
Cheung Shing Scrap Metals Recycling Ltd v Director of Lands [2009] HKEC 813, 82n77
Cheung Sou-Yat v The Queen [1979] HKLR 630, 105, 105n73, 105n76
Cheung Yick Hung v Law Society of Hong Kong [2017] 1 HKC 97, 358n43
Chiang Lily v Secretary for Justice [2009] HKEC 1562, 226n10, 235n50
Chief Constable of the North Wales Police v Evans [1982] 1 WLR 1155, 299n127
Chief Executive of HKSAR v President of the Legislative Council [2016] HKEC 2315, 28n18
Chief Executive of HKSAR v President of the Legislative Council [2016] HKEC 2487, 28n18
Chief Executive of HKSAR v President of the Legislative Council [2017] 1 HKLRD 460, 30n26, 32n37, 32n39, 61n40
Chim Shing Chung v Commissioner of Correctional Services [1995] 5 HKPLR 570, 225n4
Chim Shing Chung v Commissioner of Correctional Services [1996] 6 HKPLR 313, 225n4
China Field Ltd v Appeal Tribunal (Buildings) (No 2) [2009] 12 HKCFAR 342, 137n57
Chinluck Properties Ltd v Appeal Tribunal (Buildings) [2013] HKEC 1390, 114n35, 116n47, 116n50, 206n5, 212n41
Chit Fai Motors Co Ltd v Commissioner for Transport [2004] 1 HKC 465, 285n56, 286nn59–61, 288n72
Chiu Hung Kwan v Director of Food and Environmental Hygiene [2012] HKEC 546, 47n26
Chiu Kin Ho v Commissioner of Police [2010] HKEC 701, 44n6, 46n15, 48n31, 48n33, 48n40, 50n52
Chiu Ming Kiang v William Lee Sheung [1991] 1 HKLR 230, 138n64
Ch'ng Poh v Chief Executive of HKSAR [2003] HKEC 1441, 102n67, 168nn24–25, 169n30, 249n14, 270n145
Cho Fok Bo Ying v Cho Chi Biu [1991] 1 HKLR 348, 137n63, 138n63
Choi King Fung v Hong Kong Housing Authority [2017] HKEC 549, 361n61

Chow Sang Sang Jewellery Co Ltd v Ryoden Lift and Escalator Co Ltd [2001] HKLRD (Yrbk) 57, 335n16
Chow Shun Chiu v HKSAR [2001] HKEC 882, 40n26, 108n91
Chow Shun Yung v Wei Pih (2003) 6 HKCFAR 299, 250n19
Christian Bulao Palmis v Director of Immigration [2003] HKEC 230, 195n20
Chu Hoi Dick v Secretary for Home Affairs [2007] HKEC 1471, 59n32
Chu Hoi Dick v Secretary for Home Affairs [2007] HKEC 1640, 62n47, 63n48
Chu Kwok-fai v The Queen [1973] HKLR 107, 359n51
Chu Ping Tak v Commissioner of Police [2002] 3 HKLRD 679, 256n55, 257n61, 299n131
Chu Woan Chyi v Director of Immigration [2004] 3 HKLRD 11, 37n1, 110n3, 111n14, 115n38
Chu Woan Chyi v Director of Immigration [2007] HKEC 553, 151n32
Chu Yee Wah v Director of Environmental Protection [2011] 5 HKLRD 469, 238n73
Cinnamond v British Airports Authority [1980] 1 WLR 582, 216n67, 298n126
City of Vancouver v Registrar of Vancouver Land Registration District [1955] 2 DLR 709, 186n65
Clark v Kelly, 2003 SC (PC) 77, 269n138
Clean Air Foundation Ltd v Government of HKSAR [2007] HKEC 1356, 59, 59n31
Cocks v Thanet District Council [1983] 2 AC 286, 66, 66n7, 66n10, 68, 73, 283n44, 283n47
Commissioner for Labour v Jetex HVAC Equipments Ltd [1995] 2 HKLR 24, 282n39
Commissioners of Crown Lands v Page [1960] 2 QB 274, 184n47
Cook v Sprigg [1899] AC 572, 99n55
Council of Civil Service Unions v Minister for the Civil Service [1985] AC 374, 33n43, 75n46, 105n78, 122, 123n6, 123n8, 208n13, 215, 215n61, 226n5, 229, 229n24, 233n41, 235n50, 280n30
Crédit Suisse v Allerdale Borough Council [1997] QB 306, 70, 70n21, 188n73
Cropp v A Judicial Committee [2008] NZSC 46, 137n59
Cudgen Rutile (No 2) Pty Ltd v Chalk [1975] AC 520, 186n64
Cunningham v The Queen [1977] HKLR, 336n24

D v Director of Public Prosecutions [2015] 4 HKLRD 62, 47n28, 107n88
Dairy Farm Co Ltd v Director of Food and Environmental Hygiene [2005] HKEC 754, 108n91
Dato Tan Leong Min v Insider Dealing Tribunal [1998] 1 HKLRD 630, 173n56, 173n58, 252n30
Dato Tan Leong Min v Insider Dealing Tribunal [1999] 2 HKC 83, 307n16
David Morter v HKSAR (2004) 7 HKCFAR 53, 142n87
Davidson v Scottish Ministers (No 2) [2004] UKHL 34, 267n124, 268n128
Davy v Spelthorne Borough Council [1984] AC 262, 68n16, 72n33, 74, 301n139
DBS Bank (Hong Kong) Ltd v San-Hot HK Industrial Co Ltd [2013] 4 HKC 1, 362n67
de Freitas v Benny [1976] AC 239, 102n66
Deacons v White and Case LLP [2003] 2 HKLRD 840, 266n123, 269n137
Deacons v White & Case LLP (2003) 6 HKCFAR 322, 140n73, 266n120, 267n123

Dembele Salifou v Director of Immigration [2016] HKEC 922, 226n11
Democratic Republic of the Congo v FG Hemisphere Associates LLC (No 1) (2011) 14 HKCFAR 95, 28n15, 98n51, 99n55, 101n62
Designing Hong Kong Ltd v Town Planning Board [2017] 2 HKLRD 60, 62n45
Desmond Keane v Director of Legal Aid, CACV 49/2000, 57, 57n21, 282n41
Dimes v Proprietors of the Grand Junction Canal (1852) 3 HL Cas. 759, 264n111, 271n152
Director of Lands v Yin Shuen Enterprises Ltd (2003) 6 HKCFAR 1, 78n63, 80n65, 81n69, 153n44
Director of Public Prosecutions of the Virgin Islands v Penn [2008] UKPC 29, 134n43
Director of Public Prosecutions v Haw [2008] 1 WLR 379, 170n33
Domingo Irene Raboy v Commissioner of Registration [2011] 6 HKC 532, 138n67
Dorset Yacht Co Ltd v Home Office [1970] AC 1004, 128n19, 129n21
Dr Ip Kay Lo v Medical Council of Hong Kong [2003] 3 HKLRD 851, 256n53
Dr Kwong Kwok Hay v Medical Council of Hong Kong [2006] 4 HKC 157, 225n3
Dr Q v Health Committee of the Medical Council of Hong Kong [2012] 3 HKLRD 206, 255n49
Dr To Chun Fang Albert v Medical Council of Hong Kong [2011] HKEC 279, 238n72
Dr U v Preliminary Investigation Committee of the Medical Council of Hong Kong [2016] 4 HKLRD 31, 130n25, 132, 132n36, 133n38, 141n79
Dr U v Preliminary Investigation Committee of the Medical Council of Hong Kong [2015] HKEC 2623, 114n33
Dr Wang Tze Sam v Attorney General [1996] HKCFI 243, 364n83, 364n86
Dr Yuk Kong Lau v Medical Council of Hong Kong [2011] 5 HKC 218, 46n18
Dragon House Investment Ltd v Secretary for Transport (2005) 8 HKCFAR 668, 214n58
Durga Maya Gurung v Director of Immigration [2002] HKEC 477, 179n21, 236n55, 236n61

E v Secretary of State for the Home Department [2004] QB 1044, 195n20, 196n25, 203n56
Eastern Express Publisher Ltd v Obscene Articles Tribunal [1995] 2 HKLR 290, 259nn71–72, 260n82, 261n89, 261n91, 262n95, 262n100
Eastham v Newcastle United Football Club Ltd [1964] Ch 413, 286n62
Edwards v Bairstow [1955] 3 WLR 410 (HL), 183n45
Ellis v Dubowski [1921] KB 621, 172n48
Epoch Group Ltd v Director of Immigration [2011] 3 HKLRD H2, 159, 159n23, 177n11, 177n15, 180n29, 181n37
Equal Opportunities Commission v Apple Daily Ltd [1999] 1 HKLRD 188, 59n27
Equal Opportunities Commission v Director of Education [2001] 2 HKLRD 690, 59n28
Essex Incorporated Congregational Church Union v Essex County Council [1963] AC 808, 137n62

ET Investment Ltd (t/a Oasis Nursing Home) v Director of Health [2016] 1 HKLRD 1389, 44n8
Everbest Port Services Ltd v Employees' Compensation Assistance Fund Board [2016] 6 HKC 503, 136n52
Ever-long Securities Co Ltd v Wong Sio Po [2004] 2 HKLRD 143, 362n67

Fairland Overseas Development Co Ltd v Secretary for Justice [2007] 4 HKLRD 949, 137n58, 138n67, 183n46, 184n51, 185n54, 186, 186nn66–67, 187n71, 188n74
Falcon Private Bank Ltd v Borry Bernard Edouard Charles Ltd (2014) 17 HKCFAR 281, 266n120, 269n132
FB v Director of Immigration [2009] 2 HKLRD 346, 179nn24–25
Financial Secretary v Wong [2003] 6 HKCFAR 476, 270n146, 276nn6–8, 278n18, 292n97, 297n122
Fok Chun Wa v Hospital Authority [2011] 1 HKLRD A1, 175n4
Fok Chun Wa v Hospital Authority [2012] 15 HKCFAR 409, 162n33
Fok Ho Chiu v Chinese Temples Committee [2003] HKEC 1183, 160n25
Fraser v Chief Executive of the HKSAR [2000] 3 HKLRD 492, 82n78
Fu Lok Man (t/a Leatherware Manufacturing Co) v Chief Bailiff of the High Court [1999] 2 HKLRD 835, 129n22
Fung Elvira Binag v Secretary for Home Affairs [2014] HKEC 400, 45n9, 46n15, 48n40, 50n51
Fung Yiu Bun v Commissioner of Police [2002] 4 HKC 15, 302n145

Gammon Construction Ltd v HKSAR [2014] HKEC 1712, 108n91
George v Secretary of State for the Environment (1979) 38 P & CR 609, 257n60
George v Secretary of State for the Environment [1979] 77 LGR 689, 248n5
Gillick v West Norfolk and Wisbech Area Health Authority [1986] AC 112, 364n84
Glynn v Keele University [1971] 1 WLR 487, 299n130
Gouriet v Union of Post Office Workers [1978] AC 435, 107
Grassby v R (1989) 168 CLR 1, 133n40
Grunwick Processing Laboratories Ltd v Advisory, Conciliation and Arbitration Service [1978] AC 655, 134n42
Guaranty Trust Co of New York v Hannay, 286
Gurung Aruna v Director of Immigration [2004] HKEC 779, 216n68
Gurung Bhakta Bahadur v Director of Immigration [2001] 3 HKLRD 225, 89n8, 91n20, 93n29, 97n45, 201, 201n51
Gurung Deu Kumari v Director of Immigration [2010] 5 HKLRD 219, 160n26, 180n32, 236n56
Gurung Deu Kumari v Director of Immigration [2010] HKEC 804, 46n21

Hai Ho Tak v Attorney-General [1994] 2 HKLR 202, 101n60
Hang Wah Chong v Attorney-General of Hong Kong [1981] 1 WLR 1141, 153, 153n40
Hang Wah Chong Investment Co Ltd v Attorney-General [1981] HKLR 336, 78, 78n63
Hans Richard Mahncke v Electoral Affairs Commission [2012] HKCU 1551, 97nn42–43

Heland Investment Ltd *v* Attorney General [1994] 2 HKC 550, 282n40
Helow *v* Secretary of State for the Home Department [2008] UKHL 62, 266n118
Hin Tack Gee Ltd *v* Town Planning Board, 307n13
Hing Wong Enterprises Co Ltd *v* Director of Lands [1999] HKLRD (Yrbk) 18, 212n39, 212n44
HKSAR *v* Cheung Suet Ting [2010] 6 HKC 249, 207n12
HKSAR *v* Ho Loy (2016) 19 HKCFAR 110, 142n89
HKSAR *v* Hung Chan Wa (2006) 9 HKCFAR 614, 48n39
HKSAR *v* Incorporated Owners of No 10 Bonham Strand [2004] HKEC 675, 72n29
HKSAR *v* Joy Express Ltd (No 2) [2005] HKEC 554, 72n30
HKSAR *v* Lam Kwong Wai (2006) 9 HKCFAR 574, 136n55
HKSAR *v* Lau Ting Sing Jerome [2013] HKEC 1270, 207n12
HKSAR *v* Md Emran Hossain [2016] 19 HKCFAR 679, 266n120, 267n124, 268n129
HKSAR *v* Okafor [2012] 1 HKLRD 1041, 262n93
HKSAR *v* Sky Wide Development Ltd [2013] 1 HKLRD 613, 72n30
HKSAR *v* So Ping Chi [2016] HKEC 1399, 336n23
HKSAR *v* Tse Yee Ping [2015] HKEC 1134, 72n31
HLB Hodgson Impey Cheng *v* Hong Kong Institute of Certified Public Accountants [2010] 6 HKC 232, 296n116
HLB Hodgson Impey Cheng *v* Hong Kong Institute of Certified Public Accountants (2013) 16 HKCFAR 460, 269n138, 279n23, 296n116
Ho Chee Sing James *v* Secretary for Justice [2008] 1 HKCLRT 141, 82n78
Ho Choi Wan *v* Hong Kong Housing Authority (2005) 8 HKCFAR 628, 125n2, 213n52
Ho Choi Wan *v* Hong Kong Housing Authority [2006] HKEC 13, 62n46
Ho Choi Wan *v* Hong Kong Housing Authority (No 2) [2003] 3 HKLRD J1, 282n42
Ho Loy *v* Director of Environmental Protection [2016] HKEC 2751, 115n40
Ho Ming Sai *v* Director of Immigration [1994] 1 HKLR 21, 38n11, 109n1, 110, 110nn7–8, 111n11, 112, 115n37, 151n33, 259n73
Ho Pak Wa *v* Council of the Law Society of Hong Kong [2016] HKEC 1825, 293n102
Hong Kong Aircrew Officers Association *v* Director-General of Civil Aviation [2009] HKEC 1086, 49n44, 261n88, 361n60
Hong Kong and China Gas Co Ltd *v* Director of Lands [1997] HKLRD 1291, 44n8, 82n75, 212n39, 212nn43–44
Hong Kong and China Gas Co Ltd *v* Director of Lands [1998] HKEC 590, 212n44
Hong Kong Bar Association *v* Anthony Chua (1994) 4 HKPLR 637, 77n60, 361n61, 363n74
Hong Kong Broadband Network Ltd *v* Director of Highways [2011] HKEC 1096, 157n16
Hong Kong Polytechnic University *v* Next Magazine Publishing Limited [1996] 2 HKLR 260, 78n62
Hong Kong Rifle Association *v* Hong Kong Shooting Association (No 2) [2013] 3 HKLRD 362, 77n61

Hong Kong Television Network Ltd *v* Chief Executive in Council [2015] 2 HKLRD 1035, 183n44, 208n18
Hong Kong Television Network Ltd *v* Chief Executive in Council [2016] 2 HKLRD 1005, 183n44
Hookings *v* Director of Civil Aviation [1957] NZLR 929, 172n48
Hughes *v* Department of Health and Social Security [1985] AC 776, 177n14, 214n55
Hung Shui Fung *v* Director of Food and Environmental Hygiene, CACV 219/2004 and CACV 220/2014, 37n6, 39n17, 39n19
Hysan Development Co Ltd *v* Town Planning Board [2014] HKEC 1869, 158n19, 248n8, 252n31, 262n96

Imran Muhammad *v* Secretary for Security [2016] HKEC 2201, 44n8
Incorporated Owners of Wah Kai Industrial Centre *v* Secretary for Justice [2000] 2 HKLRD 458, 145n4, 145n8, 146n13, 156n12, 157n17
Inglory Ltd *v* Director of Food and Environmental Hygiene [2012] 3 HKLRD 603, 176n5, 176n7, 225n3
Ip Tang Hon-ying *v* Tse Hing-chun [1965] HKLR 136, 138n65
Isaacs *v* Robertson [1985] AC 97, 138n63

Jackson *v* Attorney-General [2005] UKHL 56, 32n36
James Yan *v* Director of Immigration [2010] HKEC 1331, 48n40, 294n106, 296n117
JH Rayner (Mincing Lane) Ltd *v* Department of Trade and Industry [1990] 2 AC 418, 100n56
Jill Spruce *v* The University of Hong Kong [1991] 2 HKLR 444, 200n47
Jill Spruce *v* The University of Hong Kong [1993] 2 HKLR 65, 78n62, 200n47, 249n11, 251n22
Johnson *v* Johnson [2000] HCA 48, 266n118, 267n126
Johnstone *v* Pedlar [1921] 2 AC 262, 99n55
Jones *v* First Tier Tribunal [2013] UKSC 19, 203n54
Judith Mary Longstaff *v* Medical Council of Hong Kong [1980] HKLR 858, 173n57

Kai Nam (A Firm) *v* Ma Kam Chan [1956] AC 358 (PC), 138n65
Kaisilk Development Ltd *v* Secretary for Planning, Environment and Lands [2000] HKCU 72, 168n23
Kam Lan Koon *v* Secretary for Justice [1999] HKLRD (Yrbk) 15, 82n75
Kanda *v* Malaya [1962] AC 322, 248nn7–8, 257n57
Karlo Joanani Dauz *v* Director of Immigration [2009] HKEC 850, 45n10
Keen Lloyd Holdings Ltd *v* Commissioner of Customs and Excise [2016] 2 HKLRD 1372, 145n3, 145n6, 147n14, 149, 149n23, 154n3
Kennedy *v* Charity Commission [2014] UKSC 20, 230n31
Keung Siu-Wah *v* Attorney General [1990] 2 HKLR 238, 104, 104n71, 105, 105n74
King Prosper Trading *v* Urban Renewal Authority [2010] HKEC 1975, 80n67, 81n69
Ko Hon Yue *v* Chiu Pik Yuk (2012) 15 HKCFAR 72, 141n79
Komal Patel *v* Chris Au [2016] 1 HKLRD 328, 266n123, 270nn147–148

Kong Tai Shoes Manufacturing Co Ltd v Commissioner of Inland Revenue [2012] 4 HKLRD 780, 62n45
Kong Yunming v Director of Social Welfare (2013) 16 HKCFAR 950, 361n61, 362n68
Koo Sze Yiu v Chief Executive of the HKSAR (2006) 9 HKCFAR 441, 288n73, 289n77, 290n84, 363n77
Koon Wing Yee v Insider Dealing Tribunal (2008) 11 HKCFAR 170, 73n32
Krishna Rai v Director of Immigration, HCAL 145/1999, 236n58
Kruse v Johnson [1898] 2 QB 91, 227n14, 229n20, 360n54
Kwan Shung King v Housing Appeal Tribunal [2000] 2 HKLRD 764, 91n18, 200, 201n48
Kwan Sun Chu Pearl v Department of Justice [2005] HKEC 1548, 107n88
Kwan Sun Chu Pearl v Department of Justice [2006] HKEC 986, 107n88
Kwan Wan Chee Alisa v City University of Hong Kong [2013] HKEC 232, 170n41
Kwok Cheuk Kin v Commissioner for Transport [2011] HKEC 1318, 212n42, 223n89
Kwok Cheuk Kin v Secretary for Transport and Housing [2016] HKEC 172, 62n45

Lai Hin Cheong v Long-Term Prison Sentences Review Board [2008] HKEC 1701, 155n9, 162n35
Lai Sam Hing v Commissioner of Police [2009] HKEC 99, 47n26, 49n45
Lake District Special Planning Board v Secretary of State for the Environment [1975] JPL 220, 248n5
Lam Chi Pan v Commissioner of Police [2009] HKEC 2049, 297n124
Lam Kwok Pun v Dental Council of Hong Kong [2000] 4 HKC 181, 173n58, 252n30
Lam Ping Cheung v Law Society of Hong Kong [2006] HKEC 2366, 257n62, 299n129
Lam Siu Po v Commissioner of Police [2009] 4 HKLRD 575, 253n36, 254n41, 255n49
Lam Siu Po v Commissioner of Police [2009] 12 HKCFAR 237, 276n9, 359n48
Lam Sze Ming v Commissioner of Police [2010] HKEC 1160, 45n13, 48n31
Lam Tat Ming v Chief Executive of the HKSAR [2012] 1 HKLRD 801, 249n13, 249n15, 270n141
Lam Yuet Mei v Permanent Secretary for Education and Manpower [2004] 3 HKLRD 524, 209n23, 210n28, 213n48
Lau Chi Fai v Secretary for Justice [1999] 2 HKLRD 494, 74n41, 75n45, 82n80
Lau Hon Cheong v Attorney-General [1987] 3 HKC 1, 364n81
Lau King Keung and Lau King Tong v Town Planning Board, 307n14
Lau Kong Yung v Director of Immigration (1999) 2 HKCFAR 300, 115n40, 116n48, 154n4, 160n28, 230n30, 230n33, 235n50, 237n63, 279n27
Lau Kong Yung v Director of Immigration [1999] 2 HKLRD 516, 352n1
Lau Kwok Fai v Commissioner of Police [2004] HKEC 1580, 168n24
Lau Luen Hung Thomas v Insider Dealing Tribunal [2009] HKEC 1977, 45n13
Lau Ping v The Queen [1970] HKCU 31, 360n52
Lau Shiu Ming v Correctional Services Department (2000) HCMP 320/2000, 74n42
Lau Wai Wo v HKSAR (2003) 6 HKCFAR 624, 142n84, 142n87
Lau Wong Fat v Attorney General [1997] HKLRD 533, 66n6

Law Chun Loy v Secretary for Justice [2006] HKEC 1981, 45nn9–11, 47n26, 49n46, 50n47
Law Sze Yan v Chinese Medicine Practitioners Board of the Chinese Medical Council of Hong Kong [2006] HKEC 1151, 219n78
Law Sze Yan v Chinese Medicine Practitioners Board of the Chinese Medical Council of Hong Kong [2007] HKEC 603, 219n78
Lawal v Northern Spirit Ltd [2003] UKHL 35, 265n117
Leary v National Union of Vehicle Builders [1971] Ch 34, 253n33
Lee Bing Cheung v Secretary for Justice [2013] 3 HKC 511, 101n63
Lee Miu Ling v Attorney General (No 1) (1995) 5 HKPLR 178, 75n45
Lee Miu Ling v Attorney General [1996] 1 HKC 124, 55n11
Lee Sap Pat v Commissioner of Inland Revenue [1991] 2 HKC 251, 110n6, 116n49
Lee Shing Leung v Director of Social Welfare [2011] HKEC 810, 165n8, 173n50
Lee Shing Yue Construction Co Ltd v Director of Architectural Services [2001] 1 HKLRD 715, 77n57, 80n66, 85n91
Lee Sze Chung v Commissioner of Police [2003] 3 HKLRD L1, 253nn35–36
Lee Yee Shing Jacky v Inland Revenue Board of Review [2011] HKEC 261, 190n2, 193n12, 308n19
Leung Chak Sang v Lingnan University [2001] 2 HKC 435, 78n62
Leung Chun Ying v Ho Chun Yan Albert (2013) 16 HKCFAR 735, 136n55
Leung Fuk Wah v Commissioner of Police [2001] HKEC 951, 297n124, 299n128
Leung Fuk Wah v Commissioner of Police [2002] 3 HKLRD 653, 248n6, 256n55, 257, 257n59
Leung Kwok Hung v Chief Executive in Council [2008] HKEC 780, 59n33
Leung Kwok Hung v Chief Executive of HKSAR [2006] HKEC 239, 30n25, 288, 288n74, 289n81
Leung Kwok Hung v Chief Executive of the HKSAR [2006] HKCU 731, 363n76
Leung Kwok Hung v Commissioner of Correctional Services [2017] HKCU 136, 359n49
Leung Kwok Hung v Commissioner of Correctional Services [2018] HKCA 225, 359n49
Leung Kwok Hung v HKSAR (2005) 8 HKCFAR 229, 32n42
Leung Kwok Hung v President of the Legislative Council [2007] HKEC 788, 62n47
Leung Kwok Hung v President of the Legislative Council (No 1) (2014) 17 HKCFAR 689, 32n38
Leung Kwok Hung v President of the Legislative Council (No 2) (2014) 17 HKCFAR 841, 62n45
Leung Lai Kwok Yvonne v Chief Secretary for Administration [2015] HKEC 1034, 296n116
Leung Man Cheung v Secretary for Planning and Lands [2000] HKEC 991, 168n21
Leung Sze Ho Albert v Bar Council of Hong Kong Bar Association [2015] 5 HKLRD 791, 260n82, 261n91, 262n93, 361n61, 363n74
Leung TC William Roy v Secretary for Justice [2005] HKEC 998, 46nn18–19, 112n20

Leung Tin Kei Edward *v* Electoral Affairs Commission [2016] HKCU 1765, 97nn42–43
Leung *v* Secretary for Justice [2006] 4 HKLRD 211, 72n32, 284, 284n50, 284n54, 285nn56–58
Lewis *v* Attorney-General of Jamaica [2001] 2 AC 50, 103n69
L'Huillier *v* State of Victoria [1996] 2 VR 465, 187n70
Li Kin Wah *v* Commissioner of Police [2010] HKEC 694, 50n53
Li Wai Hung Cesario *v* Administrative Appeals Board [2015] 5 HKLRD 575, 262n93
Li Yiu Kee *v* Chinese University of Hong Kong [2009] HKEC 184, 126n8
Li Yiu Kee *v* Chinese University of Hong Kong [2010] HKEC 1159, 126n9
Lian Ting Sen *v* Director of Education [2000] HKCU 1041, 170n39
Liu Pik Han *v* Hong Kong Federation of Insurers Appeals Tribunal [2005] HKEC 1046, 247n3, 249n12, 251, 251n24, 253n35, 297n124
Liu Tat Hang *v* Post-Release Supervision Board, HCAL 154/1999, 47n24
LK *v* Director of Immigration [2016] HKEC 1730, 180n32, 183n44
Lloyd *v* McMahon [1987] AC 625, 247n2, 251n23, 253n33
Lo Siu Lan *v* Hong Kong Housing Authority [2004] HKEC 1541, 42n2, 43n4, 45n12, 46n16
Lo Siu Lan *v* Hong Kong Housing Authority [2005] 8 HKCFAR 363, 125n2, 145n5
Lo Siu Lan *v* Hong Kong Housing Authority [2005] HKEC 279, 38n16, 62n46
Lo Yin Ming *v* Appeal Tribunal (Buildings) [2011] 3 HKLRD 586, 139n68, 208n14
Lo Yuet Hing *v* Hong Kong Housing Authority [2002] HKEC 1218, 181, 181n36
Locabail (UK) Ltd *v* Bayfield Properties Ltd [2000] 2 WLR 870, 265n114, 266n122, 269nn134–135
Locabail (UK) Ltd *v* Bayfield Properties Ltd [2000] QB 451, 297n122
Local Government Board *v* Arlidge [1915] AC 120, 168n22
London & Clydeside Estates Ltd *v* Aberdeen District Council [1980] 1 WLR 182, 135n47
Lord Tredegar *v* Harwood [1929] AC 72, 80n65
Lucky Chance Ltd *v* Commissioner for Television and Entertainment Licensing [2006] HKEC 2302, 128n17, 128n19
Lui Tat Hang *v* Post-Release Supervision Board, HCAL 154/1999, 287n65
Luk Ya Cheung *v* Market Misconduct Tribunal [2009] 1 HKLRD 114, 308n19

MA *v* Director of Immigration [2012] HKEC 1624, 209n21
Ma Pui Tung *v* Department of Justice [2008] HKEC 1590, 108n90
Ma Zhujiang *v* Secretary for Justice [2005] HKEC 1716, 295n111
Madam Ho Ring Mui *v* Attorney General [1982] HKEC 180, 129n20
Madam Ho Ring Mui *v* Attorney General [1982] HKEC 284, 129n20
Magapower Garments Ltd *v* Director General of Trade and Industry [2002] HKEC 301, 50n48
Mallawa Arachchi *v* Wesley Wong [2014] HKEC 1490, 47n25
Malloch *v* Aberdeen Corporation (No 1) [1971] SC (HL) 85, 82n79, 248n5
Man Fung Wing *v* Town Planning Board, 307n14
Martin Tao Ming Lee *v* Secretary for the Civil Service [2011] HKEC 1078, 44n8, 48n40

Master Zhang Chaojie v Director of Immigration, HCAL 5/2000, 57, 57n19, 58n24
Matalulu v Director of Public Prosecutions [2003] 4 LRC 712, 105n81, 238n67
Matteograssi SpA v Airport Authority [1998] 2 HKLRD 213, 81nn68–70, 153n43
Matteograssi SpA v Airport Authority [1998] 3 HKC 25, 302n143
McGettigan Brian Kevin v Municipal Services Appeals Board [2013] HKEC 1926, 281n34
McInnes v Onslow-Fane [1978] 1 WLR 1520, 248n4
MDB v Betty Kwan [2014] HKEC 497, 155n10, 190n1
Medical Council of Hong Kong v Helen Chan (2010) 13 HKCFAR 248, 173n54, 336n22
Meerabux v Attorney General of Belize [2005] 2 AC 513, 264n112
Meng Ching Hai v Attorney-General [1991] 1 HKLR 535, 145n3, 147n14, 148, 148n19, 149n21
Merchant Navy Officers' Guild – Hong Kong v Director of Marine [2003] HKEC 285, 212n40, 212n42
Mercury Communications Ltd v Director General of Telecommunications [1996] 1 WLR 48, 85n93, 86n94
Mercury Energy Ltd v Electricity Corporation of New Zealand Ltd [1994] 1 WLR 521, 80n66, 81n69, 153n43
Millar v Dickson [2002] 1 WLR 1615, 270n147
Millar v Dickson [2002] SC (PC) 30, 297n120
Mills v London County Council [1925] 1 KB 213, 172n48
Minister of State for Immigration and Ethnic Affairs v Teoh (1995) 183 CLR 273, 208n19, 209n22
Ministry of Housing and Local Government v Sharp [1970] 2 QB 223, 129n22
Mo Chun Hon v Agriculture, Fisheries and Conservation Department [2008] 1 HKCLRT 386, 177n13
Mo Chun Hon v Director of Agriculture, Fisheries and Conservation Department [2007] HKEC 445, 213n49, 215n62
Mo Kam Tong Stanley v Coroner of Hong Kong [2008] 1 HKCLRT 155, 49n40
Mo Yuk Ping v HKSAR (2007) 10 HKCFAR 386, 142n83, 143n90
Mo Yuk Ping v Secretary for Justice [2005] HKEC 1363, 108n91, 111n10, 111n12
Mohan v McElney [1983] 1 HKC 243, 358n43
Mohit v Director of Public Prosecutions of Mauritius [2006] 1 WLR 3343, 105n82
Mok Charles v Tam Wai Ho (2010) 13 HKCFAR 762, 87n2
Mok Charles Peter v Tam Wai Ho (2012) 15 HKCFAR 489, 146n13
Mok Tai Kei v Constitutional Affairs Bureau of the HKSAR [2005] 1 HKLRD 860, 55n11
MSSL v Director of Immigration [2016] HKEC 2650, 45n13, 47n22
Mui Mei Fung v Secretary for Justice [2014] HKEC 88, 45n9

Nam Tai Trading Co Ltd v Commissioner of Inland Revenue [2006] 2 HKLRD 459, 208n15
Nam Tai Trading Co Ltd v Commissioner of Inland Revenue [2006] 4 HKLRD 51, 208n15
National Assembly for Wales v Condron [2006] EWCA Civ 1573, 270n142

Nattrass v Attorney General [1996] 1 HKC 480, 307n17
Nelms v Roe [1969] 3 All ER 1379, 165n10
New Orient Development Ltd v Town Planning Board, 307n13
New Zealand Institute of Agricultural Science Inc v Ellesmere County [1976] 1 NZLR 630, 134n44
Ng Chi Keung v Secretary for Justice [2016] 2 HKLRD 1330, 108n89, 127n12, 269n135
Ng Chi Keung v Secretary for Justice [2016] HKEC 909, 237n66
Ng Chun-Kwan v Commissioner of Inland Revenue [1976] HKCU 11, 200n44
Ng Hon Keung Tommy v Public Officer [2015] 5 HKLRD 278, 180n27
Ng Ka Ling v Director of Immigration [1999] 2 HKCFAR 4, 29n21, 206n6, 289n78
Ng King Luen v Rita Fan [1997] HKLRD 757, 55n12
Ng Koon Fat v Li Wai Chi [2012] HKEC 156, 234n44
Ng Koon Fat v Li Wai Chi [2013] 2 HKLRD 109, 156n15, 233, 233n43, 234n45
Ng Man Yin v Registration of Persons Tribunal [2014] 1 HKLRD 1188, 257n62
Ng Nga Wo v Director of Health [2006] HKEC 843, 249n11, 250, 250n20, 252
Ng Siu Tung v Director of Immigration (2002) 5 HKCFAR 1, 150n27, 183n45, 202n53, 205n4, 206, 206n5, 207n12, 207nn9–10, 209n22, 210, 210n25, 210n33, 210nn28–29, 212n39, 212nn45–46, 213n47, 214n57, 215, 215n60, 215nn63–64, 216, 216n66, 216n69, 218n77, 219, 219n79, 222n85, 223, 241n87, 300, 300n135
Ng Wing Hung v Hong Kong Examinations and Assessment Authority [2010] HKEC 1471, 54n10, 57n17, 110n2, 114n33
Ng Yat Chi v Max Share Ltd (2005) 8 HKCFAR 1, 113n23
Ng Yuen-shiu v Attorney General [1981] HKLR 352, 281n36
Ngo Kee Construction Co Ltd v Hong Kong Housing Authority [2001] 1 HKC 493, 80n66, 81n69, 303n147
Ngo Thi Minh Huong v Director of Immigration [2000] HKEC 84, 155n6
Nguyen Ho v Director of Immigration [1991] 1 HKLR 576, 156n14, 194n13, 195n19, 197n29
Nguyen Tuan Cuong v Director of Immigration [1996] HKLY 24, 300n134
Nguyen Tuan Cuong v Director of Immigration [1997] 1 WLR 68, 218n77
Nguyen Tuan Cuong v Director of Immigration [1997] HKLRD 73, 300n134
Nguyen Tuan Cuong v Secretary for Justice [1999] 1 HKC 242, 302n142, 303n148
Nina Kung v Wong Din Shin (2005) 8 HKCFAR 387, 262n96
Nina T H Wang v Commissioner of Inland Revenue [1994] 1 WLR 1286, 135, 135n48, 135n50, 136n53
Nisa Azizan v Director of Immigration [2016] HKEC 891, 44n8
Noise Control Authority v Step In Ltd (2005) 8 HKCFAR 113, 142n82, 142n88, 360nn54–55

O'Neill v Scottish Joint Negotiating Committee for Teaching Staff, 1987 SLT 648, 294n104
Ong Kin Kee Tony v Commissioner for Administrative Complaints [1997] HKLRD 1191, 328n146
Onshine Securities Ltd v Stock Exchange of Hong Kong Ltd [1994] 1 HKC 319, 253n36, 294n104
O'Reilly v Mackman [1983] 2 AC 237, 66–7, 66n6, 66n9, 68, 73, 81n73, 199n41, 301n139

Oriental Daily Publisher Ltd *v* Commissioner for Television and
   Entertainment Licensing Authority (1997–1998) 1 HKCFAR 279,
   30n24, 258n66, 261, 261n89, 261nn91–92, 262n97, 263n107
Orrico Philippe *v* Municipal Services Appeals Board [2015] 4 HKLRD 111,
   307n18, 307nn15–16

Pacific Century Insurance Co Ltd *v* Insurance Claims Complaints Bureau
   [1999] 3 HKLRD 720, 77n60
Padfield *v* Minister of Agriculture, Fisheries and Food [1968] AC 997, 126,
   126n5, 259n75, 262n99
Pagtama Victorina Alegre *v* Director of Immigration [2016] HKEC 85,
   240n83
Pang Yiu Hung Robert *v* Commissioner of Police [2003] 2 HKLRD 125,
   288n69
PCCW-HKT Telephone Ltd *v* Telecommunications Authority (2005)
   8 HKCFAR 337, 132, 132n34, 133n40
PCCW-HKT Telephone Ltd *v* Telecommunications Authority [2004] HKEC
   799, 44n6, 132
PCCW-HKT Telephone Ltd *v* Telecommunications Authority [2007]
   2 HKLRD 536, 269nn138–139, 270n142, 277n12, 278,
   278nn17–19
Pearl Securities Ltd *v* Stock Exchange of Hong Kong Ltd [1999] 2 HKLRD 243,
   248n4, 259n76
Pearlman *v* Keepers and Governors of Harrow School [1979] QB 56, 198n36
Phillips *v* Eyre (1868–69) LR 4 QB 225, 271n152
Po Fun Chan *v* Winnie Cheung (2007) 10 HKCFAR 676, 37n1, 110n5,
   111n16, 112, 112n21, 113n23, 113n26, 114, 114nn28–30, 115, 115n39,
   115n42, 115n44
Pollard *v* Permanent Secretary for Security [2011] 3 HKLRD H1, 236n56,
   239n75
Polorace Investments Ltd *v* Director of Lands [1997] 1 HKC 373, 78n63,
   138n67, 206n5, 208n17
Porter *v* Magill [2001] UKHL 67, 265, 265n117, 266
Power Co Ltd *v* Gore District Council [1997] 1 NZLR 537, 188n72
Prem Singh *v* Director of Immigration (2003) 6 HKCFAR 26, 301n136
Priscilla Sit Ka Yin *v* Equal Opportunities Commission [1998] HKEC 898,
   68n16, 302n145
Project Blue Sky Inc *v* Australian Broadcasting Authority (1998) 194 CLR 355,
   134n46
Pushpanathan *v* Canada [1998] 1 SCR 982, 237n65
Pyx Granite Co Ltd *v* Ministry of Housing and Local Government [1959]
   3 WLR 346, 283n48
Pyx Granite Co Ltd *v* Ministry of Housing and Local Government [1960] AC
   260, 97n44

Qamar Zaman *v* Department of Immigration [2003] 3 HKLRD J26, 162n34

R *v* Aston University Senate, ex parte Roffey [1969] 2 QB 538, 45n11
R *v* Barnet and Camden Rent Tribunal, ex parte Frey Investments Ltd [1972] 2
   QB 342, 229n22
R *v* Bexley London Borough Council, ex parte Jones [1995] ELR 42, 180n33

R v Board of Visitors of HM Prison, the Maze, ex parte Hone [1988] AC 379, 254n40
R v Bow Street Metropolitan Stipendiary Magistrate, ex parte Pinochet Ugarte (No 2) [2000] 1 AC 119, 264, 264n112, 265n113, 270n147, 297n122
R v Bridges (No 2) (1989) 48 CCC (3d) 545, 31n34
R v Broadcasting Complaints Commission, ex parte Owen [1985] QB 1153, 157n17
R v Chester City Council, ex parte Quietlynn Ltd (1985) 83 LGR 308, 253n31
R v Chief Constable of the Merseyside Police, ex parte Calveley [1986] QB 424, 294n104
R v Chief Constable of Sussex, ex parte International Trader's Ferry Ltd [1999] 2 AC 418, 225n3, 239n76
R v Chief National Insurance Commissioner, ex parte Connor [1981] QB 758, 298, 298n125
R v Civil Service Appeal Board, ex parte Cunningham [1992] ICR 816, 110n7, 259n73, 260n81, 260n83, 261n85, 263n103
R v Commission for Racial Equality, ex parte Cottrell [1980] 1 WLR 1580, 171n45
R v Commissioner of Police [2010] HKEC 1531, 47n29
R v Commissioners of Inland Revenue, ex parte Unilever plc [1996] COD 421, 210n25
R v Criminal Injuries Compensation Board, ex parte A [1999] 2 AC 330, 45n13, 196n25
R v Criminal Injuries Compensation Board, ex parte Moore [1999] 2 All ER 90, 263n109
R v Curragh Inc [1997] 1 SCR 537, 269n136
R v Director of Immigration, ex parte Chan Heung Mui [1993] 3 HKPLR 533, 236n60
R v Director of Immigration, ex parte Do Giau [1992] 1 HKLR 287, 253n32
R v Director of Public Prosecutions, ex parte Kebilene [2000] 2 AC 326, 105n80
R v Disciplinary Committee of the Jockey Club, ex parte Aga Khan [1993] 1 WLR 909, 77n61
R v East Berkshire Health Authority, ex parte Walsh [1985] QB 152, 302n145
R v English Schools Foundation [2004] 3 HKC 343, 77n58, 360n53
R v Felixstowe Justices, ex parte Leigh [1987] QB 582, 58n26
R v Gaming Board for Great Britain, ex parte Kingsley (No 2) [1996] COD 241, 207n12
R v Gaming Board of Great Britain, ex parte Kingsley (No 3) [1996] CLY 3953, 213n48
R v Governor of Brixton Prison, ex parte Armah [1968] AC 192, 193n10
R v Governor of Brixton Prison, ex parte Soblen (No 2) [1963] 2 QB 243, 149n20
R v Governor of Pentonville Prison, ex parte Sinclair [1991] 2 AC 64, 99n53
R v Governor of Pentonville Prison, ex parte Sotiriadis [1975] AC 1, 193n10
R v Greater London Council, ex parte Blackburn [1976] 1 WLR 550, 172n48, 287n65
R v Higher Education Funding Council, ex parte Institute of Dental Surgery [1994] 1 WLR 242, 261n86
R v HM Inspectorate of Pollution, ex parte Greenpeace Ltd (No 2) [1994] 4 All ER 329, 58n26, 60n36, 60n38

R v Hong Kong Polytechnic, ex parte Jenny Chua Yee-yen [1992] 2 HKPLR 34, 78n62
R v Hull University Visitor, ex parte Page [1993] AC 682, 199n42
R v Inland Revenue Commissioners, ex parte Matrix Securities Ltd [1994] 1 WLR 334, 216n66
R v Inland Revenue Commissioners, ex parte MFK Underwriting Agents Ltd [1990] 1 WLR 1545, 216n66
R v Inland Revenue Commissioners, ex parte National Federation of Self Employed and Small Businesses Ltd [1982] AC 617, 39n21, 53n5, 54n7, 54n10, 60n35, 110n7, 111n16, 111nn13–14, 114n36
R v Inland Revenue Commissioners, ex parte Preston [1985] AC 835, 224n90, 294n105
R v Inner London Education Authority, ex parte Westminster City Council [1986] 1 WLR 28, 144n2, 145n4, 148n16
R v Legal Aid Board, ex parte Donn & Co [1996] 3 All ER 1, 79, 81n71
R v Legal Aid Board, ex parte Hughes [1992] 24 HLR 698, 110n6, 113n23, 116n49
R v Lewisham London Borough Council, ex parte Shell UK Ltd [1988] 1 All ER 938, 146n12, 152n35
R v Licensing Authority, ex parte Smith Kline & French Laboratories Ltd (No 2) [1990] 1 QB 574, 281n34
R v Liverpool Corporation, ex parte Liverpool Taxi Fleet Operators' Association [1972] 2 WLR 1262, 281n37
R v London Borough of Camden, ex parte Paddock (transcript 8 September 1994), 256n56
R v London Borough Council of Newham, ex parte Bibi [2001] EWCA Civ 607, 205n2, 206, 206n7, 210n33, 210nn26–27, 211n35, 211n37
R v Lord Chancellor [1997] 1 WLR 104, 229n26
R v Ludlow [1947] KB 634, 193n10
R v Marsham [1892] 1 QB 371, 175n3
R v Medical Appeal Tribunal, ex parte Gilmore [1957] 1 QB 574, 92n24
R v Ministry of Defence, ex parte Smith [1996] QB 517, 230n30, 236n53, 239n77, 241n86
R v Ministry of Defence, ex parte Walker [1999] 1 WLR 1209, 183n45
R v Ministry of Defence, ex parte Walker [2000] 1 WLR 806 (HL), 182n43, 212n45
R v Monopolies and Mergers Commission, ex parte Argyll Group plc [1986] 1 WLR 763, 42n2
R v Monopolies and Mergers Commission, ex parte South Yorkshire Transport Ltd [1993] 1 WLR 23 (HL), 183n45, 192n6
R v Nat Bell Liquors Ltd [1922] 2 AC 128, 193n10
R v North and East Devon Health Authority, ex parte Coughlan [2001] QB 213, 205n4, 217n72, 218, 218n73, 224n90, 239n76
R v North West Lancashire Health Authority, ex parte A [2000] 1 WLR 977, 182, 182n41
R v Panel on Take-overs and Mergers, ex parte Datafin plc [1987] QB 815, 75n44, 76, 76n48, 77n59
R v Port of London Authority, ex parteKynoch Ltd [1919] 1KB 176, 175n2, 180n31
R v Revising Barrister for the Borough of Hanley [1912] 3 KB 518, 282n40

R v Rochdale Metropolitan Borough Council, ex parte Cromer Ring Mill Ltd [1982] 3 All ER 761, 145n4
R v Secretary for the Civil Service, ex parte Association of Expatriate Civil Servants of Hong Kong (1995) 5 HKPLR 490, 58n25
R v Secretary of State for Education and Employment, ex parte B (A Minor) (2000) 1 WLR 1115, 210n26
R v Secretary of State for Education and Employment, ex parte Begbie [2000] 1 WLR 1115, 101n65, 208n16, 210n31, 211n34, 213n50
R v Secretary of State for Education and Science, ex parte Avon County Council [1991] 1 QB 558, 281n34
R v Secretary of State for Employment, ex parte Equal Opportunities Commission [1995] 1 AC 1, 59n29
R v Secretary of State for the Environment, ex parte Hammersmith and Fulham London Borough Council [1991] 1 AC 521, 239n78
R v Secretary of State for the Environment, ex parte Nottinghamshire County Council [1986] AC 240, 123n7, 151n29, 229n28, 239, 239nn78–79
R v Secretary of State for the Environment, ex parte Ostler [1977] QB 122, 94n32
R v Secretary of State for the Environment, ex parte Powis [1981] 1 WLR 584, 197n27
R v Secretary of State for the Environment, Transport and the Regions, ex parte Spath Holme Ltd [2001] 2 AC 349, 126n7
R v Secretary of State for Foreign and Commonwealth Affairs, ex parte World Development Movement Ltd [1995] 1 WLR 386, 47n23, 54n8, 58n26, 60nn35–36, 145n5, 145n7, 148n17
R v Secretary of State for the Home Department, ex parte Brind [1991] 1 AC 696, 101n60, 225n3, 240n85
R v Secretary of State for the Home Department, ex parte Bugdaycay [1987] AC 514, 240n84
R v Secretary of State for the Home Department, ex parte Doody [1994] 1 AC 351, 247n3, 249n10, 260, 260n82
R v Secretary of State for the Home Department, ex parte Khan [1984] 1 WLR 1337, 210n28
R v Secretary of State for the Home Department, ex parte Oladehinde [1991] 1 AC 254, 164n6, 165n10, 170n32
R v Secretary of State for the Home Department, ex parte Ruddock [1987] 1 WLR 1482, 47n23, 210n28
R v Secretary of State for the Home Department, ex parte Salem [1999] 1 AC 450, 286n60
R v Secretary of State for the Home Department, ex parte Tarrant [1985] QB 251, 254n43, 255n47
R v Secretary of State for the Home Department, ex parte Vafi (unreported, 2 August 1995), 303n146
R v Secretary of State for the Home Department, ex parte Venables [1998] AC 407, 178, 178n19, 179n20
R v Secretary of State for Trade and Industry, ex parte Lonhro [1989] 1 WLR 525, 262n102
R v Somerset County Council, ex parte Dixon [1998] Env LR 111, 60n37
R v Soneji [2006] 1 AC 340, 135n47
R v Southwark Crown Court, ex parte Bowles [1998] AC 641, 147n14
R v St Edmundsbury Borough Council [1985] 1 WLR 1168, 56n14

R v St Lawrence's Hospital, ex parte Pritchard [1953] 1 WLR 1158, 280n29
R v St Lawrence's Hospital Statutory Visitors, ex parte Pritchard [1953] 1 WLR 1158, 276n7
R v Sussex Justices, ex parte McCarthy [1924] 1 KB 256, 265n115
R v Taito [2003] 3 NZLR 577, 268n130
R v Tandridge District Council, ex parte al-Fayed (2000) 80 P & CR 90, 300n133
R v Wakefield Metropolitan District Council, ex parte Pearl Assurance plc [1997] EWHC (Admin) 1087, 180n28
R v Warwickshire County Council, ex parte Collymore [1995] ELR 217, 179n26, 180n35, 181, 181n38, 182n40
R v Westminster City Council, ex parte Ermakov [1996] 2 All ER 302, 263n105
R v Westminster City Council, ex parte Monahan [1990] 1 QB 87, 156n12
R v Wicks [1998] AC 92, 71n27
R v Wimbledon Justices, ex parte Derwent [1953] 1 All ER 390, 282n39
R (Beer (trading as Hammer Trout Farm)) v Hampshire Farmer's Markets Ltd [2004] 1 WLR 233, 77n57
R (Bloggs 61) v Secretary of State for the Home Department [2003] 1 WLR 2724, 128n14, 222n85
R (Corner House Research) v Director of the Serious Fraud Office [2009] 1 AC 756, 238n67
R (Davies) v Birmingham Deputy Coroner [2004] 1 WLR 2739, 307n18
R (Pretty) v Director of Public Prosecutions [2002] 1 AC 800, 284n53
R (Tucker) v Director General of the National Crime Squad [2003] EWCA Civ 57, 81n73
R (on the application of Alconbury Developments Ltd) v Secretary of State for the Environment, Transport and the Regions [2003] 2 AC 295, 154n1
R (on the application of Carson) v Secretary of State for Work and Pensions [2003] EWCA Civ 797, 238n68
R (on the application of Cart) v Upper Tribunal [2011] QB 120, 121n1
R (on the application of Chief Constable of West Midlands Police) v Gonzales [2002] EWHC (Admin) 1087, 169n28
R (on the application of Coke-Wallis) v Institute of Chartered Accountants in England and Wales [2011] UKSC 1, 141n78, 141n80, 141nn75–76
R (on the application of Haile) v Immigration Appeal Tribunal [2001] EWCA Civ 663, 194n15
R (on the application of Khatun) v Newham London Borough Council [2005] QB 37, 155n8, 162n32
R (on the application of Lumba) v Secretary of State for the Home Department [2011] UKSC 12, 199n43
R (on the application of Miranda) v Secretary of State for the Home Department [2016] 1 WLR 1505, 150n25
R (on the application of Molinaro) v Royal Borough of Kensington and Chelsea [2001] EWHC Admin 896, 84n85
R (on the application of Nadarajah) v Secretary of State for the Home Department [2005] EWCA Civ 1363, 151n29
R (on the application of ProLife Allianc) v BBC [2004] 1 AC 185, 238n68
R (on the application of al-Rawi) v Secretary of State for Foreign and Commonwealth Affairs [2008] QB 289, 155n7
R (on the application of Reckless) v Kent Police Authority [2010] EWCA Civ 1277, 171n43

R (on the application of Reprotech (Pebsham) Ltd) *v* East Sussex County Council [2003] 1 WLR 348, 128n15, 137n58
R (on the application of Vetterlein) *v* Hampshire County Council [2001] EWHC Admin 560, 154n1
R (on the application of West) *v* Parole Board for England and Wales [2002] EWCA Civ 1641, 250n18
Raider Ltd *v* Secretary for Justice (2000) 3 HKCFAR 309, 78n63
Rank Profit Industries Ltd *v* Director of Lands [2007] HKEC 390, 153n41, 278n22, 284n53, 303n146
Rank Profit Industries Ltd *v* Director of Lands [2009] 1 HKLRD 177, 78n63, 80n65, 153n40
Rao *v* Andhra Pradesh State Road Transport Corporation [1959] AIR 308, 253n31
Ras Behari Lal *v* King-Emperor [1933] All ER Rep 723, 92n24
Re an application by Harris Tsang Shing-kung [1986] HKLR 356, 67n15
Re an application by Yau Fook Hong Co Ltd [1985] HKLR 42, 67n14, 301n138
Re An Occupation Permit No 18555 Issued by the Hong Kong Housing Authority [1991] 2 HKLR 104, 49n43, 78n63
Re C (A Bankrupt) [2006] 4 HKC 582, 106nn86–87
Re Chiu Tat-Cheong [1992] 2 HKLR 57, 165n10
Re Ho Mei Ling [2011] 6 HKC 1, 46n14, 47n28, 48n34
Re Tran Quoc Cuong *v* Khuc The Loc [1991] 2 HKLR 312, 54n9, 146n11, 165n10, 167n19, 169n29
Reckley *v* Minister of Public Safety and Immigration (No 2) [1996] AC 527, 102n66
Rederiaktiebolaget Amphitrite *v* The King [1921] 3 KB 500, 184nn52–53
Rediffusion (Hong Kong) Ltd *v* Attorney-General of Hong Kong [1970] AC 1136, 32n39
Registrar of Births and Deaths *v* Syed Haider Yahya Hussain (2001) 4 HKCFAR 429, 214n54
Ridge *v* Baldwin [1964] AC 40, 247n1
Right to Inherent Dignity Movement Association *v* Government of the HKSAR [2008] HKEC 1835, 116n45, 285n57, 287n68
Right to Inherent Dignity Movement Association *v* HKSAR Government [2008] HKEC 1412, 37n2
Roberts *v* Hopwood [1925] AC 578, 126n4
Rowling *v* Takaro Properties Ltd [1988] AC 473, 129n23
Rowse *v* Secretary for Civil Service [2008] 5 HKLRD 217, 164n7, 167n17, 170n31, 170n35, 180n34, 255n45, 255n48, 255nn50–51, 257n60, 270n143, 270n145, 319, 319n103, 363n78
Roy *v* Kensington and Chelsea and Westminster Family Practitioner Committee [1992] 1 AC 624, 73, 73n35, 73n36, 73n39
Royal College of Nursing of the United Kingdom *v* Department of Health and Social Security [1981] AC 800, 364n84
Rustomjee *v* The Queen (1876) 2 QBD 69, 100n58
RV *v* Director of Immigration [2008] 4 HKLRD 529, 105, 105n79, 105n84, 106, 107n88, 108, 108n89

Sabinano II Marcel R *v* Municipal Services Appeal Board [2014] HKEC 370, 191n3, 195n16, 196n23, 197n31, 203n56, 226, 226n8, 306n7

Sabinano II Marcel R v Municipal Services Appeals Board [2014] 1 HKLRD 676, 281n34
Sabir Mohammed v Permanent Secretary for Security [2017] HKEC 154, 162n34
Salaman v Secretary of State-in-Council of India [1906] 1 KB 613, 99n54
SCA v Minister of Immigration [2002] FCAFC 397, 150n26
Sea Dragon Billiard and Snooker Association v Urban Council [1991] 2 HKLR 114, 253n34
Sean Leonard v Commissioner of Police [2008] HKCU 273, 303n147
Secan Ltd v Attorney General [1995] 2 HKC 629, 81n68
Secretary for Justice v Chan Wah [2000] 3 HKCFAR 459, 296n113
Secretary for Justice v Cheng Kam Mun [2017] HKEC 671, 31n34
Secretary for Justice v Commission of Inquiry Re Hong Kong Institute of Education [2009] 4 HKLRD 11, 56n16, 61n41, 300n132, 336n25
Secretary for Justice v Li Chau Wing [2004] HKEC 1417, 267n127
Secretary for Justice v Ocean Technology Ltd [2009] 3 HKLRD F1, 72n32
Secretary for Justice v Richard Ethan Latker [2009] HKEC 132, 72n34
Secretary for Security v Sakthevel Prabakar (2004) 7 HKCFAR 187, 158, 158n20, 165n8, 173n53, 179n24
Secretary of Justice v Li Chau Wing [2004] HKEC 1417, 295n110
Secretary of State for Education and Science v Tameside Metropolitan Borough Council [1977] AC 1014, 154n1, 193n9, 197n29, 229n27
Secretary of State in Council of India v Kamachee Boye Sahaba (1859) 13 Moo PCC 22, 99n54
Sengupta v Holmes [2002] EWCA Civ 1104, 268n129
Sharma v Brown-Antoine [2007] 1 WLR 780, 105n83, 106n85, 108, 113n23, 114n28
Shek Lai San v Securities and Futures Commission [2010] 4 HKC 168, 40n23, 40n25, 54n6, 54n8, 54n10, 56n15, 108n91, 109n1, 111n15, 114n33
Shem Yin Fun v Director of Legal Aid [2003] 1 HKC 404, 112n19
Shem Yin Fun v Director of Legal Aid [2003] 1 HKC 568, 115n41
Shiu Wing Steel Ltd v Director of Environmental Protection [2003] HKCU 1101, 361n60
Shiu Wing Steel Ltd v Director of Environmental Protection (No 2) (2006) 9 HKCFAR 478, 48n36, 202n53
Short v Poole Corporation [1926] Ch 66, 227n14, 229n25
Shum Kwok Sher v HKSAR [2002] 2 HKLRD 793, 142nn83–85
Siu Chi Wan v Secretary for Civil Service [2008] HKEC 1134, 248n6, 257n62
Siu Lan v Hong Kong Housing Authority [2004] HKEC 1898, 44n8
Sky Wide Development Ltd v Building Authority [2011] 5 HKLRD 202, 62n45
Smart Gain Investment Ltd v Town Planning Board, HCAL 12/2006, 37n6
Smart Gain Investment Ltd v Town Planning Board [2006] HKEC 384, 37n6
Smart Gain Investment Ltd v Town Planning Board [2006] HKEC 2063, 37n6, 113n24, 114n29
Smart Gain Investment Ltd v Town Planning Board [2007] HKEC 1964, 155n5, 162n34, 194, 194n14, 195, 195n20, 196n21, 196n24, 197n30, 261n88, 261n91, 262n96, 263n105, 263n109
Smith v East Elloe Rural District Council [1956] AC 736, 93n31
Smith v Kvaerner Cementation Foundations Ltd [2007] 1 WLR 370, 270n147
So Ching Yat v City University of Hong Kong [2016] 3 HKLRD 661, 114n33

Society for Protection of the Harbour Ltd *v* Chief Executive-in-Council (No 2) [2004] 2 HKLRD 902, 201n52, 241n90
Society for the Protection of the Harbour Ltd *v* Town Planning Board [2003] 2 HKLRD 787, 59n30
Solicitor (24/07) *v* Law Society of Hong Kong [2008] 11 HKCFAR 117, 200n47
South Buckinghamshire District Council *v* Porter (No 2) [2004] 1 WLR 1953, 261n91, 262n94, 262n100
South East Asia Fire Bricks Sdn Bhd *v* Non-Metallic Mineral Products Manufacturing Employees Union [1981] AC 363, 91n15, 199n39, 200, 201n51
Steadman-Byrne *v* Amjad [2007] EWCA Civ 625, 270n150
Stock Exchange of Hong Kong Ltd *v* New World Development Co Ltd (2006) 9 HKCFAR 234, 254n40, 254nn43–44, 255n46, 255n49, 256n52, 294n104, 296n112, 308n19
Stock Exchange of Hong Kong Ltd *v* Onshine Securities Ltd [1994] 1 HKC 319, 253n36
Sugar *v* British Broadcasting Corporation [2012] UKSC 4, 193n7
Sumukan Ltd *v* Commonwealth Secretariat [2007] EWCA Civ 1148, 134n44
Sunday Times *v* United Kingdom (1979–80) 2 EHRR 245, 142n84
Super Lion Enterprises Ltd *v* Commissioner of Rating and Valuation [2006] 1 HKLRD 239, 281n33, 291n89
Super Lion Enterprises Ltd *v* Commissioner of Rating and Valuation [2006] HKEC 1870, 44n8
Super Lion Enterprises Ltd *v* Commissioner of Rating and Valuation [2006] HKEC 1936, 46n20
Superb Quo Ltd *v* Lee Yuen Cheung Co Ltd [2011] 3 HKLRD G3, 269n134
Sydney Municipal Council *v* Campbell [1925] AC 338, 146n9

T *v* Commissioner of Police (2014) 17 HKCFAR 593, 136nn55–56
Tai Sen Choy *v* Municipal Services Appeals Board [2001] HKLRD (Yrbk) 9, 175n1, 177n9
Tam Chi Ming *v* Medical Council of Hong Kong [2008] 1 HKLRD 24, 165n8, 172n47, 172n49
Tam Heung Man *v* Hong Kong Institute of Certified Public Accountants [2008] 1 HKLRD 238, 154n3, 155n8, 160n24, 162n36
Tan Soon-Gin *v* Attorney General [1990] 2 HKLR 176, 105n78
Tan Soon-Gin *v* Attorney-General of Hong Kong [1992] 2 HKLR 254, 105n78
Tang Keung Hong *v* Poon Kit Sang [2005] 4 HKLRD 274, 277n12
Tang Yee-Chun *v* Attorney General [1988] 2 HKLR 408, 105n77
Taylor (formerly Kraupl) *v* National Assistance Board [1957] P 101, 92n24
Television Broadcasts Ltd *v* Communications Authority [2013] HKEC 729, 276n9, 277, 277n10, 279n24
Television Broadcasts Ltd *v* Communications Authority [2016] 2 HKLRD 41, 91n20, 201n51
Television Broadcasts Ltd *v* Communications Authority [2016] HKEC 238, 317n89, 318n97
Territorial and Auxiliary Forces Association of the County of London *v* Nichols [1949] 1 KB 35, 138n65
Tesco Stores Ltd *v* Secretary of State for the Environment [1995] 1 WLR 759, 161n31, 226n12

Table of Cases

Thai Muoi v Hong Kong Housing Authority [2000] HKCU 370, 91n17, 91n21, 92n23, 96n38, 201n50
The Queen v Director of Immigration, ex parte Do Giau [1992] 1 HKLR 287, 91n19, 110n4, 195nn19–20, 200n45, 257n60
The Queen v Town Planning Board, ex parte REDA [1996] 2 HKLR 267, 253n31
The Queen v Tsui Lai-Ying [1987] HKLR 857, 105n75
Thoday v Thoday [1964] P 181, 140, 140n75
Thompson v Randwick Municipal Council (1950) 81 CLR 87, 145n7, 148n18
To Kin Wah v Tuen Mun District Officer [2006] HKEC 95, 124n11
To Kin Wah v Tuen Mun District Officer (No 2) [2003] 4 HKC 213, 302n141, 302n144
Tong Pon Wah v Hong Kong Society of Accountants [1998] 2 HKLRD 427, 238n70, 259nn73–75, 260n80, 263n108, 264n110
Tong Tim Nui v Hong Kong Housing Authority [1999] 4 HKC 466, 303n149
Tong Wai Ting v Secretary for Education [2009] HKEC 1367, 208n20
Total Lubricants Hong Kong Ltd v De Chanterac (2014) 17 HKCFAR 296, 141n79
Town Planning Board v Society for the Protection of the Harbour Ltd [2004] 7 HKCFAR 1, 59n30, 198n32, 241n90
Town Planning Board v Society for Protection of the Harbour Ltd (No 2) (2004) 7 HKCFAR 114, 62n47
Town Planning Board v Town Planning Appeal Board (2017) 20 HKCFAR 196, 133n39
Tsan Luk Yuk Yin v Secretary for the Environment, Transport and Works [2012] HKEC 399, 137n62, 138n64
Tsang Hing Shing v Commissioner of Police [2004] HKEC 1540, 238n71
Tsang Kin Chiu v Commissioner of Police [2015] 4 HKLRD 71, 293n102, 294n108
Tsang Loi Fat v Sun Fook Kong [2011] 4 HKLRD 344, 48n40
Tsoi Kei Lung v Secretary for Justice [2000] HKEC 742, 282n39
Tsui Chun Fai Danny v Commissioner of Police [2010] HKEC 695, 50n53
Tsui Kin Kwok v Commissioner of Police [2010] HKEC 284, 48n39, 50n52
Turbo Top Ltd v Town Planning Board [2011] HKEC 1526, 133n41

Ubamaka v Secretary for Security [2011] 1 HKLRD 359, 51n55
Ubamaka v Secretary for Security [2012] 15 HKCFAR 743, 100n59, 101n60
United States of America v McVey [1992] 3 SCR 475, 99n53
University of Ceylon v Fernando [1960] 1 WLR 223, 256n56

V v Director of Immigration [2005] HKEC 1938, 297n124
Viva Magnetics Ltd v Secretary for Justice [2002] 3 HKLRD 571, 40n26, 108n91
Vu Ngoc Dung v Criminal and Law Enforcement Injuries Compensation Appeal Boards [1996] HKLY 8, 176n8

Walden v Liechtenstein, 289n79
Wan Yung Sang v Housing Authority [2011] HKEC 907, 82n74, 160n27, 193n11, 195n18, 203n56

Wandsworth London Borough Council *v* Winder (No 1) [1985] AC 461, 69n17, 69n20, 74
Weinberger *v* Inglis [1919] AC 606, 229n21
Welltus Ltd *v* Fornton Knitting Co Ltd [2013] HKEC 369, 261n84
Westminster Corporation *v* London and North Western Railway Co [1905] AC 426, 147n15, 151n31
Wheeler *v* Leicester City Council [1985] AC 1054, 151, 152n34
Winfat Enterprise (HK) Co Ltd *v* Attorney-General of Hong Kong [1985] AC 733, 99n55
Wing On Co Ltd *v* Building Authority [1996] 6 HKPLR 432, 155n5
Winnie Lo *v* HKSAR [2012] 1 HKC 537, 142n84, 142n86, 143n91
Wise Union Industries Ltd *v* Hong Kong Science and Technology Parks Corporation [2009] 5 HKLRD 620, 163n1, 170n38, 177n10, 178nn16–18, 180n30, 180n33
Wong Chi Keung *v* Commissioner of Police [2010] HKEC 809, 48n39
Wong Chi Man *v* Director of Food and Environmental Hygiene [2014] 2 HKLRD 1124, 226, 226n6
Wong Chung Ki *v* Chief Executive [2003] 1 HKC 404, 112n20, 112nn17–18
Wong Kam Kuen *v* Commissioner for Television and Entertainment Licensing [2003] 3 HKLRD 596, 2n1, 131, 131n29, 132n32
Wong Kei Kwong *v* Principal Assistant Secretary for Civil Service [2008] HKEC 261, 363n78
Wong Kim Ming *v* Commissioner of Police [1995] HKCFI 197, 146n10
Wong Pei Chun *v* Hong Kong Housing Authority [1996] 2 HKLR 293, 139n69, 152, 152n37, 153n39, 205n4, 206n8
Wong Tak Wai *v* Commissioner of Correctional Services [2010] 4 HKLRD 409, 253n32, 253n37, 266n119, 269n140, 270n145, 309n27
Wong Tak Yiu *v* Commissioner of Police [2010] HKEC 1531, 47n29, 50n52
Wong Wai Hing Christopher *v* Director of Lands [2010] HKEC 1485, 82n76
Wong Wei Man *v* Amusement Game Centres Appeal Board [2000] HKCU 790, 183n45
Wong Yui Hin *v* Hong Kong Arts Development Council [2004] HKEC 1102, 47n30, 77n56, 286n61, 286n64, 288n70, 302n142
Woomera Co Ltd *v* Commissioner for Transport [2009] HKEC 786, 179n23
Wu Hin Ting *v* Medical Council of Hong Kong [2004] 2 HKC 367, 174n59
Wu Yuk Wah Ben *v* Director of Hong Kong Observatory [2013] 2 HKLRD 1068, 212n41

X *v* Education and Accreditation Committee, Medical Council of Hong Kong [2013] 1 HKLRD 167, 271n152
X *v* Torture Claims Appeal Board [2014] HKEC 9, 40n24, 46, 47n22, 297n119

Yang Chang Chun Robert *v* Government of the United States of America [1997] 3 HKC 338, 98n48, 99n53
Yat Tung Investment Co Ltd *v* Dao Heng Bank Ltd [1975] AC 581 (PC), 141n79
Yau Kwong Man *v* Secretary for Security [2002] HKEC 1142, 317n85

Yeung Chun Pong v Secretary for Justice [2008] HKEC 40, 113n23
Yeung Chun Pong v Secretary for Justice (No 4) [2008] 2 HKC 46, 108n91, 294n107
Yim Shik Shi v Secretary for the Civil Service [2004] HKEC 640, 207n11, 211n38, 257n60
Yim Shik Shi v Secretary for the Civil Service [2004] HKEC 1813, 361n62
Yim Tat-Fai v Attorney General [1986] HKLR 873, 128n19
Ying Ho Co Ltd v Secretary for Justice [2005] 1 HKLRD 135, 78n63
Yiu Sung Chi v Commissioner of Police [2010] HKEC 693, 50n53
Yook Tong Electric Co Ltd v Commissioner for Transport [2003] HKEC 170, 212n39, 221, 221n83, 222n84, 229n29, 242n94
Young Yau Yau Cecilia v Dental Council of Hong Kong [2010] HKEC 311, 48n38, 49n41
Yu Cho Lam v Commissioner of Police [2016] 1 HKLRD 257, 248n7, 268n131
Yu Hung Hsua Julie v Chinese University of Hong Kong [2016] 5 HKLRD 393, 78n63
Yu Pik Ying v Director of Immigration [2002] 1 HKC 18, 110n9, 111, 111n13
Yue Yuen Marketing Co Ltd v Commissioner of Inland Revenue [2012] 4 HKLRD 761, 62n45, 136n53, 282n38, 282n40, 293n101
Yuen Kun-yeu v Attorney General [1987] 2 HKC 25, 129n23
Yuen Kun-Yeu v Attorney General [1987] HKLR 1154, 128n19, 292n98
Yuen Tat-Cheong v Urban Council [1987] HKLR 723, 128n19

Zahirul Islam v Torture Claims Appeal Board [2017] HKEC 129, 114n31
Zestra Asia Ltd v Commissioner for Transport [2007] 4 HKLRD 722, 230, 230n34, 231n36, 232n38
Zhang Rui Hua v Wang Lan [2016] HKEC 291, 261n90
Zhuo Cui Hao v Ting Fung Yee [1999] 3 HKC 634, 261n84
ZN v Secretary for Justice [2016] 1 HKLRD 174, 267n127, 268n128

1

Introduction

The state regulates almost every aspect of our lives. The tentacles of regulation extend far and wide: education, health, commerce, finance, employment, taxation, policing, transport, housing, telecommunications, construction, waste management, pensions, the family, science and technology, immigration, entertainment – almost no area is off limits. The complexities of administering the apparatus of state has resulted in a proliferation of departments, agencies and officials, and the emergence of an extensive and powerful bureaucracy. From the Department of Health to the Inland Revenue Department, and District Councils to licensing boards, a smorgasbord of powers are vested in a wide range of officials from the Chief Executive to junior-level administrators. These powers can doubtless be exercised for the common good, improving and enhancing the health, education, well-being, security and prosperity of the populace. The institutions, stability and resources of the state present a considerable opportunity for the advancement of the public interest and public welfare.

However, with every power conferred on an institution or official comes an opportunity for abuse or misuse; whether intentional or inadvertent. Corruption, favouritism, arbitrariness, selective enforcement of rules, pursuit of private motives in the exercise of public power, excessive and unreasonable proceduralism, oppression, unfair treatment, pursuit of ulterior motives in the exercise of discretion – these are violations not only of the rule of law but also of the ethics that inform it. Autocratic, oppressive or unreasonable behaviour among frontline officials, even when seemingly mundane, is worthy of our attention and scrutiny. The licensing or planning body which fails to treat like applications alike; the public official who refuses to answer reasonable questions which it is their duty to answer; the public body which ignores enquiries and requests; the tribunal which is biased or which does not observe procedural fairness; the police officer whose personal animosity towards a person is apparent in his official conduct; the customs official who selects for a full body search a man by reason of his ethnicity. The excesses of the state should not go unchecked, even on this more quotidian level.

Those who govern are not always, and apparently not often, driven to act in such a way. Their powers are more likely to be inadvertently misused than deliberately abused. Mistakes can be made in administrative procedures, whether determining the eligibility of an applicant for a licence, or hearing objections to a planning proposal. Decision makers can misunderstand the scope of their legal powers, and can commit errors in applying their powers. They might erroneously think that their power to award amusement game licences carries with it a power to censure the kinds of games that can be operated in amusement game premises,[1] or that by removing a professional's registration status in accordance with a disciplinary code there is no need to afford him or her an oral hearing. They might regard themselves as under no obligation to provide reasons for a decision taken, or think they are justified in making a particular decision as a result of a lack of resources. These acts and decisions might be committed unwittingly and without ill motive, and the official might genuinely be doing what he or she thinks to be right and in the public interest.

Administrative law is essentially directed at these abuses and misuses of public power. Its function is to regulate the relationship between public administrators and those who must deal with them; putting right abuse and misuse. Judicial review is one of the most potent aspects of administrative law and is the main focus of this book. It is the mechanism by which the courts ensure that bodies act in accordance with their public law duties. All decision makers face legal limits on the scope of their decision-making power. No decision maker has unlimited discretion. To govern is not to be immune from compliance with the law, a central principle of the rule of law. The courts, through judicial review, ensure that public bodies and officials act and decide lawfully; otherwise, their acts and decisions can be struck down.

This gives the courts great power, and their supervisory jurisdiction must be exercised with discipline. Importantly, judicial review is not an avenue of appeal. It is concerned with the legality of acts and decisions, not their merits.[2] Decision makers at all levels can make good decisions or bad decisions, but this is in principle not the business of the courts. The merits of decisions are matters for political accountability; through elections, public consultations, media scrutiny, protests and public discourse. The considerable power of unelected judges in judicial review is to a great extent tolerable because it is exercised with discipline: just as courts must be ready and willing to intervene whenever legal obligations have not been met, so must they refrain from interfering when the challenge is fundamentally not one of law and legal obligation.

In this way the rule of law is upheld in accordance with the separation of powers. The judiciary ensures that the legislature and the executive (and even the judiciary itself) comply with the law, and provide an avenue for legal redress where they do not. The rule of law is promoted not only by the courts measuring the legality of decision making against the Basic Law and legislation but also by the imposition of common law standards on public administration

---

[1] See *Wong Kam Kuen v Commissioner for Television and Entertainment Licensing* [2003] 3 HKLRD 596 (CA).

[2] Though it will be seen that the boundary between legality and merits is sometimes rather thin.

which are understood to promote laudable ethical conceptions of governance. Often the rule of law is used vaguely as a term, certainly in politics and perhaps also in law. Whilst there is scope for reasonable disagreement on its precise form and meaning, it is an essential concept, rather than a technical one.[3] The ways in which the term may be used, sometimes misused and perhaps even abused, should not be permitted to undermine the seriousness of the core issue, namely, the robust protection of individuals against unlawful acts of the state. Sight should not be lost of the rule of law ideal in the law and legal system, nor of how fragile the rule of law can be, and how subtly it can be eroded. Judicial review is a cornerstone of the rule of law, only gaining importance in Hong Kong. As Li CJ acknowledged, extra-judicially:

> It is not an exaggeration to say that the phenomenon of judicial review has redefined the legal landscape. . . . It would not be right for judicial review to be viewed negatively as a hindrance to government. On the contrary, it should be seen as providing an essential foundation for good governance under the rule of law.[4]

Furthermore, judicial independence is as critical to the utility of judicial review as it is to the integrity of the legal system. Without judicial independence, the promise of judicial review for the rule of law and the protection of individual rights would be seriously diminished. An effective system of legal aid is also important to ensure that individuals can access the courts within which to assert their rights and have the wrongs of public bodies subject to judicial scrutiny. These protections should be guarded against impairment and erosion.

Administrative law is broader, however, than judicial review. It includes an array of other mechanisms for holding public administrators to account in accordance with particular standards of governance. Administrative tribunals, the Ombudsman, the Legislative Council Redress System, Commissions of Inquiry, the Independent Commission Against Corruption, the Equal Opportunities Commission, the Privacy Commissioner for Personal Data and the Audit Commission are just some of the other means by which public bodies can be scrutinised and challenged, and they are also addressed in this book. The role that each of these institutions plays in making life tolerable in a democratically weak system is even more keenly felt. Regardless of one's view on the role, place and extent of democracy in the territory, Hong Kong would be a worse place without the robust system of administrative law that it presently enjoys. The system must not be taken for granted; it can be further improved and strengthened, and it should be protected against diminution. A thriving system of administrative law provides lifeblood to the rule of law, and its fortification and improvement can materially enhance fairness, transparency, accountability and justice within and against the state.

---

[3] See pp.30–31. [4] Andrew Li CJ, speech at the Ceremonial Opening of the Legal Year 2007.

Part I

The Constitutional and Administrative Context

Part 1

2

Governance and Administration in Hong Kong

Central Government

Chief Executive

The Chief Executive is firmly at the heart of government in Hong Kong,[1] retaining much of the centralised power and authority of the pre-Handover Governor. She appoints members of the Executive Council, civil servants, judges and the majority of administrative tribunal members. She has, *inter alia*, the power to conduct external affairs on behalf of the Hong Kong Special Administrative Region (HKSAR) within the scope of her remit, sign bills and budgets passed by the Legislative Council, approve the introduction of motions regarding revenue and expenditure to the Legislative Council, pardon persons convicted of criminal offences or commute their penalties, and handle petitions and complaints.[2] The Chief Executive must also act as a key link between Hong Kong and the Mainland, and is accountable to the Central People's Government.[3]

In order to be eligible for appointment as Chief Executive, the individual must be a Chinese citizen not less than forty years of age who is a permanent resident of Hong Kong with no right of abode in any foreign country, and who has ordinarily resided in Hong Kong for a continuous period of not less than twenty years.[4] The Basic Law also requires that the Chief Executive is a person of integrity, dedicated to his or her duties.[5] The manner of the Chief Executive's appointment is a source of controversy and tension in Hong Kong. The Basic Law provides that:

> The Chief Executive of the Hong Kong Special Administrative Region shall be selected by election or through consultations held locally and be appointed by the Central People's Government. The method for selecting the Chief

---

[1] Article 48(1) of the Basic Law empowers the Chief Executive to lead the Government of the HKSAR; and Article 60(1) provides that the Chief Executive shall be the head of Government in the HKSAR.

[2] These powers have the backing of the Basic Law, Arts.48 and 55. The Chief Executive nominates persons for appointment as Principal Officials, and reports the same to the Central People's Government for appointment – Basic Law, Art.48(5).

[3] *Id.*, Art.43(2). [4] *Id.*, Art.44. [5] *Id.*, Art.47(1).

Executive shall be specified in the light of the actual situation in the Hong Kong Special Administrative Region and in accordance with the principle of gradual and orderly progress. The ultimate aim is the selection of the Chief Executive by universal suffrage upon nomination by a broadly representative nominating committee in accordance with democratic procedures. The specific method for selecting the Chief Executive is prescribed in Annex I: "Method for the Selection of the Chief Executive of the Hong Kong Special Administrative Region".[6]

Annex I of the Basic Law currently provides that the Chief Executive is elected by a twelve-hundred-member Election Committee[7] comprised of members from the following sectors:

Industrial, commercial and financial sectors	300
The professions	300
Labour, social services, religious and other sectors	300
Members of the Legislative Council, representatives of members of the District Councils, representatives of the Heung Yee Kuk, Hong Kong deputies to the National People's Congress, and representatives of Hong Kong members of the National Committee of the Chinese People's Political Consultative Conference	300

A candidate for the office of Chief Executive may be nominated by not fewer than 150 members of the Election Committee, and each member may nominate only one candidate.[8] The Election Committee votes by secret ballot on a one-person, one-vote basis, and the winning candidate is elected as Chief Executive and appointed by the Central People's Government for a period of five years.[9] A person may not serve for more than two consecutive terms as Chief Executive.[10]

The approach of the Central Authorities has been cautious in the inching of the system towards electing the Chief Executive by universal suffrage. The National People's Congress Standing Committee (NPCSC) decided that the Chief Executive "has to be a person who loves the country and loves Hong Kong ... a basic requirement of the policy of 'one country, two systems'", and

---

[6] *Id.*, Art.45.
[7] The Electoral Committee comprised 1,194 members in the most recent selection of the Chief Executive, in 2017.
[8] Basic Law, Annex I; Amendment to Annex I to the Basic Law of the Hong Kong Special Administrative Region of the People's Republic of China Concerning the Method for the Selection of the Chief Executive of the Hong Kong Special Administrative Region (approved at the Sixteenth Session of the Standing Committee of the Eleventh National People's Congress on 28 August 2010); Decision of the Standing Committee of the National People's Congress on Issues Relating to the Selection of the Chief Executive of the Hong Kong Special Administrative Region by Universal Suffrage and on the Method for Forming the Legislative Council of the Hong Kong Special Administrative Region in the Year 2016 (adopted at the Tenth Session of the Standing Committee of the Twelfth National People's Congress on 31 August 2014).
[9] Basic Law, Art.46 and Annex I.
[10] *Id.*, Art.46.

proposed that the Chief Executive be selected by a nominating committee similar in composition to the existing Election Committee. The nominating committee would then nominate two to three candidates for the office of Chief Executive, with each candidate being required to have the endorsement of more than half of all members of the nominating committee. The ordinary electorate would then have the right to vote on the nominated candidates.[11] Although described by the Standing Committee as a measure implementing universal suffrage, it was an unorthodox understanding of universal suffrage, and the reform proposal was rejected by the Legislative Council in June 2015. The most recent Chief Executive election, held in March 2017, was therefore operated using the same system as that for the immediately preceding Chief Executive election. Whilst the Chief Executive is therefore technically "elected", it is election by a remarkably small and select electorate, comprising less than approximately 0.017 per cent of the Hong Kong population. The Chief Executive may be impeached by the Legislative Council, with the final decision resting with the Central People's Government.[12]

Executive Council and Chief Executive-in-Council

The Executive Council is designated by the Basic Law as "an organ for assisting the Chief Executive in policy-making".[13] Its members are appointed by the Chief Executive "from among the principal officials of the executive authorities, members of the Legislative Council and public figures".[14] They

---

[11] Decision of the Standing Committee of the National People's Congress on Issues Relating to the Selection of the Chief Executive of the Hong Kong Special Administrative Region by Universal Suffrage and on the Method for Forming the Legislative Council of the Hong Kong Special Administrative Region in the Year 2016 (adopted at the Tenth Session of the Standing Committee of the Twelfth National People's Congress on 31 August 2014). It was explained that "patriots" must be the "mainstay" of the principle of "Hong Kong people administering Hong Kong", and that there were still a "small number of people in the Hong Kong community" who do not properly understand the policy of "one country, two systems" – Explanations on the Draft Decision of the Standing Committee of the National People's Congress on Issues Relating to the Selection of the Chief Executive of the Hong Kong Special Administrative Region by Universal Suffrage and on the Method for Forming the Legislative Council of the Hong Kong Special Administrative Region in the Year 2016 (given at the Tenth Session of the Standing Committee of the Twelfth National People's Congress on 27 August 2014).

[12] The process is described in the Basic Law, Art.73(9): "If a motion initiated jointly by one-fourth of all the members of the Legislative Council charges the Chief Executive with serious breach of law or dereliction of duty and if he or she refuses to resign, the Council may, after a passing a motion for investigation, give a mandate to the Chief Justice of the Court of Final Appeal to form and chair an independent investigation committee. The committee shall be responsible for carrying out the investigation and reporting its findings to the Council. If the committee considers the evidence sufficient to substantiate such charges, the Council may pass a motion of impeachment by a two-thirds majority of all its members and report it to the Central People's Government for decision."

[13] Basic Law, Art.54.

[14] Basic Law, Art.55(1). The principal officials are the Secretaries and Deputy Secretaries of Departments, Directors of Bureaux, Commissioner Against Corruption, Director of Audit,

must be Chinese citizens who are permanent residents of the HKSAR with no right of abode in a foreign country.[15] They are capable of removal by the Chief Executive, and their term in office shall not extend beyond the expiry of the term of office of the Chief Executive who appointed them.[16] There is no prohibition on a subsequent Chief Executive reappointing existing or previous members of the Executive Council, however. At the time of writing, there were sixteen official[17] and sixteen non-official members of the Executive Council, excluding the Chief Executive.

It is clear that the Executive Council is subordinate to the Chief Executive. She is appointed by the Basic Law to preside over the Executive Council, and though she must consult the Council before making "important" policy decisions, introducing bills to the Legislative Council, making subordinate legislation or dissolving the Legislative Council,[18] she is not bound to follow their views or recommendations. If she does not accept a majority opinion of the Executive Council, she is merely required to "put the specific reasons on record".[19] In any event, as individuals enjoy membership of the Executive Council at the pleasure of the Chief Executive, they are unlikely to be appointed if they are thought likely to be disloyal, and there is little incentive for them to express vigorous disagreement with her proposals. Nevertheless, the Chief Executive-in-Council is clearly a distinct legal entity from the Chief Executive and the terms should not be used synonymously. The Chief Executive is not required to consult the Executive Council on the appointment, removal and disciplining of officials and the adoption of measures in emergencies.[20] The Chief Executive, principal officials, members of the Executive Council, members of the Legislative Council and judges are required to swear to uphold the Basic Law and to swear allegiance to the HKSAR.[21]

The Chief Executive's grip over central government expanded in 2002 with the introduction by then Chief Executive Tung Chee Hwa of the Principal

---

Commissioner of Police, Director of Immigration and Commissioner of Customs and Excise. They are nominated by the Chief Executive and appointed by the Central People's Government – Basic Law, Art.48(5).

[15] Basic Law, Art.55(2). For appointment as a principal official, a person must additionally have ordinarily resided in Hong Kong for a continuous period of not less than fifteen years – id., Art.61.

[16] Id., Art.55(1).

[17] Namely, the Chief Secretary for Administration, Financial Secretary, Secretary for Justice, Secretary for the Environment, Secretary for Innovation and Technology, Secretary for Home Affairs, Secretary for Financial Services and the Treasury, Secretary for Labour and Welfare, Secretary for the Civil Service, Secretary for Security, Secretary for Transport and Housing, Secretary for Food and Health, Secretary for Commerce and Economic Development, Secretary for Development, Secretary for Education, and Secretary for Constitutional and Mainland Affairs.

[18] Basic Law, Arts.50(2) and 56.   [19] Id., Art.56(3).   [20] Basic Law, Art.56(2).

[21] Id., Art.104; Interpretation of Article 104 of the Basic Law of the Hong Kong Special Administrative Region of the People's Republic of China by the Standing Committee of the National People's Congress (adopted by the Standing Committee of the Twelfth National People's Congress at its Twenty-Fourth Session on 7 November 2016).

Officials Accountability System. This was marketed as increasing accountability, with principal officials no longer being high-ranking civil servants, but political appointees chosen by the Chief Executive for a fixed term not exceeding that of the Chief Executive by whom they were appointed. This consolidated the power of the Chief Executive by giving him more control over, and likely increased loyalty from, the principal officials. The Political Appointment System, introduced in 2008 under then Chief Executive Donald Tsang, expanded the previous system by adding two levels of political appointees below Secretaries of Departments, namely Under Secretaries and Political Assistants.[22]

Civil Service

The civil service is administered by the Civil Service Bureau, headed by the Secretary for the Civil Service. The core frameworks under which the Bureau administers the civil service are the Public Service (Administration) Order, the Public Service (Disciplinary) Regulation and the Civil Service Regulations,[23] with additional provisions regulating specific sectors of the civil service. A number of reforms have been implemented, including on pay and conditions, conduct and discipline, performance management, and training and development. It is said that the civil service establishment reduced from around 198,000 persons in January 2000 to around 161,000 in March 2007 through "process re-engineering, procedure streamlining and organisational review",[24] and that it currently employs approximately 156,000 people.[25]

The Chief Executive appoints and removes public officeholders "in accordance with legal procedures".[26] Those serving in government departments must be permanent residents of the HKSAR,[27] although British and foreign nationals previously serving in the public service in Hong Kong, or those holding permanent identity cards in the HKSAR, may also serve as public servants in government departments. However, only Chinese citizens who are permanent residents of the HKSAR with no right of abode in any foreign country may serve as the Secretaries or Deputy Secretaries of Departments, Directors of Bureaux, Commissioner Against Corruption, Director of Audit, Commissioner of Police, Director of Immigration or Commissioner of Customs and Excise.[28] It is provided by the Basic Law that public servants "must be dedicated to their

---

[22] See further Albert H. Y. Chen, "The Controversial Appointment of Under Secretaries and Political Assistants in 2008" (2008) 38(2) *Hong Kong Law Journal* 325.
[23] There are also Civil Service Bureau Circulars and Circular Memoranda. The Public Service Commission is a statutory body advising the Chief Executive on civil service appointments, promotions and discipline – Public Service Commission Ordinance (cap.93).
[24] www.csb.gov.hk/english/admin/csr/9.html.
[25] www.gov.hk/en/about/govdirectory/govstructure.htm.   [26] Basic Law, Art.48(7).
[27] *Id.*, Art.99(1).   [28] *Id.*, Art.101(1).

duties and be responsible to the Government of the Hong Kong Special Administrative Region".[29]

A Civil Service Code was issued by way of departmental circular in 2009. The Code provides that civil servants must uphold the core values of (i) commitment to the rule of law, (ii) honesty and integrity, (iii) objectivity and impartiality, (iv) political neutrality, (v) accountability for decisions and actions, and (vi) dedication, professionalism and diligence.[30] There is a complaint and redress mechanism for civil servants who feel that they have been directed to act in a way which is improper or in conflict with the core values of the Civil Service, in breach of any government regulations including the Civil Service Regulations and regulations governing the use of public money, would conflict with their role as civil servants, or may involve possible maladministration.[31] Procedures are set out in a departmental circular for civil servants who feel that they have been directed to act in a way that is unlawful.[32] There is a separate Code for Officials under the Political Appointment System.[33] Public servants are subject to official secrets restrictions.[34]

Local Government

District Councils

Hong Kong is divided into eighteen District Council areas.[35] The District Councils were established on 1 January 2000, replacing the provisional District Boards and the District Boards by which they were preceded. There are 458 members of District Councils, of whom 431 are elected[36] and 27 are *ex officio* (the Chairs of the Rural Committees).[37] The eligibility criteria for standing as a

---

[29] *Id.*, Art.99(2).
[30] Civil Service Code, p.2. The content of these core values is set out in the Code at pp.3–5.
[31] *Id.*, pp.11–13. [32] CSB Circular No.7/2012.
[33] Code for Officials under the Political Appointment System. This adopts (pp.6–7) the same core values as the Civil Service Code, with the exception that "objectivity and impartiality" in the Civil Service Code is replaced with "impartiality in the execution of public functions". In addition, after "dedication, professionalism and diligence" are inserted the words "in serving the community".
[34] Official Secrets Ordinance (cap.521).
[35] District Councils Ordinance (cap.547), ss.3–4 and Schs.1–2. There are four on Hong Kong Island (Central and Western District Council; Eastern District Council; Southern District Council; Wan Chai District Council), five in Kowloon (Kowloon City District Council; Kwun Tong District Council; Sham Shui Po District Council; Wong Tai Sin District Council; Yau Tsim Mong District Council), eight in the New Territories (Kwai Tsing District Council; North District Council; Sai Kung District Council; Sha Tin District Council; Tai Po District Council; Tsuen Wan District Council; Tuen Mun District Council; Yuen Long District Council), and one for the outlying islands (Islands District Council).
[36] District Councils Ordinance (cap.547), Sch.3, Part 1. [37] *Id.*, ss.9 and 17.

candidate in a district council election are less restrictive than those for election as Chief Executive. To be eligible as a candidate, an individual must be at least twenty-one years of age, an elector, not disqualified from voting or being nominated, and have ordinarily resided in Hong Kong for the three years immediately preceding the nomination.[38] An elected member holds office for a period of four years.[39] As for elections to the Legislative Council, the franchise in elections to District Councils is considerably more extensive than that in Chief Executive elections. Accordingly, District Councillors arguably have a stronger democratic mandate than the Chief Executive or the functional constituency members of the Legislative Council.[40] District Council elections are statutorily provided only to be capable of being called into question by way of election petition on designated grounds.[41] Each District Council has a Chairman and a Vice Chairman elected from among its members.[42]

The statutory functions of a District Council are both advisory and administrative. It shall advise the Government on matters in the District affecting the wellbeing of people, the provision and use of public facilities and services, the adequacy and priorities of Government programmes, and on the use of public funds allocated to the District for local public works and community activities.[43] In terms of administration, the District Council is to undertake environmental improvements, promote recreational and cultural activities, and undertake community activities within the District.[44] This includes participation in the management of public facilities such as libraries, swimming pools and beaches. District Councils may regulate their own procedure by standing order.[45] Each District has a District Officer, a representative of the HKSAR Government who acts as a link between local and central government, acts as a local coordinator in the provision of relief in emergencies, and oversees the operation of the District Administration Scheme. As an aspect of this scheme, the District-led Actions Scheme has been implemented in all districts, having been piloted in Sham Shui Po and Yuen Long in 2014–2015. This has provided an administrative framework for the implementation of a variety of projects including curbing shopfront extensions, enhancing local environmental hygiene and enhancing mosquito and pest control.[46]

---

[38] *Id.*, s.20. [39] *Id.*, s.22.
[40] With the exception of the five members of the District Council (Second) functional constituency – see Albert H. Y. Chen, "An Unexpected Breakthrough in Hong Kong's Constitutional Reform" (2010) 40 *Hong Kong Law Journal* 259.
[41] District Councils Ordinance (cap.547), s.49. However, see pp.95–97. [42] *Id.*, s.62.
[43] *Id.*, s.61(a). [44] *Id.*, s.61(b). [45] *Id.*, s.68.
[46] Home Affairs Bureau, *'Legislative Council Panel on Home Affairs, District-led Actions Scheme: Progress Report'* (December 2016), LC Paper No CB(2)401/16–17(06).

Rural Committees

There are twenty-seven Rural Committees in Hong Kong,[47] elections to which are held every four years.[48] Each Rural Committee comprises two types of village representative: Indigenous Inhabitant Representatives, who are elected by indigenous inhabitants of an Indigenous Village,[49] are accountable to that constituency and deal with affairs relating to the lawful traditional rights and interests of indigenous inhabitants; and Resident Representatives, who are elected by electors of an Existing Village,[50] are accountable to the residents of the village, and shall not deal with affairs relating to the lawful traditional rights and interests of indigenous inhabitants. There are also Kaifong Representatives, who are elected by, accountable to and represent the interests of electors of Cheung Chau and Peng Chau Market Towns.[51] Together, Indigenous Inhabitant Representatives, Resident Representatives and Kaifong Representatives are called "Rural Representatives", and each holds office for a period of four years.[52] Rural representative elections are statutorily provided only to be capable of being called into question by way of election petition on designated grounds.[53] The Chair of each Rural Committee is an *ex officio* member of the relevant District Council.[54]

Heung Yee Kuk

The Heung Yee Kuk[55] is a statutory body performing a representative and advisory role to the HKSAR Government on matters affecting the New Territories including social, economic and cultural issues.[56] It is typically viewed as a relatively powerful concentration of political authority in the New Territories, established in 1926 and given a statutory footing in 1959. The Heung Yee Kuk has a functional constituency member in the Legislative Council, and occupies twenty-six seats on the Chief Executive Election Committee.

The organisation comprises a Chairman, two Vice Chairmen and a Full Council, within which there is an Executive Committee. The Chairman and Vice Chairmen are elected by the Full Council.[57] The Full Council consists of

---

[47] Cheung Chau; Lamma Island (North); Lamma Island (South); Mui Wo; Peng Chau; South Lantau; Tai O; Tung Chung; Tsing Yi; Fanling District; Sha Tau Kok District; Sheung Shui District; Ta Kwu Ling District; Hang Hau; Sai Kung; Sha Tin; Sai Kung North; Tai Po; Ma Wan; Tsuen Wan; Tuen Mun; Ha Tsuen; Kam Tin; Pat Heung; Ping Shan; San Tin and Shap Pat Heung.
[48] Rural Representative Election Ordinance (cap.576), s.20.   [49] *Id.*, s.2 and Sch.2.
[50] *Id.*, s.2 and Sch.1.   [51] *Id.*, s.2 and Sch.3A.   [52] *Id.*, s.7.
[53] *Id.*, s.39; Rural Representative (Election Petition) Rules (cap.576B). However, see pp.95–97.
[54] District Councils Ordinance (cap.547), ss.9 and 17.
[55] The name literally means "rural council".
[56] Heung Yee Kuk Ordinance (cap.1097), s.9. For historical and political background on the New Territories, see James L. Watson, 'Rural Society: Hong Kong's New Territories' (1983) 95 *China Quarterly* 480.
[57] Heung Yee Kuk Ordinance (cap.1097), s.2(2).

Ex Officio Councillors (the Chairs and Vice Chairs of Rural Committees, and New Territories Justices of the Peace), Special Councillors (not exceeding twenty-one in number, of which no more than seven shall be elected by Ex Officio Councillors of each of the three districts of Tai Po, Yuen Long and Southern District), and Co-opted Councillors (not exceeding fifteen in number).[58] The Executive Committee comprises Ex Officio Members (the Chairs of Rural Committees, and New Territories Justices of the Peace), Ordinary Members (not exceeding fifteen in number, elected by the Full Council) and all of the Co-opted Councillors.[59]

Mainland Affairs in Hong Kong

There are three major Mainland governmental presences of note in Hong Kong. The Liaison Office of the Central People's Government in the HKSAR is the official representative of the Central People's Government in the territory. The predecessor to the Office was the Hong Kong branch of the Xinhua News Agency, which served as an unofficial representative of the PRC in Hong Kong and was more than a mere news agency. It is unclear precisely what role the Office plays in the domestic affairs of Hong Kong. According to the Office's official website (in Chinese only), its functions are to:

1. Communicate with the Office of the Commissioner of the Ministry of Foreign Affairs of the PRC in the HKSAR and the Hong Kong Garrison of the People's Liberation Army.
2. Communicate with and assist relevant Mainland authorities in the management of Mainland-funded enterprises in Hong Kong.
3. Promote exchange and cooperation between Hong Kong and the Mainland in the areas of the economy, education, science, culture and sports. Communicate with Hong Kong people from all walks of life and enhance exchange between the Mainland and Hong Kong. Reflect Hong Kong residents' views on the Mainland.
4. Handle matters relating to Taiwan.
5. Conduct other tasks assigned by the Central People's Government.[60]

The Office has been entangled in controversy in its role in Hong Kong and its relationship with the HKSAR Government. Suspicions that the Office operated as a second or shadow government in Hong Kong were raised by the Director of the Office's Research Department, Cao Erbao, who wrote in a Communist Party of China newspaper that the Handover represented a shift from a single governing team (the colonial British government in Hong Kong) to two governing teams, namely the HKSAR Government and "the team of cadres of Central and Mainland Authorities carrying out Hong Kong work",

[58] *Id.*, s.3. [59] *Id.*, s.4. [60] www.locpg.hk/zjzlb/2014-01/04/c_125957082.htm

though adding that the Central and Mainland Authorities do not interfere in the internal affairs of the HKSAR.[61] This is just one of a number of such suspicions.[62] The issue is particularly sensitive as the Basic Law states that:

> No department of the Central People's Government and no province, autonomous region, or municipality directly under the Central Government may interfere in the affairs which the Hong Kong Special Administrative Region administers on its own in accordance with this Law.[63]

The second major Mainland governmental presence is the Office of the Commissioner of the Ministry of Foreign Affairs of the PRC in the HKSAR, which deals with foreign affairs in Hong Kong.[64] Its main functions are to coordinate the activities of international organisations in Hong Kong, handle international conventions and bilateral agreements relating to Hong Kong, deal with consular matters and process applications from foreign states for their aircraft and warships to access Hong Kong.[65]

The third major presence is the Hong Kong Garrison of the People's Liberation Army (PLA), in line with the Basic Law's provision that the Central People's Government shall be responsible for the defence of the HKSAR.[66] The Garrison's functions are to prepare against and resist aggression and safeguard the security of the HKSAR, carry out defence duties, administer military facilities and handle foreign-related military affairs.[67] It is further provided that:

> Military forces stationed by the Central People's Government in the Hong Kong Special Administrative Region for defence shall not interfere in the local affairs of the Region. The Government of the Hong Kong Special Administrative Region may, when necessary, ask the Central People's Government for assistance from the garrison in the maintenance of public order and in disaster relief. In addition to abiding by national laws, members of the garrison shall abide by the laws of the Hong Kong Special Administrative Region.[68]

---

[61] Cao Erbao *"Yiguo liangzhi tiaojianxia Xianggang de guanzhi Liliang"* ('Governing Forces of Hong Kong under "One Country, Two Systems"'), Xuexi shibao (Study Times), 28 January 2008.
[62] See, for example, Constitutional and Mainland Affairs Bureau, *"Role of Hong Kong deputies to the National People's Congress and Hong Kong members of the National Committee of the Chinese People's Political Consultative Conference: Position of the HKSAR Government"*, LC Paper No CB(2)1311/08–09(03).
[63] Basic Law, Art.22(1).   [64] Id., Art.13.
[65] www.fmcoprc.gov.hk/eng/zjgs/zygy/t944912.htm.   [66] Basic Law, Art.14.
[67] Law of the People's Republic of China on Garrisoning the Hong Kong Special Administrative Region (adopted at the twenty-third meeting of the Standing Committee of the Eighth National People's Congress on 30 December 1996; promulgated by the President of the PRC on 30 December 1996), Art.5.
[68] Basic Law, Art.14; see also Law of the People's Republic of China on Garrisoning the Hong Kong Special Administrative Region (adopted at the twenty-third meeting of the Standing Committee of the Eighth National People's Congress on 30 December 1996; promulgated by the President of the PRC on 30 December 1996), Art.9.

The Central People's Government is responsible for the expenditure of the Garrison,[69] which is under the direct control of the Central Military Commission,[70] and administratively associated with the PLA Southern Theater Command (formerly the Guangzhou Military Region). The HKSAR Government is under a duty to support the Garrison in its performance of defence functions and responsibilities,[71] consult the Garrison when formulating any policy or drafting any legislation which concerns the Garrison,[72] assist in protecting and maintaining the security of military facilities,[73] and seek the prior approval (which may be refused) of the Central People's Government where it aims to take land used for military purposes into public use.[74]

Hong Kong Affairs in the Mainland

Though Hong Kong is part of the PRC, due to its high degree of autonomy there are cross-border institutions which resemble consulates and economic, social and cultural exchange institutions. The HKSAR Government operates a small network of Mainland Offices. These are the Beijing Office of the HKSAR Government,[75] and Hong Kong Economic and Trade Offices in Shanghai, Guangdong, Chengdu and Wuhan. There is also a network of liaison units under the Mainland Offices, namely in Liaoning, Tianjin, Shenzhen, Fujian, Chongqing, Shandong, Hunan and Henan. The Mainland Offices are described by the Constitutional and Mainland Affairs Bureau as having the functions of strengthening communication and liaison between Hong Kong and the mainland, including enhancing government-to-government cooperation, comprehensively enhancing and promoting Hong Kong's trade and commercial relations with Mainland provinces and municipalities, fostering exchange and cooperation between Hong Kong and the Mainland, facilitating investment, promoting Hong Kong and providing support to Hong Kong people and enterprises in the Mainland.[76] There are also Immigration Divisions in the Beijing, Guangdong, Shanghai and Chengdu offices to provide assistance to Hong Kong residents such as where a resident in the Mainland

---

[69] Basic Law, Art.14.
[70] Law of the People's Republic of China on Garrisoning the Hong Kong Special Administrative Region (adopted at the twenty-third meeting of the Standing Committee of the Eighth National People's Congress on 30 December 1996; promulgated by the President of the PRC on 30 December 1996), Art.3. Before the Handover, the commander-in-chief was the Governor, as representative of the UK Crown, acting on the advice of the Commander British Forces in Hong Kong.
[71] Law of the People's Republic of China on Garrisoning the Hong Kong Special Administrative Region (adopted at the twenty-third meeting of the Standing Committee of the Eighth National People's Congress on 30 December 1996; promulgated by the President of the PRC on 30 December 1996), Art.10(1).
[72] Id., Art.10(2).   [73] Id., Art.12.   [74] Id., Art.13.
[75] Which is provided for by the Basic Law, Art.22(5).
[76] www.cmab.gov.hk/en/issues/new_official.htm

loses their identity document, requires a replacement HKSAR passport, is involved in an accident, is in need of financial assistance, is detained or arrested, or requires legal assistance. They serve, in other words, the functions of a consulate.

There is also a Hong Kong Economic, Trade and Cultural Office in Taiwan, and Hong Kong Economic and Trade Offices in Singapore, Jakarta, Tokyo, Sydney, London, Brussels, Geneva, Berlin, New York, Washington, San Francisco and Toronto. However, these offices provide no immigration or consular assistance, which is instead rendered by PRC embassies and consulates. The paradox is therefore that some of the HKSAR Government's Mainland Offices provide immigration and consular assistance in the Mainland, that is to say within the same state, but its foreign offices do not provide such assistance.

Licensing, Permits and Certification

Hong Kong operates an extensive system of licenses, permits and certifications, encountered in a wide range of areas including business, industry, transport, health and the environment. The breadth of the licensing, permit and certification system is important for recognising the extent to which the tentacles of regulation and administration reach into everyday life.

A licence is required to import or export certain articles including pesticides, pharmaceutical products, medicines, Chinese herbal medicines, rough diamonds, frozen or chilled meat, and baby milk powdered formula.[77] Certification and permission requirements are in place for the import of certain meat, meat products, poultry and eggs.[78] It is necessary to hold a licence to import, export, possess or control a specimen of designated species.[79] There are permits for the importation into Hong Kong of a human corpse, infectious agent or infected human tissue, animal tissue, blood and other substances.[80] A permit is required to import or remove sand from one part of Hong Kong to another,[81] and a person must hold a carriage licence to import or export vehicles, vehicle parts or outboard engines of a prescribed specification.[82] There are licences for the import and export of a range of strategic commodities including munitions, nuclear materials, facilities and equipment, certain electronic components, sensor and laser systems, designated marine equipment, and specified aerospace and propulsion systems, equipment and components.[83] There are also licences for the importation of radioactive substances, articles containing

---

[77] Import and Export Ordinance (cap.60), ss.6C–6D; Import and Export (General) Regulations (cap.60A), ss.3–4 and Schs.1–2.
[78] Imported Game, Meat, Poultry and Eggs Regulations (cap.132AK).
[79] Protection of Endangered Species of Animals and Plants Ordinance (cap.586), s.23.
[80] Prevention and Control of Disease Regulation (cap.599A), s.14.
[81] Sand Ordinance (cap.147), s.3.
[82] Import and Export (Carriage of Articles) Regulations (cap.60I).
[83] Import and Export (Strategic Commodities) Regulations (cap.60G).

radioactive substances or irradiating apparatus,[84] and for the import and export of dangerous drugs.[85]

In the field of environmental regulation, there is a system of licensing for a number of processes including certain works involving cement, asbestos, petroleum, glass or paint.[86] There is a permit for the conduct of open burning activity.[87] The owner, master or agent of a vessel may apply for an exemption from a prohibition on the use of non-compliant fuel for combustion purposes.[88] An environmental permit must be obtained to have constructed, construct or operate a diverse array of facilities, including roads, helipads, container terminals, reclamation works, typhoon shelters, dredging operations, submarine sewage pipelines, industrial estates, fuel storage facilities, golf courses and large open air concert venues; and for the decommissioning of the likes of airports, oil refineries, energy plants, radioactive waste facilities, bulk chemical storage facilities and shipbuilding facilities.[89] There is a system of construction and percussive piling noise permits.[90] A permit is required to dump at sea or under the seabed, scuttle a vessel, aircraft or marine structure, and related operations.[91] A permit is required to import or export specified waste,[92] with licences required for waste collection and disposal,[93] and in relation to certain discharges and deposits.[94] A permit scheme operates in relation to the manufacture, import and export of certain chemicals.[95]

One of the most commonly encountered licences is a vehicle driving licence.[96] However, there is a plethora of other transportation licences including a Passenger Service Licence for operating a public bus, private bus, public light bus, private light bus or school private light bus,[97] or to operate a taxi[98] or hire car, including hotel, tour, airport, school and private hire car services.[99] Vessels are subject to a certification and licensing regime.[100] There is a range of air transport licences,[101] such as several categories of Flight Crew Licence including a private pilot's licence, commercial pilot's licence and

[84] Import (Radiation) (Prohibition) Regulations (cap.60K).
[85] Dangerous Drugs Ordinance (cap.134), ss.10–21.
[86] Air Pollution Control Ordinance (cap.311); Air Pollution Control (Specified Processes) Regulations (cap.311F).
[87] Air Pollution Control (Open Burning) Regulation (cap.311O), s.6.
[88] Air Pollution Control (Ocean Going Vessels) (Fuel at Berth) Regulation (cap.311AA), ss.6 and 7.
[89] Environmental Impact Assessment Ordinance (cap.499), s.10 and Sch.2.
[90] Noise Control Ordinance (cap.400), s.8.   [91] Dumping at Sea Ordinance (cap.466), s.8.
[92] Waste Disposal Ordinance (cap.354), ss.20A–20B.   [93] Id., s.21.
[94] Water Pollution Control Ordinance (cap.358), ss.19–20.
[95] Hazardous Chemicals Control Ordinance (cap.595), s.10.
[96] Road Traffic (Driving Licences) Regulations (cap.374B).
[97] Road Traffic (Public Service Vehicles) Regulations (cap.374D), ss.4–12.
[98] Road Traffic (Registration and Licensing of Vehicles) Regulations (cap.374E), ss.26–29.
[99] Road Traffic (Public Service Vehicles) Regulations (cap.374D), ss.13–27.
[100] Merchant Shipping (Local Vessels) Ordinance (cap.548), ss.10–15A; Merchant Shipping (Local Vessels) (Certification and Licensing) Regulation (cap.548D), ss.4–35.
[101] Air Transport (Licensing of Air Services) Regulations (cap.448A).

airline transport pilot's licence for each of aeroplanes, helicopters, gyroplanes, balloons, airships and gliders.[102] There is an Air Operators' Certificate,[103] Aircraft Maintenance Licence[104] and Certificate of Airworthiness.[105] There is also an aerodrome licence,[106] and air traffic controllers are licensed.[107]

Licences are required to operate a wide range of premises and activities. A licence is required to operate certain food businesses including a food factory, restaurant, factory canteen, *siu mei* or *lo mei* shop, or cold store.[108] Milk factories are licensed;[109] there is a hawker licence[110] and a liquor licence.[111] The operation of an amusement game centre requires a licence,[112] as does the operation of a karaoke establishment,[113] billiard establishment, public bowling alley, public skating rink,[114] bathhouse[115] or swimming pool.[116] There are licences to operate a dancing school or public dance hall or to trade as a hawker of tobacco, cigars or cigarettes.[117] Certifications of exemption and compliance exist in relation to the operation of a social or recreational clubhouse.[118] Licences and certifications are required to operate various kinds of accommodation, from hotels and guesthouses,[119] to bedspace apartments[120] and residential care homes.[121] There are business registration frameworks,[122] both in general, and in relation to specific industries such as the trade of textiles[123] and rough diamonds.[124]

The Communications Authority operates a system of telecommunications licences including aeronautical and aircraft station licences, broadcasting licences, carrier licences, closed circuit television licences, maritime radio licences, private mobile radio licences, satellite master antenna television licences and taxi radiocommunications service licences.[125] Money service

---

[102] Air Navigation (Hong Kong) Order (cap.448C), s.20 and Sch.9.   [103] *Id.*, s.6.
[104] *Id.*, s.12.   [105] *Id.*, s.8.   [106] *Id.*, s.73.
[107] *Id.*, s.65. The Government is required to provide conditions and take measures for the maintenance of the status of Hong Kong as a centre of international and regional aviation – Basic Law, Art.128.
[108] Food Business Regulation (cap.132X), ss.31–34F.   [109] Milk Regulation (cap.132AQ).
[110] Hawker Regulation (cap.132AI).
[111] Dutiable Commodities Ordinance (cap.109), ss.6–9; Dutiable Commodities Regulations (cap.109A), ss.22–27A; Dutiable Commodities (Liquor) Regulations (cap.109B).
[112] Amusement Game Centres Ordinance (cap.435), ss.4–10.
[113] Karaoke Establishment Licence; Karaoke Establishments Ordinance (cap.573), ss.4–13; Karaoke Establishments (Licensing) Regulation (cap.573A).
[114] Public Health and Municipal Services Ordinance (cap.132), ss.92A–92E and Sch.11.
[115] Commercial Bathhouses Regulation (cap.132I).
[116] Swimming Pools Regulation (cap.132CA).
[117] Miscellaneous Licences Ordinance (cap.114).
[118] Clubs (Safety of Premises) Ordinance (cap.376), ss.4–12.
[119] Hotel and Guesthouse Accommodation Ordinance (cap.349), ss.5–12.
[120] Bedspace Apartments Ordinance (cap.447), ss.4–17.
[121] Residential Care Homes (Elderly Persons) Ordinance (cap.459).
[122] Business Registration Ordinance (cap.310); Business Registration Regulations (cap.310A).
[123] Import and Export (General) Regulations (cap.60A), s.5A.   [124] *Id.*, s.6DB.
[125] Telecommunications Ordinance (cap.106), s.7; and see the Register of Licences and General Conditions published in the Gazette by the Telecommunications Authority pursuant to the Telecommunications Ordinance (cap.106), s.7(9).

operators, namely persons operating a money changing service or remittance service, are subject to licensing requirements.[126] There are games, competitions and lotteries licences, and the licensing of premises for the playing therein of *mahjong* or *tin kau*.[127] A licence is needed to establish or continue an offensive trade,[128] as is operation as an undertaker of burials,[129] or to carry on the business of a funeral parlour.[130] There is a registration system for contractors, engineers and workers to carry out works on lifts and escalators.[131] There are also myriad permission and inspection systems in place, from the requirement that permission be obtained to operate or play a musical instrument or sing on a bathing beach,[132] and the power to impose restrictions or prohibition on the flying of kites, model aircraft, balloons and other devices in any pleasure ground,[133] to the inspection of bedspace apartments[134] and residential care homes.[135] There is, of course, a system of regulation on town and urban planning.[136]

Not only does this overview indicate the extent to which regulation pervades ordinary and commercial life,[137] it exhibits numerous areas in which powers can be abused or misused by decision makers. Indeed, with each licensing regime comes opportunities for the violation of grounds of judicial review: the form and extent of discretion conferred upon the licensing authority; in which circumstances and on what basis a licence can be granted, extended, renewed, refused, revoked, suspended, varied, cancelled, subject to conditions, modified, transferred, purchased or sold; what policies may guide such licensing decisions and how they may do so; opportunities for the generation and breach of legitimate expectations; opportunities for the commission of errors of fact and errors of law; whether and in what circumstances there is a right of appeal against the licensing authority; what ancillary powers the licensing authority might have; the scope for abuse or misuse of power; procedures from which there can be deliberate or inadvertent departure or which may go unimplemented; fairness and natural justice requirements which must be observed; and so on. For every power conferred on a public decision maker, there is a corresponding opportunity to go wrong in public law.

---

[126] Anti-Money Laundering and Counter-Terrorist Financing (Financial Institutions) Ordinance (cap.615), s.29.
[127] Gambling Ordinance (cap.148), s.22.   [128] Offensive Trades Regulation (cap.132AX).
[129] Public Health and Municipal Services Ordinance (cap.132), s.92AB and Sch.11A.
[130] Funeral Parlours Regulation (cap.132AD).   [131] Lifts and Escalators Ordinance (cap.618).
[132] Bathing Beaches Regulation (cap.132E), s.12.
[133] Pleasure Grounds Regulation (cap.132BC), s.17.
[134] Bedspace Apartments Ordinance (cap.447), s.20.
[135] Residential Care Homes (Elderly Persons) Ordinance (cap.459), s.18.
[136] Principal statutes include the Buildings Ordinance (cap.123); Town Planning Ordinance (cap.131); and Urban Renewal Authority Ordinance (cap.563).
[137] It is often an offence to participate or engage in a regulated activity without the relevant licence, permit or certification.

Public Procurement and Tendering

Hong Kong has been a signatory to the World Trade Organisation Agreement on Government Procurement (WTO GPA) since 20 May 1997. WTO GPA requirements apply to all government bureaux and departments for contracts with a value of not less than 130,000 XDR for the procurement of goods and specified services, and not less than 5,000,000 XDR for construction services.[138] They also apply to non-governmental public bodies such as the Airport Authority, Hospital Authority, Housing Authority, Housing Department and MTR Corporation Ltd for contracts with a value of not less than 400,000 XDR for procurement of goods and specified services, and 5,000,000 XDR for construction services.[139] There are also trade agreements with New Zealand[140] and Chile[141] which cover government procurement.[142]

The procurement process is regulated by the Stores and Procurement Regulations issued by the Financial Secretary.[143] Most but not all tendering is done by way of open and competitive tendering procedures where Government procurement exceeds HK$1.43 million for goods and services, or HK$7 million for construction and engineering services, to which separate procedures apply.[144] Tender notices and prequalification of tenderers for procurement covered by the WTO GPA must be published in the Gazette.[145] Where procurement is not covered by the WTO GPA, publication in the Gazette is optional and it is sufficient to publish the tender notice on the internet.[146] Different requirements apply to selective tendering, single and restricted tendering, and prequalified tendering.[147] Tenders are evaluated by the procuring entity which then submits its tender recommendations to the appropriate tender board or committee, each of which comprises not less than three persons.[148] These are:

- *Central Tender Board*: considers tenders which exceed the limits for tenders which may be considered by subsidiary tender boards and committees; at the

---

[138] XDR (Special Drawing Rights) is the unit of account for the International Monetary Fund (IMF). At the time of writing, 1 XDR was equivalent to 11.13 HKD.
[139] Financial Services and the Treasury Bureau, *"WTO Agreement on Government Procurement"* (10 December 2014), www.fstb.gov.hk/tb/en/guide-to-procurement.htm.
[140] Hong Kong, China – New Zealand Closer Economic Partnership Agreement (HKC/NZ CEPA) (29 March 2010, effective 1 January 2011).
[141] Free Trade Agreement between Hong Kong, China and Chile (HKC/CL FTA) (7 September 2012, effective 9 October 2014).
[142] See Financial Services and the Treasury Bureau, *"WTO Agreement on Government Procurement"* (10 December 2014), www.fstb.gov.hk/tb/en/guide-to-procurement.htm.
[143] Public Finance Ordinance (cap.2), s.11(1).
[144] Stores and Procurement Regulations, para.300(a)(i).   [145] *Id.*, para.340(c).
[146] *Id.*, para.340(d).   [147] *Id.*, paras.320, 325 and 330.   [148] *Id.*, para.310(a).

time of writing, this was HK$15 million for goods and general services, and HK$100 million for construction services;[149]
- *Government Logistics Department Tender Board*: considers tenders not exceeding a value of HK$15 million, except tenders considered by the Public Works Tender Board or Departmental Tender Committees;[150]
- *Public Works Tender Board*: considers tenders for works and related contracts with a value not exceeding HK$100 million;[151] and
- *Departmental Tender Committees*: considers tenders (excluding tenders for construction or engineering services) with a value not exceeding HK$5 million.[152]

Procurement and tendering covers a wide range of commodities and services including stores and supplies, public works, vehicles, transportation services, information technology equipment and services, property management services, social and community services, waste management services and educational services. Government procurement is said to be based on the principles of open and fair competition, value for money, transparency in procedure and practice, and public accountability.[153]

---

[149] Membership comprises: the Permanent Secretary for Financial Services and the Treasury (chair); the Director of Government Logistics; the Permanent Secretary for Development (Works) or a representative; a legal adviser at a rank not lower than Deputy Principal Government Counsel; and the Deputy Secretary for Financial Services and the Treasury. Members are appointed by the Financial Secretary.

[150] Membership comprises: the Director of Government Logistics (chair); the Deputy Director of Government Logistics; the Controller (Supplies Management), Government Logistics Department; and the Senior Treasury Accountant, Government Logistics Department. Members are appointed by the Secretary for Financial Services and the Treasury under authority delegated by the Financial Secretary.

[151] Membership comprises: the Deputy Director of Architectural Services (chair); the Government Quantity Surveyor; and a Government Engineer from the Highways Department, Civil Engineering and Development Department, or Drainage Services Department, on a rotational basis. Members are appointed by the Secretary for Financial Services and the Treasury under authority delegated by the Financial Secretary.

[152] Chaired by a directorate officer not lower than D2 rank. www.fstb.gov.hk/tb/en/guide-to-procurement.htm.

[153] Works Bureau, *"The Government of the HKSAR Tendering System for Public Works Contracts"* (December 1999) (LC Paper No CB(1) 586/99–00(02)).

3

The Constitutional Foundation of Judicial Review in Hong Kong

Constitutional Foundation under UK Sovereignty

During the First Opium War, in 1841, British forces occupied Hong Kong Island. Two proclamations were made, dated 1 and 2 February 1841, respectively, asserting UK sovereignty over Hong Kong Island. Under the Treaty of Nanking (1842), Hong Kong Island was ceded "in perpetuity" from the Emperor of China to the British Crown.[1] The Second Opium War, lasting from 1856 to 1860, culminated in the signing of the Convention of Peking, ceding Kowloon and Stonecutters Island to the British Crown as a "dependency of Her Britannic Majesty's Colony of Hongkong".[2] A proclamation and an Order-in-Council were both issued in 1861 by which Kowloon was declared to be part of the colony of Hong Kong.

The New Territories came under the control of the United Kingdom in a different manner. Whereas Hong Kong Island, Kowloon and Stonecutters Island were ceded, the New Territories were leased to the UK. This occurred by way of the Second Convention of Peking, signed in 1898.[3] The lease was for a period of ninety-nine years, unwittingly beginning the countdown to the resumption of Chinese sovereignty over Hong Kong. Even though the New Territories were subject to a lease rather than cession, they were declared by the New Territories Order-in-Council to be "part and parcel of Her Majesty's Colony of Hongkong in like manner and for all intents and purposes as if they had originally formed part of the said colony".

The PRC maintained that the Treaty of Nanking and the Convention of Peking were unequal treaties, in the sense that China (then under the Qing dynasty) was forced against its will to sign these treaties in a period described as China's "century of humiliation". It therefore disputed the legitimacy of the sovereign claims asserted by the British Crown over the various parts of Hong Kong. Nevertheless, the assertion of UK sovereignty over Hong Kong was a practical reality even if its legitimacy was disputed. The Letters Patent and

---

[1] Treaty of Nanking, 1842 (ratifications exchanged at Hong Kong, 26 June 1843).
[2] Convention of Peking, 1860 (signed at Beijing, 24 October 1860).
[3] Convention for the Extension of Hongkong, 1898 (signed at Beijing, 9 June 1898).

Royal Instructions, each issued a number of times, provided a local constitutional framework by which the law and legal order were framed. It was a broadly framed constitutional arrangement, characteristic of colonial constitutions,[4] with the British monarch at its head. With the Governor as a servant of the British Crown,[5] but very much the local centre of political and executive authority, a law and legal system burgeoned which bore strong resemblance to that of England and Wales. This was seen not only in the wholesale, statutory importation of English law into Hong Kong,[6] but a general modelling on English law and legal tradition, including strong deference to English jurisprudence.

The story of Hong Kong's transition from British Crown colony[7] to PRC Special Administrative Region is a familiar one. Regional and global political realities led to the UK and PRC Governments signing the Sino-British Joint Declaration on 19 December 1984, setting out the basic policies by which Hong Kong would be returned to Chinese sovereignty. A new constitutional text – the Basic Law – was drafted, adopted by the Seventh National People's Congress and promulgated by the President of the PRC on 4 April 1990. Finally, at midnight on 1 July 1997, ninety-nine years after the New Territories were leased to the UK, sovereignty over Hong Kong was transferred to the PRC, and Hong Kong became a Special Administrative Region of the PRC.[8]

The British colonial period has nevertheless left a lasting legacy; it has shaped the society that Hong Kong is today, and its laws and legal system are no exception in that regard. Administrative law in Hong Kong bears remarkable similarity to its counterpart in the UK (particularly England and Wales), and though there are questions of divergence, it is clear that, for better or worse, the English common law tradition was exported to Hong Kong and has in large part remained. Even though Hong Kong is now indisputably a Special Administrative Region under the sovereignty of the PRC, there is a great deal of legal, institutional and cultural continuity with pre-Handover Hong Kong – even constitutional continuity. As far as judicial review and the wider common law are concerned, the Handover was marked not only by change, but also by continuity.

---

[4] Yash Ghai, "The Past and the Future of Hong Kong's Constitution" (1991) 128 *China Quarterly* 794, pp.799–800.

[5] *Attorney-General v Chiu Tat-Cheong* (1992) 2 HKLR 84 (CA), p.116.

[6] Supreme Court Ordinance (No 15 of 1844), s.3. This approach was partially relaxed by the Supreme Court Ordinance (No 3 of 1873).

[7] After the British Nationality Act 1981 became effective, British Crown colonies were known as British Dependent Territories.

[8] This is a heavily abbreviated account of the constitutional history of Hong Kong. See, for more depth, G. B. Endacott, *Government and People in Hong Kong 1841–1962: A Constitutional History* (Hong Kong University Press, 1964); Peter Wesley-Smith, *Unequal Treaty 1898–1997: China, Great Britain, and Hong Kong's New Territories* (Oxford University Press, 1998); and Yash Ghai, *Hong Kong's New Constitutional Order: The Resumption of Chinese Sovereignty and the Basic Law* (2nd edn) (Hong Kong University Press, 1999).

Constitutional Foundation under PRC Sovereignty

PRC Constitution and the Basic Law

When tracing the formal constitutional foundation of judicial review under PRC sovereignty, the starting point is the PRC Constitution. Article 31 of the PRC Constitution provides for the establishment of special administrative regions:

> The State may establish special administrative regions when necessary. The systems to be instituted in special administrative regions shall be prescribed by law enacted by the National People's Congress in light of specific conditions.[9]

This formally provides the legal and constitutional basis for the establishment of the HKSAR.[10] The Basic Law was adopted by the Seventh National People's Congress (NPC) on 4 April 1990, taking effect on 1 July 1997.

The Basic Law has two incarnations, the first of which is that of an ordinary legislative act passed by the NPC. In this incarnation, the Basic Law can be modified or repealed by a legislative act of the NPC. However, at the SAR level, the Basic Law is a constitutional act which is putatively the most supreme expression of law in the jurisdiction (other than the PRC Constitution). It serves as a constitutional text by organising and delineating the institutions of state, and formally regulating the status of all other laws in the jurisdiction including legislation, common law and customary law. It also upholds the idea of "one country, two systems" and provides for significant autonomy for the HKSAR from the rest of the PRC for a period of fifty years from its becoming effective.[11]

Though the dual interpretations of the Basic Law as a constitutional and a legislative act are not mutually exclusive, they are clearly in tension. They also point to a fragility in the status of the Basic Law which does not provide the most solid constitutional foundation in which to ground judicial review. Moreover, whilst some provisions of the Basic Law may appear to provide constitutional support for judicial review, there is no explicit provision for judicial review in the Basic Law. Article 8 provides that:

> The laws previously in force in Hong Kong, that is, the common law, rules of equity, ordinances, subordinate legislation and customary law shall be maintained, except for any that contravene this Law, and subject to any amendment by the legislature of the Hong Kong Special Administrative Region.

---

[9] PRC Constitution, Art.31. The Chinese text is as follows: "国家在必要时得设立特别行政区 。在特别行政区内实行的制度按照具体情况由全国人民代表大会以法律规定".
[10] In addition to the Macau SAR.
[11] Basic Law, Arts.2 and 5. Similar guarantees appear in the Joint Declaration of the Government of the United Kingdom of Great Britain and Northern Ireland and the Government of the People's Republic of China on the Question of Hong Kong (19 December 1984).

This may be said to provide constitutional support for judicial review inasmuch as judicial review is an aspect of the common law. However, Article 8 does not specifically relate to judicial review, and if this provision is relied upon as providing the constitutional foundation of judicial review, it is liable to be undermined should Article 8 be amended or repealed. Similarly, Article 35(2) of the Basic Law might also be said to provide constitutional support for judicial review:

> Hong Kong residents shall have the right to institute legal proceedings in the courts against the acts of the executive authorities and their personnel.

Though this might include judicial review, its purview appears wider and would presumably include other proceedings against executive bodies including those in contract, tort, unjust enrichment and enforcement of property rights. It also does not address the possibility of judicial review against non-executive bodies. It is of course more preferable than not for constitutional protection for judicial review to be capable of being found in the Basic Law. However, the reality is that an attempt to source the constitutional foundation for judicial review from the Basic Law is an oblique exercise and an attempt to divine meaning from an ambiguous text.

Judicial Review and "One Country, Two Systems"

The principle of "one country, two systems" is attributed to Deng Xiaoping, leader of the PRC from 1978 to 1989. It purports to describe the constitutional relationship between the PRC and the Hong Kong SAR (and also between the PRC and the Macau SAR), simultaneously providing for the unity and integrity of the sovereign space (one country) and diversity in legal, political and social systems (two systems). Though the term did not feature in the Sino-British Joint Declaration, it appears in the preamble to the Basic Law. It was a way of constitutionally integrating Hong Kong into the PRC without severely disrupting, and by allowing for continuity in, the law, legal system, governance, institutions and way of life in Hong Kong.

In the context of judicial review (or any litigation), the principle means that one cannot appeal beyond the Court of Final Appeal. However, as far as interpretation of the Basic Law is concerned, the courts must seek an interpretation of the relevant provisions from the NPCSC where the provisions concern affairs which are the responsibility of the Central People's Government or which concern the relationship between the Central Authorities and the SAR. There is no requirement to seek an interpretation from the NPCSC where the provisions concern affairs which are within the limits of the autonomy of the SAR.[12] Interpretations can also be sought outside litigation,

---

[12] Basic Law, Art.158.

and only one of the five interpretations issued to date was sought on the request of the Court of Final Appeal.[13] Though it is provided that "judgments previously rendered shall not be affected",[14] it is possible for the HKSAR Government to request an interpretation, or the NPCSC to issue an interpretation on its own initiative, when litigation is contemplated or in motion but on which judgment has not yet been rendered.[15] This occurred during the oath-taking controversy in November 2016 in relation to Sixtus Leung Chung Hang and Yau Wai Ching when the NPCSC issued an interpretation of Article 104 of the Basic Law between the dates of two judgments in litigation.[16] The possibility for an interpretation to be issued when litigation is contemplated or in motion represents a significant opportunity for politically-motivated intervention by the executive authorities which can fundamentally change the course of the litigation. It is particularly disconcerting that the HKSAR Government can request an interpretation even when it is already, or is likely to be, a party to proceedings to which the interpretation relates.

Common Law and the Rule of Law

There are, in any event, risks associated with seeking to constitutionally ground judicial review exclusively in the text of the Basic Law. A text-dependent argument, without more, is a weak argument: if judicial review is constitutionally premised on such provisions as Articles 8 or 35 of the Basic Law, all that is needed is an amendment by the NPC under Article 159,[17] or an interpretation under Article 158 which effectively "explains away" reference to judicial review, and the argument is perhaps fatally wounded. The possibility is compounded by the fact there is no explicit reference to judicial review in

---

[13] *Democratic Republic of the Congo v FG Hemisphere Associates LLC (No 1)* (2011) 14 HKCFAR 95 (2011 interpretation of Arts.13 and 19). Two interpretations were issued on the request of the HKSAR Government (1999 interpretation of Arts.22 and 24; and 2005 interpretation of Art.53(2)), and two interpretations were made by the NPCSC on its own initiative (2004 interpretation of Art.7 of Annex I and Art.3 of Annex II; and 2016 interpretation of Art.104).

[14] Basic Law, Art.158(3).

[15] NPCSC interpretations can have retrospective effect; see Po Jen Yap and Eric Chan, "Legislative Oaths and Judicial Intervention in Hong Kong" (2017) 47 Hong Kong Law Journal 1.

[16] Interpretation of Article 104 of the Basic Law of the Hong Kong Special Administrative Region of the People's Republic of China by the Standing Committee of the National People's Congress (adopted by the Standing Committee of the Twelfth National People's Congress as its Twenty-Fourth Session on 7 November 2016). The interpretation was issued between judgment on an application for interim injunction to restrain the President of the Legislative Council from permitting Mr Leung and Ms Yau from retaking their oaths (*Chief Executive of HKSAR v President of Legislative Council* (2016) HKEC 2315, judgment dated 18 October 2016); and judgment on an application seeking declarations, certiorari and injunction (*Chief Executive of HKSAR v President of Legislative Council* (2016) HKEC 2487, judgment dated 15 November 2016).

[17] It is provided by Article 159(3) that no amendment to the Basic Law shall contravene the established basic policies of the PRC regarding Hong Kong, though it is questionable whether this would prevent the NPC from amending (or repealing) the Basic Law by legislative act.

Articles 8 or 35. This is not to suggest that textual protection for judicial review is worthless or of no practical significance; the contrary is true. It is to recognise that a purely textual approach to the constitutional foundation of judicial review is insufficient.

A more normatively compelling argument would recognise that textual protection is valuable but that the common law and rule of law tradition are a significant (non-textual) part of the constitutional foundation for judicial review in Hong Kong. Ivor Jennings attributed to A.V. Dicey the assumption that:

> English law ... better protects the individual because it does not give him worthless paper guarantees which can be torn up like any other scrap of paper, but provides him with substantive remedies enforced by the Courts. Moreover, these Courts are free, independent and unbiased.[18]

If one substitutes "the common law" for "English law" in this excerpt and adopts this as a recognition on the limits of textual guarantees, one begins to reject the fragility and contingency of textualism, allowing one to draw instead on the strength of the enduring normative values embedded in the common law method and tradition.

The common law is capable of functioning as a relatively independent constitutional foundation for judicial review. The Basic Law is merely the tip of the constitutional iceberg. It is itself subject to a common law approach when interpreted by the courts, including the values and norms that such an approach entails.[19] The courts are themselves part of the structural constitution, and are the most authoritative interpreters of the law (including the Basic Law).[20] The authoritative meaning of legislation is determined not solely by reference to the legislation, but by reference to the judicial interpretation of the legislation. The same holds true of judicial interpretation of Basic Law provisions, even when the courts are interpreting an NPCSC interpretation of those provisions.[21] This reveals courts to be generators, not only of legal norms, but of constitutional norms. Courts are capable of providing a distinct source of constitutional authority. That includes the capacity to provide a distinct source of constitutional authority for judicial review. It allows judicial review to be constitutionally grounded in the common law and the rule of law tradition applied by the courts.

The predominance of the rule of law is evident in the day-to-day interpretation and application of law by the courts. It is a central aspect of the common

---

[18] W. I. Jennings, 'In Praise of Dicey (1885–1935)' (1935) 13 Pub. Admin. 123, p.132.
[19] See, for example, *Ng Ka Ling v Director of Immigration* (1999) 2 HKCFAR 4.
[20] Subject, where appropriate, to interpretations of the NPCSC. See also Albert H. Y. Chen, "A Tale of Two Islands: Comparative Reflections on Constitutionalism in Hong Kong and Taiwan" (2007) 37 *Hong Kong Law Journal* 647, pp.670–671.
[21] See Eric C. Ip, "Interpreting Interpretations: A Methodology for the Judicial Enforcement of Legislative Interpretations of the Hong Kong Basic Law" [2017] Public Law 552.

law tradition,[22] of which judicial review is an important part. The rule of law has been said to lie at the heart of the Basic Law and to have "constitutional status".[23] The rule of law "reigns" in Hong Kong.[24] Li CJ stated that "the rule of law with an independent Judiciary is and will remain a cardinal value of our society which is immutable".[25] It is a "cornerstone of our society"[26] and an "end in itself".[27] Sir Anthony Mason NPJ said that the rule of law is the foundation of judicial review.[28]

The rule of law is an essential concept, rather than a technical one: it is the ethos of the rule of law that is key. It is a way of thinking about law, legality and justice, and should be a central principle guiding not only the judiciary, but also the legislature and the executive. A prominent aspect is equality before the law; that the law and the courts treat like persons alike. The idea is that the powerful and the weak, the wealthy and the impoverished, the governing and the governed, are subject as far as possible to equal treatment by the law and legal system.[29]

The rule of law has two principal conceptions: a formalistic and a substantive version.[30] A formalistic version requires little more than that all persons are subject to the law, and even equally subject to the law. It does not greatly matter whether the law is good or bad, just or unjust. The law may be crushingly unfair to the poor or the vulnerable; it may be discriminatory towards minorities; it may sanction violent means of law enforcement and the death penalty for minor offences; it may curtail freedom of speech, assembly, religion and privacy. For the most formalistic version of the rule of law, none of this particularly matters: provided that this is what is sanctioned by law, that the law is declared prospectively and both made and consistently applied using lawful processes, the rule of law is in force.

A more substantive version of the rule of law looks, as the name suggests, not just to the form but to the substance of the law in establishing its validity. The features of law just described would likely violate more substantive

---

[22] Pragmatism and robustness were described as characteristic of the common law – *Oriental Daily Publisher Ltd v Commissioner for Television and Entertainment Licensing Authority* (1997–1998) 1 HKCFAR 279, p.290.

[23] *Leung Kwok Hung v Chief Executive of HKSAR* (2006) HKEC 239, para.167, per Hartmann J.

[24] *Chief Executive of HKSAR v President of the Legislative Council* (2017) 1 HKLRD 460, para.24, per Cheung CJHC.

[25] Li CJ, *Chief Justice's Speech at the Ceremonial Opening of the Legal Year 2007*. Ma CJ said that "[w]e assemble here at the annual Opening of the Legal Year, this year and every year, to acknowledge the importance of the rule of law" – *Chief Justice's Speech at the Ceremonial Opening of the Legal Year 2015*.

[26] Li CJ, *Chief Justice's Speech at the Ceremonial Opening of the Legal Year 2005*.

[27] Ma CJ, *Chief Justice's Speech at the Ceremonial Opening of the Legal Year 2015*.

[28] *C v Director of Immigration* (2013) 16 HKCFAR 280, para.77.

[29] There are of course limitations on this, such as access to justice difficulties, making legal aid particularly important.

[30] Formalistic and substantive versions of the rule of law are linked by a gradient, along which sit varying degrees of emphasis on more formalistic or substantive criteria.

versions of the rule of law, which would tend to emphasise fundamental and inviolable rights, respect for human dignity, protection of minorities or the vulnerable, fairness, transparency, due process, reasonableness and accountability. The content of more substantive versions of the rule of law will vary, but a number of these values are discernible in the common law method and tradition.[31] Several are also discernible in the common law grounds of judicial review, for example in procedural fairness, legitimate expectations and *Wednesbury* unreasonableness. These are living examples of rule of law values enforced through judicial review, grounded in the common law method and tradition.

The common law tradition is a more entrenched constitutional foundation for judicial review in Hong Kong than a mere set of textual prescriptions; it is a guardian of the rule of law, and medium through which it is enforced. This does not belittle the Basic Law; it elevates its potential. As Wood J stated of the Canadian Charter of Rights and Freedoms:

> It is the rule of law which distinguishes civilized society from anarchy. Everything which we have today, and which we cherish in this free and democratic state, we have because of the rule of law ... Without the rule of law *the Canadian Charter of Rights and Freedoms* ... would be nothing but another piece of parchment adrift in the timeless evolution of man's history.[32]

The strength of judicial review derives not only and not principally from the Basic Law but more profoundly from the common law tradition and the rule of law ideal it promotes. Not only is that a more normatively compelling constitutional foundation in which to anchor judicial review, it is one which both stands up to logical scrutiny and which rejects the fragility and circumstance of textualism. One can annul a text at the stroke of a pen, but the common law and rule of law tradition, as a way of thinking about law, legality and justice – a way of living the law – cannot be so summarily erased.

Legislative Supremacy

There is no question of legislative supremacy in Hong Kong in the post-Handover period.[33] This is a significant constitutional difference from the

---

[31] Ma CJ stated that "Hong Kong's legal system is based on the common law and on that system's characteristics of fairness, transparency and access to justice" – *Chief Justice's Speech at the Ceremonial Opening of the Legal Year 2016*.

[32] *R v Bridges (No 2)* (1989) 48 CCC (3d) 545 (Supreme Court of British Columbia), pp. 547–548, per Wood J; endorsed in *Secretary for Justice v Cheng Kam Mun* (2017) HKEC 671, para.43, per Chan J.

[33] Subject to the reach of the NPC (and its Standing Committee) over Hong Kong; being a legislative body.

UK, where legislative supremacy has played a much greater role.[34] The Legislative Council has been held subject to the "supremacy" of the Basic Law, to be enforced by the courts in accordance with the constitution.[35] Even the principle of non-intervention, namely the principle that the courts will not intervene to rule on the regularity or irregularity of the internal processes of the Legislative Council,[36] was subject to requirements of constitutionality under the Basic Law.[37] It would be difficult to argue that judicial review has a substantial constitutional foundation in Hong Kong because of the intention of the Legislative Council,[38] and there is therefore little room for using the so-called *ultra vires* theory to constitutionally ground judicial review in Hong Kong.[39]

Constitutional Review, Administrative Review and Human Rights

Judicial review provides the primary mechanism by which public law challenges are brought on both constitutional and administrative law grounds. Though constitutional law and human rights are beyond the scope of this work, it is important to acknowledge the broader constitutional and human rights context in which administrative law and judicial review are set.

Proportionality plays a more prominent role in the constitutional law context which is not readily replicated in the administrative law context. It is well established that restrictions on constitutional rights, particularly in the context of the Basic Law and the Bill of Rights Ordinance (cap.383), must be proportionate.[40] By contrast, proportionality is not an independent, common law ground of judicial review in Hong Kong. It may be possible to discern elements of proportionality-style logic in some of the grounds of judicial review, or to recharacterise grounds such as procedural fairness and *Wednesbury* unreasonableness along proportionality contours, but this does not elevate proportionality to the same status as the other common law grounds of review. Proportionality can of course be advanced in an application for

---

[34] Though the concept of parliamentary supremacy is coming under increasing strain in the UK – see, in particular, *Jackson v Attorney-General* (2005) UKHL 56; and see extra-judicial writings, Lord Woolf, "*Droit Public – English Style*" [1995] Public Law 57; Laws J, "*Law and Democracy*" [1995] Public Law 72; and Sedley J, "*Human Rights: A Twenty-First Century Agenda*" [1995] Public Law 386.

[35] *Chief Executive of HKSAR v President of the Legislative Council* (2017) 1 HKLRD 460 (CA).

[36] *Leung Kwok Hung v President of the Legislative Council (No 1)* (2014) 17 HKCFAR 689, para.28.

[37] *Chief Executive of HKSAR v President of the Legislative Council* (2017) 1 HKLRD 460 (CA). See also *Rediffusion (Hong Kong) Ltd v Attorney-General of Hong Kong* (1970) AC 1136 (PC).

[38] The lack of a doctrine of legislative supremacy in Hong Kong also has significance for the manner in which, or the extent to which, other doctrines are applicable in Hong Kong, such as the *Carltona* principle; see pp.165–168.

[39] See generally Christopher Forsyth (ed), *Judicial Review and the Constitution* (Hart Publishing, 2000).

[40] See, for example, *Leung Kwok Hung v HKSAR* (2005) 8 HKCFAR 229.

judicial review where it is alleged that one or more common law grounds of review have been breached and where rights stemming from the Basic Law or Bill of Rights Ordinance are in play. An application for judicial review can advance both constitutional and administrative law grounds, but whereas there may be common issues and whilst a single act or decision might at once violate constitutional and administrative law grounds, the two technically remain distinct. It is of course possible that proportionality is developed in future as a common law ground of judicial review.[41]

Administrative law provides critical protection of human rights. In addition, human rights are protected by the Basic Law and the Bill of Rights Ordinance. The Basic Law enshrines a number of human rights, including equality before the law,[42] freedom of the person including protection from torture or arbitrary or unlawful deprivation of life,[43] inviolability of the home,[44] freedom and privacy of communication,[45] and freedom of marriage and the right to freely raise a family.[46] The Bill of Rights Ordinance, enacted in 1991, incorporated into domestic law many (but not all[47]) of the provisions of the International Covenant on Civil and Political Rights (ICCPR), which the UK ratified in 1976 both with regard to itself and Hong Kong.[48] Part II of the Bill of Rights Ordinance contains the Bill of Rights, which protects a number of human rights including the right to life,[49] prohibition of slavery and servitude,[50] liberty of movement,[51] equality before courts and tribunals,[52] prohibition of retrospective criminalisation,[53] protection of privacy, family, home and correspondence from arbitrary or unlawful interference,[54] freedom of thought, conscience and religion,[55] freedom of opinion and expression,[56] freedom of association,[57] and rights to marry and to family life.[58] The status of the ICCPR, to the extent incorporated into domestic law, is protected by Article 39 of the Basic Law.[59]

Though not a substitute for human rights instruments, it is important to note the contribution of the common law grounds of judicial review to protecting and promoting some of the values and principles of human rights. For example, procedural fairness and the rules on natural justice have protected equality, fairness and consistency in procedural treatment, seen in a range of contexts from the common law right to a fair hearing, to the rules against bias ensuring impartiality in decision-making. Error of law has ensured that public

---

[41] *Council of Civil Service Unions v Minister for the Civil Service* (1985) AC 374, p.410, per Lord Diplock.
[42] Basic Law, Art.25. [43] *Id.*, Art.28. [44] *Id.*, Art.29. [45] *Id.*, Art.30. [46] *Id.*, Art.37.
[47] Reservations were entered by the UK, such as on the right to self-determination enshrined in Art.1 of the ICCPR.
[48] The UK also ratified, in 1976, the International Covenant on Economic, Social and Cultural Rights (ICESCR) in relation to itself and Hong Kong.
[49] Bill of Rights, Art.2. [50] *Id.*, Art.4. [51] *Id.*, Art.8. [52] *Id.*, Art.10. [53] *Id.*, Art.12.
[54] *Id.*, Art.14. [55] *Id.*, Art.15. [56] *Id.*, Art.16. [57] *Id.*, Art.18. [58] *Id.*, Art.19.
[59] Article 39 also applies to the ICESCR and international labour conventions.

bodies are not judges of the extent of their own powers. Legitimate expectations have promoted certainty, predictability and accountability in decision and policy making, and compelled decision-makers to have regard to how changes in their position might frustrate existing expectations. Fettering of discretion has protected against discretionary rigidity and the executive narrowing the scope of its discretion. *Wednesbury* unreasonableness has offered protection against arbitrariness of discretion and egregious decision-making. The common law grounds of review, developed by an independent judiciary, jealous of fairness and rectitude in individual dealings with the state, have made an immense contribution to the baseline of legal protections enjoyed by the populace. They have advanced a strong framework for the rule of law, and embedded within the common law tradition an enduring worldview on the procedural and substantive protections of the governed against the government.

Part II

Judicial Review
The Leave Stage

4

The Leave Stage
Principles and Procedure

The leave stage essentially serves as a filter.[1] It is a preliminary stage at which the court determines whether an application is appropriate for judicial review and therefore whether it should proceed to a substantive hearing. Those deemed not appropriate are refused, without consuming further time and resources on the part of the parties or the court. This mitigates the negative impact that judicial review may have on public administration, effectively sheltering public bodies from review where the application is not thought fit for substantive consideration.

Leave is a statutory requirement.[2] The application for leave is made *ex parte* by filing a notice in Form No. 86 and an affidavit verifying the facts relied upon.[3] The judge may determine the application for leave without a hearing, unless a hearing is requested in the notice of application, and need not sit in open court.[4] If the applicant requests an oral hearing only in the event of the judge being minded to refuse leave, the judge initially considers the application without a hearing, and will fix a date for an oral hearing if minded to refuse leave.[5] Where leave is refused, or is granted on terms, the applicant may appeal to the Court of Appeal within fourteen days of such an order being made.[6] Where leave is granted, the court may impose such terms on

---

[1] Li CJ described the requirement for leave to apply for judicial review as an "important filter introduced by statute", *Po Fun Chan v Winnie Cheung* (2007) 10 HKCFAR 676, para.14. Rogers V-P stated that the application for leave "is a filtering, or perhaps more accurately a sieving, exercise", *Chu Woan Chyi v Director of Immigration* [2004] 3 HKLRD I1, para.8.
[2] High Court Ordinance (cap.4), s.21K; O.53, r.3. A challenge to the constitutionality of O.53, r.3, failed – *Right to Inherent Dignity Movement Association v HKSAR Government* [2008] HKEC 1412.
[3] O.53, r.3(2). [4] *Id.*, r.3(3). [5] Practice Direction SL3, para.7.
[6] High Court Ordinance (cap.4), ss.13(2) and 14A; O.53, r.3(4); O.59, r.21(1)(g). The original application for leave is made in the Court of First Instance. The appeal against refusal to grant leave is made in the Court of Appeal. If the appeal is successful and leave is granted, the substantive hearing is then heard in the Court of First Instance. For an example of this, see *Smart Gain Investment Ltd v Town Planning Board* [2006] HKEC 384; *Smart Gain Investment Ltd v Town Planning Board* [2006] HKEC 2063 (CA); and *Smart Gain Investment Ltd v Town Planning Board*, HCAL 12/2006. O.53, r.3(4), has been described by the Court of Appeal as a "unique Hong Kong provision" – *Hung Shui Fung v Director of Food and Environmental Hygiene*, CACV 219/2004 and CACV 220/2014 (CA), para.10.

costs and the giving of security as it thinks fit.[7] Leave can also act as a stay of proceedings to which the application relates if the relief sought is an order of certiorari or prohibition, or interim relief can be granted at any time in the proceedings where any other relief is sought.[8] After leave has been granted, the application for judicial review must be made by originating summons in Form No. 86A to a judge in open court or, if the judge granting leave has so ordered, to a judge sitting in chambers.[9] The originating summons must be issued within fourteen days of leave being granted.[10]

Though leave is a statutory requirement, the court has wide discretion on whether to grant or refuse leave. There is a statutory basis for refusing leave on the basis of delay, though this remains subject to significant judicial discretion.[11] There is also a statutory requirement for the court to refuse leave where it considers that the applicant does not have a sufficient interest in the matter to which the application relates, but the content and meaning of sufficient interest is again subject to judicial discretion.[12] Whilst the court is bound to have sufficient regard to delay and sufficient interest in deciding whether to grant leave, there is no fixed list of criteria which the court must take into account. It is provided, however, that the court shall not grant leave for a person to file evidence or make representations at the hearing of the application for judicial review unless it appears to the court that the applicant is a proper person to be heard at the hearing of the application.[13] In addition to delay and insufficient interest, courts are more likely to refuse leave where the case has an insufficient public (law) element, where the subject matter of the dispute is non-justiciable or non-reviewable, or where the application does not disclose an arguable case.

The court may direct there to be a rolled-up hearing. This involves a "direction for having the two stages to be heard on the same date with the leave application being heard immediately before the substantive application".[14] It does not involve – and cannot involve – circumventing the statutory requirement for leave: there is no discretion to dispense with the requirement for leave, or to dispense with a "two-stage process".[15] Instead, it is about managing the case in such a way that factors such as those found in Order 1A of the Rules of the High Court – including cost-effectiveness, expeditiousness, reasonable proportion and procedural economy, and the fair distribution of court resources – are promoted.[16]

---

[7] O.53, r.3(9).   [8] *Id.*, r.3(10).   [9] *Id.*, r.5(1).   [10] *Id.*, r.5(5).
[11] High Court Ordinance (cap.4), s.21K(6); O.53, r.4. It was suggested that the binding effect of precedent may not be as strong in relation to leave as in other areas of law – *Ho Ming Sai v Director of Immigration* [1994] 1 HKLR 21, p.27, per Litton JA.
[12] High Court Ordinance (cap.4), s.21K(3); O.53, r.3(7).
[13] O.53, r.5B. It is also provided that such an application must be made promptly – *id.*, r.5B(2).
[14] *BI v Director of Immigration* [2016] 2 HKLRD 520 (CA), para.135.   [15] *Id.*
[16] O.1A, Rules of the High Court (cap.4A). In *Lo Siu Lan v Hong Kong Housing Authority* [2005] HKEC 279 (CA), for example, a rolled-up hearing was adopted at first instance due to the urgency of the matters raised by the application.

However, if leave is refused by the Court of First Instance in a rolled-up hearing, an appeal to the Court of Appeal remains an appeal against the refusal to grant leave – the Court of Appeal is not obliged to hear full arguments on the merits in the appeal. It has been added, however, that if full arguments have been deployed in the Court of First Instance in a rolled-up hearing:

> other things being equal, as a matter of case management in light of the underlying objectives in Order 1A, it is usually appropriate for [the Court of Appeal] to allow parties to canvass full arguments on the merits in the appeal.[17]

This nevertheless does not enable the Court of Appeal to grant substantive relief in such an appeal if it agrees with the appellant on the substantive merits.[18] Due to procedural complexities that may arise, caution has been urged of judges in the Court of First Instance when deciding whether to deal with an application for judicial review by way of a rolled-up hearing.[19] Though a rolled-up hearing would typically be seen by "combining" the leave stage and substantive hearing, there is also precedent for a rolled-up hearing comprising an application to set aside leave and the substantive application for judicial review.[20]

It is worth considering whether the leave stage should be retained in its current form, even if the principles it seeks to uphold, and the rationale of filtering out inappropriate cases at an early stage, are thought commendable. There are several challenges to the suitability of the leave stage as it currently stands.

First, the leave stage is envisaged to be a relatively brief, preliminary aspect of judicial review procedure. It is not concerned so much with the merits of the application as with its amenability to review. Questions of substance are for the substantive hearing. As Lord Diplock explained:

> The discretion that the court is exercising at this stage is not the same as that which it is called upon to exercise when all the evidence is in and the matter has been fully argued at the hearing of the application.[21]

---

[17] *Hung Shui Fung v Director of Food and Environmental Hygiene*, CACV 219/2004 and CACV 220/2014 (CA) (6 June 2016), para.6(f) and (g).

[18] *Id.*, para.7. It was added (paras.14–17) that, in order to secure that as far as possible all matters in dispute between the parties are completely and finally determined and multiplicity of proceedings is avoided (see High Court Ordinance (cap.4), s.16(2)), and with regard to the objectives and duty of active case management in O.1A, the Court of Appeal could – provided only that all relevant issues could be determined in the appeal – remit the matter to the Court of First Instance and direct that judgment be entered in accordance with the Court of Appeal's judgment on all the substantive issues.

[19] *Hung Shui Fung v Director of Food and Environmental Hygiene*, CACV 219/2004 and CACV 220/2014 (CA) (6 June 2016), para.17.

[20] *AA v Securities and Futures Commission* [2016] HKEC 1718.

[21] *R v Inland Revenue Commissioners, ex parte National Federation of Self Employed and Small Businesses Ltd* [1982] AC 617, p.644.

However, it is difficult for the court to deal with these preliminary issues without considering issues of substance and the merits of the application. Undue delay is determined contextually, with no fixed time limit,[22] and is informed by the substance of the case. Whether and to what extent the applicant has a sufficient interest in the matter to which the application relates must surely involve consideration of the substance of the complaint. Whether there is a sufficient public element to the case must involve an evaluation of the substance of the decision to which the application relates. Non-justiciability can be a substantive determination. An assessment of the arguability of the application presumably requires consideration of the substantive issues raised and their merits. Questions of substance are not, it seems, invariably for the substantive hearing. Courts are sometimes quite open about the fact they are considering substantive issues at the leave stage: in one application for leave it was "important to look at the merits of the substantive issues sought to be raised", particularly in considering whether so-called academic questions should be entertained.[23] This is not necessarily fatal to the utility of the leave stage, but it does question whether it is appropriate for questions of substance to arise to any significant extent at this preliminary stage. Furthermore, the court retains the discretion to hold over so-called preliminary matters to the substantive hearing where circumstances so justify; this has been seen in relation to both delay[24] and standing.[25] The appropriateness of using judicial review proceedings, rather than a criminal appeal, has also been held over to the substantive hearing for further consideration.[26]

There is a clear benefit to the court having the means to, at an early stage, dispose expeditiously of applications thought inapposite for review. However, the question is whether the leave stage in its current form is the proper way to achieve that aim. Perhaps the court should avoid considering substantive

---

[22] Noting that a number of exceptions have been made to the provision that an application for leave should be made within three months from the date when grounds for the application first arose – see pp.45–51.

[23] *Shek Lai San v Securities and Futures Commission* [2010] 4 HKC 168, para.63, per Cheung J. It was added in the same paragraph that "in the present context of deciding how the Court's discretion to entertain, exceptionally, the 'academic' questions raised should be exercised, merits are taken into account for this reason: the stronger the merits, the more reason for the Court to entertain the questions. The converse is also true: the more marginal the case of the applicant (even though it is a reasonably arguable one), the less likely the Court would exercise its discretion to entertain the 'academic' questions, assuming everything else is equal".

[24] *X v Torture Claims Appeal Board* [2014] HKEC 9, paras.4–5.

[25] Cheung J stated that "[i]t is quite true that the question of sufficient interest is not infrequently left to the substantive hearing, and any doubt regarding standing is often resolved in favour of granting leave" – *Shek Lai San v Securities and Futures Commission* [2010] 4 HKC 168, para.62.

[26] *Viva Magnetics Ltd v Secretary for Justice* [2002] 3 HKLRD 571, paras.17–19. See further *Chow Shun Chiu v HKSAR* [2001] HKEC 882.

issues at the leave stage; perhaps the thresholds imposed at the leave stage are too stringent; perhaps the leave stage and substantive hearing could be streamlined to avoid duplication of argument. The utility and adequacy of the leave stage as a preliminary aspect of judicial review procedure depends to a great extent on how it is managed by the courts. The leave stage should be neither a formality to be cleared, nor a "fishing expedition",[27] nor unduly onerous for the applicant. This requires focus and discipline on the part of the courts, from ensuring that their wide discretion is exercised consistently, to being reasonable and realistic in terms of the requirements imposed on applicants.

---

[27] See p.116

5

Delay

The application for leave, and the substantive application for judicial review, can each be refused on the basis of delay.[1] This is justified by a number of policy reasons. Whilst judicial review plays a fundamental role in enforcing legality in public decision making and upholding the rule of law, it brings costs to bear on public administration. These costs should be no greater than are necessary to allow judicial review to play its role in the legal order, and the rules against delay mitigate such costs. Judicial review must be conducted with "proper awareness of the needs of public administration".[2]

The first way in which it mitigates these costs is in terms of the public body's consumption of resources in defending an application for judicial review. The defence of such an application will inevitably incur fact-finding costs which may become more time and resource intensive as time goes by, as the facts, materials and officials relevant to the case become more distant.

Second, the decisions of public bodies often feed into broader or multi-stage decision-making processes. The striking down of one decision may result in a chain or domino effect as the legality of other decisions is affected. The more time that elapses before the first decision in the chain is struck down, the greater the likelihood that further decisions will have been taken on the basis of the first, now unlawful, decision. The more decisions or stages in the decision-making process that are deemed unlawful, the greater the time, financial and operational consequences are likely to be for the decision maker which must retake those decisions. A prompt challenge to the legality of a decision is therefore likely to minimise the extent to which the legality of subsequent decisions is affected, and therefore mitigates unnecessary additional costs to public administration.

Third, decisions may affect a significant number of people. The number of people affected by a decision may also increase over time. Therefore, the sooner a decision of this nature is challenged, the less damage or inconvenience is likely

---

[1] For a more comprehensive account, see Stephen Thomson, "Leave without Delay: The Requirement to Make Prompt Application for Leave to Apply for Judicial Review" (2015) 45(2) *Hong Kong Law Journal* 449.

[2] *Lo Siu Lan v Hong Kong Housing Authority* [2004] HKEC 1541, para.34, per Hon Stock JA, quoting from *R v Monopolies and Mergers Commission, ex parte Argyll Group plc* [1986] 1 WLR 763, p.774, per Sir John Donaldson MR.

to be incurred by an ever greater number of people affected by an unlawful decision. For example, in 2001 there were 747,052 persons aged sixty-five or over in Hong Kong; whereas in 2011 there were 941,312 such persons.[3] If a decision was taken in relation to persons in this age group in 2001, and a person delayed for a period of ten years until challenging it by way of judicial review, then in principle an additional 194,260 people would be affected by the potentially unlawful decision. If the court proceeded to strike down the decision, significantly higher costs may be incurred as an alternative decision or arrangement is made for an additional 194,260 people in this category.

Fourth, there are issues of legal certainty in play, not only for decision-makers who may reasonably consider that their decisions will not be challenged by way of judicial review if more than three months have elapsed since their decision was taken, but for other people who rely on public decisions. Establishing the legality of a decision sooner rather than later is beneficial both to decision-makers and the public as a whole – the courts must consider not only the "rights of the applicants who may be affected by decisions", but also the "rights of the financial public to rely on announced decisions"[4] and the fact that people may have based or altered their conduct on existing decisions which may later be impugned.

There are therefore sound policy reasons why applications for judicial review should be made as promptly as possible. The courts, though eager to ensure that public bodies act lawfully, will not stand idly by and allow judicial review to be any more costly for public administration – and ultimately for the taxpayer – than is necessary.

The High Court Ordinance makes the following provision on delay:

Where the Court of First Instance considers that there has been undue delay in making an application for judicial review, the Court may refuse to grant–

(a) leave for the making of the application; or
(b) any relief sought on the application,

if it considers that the granting of relief sought would be likely to cause substantial hardship to, or substantially prejudice the rights of, any person or would be detrimental to good administration.[5]

It can be seen that the court has discretion to refuse an application at two distinct stages. First, it can refuse leave if the application suffers from undue delay. This is the most common stage of proceedings at which an application would fail by reason of delay. If leave is granted, however, the court retains discretion to refuse to grant relief on the application by reason of delay.[6]

---

[3] Census and Statistics Department, "Thematic Report: Older Persons" (February 2013), p.10.
[4] *Lo Siu Lan v Hong Kong Housing Authority* [2004] HKEC 1541, para.34, per Stock JA.
[5] High Court Ordinance (cap.4), s.21K(6).
[6] After leave has been obtained, the applicant must still act promptly and observe other time limits, otherwise the court may refuse relief. See *Anderson Asphalt Ltd v Secretary for Justice*

This chapter focuses on delay as an issue for determination at the leave stage. Order 53 makes additional provision for delay as an issue arising at this stage of proceedings:

(1) An application for leave to apply for judicial review shall be made promptly and in any event within three months from the date when grounds for the application first arose unless the Court considers that there is good reason for extending the period within which the application shall be made.
(2) Where the relief sought is an order of certiorari in respect of any judgment, order, conviction or other proceeding, the date when grounds for the application first arose shall be taken to be the date of that judgment, order, conviction or proceeding.
(3) The preceding paragraphs are without prejudice to any statutory provision which has the effect of limiting the time within which an application for judicial review may be made.[7]

The starting point is the general three-month time limit: that an application for leave shall be made within three months from the date when grounds for the application first arose.[8] This is in fact rather misleading, as the courts have made so many exceptions to the three month time period – both in its contraction and extension – that it can barely be considered a time limit in the ordinary sense. If the idea of specifying an exact time period was to engender certainty in the aspiring applicant, it engenders a false certainty, as the courts have been clear that promptness commands more importance than adherence to the three-month time limit. There is an argument to be made for replacing the statutory reference to a three-month time period with a test of promptness or undue delay, as this better reflects judicial practice. However, it could be argued that, in general, once a period of three months has elapsed from the making of a decision, the decision maker can be

---

[2009] 3 HKLRD 215, para.144; *Chiu Kin Ho* v *Commissioner of Police* [2010] HKEC 701, paras.17–19; and pp.296–297. Delay in seeking an amendment to an application already made is to be judged differently from delay in making the application itself – *PCCW-HKT Telephone Ltd* v *Telecommunications Authority* [2004] HKEC 799, para.26.

[7] O.53, r.4.

[8] It has been described as "trite" that one cannot artificially bring oneself back within time by asking the decision maker to reconsider and then characterising the response as a fresh decision – *Imran Muhammad* v *Secretary for Security* [2016] HKEC 2201, para.50; and see *Lo Siu Lan* v *Hong Kong Housing Authority* [2004] HKEC 1898 (CA), para.39; *Super Lion Enterprises Ltd* v *Commissioner of Rating and Valuation* [2006] HKEC 1870, para.218; *Martin Tao Ming Lee* v *Secretary for the Civil Service* [2011] HKEC 1078, para.8; *ET Investment Ltd (t/a Oasis Nursing Home)* v *Director of Health* [2016] 1 HKLRD 1389, para.18; and *Nisa Azizan* v *Director of Immigration* [2016] HKEC 891, paras.29–36. Nevertheless, if a public officer decides to reconsider an earlier decision made by himself or his subordinate, the decision made following that reconsideration is amenable to judicial review even if it amounts to confirmation of the earlier decision – *Hong Kong and China Gas Co Ltd* v *Director of Lands* [1997] HKLRD 1291, p.1294.

reasonably confident that the decision will not be (successfully) challenged by way of judicial review.

Promptness

Order 53, Rule 4(1) requires that an application for leave be made "promptly". The courts have been clear that promptness commands more importance than adherence to the three-month time period,[9] and applications for leave can be refused within the three month time period should they suffer from undue delay.[10] It would be inadvisable for an aspiring applicant to wait, for example, until two and a half months had passed since grounds for review first arose, before applying for leave. If the court finds there to have been undue delay, the application may be rejected even though it was technically within time. As Hartmann J warned, "sleep on your rights and, even if your cause is meritorious, you may find the gates locked against you".[11] It has even been stated that context may require that an application for leave is made "immediately or almost immediately", such that a delay of less than two weeks may even be regarded as undue delay.[12]

Reasons Justifying Extension of Time

It is clear from Order 53, Rule 4(1) that the court retains discretion to extend the period within which the application shall be made if it considers that there is good reason for doing so. The extension of time is at the court's discretion,[13]

---

[9] *Law Chun Loy* v *Secretary for Justice* [2006] HKEC 1981, para.9; *Mui Mei Fung* v *Secretary for Justice* [2014] HKEC 88, para.24; *Fung Elvira Binag* v *Secretary for Home Affairs* [2014] HKEC 400, para.11.

[10] *Law Chun Loy* v *Secretary for Justice* [2006] HKEC 1981, para.9; *Karlo Joanani Dauz* v *Director of Immigration* [2009] HKEC 850, para.13.

[11] *Law Chun Loy* v *Secretary for Justice* [2006] HKEC 1981, para.13. In *R* v *Aston University Senate, ex parte Roffey* [1969] 2 QB 538, p.555, Donaldson J stated that the "prerogative remedies are exceptional in their nature and should not be made available to those who sleep upon their rights".

[12] *Lo Siu Lan* v *Hong Kong Housing Authority* [2004] HKEC 1541, para.42, per Stock JA.

[13] *Lau Luen Hung Thomas* v *Insider Dealing Tribunal* [2009] HKEC 1977 (CFA), para.7; *Lam Sze Ming* v *Commissioner of Police* [2010] HKEC 1160, para.7. It has been said that the court should be disciplined in its exercise of discretion in this regard – *Re Thomas Lai* [2014] 6 HKC 1, para.44. The Court of Appeal stated that when an *ex parte* application for leave is made with an application for extending time, a judge has the option to (a) grant or refuse extension of time on an *ex parte* basis (and it will be open to a respondent to apply to set aside such leave at the *inter partes* hearing), (b) adjourn the leave application and the application to extend time to an *inter partes* hearing involving the putative respondent, or (c) direct a rolled-up hearing to be held – *BI* v *Director of Immigration* [2016] 2 HKLRD 520 (CA), para.136. If the respondent applies to set aside leave at the *inter partes* hearing, the court can direct that such application be heard together with the substantive judicial review application – *MSSL* v *Director of Immigration* [2016] HKEC 2650. See also *R* v *Criminal Injuries Compensation Board, ex parte A* [1999] 2 AC 330 (HL).

and the burden of proof for demonstrating good reason for the whole period of delay (rather than merely part thereof[14]) lies with the applicant.[15] There is no closed list of factors which the court will take into consideration, and the merits of extending time will be considered in the context of each individual case: indeed, whilst delay of less than two weeks may be regarded as undue delay,[16] leave has been granted where an application was made over two and a half years late.[17] The court must therefore weigh the policy reasons for an application to be made promptly against the effect of the time limit on the individual applicant and his circumstances and interests in fairness.

The court may take into account the importance of the point raised by the applicant in deciding whether to grant leave out of time. For example, in *Re Lee Yee Shing Jacky*, it was alleged that section 69 of the Inland Revenue Ordinance (cap.112) was unconstitutional. Whilst there was delay of over two and a half years, the case concerned the constitutionality of statutory provisions on taxation, thereby affecting a large number of people and, even if the court rejected the instant application as out of time, the constitutionality or otherwise of section 69 would not be settled until another applicant made the same challenge:

> if leave were to be refused in the present case, the point would not go away. For so long as s 69 remains in the statute book, it is potentially liable to be challenged by any aggrieved taxpayer. In a sense, the sooner the matter is clarified, the better.[18]

Extension of time is not automatic in cases where the legality of legislation or a constitutional or fundamental right is in issue.[19] However, it has been said that the normal principles on delay would not be too rigorously enforced in cases involving fundamental human rights,[20] and there are other cases involving constitutional issues where delay has been excused.[21] The issue being raised does not have to be one of constitutionality to be regarded as sufficiently important. For example, in *X v Torture Claims Appeal Board*, leave was

---

[14] See *Re Ho Mei Ling* [2011] 6 HKC 1, para.110.
[15] *Chiu Kin Ho v Commissioner of Police* [2010] HKEC 701, para.17; *Fung Elvira Binag v Secretary for Home Affairs* [2014] HKEC 400, para.22.
[16] *Lo Siu Lan v Hong Kong Housing Authority* [2004] HKEC 1541, para.42.
[17] *Re Lee Yee Shing Jacky* [2009] HKEC 605.
[18] *Id.*, para.25, per Cheung J. See also *Leung TC William Roy v Secretary for Justice* [2005] HKEC 998, para.40; and *Dr Yuk Kong Lau v Medical Council of Hong Kong* [2011] 5 HKC 218, paras.84–85.
[19] *Leung TC William Roy v Secretary for Justice* [2005] HKEC 998, para.40; and see *Chan Kong v Chief Executive of the HKSAR* [2008] 1 HKLRD 694.
[20] *Super Lion Enterprises Ltd v Commissioner of Rating and Valuation* [2006] HKEC 1936, para.233, per Hartmann J; endorsed in *Chan Mei Yu Paddy v Secretary for Justice (No 3)* [2008] 2 HKLRD 154, para.36.
[21] *Chan Mei Yu Paddy v Secretary for Justice (No 3)* [2008] 2 HKLRD 154; *Gurung Deu Kumari v Director of Immigration* [2010] HKEC 804. See also *Catholic Diocese of Hong Kong v Secretary for Justice* [2010] HKEC 163, para.58.

granted and the issue of delay held over to the substantive hearing where it was alleged that an adjudicator had failed to observe a high standard of procedural fairness in reviewing a failed application to be recognised as a torture claimant by the Director of Immigration.[22] The fact that an application raises issues of public importance[23] or issues that are likely to be the subject of future applications may weigh in favour of the extension of time.[24]

Leave may be granted out of time where the reason for the delay is beyond the applicant's control. An extension of time was granted due to the intermittent supply of documents from various sources and the time required to analyse them and prepare the necessary court papers.[25] Where the Legal Aid Department took four months to process a legal aid application, this would not weigh against the applicant where he promptly filed his application after granted legal aid.[26] However, the view has been expressed that there is no general proposition that difficulty or time taken in obtaining legal aid is good reason for extending time for applying for leave.[27] In order to have a realistic prospect of the extension of time due to delay on the part of the Legal Aid Department in processing a legal aid application, the applicant should have applied promptly for legal aid in the first place.[28] The applicant must otherwise act promptly, and any delay in such a case should be entirely due to the application process itself.[29] If the legal aid application is still pending as the three month time period is soon to expire, the applicant should nevertheless consider making the application for leave, if possible.[30]

Financial difficulties experienced by the applicant will not necessarily be a sufficient justification for explaining delay, even where an applicant had been

---

[22] *X v Torture Claims Appeal Board* [2014] HKEC 9. However, in *MSSL v Director of Immigration* [2016] HKEC 2650, an application for judicial review of a failed claim under the Convention Against Torture for protection from refoulement to Sri Lanka was refused where there had been delay of over three years from the date of the impugned decisions (other factors were also relevant).

[23] *R v Secretary of State for the Home Department, ex parte Ruddock* [1987] 1 WLR 1482; *R v Secretary of State for Foreign and Commonwealth Affairs, ex parte World Development Movement Ltd* [1995] 1 WLR 386.

[24] *Liu Tat Hang v Post-Release Supervision Board*, HCAL 154/1999.

[25] *BI v Director of Immigration* [2014] HKEC 64, para.2. See also *Mallawa Arachchi v Wesley Wong* [2014] HKEC 1490.

[26] *Lai Sam Hing v Commissioner of Police* [2009] HKEC 99; and see *Law Chun Loy v Secretary for Justice* [2006] HKEC 1981, paras.18–19; and *Chiu Hung Kwan v Director of Food and Environmental Hygiene* [2012] HKEC 546, para.12.

[27] *Re Thomas Lai* [2014] 6 HKC 1, para.48, per Lam J.

[28] *Re Ho Mei Ling* [2011] 6 HKC 1, para.107. Though in *D v Director of Public Prosecutions* [2015] 4 HKLRD 62, whereas the impugned decisions took place on 3 and 18 February 2015, the applicant did not apply for legal aid until 21 April 2015. Nevertheless, the court exercised its discretion to allow the application for leave to be made out of time.

[29] *AW v Secretary for Security* [2015] HKEC 134, para.13. See also *Wong Tak Yiu v Commissioner of Police* [2010] HKEC 1531; *R v Commissioner of Police* [2010] HKEC 1531, paras.35–38.

[30] See *Wong Yui Hin v Hong Kong Arts Development Council* [2004] HKEC 1102, paras.20–21 and 92–94.

refused legal aid, refused assistance by the Hong Kong Bar Association's free legal advice scheme, and subject to a bankruptcy order.[31] In one case, an applicant attributed her delay to poor health and a need to be hospitalised; the issue of delay was not specifically considered by the court, but leave was refused.[32] The argument that an applicant was exhausted due to having to care for his aged mother and younger sister with serious mental illness, and that this was a good reason for delay, was unsuccessful.[33]

An attempt to settle a dispute by alternative dispute resolution (ADR) will not automatically constitute good reason for extending time; at a minimum, it would have to be shown that the ADR mechanism had a real prospect of resolving the dispute.[34] Time taken to consult lawyers or experts, or negotiate with a decision maker in an attempt to secure a change of decision, will not normally excuse delay in applying for leave.[35] However, it was held that a reasonable period of time taken to obtain and digest an expert opinion on a complex Environmental Impact Assessment (EIA) Report weighed against a finding of undue delay.[36]

As a matter of principle, a necessary corollary of the courts' general requirement that one must have exhausted relevant statutory appeals mechanisms prior to seeking judicial review[37] is that an applicant should not be penalised where the use of an appeal mechanism takes him beyond the three month time period.[38] Where there has been a change in understanding of the law, and a previous understanding has been held to be incorrect, this will not normally constitute good reason for extending time to bring a challenge under the new legal position. It might only do so in exceptional circumstances.[39] Ignorance of the law or procedure is not generally considered a good reason for delay,[40] though it may weigh in favour of an unrepresented applicant who

---

[31] *Lam Sze Ming* v *Commissioner of Police* [2010] HKEC 1160. See also *Chiu Kin Ho* v *Commissioner of Police* [2010] HKEC 701, paras.13 and 19.
[32] *Cananola Lida Balboa* [2014] HKEC 877.
[33] *Chiu Kin Ho* v *Commissioner of Police* [2010] HKEC 701, paras.13 and 19.
[34] *Re Ho Mei Ling*, paras.96–102.
[35] *Re Chan Yu Nam* [2005] HKEC 1343, paras.63–65; and *Re Smith Bonnie Yee Lo* [2009] HKEC 1907, para.21.
[36] *Shiu Wing Steel Ltd* v *Director of Environmental Protection (No 2)* (2006) 9 HKCFAR 478, paras.88–89.
[37] See pp.293–295.
[38] See *Re Lee Yee Shing Jacky* [2009] HKEC 605, para.26. See also *Young Yau Yau Cecilia* v *Dental Council of Hong Kong* [2010] HKEC 311, paras.4–12.
[39] *HKSAR* v *Hung Chan Wa* (2006) 9 HKCFAR 614; *Wong Chi Keung* v *Commissioner of Police* [2010] HKEC 809, para.49. See also *Tsui Kin Kwok* v *Commissioner of Police* [2010] HKEC 284, paras.29–30; and Thomson, "Leave Without Delay", pp.463–464.
[40] *Chiu Kin Ho* v *Commissioner of Police* [2010] HKEC 701, para.18; *Martin Tao Ming Lee* v *Secretary for the Civil Service* [2011] HKEC 1078, para.9; *Tsang Loi Fat* v *Sun Fook Kong* [2011] 4 HKLRD 344, p.349; *Fung Elvira Binag* v *Secretary for Home Affairs* [2014] HKEC 400, paras.23 and 25; *Re Ng Muk Kam* [2010] HKEC 412 (though see *Chan Ka Man* v *Commissioner of Correctional Services* [2009] HKEC 1800); and *James Yan* v *Director of Immigration* [2010]

has delayed that she was misinformed about an applicable deadline by the High Court Registry.[41] It was said that there was "no real blame" where applicants failed to raise their challenge at an earlier stage, as they were "not aware" of the potential unconstitutionality of the statutory provision of which they now sought review until a judgment handed down by the Court of Final Appeal in a case to which they were party.[42] Whilst waiting on another party to litigation replying to a letter may not constitute good reason for delay,[43] seeking clarification from the public body regarding the legal basis of its decision may do so.[44]

There is, of course, potential for inconsistency in what the court considers good reason for delay, as illustrated by two cases in which police constables were ordered to leave the police force. In one case, the police constable was ordered to be compulsorily retired and did not apply for legal aid for the judicial review application until around three months after time had expired. The applicant proffered as his explanation for delay that he was "very upset and did not know what to do". Saunders J was sympathetic, stating that he could "well understand that a man would be very upset at being dismissed from the [police] force and may take some time to come to terms with his position". In the absence of any argument as to prejudice, the court granted leave even though the application was made out of time.[45] This may be contrasted with a case in which a police constable was directed to retire in the public interest. The delay of around five months was explained by the applicant as being due to the decision being a "big blow" to him, and that it took him some time to gather the documentation relevant to his application. Hartmann J was unpersuaded:

> [I]t is plain that the applicant, who was living in a small apartment, would have been able to gather together his papers in a matter of a day or so if he had resolved to do so... No doubt the applicant was despondent but that alone cannot excuse a delay of some five months or more in completing what must have been a relatively simple task.[46]

Such inconsistency is insightful in cases with remarkably similar facts, separated only by a little over two years.

HKEC 1331, paras.71–72. See also *Cheung Mei Yin* v *Postmaster General* [2007] HKEC 1214; and *Mo Kam Tong Stanley* v *Coroner of Hong Kong* [2008] 1 HKCLRT 155.

[41] *Young Yau Yau Cecilia* v *Dental Council of Hong Kong* [2010] HKEC 311, paras.4–12.
[42] *Re Lee Yee Shing Jacky* [2009] HKEC 605, para.11.
[43] *Re An Occupation Permit No 18555 Issued by the Hong Kong Housing Authority* [1991] 2 HKLR 104.
[44] *Hong Kong Aircrew Officers Association* v *Director General of Civil Aviation* [2009] HKEC 1086, para.9.
[45] *Lai Sam Hing* v *Commissioner of Police* [2009] HKEC 99, paras.4–7.
[46] *Law Chun Loy* v *Secretary for Justice* [2006] HKEC 1981, para.30.

No Substantial Hardship, Prejudice or Detriment

Section 21K(6) of the High Court Ordinance gives the court discretion to refuse to grant leave or any relief sought on the application for judicial review "if it considers that the granting of relief sought would be likely to cause substantial hardship to, or substantially prejudice the rights of, any person or would be detrimental to good administration". This is an important limitation on the case for extending time, and may override what might otherwise have constituted good reason shown by the applicant for an extension of time.[47] It has been said that the question of prejudice or detriment to good administration does not arise for consideration unless and until the applicant has shown good reason for delay.[48] When it does arise, the burden of demonstrating hardship, prejudice or detriment usually lies with the respondent.[49]

A fine example of this limitation is seen in *Cheng Sing Sze v Director of Lands*, a case concerning compensation payments following the clearance of Kowloon Walled City. It would have been detrimental to good administration to allow a successful challenge, as the impugned scheme had been in operation for almost twenty years, had affected more than twenty-eight thousand people, and the special committee for the administration of which had long since been dissolved.[50] Elsewhere, it would have been detrimental to good administration for HK$298 million to be prevented from being returned from the Community Care Fund to the Government's general revenue, and preventing an additional HK$745,000 being earned as interest on that sum.[51]

Other examples of hardship, prejudice or detriment could include a possible opening of floodgates to litigation, the reopening of disciplinary decisions taken more than ten years previously, the impossibility of a particular remedy sought,[52] strain placed on the limited resources of bodies and general administrative difficulties.[53] Though it might be detrimental to the good

---

[47] *Law Chun Loy v Secretary for Justice* [2006] HKEC 1981, para.8.
[48] *Magapower Garments Ltd v Director General of Trade and Industry* [2002] HKEC 301, para.26, per Chu J.
[49] See *Chan Wai Keung v Commissioner of Police* [2010] HKEC 1624.
[50] *Cheng Sing Sze v Director of Lands* [2007] 1 HKLRD 141. The applicant also failed to show good reason for the delay.
[51] *Fung Elvira Binag v Secretary for Home Affairs* [2014] HKEC 400.
[52] *Tsui Kin Kwok v Commissioner of Police* [2010] HKEC 284, para.50. See also *Chiu Kin Ho v Commissioner of Police* [2010] HKEC 701, paras.23–24; and *Wong Tak Yiu v Commissioner of Police* [2010] HKEC 1531, paras.48–52.
[53] See *Tsui Chun Fai Danny v Commissioner of Police* [2010] HKEC 695, paras.22–30. Cheung J, who delivered the judgment in this case, gave very similar judgments in *Yiu Sung Chi v Commissioner of Police* [2010] HKEC 693, and *Li Kin Wah v Commissioner of Police* [2010] HKEC 694.

administration of justice to disturb the finality of previous litigation, that would not, in itself, constitute an absolute bar.[54] In line with section 21K(6) of the High Court Ordinance, even if leave has been granted, relief can be refused at the substantive hearing on the basis of hardship, prejudice or detriment.[55]

---

[54] *Re Lee Yee Shing Jacky* [2009] HKEC 605, para.27.
[55] *Ubamaka* v *Secretary for Security* [2011] 1 HKLRD 359, para.186.

6
Standing

Standing, also known by the Latin term *locus standi* (and sometimes simply referred to as *locus*), is concerned with the applicant's relation to the subject matter of his judicial review application. The applicant must be capable of persuading the court that he or she is sufficiently interested in the subject matter of the application. There are a number of policy reasons justifying this position. First, it is a means (but not the only means[1]) of filtering out unconnected applicants and busybodies. Judicial review consumes the resources of both the court and the respondent public body. An application should generally not be entertained where the applicant raises an issue to which he is not sufficiently connected and by which he is not sufficiently affected. Even if the issue is one which legitimately arises for judicial challenge, if the person or persons who are actually affected by the issue do not seek to raise a challenge in judicial review of their own volition, it is questionable whether time and resources should be consumed by permitting an insufficiently connected applicant to do so.

This filter also serves as a means of deterring powerful interest groups and those with deep pockets from mounting challenges where they are insufficiently connected to the subject matter. Judicial review should not be the plaything of those with the time or resources to mount legal challenges against reviewable decisions, but should generally be reserved for deserving disputes where a person is affected by a real, live issue in which they have a sufficient interest. In addition, judicial review should not be a conduit for political challenges, a means of bringing political disputes into the courtroom. By imposing standing requirements, the court has a tool with which to turn away applications from political entities, non-governmental organisations and even individuals who do not raise strictly legal questions. The filter effected by standing requirements in principle reduces the number of judicial review applications which proceed to a substantive hearing. If public body respondents are not required to substantively defend judicial review applications unless an applicant comes with a sufficient interest in the matter to which

---

[1] The requirement to demonstrate an arguable case is significant in this regard.

the application relates, this protects the resources of public bodies against speculative, non-serious or otherwise inappropriate challenges, discourages a litigious culture against public bodies and discourages a culture of defensive decision-making by public bodies.

The statutory test for standing is one of sufficient interest. The High Court Ordinance, s.21K(3), provides that:

> No application for judicial review shall be made unless the leave of the Court of First Instance has been obtained in accordance with the rules of court, and the court shall not grant leave to make such an application unless it considers that the applicant has a sufficient interest in the matter to which the application relates.

Order 53, Rule 3(7), likewise provides that:

> The Court shall not grant leave unless it considers that the applicant has a sufficient interest in the matter to which the application relates.

Two aspects of these provisions are noteworthy. First, the requirement that the applicant has a sufficient interest in the matter to which the application relates is mandatory. The court has no discretion as to whether applicants are subject to such a requirement. However, second, the statutory requirement of sufficient interest is unelaborated in both the High Court Ordinance and Order 53. The scope and content of sufficient interest is left to be worked out by the courts, and it is in that context that the courts have discretion on the issue of sufficient interest. Just as the courts are more likely to grant an application for leave which is out of time when the subject matter of the application is sufficiently important,[2] it seems that technical arguments on standing are less likely to be entertained when the subject matter is sufficiently important.[3] A perceived lack of standing also appears to be capable of leading the court to exercise its discretion to refuse relief at the substantive hearing.[4]

The issue of standing is related to arguability and qualitative filtering, as the courts' assessment of whether an applicant has a sufficient interest also requires that it consider the "matter to which the application relates".[5] For example, the substance of the claim may lead the court to the conclusion that the application is spurious, and therefore that the applicant has no standing. Indeed, it would be difficult to assess the issue of standing without considering at least to some extent the substance and merits of the application for review. Nevertheless, standing has been described as a low threshold aimed essentially

---

[2] See pp.46–47.
[3] *Association of Expatriate Civil Servants of Hong Kong* v *Chief Executive of HKSAR* [1998] 1 HKLRD 615, p.628. Nevertheless, sufficient interest will still have to be capable of being established.
[4] See *Anderson Asphalt Ltd* v *Town Planning Board* [2007] 3 HKLRD 18 (CA), para.69.
[5] *R* v *Inland Revenue Commissioners, ex parte National Federation of Self-Employed and Small Businesses Ltd* [1982] AC 617, p.653.

at avoiding abuse.[6] Standing does not necessarily arise as a purely preliminary issue detached from the substance of the case. It was considered in the House of Lords to be "unfortunate" for standing to be treated as a preliminary point:

> There may be simple cases in which it can be seen at the earliest stage that the person applying for judicial review has no interest at all, or no sufficient interest to support the application: then it would be quite correct at the threshold to refuse him leave to apply ... But in other cases this will not be so. In these it will be necessary to consider the powers or the duties in law of those against whom the relief is asked, the position of the applicant in relation to those powers or duties, and to the breach of those said to have been committed. In other words, the question of sufficient interest can not, in such cases, be considered in the abstract, or as an isolated point: it must be taken together with the legal and factual context.[7]

This has included the merits of the challenge as a prominent or even dominant consideration in the determination of standing, with other factors contributing to the establishment of sufficient interest including the importance of vindicating the rule of law, the importance of the issue raised, the likely absence of any other responsible challenger and the nature of the breach of duty against which relief is sought.[8] There are cases in which matters of substance have apparently been considered at the leave stage in determining the standing of the applicant, or in which substance appears overtly to have determined standing,[9] as well as cases in which the standing of the applicant was still being considered at the substantive hearing, suggesting overspill of standing as an issue beyond the leave stage.[10]

---

[6] *Chan Kai Wah* v *HKSAR* [2011] HKEC 412 (CA), para.25, per Hartmann JA. Where a hypothetical or "academic" question is raised, an applicant may have to demonstrate a stronger sufficient interest – see *Shek Lai San* v *Securities and Futures Commission* [2010] 4 HKC 168, para.57.

[7] *R* v *Inland Revenue Commissioners, ex parte National Federation of Self Employed and Small Businesses Ltd* [1982] AC 617 (HL), p.630, per Lord Wilberforce.

[8] *R* v *Secretary of State for Foreign and Commonwealth Affairs, ex parte World Development Movement Ltd* [1995] 1 WLR 386. It was cited as a relevant factor in determining sufficient interest that no other persons in the position of the applicant had made a legal challenge against the impugned decisions – *Shek Lai San* v *Securities and Futures Commission* [2010] 4 HKC 168, para.57–62.

[9] *Re Tran Quoc Cuong* v *Khuc The Loc* [1991] 2 HKLR 312.

[10] *Anderson Asphalt Ltd* v *Town Planning Board* [2007] 3 HKLRD 18, para.59. Cheung J stated in *Shek Lai San* v *Securities and Futures Commission* [2010] 4 HKC 168, para.62, that "[i]t is quite true that the question of sufficient interest is not infrequently left to the substantive hearing, and any doubt regarding standing is often resolved in favour of granting leave". In addition, Au J stated in *Ng Wing Hung* v *Hong Kong Examinations and Assessment Authority* [2010] HKEC 1471, para.13, that the court considers at the leave stage whether a *prima facie* case of sufficient interest is made out, and if leave is granted, the court may consider again the issue of sufficient interest at the substantive hearing "when all the evidence is placed before it"; citing also in this regard *R* v *Inland Revenue Commissioners, ex parte National Federation of Self-Employed and Small Businesses Ltd* [1982] AC 617 (HL), p.644.

There is some evidence that standing can be used as a way for the courts to sidestep politically sensitive questions. An example of this was where an elector in a Legislative Council geographic constituency applied for judicial review of the functional constituency electoral framework as in violation of Article 26 of the Basic Law and Article 21 of the Bill of Rights. The Court of Appeal held that the applicant did not have standing: he would have to show that he had a sufficient interest in the functional constituency electoral framework by, for example, being an elector in a functional constituency.[11] This is unpersuasive, as the functional constituency arrangement is already controversial and the applicant presumably had little control of the fact that he was not entitled to vote in a functional constituency. It would be a serious issue requiring urgent resolution were the functional constituency arrangements in violation of constitutional provisions, perhaps even justifying a relaxation of the degree of sufficient interest required to be shown. It is conceivable that the court was rather seeking to deter challenges of this nature in the future, by sheltering the functional constituency arrangements from constitutional attack by non-functional constituency electors, and standing was a convenient way of disposing of the case.

In another case, a resident of Hong Kong applied for judicial review seeking declarations that the Provisional Legislative Council which sat in Shenzhen prior to the Handover, purporting to pass bills for Hong Kong, was acting unlawfully. The High Court held that the applicant did not have sufficient interest in the matter to which the application related. Sears J gave the following opinion:

> [T]his matter, which is said to raise important constitutional matters, if that were the position, should have been brought by the Attorney-General of Hong Kong. The Attorney-General is the legal spokesman for the Hong Kong Government. If he thought the Provisional Legislature was acting contrary to the law, I am sure that he would have brought proceedings here, but he has chosen not to do so. What it appears to me is that this applicant is seeking to utilise the court to promote his own particular political interest ... Essentially, the judiciary here is being utilised so that it would become involved in this political conflict and it would have to promote in one way or another the political interests of Mr Martin Lee's client, the Democratic Party, or those who operate the Provisional Legislature. That is wrong because that would involve and threaten the independence of the judiciary. Whatever personal views one has about these matters, judges must stand back from this type of political conflict. A judge's duty is only to be concerned with those who break the law, either in criminal matters or break the law in civil matters.[12]

---

[11] *Mok Tai Kei* v *Constitutional Affairs Bureau of the HKSAR* [2005] 1 HKLRD 860 (CA). A similar conclusion had been reached in *Lee Miu Ling* v *Attorney General* [1996] 1 HKC 124 (CA).

[12] *Ng King Luen* v *Rita Fan* [1997] HKLRD 757, p.759.

This is, respectfully, an unpersuasive judgment. There is a clear difference between an applicant raising a political issue – which is clearly not apposite for judicial determination – and an applicant raising a legal issue which has political ramifications. Sears J stated that a judge's duty is "only to be concerned with those who break the law", but the applicant's contention was precisely that the Provisional Legislative Council was acting unlawfully. The applicant was concluded to have no standing because the Attorney General was instead regarded as the appropriate party to raise proceedings of this nature. However, if the Attorney General (now the Secretary for Justice) decides not to raise proceedings, should this be a bar to other persons applying for judicial review? The idea that the legality of a public body's actions should go unchallenged because a member of the government has declined to bring proceedings sits uncomfortably with the rule of law. The concern is that standing has again been used by the court to avoid ruling on an issue which would have resulted in significant political consequences – even though it was a challenge made on the basis of legality, which is precisely the remit of judicial review.

Personal Standing

An applicant[13] may personally have an interest in the subject matter of the application. This can take a number of different forms, such as a health, educational, immigration, financial, economic, commercial or property interest.[14] He could have a substantive benefit or interest affected, whether actual or potential, such as a licence, residence permit, employment or public housing entitlement. The applicant could have been affected by a procedural or fairness expectation, such as the procedural expectation of an oral hearing. He or she could also be affected in a professional capacity, such as findings of a Commission of Inquiry criticising an individual,[15] or findings of a Commission of Inquiry affecting the government's education policy and administration, which could afford standing to the Secretary for Education.[16] The court is concerned

---

[13] Whether a natural or legal person.

[14] On qualifying interests in the context of planning permission, see *R v St Edmundsbury Borough Council* [1985] 1 WLR 1168; *Capital Rich Development Ltd v Town Planning Board* [2007] 2 HKLRD 155 (CA); and *Anderson Asphalt Ltd v Town Planning Board* [2007] 3 HKLRD 18 (CA). The burden is on the applicant to adequately demonstrate detriment where it is alleged – see *Re Chan Yu Nam* [2005] HKEC 1343.

[15] *Re Wong Chi Kin* [2014] HKEC 1590 (CA). Though elsewhere it has been held that failure to establish a "legal right", perhaps because an application is premature and a decision-making procedure has not yet run its course, can lead to the conclusion that the applicant lacks sufficient interest – *Benbecula Ltd v Attorney General* [1994] 3 HKC 238, p.241. Consider also *Shek Lai San v Securities and Futures Commission* [2010] 4 HKC 168, paras.57–62 in the context of a "legal right".

[16] *Secretary for Justice v Commission of Inquiry Re Hong Kong Institute of Education* [2009] 4 HKLRD 11.

to recognise the standing of persons who are actually affected, or likely to be affected, by an act or decision. A sufficient interest will unlikely be successfully demonstrated where a person might, but will probably not, be affected in the future.[17] It should be noted that a deliberate change of behaviour to effectively give oneself sufficient interest may be regarded as abuse of process.[18]

Personal standing is not without controversy, however. In *Master Zhang Chaojie* v *Director of Immigration*,[19] a Mainland Chinese mother who resided in Hong Kong applied for permission for her young son to reside with her. The son's residency application was rejected by the Director of Immigration. The Court of First Instance held that the mother had no independent right to seek to quash the Director's decision, Yeung J adding that:

> [I]f the court were to allow locus to anyone who may be affected by a decision of the Director to make application directly and independently to the court, the court will probably be swarmed with applications by all sort of affected parties.[20]

It is difficult to understand how the mother could not be said to have a sufficient interest in whether her young son could reside with her in Hong Kong. It is also difficult to conciliate with the approach in the near-contemporaneous case of *Desmond Keane* v *Director of Legal Aid*.[21] Mr Keane, a practising barrister, had been nominated as the choice of counsel by an applicant for legal aid. Legal aid was granted to the applicant, but different counsel was assigned to act in the case. Mr Keane alleged that this was in breach of the Legal Aid Ordinance (cap.91) and applied for judicial review of the Director of Legal Aid's decision. On the subject of Mr Keane's standing, Keith JA opined that:

> I accept without reservation that the legally aided person is the beneficiary of any right which he may have to be represented by counsel of his choice. But that does not mean that if the Director of Legal Aid declines to give effect to the legally aided person's choice of counsel, counsel is unaffected by that decision. That he is affected by it is obvious. He is denied the chance to act for the legally aided person in the proceedings to which the legal aid certificate relates, thereby losing the opportunity to earn fees and to practise his skills. Now that the courts have "adopted a more generous concept of locus standi" in applications for judicial review (per Lord Roskill in the Fleet St. Casuals case at p. 658B), it cannot be said that Mr Keane did not have sufficient standing to pursue his case as originally formulated.[22]

Though the factual context is different, the contrasting approach to the issue of personal standing in these cases does not make for a flattering comparison.

---

[17] *Ng Wing Hung* v *Hong Kong Examinations and Assessment Authority* [2010] HKEC 1471.
[18] *Id.*, para.18.   [19] *Master Zhang Chaojie* v *Director of Immigration*, HCAL 5/2000.
[20] *Id.*, p.2. The son's standing was recognised by the court.
[21] *Desmond Keane* v *Director of Legal Aid*, CACV 49/2000.   [22] *Id.*, p.19.

Whilst a Mainland Chinese mother had no sufficient interest in whether her young son could reside with her in Hong Kong, a barrister had a sufficient interest in whether he was assigned as counsel on a successfully obtained legal aid certificate. This demonstrates the considerable potential for inconsistency in the determination of sufficient interest. That is true even of cases that are near-contemporaneous: the judgments in these cases were issued less than five months apart. It also suggests that a systematic approach to the determination of personal standing has not yet been developed by the courts.

Representative Standing

Representative standing can take the form of proxy, organisational and public interest standing.[23] This distinction is not formalised in the statutory rules or in the case law, but constitutes a useful analytical taxonomy for understanding the various scenarios in which a natural or legal person can apply for judicial review even when they are not personally sufficiently connected to the subject matter of the application.

Proxy standing describes a situation in which a person (who may not personally have a sufficient interest) represents another person (who does have a sufficient interest) in the application for judicial review. There should be good reason for the person with sufficient interest being represented in this way. For example, a next friend or guardian may represent a minor or mentally incapacitated person.[24] Organisational standing is where an individual or group purports to represent a group of individuals who would be able to establish a sufficient interest. For example, a professional association had standing to challenge a decision because it represented a class of officers, at least one of whom might be affected by the impugned decision, and it being possible that at least one of them wished for the association to challenge the decision on his behalf.[25]

Public interest standing is the broadest form of standing in that the applicant purports to represent the "public interest".[26] The Equal Opportunities Commission had standing to challenge the legality of a newspaper advertisement[27]

---

[23] This broadly reflects Peter Cane's division between surrogate, associational and citizen standing – Peter Cane, *Administrative Law* (5th edn) (Oxford University Press, 2011), p.285.
[24] See O.80. Note that the mother in *Master Zhang Chaojie* v *Director of Immigration*, HCAL 5/2000, was seeking to establish standing independently of her son.
[25] *R* v *Secretary for the Civil Service, ex parte Association of Expatriate Civil Servants of Hong Kong* (1995) 5 HKPLR 490; *Association of Expatriate Civil Servants of Hong Kong* v *Chief Executive of HKSAR* [1998] 1 HKLRD 615, p.629.
[26] Prominent examples from England and Wales include *R* v *Felixstowe Justices, ex parte Leigh* [1987] QB 582; *R* v *HM Inspectorate of Pollution, ex parte Greenpeace Ltd (No 2)* [1994] 4 All ER 329; and *R* v *Secretary of State for Foreign and Commonwealth Affairs, ex parte World Development Movement Ltd* [1995] 1 WLR 386 (the "Pergau Dam case").
[27] *Equal Opportunities Commission* v *Apple Daily Ltd* [1999] 1 HKLRD 188 (CA).

and a school transfer system,[28] each alleged to be discriminatory on the basis of sex.[29] The Society for the Protection of the Harbour Ltd was treated as having standing to challenge decisions of the Town Planning Board to reject the Society's objections to proposals to reclaim part of Victoria Harbour.[30] The standing of Clean Air Foundation Ltd and an environmental advocate to challenge multiple alleged failures by the Government to tackle air pollution was not challenged or doubted by the court.[31] Nor was the standing of two legally aided persons to challenge a decision not to classify the Queen's Pier as a monument under the Antiquities and Monuments Ordinance (cap.53) called into question.[32] There was no dispute as to the standing of a Legislative Councillor to challenge a decision of the Chief Executive-in-Council not to introduce minimum wage legislation with reference to the Trade Boards Ordinance (cap.63).[33] A resident living beside the site of the West Kowloon Terminus had his standing recognised to challenge a decision of the Finance Committee of the Legislative Council to approve funding for the Guangzhou-Shenzhen-Hong Kong Express Rail Link.[34]

There are a number of justifications for allowing public interest standing in appropriate cases. Charities, non-governmental organisations, unions and similar collective entities often have better resources than individuals for making judicial challenges, in the form of both financial resources and expertise, such as previous litigation experience and legal practitioners in their employment. Public interest standing therefore allows collective entities to challenge decisions that individuals are not necessarily financially or practically equipped to challenge, or to mount such challenges in a better formulated or financed, or more knowledgeable or strategic, way. This is particularly important in the case of entities representing disadvantaged, minority or vulnerable groups, who might not have the opportunity or resources to

---

[28] *Equal Opportunities Commission v Director of Education* [2001] 2 HKLRD 690.

[29] The statutory mandate of the Commission includes working towards the elimination of sex discrimination, promoting equality of opportunity between men and women, and working towards the elimination of sexual harassment – Sex Discrimination Ordinance (cap.480), s.64 (1). See also *R v Secretary of State for Employment, ex parte Equal Opportunities Commission* [1995] 1 AC 1 (HL).

[30] *Society for the Protection of the Harbour Ltd v Town Planning Board* [2003] 2 HKLRD 787; *Town Planning Board v Society for the Protection of the Harbour Ltd* (2004) 7 HKCFAR 1.

[31] *Clean Air Foundation Ltd v Government of HKSAR* [2007] HKEC 1356.

[32] *Chu Hoi Dick v Secretary for Home Affairs* [2007] HKEC 1471. The application failed for other reasons.

[33] *Leung Kwok Hung v Chief Executive in Council* [2008] HKEC 780 (CA). The application failed for other reasons.

[34] *Chan Kai Wah v HKSAR* [2011] HKEC 412 (CA). The Court of First Instance had denied that the applicant had standing – *Re Chan Kai Wah* [2010] HKEC 789. Whilst this may appear to be an instance of personal standing, it was stated in the Court of First Instance that the applicant's interest was "no more, nor less, than that of any ordinary civic-minded person living in Hong Kong who is concerned about matters going on here" and that he had "no private interest in the outcome of the judicial review" – *id.*, para.5, per Reyes J.

challenge decisions by way of judicial review, or whose interests might otherwise not be represented well, or represented at all, in legal proceedings. An application by a single entity may also be more efficient than a number of individual applications for judicial review, with a collective pooling of resource and argument, rather than the advancement of individual or even conjoint applications for judicial review.

Moreover, there is an important rule of law argument in favour of organisational, and in particular public interest, standing being permitted in appropriate cases. This is to recognise that, on balance, it can be in the interests of justice to afford greater priority to permitting a challenge to the legality of an act or decision than to insisting on procedural formalities in terms of standing. This was adverted to by Lord Diplock:

> It would, in my view, be a grave lacuna in our system of public law if a pressure group, like the federation, or even a single public-spirited taxpayer, were prevented by outdated technical rules of *locus standi* from bringing the matter to the attention of the court to vindicate the rule of law and get the unlawful conduct stopped.[35]

In particular, there may be situations in which there does not seem to be another appropriate challenger to a particular decision, which might strengthen the standing asserted by the challenger in a specific case.[36] The motives of the applicant are also important; in particular, the application should not be made for an ill motive.[37]

There are of course limits to representative standing on an organisational or public interest basis. Crucially, the applicant must still have a sufficient interest in the matter to which the application relates, bearing in mind that this is a statutory requirement and is mandatory. It should in principle not be difficult for organisations such as Greenpeace or the World Wide Fund for Nature (WWF) to make a public interest challenge to an environmental decision,[38] whereas it might be more difficult for a trade union or a charity representing victims of domestic violence to demonstrate a sufficient interest in an environmental decision.

There are also potential drawbacks to allowing public interest standing. It has the potential to allow political or policy battles to be introduced to the courtroom, or for interest groups to pursue their own policy agenda through

---

[35] *R v Inland Revenue Commissioners, ex parte National Federation of Self Employed and Small Businesses Ltd* [1982] AC 617 (HL), p.644. See also *R v Secretary of State for Foreign and Commonwealth Affairs, ex parte World Development Movement Ltd* [1995] 1 WLR 386.

[36] See *R v HM Inspectorate of Pollution, ex parte Greenpeace Ltd (No 2)* [1994] 4 All ER 329, para.82; and *R v Secretary of State for Foreign and Commonwealth Affairs, ex parte World Development Movement Ltd* [1995] 1 WLR 386, p.395.

[37] *R v Somerset County Council, ex parte Dixon* [1998] Env LR 111, p.121, per Sedley J.

[38] See, for example, *R v HM Inspectorate of Pollution, ex parte Greenpeace Ltd (No 2)* [1994] 4 All ER 329.

judicial review. Organisations may have broader motivations for seeking judicial review, such as opposition to an administration or particular government department, organisational reputation and prestige. Such entities will not necessarily be not-for-profit organisations, and it may be considered whether and to what extent the status of an entity seeking to assert public interest (or organisational) standing as a for-profit entity should have any bearing on whether its standing is recognised. Moreover, whilst she may be motivated by political considerations, the Chief Executive has standing, essentially on a public interest basis, to bring applications for judicial review seeking enforcement of the Basic Law or other laws in force in Hong Kong. In this regard it would seem that the Chief Executive is mandated by the Basic Law to bring proceedings in such circumstances:

> The Chief Executive of the Hong Kong Special Administrative Region shall exercise the following powers and functions ... To be responsible for the implementation of this Law and other laws which, in accordance with this Law, apply in the Hong Kong Special Administrative Region.[39]

Accordingly, the Chief Executive had standing to seek an injunction by way of judicial review, under section 21J of the High Court Ordinance (cap.4), restraining the President of the Legislative Council from administering or allowing to be administered new oaths under section 19 of the Oaths and Declarations Ordinance (cap.11).[40] This concerned the oath-taking controversy of Sixtus Leung Chung Hang and Yau Wai Ching, elected as members of the Legislative Council, who purported to take their oaths in a manner sure to upset the HKSAR and Mainland Governments (and later confirmed to be an unlawful manner). Though the context and manner in which judicial review proceedings were commenced made it likely that political motives underlay the Chief Executive's judicial intervention (particularly as the Chief Executive rarely applies for judicial review in this way), legally there can be little doubt that he was entitled to commence proceedings.[41]

It is worth asking more broadly whether and to what extent a given organisation faithfully represents the interests of the cause or persons it purports to represent.[42] Does the organisation claiming to represent environmental causes faithfully do so, or is it also, or instead, motivated by social policy? Does the charity claiming to represent the elderly faithfully represent their interests? Are the interests of elderly people uniform across the board? What gives one organisation the right to claim that it represents the elderly,

---

[39] Basic Law, Art.48(2).
[40] *Chief Executive of HKSAR* v *President of the Legislative Council* [2017] 1 HKLRD 460 (CA).
[41] The standing of other government officials has also been established. In *Secretary for Justice* v *Commission of Inquiry Re Hong Kong Institute of Education* [2009] 4 HKLRD 11, the court was satisfied that the Secretary for Education had sufficient interest – *Secretary for Justice* v *Commission of Inquiry Re Hong Kong Institute of Education* [2009] 4 HKLRD 11, paras.43–45.
[42] See Cane, *Administrative Law*, pp.287–288.

and to assert a sufficient interest on that basis, whereas another organisation claiming to represent the elderly might have different views on the relevant issues, and might also apply (or might decide not to apply) for judicial review?[43] In addition, not all disadvantaged, minority or vulnerable groups are represented, or represented to the same extent, by organisations. The same applies to causes, whether environmental, scientific, educational, recreational, cultural or otherwise. Are courts at risk of taking for granted the claims made by such organisations to faithfully represent the interests of persons affected by the decision challenged in the judicial review application? How should courts make that assessment, and does this not take courts into unfamiliar, complex and potentially time-consuming territory? Moreover, it is not only organisations and collective entities that can assert public interest standing, but individuals. How should the court treat the individual who seeks to assert public interest standing?[44] The courts are not faced with an easy task in developing a systematic approach to these questions.

The usual costs rule is that the losing party is required to pay the relevant costs of the litigation.[45] However, the courts are open to making an exception in representative standing applications.[46] The exception is neither automatic nor a general immunity from the payment of costs, but a matter for the court's discretion having regard to the circumstances of the application.[47] Of particular relevance is where the litigation has apparently not been for

---

[43] Whilst judicial review is putatively confined to questions of legality, the reality is that an application for judicial review is unlikely to be made where the potential applicant is satisfied with the merits of the decision. For example, Elderly Charity A might approve of the merits of a government decision on elderly residential care provision, whilst Elderly Charity B might disapprove of its merits. All else being equal, Elderly Charity A is less likely than Elderly Charity B to contest the legality of the government decision.

[44] On public interest standing, see further Po Jen Yap, "Understanding Public Interest Litigation in Hong Kong" (2008) 37 *Common Law World Review* 257.

[45] O.62, r.3(2). However, the court has discretion in this regard. Where, for example, an applicant sought an order of certiorari, but instead obtained an order of mandamus, which they had not sought in their Form 86A notice, the court awarded the applicant 75 per cent of costs – *Yue Yuen Marketing Co Ltd v Commissioner of Inland Revenue* [2012] 4 HKLRD 761, para.70; and see also *Kong Tai Shoes Manufacturing Co Ltd v Commissioner of Inland Revenue* [2012] 4 HKLRD 780, para.68, where it was held that the applicant would be awarded 75 per cent of costs due to the applicant making an "unjustified allegation" against the respondent. On protective costs orders, see *Designing Hong Kong Ltd v Town Planning Board* [2017] 2 HKLRD 60 (CA). On costs relating to an unsuccessful leave application, see *Leung Kwok Hung v President of the Legislative Council (No 2)* (2014) 17 HKCFAR 841, para.17; and *Kwok Cheuk Kin v Secretary for Transport and Housing* [2016] HKEC 172. Tang V-P said that it takes unusual circumstances for an award of costs to be made against an applicant for leave and that the court should be sparing in the exercise of such discretion – *Sky Wide Development Ltd v Building Authority* [2011] 5 HKLRD 202, para.28.

[46] *Lo Siu Lan v Hong Kong Housing Authority* [2005] HKEC 279 (CA); *Ho Choi Wan v Hong Kong Housing Authority* [2006] HKEC 13 (CFA).

[47] See *Town Planning Board v Society for Protection of the Harbour Ltd (No 2)* (2004) 7 HKCFAR 114; *Leung Kwok Hung v President of the Legislative Council* [2007] HKEC 788; and *Chu Hoi Dick v Secretary for Home Affairs* [2007] HKEC 1640.

private gain, but for the furtherance of the public interest, noting that even a failed application can result in clarification of the law and legal rights and interests. Lam J set out general conditions to be satisfied before the court would depart from its usual costs order, subject to the court's discretion:

(a) A litigant has properly brought proceedings to seek guidance from the court on a point of general public importance so that the litigation is for the benefit of the community as a whole (understood objectively) to warrant that the costs of the litigation be borne by the public purse as costs incidental to good public administration.
(b) The judicial decision has contributed to the proper understanding of the law in question.
(c) The litigant has no private gain in the outcome.[48]

The rationale is to recognise that public interest challenges can make a positive and constructive contribution to the clarification and development of the law, and potential public interest challengers should not be deterred from applying for review merely for fear of bearing the burden of the usual costs order. However, it is questionable to what extent the possibility of this exception being made is sufficiently certain and predictable so as to ameliorate such deterrence on the part of aspiring public interest challengers. It is also important that reasonable controls are maintained on the granting of this exception so as to protect against the utilisation of judicial review as a mechanism for airing general public grievances.

---

[48] *Chu Hoi Dick* v *Secretary for Home Affairs* [2007] HKEC 1640 at para.29. These criteria are cumulative.

7

Judicial Review and the Public/Private Divide

Judicial review in Hong Kong is, as in England and Wales, concerned principally with reviewing the legality of acts and decisions of public bodies or bodies performing public functions.[1] This is consistent with the classification of administrative law (including judicial review) as a branch of public law,[2] invoking the special standards and duties which apply to bodies acting in a public (law) capacity. By contrast, the private (law) activities of public bodies generally lie beyond the reach of judicial review, and it is the nature of the function exercised – not the identity of the body exercising it – that primarily determines whether judicial review is available against the impugned act or decision. Applicants must therefore be capable of demonstrating a sufficient public element in the impugned act or decision, otherwise they may face denial of leave or the withholding of relief. As the concept of 'publicness' substantially defines the scope of review, it is necessary to consider the principles and rules on what constitutes a sufficient public element. It will be seen that, although the public/private distinction may seem intuitive, it can raise intractable difficulties such as in cases involving mixed questions of public and private law, and where powers are exercised which are close to the boundary between public and private power.

Requirement for a Sufficient Public Element

The statutory procedure regulating judicial review in Hong Kong is heavily modelled on that in England and Wales.[3] The procedure is substantially (but

---

[1] This is not strictly true in all jurisdictions. In Scotland, for example, susceptibility to judicial review is defined not by whether the body under challenge was performing a public function, but whether the body exceeded its jurisdiction. Though most of the entities captured by this test are bodies performing public functions, it also allows private bodies to be judicially reviewed, even when they are not performing a public function. Thus, there are examples of sporting associations and contractually appointed arbiters being successfully judicially reviewed. See further Stephen Thomson, 'The Doctrinal Core of the Supervisory Jurisdiction of the Court of Session' [2016] Public Law 670.
[2] Though see Stephen Thomson, 'Judicial Review and Public Law: Challenging the Preconceptions of a Troubled Taxonomy' (2017) 41(2) Melbourne University Law Review 890.
[3] Previously section 31 of the Supreme Court Act 1981 (later renamed the Senior Courts Act 1981), and Order 53 of the Rules of the Supreme Court; now Part 54 of the Civil Procedure Rules.

not entirely) remedy-driven, noting that the choice of remedy bears on the form of action:

(1) An application to the Court of First Instance for one or more of the following forms of relief –
   (a) an order of mandamus, prohibition or certiorari;
   (b) an injunction under section 21J restraining a person not entitled to do so from acting in an office to which that section applies,
   shall be made in accordance with rules of court by a procedure to be known as an application for judicial review.
(2) An application for a declaration or an injunction (not being an injunction mentioned in subsection (1)) may be made in accordance with rules of court by way of an application for judicial review, and on such an application the Court of First Instance may grant the declaration or injunction claimed if it considers that, having regard to-
   (a) the nature of the matters in respect of which relief may be granted by orders of mandamus, prohibition or certiorari;
   (b) the nature of the persons and bodies against whom relief may be granted by such orders; and
   (c) all the circumstances of the case,
   it would be just and convenient for the declaration to be made or the injunction to be granted, as the case may be.[4]

This provision is mirrored by Order 53 in the Rules of the High Court:

(1) An application for judicial review must be made if the applicant is seeking-
   (a) an order for mandamus, prohibition or certiorari; or
   (b) an injunction under section 21J of the Ordinance restraining a person from acting in any office in which he is not entitled to act.
(2) An application for judicial review may be made if the applicant is seeking-
   (a) a declaration; or
   (b) an injunction (not being an injunction mentioned in paragraph (1)(b)).
(3) An application for judicial review may include an application for an award of damages, restitution or the recovery of a sum due but may not seek such a remedy alone.[5]

Whilst the remedies of mandamus, prohibition and certiorari can only be pursued using an application for judicial review, it can be seen that declaration and injunction can be obtained either on an application for judicial review or in an ordinary action. The question is whether a declaration or injunction can be obtained in respect of "public law liability" in an ordinary action,

---

[4] High Court Ordinance (cap.4), s.21K(1) and (2).   [5] O.53, r.1.

or whether they would have to be obtained using an application for judicial review in respect of such liability.

This question was in principle resolved in *O'Reilly* v *Mackman*.[6] Four prisoners sought to challenge disciplinary decisions made by a prison authority. They sought declarations by way of ordinary action, even though the core of their respective challenges was regarded as sounding in public law. It was held by the House of Lords that it would be an abuse of process for the plaintiffs to seek protection of their public law rights by way of ordinary action, which would deny the respondents the protections afforded to them by Order 53, for example those on standing and time limits.[7] Public law issues were exclusively for transaction by way of judicial review procedure, embodied in the concept of procedural exclusivity.[8] The wrong procedure having been selected in this case, the proceedings were struck out as an abuse of process.

This was the general position, clarified by Lord Diplock in his leading judgment:

> My Lords, I have described this as a general rule; for though it may normally be appropriate to apply it by the summary process of striking out the action, there may be exceptions, particularly where the invalidity of the decision arises as a collateral issue in a claim for the infringement of a right of the plaintiff arising under private law, or where none of the parties objects to the adoption of the procedure by writ or originating summons. Whether there should be other exceptions should, in my view, at this stage in the development of procedural public law, be left to be decided on a case to case basis – a process that your Lordships will be continuing in the next case in which judgment is to be delivered today.[9]

That case was *Cocks* v *Thanet District Council*.[10] The plaintiff had applied to a local authority for permanent accommodation, but was housed in temporary accommodation. He alleged that the local authority was in breach of its statutory duty under the Housing (Homeless Persons) Act 1977, seeking declaration, injunctions and damages in that regard. The question was whether the issue should be raised by way of ordinary action or judicial review, and the plaintiff having chosen an ordinary action, the House of Lords held that the case fell within the general rule articulated by Lord Diplock in *O'Reilly* v *Mackman*.

---

[6] *O'Reilly* v *Mackman* [1983] 2 AC 237. For the principle applied to a challenge to the validity of an Ordinance under the Bill of Rights, see *Lau Wong Fat* v *Attorney General* [1997] HKLRD 533.
[7] See also *Cocks* v *Thanet District Council* [1983] 2 AC 286, pp.294–295.
[8] Christopher Forsyth described the principle of procedural exclusivity as "the principle that a litigant may on occasion be restricted to the use of only one of the two potentially applicable procedures" – C. F. Forsyth, 'Beyond *O'Reilly* v *Mackman*: The Foundations and Nature of Procedural Exclusivity' (1985) 44(3) Cambridge Law Journal 415, p.416.
[9] *O'Reilly* v *Mackman* [1983] 2 AC 237, p.285.
[10] *Cocks* v *Thanet District Council* [1983] 2 AC 286.

The plaintiff's claim fundamentally relied on a challenge to the authority's public law decision as to the circumstances of his homelessness (in particular if he had a priority need and if he was intentionally homeless), and any private law rights flowed only after a determination of the public law issue. Accordingly, the challenge should have been made by way of judicial review. Furthermore, as Lord Bridge of Harwich pointed out in the leading judgment, there could be no valid reason, where the quashing of a decision was the sole remedy sought, why it should be sought otherwise than by certiorari.[11] That remedy, under Order 53 in England and Wales, and under the High Court Ordinance and Order 53 in Hong Kong at present, must be sought by way of judicial review.[12]

It did not take long for the principle embodied in *O'Reilly* v *Mackman* to be applied in Hong Kong. It is important to note, however, the two juridical bases on which the procedural exclusivity principle was constructed: abuse of process on the one hand, and interpretation of the relevant statutory provisions on remedies on the other.[13] The principle has therefore become broader than the relatively narrow question of whether declaration or injunction can be sought in relation to public law liability using ordinary procedure, setting out in more general terms that public law issues should generally be transacted by way of judicial review, and that private law issues should generally be transacted by way of ordinary procedure.

Thus, the general principle was applied by the High Court in the Summer of 1984. A tenderer sought judicial review of the Director of Lands' rejection of its tender for a lot in Sha Tin. It was held that the issue was one of private law, namely contract, and therefore not a matter of public law and not susceptible to judicial review.[14] The following year, the High Court issued a similar judgment. The applicants had their racecourse guest badges removed by the Hong Kong Jockey Club and were barred from the racecourses for two years on the allegation that they were suspected of bookmaking in contravention of the Gambling Ordinance (cap.148). They had obtained the guest badges via friends who were members of the Jockey Club; the applicants were not, themselves, members. The applicants sought judicial review on the ground of breach of natural justice. It was held that this was a contractual matter: any rights arising from the Jockey Club's unilateral termination of the contract, such as in damages, were not of a public law nature and not subject to judicial review. Though the Jockey Club purported to exercise powers under the Gambling Ordinance, it exercised neither a judicial nor ministerial function, but discretion that was not subject to judicial review.[15]

---

[11] *Id.*, p.295.   [12] High Court Ordinance, s.21K (cap.4), s.1; O.53, r.1(1).
[13] At the time of the case this was the Supreme Court Act 1981, s.31(2) in England and Wales; at present in Hong Kong it is the High Court Ordinance (cap.4), s.21K(2).
[14] *Re an application by Yau Fook Hong Co Ltd* [1985] HKLR 42.
[15] *Re an application by Harris Tsang Shing-kung* [1986] HKLR 356.

A further example may be taken from the employment sphere. A woman employed by the Equal Opportunities Commission had her contract terminated. She claimed that her dismissal was not in accordance with the Disciplinary Policy and Procedures of the Commission and her right to a fair hearing prior to disciplinary action being taken against her, and sought leave to apply for judicial review. It was held that any rights the applicant had in relation to the Disciplinary Policy and Procedures and her putative right to a fair hearing were rights enjoyed only in private law. They flowed, if anywhere, from her contract of employment with the Commission. The court refused the application for leave, the general procedural exclusivity principle again being applied.[16]

Collateral challenge

Collateral defence

By collateral defence is meant a challenge to a public law decision which is defensive in nature and asserted in proceedings other than judicial review. In a case before the House of Lords,[17] a local council resolved to increase rents under housing legislation.[18] The council served two notices of rent increase on the plaintiff, the tenant of a council flat. The tenant continued to pay the previous level of rent, refusing to pay the increase. The council brought an ordinary action against the tenant for rent arrears and claiming possession of the flat. The tenant submitted in his defence that the rent increases were *ultra vires* and therefore void, justifying his refusal to pay the increase in rent. This constituted a challenge to the legality of what was putatively a public law decision on the part of the local council, and accordingly the council sought for the claim to be struck out as an abuse of process.

The House of Lords held that this was not an abuse of process, and that the tenant was entitled to argue the illegality of a public law decision as a defence to a private law claim. As Lord Fraser of Tullybelton explained, Order 53 cannot have swept away the right to such a challenge. The tenant could not be described as abusing or misusing the process of the court: he did not select the procedure to be adopted. Instead, he was "seeking only to exercise the ordinary right of any individual to defend an action against him on the ground that he is not liable for the whole sum claimed by the plaintiff".[19] Moreover, he

---

[16] *Priscilla Sit Ka Yin* v *Equal Opportunities Commission* [1998] HKEC 898.
[17] *Wandsworth London Borough Council v Winder (No 1)* [1985] AC 461 (HL).
[18] Housing Act 1957.
[19] Lewison J stated in the Chancery Division that where a "defendant to a claim wishes to challenge a public law decision as part of his defence, the court does not have any discretion to refuse to allow him to do so, unless either the raising of the defence is an abuse of process or it has no reasonable prospect of success" – *Bunney v Burns Anderson plc* [2007] EWHC 1240 (Ch), para.47.

"puts forward his defence as a matter of right, whereas in an application for judicial review, success would require an exercise of the court's discretion in his favour".[20]

The implications of this interpretation were extraordinary: a person subject to an *ultra vires* decision could in principle wait until the public body which made that decision pursued him by way of an ordinary action before asserting the illegality of the decision in his defence. This would enable him to avoid the time limits and other restrictions encountered in judicial review procedure, leaving the decision unchallenged until the public body brings legal proceedings against him. Meanwhile, the decision stands as ostensibly valid and potentially affects other persons in a similar situation, perhaps leading to greater resource and cost consumption when challenged at a later stage. This may be argued to defeat part of the purpose for having a separate procedure for judicial review. Furthermore, as Lord Fraser of Tullybelton pointed out, the court's award of remedies in judicial review is discretionary, whereas in an ordinary action the tenant's defence is asserted as a matter of right. Though there are risks associated with ignoring an *ultra vires* decision and waiting to be pursued in litigation by the public authority, the collateral defence asserted as a matter of right in ordinary proceedings to some extent bypasses the discretionary nature of the award of remedies had the matter been litigated by way of judicial review.

This is not to dispute the House of Lords' position on the law. Even as a matter of principle, there is an argument in the tenant's favour which would serve as a counterargument to the concerns just expressed. If a public body purports to make an *ultra vires* decision and the individual affected by it suspects it is *ultra vires* and therefore chooses to ignore it (acknowledging that this might be a risky course of action), is it not that individual's prerogative to ignore it? Why should the burden of proving the *ultra vires* nature of the purported decision, and the corresponding burden of the time and costs of litigation, be saddled upon the person affected by the purported decision, if its illegality can also be "acknowledged" by doing nothing? Would it be right or fair to exclude the individual from a remedy or from judicial protection because he chose not to proactively raise an application for judicial review, or was not able to do so?

Moreover, as a matter of legal doctrine, a conclusion other than that reached by the House of Lords would be difficult to sustain. An *ultra vires* decision is a legal nullity. The rent increases in this case were (alleged to be) a legal nullity; to have no legal effect. Could the tenant rightly be expected to apply for judicial review to challenge the legality of the rent increases *in anticipation* of being pursued in private law for rent arrears? As the rent increases were (suspected to be) a legal nullity, would it have been right as a matter of

---

[20] *Wandsworth London Borough Council v Winder (No 1)* [1985] AC 461 (HL), p.509. On the discretionary nature of remedies in judicial review, see pp.293–301.

doctrine and principle to hold that the tenant's position (and the effective status of the rent increases) had thereby been changed in law, such as by holding that the individual was barred from arguing the illegality defence in the ordinary action raised against him? Would this not undermine the idea that the purported rent increases were a legal nullity?

The collateral defence, whereby the illegality of the public body's act or decision can be pleaded in defence to an ordinary action, can produce controversial results. A prime example is found in *Crédit Suisse v Allerdale Borough Council*.[21] It is an unusual example in that the illegality defence was pleaded by the public body itself, namely as a means of contesting its own private law liability. A local authority in the north west of England desired to undertake an infrastructure project but was unable to raise sufficient funds through its normal funding allocation from central government. It was also unable to borrow the necessary funds to pay for the project. Undeterred, it established a private company, wholly owned by the local authority. The company borrowed the funds from Crédit Suisse, the funds thereafter being used to finance the infrastructure project. The local authority guaranteed the loan. When the company defaulted on the loan, Crédit Suisse called in the guarantor, namely the local authority. Crédit Suisse sought enforcement of the guarantee by way of an ordinary action.

There was, however, a major problem for Crédit Suisse: the local authority had no statutory power to guarantee the loan. The authority therefore acted *ultra vires* in purporting to guarantee the loan, rendering the guarantee void. The authority pleaded its lack of legal power to guarantee the loan as a defence to non-payment; in other words, the public body pleaded a species of collateral defence to deny its ostensible liability in private law. Controversial and even objectionable as that may be, the Court of Appeal held that the local authority had no legal power to guarantee the loan, rendering the guarantee of no legal effect and thus unenforceable. The court had little choice in terms of strict legal doctrine. The local authority was a creature of statute, from which it obtained its powers. If statute did not give the local authority the power to guarantee the loan, the court could not give it that power. It did not matter that the local authority was pleading its own collateral defence to evade contractual liability.[22] It could not be estopped from doing so. It also did not matter, as far as the strict law was concerned, that Crédit Suisse would therefore be unable to recover the loan monies.[23] It had never entered into a

---

[21] *Crédit Suisse v Allerdale Borough Council* [1997] QB 306.

[22] It is assumed – absent evidence to the contrary in the judgment – that the local authority did not act to deceive Crédit Suisse when signing the contract of guarantee, otherwise there could have been valid grounds for claiming fraudulent misrepresentation against the authority. This could sound in civil and/or criminal proceedings.

[23] It may be thought that a possible avenue of redress for Crédit Suisse would have been to sue for unjust enrichment. However, this claim could not necessarily be mounted against the local authority where the funds have been transferred to the company, not the local authority as

valid contract of guarantee with the local authority, despite appearances to the contrary.

It is not just in the civil context that the collateral defence can be seen. The illegality of an administrative decision or bylaw can also be competently mounted as a defence to a criminal prosecution.[24] Just as procedural exclusivity would not apply in a civil case where a defendant sought to defend himself by questioning the validity of a public law decision:

> One would expect a defendant in a criminal case, where the liberty of the subject is at stake, to have no lesser rights. Provided that the invalidity of the byelaw is or may be a defence to the charge a criminal case must be the paradigm of collateral or defensive challenge.[25]

As Lord Steyn explained, it may not be possible or feasible for the bylaw to be (successfully) challenged by way of judicial review:

> The defendant may, however, be out of time before he becomes aware of the existence of the byelaw. He may lack the resources to defend his interests in two courts. He may not be able to obtain legal aid for an application for leave to apply for judicial review. Leave to apply for judicial review may be refused. At a substantive hearing his scope for demanding examination of witnesses in the Divisional Court may be restricted. He may be denied a remedy on a discretionary basis. The possibility of judicial review will, therefore, in no way compensate him for the loss of *the right* to defend himself by a defensive challenge to the byelaw in cases where the invalidity of the byelaw might afford him with a defence to the charge.[26]

However, the "right" to defend oneself in criminal proceedings by way of a collateral defence is not absolute. If, for example, the statute only requires an act which appears formally valid and which has not been set aside on appeal or quashed on judicial review, then the collateral criminal defence must be read subject to the language of the statute and may not be effective.[27] However, only "clear language" in the statute could deny the right to plead a collateral criminal defence.[28]

The statutory context has been interpreted in Hong Kong to disentitle a defendant from raising a collateral criminal defence on the basis that legislative

---

such. In addition, such a claim could not necessarily be mounted against the company where it was the contract of guarantee (not the contract of loan) that was not validly concluded.

[24] *Boddington v British Transport Police* [1999] 2 AC 143 (HL), disapproving *Bugg v Director of Public Prosecutions* [1993] QB 473. Lord Steyn described the observations in *Bugg* as "contrary to authority and principle", and the consequences of that case "too austere and indeed too authoritarian to be compatible with the traditions of the common law" – *Boddington v British Transport Police* [1999] 2 AC 143 (HL), p.173.

[25] *Id.*, pp.172–173, per Lord Steyn.   [26] *Id.*, p.173. Emphasis in the original.

[27] *R v Wicks* [1998] AC 92 (HL); *Boddington v British Transport Police* [1999] 2 AC 143 (HL), p.173.

[28] *Id.*, p.162.

intention cannot have been for a "busy magistrate's court" to be the proper forum for determining public law illegality, that the statute and directions issued thereunder allowed for a reasonable time for compliance and for challenging their legality "in a more appropriate forum", and that to allow the collateral criminal defence to be pleaded would be to determine issues of considerable public importance without the relevant decision-maker having standing as a party to proceedings.[29] Relevant also is whether the defendant had an alternative procedure available by which to challenge the relevant act or decision.[30] It was stated that where there was another channel available for challenging the validity of an order in relation to which a person was now being prosecuted, permitting a defendant to use a collateral criminal defence was "something to be avoided".[31] Nevertheless, these factors will not necessarily prevent a defence being made on the basis of the unconstitutionality of the offence-creating provision.[32]

Collateral attack

The so-called collateral attack arose as an issue just one year after *O'Reilly v Mackman*, in a case described by Lord Fraser of Tullybelton as its "sequel".[33] The plaintiff was the owner of premises and was served with an enforcement notice by the local authority under town planning legislation.[34] The time limit for appealing against the notice expired without an appeal being made by the plaintiff. Thereafter, he commenced an ordinary action alleging that his failure to appeal was a result of negligent advice given to him by the local authority. He also sought an injunction restraining implementation of the enforcement notice and damages for negligence. This was essentially a private law claim. However, the defendants sought to have the claim struck out as an abuse of process. Judicial review, it was argued, would be the appropriate means of asserting a public law right.

The House of Lords held that there was no abuse of process in this case. The plaintiff was not bringing a public law challenge, but was seeking to exercise a private law right in tort. That, in addition to the fact the plaintiff was seeking damages, would have been inappropriate for pursuit by way of judicial review. The case did not fall within the scope of the rule laid down in *O'Reilly v*

---

[29] *HKSAR v Incorporated Owners of No 10 Bonham Strand* [2004] HKEC 675, paras. 17–19 and 24.
[30] *Id.*, para.19; *HKSAR v Joy Express Ltd (No 2)* [2005] HKEC 554; *HKSAR v Sky Wide Development Ltd* [2013] 1 HKLRD 613.
[31] *HKSAR v Tse Yee Ping* [2015] HKEC 1134, para.89, per Wong J.
[32] *Secretary for Justice v Ocean Technology Ltd* [2009] 3 HKLRD F1; *Secretary for Justice v Richard Ethan Latker* [2009] HKEC 132, paras.62–64 and 162–163. See also *Koon Wing Yee v Insider Dealing Tribunal* (2008) 11 HKCFAR 170; and consider *Leung v Secretary for Justice* [2006] 4 HKLRD 211 (CA).
[33] *Davy v Spelthorne Borough Council* [1984] AC 262 (HL), p.269.
[34] Town and Country Planning Act 1971.

Mackman, and could be contrasted with the facts of *Cocks v Thanet District Council*. Whereas in *Cocks* the plaintiff sought to impugn or overturn the decision made by the public body, in the present case the plaintiff was not seeking to impugn or overturn the decision. In fact, the plaintiff's "whole case on negligence depends on the fact that he has lost his chance to impugn it".[35]

In *Roy v Kensington and Chelsea and Westminster Family Practitioner Committee*,[36] a medical practitioner raised an ordinary action against his medical practice for payment that had been withheld by them on the basis that the practitioner had failed to meet a criterion in secondary legislation.[37] It was held that this was not an abuse of process as the practitioner was merely seeking to enforce a private law right, even though it comprised a collateral attack on a public law act or decision. As Lord Lowry explained, there were a number of reasons why the case should fall outside the scope of the general rule articulated in *O'Reilly v Mackman*, or for regarding it as falling within one of Lord Diplock's exceptions therein expressed. These included the fact that the medical practitioner had either a contractual or statutory private law right to remuneration, that his private law rights dominated the proceedings even if he sought to enforce performance of a public law duty, that the type of claim may involve disputed issues of fact, that an order for payment of monies could not be granted by way of judicial review,[38] and that there should not be a need for leave or a special time limit, nor should relief be discretionary, where individual, private law rights were claimed. Moreover, assuming the rule in *O'Reilly v Mackman* was one of general application, it was "subject to many exceptions based on the nature of the claim and on the undesirability of erecting procedural barriers".[39]

Lord Bridge of Harwich acknowledged doubts expressed about *O'Reilly v Mackman* and *Cocks v Thanet District Council*, but defended their underlying principle:

> The decisions of this House in *O'Reilly v Mackman* [1983] 2 AC 237 and *Cocks v Thanet District Council* [1983] 2 AC 286, have been the subject of much academic criticism. Although I appreciate the cogency of some of the arguments advanced in support of that criticism, I have not been persuaded that the essential principle embodied in the decisions requires to be significantly modified, let alone overturned. But if it is important, as I believe, to maintain the principle, it is certainly no less important that its application should be confined within proper limits. It is appropriate that an issue which

---

[35] *Davy v Spelthorne Borough Council* [1984] AC 262 (HL), pp.273–274.
[36] *Roy v Kensington and Chelsea and Westminster Family Practitioner Committee* [1992] 1 AC 624 (HL).
[37] National Health Service (General Medical and Pharmaceutical Services) Regulations 1974.
[38] Though it can now be granted: O.53, r.1(3).
[39] *Roy v Kensington and Chelsea and Westminster Family Practitioner Committee* [1992] 1 AC 624 (HL), p.654, per Lord Lowry.

depends exclusively on the existence of a purely public law right should be determined in judicial review proceedings and not otherwise. But where a litigant asserts his entitlement to a subsisting right in private law, whether by way of claim or defence, the circumstance that the existence and extent of the private right asserted may incidentally involve the examination of a public law issue cannot prevent the litigant from seeking to establish his right by action commenced by writ or originating summons, any more than it can prevent him from setting up his private law right in proceedings brought against him. I think this proposition necessarily follows from the decisions of this House in *Davy v Spelthorne Borough Council* [1984] AC 262 and *Wandsworth London Borough Council v Winder* [1985] AC 461.[40]

Moreover, it has been said that a plaintiff would only have been required to bring proceedings for judicial review if the ordinary action amounted to an abuse of process, or the defence sounded only in public law.[41] Where the central issues of the case are public law issues, even where putatively private law interests (such as financial interests) are affected, procedural exclusivity is engaged and judicial review procedure must be used.[42]"

Consent of the Parties

The second exception articulated by Lord Diplock is apparently more straightforward than the first, though not without difficulty. In principle, if the public body agrees to the use of ordinary procedure for hearing a public law challenge, then it cannot claim that the use of ordinary procedure is an abuse of process. In other words, the public body cannot claim that the applicant has opted to use ordinary procedure in order to circumvent the procedural protections from which the public body would have benefited had judicial review been used – the public body has essentially waived the procedural protections from which it would have benefited under judicial review.

However, as a matter of policy, it is less straightforward whether a public body should be able to waive its procedural protections in this way. When acting in a public (law) capacity, it generally acts, or is expected to act, in the public interest. Its resources will typically come from public funds. The effective waiver of procedural protections might be said not merely to be a waiver on the part of the public body as a distinct legal entity, but waiver of an element of the public interest, including that of public resources.[43] It is also questionable why a body would waive those procedural rights, though it could

---

[40] *Id*, pp.628–629.   [41] *Lau Chi Fai v Secretary for Justice* [1999] 2 HKLRD 494.
[42] *Lau Shiu Ming v Correctional Services Department* (2000) HCMP 320/2000.
[43] For example, if an applicant is out of time to apply for leave to seek judicial review and tries to bypass the procedural time limit by raising an ordinary action, why should the public body respondent be able to consent to such a use of procedure by "agreeing" to litigate and thereby incurring expense that will come from public finances?

be that the body seeks to deny that it is a public body or one acting in a public law capacity, and therefore disclaim the appropriateness of a challenge in judicial review.[44] A body could hardly insist that judicial review procedure should have been used by the applicant and then deny that it was acting in a public law capacity in relation to the impugned act or decision. It could also be that a respondent public body seeks to have the issue litigated under ordinary procedure for strategic reasons, such as those of time. In practice a failure by the public body to object to the use of ordinary procedure may be taken as tacit agreement to the use of that procedure,[45] thus a respondent public body which intends to deny the validity of a plaintiff's use of ordinary procedure should expressly object thereto.

Definitional Problems: The Concept of Publicness

As a sufficient public element must be capable of being shown in an application for judicial review, there must be a test for determining 'publicness'. Historically, this was essentially done by identifying whether the decision of the body under challenge was purportedly made in exercise of a statutory power.[46] First, it was generally the case that entities with statutory powers were public bodies in the orthodox understanding, such as government ministers, local authorities and statutory corporations. Private persons, companies and so on tended not to have statutory powers. Second, this would be a way of ensuring that judicial review did not over-exert its influence into all spheres of a public body's activity. In particular, contractual, commercial and employment decisions taken by public bodies would tend to be private law and non-statutory in nature,[47] thus falling outside the scope of judicial review under this test.

However, this would prove to be an inadequate test for determining this aspect of susceptibility to judicial review. Many, perhaps most, exercises of public (law) powers and functions would be carried out by a public body exercising statutory powers. However, not all public bodies, and not all bodies exercising public functions, would be acting in exercise of statutory powers. A (non-statutory) body exercising public functions might exercise non-statutory powers, yet under the pre-existing approach would not be susceptible to judicial review in exercise of those powers.

The case of *R v Panel on Take-overs and Mergers, ex parte Datain plc* in the Court of Appeal of England and Wales neatly demonstrated that inadequacy. According to Datafin plc, Norton Opax plc had acted in violation of the

---

[44] Consider *R v Panel on Take-overs and Mergers, ex parte Datafin plc* [1987] QB 815, p.845, in the broader context of the case.

[45] *Lee Miu Ling v Attorney General (No 1)* (1995) 5 HKPLR 178; *Lau Chi Fai v Secretary for Justice* [1999] 2 HKLRD 494.

[46] A prerogative power would also be susceptible to judicial review – *Council of Civil Service Unions v Minister for the Civil Service* [1985] AC 374 (HL).

[47] Though the power to contract can have a statutory basis.

City Code on Take-overs and Mergers, which regulated certain aspects of the UK financial industry. Datafin reported the alleged violation to the Panel on Takeovers and Mergers which dismissed the complaint. Datafin therefore applied for leave to seek judicial review of the Panel's dismissal. The court had to determine whether the Panel was subject to judicial review. However, on the existing test of whether a decision was taken in purported exercise of a statutory power, the decision would not be subject to review: the Panel was not a statutory body and did not have direct statutory powers. It was an "unincorporated association without legal personality" and had "no statutory, prerogative or common law powers and [was] not in [a] contractual relationship with the financial market or with those who deal in that market".[48] It was in that sense a self-regulatory body,[49] though the implications of the voluntariness of acceding to the Panel's powers might be overstated.[50]

The problem with holding the Panel's decision to be outside the scope of judicial review was that the Panel exercised:

> immense power de facto by devising, promulgating, amending and interpreting the City Code on Take-overs and Mergers, by waiving or modifying the application of the code in particular circumstances, by investigating and reporting upon alleged breaches of the code and by the application or threat of sanctions. These sanctions are no less effective because they are applied indirectly and lack a legally enforceable basis.[51]

The self-regulatory model had the support of the Government, and the Panel was supported by a periphery of statutory powers and penalties.[52] If there was no contractual, tortious or other basis in private law on which the decision could be challenged, the decision would effectively be unchallengeable in the courts. This would be a violation of the rule of law as the Panel would therefore have been beyond the reach of the civil courts. The Panel was "without doubt performing a public duty and an important one",[53] and "[s]o long as there is a possibility, however remote, of the panel abusing its great powers, then it would be wrong for the courts to abdicate responsibility".[54] Fundamentally, the Panel appeared to be acting in the capacity of a public body or to be exercising powers or functions resembling those of public bodies.

The court therefore took the opportunity to effect an important shift in emphasis from the source of the power under challenge, to the nature of the power under challenge (though this is not as radical a change as may

---

[48] *R v Panel on Take-overs and Mergers, ex parte Datafin plc* [1987] QB 815, pp.824–825, per Sir John Donaldson MR.
[49] *Id.*, p.826.   [50] *Id.*, p.846, per Lloyd LJ.   [51] *Id.*, p.826, per Sir John Donaldson MR.
[52] See *id.*, pp.834–836.   [53] *Id.*, p.838, per Sir John Donaldson MR.
[54] *Id.*, p.846, per Lloyd LJ.

initially appear[55]). Under this test, the source of the power would no longer be determinative of reviewability.[56] The source of the power could still be decisive:[57] where it was statutory, or derived from subordinate legislation,[58] the body would in principle be subject to judicial review; at the other end of the scale, contractual powers such as those applying to private arbiters would not be subject to review. However,

> between these extremes there is an area in which it is helpful to look not just at the source of the power but the nature of the power. If the body in question is exercising public law functions, or if the exercise of its functions have public law consequences, then that may... be sufficient to bring the body within the reach of judicial review.[59]

The exercise of public functions would include where a body is incorporated into a regulatory scheme or operates as an extension of Government policy.[60] Monopoly power is not enough in itself to render it public power amenable to judicial review, even where it is exercised largely at Government expense.[61] In appropriate cases, greater emphasis would therefore be placed on the nature of the power under challenge than the source of the power being exercised. This would have important consequences for situations such as outsourcing by public bodies, where the body to whom a public power or function is outsourced may be susceptible to judicial review under *Datafin* principles. However, the nature of the functions performed, and the purpose for which they are performed, has been said not to be a sufficiently comprehensive definition of what makes a body "public". Other significant factors would include the

---

[55] See generally Stephen Thomson, '*Judicial Review and Public Law: Challenging the Preconceptions of a Troubled Taxonomy*' (2017) 41(2) Melbourne University Law Review 890.

[56] *Cheng Chun-Ngai Daniel v Hospital Authority* [2004] HKCU 1315, para.19. A statutory underpinning of the body's decision or function is not vital for amenability to judicial review; see *Wong Yui Hin v Hong Kong Arts Development Council* [2004] HKEC 1102, para.36.

[57] *Lee Shing Yue Construction Co Ltd v Director of Architectural Services* [2001] 1 HKLRD 715; *R (Beer (trading as Hammer Trout Farm)) v Hampshire Farmer's Markets Ltd* [2004] 1 WLR 233.

[58] It was stated in *R v English Schools Foundation* [2004] 3 HKC 343, para.35, that if the source of the power lay in subordinate legislation, then absent any evidence of the decision-making process having its genesis in a private trust or private contract, it must follow that any decision to exercise that power must constitute the performance of a public function (per Hartmann J).

[59] *R v Panel on Take-overs and Mergers, ex parte Datafin plc* [1987] QB 815, p.847, per Lloyd LJ.

[60] *Pacific Century Insurance Co Ltd v Insurance Claims Complaints Bureau* [1999] 3 HKLRD 720. See also *Hong Kong Bar Association v Anthony Chua* (1994) 4 HKPLR 637.

[61] *Hong Kong Rifle Association v Hong Kong Shooting Association (No 2)* [2013] 3 HKLRD 362 (CA), applying *R v Disciplinary Committee of the Jockey Club, ex parte Aga Khan* [1993] 1 WLR 909. Kwan JA stated that the Hong Kong Shooting Association was "not in its origin, history, constitution or membership a public body", that there was "no public source for any of its powers", and that there was a "difference between what may affect the public and what amounts to a public duty" – *Hong Kong Rifle Association v Hong Kong Shooting Association (No 2)* [2013] 3 HKLRD 362 (CA), para.24.

nature of the body, its constitution, its links with government, the source of its funding, a measure of governmental control or monitoring of its performance, and the form and extent of public accountability; but in any event not merely that the body's functions are to be performed for public benefit and not for private profit.[62]

The *Datafin* approach already existed in the more limited context of land decisions in Hong Kong. The Privy Council held in *Hang Wah Chong Investment Co Ltd v Attorney-General* that the Director of Public Works was acting in his capacity as Government Land Agent, akin to a private landlord, when granting approval to modify a lease subject to payment of a premium.[63] This gave rise to what was later described as the "*Hang Wah Chong* principle", and is conceptually rooted in the broader idea that a public decision maker, when acting in a private law capacity, is not to be reviewed on public law criteria. Cheung J gave the following useful summary of the principle and its attendant issues in *Anderson Asphalt Ltd v Secretary for Justice*:

(a) Only a decision made in the public domain is amenable to judicial review.

(b) Whilst the nature of the source of power or discretion is by no means irrelevant, it is the nature of the functions that the decision-maker was performing when making the decision under challenge that is of crucial importance.

(c) In the absence of fraud, corruption, bad faith and breach of law, a purely commercial decision, or a decision made in the performance of a purely commercial function, is most likely a private law decision, not amenable to judicial review.

---

[62] *Hong Kong Polytechnic University v Next Magazine Publishing Limited* [1996] 2 HKLR 260, p.264. The High Court searched in this case for the meaning of "public authority" within section 7(1) of the Bill of Rights Ordinance (cap.383), but many of the same issues of principle will be involved. It was held that Hong Kong Polytechnic University was a public authority within the meaning of that section. See also *R v Hong Kong Polytechnic, ex parte Jenny Chua Yee-yen* [1992] 2 HKPLR 34. Lingnan University was "clearly a public authority amenable to judicial review" considering it had been established by statute and its objects were "clearly" public functions – *Leung Chak Sang v Lingnan University* [2001] 2 HKC 435, p.443, per Chung J. Judicial review was not regarded by the Privy Council as inappropriate in *Spruce v The University of Hong Kong* [1993] 2 HKLR 65 (PC). A university examination panel was in principle subject to judicial review, even though leave was refused – *Yu Hung Hsua Julie v Chinese University of Hong Kong* [2016] 5 HKLRD 393 (CA).

[63] *Hang Wah Chong Investment Co Ltd v Attorney-General* [1981] HKLR 336. This principle was also applied in *Canadian Overseas Development Co Ltd v Attorney General* [1991] 1 HKC 288 (CA); *Benbecula Ltd v Attorney General* [1994] 3 HKC 238; *Polorace Investments Ltd v Director of Lands* [1997] 1 HKC 373 (CA); *Raider Ltd v Secretary for Justice* (2000) 3 HKCFAR 309, pp.313–314; *Director of Lands v Yin Shuen Enterprises Ltd* (2003) 6 HKCFAR 1, para.19; *Ying Ho Co Ltd v Secretary for Justice* [2005] 1 HKLRD 135, paras.15 and 102; and *Rank Profit Industries Ltd v Director of Lands* [2009] 1 HKLRD 177. It was held that where the Housing Department issued an occupation permit, it was performing a function analogous to that of a landlord and should be characterised as an act in the private domain – *Re An Occupation Permit No 18555 Issued By The Hong Kong Housing Authority* [1991] 2 HKLR 104.

(d) Put another way, the presence of a public element(s) of sufficient significance in the decision-making process could turn an otherwise commercial decision into a public law decision, amenable to judicial review.

(e) What is sufficient is a matter of fact and degree, depending very much on individual cases. No hard and fast rule can be laid down. It is, in a borderline case, very much a matter of overall impression and one of degree: *R v Legal Aid Board, ex p Donn & Co* [1996] 3 All ER 1, p.11h, cited with approval by Mortimer V-P in *Matteograssi SpA v Airport Authority* at p.219C-D.

(f) In relation to decisions made in land transactions, the same legal principles apply. A complete statement of the *Hang Wah Chong* principle does not merely state that in lease modification cases, the Government's decisions on whether to grant a modification and on the amount of premium to be extracted (if any) are in the nature of private commercial or economic decisions of a private landlord, and therefore not susceptible to judicial review. A complete statement of the principle also says that where the Government official, in making the decision, acts in his role as protector of the public interest, his decision is almost certainly liable to judicial review.

(g) Thus understood, the so-called *Hang Wah Chong* principle is no more than a special application of the general principles on the distinction of public/private law to land matters in Hong Kong.

(h) In land matters, invariably, there are restrictive user covenants in the relevant leases or grants. Plainly, they serve the commercial and economic interests of the Government as landlord. But, equally plainly, they serve, to some extent, a purpose of town planning, which, no doubt, any responsible government must be responsible for, whether directly or indirectly.

(i) Therefore, there is always a built-in town planning element in land grants and the system of land-holding in Hong Kong, leaving aside any specific town planning legislation.

(j) That, however, is not sufficient in itself to turn a decision made by the Director in relation to modifying a restrictive user covenant in a grant or demanding a premium for the modification into a public law decision, amenable to judicial review, according to the decided cases.

(k) This illustrates that the mere presence of some public element (namely, town planning consideration) may not be sufficient to render the decision a public law decision. The crucial question is whether some additional public element(s) of sufficient weight is/are present in the decision-making process to render the decision made a public one, amenable to judicial review. Put another way, the crucial question is whether the role played or function performed by the Government official is sufficiently public to render the decision a public one, susceptible to judicial review.

(l) Again it depends on the facts, and in a borderline case, it is really a matter of overall impression and degree.[64]

---

[64] *Anderson Asphalt Ltd v Secretary for Justice* [2009] 3 HKLRD 215, para.57.

The flexibility referred to by Cheung J is at once a strength and weakness of the courts' approach. It allows the courts to take a case-by-case approach to the determination of publicness without formulating an over-restrictive definition; yet it provides little guidance on what exactly will be anticipated to be a sufficient public element in a given case. There is also the potential for inconsistencies to arise. It was stated that the Government, in its capacity as private landlord, had an "absolute right if it chooses to demand a premium, however large, for granting a modification of the terms of the lease, or to withhold its consent altogether, however unreasonably".[65] However, *Anderson Asphalt* signals a potential qualification on that "absolute right" in stating that:

> [i]n the absence of fraud, corruption, bad faith and breach of law, a purely commercial decision, or a decision made in the performance of a purely commercial function, is most likely a private law decision, not amenable to judicial review.[66]

In other words, it is unclear whether and when a Government decision on lease modification made in its capacity as private landlord becomes challengeable in public law.[67] It would seem logical that if the Government acted in violation of public law powers when deciding a lease modification issue, then the decision would be *ultra vires* and challengeable as such. An obvious example would be if the Director of Lands was statutorily permitted to demand a premium on commercial premises, but not on residential premises, and the Director nevertheless purported to demand a premium on residential premises. Despite acting in his capacity as private landlord, the Director cannot exceed his statutory powers and thus the "private law" decision on

---

[65] *Director of Lands* v *Yin Shuen Enterprises Ltd* (2003) 6 HKCFAR 1, para.19, per Lord Millett NPJ; drawing on *Lord Tredegar* v *Harwood* [1929] AC 72. See also *Rank Profit Industries Ltd* v *Director of Lands* [2009] 1 HKLRD 177.

[66] *Anderson Asphalt Ltd* v *Secretary for Justice* [2009] 3 HKLRD 215, para.57, per Cheung J. It was stated in the Privy Council that it "does not seem likely that a decision by a state enterprise to enter into or determine a commercial contract to supply goods or services will ever be the subject of judicial review in the absence of fraud, corruption or bad faith" – *Mercury Energy Ltd* v *Electricity Corporation of New Zealand Ltd* [1994] 1 WLR 521 (PC) (New Zealand), p.529. Cheung J understood that commercial decisions are in principle not subject to judicial review, unless the decision falls within these three categories – *Ngo Kee Construction Co Ltd* v *Hong Kong Housing Authority* [2001] 1 HKC 493, p.509; and see *Lee Shing Yue Construction Co Ltd* v *Director of Architectural Services* [2001] 1 HKLRD 715.

[67] A commercial decision of the Urban Renewal Authority not to purchase a particular property for the purpose of implementing a development scheme, even though the power to purchase was statutory in nature and the Authority's powers were to be exercised in the public interest, was deemed not subject to judicial review. This was because, acting on legal advice, the Authority was not satisfied that the vendor had good title in the properties considered for purchase, a matter which did "not involve any or any consideration of public element at all" and which was "essentially commercial in nature". It was, in the "absence of fraud, corruption, bad faith and breach of law", not susceptible to judicial review – *King Prosper Trading* v *Urban Renewal Authority* [2010] HKEC 1975, para.49.

the premium would be vitiated by public law constraints. Those constraints may be broad: Cheung J referred to "breach of law" as potentially rendering an otherwise private law decision amenable to judicial review.[68] However, a grey area is reached where the premium demanded is potentially *Wednesbury* unreasonable or demanded in bad faith. It is unclear whether such an exercise of discretion would bring the "private law" decision into the realm of public law and thus amenable to judicial review.[69]

Whilst the foregoing discussion outlines the approach of the courts in determining what is a sufficient public element for the purposes of reviewability, it will be apparent that the fundamental question of what makes someone or something (for example a body or function) 'public', as opposed to 'private', is essentially unanswered, even though the test of publicness substantially determines susceptibility to judicial review. The case law is lacking a systematic approach to this question: "[t]here is, of course, no universal test to determine whether a decision by a public body is amenable to judicial review. In borderline cases this is a question of impression and degree".[70] There "can be no universal test".[71] It "depend[s] very much on individual cases" and "[n]o hard and fast rule can be laid down".[72] It is "as much a matter of feel, as deciding whether any particular criteria are met".[73]

The lack of a sufficiently systematic approach to the determination of publicness has resulted in some haphazard judicial decisions. For example, where a notice to quit is served by the Hong Kong Housing Authority on a tenant who has violated the terms of his tenancy agreement, it might generally

---

[68] Eliminating the most expensive tenders for public seating at Hong Kong International Airport, and selecting among the remaining tenders based on comfort, appearance, durability and maintainability, was not in breach of law. There also being no fraud, corruption or bad faith, the Airport Authority had exercised a purely commercial function which was not subject to judicial review – *Matteograssi SpA v Airport Authority* [1998] 2 HKLRD 213 (CA).

[69] The suggestion in *Canadian Overseas Development Co Ltd v Attorney General* [1991] 1 HKC 288 (CA) and *Director of Lands v Yin Shuen Enterprises Ltd* (2003) 6 HKCFAR 1, para.19, is that it would not be subject to review for unreasonableness; but the suggestion in *Mercury Energy Ltd v Electricity Corporation of New Zealand Ltd* [1994] 1 WLR 521 (PC) (New Zealand), p.529; *Matteograssi SpA v Airport Authority* [1998] 2 HKLRD 213 (CA); *Ngo Kee Construction Co Ltd v Hong Kong Housing Authority* [2001] 1 HKC 493, p.509; *Anderson Asphalt Ltd v Secretary for Justice* [2009] 3 HKLRD 215, para.57; and *King Prosper Trading v Urban Renewal Authority* [2010] HKEC 1975, para.49, is that it would be. See also *Secan Ltd v Attorney General* [1995] 2 HKC 629 (CA).

[70] *Matteograssi SpA v Airport Authority* [1998] 2 HKLRD 213, p.219, per Mortimer V-P.

[71] *R v Legal Aid Board, ex parte Donn & Co* [1996] 3 All ER 1, p.11, per Ognall J.

[72] *Anderson Asphalt Ltd v Secretary for Justice* [2009] 3 HKLRD 215, para.57, per Cheung J.

[73] *R (Tucker) v Director General of the National Crime Squad* [2003] EWCA Civ 57, para.13, per Scott Baker LJ. Peter Cane noted that the "classification of functions and activities as public or private is ultimately a matter of value-judgment and choice" – Cane, *Administrative Law*, p.8. Christopher Forsyth noted that the *O'Reilly v Mackman* line of cases were "noteworthy for the way in which the distinction [between public and private law] is not defined but simply taken for granted" – C. F. Forsyth, "Beyond O'Reilly v Mackman: The Foundations and Nature of Procedural Exclusivity" (1985) 44(3) *Cambridge Law Journal* 415, p.427.

be expected that the Authority is acting in the capacity of a private landlord and therefore the decision to issue the notice to quit is not challengeable by way of judicial review. However, in just these circumstances it was held that the Authority, in managing the public housing estates via tenancy agreements, was discharging a public function to provide low cost housing. It would be concerned with the fair and proper distribution and use of public resources, taking this into consideration in deciding whether to issue a notice to quit, and this injected a sufficient public element to render the decision subject to judicial review.[74] Similarly, where the Director of Lands decided not to extend a New Territories special purpose lease – governed by the law of contract – the fact that he had to consider and balance competing public interests in deciding whether or not to extend the lease made his decision one in exercise of public functions and thus subject to judicial review.[75] The existence of additional statutory powers or consequences relating to the Government acting in the capacity of a landlord, which are beyond those pertaining to a private landlord, may also inject a sufficient public element.[76] It is important to stress, however, that mere consideration of public issues or benefits is not in itself sufficient to render a decision one in public law and one subject to judicial review.[77] It is a question of the sufficiency and extent of any such public elements.

Another area of uncertainty in terms of whether a sufficient public element is engaged is when a person is employed by a public body. It is clear that mere employment by a public body is not sufficient in itself to inject the public element necessary to render the employer subject to judicial review in relation to employment decisions. The employment relationship is one in contract and therefore, ordinarily, the employee's remedy will be contractual.[78] However, employment by a public body may give rise to mixed issues of public and private law. Where the terms of employment are statutorily regulated, there might be a sufficient public element to render an employment decision subject to judicial review.[79] Even in that case, however, it will not necessarily be mandatory to proceed by way of judicial review where it is not an abuse of process to use ordinary procedure and where the challenge is not purely a public law challenge.[80]

---

[74] *Wan Yung Sang* v *Housing Authority* [2011] HKEC 907.
[75] *Hong Kong and China Gas Co Ltd* v *Director of Lands* [1997] HKLRD 1291. See also *Kam Lan Koon* v *Secretary for Justice* [1999] HKLRD (Yrbk) 15 (CA).
[76] *Wong Wai Hing Christopher* v *Director of Lands* [2010] HKEC 1485.
[77] *Anderson Asphalt Ltd* v *Secretary for Justice* [2009] 3 HKLRD 215; *Cheung Shing Scrap Metals Recycling Ltd* v *Director of Lands* [2009] HKEC 813; *Chau Tam Yuet Ching* v *Director of Lands* [2013] 3 HKLRD 169 (CA).
[78] See, for example, *Fraser* v *Chief Executive of the HKSAR* [2000] 3 HKLRD 492; *Cheng Chun Ngai Daniel* v *Hospital Authority*, HCAL 202/2002; and *Ho Chee Sing James* v *Secretary for Justice* [2008] 1 HKCLRT 141.
[79] *R* v *East Berkshire Health Authority, ex parte Walsh* [1985] QB 152. See also *Malloch* v *Aberdeen Corporation*, 1971 SC (HL) 85.
[80] *Lau Chi Fai* v *Secretary for Justice* [1999] 2 HKLRD 494.

The public/private distinction can be one of great difficulty.[81] In many cases it will not arise as an issue, but there are situations in which the distinction comes into focus and which can succumb to the rigidity of formalistic public/private tests. First, where an act occurs or a decision is taken which is close to the boundary between public (law) and private (law), then precisely how the line is drawn will determine the competency of an application for judicial review. The line can be drawn in substantive or procedural terms; for example, an act is or is not sufficiently public in nature (substantive), or an applicant seeks an order of certiorari, mandamus or prohibition and therefore must seek judicial review (procedural).[82]

Second, the public/private distinction, in particular as a litmus test for the competency of judicial review, is problematic where the public or private character of an act, decision, power or function is merely ostensible. In other words, a *prima facie* public (law) act or decision may in fact be substantively private (law) in nature; or vice versa. In such cases, the risk is that an act or decision is mischaracterised by the court, such that a substantively private (law) act or decision is subject to judicial review or, worse, a substantively public (law) act or decision is wrongly shut out of judicial review. An example of an act that is difficult to characterise as public or private in nature is the contractual outsourcing by a public body of powers or functions.[83] Outsourcing can bring recognised improvements in efficiency, service delivery and value for money; for example, the government may be able to offer the same standard of prison service with cost savings where the operation of prison facilities is outsourced to a private company, or a local authority may be able to offer better and cheaper provision of public swimming pools where the operation of the pools is outsourced to a private company. Another example that is difficult to characterise as public or private in nature is government franchising, such as where central or local government awards an exclusive franchise to a transport operator. It is unclear in such situations whether and to what extent the "private" contractor assumes, or should assume, public law duties. It is also unclear how outsourcing and franchising affects the public law obligations of the public body.[84] These questions are important for delineating the scope of judicial review.

---

[81] It was described as "something of a headache" in the fourth edition of Michael Fordham, *Judicial Review Handbook* (4th edn) (Hart Publishing, 2004), p.562; though by the fifth edition it had been downgraded to a "difficult distinction" – Michael Fordham, *Judicial Review Handbook* (5th edn) (Hart Publishing, 2008), p.287.

[82] This broadly corresponds to the two juridical bases of the procedural exclusivity principle – see p.67.

[83] See Terence Daintith, "Regulation by Contract: The New Prerogative" (1979) 32(1) *Current Legal Problems* 41; and A. C. L. Davies, *The Public Law of Government Contracts* (Oxford University Press, 2008), pp.231–259.

[84] There can also be questions about whether the relationship between the individual who uses the services of such companies, particularly where the relationship is contractual, sounds (or should sound) in public law as well as in private law.

There are also contestable assumptions at play when the private sector is largely sheltered from judicial review. Where contractual powers are at issue, the tendency of the courts is to recoil from judicial review, as these are seen properly to be in the domain of private law.[85] This results in a whole category of case that is largely excluded from review. A core justification for sheltering private law relationships from judicial review is that such relationships are said to be voluntarily established.[86] This distinguishes private law obligations from public law duties, for whereas the former are voluntarily assumed (for example, no one is forced to contract), the latter are often unilaterally imposed and do not require the consent of the individual subject to the jurisdiction of public bodies. The special powers enjoyed by public bodies give rise to special obligations, hence the justification for the grounds of judicial review being directed at public functions. However, the characterisation of private law powers as voluntarily assumed risks understating the extent to which individuals are constrained by economic realities.[87] In the case of transport operated on an exclusive government franchise, a passenger contracts with the transport operator on a supposedly bilateral and voluntary basis; ostensibly as "legal equals". However, if this highly regulated marketplace, uncompetitive at the point of consumption, offers bad value for passengers,[88] a public (law) restriction has resulted in an erosion of consumer choice implicit in the concept of a private (law) marketplace in which obligations are concluded bilaterally and voluntarily. The state has created an uncompetitive market at the point of consumption, yet the customer is relegated to remedies that sound only in private law. Despite sometimes high levels of state intervention and paternalism in the regulation of the marketplace, the matter is seen to be one of private law and thus beyond the scope of judicial review.[89] It is not just in the award of government franchises that one can see an erosion of market competitiveness

---

[85] See *R (on the application of Molinaro) v Royal Borough of Kensington and Chelsea* [2001] EWHC Admin 896, para.67; and Mark Elliott, 'Judicial Review's Scope, Foundations and Purposes: Joining the Dots' [2012] New Zealand Law Review 75, p.85.

[86] Neil MacCormick, *Institutions of Law* (Oxford University Press, 2007), pp.172–176.

[87] See Stephen Thomson, "Judicial Review and Public Law: Challenging the Preconceptions of a Troubled Taxonomy" (2017) 41(2) *Melbourne University Law Review* 890, pp.902–904.

[88] The potential for this is increased by the fact that an incumbent franchisee has advantages over rival tenderers in refranchising rounds, distorting the competitiveness of the tendering process – Oliver E. Williamson, "Franchise Bidding for Natural Monopolies – In General and with respect to CATV"(1976) 7(1) *Bell Journal of Economics* 73.

[89] The state's regulatory acts and decisions might not be subject to judicial review on the conventional grounds of review, as the regulation could take the form of primary or subsidiary legislation. See Michel Rosenfeld, "Rethinking the Boundaries between Public Law and Private Law for the Twenty First Century: An Introduction" (2013) 11 *International Journal of Constitutional Law* 125, p.126.

(and an erosion of the contractual and commercial freedom that implies), but in licensing, certification, the erection of high barriers to market entry (such as in the banking and utilities sectors), inadequate consumer protection laws,[90] inadequate competition laws, inadequate mergers and acquisitions control, insufficient protection of intellectual property, economic protectionism and government subsidies.

Furthermore, various techniques can allow the government to pursue public policy objectives using the apparatus of private law. Companies in majority public ownership can be used to pursue policy objectives through and under the guise of commercial activity. The government can pursue policy objectives through the award and control of commercial tenders and franchises,[91] which may on their face appear to be characteristically commercial or economic arrangements. Public Private Partnerships (PPPs) can obscure public law, and even private law, accountability. These techniques can be used to promote "public law" objectives in a way that may reduce or evade liability in public law, typically by funnelling such liability into private law mechanisms.

The reality is that, as long as a separate procedure for judicial review is defined as the channel through which public law challenges must (with limited exceptions) be ventilated, one is forced to categorise cases as having or not having a sufficient public element.[92] It has been pointed out that it is important to "retain some flexibility as the precise limits of what is called "public law" and what is called "private law" are by no means worked out".[93] Lord Diplock's recognition that exceptions apply to the procedural exclusivity

---

[90] Though, even when such laws are in place – for example, in relation to unfair contract terms – the individual may still face access to justice barriers in challenging the legality of such terms. Economic inequality can heavily impact the result or even the existence of litigation.

[91] The argument was not accepted that the Government's decisions as to who should or should not be on their approved list of contractors was effectively the employment of an administrative technique equivalent to licensing, and that through such licensing the Government was attempting to regulate the commercial activities of a section of the public, thus providing evidence of the public nature of decisions made under a monitoring scheme. Nor was the monitoring scheme itself, under which the performance of Government contractors was monitored, anything other than purely commercial in nature, and was thus not subject to judicial review – *Lee Shing Yue Construction Co Ltd v Director of Architectural Services* [2001] 1 HKLRD 715. See Cheryl Saunders and Kevin KF Yam, "Government Regulation by Contract: Implications for the Rule of Law" (2004) 15 *Public Law Review* 51.

[92] Unless a different conceptual basis is used for determining susceptibility to review, such as the exercise of monopoly power or the confinement of bodies to jurisdiction – see Thomson, "Judicial Review and Public Law", pp.26–27.

[93] *Mercury Communications Ltd v Director General of Telecommunications* [1996] 1 WLR 48, p.57. The need to avoid excessive rigidity was also expressed in *Attorney General v Yau Kwok-Lam, Johnny* [1988] 2 HKLR 394 (CA).

principle has been described as potentially introducing some uncertainty, but a "small price to pay to avoid ... over-rigid demarcation".[94] For as long as there remains a concept of procedural exclusivity, courts and practitioners must continue to negotiate the uncertain contours of the troubled public/private distinction.[95]

---

[94] *Mercury Communications Ltd* v *Director General of Telecommunications* [1996] 1 WLR 48, p.57. It was added that "[i]t has to be borne in mind that the overriding question is whether the proceedings constitute an abuse of process of the court" (p.57).

[95] These issues are discussed in greater detail in Thomson, "Judicial Review and Public Law".

8

Statutory Exclusion of Review, Non-Justiciability and Variable Intensity of Review

Statutory Exclusion of Review

The legislature may purport to make the acts and decisions of bodies unchallengeable using ouster clauses.[1] These are statutory provisions that purport to "oust" the jurisdiction of the courts to judicially review. Such provisions can take many different forms, though a principal division can be made between exclusionary clauses and limitation clauses. With an exclusionary clause, the legislature purports to exclude judicial review as it relates to a particular decision or decision-maker. With a limitation clause, the legislature does not seek to exclude judicial review, but to limit its scope in relation to a particular decision or decision-maker. For example, it might be provided that review is possible only on a limited range of grounds, or that a body can be reviewed in a narrower range of circumstances than normal.[2] Ouster clauses can also be more explicit about the extent to which judicial review is or is not envisaged to be permitted. They may state expressly that judicial review or judicial challenge more generally is not permitted,[3] or can be more implicit, such as by

---

[1] Ouster clauses have also gone by other names, such as exclusionary clauses, privative clauses, finality clauses and preclusive clauses – see, for example, *Chan Yik Tung* v *Hong Kong Housing Authority* [1989] 2 HKC 394, p.397.

[2] Section 32 of the Chief Executive Election Ordinance (cap.569) provides that an election may be questioned only by an election petition on specified grounds, enumerated therein. Section 67(3) of the Legislative Council Ordinance (cap.542) was ruled unconstitutional as in violation of Article 82 of the Basic Law insofar as it provided for the finality of the determination of the Court of First Instance after the trial of an election petition – *Mok Charles* v *Tam Wai Ho* (2010) 13 HKCFAR 762.

[3] For example, the Airport Authority Ordinance (cap.483), s.34(3)(h) ("... in so far as the decision related to a belief described in paragraph (e)(ii) (including the belief's basis) or the absence of such a belief, it shall not be questioned in any legal proceedings"); Co-operative Societies Ordinance (cap.33), s.49(4) ("A decision of the Registrar under subsection (2) or in appeal under subsection (3) shall be final and shall not be called in question in any civil court"); Electoral Procedure (Chief Executive Election) Regulation (cap.541J), s.75 ("An election shall not be questioned only because of a defect in the appointment of a person as an electoral officer if the person was at the relevant time holding office or acting as such an officer at the election"); Housing Ordinance (cap.283), s.19(3) ("No court shall have jurisdiction to hear any application for relief by or on behalf of a person whose lease has been terminated under subsection (1) in connection with such termination") (and see also *Chan Yik Tung* v *Hong Kong Housing*

designating particular decisions or the decisions of a particular decision maker to be final or conclusive.[4]

An important question is how the courts should treat such provisions. It could be argued that, if the Legislative Council is the primary lawmaker in Hong Kong, and it is the will of the legislature that a particular body's decision is not subject to judicial review, then the will of the legislature must be respected to that effect. That argument may gain more traction in legislatures with greater democratic legitimacy than the Legislative Council: if 100 per cent, rather than 50 per cent, of the Legislative Council was elected on a geographical constituency basis, and the will of the legislature is to exclude judicial review in specified cases, then – assuming that the legislative output of the Council is an accurate reflection of the popular will – the courts must presumably respect the popular will of the people to exclude judicial review in those cases. To do otherwise would be anti-democratic.

However, this line of argumentation runs into serious difficulties. The obvious objection is to question whether and to what extent the legislative output of a legislature accurately reflects the popular will of the electorate, and even if it does, whether the legislature should be permitted to reflect such a "tyranny of the majority".[5] There are good reasons for doubting whether it should, and one of the main driving forces behind the enactment (and entrenchment) of human rights and fundamental freedoms instruments is precisely to remove or mitigate the risk of a legislature or government

---

Authority [1989] 2 HKC 394); Protection of Wages on Insolvency Ordinance (cap.380), s.20 ("No decision of the Commissioner or the Board made in exercise of any discretion under this part shall be challenged in any court").

[4] For example, the Antiquities and Monuments Ordinance (cap.53), s.16(2) ("The decision of the Chief Executive on the appeal shall be final"); Banking Ordinance (cap.155), s.119(1) ("In the event of any dispute as to whether a person is carrying on a banking business or a business of taking deposits . . . the decision of the Chief Executive in Council shall be final and conclusive for all purposes of this Ordinance"); Government Rent (Assessment and Collection) Ordinance (cap.515), Sch.1, para.2(b) (". . . shall bear the same proportion to 3% of the rateable value of the tenement as, in the opinion of the Director whose decision shall be final, the area of such part bears to the area of the whole of such tenement"); Housing Ordinance (cap.283), s.20(4) ("The decision of the tribunal shall be final"); Nurses Registration Ordinance (cap.164), s.3A ("The result of an election of members to the Council under section 3(2)(ca) may only be questioned by an election petition heard and determined by the Council"); Supplementary Medical Professions Ordinance (cap.359), s.3(3) ". . . may before the expiry of his term of office be removed from office by the Chief Executive for permanent incapacity or other sufficient cause (as to the existence of which the decision of the Chief Executive shall be final").

[5] "Tyranny of the majority" and similar terms were used by a number of writers including John Adams, *A Defence of the Constitutions of Government of the United States of America* (vol.3) (new edn) (John Stockdale, 1794), p.291; Edmund Burke, *Reflections on the Revolution in France* (J. Dodsley, 1790), in which the concept is found throughout the text; and John Stuart Mill, *On Liberty* (2nd edn) (Ticknor and Fields, 1863), p.13. Lord Hailsham referred in his 1976 Richard Dimbleby Lecture to an "elective dictatorship", referring to the specific context of the UK Government dominating Parliamentary processes.

eroding core rights and freedoms, even if their erosion has the support of a majority of the electorate.[6]

There is, however, a further series of objections to ouster clauses having unqualified effect. First, if they were to achieve the purpose they are purported to achieve, there might be an incentive for the Legislative Council to protect with ouster clauses, as a matter of course, decision makers upon whom they confer discretion. If every statutory decision maker was capable of being given blanket protection by ouster clauses, then judicial review would be seriously diminished in scope and inhibited in utility. As far as administrative action is concerned, there would barely be anything left to judicially review.

Second, if ouster clauses were capable of successfully excluding judicial review, this would be difficult to reconcile with Article 35 of the Basic Law, wherein Hong Kong residents "shall have the right to ... access to the courts... and to judicial remedies". It furthermore provides that Hong Kong residents "shall have the right to institute legal proceedings in the courts against the acts of the executive authorities and their personnel". The Legislative Council (or, in the case of subsidiary legislation, a secondary legislator) would presumably be acting in violation of the rights enshrined in Article 35 were ouster clauses to have unqualified effect – perhaps the courts would also be acting in violation of the right "to judicial remedies" were they to deny a remedy in judicial review on the basis that an ouster clause had successfully ousted their jurisdiction.

Third, there is a crucial rule of law objection. When courts conduct judicial review, they are at their core confining bodies to the lawful exercise of their powers. If a body has legal powers conferred upon it, those legal powers necessarily have limits. There is no such thing as unlimited discretion. The limits of the body's powers are defined by law, whether by statute, the common law, regulations or whatever other source of its powers. However, if an ouster clause was to successfully exclude the jurisdiction of the courts to judicially review a body acting in excess of its powers, then the rule of law would be critically undermined, as there would no longer be a way of confining the body to its legal powers. The judicial means of enforcing the limits of legality would be paralysed. The "personalities presiding on the tribunal" or any other decision-maker, "empowered with an uncontrollable jurisdiction", would become the sole judges of the validity of their own decisions.[7] The ouster clause is paradoxical: by legislating that a particular decision maker, the limits of whose powers must necessarily be defined, is not to be challenged in the courts (including by way of judicial review), the legislature is

---

[6] This encounters the so-called counter-majoritarian difficulty – see Alexander M. Bickel, *The Least Dangerous Branch: The Supreme Court at the Bar of Politics* (2nd edn) (Yale University Press, 1986).

[7] *Gurung Bhakta Bahadur* v *Director of Immigration* [2001] 3 HKLRD 225, p.236, per Hartmann J.

undermining the very means of ensuring that the decision maker complies with the limits of its powers. As Lord Wilberforce asked: "What would be the purpose of defining by statute the limit of a tribunal's powers if, by means of a clause inserted in the instrument of definition, those limits could safely be passed?".[8] The rule of law demands that ouster clauses cannot be permitted to override the limits on legal power.

The issue was notably examined in *Anisminic Ltd v Foreign Compensation Commission*. An English company owned property in Egypt which was sequestrated, and subsequently applied to the Foreign Compensation Commission in accordance with the Foreign Compensation (Egypt) (Determination and Registration of Claims) Order 1962. The provisional determination of the application was refused, and the company sought declarations that the determination was a nullity and that they were entitled to participate in the fund. It was contended by the Commission that the court had no jurisdiction to hear the claim, as the Foreign Compensation Act 1950 contained the following ouster clause:

> The determination by the Commission of any application made to them under this Act shall not be called in question in any court of law.[9]

However, the House of Lords held that this ouster clause would only protect from judicial review a "determination". It would not protect something which purported to be a determination but was in fact a nullity, and therefore not a determination. As Lord Reid added, "there are no degrees of nullity":[10]

> If you seek to show that a determination is a nullity, you are not questioning the purported determination, you are maintaining that it does not exist as a determination. It is one thing to question a determination which does exist: it is quite another thing to say that there is nothing to be questioned.[11]

Anisminic is therefore authority for a seemingly simple rule: an ouster clause will never protect a legal nullity from judicial review.[12] This approach was followed in Privy Council decisions. A statutory ouster clause did not prevent the Supreme Court of the Bahamas from assessing the legality of a minister's decision to determine whether the decision was made in excess of jurisdiction.[13] The Privy Council, on appeal from the Federal Court of Malaysia, held that the clause "an award of the [Industrial] Court shall be final and conclusive, and no award shall be challenged, appealed against, reviewed, quashed or called in question in any court of law" did not exclude

---

[8] *Anisminic Ltd v Foreign Compensation Commission* [1969] 2 AC 147 (HL), p.208.
[9] Foreign Compensation Act 1950, s.4(4).
[10] *Anisminic Ltd v Foreign Compensation Commission* [1969] 2 AC 147 (HL), p.170.   [11] *Id.*
[12] The issue can become complex, however, in determining when a purported act or decision is a nullity. This has raised particular difficulties in relation to error of law.
[13] *Attorney-General v Ryan* [1980] AC 718 (PC) (Bahamas) (Bahamas Nationality Act 1973, s.16).

the jurisdiction of the High Court of Malaysia where the Industrial Court had exceeded its jurisdiction.[14]

This approach has also been followed in Hong Kong. It was held that the ouster clause "[n]o court shall have jurisdiction" appeared to confer extensive and unreviewable power on the tribunal, but did not protect from review a tenancy termination following from decisions of the Hong Kong Housing Authority and the Tenancy Appeals Committee.[15] The provision was not clear enough to override the presumption of legislative intention that executive, tribunal and other official decisions are justiciable by way of judicial review.[16] It was "tolerably clear" that "[t]he decision of the tribunal shall be final" did not oust the tribunal's decisions from the courts' jurisdiction, and it "has been held, time and again" that exclusionary clauses of this kind do not have the "effect of eliminating the courts' power to review".[17] The ouster clause "[a] decision of the Board shall not be subject to review or appeal in any court" did not protect a purported decision that was a nullity, which was subsequently quashed.[18] The provision that "no proceedings by way of mandamus, certiorari, prohibition, injunction or other order shall be taken against the Chief Executive-in-Council" may have appeared to be comprehensive and unqualified, but it was settled law in Hong Kong that *Anisminic* principles applied to complete ouster provisions, and the purported ouster would not protect anything done by the Chief Executive-in-Council which was a nullity.[19] There is a great deal to commend the courts standing firm on this issue; as pointed out in the Court of First Instance, "[i]n any state with [the] separation of the powers, the right of the court to supervise the decisions of the executive is always zealously guarded against [*sic*]".[20]

Whilst there are compelling reasons underlying this approach, there are two phenomena which nevertheless highlight the artificiality of the approach. One is that the courts have repeatedly stated that only the clearest, most express

---

[14] *South East Asia Fire Bricks Sdn Bhd* v *Non-Metallic Mineral Products Manufacturing Employees Union* [1981] AC 363 (PC) (Malaysia) (Industrial Relations Act 1967, s.29(3)(a)).

[15] *Chan Yik Tung* v *Hong Kong Housing Authority* [1989] 2 HKC 394 (Housing Ordinance (cap.283), s.19(3)). The term "tribunal" was used "loosely to signify all bodies amenable to judicial review" – *Chan Yik Tung* v *Hong Kong Housing Authority* [1989] 2 HKC 394, p.397, per Liu J.

[16] *Thai Muoi* v *Hong Kong Housing Authority* [2000] HKCU 370, p.7, per Yeung J.

[17] *Chan Yik Tung* v *Hong Kong Housing Authority* [1989] 2 HKC 394, p.404, per Liu J (Housing Ordinance (cap.283), s.20(4)). The same conclusion on the legal effect of this provision was reached in *Kwan Shung King* v *Housing Appeal Tribunal* [2000] 2 HKLRD 764.

[18] *The Queen* v *Director of Immigration, ex parte Do Giau* [1992] 1 HKLR 287 (Immigration (Refugee Status Review Boards) (Procedure) Regulations, Clause 13F(6)).

[19] *Gurung Bhakta Bahadur* v *Director of Immigration* [2001] 3 HKLRD 225 (Interpretation and General Clauses Ordinance (cap.1), s.64(7)). See also *Television Broadcasts Ltd* v *Communications Authority* [2016] 2 HKLRD 41, paras.168–169.

[20] *Thai Muoi* v *Hong Kong Housing Authority* [2000] HKCU 370, p.7, per Yeung J.

and unambiguous language will successfully oust the jurisdiction of the courts,[21] yet statutory provisions rarely seem sufficiently clear, express and unambiguous for the court to regard them as successfully excluding their jurisdiction to review.[22] This is true even where the plain reading of an ouster clause would appear to make quite clear the intention of the legislature that the decision-maker be protected from legal challenge. This artificiality seems unnecessary: it would be a more solid and principled rule simply to hold that *ultra vires* decisions will never be statutorily immunised from review by reference, if necessary, to the rule of law.

The second phenomenon, which has been seen in the UK case law in particular, is variations on the courts' claim that "Parliament surely could not have intended" to exclude the courts' jurisdiction to judicially review where the decision-maker had acted in various unlawful ways.[23] The courts may have felt compelled to defend their intervention where some common law grounds of review were being applied, even in "contravention" of the plain text of a statutory ouster clause. For example, they might have felt the need to justify review for *Wednesbury* unreasonableness notwithstanding a statutory provision purporting to oust the courts' jurisdiction to review the decision. However, the apparent need to validate judicial review in the face of the plain text of a statutory ouster clause has likely been heightened by the doctrine of parliamentary supremacy in the UK,[24] which is not replicated in the Hong Kong context. The courts in Hong Kong therefore do not have to confront a doctrine of legislative supremacy, and can seemingly more easily justify judicial review, even where it appears to be prohibited by a statutory ouster clause, by reference to Article 35 of the Basic Law and to the rule of law as a constitutional fundamental.

It might be asked why, if ouster clauses do not protect *ultra vires* decisions from review, the legislature continues to enact such clauses. It is possible, though presumably unlikely, that legislative drafters erroneously believe that ouster clauses will successfully exclude judicial review. More likely – though the author speculates – ouster clauses are included to dissuade potential challengers from seeking judicial review, as they may erroneously (though

---

[21] Liu J said that "no court should stand by and allow an attempted encroachment on its power of review unless it is restrained by an unassailably appropriate ouster clause" – *Chan Yik Tung* v *Hong Kong Housing Authority* [1989] 2 HKC 394, p.404.

[22] It was observed in the Court of First Instance that "clauses which seek to oust the power of the court to review decisions of a lower court or an administrative tribunal on question of law are never given effect to save in the most exceptional circumstances" – *Thai Muoi* v *Hong Kong Housing Authority* [2000] HKCU 370, p.5, per Yeung J.

[23] See, for example, *Taylor (formerly Kraupl)* v *National Assistance Board* [1957] P 101, p.111; repeated in *R* v *Medical Appeal Tribunal, ex parte Gilmore* [1957] 1 QB 574, p.575. Lord Atkin said that "[f]inality is a good thing but justice is a better" – *Ras Behari Lal* v *King-Emperor* [1933] All ER Rep 723 (PC) (India), p.726.

[24] Sir John Laws described parliamentary intention as a fig leaf – John Laws, 'Law and Democracy' [1995] Public Law 72, p.79.

understandably) regard the effect of an ouster clause as excluding the availability of review. A plain reading of many ouster clauses could reasonably lead one to that conclusion. Though it would be an erroneous conclusion, it may still lead to a reduction in the number of attempted challenges. It is nevertheless interesting to consider what motivations the legislature may have for seeking to protect executive decision-makers in this way.[25]

Statutory Limitation of Review

Though statute may purport to exclude the jurisdiction of the courts to judicially review, it may instead purport to limit review rather than exclude it. This is seen in the context of temporal limitations on the availability of review and partial exclusion of review.

Time-Limited Ouster

Statute may include a time-limited ouster clause, in other words exclusion or limitation of review after a particular period of time has elapsed. The legislature thereby seeks to limit judicial review applications, either at all or on the full range of grounds, to a given period following a particular event. The time limits encountered in this context are separate from, and additional to, the procedural three-month time limit under Order 53.[26] Whereas the time limit in Order 53 is a standard component of judicial review procedure and is applicable in every application for judicial review,[27] time-limited ouster clauses apply only in the specific statutory contexts in which they appear.

The courts more readily accept the effectiveness of a time-limited ouster clause than an absolute ouster clause,[28] though even time-limited ouster clauses have drawn criticism.[29] The House of Lords held jurisdiction to effectively be ousted by a statutory provision which stated that a particular challenge by way of an application to the High Court "may" be made "within six weeks from the date on which notice of the confirmation or making the order" was first published.[30] A similar decision was made by the Court of

---

[25] It is worth noting that, as long ago as in 1932, the Committee on Ministers' Powers in the UK recommended that ouster clauses should be "abandoned in all but the most exceptional cases" – Report of the Committee on Ministers' Powers, Cmd 4060 (1932), 65.

[26] O.53, r.4(3), provides that the provisions on delay in r.4 "are without prejudice to any statutory provision which has the effect of limiting the time within which an application for judicial review may be made".

[27] Subject to the various exceptions made by the courts – see pp.45–51.

[28] *Chan Yik Tung* v *Hong Kong Housing Authority* [1989] 2 HKC 394, pp.399–400. See also *Gurung Bhakta Bahadur* v *Director of Immigration* [2001] 3 HKLRD 225, pp.238–239.

[29] See *Chan Yik Tung* v *Hong Kong Housing Authority* [1989] 2 HKC 394, pp.400 and 404.

[30] *Smith* v *East Elloe Rural District Council* [1956] AC 736 (Acquisition of Land (Authorisation Procedure) Act 1946, Sch.1), Lord Reid and Lord Somervell of Harrow dissenting.

Appeal of England and Wales, again where the period for challenge was six weeks.[31] The courts appear to be more accepting of time-limited ouster clauses as they do not deny the applicant the opportunity of challenging the relevant decision; they merely stipulate that such a challenge must be brought within a particular period of time. It has been said that time-limited ouster clauses:

> might well be regarded not as ousting the jurisdiction of the court but merely as confining the time within which it can be invoked. In other words, clauses of this type might be regarded as analogous to statutes of limitation, setting limits of time within which action must be brought. There is no judicial criticism of statutes of limitation as 'ousting the jurisdiction of the court', though this is exactly what they do ... .[32]

There can be legitimate policy reasons behind the enactment of additional time limits to those found in Order 53. It may be that the three-month time period in Order 53 is thought too short, and that a longer time limit should apply. In this situation the longer time limit will be more likely to be observed by the courts as the specific intention of the legislature, as the additional time limit is specific to a particular statutory context, whereas the Order 53 time period is a general one which applies to judicial review proceedings across the board: *generalia specialibus non derogant*.[33] It may be that three months is thought too long a period of challenge in particular circumstances, that due to public interest or resource needs a challenge must be made within, for example, two months. Again, the shorter time period is more likely to be observed by the courts. It may also be that the legislature, mindful that the time limits in Order 53 are subject to the discretion of the court, impose a strict time limit which is subject to no discretionary application in its own right by the court – it may be longer, shorter or equivalent in duration to the time limit in Order 53.[34]

The courts will not, however, accept time-limited ouster clauses slavishly and without regard for the length of time stipulated. If the time limit is so short that it cannot reasonably be complied with, then it may be tantamount

---

[31] *R v Secretary of State for the Environment, ex parte Ostler* [1977] QB 122 (Acquisition of Land (Authorisation Procedure) Act 1946, Sch.1, para.15; Highways Act 1959, Schedule 2, para.2).

[32] Sir William Wade and Christopher Forsyth, *Administrative Law* (11th edn), p.622.

[33] If the shorter time period (i.e., that found in O.53) trumped the longer time period (i.e., that in the time-limited ouster clause), it would be impossible for a time-limited ouster clause to be effective which provided for longer than that found in O.53. This would be in tension with the idea that time-limited ouster clauses should be effective provided they do not obstruct access to justice (in particular by making it unfeasible that an application for judicial review could be made within the time limit). In other words, the more generous the time limit, the more likely it is that it will be respected by the court; therefore a time limit longer than that provided for in O.53 should generally be prioritised. This may well, however, still be subject to the general rules on delay, such that a delayed application may still be denied leave even where the applicant is within time as far as the time-limited ouster clause is concerned.

[34] Again, subject to the general rules on delay, unless the statute provides otherwise.

to a standard ouster provision and should be treated as such. A time-limited ouster clause of that nature may also conflict with the protections of Article 35 of the Basic Law. Whether a time limit is too short will depend on the context of the individual statutory framework and the broader legal and constitutional context. A time limit of two months may be acceptable for some types of challenges but not others. Fewer types of challenges would be likely to be reasonably subject to a one-month time limit. As time limits are progressively shorter, the probability increases that they will be found tantamount to a standard ouster clause and treated as such; but really the question is context dependent. The nature of the alleged breach of law may also affect the question of whether a time-limited ouster clause is treated as successfully ousting the jurisdiction of the court. A court might treat its jurisdiction as ousted after the expiry of (for example) a six week time limit where the alleged defect is non-compliance with the form of a statutory process, yet the same time limit might be held not to exclude the jurisdiction of the court where a gross violation of procedural fairness has occurred or where there has been breach of a constitutional or fundamental right.

Partial Ouster

A statute may seek not to exclude judicial review, but to permit review only on a more limited range of grounds, in a more limited range of situations (for example, by limiting standing beyond the normal rules) or by requiring that a more particular form of process is used.

An example of partial ouster is seen in the case of *Re Lau San-Ching*,[35] in which three individuals had their nominations to stand as candidates in District Board Elections rejected by the Returning Officer. They sought judicial review of the rejections on the basis of the alleged non-compliance of an electoral statutory provision with the Bill of Rights Ordinance. However, it was statutorily provided that "[t]he decision of the returning officer that a nomination paper is valid or invalid is final and shall not be questioned in any proceeding whatsoever except by an election petition".[36] The High Court rejected the contention that this provision was unlawful, and if it was not unlawful then the clear wording of the provision excluded the availability of judicial review as a means of redress. This did not mean that the applicants could not pursue their claims, but that the appropriate means of doing so was by way of an election petition. In other words, it was not a complete ouster: *Re Lau San-Ching* was indeed later regarded as not providing authority for the

---

[35] *Re Lau San-Ching* [1995] 2 HKLR 14.
[36] Boundary and Election Commission (Electoral Procedure) (Geographical Constituencies) Regulations, reg.9(7); also relevant was the Electoral Provisions Ordinance (cap.367), s.30(2).

proposition that ouster clauses can generally exclude the court's jurisdiction to judicially review.[37] On appeal, Litton JA stated that, as the regulations had laid down time limits for an election to proceed, "any intermediate judicial proceeding could have unexpected and perhaps the most deleterious effect".[38] Godfrey JA, though agreeing that the appeal should be dismissed, expressed concerns about the apparent ouster effect of the provision:

> The judge decided that the remedy of judicial review was not available to any of these applicants. His view was that the law afforded them no remedy other than by way of election petition. That remedy is not available to them until after the election. It follows, if he is right, that there would be a period between the date when a candidate's cause for grievance arises and the date of the election during which there could be no intervention by the court to correct some manifest illegality, irrationality or impropriety on the part of the returning officer, not even if justice and convenience required such intervention. I recoil from this conclusion ... But no doubt it will rarely be sensible, for practical reasons, to interfere with the course of the election. Once the election has been set in motion by noticed published in the Gazette... any intervention by the court before the date of the election would, I suspect, nearly always reduce the whole process, with its carefully crafted statutory timetable, to rubble. That is something which the court should refrain from doing unless very compelling reasons exist for its doing so.[39]

Godfrey JA added that this case was not, in his view, one in which such compelling reasons existed, but he was clearly more open to making an exception to the rule that such a challenge should be mounted post-election by way of election petition. Whilst it could indeed become too disruptive to election processes for challenges to come by way of judicial review before the election is concluded – and the possibility of using judicial review to disrupt or derail an election might be too tempting for some to resist, including those who wish to make a political point out of it – it does seem prudent to be prepared to make an exception where there exist compelling reasons for intervening before the election has come to a conclusion, perhaps because the returning officer has acted in flagrant violation of the legal requirements to which he is subject. To allow those to go unchallenged until after an election might likewise produce deleterious effects. The requirement that challenges be held off until after the election is also in conflict with the general principle that the sooner a challenge is brought, the less likely it is to be disruptive to public administration or unduly consumptive of public resources.[40] Nevertheless, the view of the majority in the

---

[37] *Thai Muoi v Hong Kong Housing Authority* [2000] HKCU 370, p.9.
[38] *Re Lau San-Ching* [1995] 2 HKLR 95 (CA), p.99. See also the Chemical Weapons (Convention) Ordinance (cap.578), s.27(8).
[39] *Re Lau San-Ching* [1995] 2 HKLR 95 (CA), p.100.   [40] See pp.50–51.

Court of Appeal was followed in future cases,[41] and it was confirmed that the judicial position on election petitions applied not only to District Council elections, but also to Legislative Council elections.[42]

It is not always clear whether, where a choice of procedures has been prescribed for challenging a decision, one of which is judicial review, election for the non-judicial review procedure results in effective ouster of the courts' jurisdiction should the person subsequently seek to apply for judicial review. The courts are reluctant to allow this effect to be implied.[43] Section 64(3) of the Interpretation and General Clauses Ordinance (cap.1) provided that:

> The conferring by an Ordinance of a right of appeal or objection to the Chief Executive in Council shall not prevent any person from applying [for judicial review], instead of appealing or making an objection to the Chief Executive in Council … but no proceedings by way [of judicial review] shall be taken against the Chief Executive in Council in respect of any such appeal or objection to the Chief Executive in Council or any proceedings connected therewith.

Hartmann J held that this provision conferred an option on the aggrieved person, but not a mutually exclusive option. The language was insufficiently clear to be construed as prohibiting both procedures from being utilised; indeed, an appeal to the Chief Executive-in-Council, which can include an appeal on the merits, is distinct from an application for judicial review on the basis of legality.[44] The "true intent" of the provision was rather, as a "matter of ordinary construction", that a decision made on appeal to the Chief Executive-in-Council cannot itself be subject to judicial review;[45] though as the same court held, the Chief Executive-in-Council would still be liable to review where she exceeded her jurisdiction.

Non-Justiciability

Though statutory exclusion of review is generally not permitted when a body has exceeded its jurisdiction, an act, decision, instrument or process is unreviewable if its subject matter is non-justiciable. This can arise due to restrictions in the Basic Law or imposed at common law. Though in principle a statute could designate certain types of decisions to be non-justiciable, these

---

[41] *Tang Kai Tak* [2010] HKCU 2547, paras.24–37; *Hans Richard Mahncke v Electoral Affairs Commission* [2012] HKCU 1551, paras.3–8; *Leung Tin Kei Edward v Electoral Affairs Commission* [2016] HKCU 1765, paras.10–18.
[42] *Hans Richard Mahncke v Electoral Affairs Commission* [2012] HKCU 1551; *Leung Tin Kei Edward v Electoral Affairs Commission* [2016] HKCU 1765, para.16.
[43] *Pyx Granite Co Ltd v Ministry of Housing and Local Government* [1960] AC 260 (HL).
[44] *Gurung Bhakta Bahadur v Director of Immigration* [2001] 3 HKLRD 225, pp.232–233.
[45] *Id.*, p.233.

restrictions are likely to take the form of ouster clauses and would tend not to protect unlawful acts and decisions.

As the courts labour under the constitutional framework of which the Basic Law is formally a capstone,[46] they must comply with its provisions. If the Basic Law clearly and unambiguously provides that certain subject matter is non-justiciable, the courts have little choice but to regard themselves as prohibited from reviewing in that area. An example of subject matter rendered non-justiciable by the Basic Law is the act of state:

> The courts of the Hong Kong Special Administrative Region shall have no jurisdiction over acts of state such as defence and foreign affairs. The courts of the Region shall obtain a certificate from the Chief Executive on questions of fact concerning acts of state such as defence and foreign affairs whenever such questions arise in the adjudication of cases. This certificate shall be binding on the courts. Before issuing such a certificate, the Chief Executive shall obtain a certifying document from the Central People's Government.[47]

The act of state was described by Lord Wilberforce as a "generally confused topic".[48] It was defined by Wade as an "act of the Executive as a matter of policy performed in the course of its relations with another state, including its relations with the subjects of that state",[49] though issue has been taken with this definition, in particular the inclusion of the words "as a matter of policy".[50] Reasons for acts of state being non-justiciable range from the fact that courts are unlikely to be in possession of sufficient information and expertise to adjudicate on acts of state, to the idea that they are pure issues of policy which do not raise justiciable questions of law, at least on the domestic plane. It has also been argued that it is the executive that must ultimately be accountable for decisions relating to defence, national security, foreign affairs and so on. An additional factor in the PRC is the fact that there

---

[46] Subject, of course, to the PRC Constitution.
[47] Basic Law, Art.19(2) and (3). This would nevertheless seem to require the courts to form a view on whether an issue does or does not concern an act of state. See also the Interpretation of Paragraph 1, Article 13 and Article 19 of the Basic Law of the Hong Kong Special Administrative Region of the People's Republic of China by the Standing Committee of the National People's Congress (adopted at the Twenty Second Session of the Standing Committee of the Eleventh National People's Congress on 26 August 2011); and consider also *Yang Chang Chun Robert v Government of the United States of America* [1997] 3 HKC 338; and *Re Chong Bing Keung (No 2)* [2000] 2 HKLRD 571 (CA).
[48] *Buttes Gas & Oil Co v Hammer (No 3)* [1982] AC 888 (HL), p.930. See also Yash Ghai, *Hong Kong's New Constitutional Order* (2nd edn) (Hong Kong University Press, 1999), pp.319–320.
[49] E. C. S. Wade, "Act of State in English Law: Its Relation with International Law" (1934) 15 *British Year Book of International Law* 98, p.103.
[50] *Attorney-General v Nissan* [1970] AC 179 (HL), p.212. No objection was taken to the words "as a matter of policy" by the Court of Final Appeal, however, which emphasised the word "policy" – *Democratic Republic of the Congo v FG Hemisphere Associates LLC (No 1)* (2011) 14 HKCFAR 95, para.354.

are three constituent jurisdictions in play: if acts of state were justiciable in the Hong Kong courts, what might the legal and practical consequences be of courts in different PRC jurisdictions reaching different conclusions on the legality of acts of state? It would be incongruous if, for example, a Mainland or Macanese court was to rule in a way which recognised PRC sovereignty over the Spratly and Paracel Islands, and other disputed reefs and features in the South China Sea, but a Hong Kong court ruled to the contrary.[51]

The Basic Law provision on acts of state essentially maintains the existing common law position in Hong Kong. It was remarked by Keith J that it was "well settled" that the courts have no power to monitor the performance by parties to extradition treaties of their obligations under those treaties, because "treaty obligations are of a political character which, in the absence of statutory intervention, are the exclusive province of the executive".[52] There is longstanding authority for this idea at common law. It was stated in the Privy Council, on appeal from India, that:

> The transactions of independent States between each other are governed by other laws than those which Municipal Courts administer: such Courts have neither the means of deciding what is right, nor the power of enforcing any decision which they may make.[53]

This was echoed in the Privy Council on appeal from the Cape of Good Hope where it was described as a "well-established principle of law".[54] More recently, Lord Templeman stated in the House of Lords that:

> A treaty is a contract between the governments of two or more sovereign states. International law regulates the relations between sovereign states

---

[51] Assuming a case in which each of these respective courts had geographic jurisdiction. It might be, for example, that a court is asked to rule on a particular tax or tariff which applied for the use of machinery in the PRC, and there is a disagreement between the parties on whether the Spratly Islands, Paracel Islands and other disputed reefs and features in the South China Sea were part of the PRC. In a case of this nature, the court would apparently be required to obtain a certificate from the Chief Executive on questions of fact concerning the issue of whether these islands and features are part of the PRC.

[52] *Yang Chang Chun Robert v Government of the United States of America* [1997] 3 HKC 338, p.342; and see *R v Governor of Pentonville Prison, ex parte Sinclair* [1991] 2 AC 64, p.89, in which Lord Ackner said that "monitoring the provisions of the [Treaty] is an executive, and not a magisterial, function". See also *United States of America v McVey* [1992] 3 SCR 475 (Supreme Court of Canada).

[53] *Secretary of State in Council of India v Kamachee Boye Sahaba* (1859) 13 Moo PCC 22 (PC) (India), p.75, per Lord Kingsdown; followed in *Salaman v Secretary of State-in-Council of India* [1906] 1 KB 613.

[54] *Cook v Sprigg* [1899] AC 572 (PC) (Cape of Good Hope), p.578, per Earl of Halsbury LC. This was also cited in *Democratic Republic of the Congo v FG Hemisphere Associates LLC (No 1)* (2011) 14 HKCFAR 95, para.348. See *Johnstone v Pedlar* [1921] 2 AC 262 (HL), where Lord Summer stated (at p.290) that "Municipal Courts do not take it upon themselves to review the dealings of State with State or of Sovereign with Sovereign"; and *Winfat Enterprise (HK) Co Ltd v Attorney-General of Hong Kong* [1985] AC 733 (PC).

and determines the validity, the interpretation and the enforcement of treaties. A treaty to which Her Majesty's Government is a party does not alter the laws of the United Kingdom. A treaty may be incorporated into and alter the laws of the United Kingdom by means of legislation. Except to the extent that a treaty becomes incorporated into the laws of the United Kingdom by statute, the courts of the United Kingdom have no power to enforce treaty rights and obligations at the behest of a sovereign government or at the behest of a private individual.[55]

Lord Oliver of Aylmerton, sitting in the same case, added under the heading of the "principle of non-justiciability" that it is "axiomatic that municipal courts have not and cannot have the competence to adjudicate upon or to enforce the rights arising out of transactions entered into by independent sovereign states between themselves on the plane of international law".[56] Domestically, the power of the Crown to conclude treaties was a matter for the exercise of the royal prerogative, as confirmed in an English case on the Treaty of Nanking 1842 between the Queen of the United Kingdom and the Emperor of China.[57] These statements of principle have been endorsed by the Court of Appeal as reflecting the common law position in Hong Kong, including post-Handover.[58] The legal position on the status and treatment of international treaties by the Hong Kong courts was set out by Ribeiro PJ:

> It has long been established under Hong Kong law (which follows English law in this respect), that international treaties are not self-executing and that, unless and until made part of our domestic law by legislation, they do not confer or impose any rights or obligations on individual citizens. It is a principle of construction that where a domestic statute is ambiguous and is capable of bearing different meanings which may in turn conform or conflict with the treaty, the court will presume that the legislature intended to legislate in accordance with applicable international treaty obligations. But where the statute is clear, the court's duty is to give effect to it whether or not that would involve breach of a treaty obligation. It is furthermore clear that the courts do

---

[55] *JH Rayner (Mincing Lane) Ltd* v *Department of Trade and Industry* [1990] 2 AC 418 (HL), pp.476–477.
[56] *Id.*, p.499.
[57] See *Rustomjee* v *The Queen* (1876) 2 QBD 69, p.74, per Lord Coleridge CJ; cited in *Blackburn* v *Attorney-General* [1971] 1 WLR 1037, p.1039, per Lord Denning MR.
[58] *Re Chong Bing Keung (No 2)* [2000] 2 HKLRD 571 (CA), pp.582–583; approved in *Ubamaka* v *Secretary for Security* (2012) 15 HKCFAR 743, para.43. It was stated that "[u]nder the current judicial system and principles, the Hong Kong authorities have never exercised jurisdiction over acts of state such as defence and foreign affairs", adding that the draft of Article 19 "preserv[ed] the above principle" – Ji Pengfei (Chair of the Drafting Committee for the Basic Law), 1990 Explanation of the Draft Basic Law given to the Third Session of the Seventh National People's Congress.

not have jurisdiction to adjudicate upon rights and obligations arising out of transactions between sovereign states.[59]

There is nevertheless scope for uncertainty at the margins of acts of state, in the sense that the courts may have to decide whether a matter is or is not an act of state. Whether to seek certification from the Chief Executive under Article 19 seems to be, within reason, a matter for the courts' assessment. It has been held in the Court of Final Appeal that Article 19(3) does not deprive the court of jurisdiction to decide a case in which there is an act of state: it rather prevents the court from exercising jurisdiction over an act of state, the facts of which as certified by the Chief Executive are binding on the court.[60] The court then adopts those "facts of state", and determines their legal consequences in deciding the case in question.[61] Broad terms of the enactment background in the Preamble to the Basic Law concerning acts of state that led to the resumption of sovereignty over Hong Kong have been said not to be justiciable in the municipal courts.[62]

Variable Intensity of Review

Justiciable decisions may be subject to a greater or lesser intensity of review.[63] This is informed both by institutional considerations (including the contours of the separation of powers) and the subject matter of a particular decision.[64]

---

[59] *Ubamaka* v *Secretary for Security* (2012) 15 HKCFAR 743; and see *R* v *Secretary of State for the Home Department, ex parte Brind* [1991] 1 AC 696 (HL). Note also *Hai Ho Tak* v *Attorney-General* [1994] 2 HKLR 202 (CA), p.208: "It is trite law that mere accession to a treaty or international covenant does not give effect to its provisions in terms of domestic law" (per Nazareth JA).

[60] In addition, it does not necessarily mean that litigation cannot arise as a result of an act of state. See, for example, *Burmah Oil Co (Burma Trading) Ltd* v *Lord Advocate*, 1964 SC (HL) 117.

[61] *Democratic Republic of the Congo* v *FG Hemisphere Associates LLC (No 1)* (2011) 14 HKCFAR 95, para.344.

[62] *Lee Bing Cheung* v *Secretary for Justice* [2013] 3 HKC 511, para.155.

[63] On a greater intensity of review, see pp.240–241.

[64] Laws LJ said that the "facts of the case, viewed always in their statutory context, will steer the court to a more or less intrusive quality of review. In some cases a change of tack by a public authority, though unfair from the applicant's stance, may involve questions of general policy affecting the public at large or a significant section of it (including interests not represented before the court); here the judges may well be in no position to adjudicate save at most on a bare *Wednesbury* basis, without themselves donning the garb of policy-maker, which they cannot wear" – *R* v *Secretary of State for Education and Employment, ex parte Begbie* [2000] 1 WLR 1115, p.1130. See generally Cora Chan, "Deference and the Separation of Powers: An Assessment of the Court's Constitutional and Institutional Competences" (2011) 41 *Hong Kong Law Journal* 7.

Deference

The concept of deference is marked by the court affording greater latitude to decision-makers in the exercise of their discretion than may normally be the case. This is often seen in cases in which there is a greater policy content to the decision-making process, making it less amenable to the usual level of judicial scrutiny. In other words, the extent to which a decision is discretionary in nature may require that the court exercises particular restraint in reviewing the decision to avoid trespassing on executive discretion. Deference must be understood in this relatively narrow context – as a modification on the "normal" level of intensity of review – otherwise it would be a mere paraphrase of the separation of powers. It is a specific application of the separation of powers in relation to particular categories of discretion. It is sometimes seen across the range of grounds of judicial review, and sometimes in relation to a specific ground, in particular *Wednesbury* unreasonableness.

One area in which the courts exercise deference is in relation to the Chief Executive's power to pardon criminal offenders or commute their penalties, enshrined in Article 48(12) of the Basic Law:

> The Chief Executive of the Hong Kong Special Administrative Region shall exercise the following powers and functions: . . .
>
> (12) To pardon persons convicted of criminal offences or commute their penalties . . .

This power acts as an important safety valve where the public interest is not best served by allowing the criminal legal process to run its ordinary course. It may, for example, be exercised to prevent a perceived gross injustice arising, such as to pardon a person who has been diagnosed with a terminal illness, or to commute a penalty where the sentence is manifestly disproportionate to the criminal act committed. This power was known as the prerogative of mercy, exercised by the Governor on behalf of the monarch. Though there was authority in the Privy Council on appeal from other jurisdictions that the prerogative of mercy did not give rise to legal rights and would therefore not be justiciable,[65] in post-Handover Hong Kong this power is based not on the royal prerogative but on the power conferred by Article 48(12) of the Basic Law.[66] Hartmann J said the following on the matter:

> In my judgment, it is evident that the Basic Law, while giving the Chief Executive certain prerogative powers, does not seek to place him above the

---

[65] *de Freitas* v *Benny* [1976] AC 239 (PC) (Trinidad and Tobago); *Reckley* v *Minister of Public Safety and Immigration (No 2)* [1996] AC 527 (PC) (Bahamas).
[66] *Ch'ng Poh* v *Chief Executive of HKSAR* [2003] HKEC 1441, paras.33–34.

law; his powers are defined by and therefore constrained by the Basic Law. The Chief Executive is a creature of the Basic Law and enjoys no powers, no rights or privileges which are not afforded to him by that Law. That being the case, I do not see that his powers exercised pursuant to art.48(12) can be classified as purely personal acts of grace, a species of private acts ... To the contrary, when the Chief Executive acts pursuant to art.48(12), in my judgment, he acts within the greater constitutional scheme, a scheme which looks to the protection of the rights of all residents according to law ...

In my judgment, it would offend the Basic Law – and do so manifestly – if, for example, those advising the Chief Executive in respect of his discretion under art.48(12) were able with impunity to subvert the honesty of that advice on the basis of racial, sexual or religious grounds or were able with impunity to refuse to put before the Chief Executive evidential material which did not for whatever reason suit their private ends. If such was the case, the Chief Executive would not, in making a determination on the basis advice [sic], be discharging his obligations in terms of the Basic Law. That is because the Basic Law, as a document of constitution that safeguards the rights and freedoms of all residents in accordance with law (see art.4), does not permit such pollution of lawful process, executive or otherwise.

In the circumstances, I am satisfied that in terms of the Basic Law, while the merits of any decision made by the Chief Executive pursuant to art.48(12) are not subject to the review of the courts, the lawfulness of the process by which such a decision is made is open to review. Accordingly, the applicant's challenge in respect of art.48(12) is not vitiated by a lack of jurisdiction.[67]

The significance of this statement is to show that the courts in post-Handover Hong Kong do not regard the Chief Executive's power of pardon and commuting of sentence as non-justiciable and thus immune from review. Though the Basic Law changed the context in which this issue was considered, Privy Council jurisprudence had in any event changed course by confirming that an exercise of the prerogative of mercy would be justiciable, and that its exercise should meet the requisite standards of fairness and natural justice.[68]

Though the power of pardon and commuting of sentence is now justiciable, the courts are likely to apply a lower intensity of review in relation to the Chief Executive's decisions in exercise of this power due to its invocation of a broad and policy-laden discretion. The courts are inclined not to scrutinise the exercise of this discretion too closely in recognition of the nature of the power in question. Nevertheless, the discretion must still be lawfully exercised, and if

---

[67] *Id.*, paras.35 and 37–38.
[68] *Lewis* v *Attorney-General of Jamaica* [2001] 2 AC 50 (PC) (Jamaica).

for example an individual's interests in fairness and natural justice are compromised, or if the decision is *Wednesbury* unreasonable,[69] then the courts seem prepared to intervene.

Another area in which a lower intensity of scrutiny may be discernible is in relation to prosecutorial discretion. This includes such decisions as whether to prosecute, what charges to bring, whether to file a voluntary bill, whether there should be joint or separate trials, whether to take over a private prosecution, decisions on the immunity of witnesses, which witnesses to call to give evidence, plea bargaining decisions, and whether to end criminal proceedings by entering a *nolle prosequi* or offering no evidence. The principle of prosecutorial independence is enshrined in Article 63 of the Basic Law:

> The Department of Justice of the Hong Kong Special Administrative Region shall control criminal prosecutions, free from any interference.

In the pre-Handover period, the Court of Appeal held in *Keung Siu-Wah v Attorney General* that prosecutorial decisions of the Attorney-General were not subject to judicial review. Fuad V-P stated that there must be few subjects less suited to judicial review proceedings than the exercise of the Attorney-General's discretion on whether to institute criminal proceedings and what charge should be pursued. He pointed out difficulties in terms of the requirement for affidavit evidence and cross-examination, and potential overlap with criminal proceedings should the application for judicial review fail. It would also not be in the public interest to delay a criminal trial in order to transact the application for judicial review. In addition, the courts possessed all the necessary powers to prevent abuse of process and to ensure a fair trial.[70] It was a "constitutional imperative that the Courts do not attempt to interfere with the Attorney General's discretion to prosecute".[71]

The court was not asserting that the Attorney-General was beyond judicial control, but that trial proceedings were the appropriate place to exert such control wherein the court had an inherent power to prevent abuse of process. Fuad V-P noted previous judicial pronouncements which confirmed the subjection of the Attorney-General to judicial control, but that those pronouncements were made in judgments on appeal against conviction and not in judicial review proceedings. He could "discern nothing" in those pronouncements that "would give support to the contention that any of the decisions of the Attorney General which they were addressing could be made the subject of judicial review proceedings under RSC O.53".[72]

---

[69] Though see B. V. Harris, "Judicial Review, Justiciability and the Prerogative of Mercy" (2003) 62(3) *Cambridge Law Journal* 631, pp.656–657.
[70] *Keung Siu-Wah v Attorney General* [1990] 2 HKLR 238, pp.253–255.
[71] *Id.*, p.255, per Fuad V-P.
[72] *Id.*, p.252. It was added by Penlington JA that the "authorities are overwhelming that the decision of the Attorney General whether or not to prosecute in any particular case is not

However, these pronouncements were not so unequivocal. Though Fuad V-P noted this comment,[73] Silke JA had stated in the Court of Appeal that there may in exceptional circumstances be a "right to review" the Attorney-General's exercise of discretion in a passage in which judicial review was explicitly referenced.[74] The Court of Appeal was not prepared to accept in *Cheung Sou-yat* v *The Queen* that the Attorney-General's exercise of discretion could never be called into question.[75] It was held elsewhere that the Attorney-General's decision could, if justiciable, be reviewed where it was "outrageous".[76]

The decision in *Keung Siu-Wah* v *Attorney General* seems therefore to have been the most unyielding of judgments on the non-reviewability of prosecutorial discretion.[77] Indeed, the courts have departed from this hard-line approach and admitted that prosecutorial discretion is subject to judicial review, albeit under a lower intensity of scrutiny. It was noted in *RV* v *Director of Immigration*[78] that, in other jurisdictions, judicial review may exceptionally lie against a decision of the prosecuting authority. This was the conclusion of the House of Lords,[79] the Supreme Court of Fiji,[80] and the Privy Council on appeal from Mauritius[81] and Trinidad and Tobago.[82] In the latter three of these, as Hartmann J pointed out, the powers of the prosecuting authority were drawn from a "written constitution" and therefore limited by it.[83] The Privy Council on appeal from Trinidad and Tobago stated that the reasons for

---

subject to judicial review" and that he did "not regard the dicta of Cons and Yang, JJ. in *Cheung Sou-yat* as authority to the contrary" (pp.255–256).

[73] *Keung Siu-Wah* v *Attorney General* [1990] 2 HKLR 238, pp.251–252.

[74] *The Queen* v *Tsui Lai-Ying* [1987] HKLR 857 (CA), p.874.

[75] *Cheung Sou-Yat* v *The Queen* [1979] HKLR 630 (CA), pp. 636 (per Huggins JA), 639 (per Cons J) and 641 (per Yang J).

[76] *Tang Yee-Chun* v *Attorney General* [1988] 2 HKLR 408, pp.415–416, per Sears J. The reference to justiciability was in relation to the fact that the Attorney-General merely set in motion a procedure whereby the judge may or may not consent to the preferment of a bill of indictment without prior committal proceedings (in other words, the relevant decision was that of the judge, not the Attorney-General).

[77] The High Court gave a somewhat incoherent judgment when it held that the Attorney-General had many duties to perform in the conduct of a prosecution which "clearly are not reviewable" (before citing examples of prosecutorial decisions), but that "in the exercise of his discretion with regard to his prerogative powers, the Attorney General is not subject to judicial review, unless he comes within one of the three criteria referred to by Lord Diplock in *Council of Civil Service Unions* v *Minister for the Civil Service* of illegality, irrationality and procedural impropriety... The decision whether or not to proceed with the... charges is one to be made by the Attorney General in the exercise of his discretion which is not subject to judicial review" – *Tan Soon-Gin* v *Attorney General* [1990] 2 HKLR 176, p.182, per Jones J. The case went on appeal to the Privy Council – *Tan Soon-Gin* v *Attorney-General of Hong Kong* [1992] 2 HKLR 254 (PC).

[78] *RV* v *Director of Immigration* [2008] 4 HKLRD 529.

[79] *R* v *Director of Public Prosecutions, ex parte Kebilene* [2000] 2 AC 326 (HL).

[80] *Matalulu* v *Director of Public Prosecutions* [2003] 4 LRC 712 (Supreme Court of Fiji).

[81] *Mohit* v *Director of Public Prosecutions of Mauritius* [2006] 1 WLR 3343 (PC) (Mauritius).

[82] *Sharma* v *Brown-Antoine* [2007] 1 WLR 780 (PC) (Trinidad and Tobago).

[83] *RV* v *Director of Immigration* [2008] 4 HKLRD 529, para.44.

courts having "extreme reluctance" to judicially review decisions to prosecute included, from a review of the authorities:

(i) the great width of the prosecuting authority's discretion and the polycentric character of official decision-making in such matters including policy and public interest considerations which are not susceptible to judicial review because it is within neither the constitutional function nor the practical competence of the courts to assess their merits;

(ii) the wide range of factors relating to available evidence, the public interest and perhaps other matters which the prosecuting authority may properly take into account;

(iii) the delay inevitably caused to the criminal trial if it proceeds;

(iv) the desirability of all challenges taking place in the criminal trial or on appeal, noting that in addition to the safeguards afforded to the defendant in a criminal trial, the court has a well-established power to restrain proceedings which are an abuse of its process, even where such abuse does not compromise the fairness of the trial itself; and

(v) the blurring of the executive function of the prosecuting authority and the judicial function of the court, and of the distinct roles of the criminal and the civil courts.[84]

It was explained in the Court of Appeal that the prosecutorial independence enshrined in Article 63 of the Basic Law was a "linchpin of the rule of law".[85] However, the possibility of judicial review in exceptional circumstances was admitted:

> I apprehend that it is to such interference, that is to say, interference of a political kind, to which art 63 is directed. But the rule that ensures the Secretary's independence in his prosecutorial function necessarily extends to preclude judicial interference, subject only to issues of abuse of the court's process and, possibly, judicial review of decisions taken in bad faith ... There is also authority for the proposition that 'dishonesty, bad faith or some other exceptional circumstances' might found a basis for challenge in the courts of the exercise in a particular case of a prosecutorial prerogative ...[86]

The court in *RV v Director of Immigration* explicitly admitted the reviewability of prosecutorial discretion. Hartmann J considered that the new constitutional order under the Basic Law meant that the Secretary for Justice (assuming the role formerly exercised by the Attorney-General in matters of prosecutorial discretion) had to act within the constitutional limits on his powers and was subject in that regard to judicial review. This was "not a defiance of binding precedent", but the "recognition of a new constitutional order and the duties

---

[84] *Sharma v Brown-Antoine* [2007] 1 WLR 780 (PC) (Trinidad and Tobago), pp.788–789.
[85] *Re C (A Bankrupt)* [2006] 4 HKC 582 (CA), para.18, per Stock JA.
[86] *Id*, paras.20–22, per Stock JA.

of our courts in respect of that new order".[87] The more difficult issue for Hartmann J was not whether prosecutorial discretion was subject to judicial review, but in what circumstances:

> The more difficult question, in my view, is the determination of what are the constitutional limits, remembering that the Secretary for Justice must be able to control criminal prosecutions free of judicial encroachment ...
>
> Clearly, the Secretary would act outside of his powers if it could be demonstrated that he has done so not on an independent assessment of the merits but in obedience to a political instruction. Article 63 specifically forbids such interference with the exercise of his powers.
>
> Equally plain, in my view, is the conclusion that the Secretary would act outside of his powers if he acted in bad faith, for example, if one of his offices instituted a prosecution in return for payment of a bribe.
>
> I am also of the view that a rigid fettering of his discretion would fall outside the Secretary's constitutional powers; for example, a refusal to prosecute a specific class of offences detailed in a statute lawfully brought into law. Such an action would undermine the constitutional functioning of other organs of state: the Executive and the Legislature.
>
> It is not possible, of course, to foresee and classify every circumstance in which this Court can hold, without impermissible encroachment, that the Secretary has acted outside of his constitutional powers. There may be exceptional circumstances that arise. But this proviso is not to be read as somehow acting to reduce the role of the Secretary to that of an ordinary administrator. The prosecutorial independence of the Secretary is a linchpin of the rule of law. That is the way it has been prior to the Basic Law and the way it now remains. The exceptional circumstances of which I speak must be truly exceptional and must demonstrate that the Secretary has acted outside of his very broad powers, powers that, as Viscount Dilhorne said [in *Gouriet* v *Union of Post Office Workers* [1978] AC 435], he exercises free of direction by his ministerial colleagues and free also of the control and supervision of the courts.
>
> In summary, I am satisfied that, under the Basic Law, the Secretary's control of criminal prosecutions is amenable to judicial review but only to the very limited extent that I have described.
>
> In so far as it is still necessary to do so, I would emphasise that the remedy of judicial review will only be granted in the rarest of cases. As the Privy

---

[87] *RV* v *Director of Immigration* [2008] 4 HKLRD 529, para.68. The reviewability of prosecutorial discretion under the constitutional regime of the Basic Law arose as an issue prior to *RV* v *Director of Immigration*, but with no firm view expressed on the matter as the application was deemed "hopeless" and leave refused – *Kwan Sun Chu Pearl* v *Department of Justice* [2006] HKEC 986 (CA); though hints of a possible change of position were discernible in the Court of First Instance – *Kwan Sun Chu Pearl* v *Department of Justice* [2005] HKEC 1548 (in which the sitting judge was Hartmann J). Zervos J said in *D* v *Director of Public Prosecutions* [2015] 4 HKLRD 62, para.24, that "the principle as stated in *Keung Siu Wah* has been qualified and reviewed in a new constitutional and modern context".

Council said in *Sharma* v *Brown-Antoine* ... it is to be considered a highly exceptional remedy.[88]

Though *RV* v *Director of Immigration* was not expressly referred to in its judgment, the Court of Appeal stated in a closely following case that it would be in "extremely rare cases" and "only where the evidence points unquestionably to the desirability of there being a prosecution" that the court should interfere with the prosecuting authority's decision not to prosecute. Article 63 of the Basic Law made it all the more important that the court should exercise "extreme caution" when considering whether to review such a decision.[89] To completely insulate prosecutorial discretion from the possibility of judicial review could undermine the rule of law by rendering persons vulnerable to abuses and misuses of those powers. The adoption of a lower intensity of review in relation to prosecutorial discretion would therefore seem to be a sensible middle ground between immunising such discretion from judicial review and jeopardising the principle of prosecutorial independence. It has been suggested that the common law rules on review of prosecutorial discretion might also apply to decisions of a similar nature taken by regulatory bodies such as the Securities and Futures Commission.[90]

---

[88] *RV* v *Director of Immigration* [2008] 4 HKLRD 529, paras.69–76. The application for judicial review failed on the merits of the challenge. See also *Ng Chi Keung* v *Secretary for Justice* [2016] 2 HKLRD 1330, paras.104–110; and *Re Lau Hei Wing* [2016] 3 HKLRD 652, paras.18–21.
[89] *Ma Pui Tung* v *Department of Justice* [2008] HKEC 1590 (CA), para.10, per Rogers V-P.
[90] *Shek Lai San* v *Securities and Futures Commission* [2010] 4 HKC 168, para.79. For more general concerns about permitting judicial review in relation to criminal prosecutions, see *Dairy Farm Co Ltd* v *Director of Food and Environmental Hygiene* [2005] HKEC 754, paras.28 and 32; *Mo Yuk Ping* v *Secretary for Justice* [2005] HKEC 1363, paras.51–52; *Yeung Chun Pong* v *Secretary for Justice (No 4)* [2008] 2 HKC 46, pp.74–77; and *Gammon Construction Ltd* v *HKSAR* [2014] HKEC 1712, paras.63–64. One of the concerns is whether judicial review should be permitted when the applicant could instead appeal the case through the criminal courts – *Viva Magnetics Ltd* v *Secretary for Justice* [2002] 3 HKLRD 571, paras.18–19; *Chow Shun Chiu* v *HKSAR* [2001] HKEC 882, para.34. This is not to say, as the discussion in these cases demonstrates, that the courts are categorically unwilling to allow judicial review in the context of a criminal prosecution.

9

Arguability and Qualitative Filtering

The court will make a qualitative assessment of the applicant's case in deciding whether or not to grant leave. This is more controversial than may at first appear, as the leave stage is in principle not suited to a consideration of substantive issues. An assessment of the quality of the application for leave will, however, be difficult to conduct without at least partly examining the substance of the application and the merits of the grounds advanced therein. In addition, the courts have moved to a more rigorous examination of the quality of the application at the leave stage, which can have a tendency to encourage more detailed papers to be lodged, and arguments made, at the leave stage than was previously the case. This qualitative filter is increasingly in tension with the concept of the leave stage as a brief, procedural sift.

There are essentially two types of application that this test aims to target. One is the application that is non-serious, vexatious or for some other reason inappropriate, such as where the arguments are political rather than legal, or where the application is merely calculated to cause annoyance or inconvenience. Such applications can with relatively little controversy be dispensed with at the leave stage on the basis that they do not meet the necessary qualitative requirements. Less straightforward is the second kind of application, which is a *bona fide* application which seeks to argue a genuine point but is for some reason misconceived or deemed hopeless. Perhaps the arguments are poorly or irrelevantly framed, or the argument advanced has already failed in a previous case, or the complaint is hypothetical or speculative, or the court simply does not think that the application has a realistic chance of success.[1] This can be a more delicate assessment for the court to make, as it is already judging the merits of the application but without the benefit of the full argumentation and

---

[1] Litton JA described the intention behind the qualitative filter as "that public authorities and the like should not be vexed with hopeless applications" – *Ho Ming Sai* v *Director of Immigration* [1994] 1 HKLR 21, p.27. Where the potential impact on third parties that the relief sought would have would be such as to conclude that there is no realistic prospect of the grant of such relief at the substantive hearing, the case could be held not to be reasonably arguable – *Shek Lai San* v *Securities and Futures Commission* [2010] 4 HKC 168, paras.42–45. It was specifically stated (para.44) that the reasonably arguable case related not only to the substantive complaint, but also to the relief sought.

evidence which would be led at the substantive hearing.[2] Arguability also raises other issues, such as sufficient interest.[3]

In principle, however, the idea of a qualitative filter is a fair one, and there are certainly arguments favouring the prevention of applications of this nature from proceeding to a substantive hearing. It helps ensure that public body respondents do not needlessly incur the full time and resource costs associated with legal representation and court process at the substantive hearing. The court's time and resources are also conserved if such applications are not allowed to proceed, in terms of the substantive hearing and associated procedure, such as in relation to discovery, interrogatories, cross-examination and so on.[4] There are also implications for the smooth conduct of public administration, as public bodies and third parties affected by their decisions may face uncertainty as to the legality of decisions impugned by essentially unarguable claims.[5]

Threshold

The courts now adopt an "arguability" threshold to test the quality of the application at the leave stage. This represents a shift from the previous threshold of "potential arguability", though there was also authority for a higher threshold.[6] Kempster JA, sitting in the Court of Appeal in *Ho Ming Sai v Director of Immigration*, expressly rejected as too high the test that "it was arguable that grounds for judicial review existed".[7] Litton JA explained in the same case why it was inappropriate to erect too high a threshold for the applicant, pointing out that the applicant may have little material in hand at the leave stage and may have a complaint that the public body had "dealt with him in an oppressively secretive manner".[8] As more information may come to light after discovery, interrogatories, cross-examination and so on, to set the bar too high at the leave stage may mean that "many legitimate grievances could be screened out".[9]

---

[2] Consider *Ng Wing Hung v Hong Kong Examinations and Assessment Authority* [2010] HKEC 1471, para.13.
[3] See, for example, *Chu Woan Chyi v Director of Immigration* [2004] 3 HKLRD 11, paras.8–9.
[4] Regarding cross-examination, see *The Queen v Director of Immigration, ex parte Do Giau* [1992] 1 HKLR 287, pp.302 and 343–344.
[5] *Po Fun Chan v Winnie Cheung* (2007) 10 HKCFAR 676, para.14, per Li CJ.
[6] *R v Legal Aid Board, ex parte Hughes* (1992) 24 HLR 698; and see *Lee Sap Pat v Commissioner of Inland Revenue* [1991] 2 HKC 251, p.257.
[7] *Ho Ming Sai v Director of Immigration* [1994] 1 HKLR 21, p.23. This case applied, on point of the leave threshold, *R v Inland Revenue Commissioners, ex parte National Federation of Self Employed and Small Businesses Ltd* [1982] AC 617 (HL); and *R v Civil Service Appeal Board, ex parte Cunningham* [1992] ICR 816. In the latter case, reference was made by Lord Donaldson MR (p.823) to making out a *prima facie* case for the granting of leave.
[8] *Ho Ming Sai v Director of Immigration* [1994] 1 HKLR 21, p.27.
[9] *Id.*, per Litton JA. Uncertainty as to the appropriate threshold was expressed in *Yu Pik Ying v Director of Immigration* [2002] 1 HKC 18 (CA), pp.28–29.

Further evidence of the lower threshold was seen in later cases. Hartmann J stated that the "standard test for leave is whether the material ... discloses matters which, on further consideration, might disclose an arguable case. It is not a high test. It is intended only to eliminate vexatious or hopeless cases",[10] echoing Litton JA's expression from a decade earlier.[11] Hartmann J went on to say that there was in the instant case a "*prima facie* arguable case ... not a hopeless case".[12] Rogers V-P said in *Yu Pik Ying* v *Director of Immigration* that:

> In my view, the application for leave to bring judicial review proceedings should be a short procedure. As the cases indicate it should not involve lengthy applications. Indeed, the more the details of the case are considered, at the application stage, the more undesirable the lengthening of the proceedings becomes. The merits of the application should be considered at the hearing for judicial review, if leave be granted. It is indeed, undesirable that the merits are considered in depth until the case is fully prepared since even the expression of preliminary views can have undesirable effects. It is for this reason that in my view the application stage should be more of a weeding out process, stopping those applications doomed to failure.[13]

In another case, it was said that the applicant was not a "meddlesome busybody",[14] which is again not to set the bar particularly high.[15] On an application of the potential arguability test, it was "sufficient for [the applicant] merely to satisfy the court that on *further* consideration at a *subsequent* hearing an arguable case *might* be demonstrated".[16]

---

[10] *Mo Yuk Ping* v *Secretary for Justice* [2005] HKEC 1363, para.47.
[11] *Ho Ming Sai* v *Director of Immigration* [1994] 1 HKLR 21, p.27.
[12] *Mo Yuk Ping* v *Secretary for Justice* [2005] HKEC 1363, para.47.
[13] *Yu Pik Ying* v *Director of Immigration* [2002] 1 HKC 18 (CA), p.29. Lord Diplock described the qualitative aspect of the leave stage as to "prevent the time of the court being wasted by busybodies with misguided or trivial complaints of administrative error" – *R* v *Inland Revenue Commissioners, ex parte National Federation of Self Employed and Small Businesses Ltd* [1982] AC 617 (HL), pp.642–643.
[14] *Chu Woan Chyi* v *Director of Immigration* [2004] 3 HKLRD I1, para.9, per Rogers V-P; drawing on Lord Diplock's use of the term "busybody" in *R* v *Inland Revenue Commissioners, ex parte National Federation of Self Employed and Small Businesses Ltd* [1982] AC 617 (HL). This raises issues of sufficient interest in addition to those of arguability.
[15] It has been said, however, that the fact the applicant is not a busybody or troublemaker "may well not be sufficient to tip the scales in her favour" and persuade the court to grant leave – *Shek Lai San* v *Securities and Futures Commission* [2010] 4 HKC 168, para.57.
[16] *Po Fun Chan* v *Winnie Cheung* (2007) 10 HKCFAR 676, para.12, per Li CJ. Emphasis in the original. Lord Diplock had stated that: "The whole purpose of requiring that leave should first be obtained to make the application for judicial review would be defeated if the court were to go into the matter in any depth at that stage. If, on a quick perusal of the material then available, the court thinks that it discloses what might on further consideration turn out to be an arguable case in favour of granting to the applicant the relief claimed, it ought, in the exercise of a judicial discretion, to give him leave to apply for that relief. The discretion that the court is exercising at this stage is not the same as that which it is called upon to exercise when all the evidence is in and the matter has been fully argued at the hearing of the application" – *R* v *Inland Revenue*

For some, the bar was not high enough. Keith JA said the test set out in *Ho Ming Sai* would be appropriate "if the rationale for obtaining leave is only to weed out those cases which are obviously hopeless", but a more rigorous test would be appropriate "if it was intended that only those cases which are genuinely arguable should go to a full hearing, in which case the arguability of the case would have to be considered in a meaningful way".[17] Though stating that this was not the case in which to establish which was the correct test, he posited a flexible test in which a higher, arguability threshold should apply in cases such as those of statutory construction, but a lower, potential arguability threshold in cases of, for example, procedural fairness.[18] This more flexible approach was endorsed in a subsequent case, though not with the most persuasive argument: "[l]eave should only be granted if the point of law is arguable for it is very difficult, if not impracticable, to draw a meaningful distinction between an arguable point of law and a potentially arguable point of law".[19] Hartmann J stated that, though he had some sympathy for the view that the test of potential arguability was too weak and thus may "as often undermine the ends of justice as enhance them", he was bound to apply it.[20] That test would merely screen out the "plainly hopeless cases".[21]

In *Po Fun Chan* v *Winnie Cheung*, Li CJ gave "authoritative guidance" on the applicable threshold in leave applications:[22]

> The purpose of the leave requirement would be better served by the adoption of the arguability test instead of the potential arguability test. The granting of leave to apply for judicial review is a matter for the court's discretion to be exercised judicially. The test which should be applied is the arguability test. Under this test, arguability must mean reasonable arguability. A claim for relief which is not reasonably arguable could not be regarded as arguable. A reasonably arguable case is one which enjoys realistic prospects of success. Whilst the test adopted represents a higher threshold than the potential arguability test, claims which are reasonably arguable would be given leave

---

Commissioners, ex parte National Federation of Self Employed and Small Businesses Ltd [1982] AC 617 (HL), pp.643–644.

[17] *Wong Chung Ki* v *Chief Executive* [2003] 1 HKC 404 (CA), pp.413–414. In the same case, Godfrey V-P referred to Atkin's Court Forms (2nd edn) (Vol. 23(2), 1998 issue), p.177, which stated that "[l]eave should only be refused ... if there is no prima facie arguable case at all".

[18] *Wong Chung Ki* v *Chief Executive* [2003] 1 HKC 404 (CA), p.414.

[19] *Shem Yin Fun* v *Director of Legal Aid* [2003] 1 HKC 404 (CA), p.574, per Chu J. The case involved "construction of the statute and does not involve any investigation of fact, [therefore] the Court ought to adopt a more flexible approach". Nevertheless, it made, in that case, "no practical difference to the outcome whether the threshold test is one of arguability or potential arguability".

[20] *Leung TC William Roy* v *Secretary for Justice* [2005] HKEC 998, para.16; noting *Wong Chung Ki* v *Chief Executive* [2003] 1 HKC 404 (CA), p.417.

[21] *Po Fun Chan* v *Winnie Cheung* (2007) 10 HKCFAR 676, para.13, per Li CJ.   [22] *Id.*, para.11.

to go forward under it. It is in the public interest that challenges which are not reasonably arguable should not be given leave to proceed.[23]

Whilst this was an expression from the most senior judge and the most senior court in the jurisdiction that the threshold for granting leave should be higher,[24] it remained unclear what an arguable claim might look like as distinct from a potentially arguable claim. The description of arguability as meaning "reasonable arguability" was neither, with respect, elucidatory.[25] It was pointed out that one of the difficulties of the potential arguability threshold was uncertainty at the leave stage about what further materials and arguments may be available at the substantive hearing.[26] However, raising the threshold presumably makes it more likely that legitimate claims will fail at the leave stage merely because of the unavailability of evidence and sufficiently elaborated arguments that would and perhaps could only be presented at the substantive hearing. In any event, uncertainties appear to persist under the arguability threshold. The lack of certainty in what is required by the arguability threshold is exacerbated by the following observations made in *Re RS*:

> [I]t is necessary to point out that the mere fact that leave had previously been granted by another judge on a similar point does not necessarily mean that leave should be granted in this case. First, there may be differences in the factual matrix which call for different considerations. Second, the state of the law may have been further clarified since the grant of leave in a previous case. Third, there may be factors applicable in the instance case that are not germane in the earlier case which affect the exercise of discretionary considerations in terms of grant or refusal of leave. Fourth, the issues raised in the Forms 86 in the two cases may be different. As observed during the course of the appeal, this court must assess whether the grounds raised by the Applicant are reasonably arguable by reference to the materials placed before us and it would not be right to second-guess why leave was granted in another case.[27]

---

[23] *Id.*, para.15. The court followed in this regard *R v Legal Aid Board, ex parte Hughes* (1992) 24 HLR 698. See also *Ng Yat Chi v Max Share Ltd* (2005) 8 HKCFAR 1, para.13, and at para.20 where Li CJ described the purpose of the leave stage in judicial review proceedings as enabling "unarguable claims to be filtered out" and a "mechanism . . . for preventing abuse of process"; and *Sharma v Brown-Antoine* [2007] 1 WLR 780 (PC) (Trinidad and Tobago), p.787. The arguability threshold set out in *Po Fun Chan* was described in the Court of Appeal as a "more realistic filter" – *Yeung Chun Pong v Secretary for Justice* [2008] HKEC 40 (CA), para.17, per Stock JA.

[24] There was an indication twelve months earlier in the Court of Appeal that the lower threshold might be reconsidered; See *Smart Gain Investment Ltd v Town Planning Board* [2006] HKEC 2063, para.3, per Ma CJHC.

[25] Nevertheless, reasonableness tests are arguably part of the common law method and tradition, and emblematic of its pragmatic approach.

[26] *Po Fun Chan v Winnie Cheung* (2007) 10 HKCFAR 676, para.12.

[27] *Re RS* [2013] HKEC 1309 (CA), para.21, per Lam JA.

Li CJ rejected Keith JA's suggestion of a flexible test, stating instead that there should be a fixed threshold.[28] He also left no doubt that he was seeking to actively raise the threshold, referring to a "discarding" of the potential arguability test and an "adoption" of the arguability threshold.[29] His judgment on the issue of arguability was unanimously endorsed by the court,[30] and the arguability test as set out in *Po Fun Chan* continues to be applied by the courts.[31] In a subsequent case, it was explained that the test of "reasonable arguability" was "designed to screen out unmeritorious, frivolous, vexatious and purported challenges that are not reasonably arguable".[32] Most cases seem now to refer to "reasonable arguability",[33] though occasionally the term "arguability" is used.[34] Sometimes both phrases have been used in tandem.[35]

Issues Raised by Arguability Threshold

The purpose of the leave stage is supposed to be one of the court's "quick perusal" of the material, not one of depth, otherwise the "whole purpose of requiring that leave should first be obtained ... would be defeated".[36]

---

[28] *Po Fun Chan* v *Winnie Cheung* (2007) 10 HKCFAR 676, para.16. *Sharma* v *Brown-Antoine* [2007] 1 WLR 780 (PC) (Trinidad and Tobago), p.787, cited by Li CJ in *Po Fun Chan* v *Winnie Cheung* (2007) 10 HKCFAR 676 (paras.7–8), described the arguability test as "flexible in its application". However, Li CJ stated that the "view there expressed was not that the arguability test itself is flexible but that whether that test is satisfied in a particular case would depend on the nature and gravity of the issue raised" (para.8).

[29] *Po Fun Chan* v *Winnie Cheung* (2007) 10 HKCFAR 676, para.17. Prior to this case, the courts had still been applying the lower threshold; see *Smart Gain Investment Ltd* v *Town Planning Board* [2006] HKEC 2063.

[30] *Po Fun Chan* v *Winnie Cheung* (2007) 10 HKCFAR 676, paras.19 (per Bokhary PJ), 20 (per Chan PJ), 22 (per Ribeiro PJ) and 37 (per Litton NPJ).

[31] See, for a recent example, *Zahirul Islam* v *Torture Claims Appeal Board* [2017] HKEC 129, para.31.

[32] *Re Cheng Kar Shun* [2009] HKEC 1154, para.3, per Cheung J.

[33] See, for example, *So Ching Yat* v *City University of Hong Kong* [2016] 3 HKLRD 661, para.37; *Re Chen Hsiu Ying* [2016] HKEC 2100 (CA), para.25; and *AT* v *Director of Immigration* [2017] HKEC 136, para.60. Sometimes "reasonable arguability" has been used, but the assessment has been conducted in the language of a "realistic chance" or "realistic prospect" of success – *Ng Wing Hung* v *Hong Kong Examinations and Assessment Authority* [2010] HKEC 1471. Even though the respondents "submitted reasonable arguments", as the applicant's grounds for review were "reasonably arguable with [a] realistic prospect of success", leave was granted and a date fixed for the substantive hearing – *Dr U* v *Preliminary Investigation Committee of the Medical Council of Hong Kong* [2015] HKEC 2623, paras.21–22. There was some suggestion that a "very marginal case" might be sufficient for leave to be granted, though it was ultimately refused in the case in question – *Shek Lai San* v *Securities and Futures Commission* [2010] 4 HKC 168, paras.63–81.

[34] See, for example, *Asia Television Ltd* v *Chief Executive in Council* [2012] 3 HKLRD 1, paras.6, 8 and 16; and *Re Harvinder Singh* [2016] HKEC 2455, para.24.

[35] For example, *Chinluck Properties Ltd* v *Appeal Tribunal (Buildings)* [2013] HKEC 1390 (CA), para.28.

[36] *R* v *Inland Revenue Commissioners, ex parte National Federation of Self Employed and Small Businesses Ltd* [1982] AC 617 (HL), pp.643–644, per Lord Diplock.

The court should not, at the leave stage, entertain elaborate arguments on the facts and the law;[37] it is not the stage for sustained argument.[38] However, Li CJ was not averse to the lengthening of the leave stage. It may be necessary, he said, for more time to be spent by the judge in dealing with leave applications than was previously the case. A "quick perusal" might no longer be sufficient under the arguability threshold, and in appropriate cases the judge may require an oral hearing.[39]

It is respectfully submitted that this begins to undermine the purpose of the leave stage. The greater the time spent at the leave stage determining the arguability of the case, the lesser the justification for having a separate leave stage. Indeed, arguability must surely be capable of being determined only from an examination of the substance se of the case. It is notable that, despite the imposition of a higher arguability threshold, and the Court of Final Appeal's acknowledgement of its potential to lengthen proceedings at the leave stage, judges sometimes express frustration at the length and detail of submissions made at the leave stage.[40] Whilst no data is currently available to show an exact correlation between the raising of the arguability threshold and any corresponding increase in the length and detail of submissions made at the leave stage, and whilst practitioners must carry at least some of the responsibility for the length and detail of those submissions, it does seem that the raising of the arguability threshold by its nature encourages lengthier and more detailed submissions to be made at the leave stage.

A further issue with both the potential arguability and arguability thresholds is that it is unclear what each might mean in practice, and the extent to which a meaningful distinction can be drawn between them has been questioned.[41] Though arguability was a "higher threshold",[42] it was not a "particularly high threshold".[43] Li CJ also acknowledged in *Po Fun Chan* that there may be uncertainties at the leave stage about what further arguments and materials may be available at the substantive hearing.[44] It is therefore interesting to note a subsequent case in which arguability was said to be assessed on the presentational aspects of the arguments at the leave stage, rather than the actual arguability of the case *per se*; particularly as the case involved a

---

[37] *Ho Ming Sai* v *Director of Immigration* [1994] 1 HKLR 21, p.28, per Litton JA.
[38] *Chu Woan Chyi* v *Director of Immigration* [2004] 3 HKLRD I1, para.8, per Rogers V-P.
[39] *Po Fun Chan* v *Winnie Cheung* (2007) 10 HKCFAR 676, para.17, per Li CJ. See also Practice Direction SL3, paras.6–7.
[40] See, for example, *Ho Loy* v *Director of Environmental Protection* [2016] HKEC 2751, paras.140–142; though this also occurred before the raising of the threshold – *Lau Kong Yung* v *Director of Immigration* (1999) 2 HKCFAR 300, p.334.
[41] *Shem Yin Fun* v *Director of Legal Aid* [2003] 1 HKC 568, p.574.
[42] *Po Fun Chan* v *Winnie Cheung* (2007) 10 HKCFAR 676, para.15, per Li CJ.
[43] *Re Cheng Kar Shun* [2009] HKEC 1154, para.3, per Cheung J.
[44] *Po Fun Chan* v *Winnie Cheung* (2007) 10 HKCFAR 676, para.12.

self-represented litigant.[45] The way in which arguments are presented of course impacts upon the court's assessment of the arguability of the case – it could hardly be otherwise – but the point is that this draws into focus the fact that the court's view may not necessarily be driven by whether the application discloses an arguable case, but whether the case seems "ready" to proceed to a substantive hearing.

These issues heighten the sensitivity of applicants in terms of ensuring that they clear the heightened threshold. Cheung J explained that:

> The test does not mean that leave should be refused if there appears, on the materials before the Court, respectable counter-arguments to those relied on by the applicant. The focus is really on whether the applicant has shown, *by the materials he or she has chosen to place before the Court*, contentions that are reasonably arguable.[46]

This seems to place applicants in a difficult position: anxious to ensure they clear the higher threshold, and aware that the burden for establishing arguability lies with them,[47] they perhaps feel a natural inclination to present more, or more detailed, materials and arguments before the court at the leave stage. Yet they must, at the same time, avoid irritating the judge whom they are attempting to persuade by submitting too many, or too detailed, materials.[48] There is little to be gained, and something to be lost (in particular, time and resources), from a duplication of arguments made at the leave stage and the substantive hearing; a hearing at the leave stage should indeed not resemble the substantive hearing.[49] If an applicant attempts to run the argument that a particular ground of review is fact-sensitive and could not be resolved without full discovery and exchange of witness statements,[50] they risk facing the accusation that they are trying to resurrect the potential arguability threshold in an "attempt to fish for material on which to build a case".[51] There are both

---

[45] *Right to Inherent Dignity Movement Association* v *Government of the HKSAR* [2008] HKEC 1835, para.33.

[46] *Re Cheng Kar Shun* [2009] HKEC 1154, para.4. Emphasis added. It was also stated in this case that the application faced "significant counter-arguments" (para.7).

[47] *Chinluck Properties Ltd* v *Appeal Tribunal (Buildings)* [2013] HKEC 1390 (CA), para.51.

[48] Litton PJ condemned in strong terms in the Court of Final Appeal an application in which the grounds were covered in over 50 paragraphs in an application, and where factors relevant to the case were put in "vague and general terms" which bore "little relationship to the grounds stated in the formal application lodged by the applicants purportedly in compliance with O.53 r.3". He added that the grounds should be "stated clearly and succinctly, in a few numbered paragraphs. I would emphasise the word *few*" – *Lau Kong Yung* v *Director of Immigration* (1999) 2 HKCFAR 300, p.340, per Litton PJ.

[49] *Lee Sap Pat* v *Commissioner of Inland Revenue* [1991] 2 HKC 251, p.258, per Fuad V-P. Lord Donaldson stated in *R* v *Legal Aid Board, ex parte Hughes* (1992) 24 HLR 698, p.703, that the hearing at the leave stage is "quite different from a substantive hearing in that the respondent need only summarise its answer sufficiently to enable the judge to decide whether there is or is not an *arguable* case" (emphasis in the original).

[50] *Chinluck Properties Ltd* v *Appeal Tribunal (Buildings)* [2013] HKEC 1390 (CA), para.42.

[51] *Id.*, para.51, per Fok JA.

factors pulling in favour of, and against, the submission of more (detailed) materials at the leave stage, and this cannot be a positive state of affairs for encouraging certainty and consistency in judicial review procedure. Whilst the "burden is on the applicant to show arguable grounds for judicial review",[52] this should not be a burden in the literal sense.

---

[52] *Re Harvinder Singh* [2016] HKEC 2455, para.24.

Part III

The Grounds of Judicial Review

10
Overview of the Grounds of Judicial Review

The grounds of judicial review are the bases on which an application for judicial review can be made. They comprise categories of activity that, if violated, may result in a successful application for review. There is no fixed list of grounds, but there are three main sources for the grounds of review: (i) the Basic Law; (ii) statute; and (iii) the common law. If a relevant provision of the Basic Law is violated, this can form a legitimate ground for judicial review. It will essentially comprise "constitutional review", as the Basic Law formally has the status of a constitutional document. Statutes have created many and varied grounds of judicial review. The courts have created and developed grounds of review over centuries of jurisprudence in England and Wales in particular, and these have largely been incorporated into the law of Hong Kong. The common law grounds are neither fixed nor static, and they continue to be developed by the courts. Just as judges could change the rules on standing to meet the need to preserve the integrity of the rule of law, so could they change the substantive principles of judicial review.[1] Some grounds – for example aspects of procedural impropriety – are of longstanding pedigree, whilst others, such as breach of legitimate expectations (especially substantive expectations) are more recent innovations. The common law grounds of review are the focus of this part of the book, as they are available across the whole range of reviewable decisions, whereas statutory grounds in particular take different, discrete forms which are specific to individual statutory contexts. The Basic Law is of course an important source of rights, and of potential grounds of judicial review, but is rather for analysis in a text on constitutional law.

Judicial review can be used to mount a more procedural or substantive form of challenge. Where a more procedural form of challenge is made, the applicant will usually be seeking judicial review of a process by which a decision is made. Where a more substantive form of challenge is made, the applicant will usually be seeking review of a substantive act or decision. These are not discrete categories of review, and issues of procedure and substance are often

---

[1] *R (on the application of Cart)* v *Upper Tribunal* [2011] QB 120, pp.168–169, per Sedley LJ.

intertwined.[2] Nevertheless, some grounds of review are more typically utilised to attack procedure (such as procedural impropriety), whilst others are more typically utilised to attack substance. A number of grounds can be equally useful to attack procedure or substance, such as breach of legitimate expectations.[3] If a decision-making process is found to be unlawful, this will usually also vitiate the legality of the decision resulting from that process.

There is no fixed list of common law grounds of review. Variations in terminology will be found among different cases and texts. Some will treat as distinct two grounds of review which may elsewhere be considered to combine as a single ground, or vice versa. For example, some texts are more prepared than others to recognise breach of legitimate expectations as a distinct ground of review. Some refer to (*Wednesbury*) unreasonableness rather than irrationality, or vice versa. Whereas one text may specify procedural impropriety as a ground of review, another may label it breach of procedural fairness, or natural justice. The common law grounds of review are neither discrete nor mutually exclusive: they are often interrelated, overlapping, complementary, interacting and conceptually interdependent. However, some structure must be brought to bear on the grounds; conceptually, doctrinally and practically. The categorisations and typologies found in the case law and literature are attempts to make sense of, and give structure to, an array of different bases on which judicial review can be sought; to bring order to a wide range of angles of attack. Categorisation is an "indispensable tool in the search for rationality and coherence in law".[4]

One of the classic statements on the grounds of review was given by Lord Diplock in *Council of Civil Service Unions* v *Minister for the Civil Service*:

> Judicial review has I think developed to a stage today when without reiterating any analysis of the steps by which the development has come about, one can conveniently classify under three heads the grounds upon which administrative action is subject to control by judicial review. The first ground I would call "illegality", the second "irrationality" and the third "procedural impropriety". That is not to say that further development on a case by case basis may not in course of time add further grounds. I have in mind particularly the possible adoption in the future of the principle of "proportionality" which is recognised in the administrative law of several of our fellow members of the European Economic Community; but to dispose

---

[2] It has been said that the distinction between substantive and procedural invalidity will often be difficult or impossible to draw and that the grey area between them may cover considerable terrain – *Boddington* v *British Transport Police* [1999] 2 AC 143 (HL), p.170, per Lord Steyn.

[3] Lord Steyn stated that the taking into account of extraneous considerations is variously treated as substantive or procedural – *id.*

[4] *Id.*, per Lord Steyn.

of the instant case the three already well-established heads that I have mentioned will suffice.[5]

Whether or not Lord Diplock intended this to be or become a definitive statement of the grounds of review, it has become much-recycled in the case law and literature. Lord Scarman described Lord Diplock's statement as a "valuable, and already 'classical', but certainly not exhaustive analysis" of the grounds of judicial review.[6] It is indeed not exhaustive, not only because other grounds of review may in future develop, or because existing grounds might change so as to insufficiently fit within this framework. It is also unclear where some grounds of review, such as breach of legitimate expectations or fettering of discretion, would fit under this categorisation. Furthermore, the terms used are problematic. This is principally seen in the term "illegality", which is over-broad and chronically unspecific – violation of any of the grounds of review could be described as "illegal". Lord Diplock described illegality as meaning that the "decision-maker must understand correctly the law that regulates his decision-making power and must give effect to it".[7] Instances of "irrationality" or "procedural impropriety" could easily enough be accommodated within this description. Rather than being an elastic category, this borders on the meaningless as far as categorisation is concerned. Furthermore, the term "irrationality" is potentially problematic.[8] It is doubtful how useful is this tripartite categorisation, and questionable whether it ought to be used as a taxonomy of the grounds of review. It is neither particularly accurate nor elucidatory, and does not form the basis on which the grounds of review are organised in this book. As Lord Hoffmann explained:

> The principles of judicial review, the ceaseless struggle to delimit the boundaries which the law has set to the power of the State, cannot be captured even by Lord Diplock in three or four bullet points with single word headings elucidated by a single sentence of explanation. It is a far more subtle and complex subject. Judges tend to support their decisions in a particular case by appropriate rhetoric. In a case in which the court has decided that judicial intervention is inappropriate, there is a temptation to emphasize in the most general terms the reluctance of the courts to intervene. And there is always a tendency to reductionism, to trying to squeeze the diversity of life into single formula which can be made to yield an answer in every case.[9]

---

[5] *Council of Civil Service Unions* v *Minister for the Civil Service* [1985] AC 374, p.410, per Lord Diplock.
[6] *R* v *Secretary of State for the Environment, ex parte Nottinghamshire County Council* [1986] AC 240, p.249, per Lord Scarman.
[7] *Council of Civil Service Unions* v *Minister for the Civil Service* [1985] AC 374, p.410, per Lord Diplock.
[8] See Chapter 18, and pp.242–245 in particular.
[9] Lord Hoffmann, "A Sense of Proportion" in Mads Andenas and Francis Jacobs (eds), *European Community Law in the English Courts* (Clarendon Press, Oxford, 1988), p.153.

Lord Irvine of Lairg added in the context of Lord Diplock's classification that:

> Categorisation of types of challenge assists in an orderly exposition of the principles underlying our developing public law. But these are not watertight compartments because the various grounds for judicial review run together. The exercise of a power for an improper purpose may involve taking irrelevant considerations into account, or ignoring relevant considerations; and either may lead to an irrational result. The failure to grant a person affected by a decision a hearing, in breach of principles of procedural fairness, may result in a failure to take into account relevant considerations.[10]

The grounds of review discussed in this book are presented as neither exhaustive nor mutually exclusive, but as an attempt to distil the broad range of bases on which decisions and decision-making processes can be challenged and to organise the grounds in a coherent and structured manner.

---

[10] *Boddington* v *British Transport Police* [1999] 2 AC 143 (HL), p.152, per Lord Irvine of Lairg LC; approved in *To Kin Wah* v *Tuen Mun District Officer* [2006] HKEC 95 (CA), para.37. Lord Greene MR pointed out that different grounds of review "run into one another" and "overlap to a great extent" – *Associated Provincial Picture Houses Ltd* v *Wednesbury Corporation* [1948] 1 KB 223, p.229.

11

Excess of Power, the Limits of Discretionary Power and Non-Compliance with Statute

Authority and Agency

Decision makers must be careful to remain within the bounds of their legal powers. Exceeding those powers may result in actions and decisions being struck down as *ultra vires*,[1] and there may be additional liability such as in contract or tort depending on the circumstances of the case. Every act or decision of the body must be capable of being traced to a source of legal power; typically, this will be statutory. The capacity of a statutory corporation must be ascertained from a proper interpretation of the statute, and it would be a mistake to begin by assuming that the legislature meant to create a corporation with a capacity resembling that of a natural person, and then to ask whether the language of the statute cuts down that capacity.[2] Legal powers need not always be explicitly conferred: as noted in the following section, bodies can often exercise ancillary and implied powers.

However, there are of course limits to those powers, and every body's power is limited by law. There is, in particular, no such thing as unfettered discretion. The use of broad or subjective language in statute, such as the conferral on a body of discretion to be exercised "as it thinks fit", does not confer unlimited

---

[1] In addition, if the *ultra vires* act or decision is one that should properly have been done or made by another body, that other body will not ordinarily be bound by the *ultra vires* act or decision.

[2] *Lo Siu Lan* v *Hong Kong Housing Authority* (2005) 8 HKCFAR 363, para.32, applying *Bonanza Creek Gold Mining Co Ltd* v *The King* [1916] 1 AC 566 (PC) (Canada), pp.577–578. In construing statutory language, the court's task is to ascertain and give effect to legislative intention. The purpose of legislation has been said to remedy a perceived mischief or defect in the existing legislation, and it should be presumed that legislation was not intended to be wider in its operation than necessary to remedy the relevant mischief or defect. General terms must be narrowly construed so as to give effective to legislative intention but not go beyond it – *Ho Choi Wan* v *Hong Kong Housing Authority* (2005) 8 HKCFAR 628, para.109. Note, however, section 19 of the Interpretation and General Clauses Ordinance (cap.1), which states that an "Ordinance shall be deemed to be remedial and shall receive such fair, large and liberal construction and interpretation as will best ensure the attainment of the object of the Ordinance according to its true intent, meaning and spirit".

discretion on the body.[3] Statutory discretion must, for example, be exercised reasonably.[4] It must also exercised so as to promote the policy and objects of the statute,[5] though there may be more than one way in which to promote its policy and objects.[6] As Lord Nicholls of Birkenhead put it:

> No statutory power is of unlimited scope. The discretion given by Parliament is never absolute or unfettered. Powers are conferred by Parliament for a purpose, and they may be lawfully exercised only in furtherance of that purpose ... The purpose for which a power is conferred, and hence its ambit, may be stated expressly in the statute. Or it may be implicit. Then the purpose has to be inferred from the language used, read in its statutory context and having regard to any aid to interpretation which assists in the particular case. In either event, whether the purpose is stated expressly or has to be inferred, the exercise is one of statutory interpretation.[7]

This principle cannot be used to create ambiguity in the meaning of the provisions that are being construed,[8] nor can an applicant seek to achieve through "the back door of *Padfield*" that which he could not achieve through "the front door of statutory interpretation".[9] Furthermore, courts cannot give powers to bodies which they do not already enjoy; and specifically, courts cannot extend the scope of statutory powers beyond that provided for in the statute (or, where relevant, the Basic Law). There must be legal authority for every act performed, thing done or decision made.

Second, there is the issue of agency. A person acting on behalf of a body in a public law context will represent that body and be capable of binding it in public law. For example, the failure of an official in the Inland Revenue Department to provide reasons for a decision, where the law deems reasons to be required, will in law comprise a failure on the part of the Inland Revenue Department to provide reasons. A representation made by an immigration official will, subject to the relevant legal requirements being established, be capable of generating a legitimate expectation on the part of the Immigration Department. This is essentially vicarious liability in public law.

However, it is an important limitation that this form of agency in public law remains subject to the restrictions on legal authority. Under strict legal doctrine, legal validity cannot be given to anything the public body or one of

---

[3] This applies "no matter how widely expressed" the statutory discretionary power may be – C v Director of Immigration (2013) 16 HKCFAR 280, para.72.
[4] *Roberts* v *Hopwood* [1925] AC 578 (HL).
[5] *Padfield* v *Minister of Agriculture, Fisheries and Food* [1968] AC 997 (HL).
[6] *Chan Noi Heung* v *Chief Executive in Council* [2007] HKEC 885.
[7] *R* v *Secretary of State for the Environment, Transport and the Regions, ex parte Spath Holme Ltd* [2001] 2 AC 349, p.397.
[8] *Li Yiu Kee* v *Chinese University of Hong Kong* [2009] HKEC 184, para.44, per Cheung J.
[9] *Id.*, para.112, per Cheung J; affirmed in *Li Yiu Kee* v *Chinese University of Hong Kong* [2010] HKEC 1159 (CA).

its officials says or does which would have the effect of unlawfully expanding their powers or taking them beyond their jurisdiction. An employee or representative of a public body cannot bind that body in public law when to do so would take the body beyond its legal powers. Were it otherwise, either the employee or representative – or the courts in litigation – would be capable of effectively extending the legal powers of public bodies. This would be particularly objectionable where it involved the extension of statutory powers. It is also not within the discretion of a public body to relax or abrogate compliance with the law.

This can, of course, lead to some undesirable outcomes. If a Hong Kong non-permanent resident is told by an immigration official at Hong Kong International Airport that he will enjoy the right to land on an indefinite basis, and the resident relies on that statement – only for it to transpire that the Immigration Department had no statutory power to make that assurance and that the statement is of no legal effect – the resident may suffer material loss or detriment to his plans or intentions.[10] That is in addition to the feelings of disappointment and unfair treatment that he will likely experience. If a person who intends to establish a restaurant business is told by the Business Registration Office of the Inland Revenue Department that he meets the requirements for a General Restaurant Licence, but his subsequent application for such a licence to the Director of Food and Environmental Health is rejected, the Business Registration Office is not capable of binding the Director of Food and Environmental Health as to his licensing decisions and the licence application may lawfully be rejected.[11] The applicant may likewise suffer material loss or detriment to his plans or intentions, again in addition to the likely feelings of disappointment and frustration. In each of these cases, however, it is (in public law) simply too bad for the person affected: the necessary legal authority is lacking in the relevant decision maker for public law liability to result. It was recently stated *obiter* that "an officer of a government department or a public body may bind the latter only if he acts on actual or ostensible authority".[12] Whether an entity has actual or ostensible authority will be taken from the evidence,[13] including of course the relevant statutory context.

In the context of legitimate expectations, a police informant who was imprisoned was told by police that if he was accepted into the protected witness unit scheme he would remain in it for the whole of his sentence, and he was subsequently accepted into it but later removed and returned to the general prison population. It was held that the police had no actual or ostensible authority to treat the claimant as a protected witness, as decision-making

---

[10] This is subject to the law on breach of legitimate expectations, but that itself brings limitations to bear on such statements.
[11] See pp.221–223.
[12] *Ng Chi Keung* v *Secretary for Justice* [2016] 2 HKLRD 1330, para.41, per Li J.
[13] See, for example, *id.*, para.42.

power on the scheme lay with the Prison Service. Accordingly, the Prison Service would not be estopped from removing the informant from the scheme. This rendered the purported expectation not legitimate,[14] but the underlying distinction between "private law estoppel" and the "public law concept of a legitimate expectation" must be retained, not least because the general public interest must be taken into account when considering remedies against a public body.[15]

Not all is lost in such cases, however, for there may be liability in tort. It would of course seem grossly unfair for a person to detrimentally rely on a statement or representation made by a public body, only to later discover the statement or representation is itself unlawful or a false representation of the true legal position, and thereby suffer harm, loss or damage as a result thereof. One solution which preserves the *ultra vires* principle is to attach no strict legal effect in public law to the statement or representation, but to allow the person affected to sue for the tort of negligent misrepresentation, and thereby for compensation.[16] Tort could provide a remedy not only where false or misleading representations have been made, but where other wrongs have been committed.

Most examples would probably not give rise to an actionable claim in tort,[17] particularly as negligence would typically have to be established,[18] which may be a higher threshold to satisfy than breach of law in a public law sense.[19] However, to use the aforementioned examples, if the immigration official had been negligent in telling the non-permanent resident that he would enjoy the right to land on an indefinite basis, or if the Inland Revenue Department had been negligent in telling the applicant that he met the requirements for a

---

[14] *R (Bloggs 61) v Secretary of State for the Home Department* [2003] 1 WLR 2724.

[15] *R (on the application of Reprotech (Pebsham) Ltd) v East Sussex County Council* [2003] 1 WLR 348 (HL), p.358, per Lord Hoffmann. It was also stated, in the same place, that "in this area, public law has already absorbed whatever is useful from the moral values which underlie the private law concept of estoppel and the time has come for it to stand upon its own two feet".

[16] See Sir William Wade and Christopher Forsyth, *Administrative Law* (11th edn), pp.284–285.

[17] It may also be considered that a statutory provision is considered not to give rise to a private cause of action – *Lucky Chance Ltd v Commissioner for Television and Entertainment Licensing* [2006] HKEC 2302.

[18] Unless there is provision for strict liability.

[19] For example, a duty of care would have to be established – see *Yim Tat-Fai v Attorney General* [1986] HKLR 873; and *Yuen Kun-Yeu v Attorney General* [1987] HKLR 1154 (PC), in which the facts were distinguished from those in *Dorset Yacht Co Ltd v Home Office* [1970] AC 1004 (HL). Where a duty of care exists, it would have to be established that the duty has been breached – see *Yuen Tat-Cheong v Urban Council* [1987] HKLR 723, in which a young child was badly injured during a raid on unlicensed hawkers carried out by the General Duties Team of the Urban Council; and *Lucky Chance Ltd v Commissioner for Television and Entertainment Licensing* [2006] HKEC 2302, para.50. Though negligence may be a higher threshold to satisfy than breach of law in a public law sense, a common law duty of care may be wider in scope than a statutory duty – *Lucky Chance Ltd v Commissioner for Television and Entertainment Licensing* [2006] HKEC 2302, para.22. Furthermore, some grounds of review may require a higher threshold than negligence, for example the traditional *Wednesbury* threshold.

General Restaurant Licence, then it may be possible for the affected persons to sue the Immigration Department and the Inland Revenue Department, respectively, in tort.[20] In a well-known English case, the House of Lords held that custodial officers owed a duty of care to the owners of a nearby yacht moored offshore, and that public policy did not give them immunity in their defence where they negligently failed to prevent young offenders within their custody from damaging the yacht.[21] There can, indeed, be vicarious liability where an employee of a public body was negligent, so that the public body would be liable in negligence.[22] It is an important aspect of the rule of law that public bodies are accountable in tort. Provided that the restrictions on suing in tort are appropriate to protect against abuse or a compensation culture sought of public authorities, and that overkill is avoided so that the imposition of liability does not lead to harmful consequences,[23] the individual would be in an appalling position if public bodies were able to claim immunity from suit in tort merely by virtue of their purporting to act in a public law capacity.

Ancillary and Implied Powers

Generally, all ancillary powers are granted which are necessary to achieve the fulfilment of the principal powers conferred, as provided in the Interpretation and General Clauses Ordinance:

> 40. Construction of enabling words
>
> (1) Where any Ordinance confers upon any person power to do or enforce the doing of any act or thing, all such powers shall be deemed to be also conferred as are reasonably necessary to enable the person to do or enforce the doing of the act or thing.
>
> (2) Without prejudice to the generality of subsection (1), where any Ordinance confers power –
>   (a) to provide for, prohibit, control or regulate any matter, such power shall include power to provide for the same by the licensing thereof and power to prohibit acts whereby the prohibition, control or regulation of such matter might be evaded;

---

[20] However, a person might not necessarily be able to recover losses caused by the *ultra vires* act of a public officer – *Attorney-General* v *Ng Kee* [1978] HKLR 52 (CA). See also *Madam Ho Ring Mui* v *Attorney General* [1982] HKEC 284 (HC), in which liability in negligence was not contested; the appeal on quantum of damages was dismissed – *Madam Ho Ring Mui* v *Attorney General* [1982] HKEC 180 (CA). On tortious liability for misleading advice, see the discussion and authorities referred to in Wade and Forsyth, *Administrative Law* (11th edn), pp.648–649.

[21] *Dorset Yacht Co Ltd* v *Home Office* [1970] AC 1004 (HL).

[22] *Ministry of Housing and Local Government* v *Sharp* [1970] 2 QB 223, followed in *Fu Lok Man (t/a Leatherware Manufacturing Co)* v *Chief Bailiff of the High Court* [1999] 2 HKLRD 835 (CA).

[23] *Yuen Kun-yeu* v *Attorney General* [1987] 2 HKC 25 (PC), p.39; *Rowling* v *Takaro Properties Ltd* [1988] AC 473 (PC) (New Zealand), p.502.

(b) to grant a licence, Government lease, permit, authority, approval or exemption, such power shall include power to impose reasonable conditions subject to which such licence, Government lease, permit, authority, approval or exemption may be granted;

(c) to approve any person or thing, such power shall include power to withdraw approval thereof;

(d) to give directions, such power shall include power to couch the same in the form of prohibitions.[24]

It is also the position at common law that decision makers have whatever powers are reasonably necessary to enable them to effectively carry out their statutory functions.[25]

However, the question of what powers are conferred by statute is not always straightforward. In *Re Sea Dragon Billiard and Snooker Association*, the applicant operated a billiard and snooker club in an industrial building in Kowloon. The Director of Fire Services purported to serve a Fire Hazard Abatement Notice (FHAN) on the applicant. The FHAN stated that a fire hazard was considered to exist due to the operation of the club in industrial premises, and required the applicant within a period of thirty days to abate the fire hazard, which could essentially only be achieved by ceasing its business at the premises in question.

The High Court considered whether the Director had the power to effectively compel the cessation of the business through the issuance of a FHAN. The issue turned on an interpretation of section 9(1) of the Fire Services Ordinance, which empowered the serving of a FHAN if the Director was "satisfied of the existence in or on any premises of any fire hazard". Kaplan J concluded that the Director's serving of the FHAN was *ultra vires*. On a proper interpretation of the statute, for a fire hazard to exist, the "person against whom it is alleged must have done something which constitutes a fire hazard other than the lawful running of a business on the premises".[26] Moreover, there was nothing "in or on" the premises which amounted to a fire hazard. Section 9(1) was directed at the abatement of fire hazards which were in fact capable of abatement, not cessation of business. It would stretch the language of the statute too far to include within the section the use to which premises were put, and if it had been intended that this was to be included within the scope of the section, Kaplan J would have expected to see such powers set out in the clearest language. As a matter of statutory interpretation, section 9(1) was purportedly being used to achieve a wider purpose than that contemplated by the language of the section itself.[27] The power to effectively compel the cessation of business at the premises was not ancillary to the power to issue a FHAN.

---

[24] Interpretation and General Clauses Ordinance (cap.1), s.40. See also ss.41–42.
[25] *Dr U v Preliminary Investigation Committee of the Medical Council of Hong Kong* [2016] 4 HKLRD 31, para.108.
[26] *Re Sea Dragon Billiard and Snooker Association* [1991] 1 HKLR 711 (HC), p.719, per Kaplan J.
[27] *Id.*, p.720.

Important issues of public policy or the public interest can sometimes override other legal obligations of public bodies, such as overriding considerations defeating otherwise legitimate expectations, and the executive necessity doctrine as a means of unshackling Government entities from contractual obligations in exceptional circumstances. One might have expected that in *Re Sea Dragon Billiard and Snooker Association*, there might have been public interest considerations overriding the alleged unlawfulness of the FHAN. After all, the FHAN stated that there was considered to exist in the premises "materially increased... danger to life and property that would result from the outbreak of fire or the occurrence of any other calamity". However, the High Court held that merely because it may have been in the public interest for the current use of the premises to cease, that did not in itself confer the necessary jurisdiction on the Director of Fire Services to effectively order cessation of business at that location. The proper solution would be for the legislation to be changed. Kaplan J stated that he "cannot allow this power to come in by the back door by reason of a strained construction" of the Ordinance.[28] It should nevertheless be emphasised that the evidence did not show that the applicant had actually done or permitted something in or on the premises which constituted a fire hazard.

In *Wong Kam Kuen* v *Commissioner for Television and Entertainment Licensing*,[29] the Commissioner had the power to regulate licences for amusement game centres. The Amusement Games Centres Ordinance stated that the Commissioner "may grant a licence, and may impose such conditions in relation to the operation, keeping or other control of the amusement games centre as he thinks fit",[30] and that a "licence shall authorise the licensee to operate an amusement game centre for the playing of such type of games by persons of such category or description as shall be indicated therein".[31] Where the Commissioner purported to suspend the applicant's licence due to alleged violations of the terms of the licence, including the playing of unapproved games, this was held by the Court of Appeal to be *ultra vires*. In the absence of clear language to the contrary, the statutory provisions were not considered to confer the ancillary power of censorship over the types of games played in the amusement game centre "under cover of an unspecific power which was intended to regulate the management of premises". Yuen JA offered the following analogy:

> it is as if a restaurant licensing authority is seeking to exercise control over the food served, by including in the licence a condition requiring the ingredients of each item on the menu to be approved by him first. In the absence of clear

---

[28] *Re Sea Dragon Billiard and Snooker Association* [1991] 1 HKLR 711 (HC), pp.720–721, per Kaplan J.
[29] *Wong Kam Kuen* v *Commissioner for Television and Entertainment Licensing* [2003] 3 HKLRD 596 (CA).
[30] Amusement Games Centres Ordinance (Cap.435), s.5(3).   [31] *Id.*, s.5(7).

language, and given that public morals are already protected by the [Control of Obscene and Indecent Articles] Ordinance, I am not persuaded that s.5(3) gives the Commissioner such authority.[32]

An issue that has arisen in the case law is whether a decision maker has an ancillary or implied power to review its own decisions. If there is an express statutory power conferred upon the decision maker to review its own decisions, then generally it will have the power to do so.[33] Likewise, an express statutory prohibition on the decision maker will prevent it from reviewing its own decision. However, the statute will not necessarily give an express conferral of, nor prohibition on, this power, and the question is whether the decision maker enjoys the power to review its own decisions in such circumstances.

This matter arose in *PCCW-HKT Telephone Ltd v Telecommunications Authority*,[34] in which the question was whether the Telecommunications (Competition Provisions) Appeal Board, which had the statutory power to determine appeals by upholding, varying or quashing decisions subject to appeal, and to make such consequential orders as may be necessary, also had the ancillary power to suspend its own direction pending appeal. The Court of Final Appeal held that the Board did have such a power. As Bokhary PJ pointed out, if a decision under appeal had not been suspended pending appeal, failure to act in conformity with the decision pending appeal could have serious consequences, including breach of the Ordinance. In the present case, breach could result in the telecommunications licence being suspended for up to twelve months or even being cancelled. In the overall context of the case, the Board had, by statutory implication and for the effective exercise of its express jurisdiction, an ancillary power to suspend a decision pending appeal.[35]

The issue again arose in *Dr U v Preliminary Investigation Committee of the Medical Council of Hong Kong*,[36] in which a medical patient had complained to the Medical Council of Hong Kong about a doctor's conduct. The investigation committee of the Council dismissed the complaint in accordance with the relevant regulations.[37] The complainant's solicitors thereafter

---

[32] *Wong Kam Kuen v Commissioner for Television and Entertainment Licensing* [2003] 3 HKLRD 596 (CA), para.56, per Yuen JA. The fact that the Control of Obscene and Indecent Articles Ordinance (cap.390) already provided for the regulation and censorship of obscene materials assisted the court in its interpretation of the relevant statutory provisions.

[33] Assuming it is lawful and appropriate to do so. For example, if the applicant needs a question of law to be addressed, but the decision maker only has the power to address questions of fact and merits, then another form of challenge (such as judicial review) will be more appropriate.

[34] *PCCW-HKT Telephone Ltd v Telecommunications Authority* (2005) 8 HKCFAR 337.

[35] *Id.*, paras.45–50, per Bokhary PJ. It was added (para.30, per Bokhary PJ) that this discretionary power "will not paralyse administrative action", quoting *Anglo Starlite Insurance Co Ltd v Insurance Authority* [1992] 2 HKLR 31, p.36, per Bokhary J.

[36] *Dr U v Preliminary Investigation Committee of the Medical Council of Hong Kong* [2016] 4 HKLRD 31.

[37] Medical Practitioners (Registration and Disciplinary Procedure) Regulations (cap.161E).

requested reconsideration of the decision, and submitted additional materials in support of the complaint. The complaint was reviewed by a new chair of the committee and its deputy chair, who referred the complaint to the investigation committee, which in turn referred it to the Council for further investigation. It was contended that the committee had no power to review its own decisions. However, there was no statutory provision expressly prohibiting review of its own decisions, and it appeared to the court that such a power would be reasonably necessary to allow the committee to perform its statutory duty and function, and to promote the overall objectives of the statute, namely the protection of the public from the risk of medical practitioners who lack the competence or fitness to practice, and to maintain and sustain the reputation of, and public confidence in, the medical profession.[38]

Where the Town Planning Board had a statutory power to review its own decisions, this was held by the Court of Final Appeal to include review of decisions made where permission was refused or permission was approved subject to conditions, but not to other decisions.[39] It has been said that the correct test for determining whether an inferior court or tribunal has an implied power is that an "inferior court or tribunal has such ancillary powers as are derivable by statutory implication and are required for the effective exercise of jurisdiction expressly conferred upon it".[40] In determining the limits of a (statutory) body's powers, it is necessary to examine the statute as a whole, and a putative applicant cannot purport to rely on one part of the statute in isolation.[41]

Effect of Non-Compliance with Statutory Requirements

A distinction has been drawn between statutory provisions that impose mandatory requirements and those that impose directory requirements. Whereas failure to comply with a mandatory requirement will result in the invalidity of the act done or decision made, failure to comply with a directory requirement will not result in invalidity.

It might generally be thought that the distinction should be obvious from the language used in the statute. For example, if it is provided that a decision maker "must", "shall", "should" or "will" do a certain thing, then it is a mandatory requirement. By contrast, if a decision maker "can" or "may" do a certain thing, then it is a directory requirement. However, the matter is not as straightforward in practice, and sometimes a word which might appear to

---

[38] *Dr U* v *Preliminary Investigation Committee of the Medical Council of Hong Kong* [2016] 4 HKLRD 31, paras.102–140.
[39] *Town Planning Board* v *Town Planning Appeal Board* (2017) 20 HKCFAR 196.
[40] *PCCW-HKT Telephone Ltd* v *Telecommunications Authority* (2005) 8 HKCFAR 337, para.36, per Bokhary PJ. See also *Grassby* v *R* (1989) 168 CLR 1 (High Court of Australia), p.17.
[41] See *Turbo Top Ltd* v *Town Planning Board* [2011] HKEC 1526.

be mandatory can be construed as directory.[42] Lord Mance stated in the Privy Council, on appeal from the Court of Appeal of the British Virgin Islands, that the modern tendency is no longer to identify or distinguish between mandatory and directory requirements, but to ascertain legislative intention on the effect of non-compliance with a particular statutory direction.[43] Though the distinction has been criticised – Sedley J stated that the "significance of a departure from a prescribed process has been bedevilled in modern public law by an opaque distinction between mandatory and directory requirements"[44] – some have defended it. Wade and Forsyth, for example, explained that:

> properly understood [the distinction] simply expresses in a convenient way the conclusion reached whether the defect in the procedure leads to invalidity or not. The terminology is not (if it ever was) a way in which the validity or invalidity of an act may be decided upon without recourse to the relevant statute.[45]

As they pointed out, it was stated in the High Court of Australia that classification as mandatory or directory should come at the end of the inquiry, not the beginning:

> That being so, a court, determining the validity of an act done in breach of a statutory provision, may easily focus on the wrong factors if it asks itself whether compliance with the provision is mandatory or directory and, if directory, whether there has been substantial compliance with the provision. A better test for determining the issue of validity is to ask whether it was a purpose of the legislation that an act done in breach of the provision should be invalid.[46]

It is questionable whether there is really a fundamental distinction between the two approaches, as both involve an assessment of the statutory language and an attempt to ascertain legislative intention in the context of the relevant statutory framework. Each is an exercise in statutory interpretation. Lord Hailsham of St Marylebone LC opined, in a Scottish appeal to the House of Lords, that although expressions such as *mandatory, directory, void, voidable, nullity* and *purely regulatory* were useful:

> [i]t may be that what the courts are faced with is not so much a stark choice of alternatives but a spectrum of possibilities in which one compartment or description fades gradually into another. At one end of this spectrum there

---

[42] See *Grunwick Processing Laboratories Ltd* v *Advisory, Conciliation and Arbitration Service* [1978] AC 655, pp.698–699.
[43] *Director of Public Prosecutions of the Virgin Islands* v *Penn* [2008] UKPC 29 (PC) (British Virgin Islands), para.18, per Lord Mance.
[44] *Sumukan Ltd* v *Commonwealth Secretariat* [2007] EWCA Civ 1148, para.42, per Sedley LJ. See also *New Zealand Institute of Agricultural Science Inc* v *Ellesmere County* [1976] 1 NZLR 630; and *British Columbia (Attorney General)* v *Canada (Attorney General), Re An Act Respecting the Vancouver Island Railway* [1994] 2 SCR 41 (Supreme Court of Canada).
[45] Wade and Forsyth, *Administrative Law* (11th edn), p.184, fn.68.
[46] *Project Blue Sky Inc* v *Australian Broadcasting Authority* (1998) 194 CLR 355, para.93.

may be cases in which a fundamental obligation may have been so outrageously and flagrantly ignored or defied that the subject may safely ignore what has been done and treat it as having no legal consequences upon himself ... At the other end of the spectrum the defect in procedure may be so nugatory or trivial that the authority can safely proceed without remedial action, confident that, if the subject is so misguided as to rely on the fault, the courts will decline to listen to his complaint ... I do not wish to be understood in the field of administrative law and in the domain where the courts apply a supervisory jurisdiction over the acts of subordinate authority purporting to exercise statutory powers, to encourage the use of rigid legal classifications. The jurisdiction is inherently discretionary and the court is frequently in the presence of differences of degree which merge almost imperceptibly into differences of kind.[47]

The stark classification as mandatory or directory was avoided by the Privy Council in *Nina T H Wang* v *Commissioner of Inland Revenue*.[48] It was provided by statute that:

On receipt of a valid notice of objection under subsection (1) the Commissioner shall consider the same and within a reasonable time may confirm, reduce, increase or annul the assessment objected to ...[49]

The question was whether, if the Commissioner had not acted "within a reasonable time", then the Commissioner lacked jurisdiction to make any determination. The applicant contended that the duty imposed by statute was mandatory, and therefore that failure to act within a reasonable time rendered any subsequent, purported determination automatically null and void. The Privy Council stated that, where there is an alleged failure to comply with a statutory time provision, it is "simpler and better to avoid these two words "mandatory" and "directory" and to ask two questions":

The first is whether the legislature intended the person making the determination to comply with the time provision, whether a fixed time or a reasonable time. Secondly, if so, did the legislature intend that a failure to comply with such a time provision would deprive the decision maker of jurisdiction and render any decision which he purported to make null and void?[50]

The legislature did intend the Commissioner to make a determination within a reasonable time, and if he failed to do so, he could be compelled to make a determination by order of mandamus. However, it did not follow that the Commissioner's jurisdiction to make a determination disappeared the moment a reasonable time had elapsed: it would be "surprising" if, in the context, the

---

[47] *London & Clydeside Estates Ltd* v *Aberdeen District Council* [1980] 1 WLR 182 (HL), pp.189–190. See also *R* v *Soneji* [2006] 1 AC 340 (HL), pp.352–353.
[48] *Nina T H Wang* v *Commissioner of Inland Revenue* [1994] 1 WLR 1286 (PC).
[49] Inland Revenue Ordinance (cap.112), s.64(2).
[50] *Nina T H Wang* v *Commissioner of Inland Revenue* [1994] 1 WLR 1286 (PC), p.1296.

Commissioner had jurisdiction to make a determination immediately before the expiry of a reasonable time, but not immediately after its expiry.[51] A result of that kind would deprive the Government of revenue, and therefore be unfair to other taxpayers who would shoulder the burden in lieu of the tax which had failed to be recovered. Accordingly, in the context of the legislation, failure to act within a reasonable time would neither deprive the Commissioner of jurisdiction nor make his determination null and void.[52] The approach was to ascertain the legislature's intention for what should happen in the event that the Commissioner failed to make a determination within a reasonable time. The expression "shall" nevertheless retains some of its ordinary meaning, as the courts have judged the appropriate remedy to be one of mandamus, compelling the Commissioner to perform his statutory duty.[53] A similar approach was taken to the decision in *Wang* by the Privy Council on appeal from the Court of Appeal of Trinidad and Tobago.[54]

Statutory interpretation involves not only looking at the individual provision being interpreted, but its context in the broader statute of which it is a part and the existing state of the law. A contextual and purposive approach to statutory interpretation is appropriate not only when ambiguity arises;[55] it is primarily driven by an attempt to ascertain the legislative intention of the statutory language.[56] Millett NPJ emphasised:

> There can be no quarrel with the principle that statutory provisions should be given a purposive interpretation, but there has been a distressing development by the courts which allows them to distort or even ignore the plain meaning of the text and construe the statute in whatever manner achieves a result which they consider desirable. It cannot be said too often that this is not permissible. Purposive construction means only that statutory provisions are to be interpreted to give effect to the intention of the legislature, and that intention must be ascertained by a proper application of the interpretative process. This does not permit the Court to attribute to a statutory provision a

---

[51] *Id.*, p.1296.
[52] *Id.*, pp.1296–1297. See also *Everbest Port Services Ltd v Employees' Compensation Assistance Fund Board* [2016] 6 HKC 503.
[53] *Nina T H Wang v Commissioner of Inland Revenue* [1994] 1 WLR 1286 (PC), p.1296. This approach was also taken in *Yue Yuen Marketing Co Ltd v Commissioner of Inland Revenue* [2012] 4 HKLRD 761.
[54] *Charles v Judicial and Legal Service Commission* [2002] UKPC 34 (PC) (Trinidad and Tobago). It was pointed out that, in a complaint about non-compliance with a time limit, the grant of relief would usually be discretionary, and accordingly that breach of time limits or similar procedural defects were not generally susceptible to rigid classification – *Charles v Judicial and Legal Service Commission* [2002] UKPC 34 (PC) (Trinidad and Tobago), para.17, per Tipping J.
[55] *HKSAR v Lam Kwong Wai* (2006) 9 HKCFAR 574, para.63; *Leung Chun Ying v Ho Chun Yan Albert* (2013) 16 HKCFAR 735, para.12; *T v Commissioner of Police* (2014) 17 HKCFAR 593, paras.48 and 194.
[56] *T v Commissioner of Police* (2014) 17 HKCFAR 593, para.195.

meaning which the language of the statute, understood in the light of its context and the statutory purpose, is incapable of bearing ...[57]

Estoppel, Acquiescence, Waiver and Consent

No public body or public official can extend the limitations placed on their statutory powers by way of estoppel.[58] Sir William Wade and Christopher Forsyth stated, in a passage approved by the Supreme Court of New Zealand,[59] that:

> The primary rule is that no waiver of rights and no consent or private bargain can give a public authority more power than it legitimately possesses. Once again, the principle of ultra vires must prevail when it comes into conflict with the ordinary rules of law.[60]

This is seen, for example, in the context of a public body purporting to enter a contract in a way that exceeds or conflicts with its powers, with the result that, if the body acted *ultra vires* in its purporting to contract in this way, the contract is void.[61] Lord Reid said that:

> it is a fundamental principle that no consent can confer on a court or tribunal with limited statutory jurisdiction any power to act beyond that jurisdiction, or can estop the consenting party from subsequently maintaining that such court or tribunal has acted without jurisdiction.[62]

This principle was applied in the Court of Appeal where a matrimonial consent order was made by a District Court judge which was *ultra vires* the Matrimonial Proceedings and Property Ordinance (cap.192). The order was deemed void for want of jurisdiction "regardless of the attitude of the parties".[63] It has

---

[57] *China Field Ltd v Appeal Tribunal (Buildings) (No 2)* (2009) 12 HKCFAR 342, para.36, per Millett NPJ.

[58] *Fairland Overseas Development Co Ltd v Secretary for Justice* [2007] 4 HKLRD 949, para.91, per Recorder Gerard McCoy SC, citing with approval Lord Hoffmann in *R (on the application of Reprotech (Pebsham) Ltd) v East Sussex County Council* [2003] 1 WLR 348 (HL), pp.357–358.

[59] *Cropp v A Judicial Committee* [2008] NZSC 46, para.20.

[60] Wade and Forsyth, *Administrative Law* (11th edn), p.198.   [61] See pp.70–71 and 184–185.

[62] *Essex Incorporated Congregational Church Union v Essex County Council* [1963] AC 808, pp.820–821. See also *Tsan Luk Yuk Yin v Secretary for the Environment, Transport and Works* [2012] HKEC 399, para.60, where it was said that it is a "fundamental principle that a party cannot be stopped from subsequently maintaining that a court or tribunal has acted without jurisdiction".

[63] *Cho Fok Bo Ying v Cho Chi Biu* [1991] 1 HKLR 348 (CA), p.351, per Kempster JA. It follows that it is not strictly necessary for the validity of an act or decision to be challenged by way of judicial review in order for it to be held – or at least treated – as void: see *Cho Fok Bo Ying v Cho Chi Biu* [1991] 1 HKLR 348 (CA), p.350. Though agreeing with the overall finding of the court, Clough JA stated that he would prefer the consent order not to be considered a complete nullity, but the point had not been explored in the proceedings – *Cho Fok Bo Ying v Cho Chi Biu* [1991] 1 HKLR 348 (CA), pp.351–352, per Clough JA. See, on the distinction between void and voidable court orders, *Isaacs v Robertson* [1985] AC 97, pp.102–103 (PC) (St Vincent and the Grenadines).

been part of the law of Hong Kong for some time that a statutory tribunal can act only in accordance with its statutory powers, and that resort to concepts of estoppel, waiver, acquiescence or even express consent cannot confer jurisdiction on the tribunal.[64]

It was confirmed by the Privy Council that a party who makes a representation of law is not estopped from claiming inconsistently with that representation, where the latter position was correct in law. Shop premises had been constructed on the site of properties in Wan Chai which had been almost completely destroyed during the Pacific War. The landlord purported to terminate the tenancies over the premises and sought possession, claiming that the premises were "entirely new" buildings and therefore excluded from the scope of the Landlord and Tenant Ordinance 1947. The tenants argued that the landlord was estopped from claiming that the buildings were "entirely new", as the landlord had served notices of increased rent under the Ordinance. The Privy Council held that the landlord was not estopped by having purported to serve the notices under the Ordinance and thereafter receiving the increased rent, and that if the documents relied on were regarded as containing representations, they were merely representations of law (not fact) which could not found an estoppel.[65] Though neither of the parties was a public body, the case is authority for a broader principle of estoppel which would apply to a public body which made a representation of law.[66]

The concept of estoppel is also relevant in asking whether a public body can be estopped by their prior statements or representations. This is related to the law on breach of legitimate expectations; it was stated in the Court of First Instance that the invocation of estoppel by an applicant against a public body in public law litigation has largely, if not wholly, been overtaken by the development of the doctrine of legitimate expectations and the requirements of procedural fairness.[67] For example, the Building Authority issued demolition orders against certain balconies which did not appear on approved building plans and were deemed to be unlawful structures. However, several inspections

---

[64] *Chiu Ming Kiang* v *William Lee Sheung* [1991] 1 HKLR 230; and *Tsan Luk Yuk Yin* v *Secretary for the Environment, Transport and Works* [2012] HKEC 399, in which a tribunal with a statutory power to extend a time limit had no jurisdiction to extend time other than in accordance with the statute – regardless of any attempt by a third party to waive, acquiesce or even expressly consent otherwise.

[65] *Kai Nam (A Firm)* v *Ma Kam Chan* [1956] AC 358 (PC), applying *Territorial and Auxiliary Forces Association of the County of London* v *Nichols* [1949] 1 KB 35. See also *Ip Tang Hon-ying* v *Tse Hing-chun* [1965] HKLR 136.

[66] Though the *ultra vires* principle would apply to such an act of a public body; depending on the facts of the case, so might the rules on error of law.

[67] *Domingo Irene Raboy* v *Commissioner of Registration* [2011] 6 HKC 532, para.23, per Lam J. It has been stated that "[p]rivate law is the exclusive home of estoppel; legitimate expectation exists only in public law. There is an analogy between them but cross-fertilisation is prohibited" – *Fairland Overseas Development Co Ltd* v *Secretary for Justice* [2007] 4 HKLRD 949, para.91, per Recorder Gerard McCoy SC. See also *Polorace Investments Ltd* v *Director of Lands* [1997] 1 HKC 373 (CA).

had been conducted by the Authority to determine whether the building was constructed in accordance with the building plans whilst the balconies were present, and the Authority thereafter issued an occupation permit. Rather than this being characterised as the Authority being estopped from issuing demolition orders, it was held that a legitimate expectation had been generated that the Authority approved of the balconies' construction and that they were lawfully constructed.[68] A body may be estopped from reneging on promises previously made, but whilst this could not prevent the body from exercising its statutory function, a remedy may sound in damages.[69] Estoppel is also related to unlawful delegation. An additional element is that of agency and the extent to which a person or body making a statement has the authority to do so.

Notwithstanding the general principle that a body cannot, by estoppel, acquiescence, waiver or consent, arrogate to itself more powers than it has in law, or be given such powers by a third party, a form of estoppel does appear to operate in relation to bias and insufficient impartiality. If a party who is subject to the jurisdiction of a decision maker has knowledge of or suspects bias or insufficient impartiality during proceedings or during a decision-making process, and fails to object to the participation of that decision maker at a suitably early stage, he can be taken to have waived his right to complain about bias or insufficient impartiality.[70] This has been rationalised on the basis that the bias or insufficient impartiality goes to jurisdiction, and the resulting decision is void; but that the decision maker does not lose jurisdiction if and until the objection is made to his participation in proceedings at an appropriately early stage.[71] This runs into intractable difficulties of voidness and voidability; it seems to assume that a decision which might be tainted by bias or insufficient impartiality is voidable, as it would only become void if and when it is appropriately challenged. However, this would not square with the contention that such a decision is void (rather than voidable).[72]

A possible route around this logical conundrum is to regard bias and insufficient impartiality as not going to jurisdiction, but still retaining the capacity to contaminate the legality of a decision (indeed, it is not imperative that it is viewed as a matter of jurisdiction). In this way, estoppel would not be regarded as expanding the jurisdiction of the biased or insufficiently impartial decision maker, by turning an otherwise "void" decision into one that is valid in law. It would seem unsatisfactory to resort to a further possibility, and one which can retain the concept of bias and insufficient impartiality going to

---

[68] *Lo Yin Ming* v *Appeal Tribunal (Buildings)* [2011] 3 HKLRD 586.
[69] *Wong Pei Chun* v *Hong Kong Housing Authority* [1996] 2 HKLR 293. Sears J (at p.299) did not consider, however, that the case could found a legitimate expectation. See pp.152–153.
[70] See pp.270–271.   [71] Wade and Forsyth, *Administrative Law* (11th edn), p.200.
[72] See *id*; and Christopher Forsyth, "'The Metaphysic of Nullity': Invalidity, Conceptual Reasoning and the Rule of Law" in Christopher Forsyth and Ivan Hare, *The Golden Metwand and the Crooked Cord* (Clarendon Press, 1998), pp.141–160. In fact, similar observations could be made with regard to other grounds.

jurisdiction, that even if a decision maker acts outside jurisdiction, the putative applicant is simply estopped from challenging the decision. This would presumably see the decision continuing to be *ultra vires*, as it was made beyond jurisdiction, yet the applicant is incapable of having it declared as such due to the operation of estoppel.[73] Apart from this leaving the decision in a state of legal limbo, where its invalidity cannot be proved in court due to the operation of estoppel, yet where the *ultra vires* decision cannot in law have legal effect (again invoking the problematic voidness and voidability distinction[74]), it could also run into difficulties with constitutional rights and fundamental notions of the certainty of law and whether and to what extent one is legally affected by a decision. That being said, if insufficient unfairness has resulted from the unlawful act – because, for example, the putative applicant failed to challenge the bias or insufficient impartiality at an appropriately early stage – then he might simply be personally estopped from having a court rule in his favour on bias or insufficient impartiality.

Res judicata: Cause of Action Estoppel

The concept of *res judicata* is typically used in the context of court proceedings, but also finds application in other adjudicatory processes, such as those of tribunals. *Res judicata* has two sub-categories, set out by Diplock LJ in *Thoday* v *Thoday*:

> The first species, which I will call "cause of action estoppel", is that which prevents a party to an action from asserting or denying, as against the other party, the existence of a particular cause of action, the non-existence or existence of which has been determined by a court of competent jurisdiction in previous litigation between the same parties. If the cause of action was determined to exist, i.e., judgment was given upon it, it is said to be merged in the judgment, or, for those who prefer Latin, *transit in rem judicatem*. If it was determined not to exist, the unsuccessful plaintiff can no longer assert that it does; he is estopped *per rem judicatem*.[75]

---

[73] Paul Craig pointed out that the "sanctity of the *ultra vires* principle is compromised by the balancing process inherent within the time limits for remedies, and in the rules concerning delay, acquiescence and the effect of alternative remedies" – Paul Craig, *Administrative Law* (8th edn) (Sweet and Maxwell, 2016), p.751, fn.99. See also *Deacons* v *White & Case LLP* (2003) 6 HKCFAR 322 in the context of the issue becoming "academic".

[74] Though Paul Craig saw no inconsistency in admitting a doctrine of waiver and regarding a procedural defect if not waived as producing a void decision – Craig, *Administrative Law*, p.752.

[75] *Thoday* v *Thoday* [1964] P 181, p.198, per Diplock LJ. The second sub-category, "issue estoppel", is described in the same place. Whilst cause of action estoppel creates an absolute bar, issue estoppel does not – *R (on the application of Coke-Wallis)* v *Institute of Chartered Accountants in England and Wales* [2011] UKSC 1, para.26, per Lord Clarke.

This issue arose in the UK Supreme Court, where it was held that *res judicata* applied to a second set of disciplinary proceedings, essentially on the same issue, before a disciplinary committee of the Institute of Chartered Accountants in England and Wales. The committee's dismissal of the first complaint was a final determination on the merits and was therefore an absolute bar to the second complaint.[76] In the course of judgment, the following constituent elements of a case based on cause of action estoppel were endorsed from *Spencer Bower & Handley, Res Judicata*:[77]

(i) the decision, whether domestic or foreign, was judicial in the relevant sense;
(ii) it was in fact pronounced;
(iii) the tribunal had jurisdiction over the parties and the subject matter;
(iv) the decision was –
   (a) final;
   (b) on the merits;
(v) it determined a question raised in the later litigation; and
(vi) the parties are the same or their privies, or the earlier decision was *in rem*.[78]

This classification was recently accepted in Hong Kong, though in that case the constituent elements of *res judicata* were not satisfied.[79] If these criteria are satisfied in a future case of judicial review against an adjudicator in Hong Kong, then *res judicata* would apply. It was argued in the UK Supreme Court that a public interest exception should be made to the strict application of cause of action estoppel in the context of disciplinary proceedings, namely where the strict operation of the rule would put public safety at risk. Though this found sympathy with the court, it was opined that if such an exception was to be introduced, it would be for the legislature to introduce it.[80]

---

[76] *R (on the application of Coke-Wallis) v Institute of Chartered Accountants in England and Wales* [2011] UKSC 1.
[77] Kenneth R. Handley (ed), *Spencer, Bower and Handley: Res Judicata* (4th edn) (Lexis Nexis, 2009), para.1.02.
[78] *R (on the application of Coke-Wallis) v Institute of Chartered Accountants in England and Wales* [2011] UKSC 1, para.34.
[79] *Dr U v Preliminary Investigation Committee of the Medical Council of Hong Kong* [2016] 4 HKLRD 31. See also *Total Lubricants Hong Kong Ltd v De Chanterac* (2014) 17 HKCFAR 296. On *res judicata* more generally, see *Yat Tung Investment Co Ltd v Dao Heng Bank Ltd* [1975] AC 581 (PC); and *Ko Hon Yue v Chiu Pik Yuk* (2012) 15 HKCFAR 72.
[80] *R (on the application of Coke-Wallis) v Institute of Chartered Accountants in England and Wales* [2011] UKSC 1, paras.48–50, per Lord Clarke.

Ambiguity and Uncertainty as a Ground of Judicial Review

Acts, decisions and instruments can be impugned on the basis of their ambiguity and uncertainty. This is seen, for example, in relation to subsidiary legislation.[81] The Court of Final Appeal has set out the following principle based on an analysis of the case law in other jurisdictions:

> challenges to statutory instruments on the grounds of uncertainty and irrationality depend upon the scope of the power to make the instrument, not on a judicial policy or a free-standing common law rule. Provided the impugned instrument is not so uncertain in its terms as to be meaningless, uncertainty or unreasonableness in application or inconsistency with the general law are relevant to validity only insofar as they assist in answering the question whether the instrument falls within or without the power to make it.[82]

Whilst this is a matter of statutory interpretation, an important factor in the Hong Kong context is the constitutional principle of legal certainty. This has been described as incorporated in the expressions "prescribed by law" in Article 39 of the Basic Law, and "according to law" in Article 11(1) of the Bill of Rights.[83] It was stated in the Court of Final Appeal that the "principle of legal certainty requires that a law must be sufficiently precise to enable a citizen to foresee, to a degree that is reasonable in the circumstances, the consequences that a given action may entail".[84] It was accepted, however, that the degree of precision required will vary according to the legal context:[85] absolute certainty at all times is unattainable.[86] Whereas it was held that the wording of bind-over orders failed to meet the level of precision necessary to satisfy the principle of legal certainty,[87] the terms of a noise abatement notice were sufficiently certain to satisfy the principle.[88] A road traffic sign was not insufficiently certain in its meaning because the Road Traffic (Traffic Control) Regulations (cap.374G) provided a clear and unambiguous explanation of the requirement of the sign.[89] The criminal offence of conspiracy to defraud did

---

[81] See p.360.
[82] *Noise Control Authority* v *Step In Ltd* (2005) 8 HKCFAR 113, para.40, per Sir Gerard Brennan NPJ.
[83] *Shum Kwok Sher* v *HKSAR* [2002] 2 HKLRD 793 (CFA), para.60, per Sir Anthony Mason NPJ; see also *Mo Yuk Ping* v *HKSAR* (2007) 10 HKCFAR 386.
[84] *Lau Wai Wo* v *HKSAR* (2003) 6 HKCFAR 624, para.36, per Lord Scott of Foscote NPJ. This closely followed the wording of the European Court of Human Rights in *Sunday Times* v *United Kingdom* (1979–80) 2 EHRR 245, para.49, itself cited in *Shum Kwok Sher* v *HKSAR* [2002] 2 HKLRD 793 (CFA), para.63. See also *Winnie Lo* v *HKSAR* [2012] 1 HKC 537 (CFA), para.19.
[85] *Shum Kwok Sher* v *HKSAR* [2002] 2 HKLRD 793 (CFA), para.89.
[86] *Winnie Lo* v *HKSAR* [2012] 1 HKC 537 (CFA), para.20.
[87] *Lau Wai Wo* v *HKSAR* (2003) 6 HKCFAR 624; followed in *David Morter* v *HKSAR* (2004) 7 HKCFAR 53.
[88] *Noise Control Authority* v *Step In Ltd* (2005) 8 HKCFAR 113.
[89] *HKSAR* v *Ho Loy* (2016) 19 HKCFAR 110, para.42.

not infringe the principle of legal certainty;[90] likewise, torts and crimes of maintenance and champerty were also sufficiently certain as to be constitutionally compliant.[91] Nevertheless, the greater the extent to which a legal requirement affects a fundamental right or freedom, the greater the degree of definitional certainty required.[92]

---

[90] *Mo Yuk Ping* v *HKSAR* (2007) 10 HKCFAR 386.
[91] *Winnie Lo* v *HKSAR* [2012] 1 HKC 537 (CFA).
[92] See *id.*, para.21.

12

Improper Purposes, Improper Motives and Abuse of Power

When discretion is exercised, the decision maker must not be driven by improper purposes or motives.[1] If improper purposes or motives underlie a decision, or if power is abused or exercised in bad faith, the resulting decision may be struck down as unlawful – even if it otherwise appears to be lawful.[2] A principal objective of this rule is not only to prevent decision makers abusing their discretion, but to reduce the opportunities for decisions to be made which appear on their face to be lawful decisions, but which are reached with improper objects or purposes in mind. For example, an immigration application may be refused on *prima facie* lawful grounds, but if it is established that those grounds are substantially a facade, that the ulterior motive behind refusing the application was, for example, because of the applicant's ethnicity, then the decision is contaminated by an unlawful purpose even though the decision was one which was substantively within the range of decisions which could lawfully be made.

This ground is closely related to the relevance of considerations, inasmuch as the motives or objects for a decision on the one hand, and the considerations taken into account in the course of decision-making on the other, are often overlapping. Nevertheless, a distinction can be drawn. The relevance of considerations ground is primarily about establishing that the decision maker made his decision on the basis of the wrong reasons or factors taken into account, or the right reasons or factors not taken into account. On the other hand, improper purposes and motives is about establishing that the discretion was exercised with the wrong motivations or objects in mind. It is possible for a decision to be made in good faith and be driven by proper purposes and motives, but for irrelevant considerations to have been taken into account. It is also possible for a decision to have been made in bad faith and be driven by

---

[1] It has been claimed that the designation of a purpose as "improper" has a connotation of moral impropriety – Lord Woolf et al, *De Smith's Judicial Review* (8th edn) (Sweet and Maxwell, 2018 p.291). However, it need not carry a connotation of moral impropriety, an improper purpose or motive simply being one that is not in accordance with law. This would therefore cover purposes and motives pursued in good faith and those pursued in bad faith.

[2] R v *Inner London Education Authority, ex parte Westminster City Council* [1986] 1 WLR 28.

improper purposes and motives, but with only relevant considerations taken into account. Nevertheless, the significant degree of overlap between the grounds does mean that either test can sometimes lead to the same conclusion on the legality of the manner in which discretion has been exercised,[3] and as a result the grounds are sometimes used interchangeably or in parallel to establish one or other of the grounds being violated.[4]

In determining the permitted purposes for which discretion may be exercised, the starting point is (assuming the powers to be statutory in nature) interpretation of the relevant statutory provisions, and to ascertain what is expressly or impliedly permitted thereby.[5] Establishing the purpose for which a power was exercised or a decision made is a matter of evidence, including representations made by the decision maker as to what was their purpose or intention,[6] and inference from other conduct of the decision maker.[7] The burden lies with the applicant to establish that a decision maker sought to exercise powers for an ulterior purpose, rather than the professed purpose.[8]

It was an improper purpose where Sydney Municipal Council exercised powers for the compulsory purchase of land solely to gain financially from the extension of a particular highway, and not for the statutory purpose of "carrying out improvements in or remodelling any portion of the city". Duff J stated that the Council was not permitted to exercise its statutory powers for purposes other than those permitted by the statute, and if it attempted to do

---

[3] *Re Kelly's Application for Judicial Review* [2000] NI 103 (Court of Appeal, Northern Ireland), in which Carswell LCJ stated: "[w]hether one applies the test of true or dominant purpose or that of irrelevant considerations having a material or substantial influence upon the decision, one must in our opinion reach the same conclusion". This was cited with approval in *Keen Lloyd Holdings Ltd v Commissioner of Customs and Excise* [2016] 2 HKLRD 1372 (CA), paras.134–140 and 167, where it was stated (at para.167) that the "dominant purpose test would be satisfied in this instance, and if one is to test this by the alternative test of an irrelevant consideration having a material influence on the decision, the same result would be arrived at" – *Keen Lloyd Holdings Ltd v Commissioner of Customs and Excise* [2016] 2 HKLRD 1372 (CA). See also *Meng Ching Hai v Attorney-General* [1991] 1 HKLR 535 (CA), p.549; and Chapter 13.

[4] See, for example, *R v Rochdale Metropolitan Borough Council, ex parte Cromer Ring Mill Ltd* [1982] 3 All ER 761, p.770; and *Incorporated Owners of Wah Kai Industrial Centre v Secretary for Justice* [2000] 2 HKLRD 458, pp.476–477. See also *R v Inner London Education Authority, ex parte Westminster City Council* [1986] 1 WLR 28.

[5] *R v Secretary of State for Foreign and Commonwealth Affairs, ex parte World Development Movement Ltd* [1995] 1 WLR 386; *Lo Siu Lan v Hong Kong Housing Authority* (2005) 8 HKCFAR 363, paras.32 (on which, see p.125); *C v Director of Immigration* (2013) 16 HKCFAR 280, para.72.

[6] *Keen Lloyd Holdings Ltd v Commissioner of Customs and Excise* [2016] 2 HKLRD 1372 (CA).

[7] *Thompson v Randwick Municipal Council* (1950) 81 CLR 87 (High Court of Australia): "Upon consideration of the scheme as whole, the conclusion seems irresistible that, with respect to so much of the land included in the scheme as is not required for the new road, profit-making is a substantial purpose actuating the Council in deciding upon the proposed resumptions" (p.107). See also *R v Secretary of State for Foreign and Commonwealth Affairs* [1995] 1 WLR 386.

[8] *Incorporated Owners of Wah Kai Industrial Centre v Secretary for Justice* [2000] 2 HKLRD 458, p.477.

so, the court would interfere.[9] Where a Force Discipline Officer in the police force was acting in a judicial capacity under the Police (Discipline) Regulations, but assumed what appeared to be a more prosecutorial role, this would be unlawful as the use of his powers for an improper purpose.[10] In another case, two Vietnamese asylum seekers challenged a decision to move them from a detention centre to facilities which were also used as a prison. It was contended for the applicants that, *inter alia*, the purpose of moving them to prison facilities was punitive. Once it was established that the move was lawful, the court was persuaded that the purpose of the move was not punitive, but managerial and in particular for the maintenance of good order. This was a lawful purpose.[11]

Multiple Purposes or Motives

In reality, a decision maker might be motivated by more than one purpose. If all the purposes motivating his decision are lawful then, all else being well, the decision will be lawful. If all the purposes are unlawful, then clearly the resulting decision will be unlawful. Where a decision is motivated by a mixture of lawful and unlawful purposes, the courts endeavour to identify and assess the true or dominant purpose: if the true or dominant purpose of the decision is lawful, then the resulting decision will be lawful even if one or more of the ancillary or secondary purposes was unlawful. Likewise, if the true or dominant purpose of the decision is unlawful, then the resulting decision will be unlawful even if one or more of the ancillary or secondary purposes was lawful. This is assuming that the purposes can be disentangled. If they cannot be disentangled, and one of them is unlawful, then the purposes as a whole will be contaminated and the resulting decision will be unlawful.[12] The question of plurality of purposes has been described as a "legal porcupine which bristles with difficulties as soon as it is touched".[13]

Sir William Wade and Christopher Forsyth explained this area of law in a passage that has been cited with approval in the English and Hong Kong courts:

---

[9] *Sydney Municipal Council* v *Campbell* [1925] AC 338 (PC) (Australia), p.343, per Duff J.
[10] *Wong Kim Ming* v *Commissioner of Police* [1995] HKCFI 197.
[11] *Re Tran Quoc Cuong* v *Khuc The Loc* [1991] 2 HKLR 312 (HC).
[12] See *R* v *Lewisham London Borough Council, ex parte Shell UK Ltd* [1988] 1 All ER 938, p.951.
[13] Lord Woolf et al, *De Smith's Judicial Review* (8th edn), p.302; earlier edition quoted in *Incorporated Owners of Wah Kai Industrial Centre* v *Secretary for Justice* [2000] 2 HKLRD 458, p.476, per Cheung J. It was also said that in "determining *purpose* the court is entering a grey area where many factors have to be weighed" and that "[w]here the facts of a case lie close to the borderline, two tribunals of fact could legitimately come to different conclusions" – *Mok Charles Peter* v *Tam Wai Ho* (2012) 15 HKCFAR 489, para.90, per Litton NPJ (emphasis in the original).

Sometimes an act may serve two or more purposes, some authorised and some not, and it may be a question whether the public authority may kill two birds with one stone. The general rule is that its action will be lawful provided that the permitted purpose is the true and dominant purpose behind the act, even though some secondary or incidental advantage may be gained for some purpose which is outside the authority's powers. There is a clear distinction between this situation and the opposite, where the permitted purpose is a mere pretext and a dominant purpose is ultra vires.[14]

A power to construct public toilets under a street was lawfully exercised even where an incidental purpose or consequence may have been that pedestrians could use the subway as a means of passing from one side of the street to the other. This was because the true or dominant purpose was shown on the evidence to be the construction of public toilets under the street, which was a lawful purpose in accordance with the body's statutory powers:

> It appears to me impossible to contend that these conveniences are not the things authorized by the Legislature. It seems to me that the provision of the statute itself contemplates that such conveniences should be made beneath public roads, and if beneath public roads some access underneath the road level must be provided; and if some access must be provided, it must be a measure simply of greater and less convenience, when the street is a wide one, whether an access should be provided at only one or at both sides of the street. That if the access is provided at both sides of the street, it is possible that people who have no desire or necessity to use the convenience will nevertheless pass through it to avoid the dangers of crossing the carriageway seems to me to form no objection to the provision itself; and I decline altogether to sit in judgment upon the discretion of the local authorities upon such materials as are before us ... [I]f there be the express provision, as I think there is, to make a tunnel under the street for the purpose of these conveniences, then I think the question of its extent or cost is a matter with which neither a Court of law or equity has any concern, *since the thing contemplated by statute has been done, and done in the way which the statute contemplated it might be done. That the public may use it for a purpose beyond what the statute contemplated is nothing to the purpose.*[15]

Where a local education authority in England had the power to expend funds on a public advertising campaign for informational purposes, it would

---

[14] Wade and Forsyth, *Administrative Law* (11th edn), p.352. Earlier editions cited with approval in, inter alia, *Meng Ching Hai v Attorney-General* [1991] 1 HKLR 535 (CA), p.548; *R v Southwark Crown Court, ex parte Bowles* [1998] AC 641 (HL), p.651; and see *Keen Lloyd Holdings Ltd v Commissioner of Customs and Excise* [2016] 2 HKLRD 1372 (CA), paras.137–138.

[15] *Westminster Corporation v London and North Western Railway Co* [1905] AC 426 (HL), pp.427–428, per Earl of Halsbury LC. Emphasis added.

be unlawful to fund advertising the dominant purpose of which was for persuading the public on a political point about funding cuts to education provision, even though the informational purpose was also being pursued. The authority had pursued an unauthorised purpose which materially influenced its making of the decision which would otherwise have been lawful.[16] Where the UK Secretary of State for Foreign and Commonwealth Affairs approved financial aid for the construction of a hydroelectric power station (the "Pergau Dam") in Malaysia, despite it being deemed uneconomic, this was unlawful given that the dominant purpose of the funding decision was the credibility of the UK, rather than the purpose authorised by statute, namely promoting the development or maintenance of the economy of a non-UK country or territory or the welfare of its people.[17]

In a case in the High Court of Australia, a local authority in the Eastern suburbs of Sydney made a statutory application for the resumption of vacant land within its municipality for the statutory purpose of the "improvement and embellishment of the area". However, the local authority was planning to sell part of the acquired land and was therefore substantially motivated by profit-making. It was also planning merely to subdivide and sell that land, not performing any work thereon, and therefore not in accordance with the statutory purpose of the improvement and embellishment of the area. The evidence:

> establishes that one purpose at least of the Council in attempting to acquire the land not required to construct the new road is to appropriate the betterments arising from its construction ... [It is] an abuse of the Council's powers if such a purpose is a substantial purpose in the sense that no attempt would have been made to resume this land if it had not been desired to reduce the cost of the new road by the profit arising from its re-sale.[18]

In *Meng Ching Hai v Attorney-General*,[19] the applicant was a Taiwanese national who had been ordered to be deported from Hong Kong following the expiry of his prison sentence for entering Hong Kong on a forged Singaporean passport. The Director of Immigration exercised his statutory discretion to deport the applicant to Taiwan. However, the applicant wanted to be removed either to Mainland China or the Philippines. The applicant, it emerged, was wanted in Taiwan as a suspect of serious commercial crime. The Director claimed that Taiwan was selected as the jurisdiction for deportation based on the applicant's connections with Taiwan and that it indicated it would accept the applicant as a deportee. Meanwhile, it was contended for the applicant that the deportation order was an unlawful extradition in disguise – that the

---

[16] R v *Inner London Education Authority, ex parte Westminster City Council* [1986] 1 WLR 28.
[17] R v *Secretary of State for Foreign and Commonwealth Affairs, ex parte World Development Movement Ltd* [1995] 1 WLR 386.
[18] *Thompson v Randwick Municipal Council* (1950) 81 CLR 87 (High Court of Australia), p.106.
[19] *Meng Ching Hai v Attorney-General* [1991] 1 HKLR 535 (CA).

deportation was merely a pretext to achieve the ulterior motive of extradition. The Court of Appeal noted Lord Denning MR's observation that if the removal was "done for an authorised purpose, but in fact for a different purpose with an ulterior object, it was unlawful".[20] It concluded that, on the evidence, "[n]o bad faith had been shown" and that the "Director proposed to exercise the discretionary power given to him in accordance with the provisions of the Ordinance and for a proper purpose".[21] It had been similarly concluded, in a recently preceding case, that a decision to remove two persons to Mainland China had not been made for the purpose of extradition, even though the judge was in "no doubt" that the relevant immigration officer had taken into account the fact that there had been a request from Mainland China for the extradition of these persons.[22]

A more recent illustration of the true or dominant purpose test in Hong Kong is in *Keen Lloyd Holdings Ltd* v *Commissioner of Customs and Excise*.[23] The Customs and Excise Department was engaged in a joint operation with Huangpu Customs in the Mainland in relation to suspected cross-border smuggling of goods and money laundering by the applicant company and its subsidiaries. The Department provided copies of seized documents and materials to Huangpu Customs, in furtherance of an allegedly improper purpose. However, the Court of Appeal was satisfied that the Department would still have provided this information to Huangpu Customs if the Department had not desired concurrently to pursue the impermissible purpose of assisting the Mainland investigation. It held that even though the decision to provide this information to Huangpu Customs may have served both permissible and impermissible purposes, the impermissible purpose was merely an incidental consideration, and the Department's purpose of furthering its own investigation far outweighed the impermissible purpose. The "true or dominant purpose for the decision to provide copies of some of the seized materials to the Mainland Customs was to further [the Department's] investigation";[24] in other words the true or dominant purpose was a lawful decision, so any ancillary, impermissible benefit accruing would not contaminate the legality of the decision to provide this information to Huangpu Customs. This had

---

[20] *R* v *Governor of Brixton Prison, ex parte Soblen (No 2)* [1963] 2 QB 243, p.302, per Lord Denning MR. The case concerned a challenge to the lawfulness of a deportation order, *inter alia* on the ground that it was being used for the unlawful purpose of extradition for a non-extraditable offence and that the order was therefore a sham and not made in good faith. The challenge failed.

[21] *Meng Ching Hai* v *Attorney-General* [1991] 1 HKLR 535 (CA), p.550. It was also stated that the Director had not been shown to have taken irrelevant considerations into account or to have ignored relevant considerations, in addition to him not being shown to have acted capriciously or unreasonably – *Meng Ching Hai* v *Attorney-General* [1991] 1 HKLR 535 (CA), pp.549–550.

[22] *Re Lee Ching Ming* [1990] HKEC 517, para.14, per Sears J.

[23] *Keen Lloyd Holdings Ltd* v *Commissioner of Customs and Excise* [2016] 2 HKLRD 1372 (CA).

[24] *Id.*, para.171.

parallels with an English case in which it was held that the exercise of a police power under the Terrorism Act 2000 which also promoted a different but overlapping purpose, namely one of the Security Service, did not mean that the police power had not been exercised for the purpose of the legislation, and would not be rendered unlawful by reason of it also incidentally promoting the Security Service's purpose.[25]

Abuse of Power and Misuse of Power

Sir William Wade and Christopher Forsyth have been critical of the use of the terms "good faith" and, in particular, "bad faith" in the context of administrative law:

> It is extremely rare for public authorities to be found guilty of intentional dishonesty: normally they are found to have erred, if at all, by ignorance or misunderstanding. Yet the courts constantly accuse them of bad faith merely because they have acted unreasonably or on improper grounds. Again and again it is laid down that powers must be exercised reasonably and in good faith. But in this context 'in good faith' means merely 'for legitimate reasons'. Contrary to the natural sense of the words, they impute no moral obliquity ... The courts no less frequently use the word 'good faith' in their ordinary sense, implying personal honesty and good intentions ... [an] order was held to be 'an abuse of power and a flagrant invasion of private rights which the council has tried to cover up by means which do them no credit'. But the Court of Appeal decided that it was not necessary to go so far as to hold the council 'guilty of bad faith'. Elsewhere in this case 'mala fide' was used merely to mean 'for an unauthorised purpose'. Such opprobrious terms would be more suitably restricted to the rare cases of actual dishonesty ... The various categories of ultra vires can more fittingly be described by words which do not impute dishonesty.[26]

The point is illustrated in a joint judgment of four judges in the Court of Final Appeal that failure to honour a substantive legitimate expectation may "result in such unfairness to individuals as to amount to an abuse of power".[27] Bokhary J stated in the same case that:

---

[25] *R (on the application of Miranda)* v *Secretary of State for the Home Department* [2016] 1 WLR 1505. The case involved David Miranda, a Brazilian citizen who was married to a journalist working for the *Guardian* newspaper, who was stopped in transit at London Heathrow Airport en route from Berlin to Rio de Janeiro on suspicion of possessing material relevant to UK national security which had allegedly been leaked by Edward Snowden.

[26] Wade and Forsyth, *Administrative Law* (11th edn), pp.354–356. The imputation of dishonesty by a claim of bad faith was also recognised in *SCA* v *Minister of Immigration* [2002] FCAFC 397, para.19.

[27] *Ng Siu Tung* v *Director of Immigration* (2002) 5 HKCFAR 1, para.92 (joint judgment of Li CJ, Chan PJ, Ribeiro PJ and Sir Anthony Mason NPJ).

The essential function of the doctrine commonly called "the doctrine of legitimate expectation" is to give judicial relief against abuse of executive power. If one were to name this doctrine after its raison d'être, it could be called "the doctrine against abuse of power". But it has been named after the thing which it would be an abuse of power to ignore. And I will call it by that name.[28]

Legitimate expectations can certainly be breached due to an abuse of power, such as where an authority promises a benefit in the knowledge that the recipient of the promise is not entitled to that benefit, and thereafter reneges on the promise. However, it is questionable whether it is typical for breaches of legitimate expectations to be characterised by abuse of power. An authority may fail to honour a previous representation due to an error or misunderstanding, or due to a change in practice or policy. These will often be better explained as misuses of power rather than abuses of power. It is not even clear that failure to honour a previous representation due to incompetence is an abuse of power. Abuse necessarily includes misuse; but misuse need not include abuse. Over-broad definition of abuse of power has been seen in the English case law,[29] whilst in Hong Kong improper purposes or motives have been described as abuse of power,[30] as have bias and bad faith,[31] and discretionary powers it was said could not be abused by acting "illegally or irrationally".[32] Rather more on point, a public official who refused to consider an exercise of his powers in favour of an affected person unless bribed to do so would fittingly be described as in abuse of power.[33]

In *Wheeler* v *Leicester City Council*, a city council discontinued permission for a rugby club to use its facilities for games and training purposes. The decision was taken because three members of the team agreed to serve in the English Rugby Football Union team on a tour of South Africa, where the government administered a policy of apartheid. The tour was alleged to be an endorsement of the apartheid policies of the South African government, and

---

[28] *Id.*, para.330, per Bokhary PJ.
[29] For example, Lord Scarman stated that "[p]ower can be abused in a number of ways: by a mistake of law in misconstruing the limits imposed by statute (or by common law in the case of a common law power) upon the scope of the power; by procedural irregularity; by unreasonableness in the *Wednesbury* sense; or by bad faith or an improper motive in its exercise" – *R v Secretary of State for the Environment, ex parte Nottinghamshire County Council* [1986] AC 240, p.249. Laws LJ stated that "[a]buse of power is a name for any act of a public authority that is not legally justified" and that it is a "useful name, for it catches the moral impetus of the rule of law" – *R (on the application of Nadarajah) v Secretary of State for the Home Department* [2005] EWCA Civ 1363, para.67.
[30] *Chan Kai Wah v HKSAR* [2011] HKEC 412, para.28, per Hartmann JA.
[31] *C v Director of Immigration* (2013) 16 HKCFAR 280, para.72, per Sir Anthony Mason NPJ. Lord Macnaghten stated that a public body invested with statutory powers must act in good faith – *Westminster Corporation v London and North Western Railway Co* [1905] AC 426, p.430.
[32] *Chu Woan Chyi v Director of Immigration* [2007] HKEC 553, para.71, per Hartmann J.
[33] *Ho Ming Sai v Director of Immigration* [1994] 1 HKLR 21 (CA), p.30, per Godfrey J.

the council claimed that in taking its decision it was exercising its statutory duty under the Race Relations Act 1976 to promote good race relations. The House of Lords held that the rugby club had done nothing legally wrong, and that the council's purported exercise of its statutory power was a misuse of that power and therefore unlawful.[34]

Similarly, a local authority in London purported by resolution to boycott Shell products due to the corporate group's doing business in South Africa. The boycott was driven by the local authority's opposition to the apartheid policy of the South African government, and purportedly justified in terms of its statutory duty under the Race Relations Act 1976. Neill LJ concluded that the authority "cannot use its statutory powers in order to punish a body or person who has done nothing contrary to English law". Nor could it "exercise its statutory powers in a way which involves some procedural impropriety or some unfairness towards a body or person who has acted reasonably and in no way in a hostile attitude" towards the authority.[35] Even if an attempt to promote good race relations was part of the authority's decision to boycott Shell products, the dominant purpose appeared to be to put pressure on the Shell group to withdraw its business from South Africa.[36]

The potential for overlap with other grounds of review is clear. If power is abused, this can be struck down as *Wednesbury* unreasonable. It could be an abuse of power to fetter one's discretion. The taking into account of irrelevant considerations could constitute abuse of power. In *Wong Pei Chun v Hong Kong Housing Authority*,[37] a large number of Chinese refugees (especially former Kuomintang soldiers and their families) were moved to Rennie's Mill (Tiu Keng Leng) where a village was constructed. The Commissioner for Resettlement issued a letter to residents of Rennie's Mill in 1961 stating that "most residents in the area will be allowed to continue to reside in their existing buildings indefinitely", followed by another letter containing a "solemn assurance" essentially of preserving their residence in Rennie's Mill. In 1988, Government approval was given for the development of Junk Bay New Town Development, which would have obliterated Rennie's Mill village. Compensation was negotiated with some residents, but notices to quit were served on the remaining residents, some of whom sought judicial review of the decisions to serve the notices to quit. The High Court held that the 1961 letters constituted promises to the residents that they would not be moved away from Rennie's Mill. Though not regarding this as breach of a legitimate expectation,[38] the decision of the Hong Kong Housing Authority to act in breach of these promises was an abuse of power. The court ultimately determined that

---

[34] *Wheeler v Leicester City Council* [1985] AC 1054 (HL).
[35] *R v Lewisham London Borough Council, ex parte Shell UK Ltd* [1988] 1 All ER 938, p.951, per Neill LJ.
[36] *Id.*, p.952.   [37] *Wong Pei Chun v Hong Kong Housing Authority* [1996] 2 HKLR 293 (HC).
[38] *Id.*, p.299. The case could also be considered as one of estoppel.

the residents would be entitled to damages, as the court considered that it could not prevent the Housing Authority from exercising its statutory function to provide new housing in the area.[39]

The Privy Council held in *Hang Wah Chong* v *Attorney-General of Hong Kong* that the Director of Public Works' demand of a premium for obtaining Crown consent to the modification of lease conditions was not an abuse of power.[40] The principle flowing from that case, described by Hartmann J as the "*Hang Wah Chong* principle",[41] was explained by the Court of First Instance to more broadly mean that Government decisions taken in the capacity of land agent – essentially private landlord – were not subject to judicial review.[42] However, it was added that though a purely commercial decision, or a decision made in the performance of a purely commercial function, is likely a private law decision and not subject to judicial review, this was in the "absence of fraud, corruption, bad faith and breach of law", a qualification used also by the Court of Appeal.[43] This is notwithstanding a statement in the Court of Final Appeal that the Government acting in its private law capacity of landlord had an "absolute right if it chooses to demand a premium, however large, for granting a modification of the terms of the lease, or to withhold its consent altogether, however unreasonably".[44] These qualifications appear to suggest that if a public body (even when acting in a private law capacity) acts in an oppressive way that only a public body might be able to, this may inject a sufficient public element and thus render the body's decision or conduct subject to judicial review. If correct, abuse of power by a public body may, depending on the circumstances, be subject to judicial review even where the body purported to act in a private law capacity.

---

[39] Though the issuance of occupation permits (and notices to quit) would typically be a matter of private law between the Housing Authority and the occupier, it was explained by Sears J that the promises were given by the Government "and most probably the Governor". The promises were not given by the Government as landlord, and Sears J was satisfied that the issue was susceptible to judicial review. See *Wong Pei Chun* v *Hong Kong Housing Authority* [1996] 2 HKLR 293 (HC), p.300.

[40] *Hang Wah Chong Investment Co Ltd* v *Attorney-General of Hong Kong* [1981] 1 WLR 1141 (PC). See also *Rank Profit Industries Ltd* v *Director of Lands* [2009] 1 HKLRD 177 (CA).

[41] *Rank Profit Industries Ltd* v *Director of Lands* [2007] HKEC 390, para.62, per Hartmann J.

[42] See *Anderson Asphalt Ltd* v *Secretary for Justice* [2009] 3 HKLRD 215, pp.236–237.

[43] *Id.*, p.236, per Cheung J. This mirrored the discussion in *Matteograssi SpA* v *Airport Authority* [1998] 2 HKLRD 213 (CA); and comments of Lord Templeman in *Mercury Energy Ltd* v *Electricity Corporation of New Zealand Ltd* [1994] 1 WLR 521 (PC) (New Zealand), p.529.

[44] *Director of Lands* v *Yin Shuen Enterprises Ltd* (2003) 6 HKCFAR 1, para.18, per Lord Millett NPJ.

13

Relevance of Considerations

In the course of exercising their discretion, decision makers must be guided by lawful considerations, and must not be guided by unlawful considerations.[1] This ensures that decisions are made in accordance with appropriate criteria and factors and comprises both a procedural and substantive control on discretion. It is closely related to improper purposes as a ground of review, but is nevertheless distinguishable. Whereas an averment of improper purposes is about establishing that discretion has been exercised with the wrong motivations or objects in mind, irrelevant considerations is about establishing that the decision maker made a decision on the basis of the wrong reasons or factors taken into account.[2]

This ground of review comprises two alternative or complementary parts: the first is where a decision maker has taken into account an irrelevant consideration.[3] The second is where he or she has failed to take into account a relevant consideration. Each may lead to the decision being unlawful, though the lawfulness of the decision will not be automatically tainted. The relevance of considerations will typically be assessed according to the appropriate statutory provisions,[4] though the factual, legal and policy context of the case, including that of departmental circulars, policy documents, practical

---

[1] *Associated Provincial Picture Houses Ltd* v *Wednesbury Corporation* [1948] 1 KB 223, p.229, per Lord Greene MR (discussing the relevance of considerations under the head of unreasonableness); *Secretary of State for Education and Science* v *Tameside Metropolitan Borough Council* [1977] AC 1014, p.1065, per Lord Diplock; *R (on the application of Vetterlein)* v *Hampshire County Council* [2001] EWHC Admin 560, para.22; *R (on the application of Alconbury Developments Ltd)* v *Secretary of State for the Environment, Transport and the Regions* [2003] 2 AC 295, para.50, per Lord Slynn of Hadley; *Capital Rich Development Ltd* v *Town Planning Board* [2007] 2 HKLRD 155.

[2] See also pp.144–145.

[3] The phrases "impermissible consideration" (*Building Authority* v *Appeal Tribunal (Buildings)* (2015) 18 HKCFAR 317, para.20; *Keen Lloyd Holdings Ltd* v *Commissioner of Customs and Excise* [2016] 2 HKLRD 1372 (CA), para.132) and "extraneous consideration" (*Tam Heung Man* v *Hong Kong Institute of Certified Public Accountants* [2008] 1 HKLRD 238, para.193; *C* v *Director of Immigration* (2013) 16 HKCFAR 280, para.72) have also made an appearance.

[4] *Lau Kong Yung* v *Director of Immigration* (1999) 2 HKCFAR 300, p.339. Statutory provisions will not necessarily be narrowly construed in this regard – *Building Authority* v *Appeal Tribunal (Buildings)* (2015) 18 HKCFAR 317.

considerations and the common law, are also relevant.[5] That assessment will often be a point of contention between the litigants where this ground is argued in an application for judicial review, and the court will ultimately have to form its own view on the matter.[6] It has been said that where a statute conferring discretionary power has not spelled out the matters to be treated as relevant by the decision maker, then it is for the decision maker and not the court to conclude what is relevant[7] subject only to a finding of *Wednesbury* unreasonableness.[8]

Decision makers may be able to pre-empt successful review on the head of irrelevant considerations taken into account, or failure to take relevant considerations into account, by providing reasons for their decisions. In the absence of reasons for a "surprising" decision, a body may be assumed by the court to have taken account of irrelevant considerations and to have failed to take into account relevant considerations.[9] Failure to give reasons at all, or on a particular point of contention, may suggest either that the decision maker failed to take relevant considerations into account, or if the decision maker had in fact taken those considerations into account, he or she had failed to give adequate reasons for his or her decision.[10] Nevertheless, if the decision maker take an irrelevant consideration into account, or fail to take a relevant consideration into account, this can be apparent from the reasons given.

Insufficiently Relevant Considerations

The case of *Capital Rich Development Ltd v Town Planning Board*[11] gives an example of an irrelevant consideration being taken into account and illustrates why this threshold may be too "hard-edged". The Urban Renewal Authority published a Development Scheme for a residential area, and a draft plan was submitted to the Town Planning Board. Objections were made by the owners of various buildings within the proposed development area, who wanted their

---

[5] Apprehension of a decision maker setting an undesirable precedent could, depending on the facts, be a relevant consideration – *Smart Gain Investment Ltd v Town Planning Board* [2007] HKEC 1964, para.109, per Cheung J. See also *Wing On Co Ltd v Building Authority* (1996) 6 HKPLR 432, p.439.

[6] See, for example, *Ngo Thi Minh Huong v Director of Immigration* [2000] HKEC 84.

[7] *BH v Director of Immigration* [2015] 4 HKC 107, para.64, citing with approval *R (on the application of al-Rawi) v Secretary of State for Foreign and Commonwealth Affairs* [2008] QB 289, p.341.

[8] *R (on the application of Khatun) v Newham London Borough Council* [2005] QB 37, para.35, per Laws LJ. Though see *Tam Heung Man v Hong Kong Institute of Certified Public Accountants* [2008] 1 HKLRD 238, in which the court decided what constituted relevant considerations, which were held not to have been taken into account, supporting a finding of irrationality or unreasonableness.

[9] See *Lai Hin Cheong v Long-Term Prison Sentences Review Board* [2008] HKEC 1701, particularly at para.65.

[10] *MDB v Betty Kwan* [2014] HKEC 497, paras.63–68.

[11] *Capital Rich Development Ltd v Town Planning Board* [2007] 2 HKLRD 155.

site to be excluded from the proposed development area. The Board refused to change the Development Scheme. The evidence suggested that the Board relied on financial implications which would follow from excluding the objectors' site from the Scheme as a consideration in refusing to change the Scheme. The court regarded financial viability as a relevant consideration;[12] however Cheung JA opined that when the Board relied on financial viability as its basis for asserting that the Scheme would be jeopardised there was "insufficient evidence for it to come to such a conclusion". Accordingly, "[i]n the context of public law the [Board] had taken an irrelevant consideration into account".[13]

This is a somewhat odd line of reasoning: an ostensibly relevant consideration (financial viability) was taken into account, but as there was insufficient evidence to support the contention that the Scheme would be financially jeopardised, the ostensibly relevant consideration (financial viability) was concluded to be an irrelevant consideration. There may have been more intuitive ways of reasoning through these facts. For example, it could have been held that a material error of fact was committed when assessing financial viability,[14] or that the assessment of financial viability was either irrational or *Wednesbury* unreasonable. On *Wednesbury* unreasonableness, one should note in particular the lower threshold applied in the Court of Appeal where a decision was struck down as unreasonable on the basis that a decision was made which was not supported by the material put before the decision maker.[15]

It is submitted that a better expression in this case would have been not the taking into account of an irrelevant consideration, but the taking into account of an insufficiently relevant consideration. Whilst the former is more euphonious, the latter has greater accuracy in this case. Indeed, a binary division between relevant and irrelevant considerations seems too stark: whilst some decisions will be plainly relevant, and others will be plainly irrelevant, there will be some which occupy the middle ground and the (ir)relevance of which may be less clear. The test in such a case may be more appropriately set as the taking into account of an insufficiently relevant consideration – arguably the threshold of irrelevant consideration may be set too high (though in this case the test of an irrelevant consideration was said to be established even though the consideration was not plainly irrelevant). This lower threshold would therefore permit to be struck down decisions supported by considerations which are,

---

[12] Citing, in support, *R v Westminster City Council, ex parte Monahan* [1990] 1 QB 87, p.111. Financial considerations may generally be a relevant factor – *Incorporated Owners of Wah Kai Industrial Centre v Secretary for Justice* [2000] 2 HKLRD 458, p.478.

[13] *Capital Rich Development Ltd v Town Planning Board* [2007] 2 HKLRD 155, para.63, per Cheung JA.

[14] Sir Derek Cons V-P stated in *Nguyen Ho v Director of Immigration* [1991] 1 HKLR 576, p.583: "if the Court may properly interfere when the inferior tribunal has not taken into account some matter which it should have done, the Court must also be able to do so when the inferior tribunal has got that matter wrong".

[15] *Ng Koon Fat v Li Wai Chi* [2013] 2 HKLRD 109; discussed at pp.233–235.

viewed objectively, insufficiently relevant to the decision being made. In *Capital Rich Development*, financial viability was confirmed as a relevant consideration. Its being improperly or incompletely assessed does not render it an irrelevant consideration; rather, it is a relevant consideration which is tainted by some inadequacy of fact or methodology. In such a case, the label irrelevant consideration does not quite seem to fit; but insufficiently relevant consideration would fit, as financial viability remains a relevant consideration, albeit one which was not sufficiently relevant due to its improper means of its assessment. The modified test could therefore not only be of benefit in marginal cases, but perhaps also result in a more focused test being applied in cases such as *Capital Rich Development*.

For example, assume that a decision is being made on whether to grant a licence to a person seeking to operate a restaurant. Whether the applicant has the necessary health and hygiene certification appears plainly relevant as a consideration in whether to grant the licence. On the other hand, whether the applicant has black hair or brown hair appears plainly irrelevant as a consideration. However, whether the applicant has long hair or short hair might be a relevant consideration, as it might be unhygienic for a person with long hair to be involved in the preparation and serving of food. It might be concluded that the length of the applicant's hair is not a sufficiently relevant consideration, as they might tie their hair tightly behind their head, or wear a hat or hair net. However, that would not necessarily render the length of the applicant's hair irrelevant; it would rather depend on how that consideration was being used by the decision maker.

A decision is not automatically vitiated because an irrelevant consideration is taken into account. In order for the irrelevant consideration to vitiate the decision, the consideration must have been material or substantial in the course of making the decision.[16] This stands to reason, as if an irrelevant consideration was one of a number of considerations taken into account, but the irrelevant consideration was not material or substantial to the decision being made, then the same decision would presumably have been made had the irrelevant consideration not been taken into account.[17] It does not appear to be necessary for the irrelevant consideration to be the sole or even dominant consideration.[18] Where an irrelevant consideration has been taken into account and it is not known whether the decision maker would have reached

---

[16] *Capital Rich Development Ltd v Town Planning Board* [2007] 2 HKLRD 155, paras.70–77; *Hong Kong Broadband Network Ltd v Director of Highways* [2011] HKEC 1096, paras.47 and 72.

[17] *R v Broadcasting Complaints Commission, ex parte Owen* [1985] QB 1153, p.1177, per May LJ; *Incorporated Owners of Wah Kai Industrial Centre v Secretary for Justice* [2000] 2 HKLRD 458, p.477, per Cheung J. See also *Anderson Asphalt Ltd v Town Planning Board* [2007] 3 HKLRD 18, para.57.

[18] Lord Woolf et al, *De Smith's Judicial Review* (8th edn), p.306, earlier edition cited with approval in *Capital Rich Development Ltd v Town Planning Board* [2007] 2 HKLRD 155, para.70.

the same decision had the irrelevant consideration not been relied upon, the legality of the resulting decision can be tainted.[19]

Relevant Considerations

Failure to Take into Account a Relevant Consideration

An example of a decision being struck down on the basis of a decision maker failing to take into account relevant considerations can be seen in *Secretary for Security* v *Sakthevel Prabakar*.[20] Mr Prabakar was a citizen of Sri Lanka who had fled the country after allegedly having been tortured there by security forces. He obtained a forged Canadian passport which he intended to use to enter Canada and thereafter apply for asylum. Mr Prabakar began his journey to Canada and, on arrival at Hong Kong International Airport, was questioned by immigration officers who subsequently discovered his forged Canadian passport and arrested him. In due course, the Secretary for Security made a deportation order against Mr Prabakar for his removal to Sri Lanka.

The Court of Final Appeal noted that no consideration had been given by the Secretary for Security to whether Mr Prabakar's claim that he would be subjected to torture on his return to Sri Lanka was well founded. Relevant considerations for the Secretary would have included any evidence of gross violations of human rights in Sri Lanka, whether the potential deportee had been tortured there in the past, and whether there was medical or other evidence to support the claim of torture. Rather than taking these considerations into account, the Secretary had merely relied on the United Nations High Commissioner for Refugees' (UNHCR) decision to refuse refugee status for Mr Prabakar. The court pointed out that the UNHCR's determination might for a variety of reasons not be relevant to the decision which had to be made by the Secretary, and that the Secretary had not verified why the UNHCR rejected the refugee application. The UNHCR determination might be a relevant consideration, but it could not be the only consideration. The Secretary had to make her own assessment of the materials and come to an independent judgment, taking into account relevant considerations, and not merely relying on the UNHCR determination. Having failed to do so, the decision of the Secretary was unlawful.[21] Similarly, it was held by the Court of

---

[19] *Hysan Development Co Ltd* v *Town Planning Board* [2014] HKEC 1869 (CA), para.164. There appears to be overlap in the point about being unable to disentangle relevant from irrelevant considerations, and proper from improper purposes; see *Capital Rich Development* v *Town Planning Board* [2007] 2 HKLRD 155, paras.70–77; and p.146.

[20] *Secretary for Security* v *Sakthevel Prabakar* (2004) 7 HKCFAR 187; followed in *CH* v *Director of Immigration* [2011] HKEC 1595.

[21] In merely relying on the UNHCR determination instead of making her own independent assessment of the facts, the Secretary had also divested or relinquished her discretion.

Final Appeal that the Director of Immigration must, in deciding whether to make a removal order against a refugee claimant, consider the individual circumstances of the claimant, including whether his claim for refugee status is well-founded. This would be a relevant consideration. The Director would be entitled to give weight to a Refugee Status Determination by the UNHCR, but the Director must make his own determination in accordance with high standards of fairness.[22]

Another example of a failure to take into account relevant considerations occurred in *Epoch Group Ltd v Director of Immigration*.[23] Epoch was a newspaper publisher associated with Falun Gong, which invited a performing arts group called Shen Yun from New York to give seven shows in Hong Kong. Epoch submitted ninety-five employment visa applications to the Immigration Department on behalf of Shen Yun, and these were submitted under the Department's general employment category as no specific category existed for travelling performance arts or music groups. A total of eighty-nine applications relating to dancers and musicians were approved, whilst six applications relating to lighting and audio technicians were rejected. Shen Yun regarded the six rejected applicants as key to their ability to perform the show, and therefore cancelled the shows and began taking steps to refund over HK$5 million of ticket sales.

The Director of Immigration had given near identical reasons for refusing each of the six unsuccessful applications:

> Under existing policy, a person seeking to enter the Hong Kong Special Administrative Region for employment should, among other things, possess a special skill, knowledge or experience of value to and not readily available in the HKSAR. Besides, other criteria to be considered include whether the job can be filled locally and whether it is justified for the employment to bring in an expatriate staff [*sic*]. Having considered the information made available and all circumstances of the case, we are not satisfied that [the applicant's] case meets the aforesaid criteria. His application is therefore refused.

The approach taken by the Director was essentially that audio and lighting technicians were available in Hong Kong, and there was accordingly no need to bring in such technicians from elsewhere. However, the court regarded this as a flawed approach whereby the Director was asking himself the wrong question. Rather than asking whether audio and lighting technicians were available in Hong Kong, he should instead have asked himself whether the applicant audio and lighting technicians played such an integral role in the work and practice of the performing arts group that they would be justifiably distinguished from local technicians. Considerations such as the fact that the technicians had previously supported the performances, the

---

[22] *C v Director of Immigration* (2013) 16 HKCFAR 280.
[23] *Epoch Group Ltd v Director of Immigration* [2011] 3 HKLRD H2.

performing artists trusted their abilities and experience, they had worked together previously in rigorous rehearsals and so on, were not properly taken into account by the Director. As such, the Director failed to take into account relevant considerations, and his decisions to reject the applications were quashed.

Where 80 per cent of members of the Hong Kong Institute of Certified Public Accountants were electors in the accountancy functional constituency of the Legislative Council, but open disagreements emerged between the Institute and the accountancy functional constituency member, the Institute resolved to stop distributing her newsletters to its members. It was held that the Institute failed to adequately take into account two relevant considerations. First, it failed to adequately take into account the fact that its register of members provided the only available link between the Legislative Council member and the electorate. Second, it failed to adequately take into account the effect of its requirement that every newsletter's cover bear a disclaimer stating that the views expressed in the newsletter were not those of the Institute. It was also held that two irrelevant considerations had been taken into account, namely the difference of political opinion between the Institute and the Legislative Council member, and an erroneous reliance on the Personal Data (Privacy) Ordinance (cap.486) in purported justification of its decision.[24]

There have of course been cases in which the relevance of considerations argument has been unsuccessful. This can occur for a variety of reasons. It may be that the relevant consideration has already been taken into account.[25] It may be that the consideration had never become relevant in the first place, such as where financial considerations relating to an application to the Director of Immigration for dependent status had never become relevant because the applicant did not fall into any of the established categories under the dependant policy, only after which such consideration would become relevant.[26] In addition, there does not have to be a direct relationship between the factor being considered and the decision being made in order for the consideration to be relevant – an indirect connection may be sufficient.[27] Nevertheless, failure to take into account a relevant consideration can only be successfully established if the decision maker was bound to take that consideration into account.[28] The court cannot infer

---

[24] *Tam Heung Man* v *Hong Kong Institute of Certified Public Accountants* [2008] 1 HKLRD 238.
[25] *Fok Ho Chiu* v *Chinese Temples Committee* [2003] HKEC 1183; *BI* v *Director of Immigration* [2016] 2 HKLRD 520 (CA).
[26] *Gurung Deu Kumari* v *Director of Immigration* [2010] 5 HKLRD 219.
[27] *Wan Yung Sang* v *Hong Kong Housing Authority* [2011] HKEC 907.
[28] *Lau Kong Yung* v *Director of Immigration* (1999) 2 HKCFAR 300, pp.332 and 339. The Director of Immigration was in that case not bound to take into account humanitarian considerations when deciding whether to make a removal order, though it was open for him to do so if he thought fit (Bokhary PJ dissenting). The same point was made in *BI* v *Director of Immigration*

that the decision maker failed to take a relevant consideration into account merely because a decision was made which was adverse to such a consideration.[29] Clearly the court can simply disagree with the averment that a given consideration was irrelevant.[30] Though a body may be required to take into account relevant considerations, which might include the views or objections of particular persons, the body must still make its own decision so as to avoid fettering, divesting or relinquishing its discretion.

Intensity of Review if Relevant Consideration Taken into Account

The courts have stated that once a decision maker has taken into account a relevant consideration, it is within his discretion as to what weight should be attached to that consideration. The question of weight has been stated not to be a matter for the courts, provided that the decision maker does not lapse into *Wednesbury* unreasonableness. This is reflected in two well-known statements made in the House of Lords, first by Lord Keith of Kinkel:

> It is for the courts, if the matter is brought before them, to decide what is a relevant consideration. If the decision maker wrongly takes the view that some consideration is not relevant, and therefore has no regard to it, his decision cannot stand and he must be required to think again. But it is entirely for the decision maker to attribute to the relevant considerations such weight as he thinks fit, and the courts will not interfere unless he has acted unreasonably in the *Wednesbury* sense ...[31]

Lord Hoffmann added:

> The law has always made a clear distinction between the question of whether something is a material consideration and the weight which it should be given. The former is a question of law and the latter is a question of planning judgment, which is entirely a matter for the planning authority. Provided that the planning authority has regard to all material considerations, it is at liberty (provided that it does not lapse into *Wednesbury* irrationality) to give them whatever weight the planning authority thinks fit or no weight at all. The fact that the law regards something as a

---

[2016] 2 HKLRD 520, p.553. If, however, humanitarian considerations had been taken into account, the court could intervene if there was procedural unfairness – *BI v Director of Immigration* [2016] 2 HKLRD 520, pp.557–558. See also *BH v Director of Immigration* [2015] 4 HKC 107, para.70.

[29] *BI v Director of Immigration* [2016] 2 HKLRD 520, pp.558–559.

[30] See, for example, *Anderson Asphalt Ltd v Town Planning Board* [2007] 3 HKLRD 18, paras.49–57; and *Anderson Asphalt Ltd v Secretary for Justice* [2009] 3 HKLRD 215, paras.94–101. Further discussion on the relevance of considerations can be found in *Building Authority v Appeal Tribunal (Buildings)* [2013] 1 HKLRD 101.

[31] *Tesco Stores Ltd v Secretary of State for the Environment* [1995] 1 WLR 759 (HL), p.764, per Lord Keith of Kinkel.

material consideration therefore involves no view about the part, if any, which it should play in the decision-making process.[32]

The position has also been taken in Hong Kong that the weight attached by the decision maker to a relevant consideration is, subject to *Wednesbury* unreasonableness, a matter within the decision maker's discretion:[33]

> It is of course true to say, as has been pointed out by Laws LJ in *R (Khatun)* v *Newham London Borough Council* [2005] QB 37, 55 (para 35), that it is for the decision maker and not the courts, subject to *Wednesbury* review, to decide upon the manner and intensity of inquiry to be undertaken into any relevant factor accepted or demonstrated as such.[34]

The distinction is perhaps not quite as clean as the courts suggest. First, the courts wield significant power in deciding what does and does not qualify as a relevant consideration, which can also involve assessments of factual issues, policy realities and common law requirements, in addition to express statutory requirements. Second, the decision maker may have to prove that it took a particular (relevant) consideration into account, as without reasons attesting to that consideration, the court may assume that the relevant consideration was not taken into account.[35] Third, noting that some recent cases appear to have lowered the threshold of *Wednesbury* unreasonableness, the notion that the weight to be attached to a relevant consideration is one for the decision maker, and not the courts, could become rather thin. It has indeed been held that failure to give proper weight to the consequences of a requirement can support a finding of irrationality.[36] As the courts have seemed willing to impose increasingly rigorous rationality standards on decision-making processes, it is conceivable that it would take less than it previously did for a court to assess the legality of the weight attached to a relevant consideration.

---

[32] *Id.*, p.780, per Lord Hoffmann. See also *R (on the application of Khatun)* v *Newham London Borough Council* [2005] QB 37, para.35, per Laws LJ.
[33] *Fok Chun Wa* v *Hospital Authority* (2012) 15 HKCFAR 409, paras.97–98.
[34] *Smart Gain Investment Ltd* v *Town Planning Board* [2007] HKEC 1964, para.87, per Cheung J. It was also said (at para.82) that "the individual characteristics of the sites are relevant considerations. How much weight one should place on them... is a matter of planning judgment which should primarily be a matter for the Board, not the courts. However, the individual characteristics remain material factors to be taken into account". The approach is also seen in *Qamar Zaman* v *Department of Immigration* [2003] 3 HKLRD J26, paras.17–18; and "reiterate[d] categorically" in *BI* v *Director of Immigration* [2016] 2 HKLRD 520, p.558. See also *Sabir Mohammed* v *Permanent Secretary for Security* [2017] HKEC 154, paras.41 and 59.
[35] See *Lai Hin Cheong* v *Long-Term Prison Sentences Review Board* [2008] HKEC 1701, particularly at para.65; and p.262.
[36] *Tam Heung Man* v *Hong Kong Institute of Certified Public Accountants* [2008] 1 HKLRD 238, para.192.

14

Insufficient Retention of Discretion
Unlawful Delegation, Divestiture and Relinquishment

Where legislation confers discretion on a specified decision maker, discretion should in general be exercised by that decision maker and not by some other person. This is because all bodies must be able to base their acts and decisions in law, thus absent legal authority to delegate, delegation will be unlawful. There are nevertheless three important qualifications on this general legal position.

The first is that some statutes permit delegation of power.[1] This may be express or implied, and the usual principles of statutory interpretation will apply. Where an Ordinance confers the power to delegate powers or duties, this does not preclude the delegator from exercising those powers or performing those duties.[2] The second is that it is statutorily provided that a specified public officer may delegate powers or duties to another public officer or person, effective by notice of the Chief Executive-in-Council in the Gazette.[3] This does not, however, permit delegation of the power to make subsidiary legislation or to hear any appeal.[4] Where a power is conferred or a duty is imposed on a specified public officer and is performed by any other public officer, the specified public officer shall be deemed to have delegated the power or duty unless the contrary is proved.[5]

The third qualification is the *Carltona* principle. This is different from the other qualifications, as whilst the first and second qualifications described above constitute delegation of powers or duties, the *Carltona* principle does not strictly involve delegation.[6] This will be seen to be a legal basis on which

---

[1] Statutory provisions authorising delegation of power include the Child Care Services Ordinance (cap.243), s.4; and the Housing Ordinance (cap.283), s.10. Sub-delegation can also be authorised: see Hong Kong Science and Technology Parks Corporation Ordinance (cap. 565), s.11(3) and (4); and *Wise Union Industries Ltd v Hong Kong Science and Technology Parks Corporation* [2009] 5 HKLRD 620.

[2] Interpretation and General Clauses Ordinance (cap.1), s.44(1)(a).

[3] *Id.*, s.43(1) and (4). See, for example, Gazette notices L.N. 192 of 2003 (specification of Secretary for Home Affairs for provisions in six Ordinances) and L.N. 99 of 2009 (specification of Commissioner for Transport for provisions in one Ordinance and two Regulations, and specification of Director of Highways for provisions in one Ordinance and one Regulation).

[4] Interpretation and General Clauses Ordinance (cap.1), s.43(2).   [5] *Id.*, s.43(3)

[6] Wade and Forsyth, *Administrative Law* (11th edn), pp.266–267. It has been described as a "common law constitutional power . . . which is capable of being negatived or confined by

officials in central government departments can exercise powers on behalf of and in the name of a specified decision maker within that government department. It has been legitimated on the basis of a specific constitutional justification in the UK which is absent in Hong Kong and questions whether and to what extent the principle should be capable of operating in Hong Kong.

The possibility of delegation and the taking of decisions under the *Carltona* principle are important for the practical realities of public administration. In particular, persons upon whom decision-making powers are conferred by legislation are often recipients of a large or unmanageable volume of such powers. This especially applies to the heads of government departments. Powers and duties may be so multitudinous or consuming of resources that they are practically incapable of being exercised solely by the decision maker specified by statute. However, neither delegation nor decisions made under the *Carltona* principle derogate from the cardinal principle that a public body or official must ground all of its acts and decisions in law. Accordingly, delegation will be unlawful unless a specific legal basis can be found in its favour.

The courts have therefore developed rules on how and in what circumstances discretion may be delegated at common law. Failure to comply with these rules will (assuming there is no statutory basis for delegation) constitute unlawful delegation and may result in both the purported delegation, and the decision purportedly delegated, being struck down as *ultra vires*.[7] Rules have also been developed on divestiture and relinquishment of discretion, namely where a body on whom discretion is conferred unlawfully shares its discretion with an unauthorised body, or gives it up completely. This may result in the decision being struck down on the basis that discretion was not properly retained by the decision-making body, or – particularly where discretion is divested or relinquished – the purported decision taken by the unauthorised body is unlawful as in excess of power.

It is in the interests of bodies susceptible to judicial review to properly understand their legal obligations in this field, not only in terms of avoiding liability in public law for "getting it wrong", but in terms of the potential magnitude of the practical consequences of important, complex or a large number of decisions having to be retaken. For the person subject to decisions of public bodies, these rules and principles are important not only for ensuring that decision makers comply with their legal obligations, but in ensuring that

---

express statutory provisions" – *R v Secretary of State for the Home Department, ex parte Oladehinde* [1991] 1 AC 254, p.282, per Lord Donaldson MR. This case referred to "devolution" rather than "delegation" of powers or duties under the *Carltona* principle. Some statutes do not expressly delegate power to other officials within the relevant central government department, but define the principal decision maker in such a way as to include subordinate officials. For example, section 2(1) of the Immigration Ordinance defines the "Director" to mean the Director of Immigration, the Deputy Director of Immigration, any assistant director of immigration and any member of the Immigration Service of the rank of senior principal immigration officer.

[7] See, for example, *Rowse v Secretary for Civil Service* [2008] 5 HKLRD 217, para.232.

public decision makers are properly accountable for their decisions. It is not only legally objectionable, but also politically objectionable, for decision makers upon whom discretion is conferred to freely delegate or relinquish those powers to others, in particular where the decision maker fails to retain sufficient control over the exercise of that discretion. Unlawful delegation can be closely linked to, or in some cases resemble, other grounds such as failure to take into account relevant considerations or fettering of discretion.[8]

Unlawful Delegation

Carltona Principle

Lord Greene MR made the following statement on the exercise of powers in public administration in *Carltona Ltd* v *Commissioners of Works*:

> In the administration of government in this country the functions which are given to ministers (and constitutionally properly given to ministers because they are constitutionally responsible) are functions so multifarious that no minister could ever personally attend to them ... The duties imposed upon ministers and the powers given to ministers are normally exercised under the authority of ministers by responsible officials of the department. Public business could not be carried on if that were not the case.[9]

The *Carltona* principle is a qualification on the general rule against delegation of powers or duties by which specified decision makers in central government departments can "delegate" (or devolve) powers or duties within their departments. As noted above, this is formally not delegation at all, as the powers or duties are exercised on behalf of and in the name of the specified decision maker (the "minister"). The official acts as the alter ego of the minister.[10]

The constitutional context is a key aspect of the justification for the *Carltona* principle. Not only is the principle of significant practical benefit for the day-to-day operation of public administration, Lord Greene MR explained that, when an official exercises discretion under the principle, the decision formally remains one of the minister:

> Constitutionally, the decision of such an official is, of course, the decision of the minister. The minister is responsible. It is he who must answer before Parliament for anything that his officials have done, under his authority, and,

---

[8] Consider, for example, *Secretary for Security* v *Sakthevel Prabakar* (2004) 7 HKCFAR 187; *Tam Chi Ming* v *Medical Council of Hong Kong* [2008] 1 HKLRD 24; and *Lee Shing Leung* v *Director of Social Welfare* [2011] HKEC 810.
[9] *Carltona Ltd* v *Commissioners of Works* [1943] 2 All ER 560, p.563, per Lord Greene MR.
[10] *Nelms* v *Roe* [1969] 3 All ER 1379, p.1382; *R* v *Secretary of State for the Home Department, ex parte Oladehinde* [1991] 1 AC 254, p.284; *Re Tran Quoc Cuong* v *Khuc The Loc* [1991] 2 HKLR 312, p.337; *Re Chiu Tat-Cheong* [1992] 2 HKLR 57, p.70. See also fn.6.

if for an important matter he selected an official of such junior standing that he could not be expected competently to perform the work, the minister would have to answer for that in Parliament. The whole system of departmental organisation and administration is based on the view that ministers, being responsible to Parliament, will see that important duties are committed to experienced officials. If they do not do that, Parliament is the place where complaint must be made against them.[11]

The necessary systemic protections were in place because, if decisions were made by government officials in the name of, and as the alter ego of, the minister heading the department, the minister – as a member of Parliament – was constitutionally accountable to Parliament for those decisions. In other words, political accountability would not be lost, and (in theory at least) the minister had a sufficient incentive to ensure those decisions were properly taken, otherwise he would be accountable to Parliament for any deficiencies in the taking of those decisions. Nevertheless, the *Carltona* principle is not a blank cheque for the manner in which powers or duties are devolved within a department. This may be subject, at a minimum, to scrutiny for *Wednesbury* unreasonableness.[12]

Whether or not a constitutional justification of this kind is regarded as adequate in the UK, it is questionable whether the *Carltona* principle is constitutionally relevant and appropriate in Hong Kong. The approximate equivalent to UK government ministers in Hong Kong are members of the Policy Committee. This comprises the Chief Secretary for Administration, the Financial Secretary, the Secretary for Justice and the Secretaries of Bureaux, who collectively comprise the official members of the Executive Council.[13] They are appointed and removed by the Chief Executive, and whilst they may be appointed from among members of the Legislative Council, there is no requirement that they must be so appointed.[14] At the time of writing, none of the sixteen official members of the Executive Council was concurrently serving as a member of the Legislative Council. This means that members of the Policy Committee are not accountable to the legislature in a way that resembles ministerial accountability to the UK Parliament.[15]

---

[11] *Carltona Ltd* v *Commissioners of Works* [1943] 2 All ER 560, p.563.
[12] Lord Woolf et al, *De Smith's Judicial Review* (8th edn), p.336.
[13] The Executive Council, presided over by the Chief Executive, also comprises part-time non-official members, who are not members of the Policy Committee. The members of the Policy Committee constitute the Principal Officials of the Hong Kong SAR, excluding the Commissioner of Police, the Commissioner of the Independent Commission Against Corruption, the Director of Audit, the Commissioner of Customs and Excise, and the Director of Immigration.
[14] Basic Law, Art.55.
[15] Though there is formal provision for some degree of accountability. Article 62(6) of the Basic Law provides that the Government shall designate officials to sit in on meetings of the Legislative Council and to speak on behalf of the Government. It is also provided by Article 73(10) of the Basic Law that the Legislative Council may summon persons to testify or

Furthermore, whereas the orthodox constitutional position in the UK is formally one of legislative supremacy, which again explains the importance attached to ministerial accountability to Parliament, the Legislative Council cannot feasibly be formally regarded as constitutionally supreme in Hong Kong. Whilst there is some accountability of the Chief Executive and members of the Policy Committee to the Legislative Council, providing some support for the system of checks and balances, it arguably does not enjoy the constitutional significance of ministerial accountability to the UK Parliament.[16] Whilst the *Carltona* principle still provides an important legal basis on which decision makers in central government departments in Hong Kong can devolve certain of their powers in maintaining the overall manageability of public administration, it seems that the principal justifications are practical rather than constitutional.[17] It should also be recognised that the heads of many bodies susceptible to judicial review in Hong Kong are not members of the Policy Committee and are not directly accountable to the Legislative Council.[18] In any event, the *Carltona* principle is said to be limited to central government departments, thus other public bodies cannot necessarily benefit from the principle.[19] Even if implied delegation exists in public bodies outside the departments of central government, those bodies cannot rely on the constitutional justifications for the *Carltona* principle. It might even be asked whether central government departments in Hong Kong do not benefit from the *Carltona* principle, for reasons of constitutional difference, but rather a form of implied delegation. Operation of the *Carltona* principle can be

---

give evidence before it. The Chief Secretary for Administration, Financial Secretary and Secretary for Justice may attend any meeting of the Legislative Council or its committees, but are not generally required to do so – Rules of Procedure of the Legislative Council, r.10(3). Similar provision is made for the Chief Executive, whose attendance for the purpose of addressing the Legislative Council, answering questions put to her by members of the Legislative Council on the work of the Government, and proposing any policy, measure, bill, resolution, motion or question for debate is at her discretion – Rules of Procedure of the Legislative Council, r.8.

[16] It could be pointed out that, as half of the Legislative Council membership is elected on a functional constituency basis, there is not the same popular accountability to the Hong Kong legislature as there is to the UK legislature. However, it would have to be remembered that ministerial accountability to Parliament in the UK is in practice accountability to the House of Commons, as government ministers are nowadays usually drawn from the House of Commons. Parliament also comprises the House of Lords and the Monarch, neither of which is elected and neither of which is as popularly accountable as are members of the House of Commons. In purely numerical terms, a greater proportion of Legislative Council members is elected by geographical constituency (35 of 70 members) than is the case for the UK Parliament (650 of around 1,450 members at the time of writing).

[17] Consider *Rowse v Secretary for Civil Service* [2008] 5 HKLRD 217, para.228.

[18] However, that is also largely true in the UK, *mutatis mutandis*.

[19] This can be inferred from *Re Tran Quoc Cuong v Khuc The Loc* [1991] 2 HKLR 312, pp.336–337.

expressly excluded by legislation,[20] which stands to reason as a statutory rule taking precedence over a common law rule.

The idea that ministers, or heads of central government departments, are entitled to rely on the collective knowledge, experience and expertise of public officers best positioned to advise them, in particular (but not exclusively[21]) those working in their own department, is one of long standing.[22] This principle was regarded as applying also to Hong Kong, even when it did not have a ministerial system of government.[23] This justified the Chief Executive consulting public advisers, again during a period in which there was no ministerial system of government in Hong Kong.[24] However, Hartmann J's assertion that "the office of the Chief Executive is an elected office" and that "[f]undamentally therefore the manner in which he attains office is comparable to the manner in which a minister attains office in the United Kingdom"[25] is, with respect, fanciful.[26] Whilst the general principle might support the Chief Executive or other departmental heads relying on the collective knowledge, experience and expertise of advisers and staff in their respective offices and departments, the Chief Executive and other departmental heads are in practical terms far less accountable to the legislature and the electorate than their UK counterparts, so again the primary justification in Hong Kong would seem to be practical rather than constitutional as such.[27]

Status of Delegator and Delegate

One of the factors relevant for determining the legality of a purported delegation is the status of the person purporting to delegate discretion, and the status of the person to whom they purport to delegate it. The relative seniority of the delegator and delegate is particularly important. In principle, the greater the difference in seniority between the delegator and the delegate, the less likely it

---

[20] Lord Woolf et al, *De Smith's Judicial Review* (8th edn), p.336.
[21] *Leung Man Cheung* v *Secretary for Planning and Lands* [2000] HKEC 991.
[22] See, for example, *Local Government Board* v *Arlidge* [1915] AC 120, p.133, per Viscount Haldane LC; and *Bushell* v *Secretary of State for the Environment* [1981] AC 75, p.95, per Lord Diplock.
[23] *Kaisilk Development Ltd* v *Secretary for Planning, Environment and Lands* [2000] HKCU 72, p.8, per Cheung J.
[24] *Ch'ng Poh* v *Chief Executive of HKSAR* [2003] HKEC 1441, paras.19–20. This line of authority was supported in *Lau Kwok Fai* v *Commissioner of Police* [2004] HKEC 1580, paras.75–78.
[25] *Ch'ng Poh* v *Chief Executive of HKSAR* [2003] HKEC 1441, para.20, per Hartmann J.
[26] It was stated in the pre-Handover constitutional context that "a Colonial Governor is not to be equated with a minister in the United Kingdom" in the context of a discussion of the Carltona principle – *Attorney General* v *Chiu Tat-Cheong* [1992] 2 HKLR 84 (CA), p.108, per Kempster JA. However, elections to the office of Chief Executive are far more restrictive than for members of the UK Parliament who are subsequently appointed as government ministers.
[27] See Wade and Forsyth, *Administrative Law* (11th edn), pp.266–269; and see also Mark Freedland, 'The Rule Against Delegation and the Carltona Doctrine in an Agency Context' [1996] Public Law 19.

is that delegation will be lawful. If a senior decision maker delegates to another senior decision maker, or if a junior decision maker delegates to another junior decision maker, then delegation is more likely to be lawful. In both examples, the decision is still taken by a person of appropriate seniority. However, if a senior decision maker delegates to a junior decision maker, then the decision may (depending on the nature of the power) no longer be taken by a person of appropriate seniority, and this attempt to delegate is more likely to be unlawful.[28]

Of course, there are no automatic rules in this regard and it is a question of context in individual cases. It can be lawful for a decision maker to delegate powers outside his own department in which case the *Carltona* principle would not apply.[29] The nature of the delegated power also matters: the Chief Executive may be required to make a decision, and she may be under a statutory duty to provide that decision in writing, but it will probably not be unlawful for her to ask her secretary to assist with the phraseology of her decision. This is because she is advised on, or "delegates", only the administrative, clerical or stylistic aspect of the written decision, does not delegate the substance of the decision to be made, and retains an appropriate degree of control over the decision as a whole. Accordingly, the status of the delegator and the delegate is not determinative of legality, but can materially affect it.

Nature of Delegated Power

The nature of the power to be delegated is relevant for determining the legality of the delegation. The more serious or important the power, the less likely it is that the power can lawfully be delegated. Thus, it will be less likely to be lawful for a decision to pardon a criminal offender to be lawfully delegated,[30] or a power to determine an appeal from a civil servant subject to serious

---

[28] It is of course possible – though improbable – for a more junior decision maker to "delegate" his discretion to a more senior decision maker. Context would dictate whether or not this is lawful. For example, there might be reasons why the more junior decision maker was invested with the power, such as to avoid the more senior decision maker exercising the power if a potential conflict of interests could arise, or if there are "firewalls" erected within a department or organisation in order to segregate information channels. It may also be improper to "delegate" a function to a more senior decision maker if the more junior decision maker possesses specialised skills or competences which are not possessed by the more senior decision maker. For example, an employee in an intelligence agency might have the capacity to decide whether a wiretapped telephone conversation in a foreign language raises security concerns, whereas the head of the intelligence agency might not have the skills (including foreign language skills) necessary to make that decision. Indeed, it is not only the relative seniority of the delegate that is important, but also issues of resource, availability, skill, contacts, experience and knowledge – *R (on the application of Chief Constable of West Midlands Police) v Gonzales* [2002] EWHC (Admin) 1087, para.18.

[29] *Re Tran Quoc Cuong v Khuc The Loc* [1991] 2 HKLR 312, pp.336–337.

[30] The Chief Executive enjoys this power under the Basic Law, Art.48(12). Though see *Ch'ng Poh v Chief Executive of HKSAR* [2003] HKEC 1441, para.21.

disciplinary measures.[31] In combination with the relative seniority of the delegator and the delegate, the more serious or important the power, the less likely it is that the power can lawfully be delegated far down the hierarchical chain. Thus, a deportation decision may be delegated from a departmental head to a person of appropriate seniority in the department,[32] but clearly the same decision could not be delegated to a clerical assistant. Unless delegation between the two officials in question is expressly permitted by statute, or unless delegation is expressly prohibited, the assessment of the legality of the purported delegation will often be informed both by the relative seniority of the delegator and delegate, and by the nature of the power being delegated.[33]

Where the power that is sought to be delegated resembles a judicial or quasi-judicial power, such as disciplinary or appellate powers, there is a presumption against lawful delegation,[34] unless there is express authority to the contrary. Accordingly, though it was "an established arrangement for the Chief Executive to delegate some of his functions to senior officials as he sees fit", and though delegation of a power under section 20 of the Public Service (Administration) Order to determine appeals was not prohibited by the Order,[35] the Chief Executive could not lawfully delegate to the Chief Secretary a power to consider appeals under that Order.[36]

Where the power is a substantive power, and not merely an ancillary, peripheral or incidental power, it is less likely to be regarded as lawfully delegated.[37] Merely administrative or clerical work may, depending on the context, be capable of lawful delegation.[38] Notwithstanding the status of the delegator and delegate, and the nature of the delegated power, there is less likely to be unlawful delegation where sufficient control is retained by the delegator.[39] Retention of control by an entity, including the power to revoke the authority of the delegate, would indicate delegation (which, other criteria being satisfied, will be lawful) rather than (unlawful) divestiture or relinquishment.[40] Where a power has been conferred on a specified body, but without a corresponding power to delegate that power, it cannot subsequently ratify an *ultra vires* delegation.[41]

---

[31] See *Rowse v Secretary for Civil Service* [2008] 5 HKLRD 217, paras.229–232.
[32] *R v Secretary of State for the Home Department, ex parte Oladehinde* [1991] 1 AC 254.
[33] *Director of Public Prosecutions v Haw* [2008] 1 WLR 379, para.29.
[34] *Barnard v National Dock Labour Board* [1953] 2 QB 18.
[35] See *Rowse v Secretary for Civil Service* [2008] 5 HKLRD 217, para.212.
[36] *Id.*, paras.230–231.   [37] See *id.*, paras.229 and 231.
[38] *Wise Union Industries Ltd v Hong Kong Science and Technology Parks Corporation* [2009] 5 HKLRD 620, paras.95–98.
[39] *Lian Ting Sen v Director of Education* [2000] HKCU 1041, pp.25–27.
[40] See Lord Woolf et al, *De Smith's Judicial Review* (8th edn), p.328.
[41] *Kwan Wan Chee Alisa v City University of Hong Kong* [2013] HKEC 232, para.21; see also *Barnard v National Dock Labour Board* [1953] 2 QB 18.

Agency and Delegation

Related to unlawful delegation is the concept of unlawful agency. Wade and Forsyth suggested that the distinction is not necessarily a technical difference between agency and delegation but between the different degrees of devolution which either term can cover.[42] Though a distinction probably can be made, Wade and Forsyth are correct to suggest that the distinction is a fine one. Where a selection panel conducted interviews and recommended to an appointing body a single candidate from thirty-four applications for appointment by a police authority, this was treated as not comprising delegation, particularly as the appointing body could reject the recommendation, seek further information or defer the appointment decision.[43] The decision would ultimately be taken by the appointing body.

This might be characterised as a form of agency, as the appointing body was under a statutory duty to appoint members from a shortlist of candidates "prepared by a selection panel". The selection panel therefore had the statutory authority to act as a form of agent for a limited purpose, rather than exercising powers delegated to it by the appointing body. However, one could argue that it is not agency either, and Carnwath LJ took the view that the process was "simply an exercise of their implied power to take steps to obtain the information necessary to perform [its statutory function]".[44] The argument that this was effectively a situation of agency nevertheless seems more plausible than one of delegation.

This case is distinguishable from one in which there was an express statutory basis for delegating the power to collect information to staff in a commission. It would then be proper for the commission to act upon the reports produced by those staff. This appears to be an instance of delegation, as the "nominated commissioners are clearly intended to be an extension of the personality of the whole commission".[45] However, this may also be capable of characterisation as agency. The distinction between delegation and agency can therefore be seen to be a fine one and in some cases it is less clear than in others whether one is dealing with an instance of delegation, agency or a body's being assisted in the performance of its functions.

Divestiture and Relinquishment

There is a difference of principle between a decision maker delegating discretion, and a decision maker divesting or relinquishing discretion.[46] In the case

---

[42] Wade and Forsyth, *Administrative Law* (11th edn), p.260.
[43] *R (on the application of Reckless) v Kent Police Authority* [2010] EWCA Civ 1277.
[44] *Id.*, para.29.
[45] *R v Commission for Racial Equality, ex parte Cottrell* [1980] 1 WLR 1580, p.1583, per Lord Lane CJ.
[46] The terminology used by Wade and Forsyth, *Administrative Law* (11th edn), p.269, is that of surrender, abdication and dictation.

of delegation, the decision maker retains (or should retain) a sufficient degree of control over the exercise of the delegated discretion, whereas in the case of divestiture or relinquishment, there is no control, or insufficient control, over the exercise of the divested or relinquished discretion. As sufficient retention of control is a necessary precondition to lawful delegation, insufficient retention may move a purported transfer of discretion out of the category of delegation and into the category of divestiture or relinquishment.

Divestiture and relinquishment is essentially characterised by insufficient retention of discretion. The decision maker who should have decided has shared his decision-making power with an unauthorised body, or allowed or acquiesced to an unauthorised body determining the substance of the decision. It is conceptually associated with fettering of discretion, in the sense that a power to decide carries with it an obligation to decide, and failure to exercise discretion effectively constitutes a fetter on the proper exercise of that discretion. However, divestiture and relinquishment can be distinguished on the basis that, as in the case of delegation, the substance of the decision is being decided by another party. Whereas delegation of discretion can be lawful, however, divestiture and relinquishment is categorically unlawful.

Divestiture and relinquishment can take a number of different forms. It could comprise a body with authority to make a decision acting as a mere rubber stamp to a third party's decision or evaluation.[47] There may be such an over-reliance on the views of technical experts or third parties that it is tantamount to a divestiture of discretion in favour of those experts or third parties. It could take the form of a body giving an unauthorised third party an effective veto over the body's decisions or to effectively permit the third party to dictate the decision in question,[48] or a body responsible for making a decision acting as though it was bound by the decision of a third party by whose decision it is not legally bound.

The case law does not readily, or not readily enough, draw a sufficient distinction between unlawful delegation, and divestiture and relinquishment. Where a committee of the Medical Council of Hong Kong failed to make a sufficiently independent evaluation of the merits in a decision-making process, apparently relying instead on the Hong Kong College of Cardiology's views of the merits, the court quashed the Council's decision on the basis of "*ultra vires* delegation and abdication".[49] Although the court acknowledged that the two are closely connected, though apparently thought fit to make the distinction, the case was rather one of divestiture or relinquishment (abdication), as

---

[47] *Tam Chi Ming* v *Medical Council of Hong Kong* [2008] 1 HKLRD 24.
[48] *Ellis* v *Dubowski* [1921] KB 621. Though see *Mills* v *London County Council* [1925] 1 KB 213; *R v Greater London Council, ex parte Blackburn* [1976] 1 WLR 550; and *Hookings* v *Director of Civil Aviation* [1957] NZLR 929.
[49] *Tam Chi Ming* v *Medical Council of Hong Kong* [2008] 1 HKLRD 24.

the Council had not purported to delegate its discretion to the College of Cardiology. If the case was to be characterised as one of delegation, it would at a minimum have to be regarded as an attempted implied and effective delegation, rather than express and actual delegation, though this is probably to stretch the concept of delegation too far.

By contrast, where the Director of Social Welfare determined eligibility to Normal Disability Allowance having taken into account a medical assessment undertaken by a medical officer – in compliance with policy – the Director could not be regarded as surrendering judgment to a third party.[50] The argument was framed as one of unlawful delegation or dictation (essentially divestiture or relinquishment),[51] but the argument would fail on both grounds for the same reason: the medical officer did not take the decision. The Director neither delegated nor surrendered the discretion that was for him to exercise, but rather, in accordance with policy, had regard to the medical officer's assessment in the course of exercising his overall discretion.[52] Where the Secretary for Security failed to make an independent assessment of a torture claim, relying instead on the refusal of the United Nations High Commissioner for Refugees to grant refugee status to the torture claimant, the Secretary would be relinquishing her own discretion, allowing her decision effectively to be dictated by the High Commissioner.[53]

It would not be a divestiture or relinquishment of discretion, or delegation, where a legal adviser was present at tribunal proceedings and prepared a draft decision which embodied the views of the tribunal and which was submitted to the tribunal for scrutiny and modification.[54] Nor would the presence and preparation of a draft decision by the legal adviser adversely impact on the competence, independence or impartiality of the tribunal.[55] However, it may be necessary to distinguish the legal adviser's participation to this extent from sharing in the tribunal's judicial function without an express statutory power to do so.[56] The presence of a legal adviser can keep the tribunal right in law,[57] though care should be taken as to how they participate in decision-making proceedings,[58] and

---

[50] *Lee Shing Leung* v *Director of Social Welfare* [2011] HKEC 810.   [51] *Id.*, para.10.
[52] See *id.*, para.64.
[53] *Secretary for Security* v *Sakthevel Prabakar* (2004) 7 HKCFAR 187. The Court of Final Appeal did not use these terms, but could and perhaps should have done.
[54] *Medical Council of Hong Kong* v *Helen Chan* (2010) 13 HKCFAR 248.   [55] *Id.*
[56] *Dato Tan Leong Min* v *Insider Dealing Tribunal* [1998] 1 HKLRD 630; *Au Wing Lun* v *Solicitors Disciplinary Tribunal* [2002] HKEC 1141.
[57] *Judith Mary Longstaff* v *Medical Council of Hong Kong* [1980] HKLR 858, p.865, per Huggins V-P.
[58] *Dato Tan Leong Min* v *Insider Dealing Tribunal* [1998] 1 HKLRD 630; *Lam Kwok Pun* v *Dental Council of Hong Kong* [2000] 4 HKC 181.

the view has been expressed that it would be preferable for the tribunal to deliberate on its own and only call on the legal adviser should his advice be required.[59] If the legal adviser improperly shares in the tribunal's discretion, absent the requisite authority, the tribunal would open itself to a claim of divesting or relinquishing discretion to the legal adviser.

---

[59] *Wu Hin Ting* v *Medical Council of Hong Kong* [2004] 2 HKC 367, p.385, per Ma CJHC.

15

Fettering of Discretion

The conferral of discretion on a decision maker conveys a power to arrive at a range of legally permitted decisions. However, discretion is not only permissive; it is also obligatory. The power to exercise discretion carries with it an obligation to exercise discretion. It is a fundamental rule that discretion must be brought appropriately to bear on every case.[1] This has two principal dimensions. First, a decision maker must decide: they cannot ordinarily refuse to decide or abstain from deciding. Second, a decision maker must actively make a decision, and cannot resolve at a given time what decisions will be made in the future. The latter is often, but not exclusively, seen in the context of policies on how discretion will be exercised at a later stage.

Obligation to Decide

If a decision maker refuses to exercise discretion, this is tantamount to an abrogation of jurisdiction.[2] It bears some similarity to divestiture or relinquishment of discretion, but that arises in the context of unlawfully transferring discretion to a third party, or effectively permitting a third party to exercise discretion in its place. In the case of fettering, the decision maker does not cede discretion to a third party, nor permit or allow a third party to exercise discretion in his place, but simply does not exercise that discretion (which need not implicate any other party).

If, for example, a decision maker refuses to hear certain evidence in the course of a decision-making process, this may amount to a refusal to exercise discretion.[3] However, what is essentially unlawful is a refusal to exercise discretion, or, for example, a refusal to sufficiently consider exercising statutory discretion.[4] This must be distinguished from the non-exercise of a statutory power, even for a long period of time, which does not necessarily

---

[1] *Tai Sen Choy* v *Municipal Services Appeals Board* [2001] HKLRD (Yrbk) 9, para.39, per Yeung J.
[2] Consider *R* v *Port of London Authority, ex parte Kynoch Ltd* [1919] 1 KB 176.
[3] *R* v *Marsham* [1892] 1 QB 371.
[4] See *Fok Chun Wa* v *Hospital Authority* [2011] 1 HKLRD A1.

lead to the conclusion that the decision maker has renounced the power, or failed to exercise discretion.[5] Where a statutory power was conferred on the Chief Executive-in-Council to fix minimum rates of wages for any trade "at any time he thinks fit" if satisfied that the wages being paid to workers in that trade were unreasonably low, this did not mean that he was statutorily bound to fix minimum wages. Where his administration decided to pursue a pragmatic policy of encouragement and voluntary participation by employers for a period of two years, after which, if the policy had failed to yield satisfactory results, preparations would be made for the introduction of minimum wage legislation, he had not refused to exercise his discretion, but merely adopted other measures.[6] Likewise, where the Director of Food and Environmental Hygiene decided not to cancel a hawker licence due to contraventions of the licence conditions, but instead took other enforcement action, he was not fettering his discretion. The Director did not rule out cancellation of the licence and demonstrated flexibility in adopting other measures to deal with the contraventions.[7]

Obligation to Decide with a Sufficiently Open Mind

When a decision maker is making a decision, it must be made with a sufficiently open mind or be deemed unlawful on the basis of fettered discretion. This means that the decision maker cannot actually or effectively resolve in advance what decision will be made in the future, for the basic principle is that the relevant time at which the decision should be made is when a decision is required or entitled to be made. There are several aspects of the obligation to decide with a sufficiently open mind, demonstrating the interplay and overlap between various grounds of review. A decision maker who is biased or insufficiently impartial will not have a sufficiently open mind, but this would more likely be challenged under the heading of procedural impropriety or a breach of procedural fairness or natural justice. A decision maker who decides pursuant to an improper purpose could be argued to have an insufficiently open mind, as could a decision maker who fails to take into account a legitimate expectation as a relevant consideration. If a body restricts itself to too few considerations in its decision-making process, and thereby fails to take into account a sufficiently broad range of considerations, this may constitute failure to independently exercise discretion.[8] Each of these could also, depending on the context, qualify as *Wednesbury* unreasonable conduct. Where a statutory appeal lies to an appeals body, the appeals body must

---

[5] *Inglory Ltd v Director of Food and Environmental Hygiene* [2012] 3 HKLRD 603, para.42.
[6] *Chan Noi Heung v Chief Executive-in-Council* [2007] HKEC 885.
[7] *Inglory Ltd v Director of Food and Environmental Hygiene* [2012] 3 HKLRD 603.
[8] *Vu Ngoc Dung v Criminal and Law Enforcement Injuries Compensation Appeal Boards* [1996] HKLY 8.

exercise discretion in its own right and should not be unduly influenced by the decision of the body from which appeal was made[9]; this treads a fine line between fettering discretion, and divesting or relinquishing discretion.

One of the quintessential scenarios in which discretion is fettered is in the adoption and application of policies. It is commonplace for public bodies to adopt policies in the course of public administration, and there is nothing inherently wrong with this. In fact, policies can enhance the quality, consistency and efficiency of public administration and adjudication.[10] Policies can help ensure that consistent criteria or practices are applied in cases of wide discretion,[11] or that criteria or practices are consistently applied over time or by a large number of officials across a department or organisation. They can promote certainty and administrative efficiency.[12] They can also ensure that decisions are made pursuant to relevant considerations, focusing the minds of decision makers and enhancing the rational basis on which decisions are made. A public body might even be obligated to introduce (new) policies and appropriate requirements to meet changing circumstances, such as in response to developments in the threat posed by avian influenza,[13] and the liberty to change administrative policies with changing circumstances is "inherent in our constitutional form of government".[14]

The advantages of the adoption of policies are not only administrative in nature, but also legal. For example, if policies are properly applied, and decisions made pursuant to those policies are thereby more consistent, focused and rational, this can protect against liability in public law. There may be a reduction in the likelihood of successful arguments being mounted by aspiring applicants for judicial review that irrelevant considerations were taken into account, or that there was a failure to consistently follow decision-making procedures, or that an unreasonable decision was made, and so on. Generally speaking, public bodies should be encouraged to adopt policies.[15]

However, policies also bring risks, and if not properly handled, can lead to violation of grounds of judicial review, including fettering of discretion. First, the policies themselves must be lawful, in compliance with constitutional, statutory and common law requirements. In the event that a policy is found to be unlawful, both the policy and decisions taken thereunder may be struck down. Second, the policy may be lawful, but be applied or adhered to in a

---

[9] *Tai Sen Choy* v *Municipal Services Appeals Board* [2001] HKLRD (Yrbk) 9.
[10] See *Wise Union Industries Ltd* v *Hong Kong Science and Technology Parks Corporation* [2009] 5 HKLRD 620, para.31, per Cheung J.
[11] *Epoch Group Ltd* v *Director of Immigration* [2011] 3 HKLRD H2, para.46.
[12] *C* v *Director of Immigration* (2013) 16 HKCFAR 280, para.74.
[13] *Mo Chun Hon* v *Agriculture, Fisheries and Conservation Department* [2008] 1 HKCLRT 386 (CA).
[14] *Hughes* v *Department of Health and Social Security* [1985] AC 776, p.788, per Lord Diplock.
[15] Though the court cannot force the decision maker to adopt policies or determine their content unless some statutory or other duty requires otherwise – see *Epoch Group Ltd* v *Director of Immigration* [2011] 3 HKLRD H2, para.47.

way that is unlawful. In this scenario, the policy will stand as valid, but decisions taken thereunder may be quashed. Accordingly, a decision maker must not apply his or her policy blindly and rigidly. The policy must not preclude the decision maker from departing therefrom, nor preclude him from taking into account the circumstances and merits of individual cases,[16] nor should it be implemented as if it was such a policy.[17] The legality of the policy and the practical way in which the policy is implemented are therefore both of relevance.[18]

Unlawful Policies

Lord Browne-Wilkinson set out a general statement of this area of law in the English case of *R v Secretary of State for the Home Department, ex parte Venables*:

> When Parliament confers a discretionary power exercisable from time to time over a period, such power must be exercised on each occasion in the light of the circumstances at that time. In consequence, a person on whom the power is conferred cannot fetter the future exercise of his discretion by committing himself now to the way in which he will exercise his power in the future. He cannot exercise the power *nunc pro tunc*. By the same token, the person on whom the power has been conferred cannot fetter the way he will use that power by ruling out of consideration on the future exercises of that power factors which may then be relevant to such exercise.
>
> These considerations do not preclude the person on whom the power is conferred from developing and applying a policy as to the approach which he will adopt in the generality of cases... But the position is different if the policy adopted is such as to preclude the person on whom the power is conferred from departing from the policy or from taking into account circumstances which are relevant to the particular case in relation to which the discretion is being exercised. If such an inflexible and invariable policy is adopted, both the policy and the decision taken pursuant to it will be unlawful ...[19]

The House of Lords held in this case that the Secretary of State for the Home Department had, by adopting a policy which precluded himself and the Parole Board from having any regard to the circumstances and welfare of child

---

[16] *Wise Union Industries Ltd v Hong Kong Science and Technology Parks Corporation* [2009] 5 HKLRD 620, para.31.
[17] *Aita Bahadur Limbu v Director of Immigration* [1999] HKEC 788; *Wise Union Industries Ltd v Hong Kong Science and Technology Parks Corporation* [2009] 5 HKLRD 620, para.35.
[18] *Wise Union Industries Ltd v Hong Kong Science and Technology Parks Corporation* [2009] 5 HKLRD 620, para.35.
[19] *R v Secretary of State for the Home Department, ex parte Venables* [1998] AC 407, pp.496–497, per Lord Browne-Wilkinson.

murderers for a period of twelve years' detention, unlawfully fettered his discretion.[20] The policy was unlawful and so was the decision taken thereunder.

It has been described in Hong Kong as "axiomatic that a public body must not surrender its function, for example, by operating an inflexible policy,"[21] and that the "objection to the operation of an inflexible policy is that it automatically determines the outcome, thus representing a closed mind".[22] This includes the adoption of a policy or criteria which are narrower or more restrictive than permitted or envisaged by statute. Thus, where the Commissioner for Transport imposed a strict time limit (such time limit not being mandatory in the enabling legislation) on applications for a Personalised Vehicle Registration Mark, after which the allocation of the Mark must be cancelled, the Commissioner had unlawfully fettered his discretion.[23]

The policy must not be inflexible, not only with regard to formal, statutory requirements, but also common law requirements such as those on procedural fairness. Thus it was held that a blanket policy that Convention Against Torture claimants would not be entitled to have a lawyer present whilst completing an eligibility questionnaire or taking an eligibility interview, and a blanket policy that no free legal advice would be provided to the claimant, were unlawful in violation of high standards of procedural fairness.[24] The fact that "two plainly *ad hoc* exceptions have been granted to the policy does not detract from the blanket nature of that policy", particularly as there was no evidence of a case-by-case consideration of whether such exceptional circumstances existed as to warrant the making of an exception to the policy.[25] Where exceptions are provided for, if they are too extraordinary and appear not to feasibly admit of exceptions, the body may be regarded as having instituted something very close to a blanket policy, which would be unlawful.[26]

Unlawful Application of Lawful Policies

Even where a lawful policy is adopted, it must not be applied in a way that is unlawful. In particular, the decision maker must show that, notwithstanding the policy and its application, he or she retains a sufficiently open mind and can still properly be said to have exercised discretion. The policy should guide

---

[20] *R v Secretary of State for the Home Department, ex parte Venables* [1998] AC 407.
[21] *Durga Maya Gurung v Director of Immigration* [2002] HKEC 477, para. 29, per Le Pichon JA.
[22] *Id.*, per Le Pichon JA.
[23] *Woomera Co Ltd v Commissioner for Transport* [2009] HKEC 786.
[24] *FB v Director of Immigration* [2009] 2 HKLRD 346. See also *Secretary for Security v Sakthevel Prabakar* (2004) 7 HKCFAR 187.
[25] *FB v Director of Immigration* [2009] 2 HKLRD 346, para.123–124, per Saunders J.
[26] *R v Warwickshire County Council, ex parte Collymore* [1995] ELR 217.

the decision-making process, not dictate it.[27] Guidelines constitute "guidance and not tramlines",[28] and a decision maker who "allows his guidelines to blind him from matters and circumstances which he ought to have regard to" also risks failing to take into account relevant considerations.[29]

One of the ways in which a decision maker can demonstrate that a policy is being applied with a sufficiently open mind is by showing that individual cases are still decided on their own merits and, in so doing, demonstrating a genuine willingness to make exceptions to the general policy. The decision maker can adopt a policy "provided that the authority is always willing to listen to anyone with something new to say",[30] in other words when an applicant can demonstrate that his or her circumstances or the merits of his or her case are not adequately captured by the existing policy. The body in question could not "shut [its] ears to an application".[31] The rule against fettering of discretion does not mean that a decision maker cannot adhere to a policy, such as one in which a line was drawn as to the age for eligibility to dependant immigration status, provided that an open mind was given to potentially exceptional circumstances.[32]

However, the decision maker cannot simply pay lip service to a willingness to grant exceptions. There must be an "exceptions procedure worth the name".[33] Indeed, there is a distinction to be made between lawfully operating a policy which admits of exceptions, and unlawfully adhering to a policy unless exceptional circumstances can be made out in a manner which might conflict with fairness requirements.[34] The latter tends to demonstrate that the decision maker does not have a sufficiently open mind and is not considering the circumstances and merits on a case-by-case basis. It also approaches the near-blanket adoption or application of a policy.[35]

If a policy is adopted which is not, on the face of it, so inflexible as to preclude the body from ever taking into account any other relevant considerations in the

---

[27] Consider, for example, *Ng Hon Keung Tommy v Public Officer* [2015] 5 HKLRD 278.
[28] *R v Wakefield Metropolitan District Council, ex parte Pearl Assurance plc* [1997] EWHC (Admin) 228, para.9, per Jowitt J.
[29] *Epoch Group Ltd v Director of Immigration* [2011] 3 HKLRD H2, para.40.
[30] *British Oxygen Co Ltd v Board of Trade* [1971] AC 610, p.625, per Lord Reid, quoted with approval in *Wise Union Industries Ltd v Hong Kong Science and Technology Parks Corporation* [2009] 5 HKLRD 620, para.31. See also *Re Sea Dragon Billiard and Snooker Association* [1991] 1 HKLR 711.
[31] *British Oxygen Co Ltd v Board of Trade* [1971] AC 610, p.625, per Lord Reid, adapting from *R v Port of London Authority, ex parte Kynoch Ltd* [1919] 1 KB 176, p.183, per Bankes LJ.
[32] *Gurung Deu Kumari v Director of Immigration* [2010] 5 HKLRD 219. See also *LK v Director of Immigration* [2016] HKEC 1730; and consider *Baynham Paul v Liquor Licensing Board* [2010] HKEC 1329.
[33] *R v Bexley London Borough Council, ex parte Jones* [1995] ELR 42, per Leggatt LJ, quoted with approval in *Wise Union Industries Ltd v Hong Kong Science and Technology Parks Corporation* [2009] 5 HKLRD 620, para.31.
[34] See *Rowse v Secretary for Civil Service* [2008] 5 HKLRD 217.
[35] *R v Warwickshire County Council, ex parte Collymore* [1995] ELR 217, p.227.

exercise of its statutory discretion, it will nevertheless be unlawful if the evidence shows that, in practice or implementation, the body was so affected by the policy, or it was so rigidly adhered to that there was no consideration of other relevant factors in its decision-making process. Thus, in *Lo Yuet Hing* v *Hong Kong Housing Authority*, the Housing Authority served a notice to quit on a disabled, elderly lady due to dangerous drugs being found in her flat, in accordance with a policy whereby the use of a Public Rental Housing flat for any unlawful activities was a serious breach of tenancy conditions which warranted termination of the lease by notice to quit. The lady's adopted son had stored the drugs in his room in the flat and had been convicted of an offence for unlawful trafficking in dangerous drugs. However, the lady maintained that she knew nothing of the adopted son's criminal activities, who had a clear criminal record prior to his conviction for this offence. Whilst the Housing Authority had statutory discretion to terminate the lease by serving a notice to quit, it operated its policy of termination in these cases in such an inflexible manner (such as by taking inadequate account of the lady's ignorance of the adopted son's unlawful conduct) as to amount to a fetter on discretion – supported by evidence which showed that, in the preceding forty-four months, there had been 103 cases in which dangerous drugs were found in different housing estate units, and in all 103 cases a notice to quit was served.[36] In addition to a policy or guidelines too rigidly applied potentially causing a failure to take into account relevant considerations, it may also cause the taking into account of irrelevant considerations.[37]

Whilst there is no rule that a fixed proportion of exceptions must be made, there are risks associated with never, in practice, making an exception. In *R* v *Warwickshire County Council, ex parte Collymore*,[38] a local education authority adopted a policy whereby there would be no provision for new discretionary awards due to a deterioration in the finances of the authority. The policy provided that a decision on an application for an award would only be amended in extraordinary circumstances. Whilst, on paper, there appeared to exist a mechanism for making exceptions, save for two cases where the authority honoured existing commitments, approximately three hundred appeals were made over a three-year period, not one of which was successful. In view of this, it was "impossible to escape the conclusion that in practice the policy has been implemented far too rigidly and that, as a result, [the applicant's] application was not properly considered".[39] This was in line with *De Smith's* observation that a "course of conduct involving the consistent rejection of applications belonging to a particular class may justify an

---

[36] *Lo Yuet Hing* v *Hong Kong Housing Authority* [2002] HKEC 1218. See also *Chan Ming Yan* v *Hong Kong Housing Authority* [2000] HKEC 798.
[37] *Epoch Group Ltd* v *Director of Immigration* [2011] 3 HKLRD H2, para.50.
[38] *R* v *Warwickshire County Council, ex parte Collymore* [1995] ELR 217.
[39] *Id.*, p.227, per Judge J.

inference that the competent authority has adopted an unavowed rule to refuse all".[40] The policy was unlawful, principally due to the manner of its implementation and its near-blanket nature, and so was the decision resulting therefrom.

Similarly, in *R v North West Lancashire Health Authority, ex parte A*,[41] a local health authority had a policy of assigning low resource allocation priority to gender reassignment surgery, as the effectiveness, ineffectiveness or harmfulness of this form of surgery was considered by the authority to be unclear. The evidence also showed that the authority was sceptical that gender identity dysphoria was an illness requiring medical treatment. The authority gave the Director of Public Health and Health Policy the power to consider exceptions on the basis of overriding clinical need, but stipulated that "such exceptions will be rare, unpredictable and will usually be based on circumstances that could not have been predicted at the time when the policy was adopted". In the view of Auld LJ:

> a policy to place transsexualism low in an order of priorities of illnesses for treatment and to deny it treatment save in exceptional circumstances such as overriding clinical need is not in principle irrational, provided that the policy genuinely recognises the possibility of there being an overriding clinical need and requires each request for treatment to be considered on its individual merits.[42]

However, the policy did not sufficiently permit or encourage the attachment of proper weight to the authority's acknowledgement of gender identity dysphoria as an illness, the application of that weighting when setting its level of priority for treatment, and the making of effective provision for exceptions in individual cases from any general policy restricting the funding of treatment. The policy, and the decisions made thereunder, were quashed. Again, it is possible that, had the implementation of the policy been different, and had it been shown that the authority was genuinely open to making exceptions, the policy may not have been found to be unlawful.

The flip side of the rigid adoption of a policy is failure to apply a policy. This could occur in various ways, such as by ignoring the policy, which could constitute failure to take into account a relevant consideration or breach of a legitimate expectation that the policy would form the basis of a decision-making process.[43] Departure from a stated policy by reason of

---

[40] Lord Woolf et al, *De Smith's Judicial Review*, p.527; earlier edition cited with approval in *R v Warwickshire County Council, ex parte Collymore* [1995] ELR 217, p.227.
[41] *R v North West Lancashire Health Authority, ex parte A* [2000] 1 WLR 977.
[42] *Id.*, p.991, per Auld LJ.
[43] *R v Ministry of Defence, ex parte Walker* [2000] 1 WLR 806 (HL), p.816.

misinterpreting or misunderstanding the policy can be unlawful.[44] The policy could also be misinterpreted or accorded a meaning so aberrant that it is classed as *Wednesbury* unreasonable, whilst recognising that different decision makers could legitimately reach differing conclusions on the precise interpretation of the policy and that the courts should afford them latitude in that regard.[45]

Fettering Discretion through Contract

The general principle that public bodies may not fetter their discretion applies also when they enter into contracts. It is now commonplace for public bodies to contract with private entities, for a range of different purposes. Notable among contracts concluded by public bodies are those for public procurement, ranging from large-scale acquisitions such as construction of a public hospital by a private company, to more routine purchases such as office equipment for government departments, procurement of information technology services or payment to a private company for cleaning public streets. Employment contracts are commonplace within public bodies. Contracts may also be made in other situations, such as in agreements between public bodies and private persons for compensation, or in government investments using public money. The capacity of public bodies to enter into contracts can enable them to act and operate more effectively and efficiently in serving the public interest. They would, apart from anything else, be put at a significant disadvantage to private enterprise if there was a rule prohibiting public bodies from entering into contracts.[46]

In the course of contracting with other entities, public bodies may commit themselves to act, or refrain from acting, in particular ways. They may also restrict the scope of their discretion. This is potentially problematic as they may not only be committing themselves within the four corners of the contractual relationship, but in a way that affects their public law powers

---

[44] *Hong Kong Television Network Ltd v Chief Executive in Council* [2015] 2 HKLRD 1035, para.37. Though there is clearly scope for disagreement on whether the body has misinterpreted or misunderstood the policy – *Hong Kong Television Network Ltd v Chief Executive in Council* [2016] 2 HKLRD 1005 (CA); *LK v Director of Immigration* [2016] HKEC 1730, paras.53–73.

[45] *Edwards v Bairstow* [1955] 3 WLR 410 (HL); *R v Monopolies and Mergers Commission, ex parte South Yorkshire Transport Ltd* [1993] 1 WLR 23 (HL), p.32; *Ng Siu Tung v Director of Immigration* (2002) 5 HKCFAR 1, paras.195–198. It was stated that where a policy had been misinterpreted, the misinterpretation may render the decision just as flawed as if the policy had been overlooked or ignored altogether – *Wong Wei Man v Amusement Game Centres Appeal Board* [2000] HKCU 790, p.10, per Stock J, reflecting the statement in *R v Ministry of Defence, ex parte Walker* [1999] 1 WLR 1209, p.1216 (where it was also said that the "true meaning" of a policy is for the court to determine); *Ng Siu Tung v Director of Immigration* (2002) 5 HKCFAR 1, para.194; and see for an example thereof, *BI v Director of Immigration* [2016] 2 HKLRD 520.

[46] See *Ansett Transport Industries (Operations) Pty Ltd v Commonwealth of Australia* (1977) 139 CLR 54 (HCA), pp.74–75; and *Fairland Overseas Development Co Ltd v Secretary for Justice* [2007] 4 HKLRD 949, paras.50 and 79.

and duties or the broader public interest. It must also be remembered that contractual payments made by public bodies will often be funded by the taxpayer or general revenue.

As a general principle, any fetter on a public body's discretion brought about by contractual obligations will be unlawful.[47] A contractual provision which acts as a fetter on the public body's exercise of statutory discretion, or the performance of a statutory duty, may either be severed from the contract or result in the whole contract being set aside. One of the authorities in this area is *Ayr Harbour Trustees* v *Oswald*,[48] a Scottish appeal to the House of Lords. Statutory harbour trustees had a power of compulsory purchase, and gave an undertaking to the previous owner of land that he would have unobstructed access to the harbour in order to reduce the compensation payable to him. This was held to be incompetent, as it would commit and restrict the harbour trustees in the future exercise of their discretion. Lord Blackburn explained that the statutory conferral of compulsory purchase powers was for the public good, and "a contract purporting to bind them and their successors not to use those powers is void".[49] Lord Fitzgerald added that the harbour trustees "have no power in law to preclude themselves or their successors from the exercise of their statutable powers over it, as should be from time to time required for the purposes of the harbour",[50] a statement more recently regarded in Hong Kong as "much more illustrative of the real modern principle".[51]

The principle is also seen in an early English case, in which the UK Government made an undertaking during the First World War to neutral shipowners not to detain their ship with a particular class of cargo when docked at British ports. It was held that, whilst "[n]o doubt the Government can bind itself through its officers by a commercial contract, and if it does so it must perform it like anybody else or pay damages for the breach",[52] this was not an enforceable contract. It was merely an expression of intent to act in a particular way, and could not be binding, as:

> it is not competent for the Government to fetter its future executive action, which must necessarily be determined by the needs of the community when the question arises. It cannot by contract hamper its freedom of action in matters which concern the welfare of the State.[53]

---

[47] *Commissioners of Crown Lands* v *Page* [1960] 2 QB 274, p.287, per Devlin LJ; *Ansett Transport Industries (Operation) Pty Ltd* v *Commonwealth of Australia* (1977) 139 CLR 54 (High Court of Australia), p.74, per Mason J.
[48] *Ayr Harbour Trustees* v *Oswald* (1883) 8 App Cas 623.   [49] *Id.*, p.634, per Lord Blackburn.
[50] *Id.*, p.640, per Lord Fitzgerald.
[51] *Fairland Overseas Development Co Ltd* v *Secretary for Justice* [2007] 4 HKLRD 949, para.66, per Recorder Gerard McCoy SC.
[52] *Rederiaktiebolaget Amphitrite* v *The King* [1921] 3 KB 500, p.503, per Rowlatt J.
[53] *Id.* See also *Board of Trade* v *Temperley Steam Shipping Co Ltd* (1927) 27 Ll L Rep 230.

Government does not need statutory authority to enter into contracts, but it must enter and make its contracts lawfully.[54] The following statement was made in the Court of First Instance of the legal position in Hong Kong:

> The Government is bound by constitutional law not to enter a contract which is incompatible with the future exercise of public law powers. Such a contract would impermissibly constrain or fetter valid public law decision-making. It would bind now for the future: so that it amounted to an unlawful predetermination of the outcome, in relation to factors that must be genuinely evaluated at the very time whenever such a decision must properly be made. The Government official in law would have wrongly abdicated his statutory duties by a prior agreement. A contractual provision that divests the Government official from exercising a public law discretion in the future, regardless of the circumstances, is incompatible with genuine commitment to proper statutory purpose and is therefore void. The Government official would have wrongly and unwittingly sacrificed the public interest, as the contract would sanction a breach of the irrefragable duty to always exercise a power or discretion in accordance with the law.[55]

It was continued that:

> The pre-eminent responsibility of the Government is to improve the common weal: to exercise power for the public good. The exercise of Government power of the type which requires a continuous reappraisal of the circumstances, cannot be stultified by a cloying contract as to its fixed future use. It would unconstitutionally surrender the power of the relevant Government official to the vicissitudes of a fortuneteller. It would subvert public law power.[56]

A middle ground must therefore be struck between prohibiting public bodies from entering into contracts, and allowing public bodies to freely enter into contracts without condition or limitation. The compatibility of statutory powers and contractual objectives is key for determining the legal validity of contractual obligations into which public bodies purport to enter:[57] in other words, the determination of whether a contractual restriction placed upon a public body is consistent with its statutory powers. It should be noted that the threshold is somewhat higher than a test of mere inconsistency; it is agreements that have a "more fundamental disabling effect" than inconsistency that are *ultra vires*.[58]

---

[54] *Fairland Overseas Development Co Ltd v Secretary for Justice* [2007] 4 HKLRD 949, paras.44–46. It was explained (at para.44) that the Government is, by the Basic Law, "a special juridical person possessed therefore with both prerogative and common law powers apart from any statutory powers that may be conferred".
[55] *Id.*, para.47, per Recorder Gerard McCoy SC.
[56] *Id.*, para.75, per Recorder Gerard McCoy SC.   [57] See *id.*, paras.60–79.
[58] S. H. Bailey, *Cases, Materials and Commentary on Administrative Law* (4th edn) (Sweet and Maxwell, 2005), p.496.

Accordingly, the House of Lords distinguished *Ayr Harbour Trustees* in the case of *Birkdale District Electric Supply Co Ltd* v *Corporation of Southport*.[59] It was said that the Ayr Harbour Trustees had purported to "sterilize" part of their acquisition of the land,[60] and in so doing "renounced a part of their statutory birthright".[61] In *Birkdale*, a statutory electricity company had agreed with a local authority not to charge higher prices than those charged in the adjoining borough. When the company began charging higher prices than those in the adjoining borough, the local authority tried to restrain the breach of contract. The electricity company argued that the contract was *ultra vires* of its statutory powers, in effect to escape its contractual obligations in this regard. However, the House of Lords held that the contract was compatible with the company's statutory powers, which had a statutory right to sell electricity provision and should be able to conclude contracts in execution of those statutory powers. The contractual provisions "suggest rather an enforcement of the company's powers than a denudation of them".[62]

A similar approach was taken by the High Court of New Zealand in a case in which the New Zealand Wool Board had contracted for several years for the entirety of its produce to be exported by a particular shipping company. This was found to be compatible with the relevant statutory powers, and to be a permissible exercise of discretion, rather than a fetter on discretion.[63] By contrast, a government minister purporting to bind himself by contract as to how he would later use statutory powers would constitute unlawful fettering, incompatible with the nature of statutory discretion. The statutory powers must be exercised at the time, and in the manner, prescribed by statute; otherwise anticipatory contractual obligations on the future exercise of statutory powers would be incompatible with the statute itself.[64] Contractual obligations of this nature have been described as contrary to public policy.[65]

These issues had not previously arisen in a Hong Kong case concerning a government contract[66] until *Fairland Overseas Development Co Ltd* v *Secretary for Justice*.[67] The applicant owned a private road connecting a residential development with Castle Peak Road, a major public road in the western New Territories. The Government proposed to resume part of the private road to construct a drainage channel and ancillary roads. The applicant objected to the proposal, primarily due to a concern that there would be a significant increase in traffic on the private road, particularly of container

---

[59] *Birkdale District Electric Supply Co Ltd* v *Corporation of Southport* [1926] AC 355, p.371.
[60] *Id.*, per Lord Sumner. [61] *Id.*, p.372, per Lord Sumner.
[62] *Id.*, p.363, per Earl of Birkenhead.
[63] *ABC Containerline NV* v *New Zealand Wool Board* [1980] 1 NZLR 372, p.383.
[64] *Cudgen Rutile (No 2) Pty Ltd* v *Chalk* [1975] AC 520 (PC) (Australia).
[65] *City of Vancouver* v *Registrar of Vancouver Land Registration District* [1955] 2 DLR 709 (Court of Appeal of British Columbia), p.713, per Davey JA.
[66] *Fairland Overseas Development Co Ltd* v *Secretary for Justice* [2007] 4 HKLRD 949, para.92.
[67] *Fairland Overseas Development Co Ltd* v *Secretary for Justice* [2007] 4 HKLRD 949.

vehicles. A contract was formed between the applicant and the Government whereby the applicant would withdraw its objection, and the Government would erect traffic signs which would effectively prohibit container vehicles using the road. The Government later decided to postpone the erection of the traffic signs, the power to erect those signs being a statutory power of the Commissioner for Transport. The applicant sued for specific performance of the contract. However, the court held that the contract would unlawfully fetter the discretion of the Commissioner. It would permit a contract to rule out future public interest considerations on the erection of traffic signs, and the "merits of any other competing future decision were already eliminated".[68] As Recorder Gerard McCoy SC concluded:

> The regulation of traffic is not a commodity that is for sale any more than is road safety. These public interests simply transcend the notion of private enterprise ... For a public law decision maker to abdicate by contract the right to change his mind about the exercise of a public power or duty in the future, no matter what happens, is in constitutional law terms to sell your soul – the transaction of Mephistopheles.[69]

The issue is one of degree. At one end of the scale are contracts which would plainly fetter discretion by committing the body in advance as to how it must exercise discretion in the future, these being unlawful. At the other end of the scale are contracts for the execution of routine commercial transactions which bind the public body but which are not incompatible with its statutory duties. The difficulty lies in where the line is drawn between these extremes. The determination of whether the purported exercise of discretion is *intra* or *ultra vires* has been described as whether the discretion was properly exercised at the time the contract was purportedly made – not whether the contract would impede the due exercise of discretion at some later date.[70] This has been said to accord with the idea that a public body cannot resile from contractual obligations at a later date on the basis that the contract is discovered not to be as commercially advantageous as anticipated.[71]

It is important that – with very limited exceptions where overriding public interest considerations are in play – public bodies are treated, as far as possible, in the same way as any other contracting party. This is consistent with the rule

---

[68] *Id.*, para.94.
[69] *Id.*, para.95, per Recorder Gerard McCoy SC. On the applicant's subsequent claim that the Government had been "permitted to escape from its own error" and that a costs order should therefore be made in favour of the applicant, Recorder Gerard McCoy SC pointed out that the Government had succeeded in the case and properly relied on a plea of *ultra vires* for the unenforceability of the contract. A costs order was therefore made in favour of the Government.
[70] *L'Huillier v State of Victoria* [1996] 2 VR 465 (Court of Appeal of Victoria), pp.479–480, per Callaway JA.
[71] *Fairland Overseas Development Co Ltd v Secretary for Justice* [2007] 4 HKLRD 949, paras.85–88, per Recorder Gerard McCoy SC.

of law. It would be undesirable as a matter of policy to exempt public bodies from the binding nature of contractual commitments just because the view is later taken that the contract (provided it was lawfully concluded) offered poor value. The public interest in permitting public bodies to contract must be balanced with the interests of private persons with whom they contract, and that in itself feeds into the broader public interest. It would be a gross disincentive to contract with a public body if one knew that, should it later be discovered that the contract offered poor value for the taxpayer, or that a better deal could have been had elsewhere, the enforceability of the contract was at risk. Public bodies therefore cannot escape contracts merely on the ground that they were not as commercially beneficial as might have been desired.[72]

There is, however, a fundamental difference between a lawfully concluded contract which is for some reason objectionable, and a so-called contract which was never validly concluded in the first place because the public body had no capacity to act beyond its powers, including because its conclusion of such a contract would have constituted unlawful fettering of discretion. A "contract" of this nature:

> exists in fact but not in law. It is legal nullity. The purported contract which is in truth not a contract does not confer any legal rights on either party. Neither party can sue upon it. This conclusion gives rise to no conflict between public law and private law principles. The role of public law is to answer the question: what is the capacity of the [public body] to contract? The role of private law is to answer the question: when one of the parties to a supposed contract lacks contractual capacity, does the supposed contract give rise to legal obligations? ... Any defence raised by the defendant must be one which is recognised by private law. Lack of capacity to contract is a defence recognised by private law.[73]

Though Government entities will generally be bound by the terms of lawfully concluded contracts, as an embodiment of the state it retains a narrow power to escape contractual liability where overriding public interest considerations are in play. This has been termed the executive necessity doctrine, by which the Government retains "a supervening power to be unshackled from threatening contractual obligations", but only in "extreme circumstances".[74] The contract or its enforceability would have to be "contrary to the national interest",[75] such as where national security, public safety or public health would be at risk.

---

[72] *Attorney General* v *Lindegren* (1819) 6 Price 287, pp.303–304; *Ansett Transport Industries (Operations) Pty Ltd* v *Commonwealth of Australia* (1977) 139 CLR 54 (HCA), pp.74–75; *Power Co Ltd* v *Gore District Council* [1997] 1 NZLR 537 (Court of Appeal of New Zealand).
[73] *Crédit Suisse* v *Allerdale Borough Council* [1997] QB 306, p.350, per Hobhouse LJ.
[74] *Fairland Overseas Development Co Ltd* v *Secretary for Justice* [2007] 4 HKLRD 949, para.55, per Recorder Gerard McCoy SC.
[75] Philip A. Joseph, *Constitutional and Administrative Law in New Zealand* (4th edn) (Brookers, 2014), p.969, which added that the contract may be "unconscionable".

It remains to note that some of the discussion in the case law has referred to the Government purporting to fetter discretion by contract, rather than public bodies more broadly defined. The issues are not entirely the same, particularly as they relate to the source of the body's powers. For example, government departments might act on the basis of prerogative powers, whereas non-governmental public bodies will tend to be creatures of statute. The underlying rule against fettering nevertheless applies to both, and a decision maker can be held to unlawfully fetter its discretion by contract whether it be a department of central government or a non-governmental public body which is susceptible to judicial review.

16

Error of Fact and Error of Law

A decision maker may commit an error of fact or error of law when purporting to exercise discretion. There are particular complexities in this area of judicial review. On the one hand, one of the core principles of judicial review is that a decision maker must not exceed his or her jurisdiction. Should the decision maker err in fact or err in law and in doing so exceed the boundaries of his or her jurisdiction, the decision maker acts ultra vires and his or her decision is liable to be struck down by the courts. However, it must be determined whether and when an error of fact or error of law takes the decision maker beyond his or her jurisdiction, and to what extent errors of fact and errors of law can be committed in a way that does not take the decision maker in excess of jurisdiction but which nevertheless fall to be judicially reviewed. Indeed, so-called non-jurisdictional errors can also lead to the decision being struck down.

With such difficulties, there is a regrettable but not surprising lack of clarity in the case law. The difficulties are exacerbated by the fact that both errors of fact and errors of law are sometimes characterised as breach of other grounds of review.[1] In addition, the courts in Hong Kong have been inconsistent in their treatment of the distinction between jurisdictional and non-jurisdictional errors of law, including sympathising with an alternative line of authority stemming from the Privy Council on appeal from the Federal Court of Malaysia.

Error of Fact

Not all errors of fact are unlawful, and it has been said that the court's supervisory jurisdiction has a limited role in relation to findings of fact.[2]

---

[1] For example, it was held in *MDB v Betty Kwan* [2014] HKEC 497 that what were essentially errors of fact, failure to take into account relevant considerations or failure to provide adequate reasons for the decision amounted to error of law. Whilst there will often be overlap between grounds of review, error of law would be best understood in a narrower, more technical sense, to improve the coherence and consistency of application of the ground. It is not helpful to describe violation of other grounds as giving rise to error of law, unless they aggregate to error of law in a particular and distinct way.

[2] *Lee Yee Shing Jacky v Inland Revenue Board of Review* [2011] HKEC 261, para.76.

Nevertheless, the factual basis of a decision has been described as "fundamental".[3] There appear to be two broad situations in which an error of fact will be unlawful: first, if the decision maker has committed a jurisdictional error of fact, in other words a factual error which carries the decision maker beyond his or her jurisdiction; second, if the decision maker has committed a non-jurisdictional error of fact in certain circumstances, such as a decision based on evidence that is non-existent or not reasonably capable of supporting the decision, or where the "fact" on which the decision is based is wrong, misunderstood or ignores the factual reality of the situation.

Jurisdictional Error of Fact

Some errors of fact will not affect the jurisdictional basis of a decision-making power. For example, a licensing body might misspell the name of an applicant for a licence and reject the application. This is an error of fact as to the name of the applicant, but it is unlikely to taint the jurisdiction of the decision maker because it has still exercised discretion in a manner consistent with its legal powers. If the licensing body receives another application in which no such error is made, but in which the body reaches certain conclusions on, for example, the health and safety credentials of the applicant and the commercial viability of the application (assuming that these are relevant considerations), these questions do not affect the central jurisdiction of the licensing body; they merely guide the exercise of its discretion. Facts of this kind may be considered non-jurisdictional: even if they are "wrong", they do not take the decision maker beyond his or her jurisdiction, and judicial review would under this head be unlikely to succeed.

Assume, by contrast, that an air transport licensing body has the statutory power to impose conditions only on airlines operating scheduled passenger services. The body purports to impose conditions on an airline that operates only cargo services, in the mistaken belief that it operates scheduled passenger services. The licensing body's error of fact as to the nature of the airline's business has taken the body outside its jurisdiction, because it does not have the power to impose conditions on airlines operating only cargo services. For this reason its error of fact may be described as jurisdictional: the error of fact goes to jurisdiction. In this situation the airline may apply for judicial review on the basis that a jurisdictional error of fact has been committed which makes the purported imposition of conditions *ultra vires*. It must be for the court – not the decision maker – to rule conclusively on jurisdictional facts; otherwise the decision maker "could by its own error give itself powers which were never conferred upon it by Parliament".[4] The decision maker is confined by his or

---

[3] *Sabinano II Marcel R v Municipal Services Appeal Board* [2014] HKEC 370, para.26, per Zervos J.
[4] Wade and Forsyth, *Administrative Law* (11th edn), p.208.

her jurisdiction, and cannot rule definitively on the extent of his or her own jurisdiction which is a matter of law for the court. Where an error of fact is committed which takes the body outside its jurisdiction – a so-called jurisdictional error of fact – the courts can intervene on the basis that the decision maker is in excess of jurisdiction.

This principle seems fairly straightforward, but one is not always faced with such straightforward facts. To continue the above example, it would not usually be difficult to establish whether an airline does or does not operate scheduled passenger services. Either it does or it does not.[5] However, the existence or state of a fact is not always objectively and incontrovertibly verifiable. Absent some statutory or regulatory provision to the contrary, it might be difficult to establish whether an airline is a low cost carrier, and this might be relevant if, for example, the licensing body is able to subject low cost carriers to different treatment from other carriers. The House of Lords pointed out that whether the statutory requirement that a particular area constituted a "substantial part of the United Kingdom" was open to interpretation and different decision makers might validly reach different conclusions on whether a given area did or did not comprise a substantial part of the United Kingdom.[6] This is not to say that the evaluation of whether an area did comprise such a substantial part is immune from review. Assume that a similar statute referred to an area comprising a "substantial part of the Hong Kong SAR". If the relevant area comprised Kowloon and the New Territories, this comprises a substantial part of the Hong Kong SAR in terms of territory and population. If, however, the relevant area comprised only the island of Tung Ping Chau, this is unlikely to be capable of being defined as a substantial part of the Hong Kong SAR so that a decision to classify it as such would likely be struck down as a material error of fact or *Wednesbury* unreasonable. Less clear, however, is if the relevant area comprised, for example, the island of Lantau. This is the largest island in Hong Kong and makes up a reasonable proportion of the territory of Hong Kong, but is sparsely populated. Decision makers may reasonably reach different conclusions on whether Lantau comprises a substantial part of the Hong Kong SAR.

Another example from England and Wales saw the Queen's Bench Division considering the statutory categorisation "held for purposes other than those of journalism, art or literature". The statute did not define "journalism", "art" or "literature", and the view was taken that the meaning of these terms was not one of hard-edged jurisdictional fact. It was therefore open to the relevant decision maker to exercise his judgment on whether a case did or did not fall

---

[5] There are of course issues of detail which might arise, but legally there are only two possibilities: the airline does operate scheduled passenger services, or the airline does not operate scheduled passenger services.
[6] *R v Monopolies and Mergers Commission, ex parte South Yorkshire Transport Ltd* [1993] 1 WLR 23 (HL).

within the meaning of those terms, providing that he did so rationally.[7] The courts will nevertheless assess the legality, including the rationality, of such a decision within the relevant statutory context.

Non-Jurisdictional Error of Fact

It was stated in a Hong Kong case at the end of the 1970s that no case had been cited to the court to suggest that certiorari would issue against an administrative tribunal on the ground of error of fact where the fact decided did not directly involve the question of the tribunal's own jurisdiction.[8] However, error of fact can be committed in a way which does not take the decision maker beyond its jurisdiction, but which nevertheless taints the validity of the decision.

Lord Wilberforce stated that:

> If a judgment requires, before it can be made, the existence of some facts, then, although the evaluation of those facts is for the Secretary of State alone, the court must inquire whether those facts exist, and have been taken into account, whether the judgment has been made upon a proper self-direction as to those facts, whether the judgment has not been made upon other facts which ought not to have been taken into account. If these requirements are not met, then the exercise of judgment, however bona fide it may be, becomes capable of challenge . . .[9]

A lack of evidence was traditionally not considered a matter of jurisdiction.[10] However, it is now the case that the courts are prepared to review non-jurisdictional errors of fact where the evidence on which they are based is non-existent or not reasonably capable of supporting the decision. It was said to be well established in public law that where there was no evidence to support the material finding of facts relevant to the impugned decision, the court is entitled to quash the decision.[11] The sufficiency and rationality of evidence for material findings of fact is open to review by the courts.[12]

A slightly different scenario from one in which there is no evidence or there is evidence which is not reasonably capable of supporting the decision, is where the evidential basis of the decision is wrong, misunderstood or has been ignored. The Court of Appeal stated that if the court can interfere when an

---

[7] *British Broadcasting Corporation v Sugar* [2007] 1 WLR 2583. Though see *Sugar v British Broadcasting Corporation* [2012] UKSC 4, para.80.
[8] *In an Application by Tse Cho for Orders of Certiorari and Prohibition* [1979] HKLR 339, p.343.
[9] *Secretary of State for Education and Science v Tameside Metropolitan Borough Council* [1977] AC 1014 (HL), p.1047, per Lord Wilberforce.
[10] *R v Nat Bell Liquors Ltd* [1922] 2 AC 128 (PC) (Canada), pp.151–152 (regarded as "good law" in *In an Application by Tse Cho for Orders of Certiorari and Prohibition* [1979] HKLR 339, p.343); *R v Ludlow* [1947] KB 634; *R v Governor of Brixton Prison, ex parte Armah* [1968] AC 192, p.234; *R v Governor of Pentonville Prison, ex parte Sotiriadis* [1975] AC 1, p.30.
[11] *Wan Yung Sang v Housing Authority* [2011] HKEC 907, para.43.
[12] *Lee Yee Shing Jacky v Inland Revenue Board of Review* [2011] HKEC 261, para.95.

inferior tribunal has not taken into account some matter which it should have done, the court must be able to interfere when the inferior tribunal has got the matter wrong. It could only do so, however, when the matter was "plainly wrong" or "established unassailably to be erroneous", and could not see the courts evaluating facts that were properly within the exclusive jurisdiction of the tribunal.[13]

An example of a case falling under this heading is *Smart Gain Investment Ltd v Town Planning Board*.[14] The case related to an Outline Zoning Plan (OZP) for the Clear Water Bay peninsula. The applicant objected to the Town Planning Board about the OZP, which dismissed the objection noting that the "objection sites comprise wooded slopes and river valley". It added that "[t]he 'Conservation Area' zoning of the objection sites is appropriate to protect the natural landscape, the topographical features and the sensitive natural system in the area". In fact, the objection sites did not comprise wooded slopes and river valley. The Town Planning Board had erred in fact. It should be noted that it did not err in a way that fundamentally affected its jurisdiction; in other words, it still had jurisdiction over the sites in question. Instead, the evidential basis for the Board's decision was simply incorrect: its understanding of the landscape and features of the objection sites was verifiably wrong. Cheung J stated that:

> [G]iven that a mistake of fact giving rise to unfairness is a valid ground of challenge, fresh evidence must be admissible in appropriate circumstances to enable the aggrieved party to demonstrate to the court that the tribunal below has made a mistake on the facts ... [O]nce the further evidence is admitted, it is quite plain that a material mistake of fact has been made ... [and gives] rise to objective fairness.[15]

Another example of reliance on factually incorrect evidence was where the Liquor Licensing Board (LLB) made errors of fact which were inherited by the Municipal Services Appeals Board (MSAB) in a statutory appeal. Additional conditions had been imposed by the LLB in the context of noise complaints relating to the iCON bar on Wyndham Street, Central. Three errors of fact were committed by the LLB: first, it was incorrect that most of the bars in the neighbourhood were required to keep their doors and windows closed after 11 PM or earlier; second, it was incorrect that other licensed premises free from additional licensing conditions ceased operation by 11 PM; and third, it was incorrect that there was a common wall shared by the building in which iCON bar was located and that of the resident objectors. The errors of fact, inherited by the MSAB, seriously flawed its decision, playing a material part in

---

[13] *Nguyen Ho v Director of Immigration* [1991] 1 HKLR 576 (CA), p.583.
[14] *Smart Gain Investment Ltd v Town Planning Board* [2007] HKEC 1964.
[15] *Id.*, paras.94 and 98, per Cheung J. See also *R (on the application of Haile) v Immigration Appeal Tribunal* [2001] EWCA Civ 663.

its reasoning and giving rise to objective unfairness.[16] Again, none of these errors of fact was jurisdictional.

In *Chan Chi Shing* v *Symon Wong*, the Revising Officer decided that certain persons were indigenous inhabitants of the village of Luk Keng Chan Uk, off Starling Inlet in the Northern New Territories, in the context of indigenous inhabitant representative elections. The Revising Officer was shown to have committed a material error of fact on the basis of genealogical evidence. Au J described the material error of fact as "unreasonable or irrational".[17] The irrationality label was also given to a material error of fact in a case on building regulations. The Appeal Tribunal (Buildings) erred on the usable floor area of a building, and erred in concluding that the building was not a single staircase building. Though these errors of fact were non-jurisdictional, the court quashed the determination of the Tribunal.[18]

The factual error should be material to the decision made. Previously, it seemed to be a requirement that the error must be material and decisive before judicial review would lie for error of fact:

> If it is demonstrated that a decision maker made a material and decisive error of fact, which although not actually known to him or available in his department but was then easily available, generally known and unquestionably true, so that by inference it must be assumed to have been within the knowledge of the department, then if the other conditions are satisfied, this may be sufficient to show that the decision was flawed. But much depends upon the facts of the case. I would just add this that usually a material or decisive fact will be one which is a condition precedent to jurisdiction; or one which is the only or the primary basis for the decision, or a fact which the tribunal had to take into account in order to reach its decision.[19]

Materiality and decisiveness are distinguishable, however, and it now seems unnecessary to prove to the court that a different decision would have been reached had the correct facts formed the basis of the decision.[20] In *Smart Gain Investment Ltd* v *Town Planning Board* the relevant finding of fact was material because it constituted a relevant consideration for the decision

---

[16] *Sabinano II Marcel R* v *Municipal Services Appeal Board* [2014] HKEC 370, paras.25–33.
[17] *Chan Chi Shing* v *Symon Wong* [2011] HKEC 591, para.76.
[18] *Building Authority* v *Appeal Tribunal (Buildings)* [2005] HKEC 1963, para.33, per C Chu J. The irrationality/perversity label in relation to error was seen again in *Wan Yung Sang* v *Housing Authority* [2011] HKEC 907, para.43.
[19] *The Queen* v *Director of Immigration, ex parte Do Giau* [1992] 1 HKLR 287, p.302, per Mortimer J; and see *Nguyen Ho* v *Director of Immigration* [1991] 1 HKLR 576 (CA), p.583.
[20] *E* v *Secretary of State for the Home Department* [2004] QB 1044, para.66; *Smart Gain Investment Ltd* v *Town Planning Board* [2007] HKEC 1964, paras.98–99. Cf *The Queen* v *Director of Immigration, ex parte Do Giau* [1992] 1 HKLR 287, pp.301–302. Hartmann J had described it as settled law that a material error of fact may vitiate the decision if there is a real likelihood that, if the truth had been known, a different decision would or might have been reached – *Christian Bulao Palmis* v *Director of Immigration* [2003] HKEC 230, para.61.

maker: how much weight should be placed on that consideration was a matter of planning judgment for the Board, not the courts. The physical characteristics of the objection sites were nevertheless material factors which had to be taken into consideration.[21] The Appeal Tribunal (Buildings) was mistaken as to the usable floor area of a building and staircase provision therein, and this was material to its determination on the applicability of a code of practice on the means of escape from fire.[22] The errors of fact inherited by the MSAB from the LLB in relation to iCON bar played a material part in the MSAB's reasoning, for which the applicant was not responsible.[23]

The factual error may give rise to unfairness. It is not clear whether the error must give rise to unfairness for breach of the ground of review to be established,[24] but if unfairness does follow from the factual error, the applicant's challenge may be strengthened. Carnwath LJ stated in the Court of Appeal of England and Wales that:

> In our view, the time has now come to accept that a mistake of fact giving rise to unfairness is a separate head of challenge in an appeal on a point of law, at least in those statutory contexts where the parties share an interest in co-operating to achieve the correct result. Asylum law is undoubtedly such an area. Without seeking to lay down a precise code, the ordinary requirements for a finding of unfairness are apparent from the above analysis of the *Criminal Injuries Compensation Board* case. First, there must have been a mistake as to an existing fact, including a mistake as to the availability of evidence on a particular matter. Secondly, the fact or evidence must have been "established", in the sense that it was uncontentious and objectively verifiable. Thirdly, the appellant (or his advisers) must not have been responsible for the mistake. Fourthly, the mistake must have played a material (not necessarily decisive) part in the tribunal's reasoning.[25]

It is unclear why unfairness should comprise part of this test. The courts state that there is no such thing as technical breach of natural justice,[26] and unfairness would seem unnecessary to ground an application for review of a jurisdictional error of fact, but error of fact is in any event capable of standing on its own two feet as a ground of review. If the factual error is material, this should presumably be sufficient to render the decision subject to review without additionally having to show that the error has given rise to unfairness. It would seem to go to the rationality of the decision rather than procedural

---

[21] *Smart Gain Investment Ltd* v *Town Planning Board* [2007] HKEC 1964, para.82.
[22] *Building Authority* v *Appeal Tribunal (Buildings)* [2005] HKEC 1963.
[23] *Sabinano II Marcel R* v *Municipal Services Appeal Board* [2014] HKEC 370, paras.25–33.
[24] See *Smart Gain Investment Ltd* v *Town Planning Board* [2007] HKEC 1964, para.93.
[25] *E* v *Secretary of State for the Home Department* [2004] QB 1044, para.66, per Carnwath LJ; and see *R* v *Criminal Injuries Compensation Board, ex parte A* [1999] 2 AC 330 (HL).
[26] See pp.247–248.

fairness. It is, in addition, more difficult to frame a consistent judicial test on fairness than one of materiality; whereas the former is heavily context-dependent, the latter appears capable of operating more mechanically, and therefore potentially more predictably.

Admission of Fresh Evidence

In order to assess whether the evidential basis of the decision is not reasonably capable of supporting the decision, or is wrong, misunderstood or has been ignored, it may be necessary to admit fresh evidence in judicial review. The principles set out by the Court of Appeal of England and Wales[27] were accepted by the Court of Appeal in Hong Kong:[28]

> They are (1) that the court can receive evidence to show what material was before the minister or inferior tribunal . . .; (2) where the jurisdiction of the minister or inferior tribunal depends on a question of fact or where the question is whether essential procedural requirements were observed, the court may receive and consider additional evidence to determine the jurisdictional fact or procedural error . . .; and (3) where the proceedings are tainted by misconduct on the part of the minister or member of the inferior tribunal or the parties before it. Examples of such misconduct are bias by the decision making body, or fraud or perjury by a party. In each case fresh evidence is admissible to prove the particular misconduct alleged . . .

This primarily goes to jurisdictional errors of fact: fresh evidence may be admitted to show that the body acted in excess of jurisdiction. It would not have been permissible, for example, to admit fresh evidence to demonstrate *Wednesbury* unreasonableness, which could only be judged with regard to what was known to the decision maker at the time.[29] However, the courts appear to have moved to a more liberal position on the admission of fresh evidence to demonstrate error of fact. The Court of First Instance allowed fresh evidence to be admitted to show that a material error of fact had been committed by the Town Planning Board giving rise to unfairness, even though the error was non-jurisdictional.[30] Fresh evidence appears also to have been admitted to show that non-jurisdictional errors of fact were committed by the LLB and MSAB.[31]

---

[27] *R v Secretary of State for the Environment, ex parte Powis* [1981] 1 WLR 584, p.595.
[28] *Re Lo Wing-Tong* [1990] 1 HKLR 325 (CA).
[29] *Nguyen Ho v Director of Immigration* [1991] 1 HKLR 576 (CA), pp.581–582; and see *Secretary of State for Education and Science v Tameside Metropolitan Borough Council* [1977] AC 1014 (HL), p.1076.
[30] *Smart Gain Investment Ltd v Town Planning Board* [2007] HKEC 1964, paras.94–98.
[31] *Sabinano II Marcel R v Municipal Services Appeal Board* [2014] HKEC 370, paras.25–33.

Error of Law

Just as a decision maker can make an error of fact when exercising their discretion, so can they make an error of law. For example, where the Town Planning Board misinterpreted the Protection of the Harbour Ordinance (cap.531) when submitting to the Chief Executive-in-Council a land reclamation plan for part of Victoria Harbour, it erred in law and its decisions fell to be quashed.[32] Decisions of the Privacy Commissioner for Personal Data and the Administrative Appeals Board which were based on an incorrect construction of one of the Data Protection Principles were quashed.[33]

The common law on errors of law changed in England and Wales with the *Anisminic* line of jurisprudence. After *Anisminic*, all errors of law were deemed to take a decision maker beyond their jurisdiction; in other words, all errors of law are jurisdictional and render the resulting decision *ultra vires*. Anisminic Ltd applied for compensation from the Foreign Compensation Commission, which was tasked with administering funds under the Egyptian Compensation Fund. The application for compensation was refused. Anisminic sought declarations that the determination of the Commission was a nullity on the basis that it misconstrued the Order-in-Council which detailed eligibility for compensation.[34] It was held by a majority in the House of Lords that the Commission had essentially asked itself the wrong question, imposing a requirement which it was not within its jurisdiction to impose, and accordingly its decision was a nullity. The Commission had therefore committed an error of law which took it beyond its jurisdiction.[35]

Subsequent interpretation of the case was that it practically obliterated the previous distinction between errors of law within jurisdiction and errors of law without jurisdiction. *Anisminic* was applied in a case in which a judge in the county court had misconstrued a provision in the Housing Act 1974 and accordingly committed an error of law capable of being struck down.[36] Lord Denning MR described the distinction between jurisdictional and non-jurisdictional errors as "very fine... [s]o fine indeed that it is rapidly being eroded".[37] The distinction, he suggested, should now be discarded:

> The High Court has, and should have, jurisdiction to control the proceedings of inferior courts and tribunals by way of judicial review. When they go wrong in law, the High Court should have power to put them right. Not only in the instant case to do justice to the complainant. But also so as to secure that all courts and tribunals, when faced with the same point of law, should

---

[32] *Town Planning Board* v *Society for the Protection of the Harbour Ltd* (2004) 7 HKCFAR 1.
[33] *Cathay Pacific Airways Ltd* v *Administrative Appeals Board* [2008] 5 HKLRD 539.
[34] Foreign Compensation (Egypt) (Determination and Registration of Claims) Order 1962.
[35] *Anisminic Ltd* v *Foreign Compensation Commission* [1969] 2 AC 147 (HL).
[36] *Pearlman* v *Keepers and Governors of Harrow School* [1979] QB 56.
[37] *Id.*, p.69, per Lord Denning MR.

decide it in the same way. It is intolerable that a citizen's rights in point of law should depend on which judge tries his case, or in which court it is heard. The way to get things right is to hold thus: no court or tribunal has any jurisdiction to make an error of law on which the decision of the case depends. If it makes such an error, it goes outside its jurisdiction and certiorari will lie to correct it.[38]

Whilst there was a dissenting opinion on the implications of *Anisminic*,[39] Lord Denning MR's approach was consolidated in future cases, with Lord Diplock describing the distinction between errors of law going to jurisdiction and errors of law that did not "for practical purposes abolished" in a "breakthrough made by *Anisminic*",[40] and an "esoteric distinction" from which English public law had been "liberated".[41] Lord Irvine of Lairg LC later described *Anisminic* as having "made obsolete the historic distinction between errors of law on the face of the record and other errors of law", having done so by "extending the doctrine of ultra vires, so that any misdirection in law would render the relevant decisions ultra vires and a nullity".[42] It "established that both species of error render an executive act ultra vires, unlawful and a nullity", and that "there was a single category of errors of law, all of which rendered a decision *ultra vires*".[43]

The Hong Kong courts have treated the distinction between jurisdictional and non-jurisdictional errors of law inconsistently in the post-*Anisminic* period. It was held that the Licensing Authority had acted unlawfully by presuming guilt from circumstances amounting only to a *prima facie* case of breach of the relevant regulations or of licence conditions. However, the High Court avoided the issue of whether an error of law amounted to excess of jurisdiction, and preferred to ask whether the error was of such a fundamental character as to render the Authority's decision a nullity, rather than view this through a jurisdictional lens.[44] The High Court later reviewed the English

---

[38] *Id.*, p.70, per Lord Denning MR.
[39] *Id.*, pp.74–76, per Geoffrey Lane LJ; this view was preferred by the Privy Council on appeal from the Federal Court of Malaysia – *South East Asia Fire Bricks Sdn Bhd* v *Non-Metallic Mineral Products Manufacturing Employees Union* [1981] AC 363 (PC) (Malaysia).
[40] *Re Racal Communications Ltd* [1981] AC 374 (HL), p.383.
[41] *O'Reilly* v *Mackman* [1983] 2 AC 237 (HL), p.278. It was added that if a tribunal "mistook the law applicable to the facts as it had found them, it must have asked itself the wrong question, i.e. one in which it was not empowered to inquire and so had no jurisdiction to determine. Its purported 'determination', not being a 'determination' within the meaning of the empowering legislation, was accordingly a nullity".
[42] *Boddington* v *British Transport Police* [1999] 2 AC 143 (HL), p.154. See also *R* v *Hull University Visitor, ex parte Page* [1993] AC 682 (HL), p.701, in which Lord Browne-Wilkinson had made a similar statement.
[43] *R (on the application of Lumba)* v *Secretary of State for the Home Department* [2011] UKSC 12, para.66, per Lord Dyson.
[44] *In an Application by Tse Cho for Orders of Certiorari and Prohibition* [1979] HKLR 339, p.344. Whilst Leonard J characterised the Authority as having committed an error of law (p.361), McMullin J characterised the Authority as having breached the rules of natural justice (p.353).

authorities but still referred to jurisdictional errors,[45] and it did not address the issue head on when it held that *Anisminic*-type arguments could be mounted in an election petition, but not in judicial review, due to the operation of an ouster clause and the provision of alternative machinery for challenge.[46] However, the Court of Appeal expressly sided with the *South East Asia Fire Bricks* line of authority rather than that represented by *Re Racal* and other cases:

> We are bound by Privy Council authority to find that error of law on the face of the record does not necessarily import excess of jurisdiction on the part of the University albeit there is strong and almost contemporaneous House of Lords persuasive authority to the contrary. South East Asia Fire Bricks Sdn. Bhd. v. Non-Metallic Mineral Products Manufacturing Employees Union [1981] AC 363; In re Racal Communications Ltd. [1981] AC 374 at p.383 *per* Lord Diplock. The error in the present instance is not one which goes to jurisdiction and accordingly the decision of the Council remains *intra vires* and effective until and unless quashed ...[47]

It was, in other words, a non-jurisdictional error of law. A seemingly less equivocal statement on the applicability of *Anisminic* in Hong Kong on this point of law was seen in *Kwan Shung King* v *Housing Appeal Tribunal*, where Yeung J stated that:

> The principle that the High Court has jurisdiction to review a decision of an administrative tribunal on a question of law is so well established, particularly in *Anisminic Ltd* v *Foreign Compensation Commission (No 2)* [1969] 2 AC 147 when it was held that as respects administrative tribunals and authorities, the old distinction between errors of law that went to jurisdiction and errors of law that did not, was for practical purposes abolished. Any error

---

In a similar period, Huggins J did not doubt the correctness of the principle articulated by Lord Reid in *Anisminic*, but did not elaborate on the point – *Ng Chun-Kwan* v *Commissioner of Inland Revenue* [1976] HKCU 11.

[45] *Chan Yik Tung* v *Hong Kong Housing Authority* [1989] 2 HKC 394. Whilst *The Queen* v *Director of Immigration, ex parte Do Giau* [1992] 1 HKLR 287 was primarily concerned with error of fact rather than error of law, in the context of the court's discussion of *Anisminic* and *South East Asia Fire Bricks*, a jurisdictional view was taken of the decision maker's powers (see, for example, p.319).

[46] *Re Lau San-Ching* [1995] 2 HKLR 14. See also pp.95–97. Consider also *Re Chong Bing Keung (No 2)* [2000] 2 HKLRD 571 (CA).

[47] *Jill Spruce* v *The University of Hong Kong* [1991] 2 HKLR 444 (CA), p.452. The Privy Council, on appeal, disagreed that there had been an error of law, but did not disapprove of the Court of Appeal's view on jurisdictional and non-jurisdictional errors of law – *Jill Spruce* v *The University of Hong Kong* [1993] 2 HKLR 65 (PC). *South East Asia Fire Bricks* was also applied in the High Court in *Re Chang Wing Tai* [1987] HKCU 90; and was cited in support of review of jurisdictional complaints in *Attorney General* v *Chino Industries (In Voluntary Liquidation)* [1997] HKLRD 833, p.839. The Court of Appeal in *Spruce* was incorrect to regard itself as bound by a Privy Council decision on appeal from a jurisdiction other than Hong Kong – see *Solicitor (24/07)* v *Law Society of Hong Kong* (2008) 11 HKCFAR 117, paras.6–14.

of law that could be shown to have been made by them in the course of reaching their decision on matters of fact or of administrative policy would result in their having asked themselves the wrong question with the result that the decision they reached would be a nullity.[48]

However, the same court:

> accept[ed] that in circumstances where the legislation clearly confers upon a court the exclusive jurisdiction to deal with a question of law and oust the jurisdiction of the High Court to review the decision, then such decision may not be amenable to judicial review unless the decision exceeds the jurisdiction of the court.[49]

This readmits the distinction between jurisdictional and non-jurisdictional errors of law. Nevertheless, a contemporaneous decision noted that there "used to be" a distinction between jurisdictional and non-jurisdictional errors of law, but that such distinction had become "blur[red]" as the principles developed in the case law.[50] Hartmann J held in *Gurung Bhakta Bahadur v Director of Immigration* that an ouster clause did not to exclude the jurisdiction of the court to review a nullity. Though it was "now settled law" in Hong Kong that *Anisminic* principles applied, and it was "clear that [*Anisminic*] remains good law", the distinction between jurisdictional and non-jurisdictional errors again seems to have been admitted, as the court applied the principles set out in *South East Asia Fire Bricks* and specifically cited Lord Fraser of Tullybelton's passage stating that jurisdictional errors would not be protected by an ouster clause, but that non-jurisdictional errors of law would be so protected.[51] Hartmann J seemed to reaffirm the distinction between jurisdictional and non-jurisdictional errors in stating that an "error of law in reaching an administrative decision may vitiate that decision or it may not",[52]

---

[48] *Kwan Shung King v Housing Appeal Tribunal* [2000] 2 HKLRD 764, p.771.   [49] *Id.*, p.770.

[50] *Thai Muoi v Hong Kong Housing Authority* [2000] HKCU 370, pp.3–4, per Yeung J. *South East Asia Fire Bricks* was purportedly distinguished in the same judgment (at p.6) on the basis that it concerned the decision of a court, rather than the decision of a statutory body or administrative tribunal.

[51] *Gurung Bhakta Bahadur v Director of Immigration* [2001] 3 HKLRD 225, citing *South East Asia Fire Bricks Sdn Bhd v Non-Metallic Mineral Products Manufacturing Employees Union* [1981] AC 363 (PC) (Malaysia), p.370. The difficulty with stating that "*Anisminic* principles" apply in Hong Kong is that there are different interpretations of the import of *Anisminic* on errors of law, and the interpretation that has prevailed in England and Wales is that *Anisminic* practically abolished the distinction between jurisdictional and non-jurisdictional errors of law. As noted, however, this was not the only interpretation of *Anisminic*, and the interpretation that it maintained the distinction was supported in *South East Asia Fire Bricks*, which has been followed in the courts of Hong Kong. The position in *Gurung Bhakta Bahadur* was referenced in *Television Broadcasts Ltd v Communications Authority* [2016] 2 HKLRD 41, para.169, and again raises the possibility of a distinction between jurisdictional and non-jurisdictional errors.

[52] *Society for Protection of the Harbour Ltd v Chief Executive-in-Council (No 2)* [2004] 2 HKLRD 902, para.87.

in a judgment in which the Chief Executive-in-Council was deemed to have jurisdiction to determine whether an error of law committed in the Town Planning Board's preparation of an Outline Zoning Plan so vitiated its integrity that it could no longer stand and had to be remitted to the Board.[53]

Distinction between Error of Fact and Error of Law

The distinction between an error of fact and an error of law is not one that can always be cleanly made. Sometimes it is unclear whether an error is one of fact or law; or both. This would in principle appear to be more problematic in England and Wales than in Hong Kong. In England and Wales, whereas errors of fact can be jurisdictional or non-jurisdictional, all errors of law are jurisdictional. Whether an error is classed as one of fact or law can therefore affect whether it is *intra* or *ultra vires*. In Hong Kong, where the *South East Asia Fire Bricks* line of authority has been followed, it appears that errors of fact and errors of law can both be jurisdictional or non-jurisdictional (or at least the courts have not categorically written off the possibility of a non-jurisdictional error of law). However, to the extent that different rules or principles are applied as between errors of fact and errors of law, the distinction may also be problematic in Hong Kong. For example, the tests of materiality and error giving rise to unfairness are aspects of error of fact, but not error of law. The distinction is also important because, particularly in relation to administrative tribunals, appeals may be permitted on a point of law but not on a point of fact, or vice versa, and so classification as fact or law determines whether appeal could competently lie to an administrative tribunal.

The difficulty of the distinction has been acknowledged by the UK Supreme Court:

[I]t is primarily for the tribunals, not the appellate courts, to develop a consistent approach to [issues of law and fact], bearing in mind that they are peculiarly well fitted to determine them. A pragmatic approach should be

---

[53] The distinction is nevertheless problematic: for example, the Court of Final Appeal stated that if the "meaning of a policy is clear, and if the government has misinterpreted it, the misinterpretation amounts to an error of law. Where the meaning is not clear, or the policy is susceptible of more than one meaning, and the government has adopted a particular meaning, it is for the court to consider whether the adoption of that meaning is such as to be "so aberrant that it cannot be classed as rational" . . . [T]he consequence is that a decision occasioned by a misinterpretation of policy which is either an error of law or is irrational or by a misapplication of policy which is irrational, will be quashed" – *Ng Siu Tung* v *Director of Immigration* (2002) 5 HKCFAR 1, paras.195 and 197. However, misinterpretation of a policy can presumably be a non-jurisdictional error of law as the error does not necessarily carry the body beyond its jurisdiction. It may for example lead to breach of a legitimate expectation that the decision would be taken in accordance with the policy – which need not be jurisdictional – or could be *Wednesbury* unreasonable or irrational (and which might fall into the category of a nullity). Consider also, in the context of error of law, *Shiu Wing Steel Ltd* v *Director of Environmental Protection (No 2)* (2006) 9 HKCFAR 478.

taken to the dividing line between law and fact, so that the expertise of tribunals ... can be used to best effect. An appeal court should not venture too readily into this area by classifying issues as issues of law which are really best left for determination by the specialist appellate tribunals.[54]

As has been pointed out, however, a pragmatic approach to the dividing line between law and fact does not sit squarely with so-called objective limitations on questions of jurisdiction, which are determined by the courts.[55] Furthermore, the issue is confounded by the courts holding that an error of fact can amount to an error of law.[56]

---

[54] *Jones* v *First Tier Tribunal* [2013] UKSC 19, para.16, per Lord Hope of Craighead. Noting that, in England and Wales, all errors of law are jurisdictional.

[55] Wade and Forsyth, *Administrative Law* (11th edn), p.217.

[56] See *In an Application by Tse Cho for Orders of Certiorari and Prohibition* [1979] HKLR 339, pp.342–343; *E* v *Secretary of State for the Home Department* [2004] QB 1044; and *Sabinano II Marcel R* v *Municipal Services Appeal Board* [2014] HKEC 370, para.31. Au J stated that it is "well established in public law that where there is no evidence to support the material finding of facts relevant to the decision under challenge, it amounts to an error of fact and law, or that it renders the decision 'irrational' or 'perverse'" – *Wan Yung Sang* v *Housing Authority* [2011] HKEC 907, para.43.

17

Legitimate Expectations

A public body may conduct itself in a way that gives rise to a legitimate expectation that it will behave in a particular way in the future or that a particular event or state of affairs will occur. The conduct creating the expectation can arise from a representation or from previous conduct. As persons may rely on the expectation, perhaps to their detriment, and more generally be guided by the representations of public bodies, it is important that public bodies are not able to freely change their conduct or position without regard for the ways in which that change might affect persons who had a legitimate expectation of different conduct based on the previous representation or conduct. It was stated by the Privy Council that:

> when a public authority has promised to follow a certain procedure, it is in the interest of good administration that it should act fairly and should implement its promise, so long as implementation does not interfere with its statutory duty.[1]

Legitimate expectations are therefore about judicial control of public bodies which change their conduct or position – departing from a previous representation or conduct – by imposing requirements on how that change can, and cannot, lawfully come about.

From a separation of powers perspective, the courts must tread a careful line between (i) finding a body liable in public law where it has breached a legitimate expectation, and (ii) trespassing on the capacity of the executive to alter its conduct or position, particularly on policy issues. Indeed, there can be legitimate reasons why a public body departs from its previous representation or conduct. Perhaps the body has announced a financial commitment to the expansion of public housing, but later seeks to resile from that commitment on the basis that new economic conditions make the financial commitment untenable. Perhaps a licensing authority has indicated that, if certain conditions are fulfilled, applications to open specified types of retail outlet in a licensing zone will be approved – but later, as several retail outlets of that type

---

[1] *Attorney-General of Hong Kong* v *Ng Yuen Shiu* [1983] 2 AC 629 (PC), p.638.

open in the zone, the body feels that, as a matter of policy and to ensure sufficient diversity of retail outlets in the zone, it should now prioritise applications from retail outlets of a different nature. The economic, social, policy and scientific context may change in a way that gives public bodies legitimate reason to change course – and it might be politically and even legally objectionable were the body not to change course or consider changing course in the context of such changes.

The separation of powers also dictates that courts refrain from ordering public bodies which specific decision to make. This would be tantamount to the court substituting its own decision for the decision about which the applicant is complaining. Accordingly, the court typically adopts a less invasive approach, requiring that public bodies show, prior to or in the course of changing their decision, that they have taken into account as a relevant consideration parties' legitimate expectations arising from the body's previous position. In addition, the body should give reasons for the departure from its previous position. Providing it does those things to the satisfaction of the courts, and meets various other requirements, the body's change of position will be lawful.[2] This is arguably a necessary compromise between holding public bodies (legally) accountable for departing from previous representations, and respecting the limits of the separation of powers.

Legitimate expectations can be procedural or substantive in nature. Procedural expectations are those by which the applicant expects to be treated, as a matter of procedure, in a particular way. For example, an applicant might have the expectation of an oral hearing or being given the opportunity to make representations prior to a decision being made.[3] Substantive expectations, a more recent innovation in the law of Hong Kong,[4] are those by which the applicant expects to receive a particular substantive outcome. For example, an applicant might expect to receive a licence, residence status or social housing entitlement. Both procedural and substantive expectations are protected by the law of Hong Kong, though the courts have set out a number of conditions and requirements on how and when a person can successfully claim breach of a legitimate expectation.

---

[2] *R v London Borough Council of Newham, ex parte Bibi* [2001] EWCA Civ 607.
[3] See, for example, *Attorney-General of Hong Kong* v *Ng Yuen Shiu* [1983] 2 AC 629 (PC); and *Re Sea Dragon Billiard and Snooker Association* [1991] 1 HKLR 711.
[4] Recognised as part of the law in Hong Kong in *Ng Siu Tung* v *Director of Immigration* (2002) 5 HKCFAR 1. See also *R v North and East Devon Health Authority, ex parte Coughlan* [2001] QB 213; and an indication of the earlier view in *Wong Pei Chun* v *Hong Kong Housing Authority* [1996] 2 HKLR 293, p.299, where it was said that the principle of legitimate expectations was reserved for "a procedural as opposed to a legal right which might exist" (per Sears J). In a similar period, Kaplan J described the law on legitimate expectations as "of limited scope" – *Benbecula Ltd* v *Attorney General* [1994] 3 HKC 238.

The Court of Final Appeal set out a multi-stage test for establishing breach of legitimate expectations in *Ng Siu Tung v Director of Immigration*.[5] The case concerned Art. 24(2)(3) of the Basic Law, which conferred permanent residence and the right of abode on persons of Chinese nationality born outside Hong Kong, to permanent residents who were Chinese citizens born in Hong Kong, or who ordinarily resided in Hong Kong for not less than seven years prior to the establishment of the HKSAR. Certain amendments were made to the Immigration Ordinance (cap.115), and a number of Mainland children born to Hong Kong permanent residents challenged the constitutionality of those amendments and claimed permanent resident status. Over five thousand claimants sought legal aid for this purpose, and were told by the Legal Aid Department and the Secretary for Security that they did not have to initiate fresh legal proceedings or join existing proceedings due to two test cases.[6]

The Court of Final Appeal effectively confirmed eligibility to the right of abode in the two test cases. However, on the request of the HKSAR Government, the NPCSC issued an Interpretation which had the effect of reversing those judgments (though not disturbing their finality, under Art. 158 of the Basic Law). On the same day, the HKSAR Government made a public announcement that persons arriving in Hong Kong between 1 July 1997 and 29 January 1999, who had claimed the right of abode, would have their status as permanent residents verified in accordance with *Ng Ka Ling* and *Chan Kam Nga*. The question was whether the HKSAR Government's representations created a legitimate expectation that (i) the five thousand applicants who were refused legal aid or discouraged from applying for legal aid and received specific representations, and (ii) the six hundred thousand people putatively eligible for the right of abode who purported to rely only on general representations, would receive the same treatment as the applicants in *Ng Ka Ling* and *Chan Kam Nga*.

The court followed the reasoning of the Court of Appeal of England and Wales in *R v London Borough Council of Newham, ex parte Bibi*.[7] It stated that, in order for breach of a legitimate expectation to be established, there would first have to be a legitimate expectation arising from a promise or representation,[8] the expectation being that the promise or representation would be honoured and be properly taken into account in the decision-making

---

[5] *Ng Siu Tung v Director of Immigration* (2002) 5 HKCFAR 1. This is often cited as an authority on legitimate expectations in Hong Kong – see, for example, *Chinluck Properties Ltd v Appeal Tribunal (Buildings)* [2013] HKEC 1390, para.29. A legitimate expectation argument could not be mounted against a public body by originating summons – *Polorace Investments Ltd v Director of Lands* [1997] 1 HKC 373 (CA), p.380.
[6] Namely *Ng Ka Ling v Director of Immigration* (1999) 2 HKCFAR 4; and *Chan Kam Nga v Director of Immigration* (1999) 2 HKCFAR 82.
[7] *R v London Borough Council of Newham, ex parte Bibi* [2001] EWCA Civ 607.
[8] Though not every instance of resiling from a promise, even if successfully judicially reviewed, has been classed as breach of a legitimate expectation – see *Wong Pei Chun v Hong Kong Housing Authority* [1996] 2 HKLR 293; and the discussion thereon at pp.152–153.

process so long as to do so falls within the power, statutory or otherwise, of the decision maker. Second, the representation should be made effective unless there are reasons recognised by law for failing to do so. In addition, where the representation is not honoured, fairness requires that reasons should be given as to why. Third, decision makers should make decisions with consideration for parties' legitimate expectations. Finally, if the decision maker fails to do so, the decision will be vitiated by reason of failure to take into account a relevant consideration. It would only be in an exceptional case that the court would be satisfied that the failure to take into account a relevant consideration did not affect the decision. If the court was satisfied that the outcome would not have been different had the relevant consideration been taken into account, it will not quash the decision.[9]

This is an important statement of the law, but it does not provide the whole picture as other tests also apply for the establishment of breach of a legitimate expectation. Indeed, the court's decision that the applicants who received specific representations in the legal aid pro forma replies and in a letter received from the Secretary for Security should have their legitimate expectations protected, whilst the larger and broader class of people putatively eligible for the right of abode who purported to rely only on general representations would not,[10] is informed by other requirements.

Representation Made by a Public Body

The first necessary element is that a representation has been made by a public body. The representation can take a more direct form, such as a statement made by letter, email, telephone, in a media statement or in a departmental circular or guidelines;[11] or a more implied or indirect form, such as previous conduct.[12] This is an objective standard, and the court will form a view on whether a representation was indeed made by the body. An example of previous conduct generating a legitimate expectation was where a government minister had a practice of consulting a trade union on proposed changes to the employment terms of employees at a national intelligence agency, which was

---

[9] *Ng Siu Tung* v *Director of Immigration* (2002) 5 HKCFAR 1, paras.94–98. It was stated (at para.97) that failure to take into account the legitimate expectation as a relevant consideration "constitutes abuse of power", however it should arguably not be described in this way – see pp.150–151.

[10] See *Ng Siu Tung* v *Director of Immigration* (2002) 5 HKCFAR 1, paras.134–140.

[11] On departmental guidelines creating a legitimate expectation, see *Yim Shik Shi* v *Secretary for the Civil Service* [2004] HKEC 640, paras.9–11.

[12] *Ng Siu Tung* v *Director of Immigration* (2002) 5 HKCFAR 1, para.102; *R* v *Gaming Board for Great Britain, ex parte Kingsley (No 2)* [1996] COD 241, p.242. It has been said, for example, that prolonged and unjustified delay in commencing criminal proceedings might give an offender a legitimate expectation that he would not be further pursued – *HKSAR* v *Lau Ting Sing Jerome* [2013] HKEC 1270, para.95, per Pang J; and *HKSAR* v *Cheung Suet Ting* [2010] 6 HKC 249, para.24, per Mackintosh J.

held to create a legitimate expectation that the minister would continue the practice of consultation.[13] In another example, inspectors from the Building Authority had on several occasions inspected a property where balconies had been constructed in non-confirmity with the approved building plans. The Authority thereafter issued an occupation permit, but later claimed that the balconies had been unlawfully constructed and must be demolished. It was held that the inspections that took place whilst the balconies were being constructed, and the issuance of the occupation permit, generated a legitimate expectation that the balconies were lawfully constructed, and the demolition order was of no legal effect[14]; in other words, the failure of the building inspectors to properly note and object to the balconies during their inspections, and the Authority's subsequent certification by issue of the occupation permit, was sufficient to constitute a representation by the Authority. However, not all previous conduct will generate a legitimate expectation, such as the Commissioner of Inland Revenue's year to year treatment of holdover of tax.[15]

The representation must have been made by a public decision maker, that is to say by an entity acting in the capacity of a public decision maker. A pre-election manifesto promise cannot generate a legitimate expectation as it is not made in the capacity of a public decision maker, but rather in the capacity of a candidate or party seeking election to public office.[16] Representations made by a public body in a private law context would not necessarily be capable of challenge under the doctrine of legitimate expectations.[17] By contrast, a Government policy announcement is capable of generating a legitimate expectation, as it is made in the capacity of a public decision maker.[18]

A representation can be implicit: for example, if a state or territory ratified an international treaty, this can give rise to a legitimate expectation that the relevant public authorities will act in conformity with the treaty provisions.[19] However, this might not work where the treaty provisions were merely aspirational rather than creative of obligations,[20] and would

---

[13] *Council of Civil Service Unions* v *Minister for the Civil Service* [1985] AC 374. The expectation was defeated by public policy considerations.

[14] *Lo Yin Ming* v *Appeal Tribunal (Buildings)* [2011] 3 HKLRD 586. Note that the balconies were not deemed unsafe, in which case this would likely have been an overriding consideration defeating the legitimate expectation.

[15] *Nam Tai Trading Co Ltd* v *Commissioner of Inland Revenue* [2006] 2 HKLRD 459; and the failed appeal at *Nam Tai Trading Co Ltd* v *Commissioner of Inland Revenue* [2006] 4 HKLRD 51.

[16] *R* v *Secretary of State for Education and Employment, ex parte Begbie* [2000] 1 WLR 1115.

[17] Consider *Polorace Investments Ltd* v *Director of Lands* [1997] HKLY 491.

[18] *Hong Kong Television Network Ltd* v *Chief Executive in Council* [2015] 2 HKLRD 1035 (decision reversed on appeal, though not on this point, in [2016] HKEC 785).

[19] See *Minister of State for Immigration and Ethnic Affairs* v *Teoh* (1995) 183 CLR 273 (High Court of Australia).

[20] *Chan To Foon* v *Director of Immigration* [2001] 3 HKLRD 109; *Tong Wai Ting* v *Secretary for Education* [2009] HKEC 1367, para.115.

not work in relation to treaty provisions with regard to which the state or territory made reservations.[21]

Knowledge and Reliance

It seems reasonably settled that the applicant must have had knowledge of the representation in order to claim a legitimate expectation.[22] This can logically be considered an integral part of establishing whether an expectation has been generated. If a body made a representation in, for example, a departmental circular which was not made publicly available and knowledge of which never transcended that of departmental officials, it is difficult to regard an expectation as having been generated. There would appear to be relatively few situations in which a person would be able to claim that a legitimate expectation had been breached if they did not have knowledge of the representation on which the expectation is founded. It would seem in most cases to be unlikely that a claim for breach of legitimate expectations would proceed if the applicant did not have knowledge of the representation. However, first, there is at least one such case in Hong Kong.[23] Second, the question is whether the applicant had knowledge at the relevant time in the timeline of events; they may subsequently come to have knowledge of the representation and on that basis seek judicial review. This might occur where, for example, a general policy has been announced. It is worth asking whether, if ignorance of the law is usually no excuse in terms of avoiding legal liability, then ignorance of the law should not operate against a person who was ignorant of a representation. Conceivably, it could be argued that it is not reasonable to deny the applicant the benefit of the expectation even if it only came into their knowledge at some later point in time. However, it could also be argued that just as there is no such thing as technical breach of procedural fairness, so might there be no such thing as technical generation of a legitimate expectation; in other words, that an expectation has theoretically, but not actually, been generated. However, if a person was not entitled to claim a legitimate expectation because

---

[21] *Chan To Foon* v *Director of Immigration* [2001] 3 HKLRD 109. See also *MA* v *Director of Immigration* [2012] HKEC 1624.

[22] Wade and Forsyth stated that "[i]f a person did not expect anything, then there is nothing that the doctrine [of legitimate expectations] can protect. So a person unaware of an undertaking made by a public authority, cannot expect compliance with that undertaking" – Wade and Forsyth, *Administrative Law* (11th edn), p.455. There is, however, some disagreement on this point: *Minister of State for Immigration and Ethnic Affairs* v *Teoh* (1995) 183 CLR 273, pp.291 and 301; *Ng Siu Tung* v *Director of Immigration* (2002) 5 HKCFAR 1, para.355.

[23] In *Lam Yuet Mei* v *Permanent Secretary for Education and Manpower* [2004] 3 HKLRD 524, the evidence filed did not show when the letter which allegedly generated a legitimate expectation – and which was not addressed to the applicant – came to the attention of the applicant. There is of course a distinction to be drawn between the applicant having had no actual knowledge of the representation, and the applicant being unable to show on the evidence that they had knowledge of the representation. The former is a matter of fact, whilst the latter is a matter of evidence.

of a lack of knowledge, this might incentivise concealment or suppression of the representation by the public body.[24]

Arguably more contentious is whether reliance on the representation is necessary, and whether that reliance must be detrimental.[25] Whereas knowledge will usually be essential to demonstrating a claim of breach of a legitimate expectation, reliance is not essential[26] but strengthens the claim, and detrimental reliance is also not essential but further strengthens the claim.[27] The Court of Final Appeal did not take the opportunity in *Ng Siu Tung* to explore the issue of whether detrimental reliance was necessary to ground a legitimate expectation,[28] though whether representations were calculated to induce reliance was noted as relevant.[29] Detrimental reliance might be necessary in a limited class of case, such as where government policy was misrepresented through incompetence, but was corrected five weeks later. Laws LJ said that had there been "reliance and detriment in consequence, I would have been prepared to hold that it would be abusive for the Secretary of State not to make the earlier representations good".[30] There had been no detrimental reliance and, though disappointing for the applicant, this was not enough to "elevate the Secretary of State's correction of his error into abuse of power".[31]

Assessment of detrimental reliance is not straightforward, however.[32] Though in most cases where unfairness is said to result from breach of a

---

[24] Though this may constitute abuse of power or *Wednesbury* unreasonableness. It has also been said that public authorities must act in a high-principled way and with scrupulous fairness in their dealings with the public – *Ng Siu Tung v Director of Immigration* (2002) 5 HKCFAR 1, para.365, per Bokhary PJ, citing *R v Commissioners of Inland Revenue, ex parte Unilever plc* [1996] COD 421, p.423.

[25] Contrast, for example, *R v London Borough Council of Newham, ex parte Bibi* [2001] EWCA Civ 607, paras.28–32; with *R v Secretary of State for Education and Employment, ex parte B (A Minor)* (2000) 1 WLR 1115, p.1124.

[26] *R v London Borough Council of Newham, ex parte Bibi* [2001] EWCA Civ 607, para.28.

[27] See, for example, *Lam Yuet Mei v Permanent Secretary for Education and Manpower* [2004] 3 HKLRD 524. On detrimental reliance appearing not to be essential, see *Ng Siu Tung v Director of Immigration* (2002) 5 HKCFAR 1, para.358, per Bokhary PJ. See also *Attorney-General of Hong Kong v Ng Yuen Shiu* [1983] 2 WLR 735 (PC); *R v Secretary of State for the Home Department, ex parte Khan* [1984] 1 WLR 1337; and *R v Secretary of State for the Home Department, ex parte Ruddock* [1987] 1 WLR 1482.

[28] *Ng Siu Tung v Director of Immigration* (2002) 5 HKCFAR 1, para.110.   [29] *Id.*

[30] *R v Secretary of State for Education and Employment, ex parte Begbie* [2000] 1 WLR 1115, p.1131, per Laws LJ.

[31] *Id.*, per Laws LJ. See also the same case, p.1127, per Peter Gibson LJ.

[32] By detrimental reliance, one would typically look for legal detriment (such as the loss of a right or entitlement) or economic detriment (such as the loss of money, housing or opportunity). However, it has also been said that there can be moral detriment "which should not be dismissed lightly ... [T]hese things matter in public law, even though they might not found an estoppel or actionable misrepresentation in private law, because they go to fairness and through fairness to possible abuse of power" – *R v London Borough Council of Newham, ex parte Bibi* [2001] EWCA Civ 607, para.55, per Schiemann LJ. It was added by Bokhary PJ in his partially dissenting judgment in *Ng Siu Tung v Director of Immigration* (2002) 5 HKCFAR 1, para.360, that "where representations are addressed to a wide audience including some quite unsophisticated persons, the courts should not be astute to find ambiguity or qualification.

legitimate expectation there will probably be some form of detrimental reliance,[33] as Schiemann LJ pointed out in the Court of Appeal of England and Wales:

> The fact that someone has not changed his position after a promise has been made to him does not mean that he has not relied on the promise. An actor in a play where another actor points a gun at him may refrain from changing his position just because he has been given a promise that the gun only contains blanks.[34]

A public housing tenant who lives in unsatisfactory living conditions might tolerate those conditions in reliance on a promise from the local housing authority that he will in six months' time be moved to new accommodation. However, if the authority resiles from its promise, and the tenant is left in the unsatisfactory living conditions, it cannot be said that he did not detrimentally rely on the authority's promise simply because he did not change his position. He might have abstained from making alternative living arrangements, though this may be difficult or even impossible to prove.[35] It would therefore be undesirable as a matter of policy to hold that the tenant had not detrimentally relied on the authority's promise merely because he cannot prove he abstained from changing his position. Moreover, a person might not be able to change his position; perhaps the tenant was incapable of making alternative living arrangements due to adverse financial circumstances. It would hardly be a fair response if the courts penalised the tenant for not changing his position, as he was financially incapable of doing so – potentially putting him at a legal disadvantage to a party who had the means to change his position.[36] Nevertheless, "technical" breach of a legitimate expectation has not been protected where material prejudice was not caused to the applicant.[37]

With fairness as the touchstone, the courts should then look at the real impact of the representation".

[33] *R v Secretary of State for Education and Employment, ex parte Begbie* [2000] 1 WLR 1115, p.1124, per Peter Gibson LJ.

[34] *R v London Borough Council of Newham, ex parte Bibi* [2001] EWCA Civ 607, para.53, per Schiemann LJ.

[35] *De Smith's Judicial Review* pointed out that, though detrimental reliance should not be a condition precedent to the protection of a substantive legitimate expectation, it might provide evidence of the existence or extent of an expectation, and it may affect the weight of the expectation and the issue of the fairness of disappointing the expectation – Lord Woolf et al, *De Smith's Judicial Review* (8th edn), p.694.

[36] See *R v London Borough Council of Newham, ex parte Bibi* [2001] EWCA Civ 607, para.55, where Schiemann J said that "[t]o disregard the legitimate expectation because no concrete detriment can be shown would be to place the weakest in society at a particular disadvantage. It would mean that those who have a choice and the means to exercise it in reliance on some official practice or promise would gain a legal toehold inaccessible to those who, lacking any means of escape, are compelled simply to place their trust in what has been represented to them".

[37] *Yim Shik Shi v Secretary for the Civil Service* [2004] HKEC 640.

Legitimacy of Expectation

If an expectation has been generated by a public body, the court will examine the expectation to assess its legitimacy. This is an open-ended test which could be failed in a variety of ways, and an exhaustive list of factors cannot be given.

One requirement is that the representation must have been clear and unambiguous,[38] even if the expectation is implied.[39] The existence and content of the representation should be objectively and not just subjectively apparent,[40] and a legitimate expectation cannot arise merely from a person's general expectation of what they think should or ought to happen.[41] This has been framed as an element of the legitimacy of an expectation,[42] and is doubtless a critical requirement to the integrity of this ground of review, otherwise public bodies could be subject to a large volume of claims that legitimate expectations had been generated in the subjective view of applicants. A statement of general intention that certain decisions favourable to applicants would be taken, but which clearly states or implies that individual decisions will be taken on a case-by-case basis, will not generate a legitimate expectation that a decision will necessarily be made which is favourable to the applicant.[43] Indeed, prematurely assuring applicants of how discretion will be exercised in the future, or resolving in advance how discretion will later be exercised, could constitute a fetter on discretion, and whether an expectation is legitimate is constrained by the statutory and broader legal context. However, where a representation is reasonably capable of competing constructions, the courts have stated that the correct approach is to accept the interpretation applied by the public body, subject to the test of *Wednesbury* unreasonableness.[44]

To be legitimate, an expectation must be reasonable.[45] It has been stated in the Court of Final Appeal that:

> to be legitimate, the expectation must be reasonable ... that is, reasonable in the light of the official conduct which is said to have given rise to the

---

[38] *Hong Kong and China Gas Co Ltd v Director of Lands* [1997] HKLRD 1291, pp.1296–1297; *Hing Wong Enterprises Co Ltd v Director of Lands* [1999] HKLRD (Yrbk) 18; *Ng Siu Tung v Director of Immigration* (2002) 5 HKCFAR 1, paras.103–104 and 360; *Yook Tong Electric Co Ltd v Commissioner for Transport* [2003] HKEC 170.
[39] *Merchant Navy Officers' Guild – Hong Kong v Director of Marine* [2003] HKEC 285, para.41.
[40] See *Wu Yuk Wah Ben v Director of Hong Kong Observatory* [2013] 2 HKLRD 1068; and *Chinluck Properties Ltd v Appeal Tribunal (Buildings)* [2013] HKEC 1390.
[41] *Merchant Navy Officers' Guild – Hong Kong v Director of Marine* [2003] HKEC 285, paras.41–42. See also *Kwok Cheuk Kin v Commissioner for Transport* [2011] HKEC 1318.
[42] *Hong Kong and China Gas Co Ltd v Director of Lands* [1997] HKLRD 1291, p.1297
[43] *Hong Kong and China Gas Co Ltd v Director of Lands* [1997] HKLRD 1291, affirmed in *Hong Kong and China Gas Co Ltd v Director of Lands* [1998] HKEC 590 (CA); *Hing Wong Enterprises Co Ltd v Director of Lands* [1999] HKLRD (Yrbk) 18.
[44] *R v Ministry of Defence, ex parte Walker* [2000] 1 WLR 806 (HL), p.813, per Lord Slynn of Hadley; *Ng Siu Tung v Director of Immigration* (2002) 5 HKCFAR 1, para.104.
[45] *Attorney-General of Hong Kong v Ng Yuen Shiu* [1983] 2 AC 629 (PC), p.636; *Ng Siu Tung v Director of Immigration* (2002) 5 HKCFAR 1, paras.101 and 360.

expectation. Whether an expectation is legitimate in this sense depends, at least in part, upon the conduct of the relevant public authority and what it has committed itself to. Whether an expectation is legitimate, and to what extent, must also depend upon what the applicants are *entitled* to expect. The requirement of legitimacy means that judicial decisions "must be founded not only on what the claimant *factually* expected, but also on what the claimant, bearing in mind any relevant considerations of policy and principle, was *entitled* to expect".[46]

It has also been said that an expectation will not be reasonable if it could reasonably have been foreseen that the subject matter of the representation was likely to change, that it was not likely to be respected by the decision maker (though this surely cannot be deployed by public bodies to justify a practice of frequent departure from representations), or the applicant knew that the decision maker did not intend his statement to create an expectation.[47] Falling under the first, and perhaps to a lesser extent the second, of these categories is where it could have been foreseen that, in the context of the outbreak of avian influenza, and associated stricter public hygiene and environmental protection regulation, a licensing system for poultry farming would become much more rigorous.[48]

Representations are made by public bodies in a particular legal and broader societal context. Effect will clearly not be given to a legitimate expectation if it would require a body to act contrary to statute.[49] This would not only affect the reasonableness of the expectation, but the legality of its enforcement. Importantly, broader legal, economic, social, scientific and policy conditions can change. If the law itself changes, a body cannot be bound by a representation made prior to the change in the law, where the representation, if presently made effective, would be unlawful[50] or, perhaps, inappropriate as a matter of policy. For example, the Housing Authority's practices in relation to public rent levels under a previous statutory regime would not create a legitimate expectation that the same practices would be adopted under a new statutory regime.[51] Nor would their adoption of practices when the economy was inflationary create a legitimate expectation that the same practices would be

---

[46] *Ng Siu Tung v Director of Immigration* (2002) 5 HKCFAR 1, p.101, citing Mark Elliott, 'The Human Rights Act 1998 and the Standard of Substantive Review' [2001] CLJ 301, p.319. Emphasis in the original.
[47] Craig, *Administrative Law*, pp.679–680; *R. v Gaming Board of Great Britain, ex parte Kingsley (No 3)* [1996] CLY 3953 – earlier edition cited with approval in *Lam Yuet Mei v Permanent Secretary for Education and Manpower* [2004] 3 HKLRD 524, para.75.
[48] *Mo Chun Hon v Director of Agriculture, Fisheries and Conservation Department* [2007] HKEC 445.
[49] *R v Secretary of State for Education and Employment, ex parte Begbie* [2000] 1 WLR 1115.
[50] See *Attorney-General of Hong Kong v Ng Yuen Shiu* [1983] 2 AC 629 (PC), p.638.
[51] *Ho Choi Wan v Hong Kong Housing Authority* (2005) 8 HKCFAR 628.

adopted when the economy was deflationary.[52] It could not be argued that a previous legal regime on immigration gave rise to a legitimate expectation that the law would never change: "[l]egitimate expectation can never be invoked to limit the powers of the Legislature".[53] A legitimate expectation may also be extinguished when policies change[54] – and public bodies must be given latitude to change their policies[55] – but this does not mean that an expectation is "erased simply by the fact of a decision which disappoints it".[56]

An executive promise to change the law cannot, as a simple matter of the separation of powers, generate a legitimate expectation that the law will change. It is for the legislature to change the law as primary lawmaker, and it cannot be bound by executive promises that the law will be changed.[57] It is less clear whether a promise made by a secondary legislator to change the law, when the necessary power to change the law is his own, could generate a legitimate expectation to that effect – for example, whether an executive decision maker with the power to make subsidiary legislation could generate a legitimate expectation that the law would be changed by them in the future exercise of their secondary legislative power. However, it could be argued that the decision maker in question has two capacities – that of executive decision maker and that of secondary legislator – such that a representation made in one capacity does not necessarily bind his actions in the other capacity. Even if the two capacities are collapsed into one, it could be a fetter on discretion to make a representation on how discretion will in future be exercised.

Body Failed to Take into Account Legitimate Expectation as a Relevant Consideration

Once it has been established that a legitimate expectation was generated by the public body, and that the affected person had knowledge of (and perhaps reliance on) the representation, the court will seek to establish whether the body failed to take into account the legitimate expectation as a relevant consideration. Failure to take into account a relevant consideration can render a decision unlawful, and this is the primary basis on which breach of the legitimate expectation is likely to be deemed unlawful. It would be controversial, particularly from a separation of powers perspective, for the court to force the decision maker to implement the substantive expectation, though exceptionally

---

[52] *Id.*
[53] *Registrar of Births and Deaths* v *Syed Haider Yahya Hussain* (2001) 4 HKCFAR 429, para.60, per Litton NPJ. However, when an unlawful decision is made which frustrates a legitimate expectation, the public body should not be able to rely on a later change in the law for the expectation to remain frustrated – *Re Heland Investment Ltd* [1995] 2 HKLR 158.
[54] *Hughes* v *Department of Health and Social Security* [1985] AC 776, p.788, per Lord Diplock.
[55] See p.177.   [56] *Ng Siu Tung* v *Director of Immigration* (2002) 5 HKCFAR 1, para.354.
[57] *Dragon House Investment Ltd* v *Secretary for Transport* (2005) 8 HKCFAR 668, para.55.

this has been done.[58] The less controversial course for the courts to adopt, as a matter of the separation of powers, is to conclude that the decision maker failed to take into account the affected person's legitimate expectation as a relevant consideration. The decision would therefore be unlawful and require to be retaken, this time having sufficient regard for the affected person's legitimate expectation. This would presumably require the body to give serious consideration as to whether to revise its treatment of the affected person, or ways in which it could minimise or mitigate the adverse effect of its decision on affected persons.

Overriding Policy Considerations

There are clear policy reasons in favour of courts supervising public bodies for breach of legitimate expectations, and imposing public law liability in appropriate cases. However, there may sometimes be policy reasons outweighing the advantages of holding the body liable in public law, even if it breached an otherwise legitimate expectation. In cases where such overriding considerations are established, the legitimate expectation may be defeated.

Overriding considerations can take many forms, and can apply in cases of either procedural or substantive expectations.[59] In *Council of Civil Service Unions* v *Minister for the Civil Service*, though a legitimate expectation of consulting a trade union had been established, the national security implications of consultation were regarded as an overriding consideration which defeated the expectation.[60] The consideration can be one of public health, such as where concerns about the containment of avian influenza outweighed a poultry farmer's treatment under a licensing scheme.[61] There can be overriding public resource considerations, as in *Ng Siu Tung* v *Director of Immigration*, where the "overwhelming force" of immigration policy could override general representations on the right of abode made by the government purportedly relied on by some six hundred thousand persons.[62] It would be an overriding consideration where a legitimate expectation, if recognised, would impede or frustrate the statutory framework[63] or a public body's performance of its functions and duties.[64]

The conduct of the applicant can defeat a legitimate expectation, a specific application of the general principle that the award of remedies in judicial review is discretionary and that remedies can be withheld where the court

---

[58] See pp.217–219.
[59] See *Ng Siu Tung* v *Director of Immigration* (2002) 5 HKCFAR 1, para.362–363.
[60] *Council of Civil Service Unions* v *Minister for the Civil Service* [1985] AC 374.
[61] *Mo Chun Hon* v *Director of Agriculture, Fisheries and Conservation Department* [2007] HKEC 445, [2008] 1 HKCLRT 386.
[62] *Ng Siu Tung* v *Director of Immigration* (2002) 5 HKCFAR 1, para.284.
[63] Consider *Ng Siu Tung* v *Director of Immigration* (2002) 5 HKCFAR 1, especially para.134.
[64] See *Cheung Shing Ki* v *Housing Appeal Panel* [2001] HKEC 216.

finds that the applicant's conduct is such as not to justify the award of a remedy. This may arise if, for example, the applicant has not been candid,[65] or has wilfully flouted regulations and generally been disobedient.[66] In such cases it will tend to become increasingly difficult to argue that the applicant has suffered unfairness as a result of their legitimate expectation being breached, and the court's impetus to exercise its discretion to award relief is eroded. The issue can also arise in situations which do not comprise misconduct, but in which the conduct of the applicant is relevant for evaluation of their entitlement to a benefit.[67]

Bokhary PJ likened legitimate expectations to rights in his partially dissenting judgment in *Ng Siu Tung*, but pointed out that the:

> practical difference between legitimate expectations and rights is that a legitimate expectation, unlike a right, can be made to give way to what the executive manages to justify as an overriding public interest. This practical difference dovetails with the conceptual difference involved ... A person's entitlement under a legitimate expectation is not correlative to the executive's duty thereunder. For, as the separation of powers requires, not performing the duty otherwise owed under a legitimate expectation can be justified by an overriding public interest in its non-performance.[68]

With respect, it is not entirely correct to say that rights, unlike legitimate expectations, cannot be made to yield to overriding public interest considerations. If a person enters into a lawfully concluded contract with a government department, he has contractual rights, including rights of enforcement. However, under the executive necessity doctrine, the department can be unshackled from its contractual obligations in extreme circumstances such as where national security, public health or public safety is at risk.[69] In this situation, the person's contractual rights yield to overriding public policy considerations. Though the range of situations in which the executive necessity doctrine would apply would likely be narrower than those under which public policy considerations might override an otherwise legitimate expectation, it is not conceptually sound to distinguish legitimate expectations from rights on this basis. Legitimate expectations would in any event not generate rights in judicial review, noting the discretionary nature of the award of remedies under judicial review procedure.[70]

---

[65] *R v Inland Revenue Commissioners, ex parte MFK Underwriting Agents Ltd* [1990] 1 WLR 1545, p.1569, per Bingham LJ, cited with approval in *R v Inland Revenue Commissioners, ex parte Matrix Securities Ltd* [1994] 1 WLR 334 (HL), p.352, per Lord Jauncey of Tullichettle; and *Ng Siu Tung* v *Director of Immigration* (2002) 5 HKCFAR 1, para.361, per Bokhary PJ.
[66] *Cinnamond* v *British Airports Authority* [1980] 1 WLR 582.
[67] See, for example, *Gurung Aruna* v *Director of Immigration* [2004] HKEC 779.
[68] *Ng Siu Tung* v *Director of Immigration* (2002) 5 HKCFAR 1, para.364, per Bokhary PJ.
[69] See p.188.
[70] Though public law liability can of course be litigated in an ordinary action in some circumstances.

Judicial Protection of Legitimate Expectations

Procedural and Substantive Expectations

Where a court finds there to be breach of a legitimate expectation, with each of the relevant criteria and requirements being satisfied, it remains to decide how to protect the expectation, if the court exercises its discretion to grant relief:

> The court's task in all these cases is not to impede executive activity but to reconcile its continuing need to initiate or respond to change with the legitimate interests or expectations of citizens or strangers who have relied, and have been justified in relying, on a current policy or an extant promise. The critical question is by what standard the court is to resolve such conflicts.[71]

The less contentious form of protection is achieved by imposing procedural requirements on the body to ensure that the expectation is properly recognised and protected. Procedural protection applies not only in relation to procedural expectations, but also substantive expectations. Where a procedural expectation exists, such as the expectation of an oral hearing, this can be procedurally protected by the court ordering an oral hearing to be given, for example by order of mandamus. However, even where a substantive expectation exists, such as the expectation of a public housing entitlement based on a promise to be provided with the same, this can be procedurally protected by requiring the body to take into account as a relevant consideration the applicant's substantive expectation, and perhaps attaching substantial weight thereto, again by order of mandamus or by declaration. This is relatively uncontroversial because, under the separation of powers, the court rights the legal wrong whilst still allowing the executive decision maker to arrive at his own substantive decision.

More controversial is for the court to substantively protect the expectation. Where the expectation is substantively protected, the court will order for the substantive benefit to be conferred, maintained or otherwise protected. This is more controversial from a separation of powers perspective because the court dictates what substantive decision must be made by the decision maker, or what is the substantive effect of the decision made. It should arguably only be awarded by courts in exceptional circumstances, such as where an applicant would suffer serious, perhaps irreparable, detriment were substantive protection not to be afforded. It might also be asked whether the applicant would stand to suffer greater detriment than the decision maker or the wider public interest were substantive protection not to be afforded.

---

[71] *R v North and East Devon Health Authority, ex parte Coughlan* [2001] QB 213, para.65, per Lord Woolf MR.

R v North and East Devon Health Authority, ex parte Coughlan,[72] decided by the Court of Appeal of England and Wales, was a major case on substantive legitimate expectations. The applicant was a severely disabled lady who, along with seven similarly disabled patients, was moved from a public hospital to a public nursing home for the long-term disabled. The local health authority persuaded the patients to move from the hospital, which it wanted to close, to the nursing home as their "home for life". Around five years after the applicant was moved to the nursing home, the authority decided to close it. The applicant sought judicial review of the closure decision, which the court granted as in breach of a legitimate expectation that the nursing home would be the applicant's home for life. The court concluded that the decision to close the nursing home was an unjustified breach of the promise of the home for life and constituted unfairness amounting to an abuse of power, and the decision to close the home was quashed.

Enforcement of a substantive expectation would most likely arise in cases in which the expectation is confined to one person or a small number of people, "giving the promise or representation the character of a contract".[73] This view has been criticised on the argument that, the more people that are affected by breach of a substantive legitimate expectation caused by a change in policy, the greater the damage caused to legal certainty and public trust in the government.[74] However, this view is open to challenge. Not only can resource implications be much greater if a court protects the substantive legitimate expectations of a large number of people – which could be a drain on the public finances and therefore on the public resources of the community at large – unlawful conduct should be accounted for in court regardless of the number of people adversely affected, resource constraints notwithstanding. There are clearly difficult legal and policy issues at play in deciding whether and when a legitimate expectation should be substantively protected.

It is also important to note the test of inevitability.[75] Where the court is satisfied that, even if the decision maker failed to take into account a legitimate expectation as a reasonable consideration, the decision maker would have arrived at the same decision had the expectation been properly taken into account – in other words, the decision reached was inevitable – the court retains discretion to refrain from quashing the decision, and therefore to refuse relief.[76] This is a specific application of the court's discretion on whether to award relief in judicial review, but a court will and should not lightly conclude that the inevitability test is satisfied. It is interesting to consider

---

[72] *R v North and East Devon Health Authority, ex parte Coughlan* [2001] QB 213.
[73] *Id.*, para.59, per Lord Woolf MR.
[74] Kevin Yam and Benny Tai, "The Advent of Substantive Legitimate Expectations in Hong Kong: Two Competing Visions" [2002] Public Law 688, p.696.
[75] See pp.300–301.
[76] *Nguyen Tuan Cuong* v *Director of Immigration* [1997] 1 WLR 68 (PC), pp.76–77; *Ng Siu Tung* v *Director of Immigration* (2002) 5 HKCFAR 1, para.352.

whether, if the local health authority in *Coughlan* had no legal or physical option but to close the nursing home (for example, if it was impossible for the authority to continue funding the home or if it was deemed to be unsafe in a manner that could not be repaired or remedied), then the court would have refrained from substantively protecting the expectation; perhaps only protecting it procedurally (in other words, leaving the authority to decide whether or not to close the nursing home, but taking into account as a relevant consideration the expectation of the patients to whom the "home for life" promise had been made). These circumstances would probably count as overriding considerations which could defeat the otherwise legitimate expectation, but accordingly, the threshold for such considerations to be established would be high.

The courts are more likely to uphold representations made to a specific group of persons, than representations generally made.[77] This can be motivated by resource or policy considerations, but it can also form the basis of protecting the rationale of a broader statutory scheme. For example, in *Ng Siu Tung* v *Director of Immigration*, specific representations had been made to a group of persons who were the recipients of representations calculated to induce reliance. The Court of Final Appeal protected their expectations. However, the approximately six hundred thousand persons putatively eligible for the right of abode, who received general representations, were not protected. Their interests were overridden by the "overwhelming force" of immigration policy, and protecting their expectations would have undermined the legislative scheme as a whole.[78]

The Court of Final Appeal protected the expectations of the specific class of persons, who were deemed to form a discrete and ascertainable class, by quashing the removal orders which had been issued against the applicants in the specific representation class, such that the Director of Immigration would be required to retake the decisions. It also issued a declaration that the Director should reconsider the cases of those applicants in light of the Court's judgment and of his statutory discretionary powers, "giving substantial weight to the need to mitigate the unfairness of resiling from representations which have given rise to the legitimate expectation in question".[79] This is essentially an order of the Court requiring the decision maker to take into account the applicants' legitimate expectations as a relevant consideration, and to attach substantial weight to that consideration, but still does not comprise the Court directing the decision maker which decision to make, thus avoiding the taboo

---

[77] Where a representation is addressed to a specific class of persons, a more general class of persons cannot ordinarily ground a legitimate expectation on the content of that representation – see *Law Sze Yan* v *Chinese Medicine Practitioners Board of the Chinese Medical Council of Hong Kong* [2006] HKEC 1151, the point not pursued on appeal at *Law Sze Yan* v *Chinese Medicine Practitioners Board of the Chinese Medical Council of Hong Kong* [2007] HKEC 603 (CA).

[78] *Ng Siu Tung* v *Director of Immigration* (2002) 5 HKCFAR 1, para.284.

[79] *Id.*, paras.142 and 284.

of trespassing into the territory of substantive executive decision-making. In other words, the court refrained from a substantive protection of the applicants' expectations. As Bokhary PJ stated, it is "when they enforce legitimate expectations substantively (rather than merely procedurally) that the courts must take particular care to avoid trespassing upon the policy preserve of the executive".[80]

Bokhary PJ stated in his partially dissenting judgment that if a body decides against the holder of a substantive expectation without taking the expectation into account, and if the court "feels sure" that once the expectation is duly taken into account an end result favourable to the holder of the expectation will be reached by the body or by an administrative tribunal or the courts, then the court may both quash the decision and substantively enforce the expectation:

> I do not think that [the court] would be bound to follow the circuitous course of leaving it to the administrative decision maker to make a fresh decision, knowing that it will undoubtedly intervene again if he or an administrative appeal tribunal were to decide in any way other than favourably to the holder of the expectation. That would cause pointless delay. It would also be to insist that the administrative decision maker assume the undignified role of a rubber stamp. In my view, the courts would be entitled, in the extreme circumstances postulated, to proceed directly to substantive enforcement: for example by an appropriate declaration.[81]

Though Bokhary PJ was plainly attuned to the separation of powers issues in this area, as his comments above show, this does place strain on the separation of powers model. It also detracts from the important symbolism of the courts acting as bodies of review and not appeal. Though an argument could potentially be made that the court might proceed directly to substantive enforcement as an emergency measure in a situation where the delay caused by remitting the decision to the body to take afresh would irreparably frustrate the applicant's legitimate expectation, this could raise several potential problems. Perhaps most notably, the court might, to use Bokhary PJ's terminology, "feel sure" that once the expectation is duly taken into account, an end result favourable to the holder of the expectation will be reached by the body or by an administrative tribunal or the courts. However, if the court is mistaken in that assessment, it will have committed a manifest violation of the separation of powers. The court, in most cases less experienced in a given area of executive decision-making, will have interfered with the decision-making process on the basis of conjecture (even if educated and well-meaning conjecture), stepping into the shoes of, and to a great extent assuming the role of, the decision maker. The decision maker must get a decision right in law, and the

---

[80] *Id.*, para.347. [81] *Id.*, para.353.

role of the courts in judicial review is to ensure that this occurs, but the decision maker must be left able, in all matters of non-law, to go wrong. It is, after all, the decision maker who must answer to the broader community as a matter of political accountability, and the courts must exercise discipline by confining themselves to issues of legality.

Ultra vires Representations and Legitimate Expectations

The question of whether *ultra vires* representations can generate legitimate expectations raises difficult issues of legal policy. The controversy is well illustrated by the case of *Yook Tong Electric Co Ltd v Commissioner for Transport*.[82] The Commissioner for Transport designated part of a street in Wan Chai a pedestrian-only zone during business hours. The owner of Yook Tong Electric Co Ltd, who required delivery access to his shop premises during business hours, claimed that a legitimate expectation was generated that he would have vehicular access to his shop during business hours by a letter received from the Urban Services Department in the 1980s, which read:

> An investigation carried out by my staff has revealed that a width of about 9 feet has been provided in front of Yook Tong Electric Co. Ltd. of No. 5 Tai Yuen Street, Wan Chai, your client's shop. This is considered good enough for loading and unloading purposes and no obstruction to the premises in question is considered to arise.

The first potential problem is that this representation was made a number of years before the decision was made to pedestrianise the street, the passage of time potentially giving the authority increased latitude to adjust its policy. It was arguably also not sufficiently clear and unambiguous in terms of guaranteeing vehicular access, rather confirming that the street was considered wide enough for that purpose.

However, the real problem for the applicant was that it was not made by the party with legal authority to regulate vehicular access. The party with proper legal authority for taking such decisions was the Commissioner for Transport, who now sought to exercise that decision-making power, whereas the original representation was made by the Urban Services Department. These must be recognised as distinct entities, as Hartmann J indicated:

> in looking to the nature and extent of any representation, the fact that it was made by one arm of the Executive, which perhaps has only limited authority, can properly be taken into account if it is alleged that the representation binds another or all arms of the Executive. Government today is not a

---

[82] *Yook Tong Electric Co Ltd v Commissioner for Transport* [2003] HKEC 170.

monolith; it has many divisions, departments, boards, offices and the like, all with their own powers.[83]

This is potentially a controversial decision: how, in the first place, is the ordinary person reasonably expected to know whether a public body making a representation has the legal authority over that which it purports to regulate? In some cases, the answer should be clear enough, such as if an official in an immigration agency purported to regulate road traffic, or if a university purported to regulate air transport licences. However, the Commissioner for Transport and the Urban Services Department could both reasonably be considered to have the power to regulate vehicular access. This arguably leaves individuals is a fairly vulnerable position, unsure of which body has the necessary legal authority to conduct the task in question.[84] In addition, it would seem to exonerate disorganisation among public bodies. If a body makes a representation that is *ultra vires*, it has made an error (perhaps deliberate, more likely inadvertent) on the scope of its own legal powers. This decision would however result in the body being found not to be in breach of a legitimate expectation, perhaps insufficiently incentivising a more careful assessment by the body of its legal powers prior to making such representations.[85]

The decision in *Yook Tong Electric* would seem, nevertheless, to be the right one in law, and the necessary one in policy.[86] If the court took the opposite view, that an *ultra vires* representation of the Urban Services Department could bind the Commissioner for Transport, then the legal and policy implications would be far-reaching. *Ultra vires* representations would be capable of generating legally valid expectations, effectively converting *ultra vires* representations into *intra vires* representations. Bodies without a particular power would be capable of binding, or generating liability

---

[83] *Yook Tong Electric Co Ltd* v *Commissioner for Transport* [2003] HKEC 170, para.45.
[84] Consider, in this regard, Bokhary PJ's statement that "even unsophisticated persons must be candid", but that "in judging whether or not they have been candid, their lack of sophistication should in all fairness to them be borne in mind" – *Ng Siu Tung* v *Director of Immigration* (2002) 5 HKCFAR 1, para.361. See also *R (Bloggs 61)* v *Secretary of State for the Home Department* [2003] 1 WLR 2724, in which the police had no actual or ostensible authority to bind the Prison Service and thus a representation by the police would not generate a legitimate expectation on the part of the Prison Service.
[85] Though liability in tort might attach to the body making the representation – see pp.128–129. Another possibility is to award compensation to the representee as an alternative to holding an *ultra vires* representation to bind the public body, though this brings its own difficulties – see Craig, *Administrative Law*, para.22–052.
[86] However, Paul Craig argued that, where the harm caused to the public by a court holding an *ultra vires* representation to bind is minimal compared to the harm caused to the individual representee by a court holding the representation not to bind, there is "good reason to consider allowing the representation to bind" – Craig, *Administrative Law*, para.22–047; and see his broader discussion at paras.22–032 to 22–052.

for, bodies with that power.[87] This could have profound consequences for the conduct of public administration, legal and political accountability, and the consumption of public resources. It could also, depending on how it was framed, result in the court giving powers to a body which does not properly enjoy those powers in law, this being strictly taboo. In addition, the Court of Final Appeal's test in *Ng Siu Tung* v *Director of Immigration* would also be less workable, as the court has stated that it will not usually interfere where a body has departed from its previous representation, provided that the body has taken the party's legitimate expectation into account and given reasons for its departure. It is unclear how this would work where an *ultra vires* representation could generate a legitimate expectation, and whether it is the body with or without lawful authority to generate that expectation which must take the party's legitimate expectation into account. Finally, it is important to note that a legitimate expectation is unlikely to be protected where this would result in the body violating another ground of review. For example, a representation which would cause a decision maker to fetter his or her discretion at a later date might not successfully ground liability for breach of a legitimate expectation.[88]

Legitimate Expectations and Other Grounds of Review

Whilst breach of legitimate expectations may be considered a ground of review in its own right, it is bound up with other grounds. This is seen, for example, in the Court of Final Appeal's test in *Ng Siu Tung* v *Director of Immigration* that, provided a body has taken into account a party's legitimate expectation as a relevant consideration, and given reasons for departing from its previous representation, the court will usually not interfere. This test therefore feeds into two other grounds of review, namely the relevance of considerations and procedural impropriety (the giving of reasons).

Moreover, a party's expectation may be interlinked with another ground of review. For example, a party might have a (procedural) legitimate expectation of an oral hearing, which invokes procedural impropriety (the right to a hearing); or a (substantive) legitimate expectation that no reasonable body in a given situation would have rejected the authenticity of a torture claim, which invokes *Wednesbury* unreasonableness.

There are various weapons in the judicial review armoury which may be used to strike down decisions in breach of legitimate expectations. These include the possibility of finding breach of the expectation to be an abuse of

---

[87] It was stated that a "legitimate expectation can only arise on the basis of a lawful promise, representation or practice" – *al-Fayed* v *Commissioners of Inland Revenue*, 2004 SC 745, para.119.
[88] *Kwok Cheuk Kin* v *Commissioner for Transport* [2011] HKEC 1318; and see *Attorney-General for the State of New South Wales* v *Quin* (1989–90) 170 CLR 1, pp.17–18.

power, unfair, *Wednesbury* unreasonable or a combination thereof.[89] These can variably be used to protect either procedural or substantive expectations, and may allow for the decision to be quashed and retaken, perhaps with a requirement that sufficient weight be attached to the expectation. Another possibility is to recognise breach of legitimate expectations as a ground of review in its own right, and to quash a decision in breach thereof, without resorting to other grounds.

---

[89] See the discussion in *R v Inland Revenue Commissioners, ex parte Preston* [1985] AC 835; and *R v North and East Devon Health Authority, ex parte Coughlan* [2001] QB 213.

18

Unreasonableness and Irrationality

Unreasonableness is primarily a qualitative control on discretion, assessing the decision or decision-making process according to minimum standards of rationality and reasoning. The standard of review is often known as *Wednesbury* unreasonableness, named after the case of *Associated Provincial Picture Houses* v *Wednesbury Corporation*,[1] in which Lord Greene MR asked whether Wednesbury Corporation had made a decision so unreasonable that no reasonable decision maker would have made it. Lord Greene held the Corporation not to have violated this standard, and it has been said that the birth of the test may have been unintended.[2] Nevertheless, the standard has persisted and is still cited as the standard of unreasonableness in Hong Kong.

There are obvious difficulties and issues of circularity with such a standard. What qualifies as a decision so unreasonable that no reasonable decision maker would have made it? Who or what is a reasonable decision maker? Are there different standards of reasonableness depending on the nature of the decision maker or the nature of the decision? Can the court satisfactorily answer these questions in a way that does not jeopardise adherence to the separation of powers? It should be noted, in particular, that a judicial assessment of reasonableness comes particularly close to merits review, even if the courts insist that they are only reviewing for legality.[3] Courts must take care to avoid merits review, such as on the effectiveness of a policy,[4] though if the

---

[1] *Associated Provincial Picture Houses Ltd* v *Wednesbury Corporation* [1948] 1 KB 223.
[2] It was also highly unspecific; see Anthony Lester and Jeffrey Jowell, *'Beyond Wednesbury: Substantive Principles of Administrative Law'* [1987] Public Law 368, pp.369–370.
[3] If unreasonableness carries risks for the separation of powers, proportionality may carry even greater risks. See James Goodwin, "The Last Defence of Wednesbury" [2012] Public Law 445; and *R* v *Secretary of State for the Home Department, ex parte Brind* [1991] 1 AC 696 (HL). Though see *R* v *Chief Constable of Sussex, ex parte International Trader's Ferry Ltd* [1999] 2 AC 418 (HL). Whilst unreasonableness and proportionality may overlap, they are clearly distinguishable – *Dr Kwong Kwok Hay* v *Medical Council of Hong Kong* [2006] 4 HKC 157, paras.94–99. The finding that a decision maker acted proportionately can support a finding that he did not act unreasonably in the *Wednesbury* sense; see *Inglory Ltd* v *Director of Food and Environmental Hygiene* [2012] 3 HKLRD 603, paras.56–61.
[4] See *Chim Shing Chung* v *Commissioner of Correctional Services* (1995) 5 HKPLR 570; and the appeal at *Chim Shing Chung* v *Commissioner of Correctional Services* (1996) 6 HKPLR 313 (CA).

decision is egregious the court may treat it as unlawful. Moreover, the standard is framed in such a way as to raise uncertainty in its scope of application and concerns about how consistently the standard can or will be applied. Lord Diplock claimed that "[w]hether a decision falls within this category is a question that judges by their training and experience should be well equipped to answer, or else there would be something badly wrong with our judicial system".[5] This may be a somewhat idealistic view of the matter: there are large and difficult grey areas, possibilities for subjectivity on the part of courts, and intractable conundrums in the legality/merits divide.

Whilst unreasonableness is a ground of review in its own right, the courts sometimes describe violation of another ground as being unreasonable. For example, failure to take into account a relevant consideration, exercise of discretion for an improper purpose or fettering of discretion may each be deemed unreasonable. In *Wong Chi Man* v *Director of Food and Environmental Hygiene*,[6] the Director of Food and Environmental Hygiene, and the Municipal Services Appeals Board in affirming the Director's decision, erred in fact, erred in law and failed to take into account a relevant consideration. It was held that "[f]or these reasons, the decisions of the Director and the Board may be impugned as irrational, or perverse, and unreasonable in the *Wednesbury* sense".[7] This was not a violation of *Wednesbury* unreasonableness in its own right, but violation of other grounds which were held to aggregate to unreasonableness.

Similarly, in *Sabinano II Marcel R* v *Municipal Services Appeal Board*, the respondent erred in fact and failed to take into account relevant considerations.[8] These were cumulatively regarded as violating *Wednesbury* unreasonableness as a further ground of review.[9] Elsewhere, it was said that unreasonableness could follow from bad faith, taking into account extraneous factors, failing to take into account relevant considerations or disregarding public policy.[10] In addition, it has been specifically asked whether it was *Wednesbury* unreasonable for a decision maker to have taken a particular consideration into account,[11] and even if one had been, the court might still intervene if the weight placed on that consideration was *Wednesbury* unreasonable.[12] Lord Greene MR even referred in *Wednesbury* itself to overlap between unreasonableness and the relevance of considerations.[13]

Though the grounds of review are not entirely discrete and shade into each other, it is questionable whether courts should be conducting their analysis

---

[5] *Council of Civil Service Unions* v *Minister for the Civil Service* [1985] AC 374, p.410.
[6] *Wong Chi Man* v *Director of Food and Environmental Hygiene* [2014] 2 HKLRD 1124.
[7] *Id.*, para.28.   [8] *Sabinano II Marcel R* v *Municipal Services Appeal Board* [2014] HKEC 370.
[9] *Id.*, para.59.   [10] *Chiang Lily* v *Secretary for Justice* [2009] HKEC 1562, para.30.
[11] *Dembele Salifou* v *Director of Immigration* [2016] HKEC 922, paras.94–95.
[12] *Tesco Stores Ltd* v *Secretary of State for the Environment* [1995] 1 WLR 759, pp.764 and 780.
[13] *Associated Provincial Picture Houses Ltd* v *Wednesbury Corporation* [1948] 1 KB 223, pp.228–229.

on the basis of other grounds being violated, and then concluding that the decision maker has therefore acted unreasonably. If the court is minded to draw this conclusion, it should conduct a proper scrutiny of the impugned decision or decision-making process on *Wednesbury* terms, as unreasonableness is – notwithstanding the non-exclusivity of the grounds of review – a ground in its own right. It has (or should have), in particular, a high threshold of review, and whilst in some cases a body's violation of other grounds may be so egregious as to amount to *Wednesbury* unreasonableness, in most cases it will not. This practice only encourages applicants to "throw in" unreasonableness as an additional and unelaborated ground of review in their applications, which is not only to ignore the content and logic of *Wednesbury* unreasonableness in its own right, but might be disadvantageous to the applicant, as the courts are sometimes irked by what are perceived to be unduly expansive or insufficiently focused applications.

A related concern is a potential lowering of the *Wednesbury* threshold in Hong Kong. It should also be noted that the term "irrationality" is often used synonymously with unreasonableness, though it is questionable whether it ought to be so used noting that there are important conceptual and logical differences between them.

Standard of Review: *Wednesbury* Unreasonableness

Wednesbury is the natural starting point for discussion of this ground, though it was not the first case in which there was reference to a form of reasonableness review.[14] The case concerned the Sunday Entertainments Act 1932 which made it lawful for cinemas to be open on a Sunday. Under the Act, the relevant licensing authority was empowered to license the opening of cinemas subject to such conditions as it thought fit to impose. Wednesbury Corporation imposed on the applicant the condition that "no children under the age of fifteen years shall be admitted to any entertainment, whether accompanied by an adult or not". Lord Greene MR held that, on the face of it, the authority had acted lawfully in imposing the requirement. He found the contention that the court is the ultimate arbiter of what is and is not reasonable, rather than the local authority itself, to be an unsound argument. The licensing authority was entrusted by Parliament with particular powers on a matter with which the knowledge and experience of the authority could be best trusted to deal. The authority had exercised its discretion and a decision had been made.

However, Lord Greene effectively contradicted his own position that the court would not be the ultimate arbiter of what would and would not be reasonable, in stating that "[i]t is true to say that, if a decision on a competent

[14] See, for example, *Kruse v Johnson* [1898] 2 QB 91, pp.99–100, per Lord Russell of Killowen CJ; and *Short v Poole Corporation* [1926] Ch 66, pp.87–88 (per Lord Pollock MR), 91 (per Warrington LJ) and 95 (per Sargant LJ).

matter is so unreasonable that no reasonable authority could ever have come to it, then the courts can interfere", even though its establishment would require "something overwhelming" and in the present case "the facts do not come anywhere near anything of that kind".[15]

Lord Greene recognised the sensitivity of this proposition:

> It is not what the court considers unreasonable, a different thing altogether. If it is what the court considers unreasonable, the court may very well have different views to that of a local authority on matters of high public policy of this kind. Some courts might think that no children ought to be admitted on Sundays at all, some courts might think the reverse, and all over the country I have no doubt on a thing of that sort honest and sincere people hold different views. The effect of the legislation is not to set up the court as an arbiter of the correctness of one view over another. It is the local authority that are set in that position and, provided they act, as they have acted, within the four corners of their jurisdiction, this court, in my opinion, cannot interfere.[16]

However, it is unclear how this is fundamentally different from asking whether the decision of an authority is "unreasonable in the sense that the court considers it to be a decision that no reasonable body could have come to".[17] The court may well be reluctant to interfere on the basis of unreasonableness, and it is conceivable that there are some decisions which would, with little controversy, be unreasonable to the point that few people would object to them being deemed unlawful. However, this still implicates the court as arbiter of what is and is not reasonable. Lord Greene was expressly affirming substantive review of decisions when he concluded that:

> it may be still possible to say that, although the local authority have [sic] kept within the four corners of the matters which they ought to consider, they have nevertheless come to a conclusion so unreasonable that no reasonable authority could ever have come to it.[18]

Whilst he added that the "power of the court to interfere in each case is not as an appellate authority to override a decision of the local authority",[19] this is not the same as categorically ruling out review on the merits, for it is possible to declare unlawful a decision on its merits and remit the decision back to the decision maker to be retaken. Whilst this would be a controversial form of review, it would still not implicate the court in an appellate function for it would not be substituting its decision in place of the decision maker. In any event, even if the court is restrained and takes steps to distance itself from merits review, determining what is unreasonable in a legal sense still positions the court as an arbiter of reasonableness, and takes it controversially close to

---

[15] *Associated Provincial Picture Houses Ltd v Wednesbury Corporation* [1948] 1 KB 223, p.230.
[16] *Id.*, pp.230–231.   [17] *Id.*, p.230.   [18] *Id.*, p.234.   [19] *Id.*

merits review. This does not mean, however, that *Wednesbury* unreasonableness is not an important or defensible ground in the judicial review armoury. It is valuable and can be justified, but the courts must exercise significant caution and discipline in its exercise.

Substantive Review

The classic formulation of unreasonableness, including in the cases leading up to *Wednesbury*, was primarily substantive in the sense that it focused on the extent to which the decision was so outstandingly bad that it should be regarded as unlawful. This tended to be framed in the language of decisions that were "manifestly unjust",[20] "arbitrary and capricious",[21] "capricious and vexatious",[22] "frivolous or vexatious"[23] and so on. It is also what prompted Lord Diplock to speak in *Council of Civil Service Unions* v *Minister for the Civil Service* of decisions "so outrageous in [their] defiance of logic or of accepted moral standards that no sensible person who had applied his mind to the question to be decided could have arrived at it".[24] It is encapsulated in Warrington LJ's example of dismissing a teacher because she had red hair "or for some equally frivolous and foolish reason".[25] Unreasonable decisions were those that would "jump off the page at you",[26] or those "so wrong that no reasonable person could sensibly take that view".[27] A decision maker taking an unreasonable decision might appear to have "taken leave of his senses".[28]

However, the language of the courts has not always been so colourful or invoked a sense of decisions so outstandingly bad that they should be struck down as unlawful. This is perhaps a reflection of the fact that there will be relatively few real life examples of decisions which would attract such universal condemnation that their being struck down as unlawful would be roundly and uncontroversially accepted. Most public administrators would presumably not lack the competence, experience, self-awareness and good judgment necessary to avoid making such egregious decisions. Hartmann J described *Wednesbury* unreasonable decisions as those "so flawed that no reasonable decision maker could have reached those decisions".[29] Litton PJ was even milder in tone, describing the basis for the court's intervention on unreasonableness as arising "only where the administrator has acted beyond the range of responses

---

[20] *Kruse* v *Johnson* [1898] 2 QB 91, pp.99–100.   [21] *Weinberger* v *Inglis* [1919] AC 606, p.626.
[22] *R* v *Barnet and Camden Rent Tribunal, ex parte Frey Investments Ltd* [1972] 2 QB 342.
[23] *Id.*   [24] *Council of Civil Service Unions* v *Minister for the Civil Service* [1985] AC 374, p.410.
[25] *Short* v *Poole Corporation* [1926] Ch 66, p.91.
[26] *R* v *Lord Chancellor* [1997] 1 WLR 104, p.109.
[27] *Secretary of State for Education and Science* v *Tameside Metropolitan Borough Council* [1977] AC 1014, pp.1025–1026.
[28] *R* v *Secretary of State for the Environment, ex parte Nottinghamshire County Council* [1986] AC 240, p.247.
[29] *Yook Tong Electric Co Ltd* v *Commissioner for Transport* [2003] HKEC 170, para.66.

reasonably open to him under the statutory scheme".[30] *Wednesbury* unreasonableness was described as meaning "beyond rational justification"[31] and a decision which the decision maker "could not have reached if it was applying its mind to the issues in a fair, balanced and reasonable way".[32] Nevertheless, the allegation of substantive unreasonableness is "often asserted but seldom with success".[33] This will predominantly be because of the high threshold attaching to the standard of unreasonableness, though where *Wednesbury* unreasonableness is used as a qualitative assessment of procedural review, a potentially lower threshold of review seems to be discernible.

Procedural Review

Despite the rhetoric of the courts about unreasonableness being reserved as a ground for marginal cases in which the decision maker has egregiously violated acceptable parameters of decision making, the courts have been willing to strike down decisions that have fallen significantly short of such offending standards. This has been seen in relation to procedural review rather than substantive review. This will be somewhat easier to establish for two related reasons. First, as noted, there should be relatively few real-life situations where a decision maker has made a decision which is so egregious that it falls foul of *Wednesbury* unreasonableness as a substantive control on discretion. Second, it is easier as a matter of principle to examine the decision-making process and to identify procedural deficiencies which can be regarded as unreasonable. Importantly, this appears to maintain some distance between the courts and merits review, as substantive review is replaced by a critique of process. This might translate into less judicial reluctance to intervene under this head of review. In other words, the court can avoid or preempt criticism that it is trespassing on the domain of executive decision makers by affirming that the decision maker was free to exercise its discretion, but that it has departed from what is procedurally reasonable and would therefore be required to retake the decision.

An example which illustrates *Wednesbury* unreasonableness as a ground of procedural review – and with a lower threshold of review – is *Zestra Asia Ltd* v *Commissioner for Transport*.[34] The Commissioner for Transport could refuse an application for a Personalized Vehicle Registration Mark (PVRM) "if, in his opinion, the proposed personalized registration mark... is likely to be offensive to a reasonable person, or has a connotation offensive to good taste

---

[30] *Lau Kong Yung* v *Director of Immigration* (1999) 2 HKCFAR 300, p.334. This was reminiscent of language used by Sir Thomas Bingham MR in *R* v *Ministry of Defence, ex parte Smith* [1996] QB 517, p.554.
[31] *Kennedy* v *Charity Commission* [2014] UKSC 20, para.132.
[32] *Ala* v *General Medical Council* (2000) WL 1720374, para.9.
[33] *Lau Kong Yung* v *Director of Immigration* (1999) 2 HKCFAR 300, p.335.
[34] *Zestra Asia Ltd* v *Commissioner for Transport* [2007] 4 HKLRD 722.

or decency".[35] Zestra Asia Ltd was a Hong Kong seller, marketer and distributor of a female sexual arousal oil which was recognised by various professional journals as an effective product used in the treatment of, or as a therapy for, female sexual arousal disorder or dysfunction. The company applied for a PVRM in the form of "ZESTRA". The Commissioner purported to reject Zestra's application in accordance with the Regulations on the basis that the proposed PVRM was likely to be offensive to a reasonable person, or had a connotation offensive to good taste or decency.

Despite the Commissioner's decision being substantively permitted by the Regulations, the decision was held to be *Wednesbury* unreasonable and quashed. The problem lay not in the substantive decision as such, but in the process by which the decision was made. In coming to its conclusion, the court accepted that whether the proposed PVRM was likely to be offensive or have a connotation offensive to good taste or decency was a matter for the Commissioner, but identified factors which in its view vitiated the process by which the decision was made.

First, the court referred to evidence that the Commissioner regarded the general community in Hong Kong to be socially conservative and that it would therefore find an open reference to sexual intercourse to be objectionable and offensive to good taste or decency. However, the Commissioner had "not explained the objective basis for his view", there being no automatic conclusion from the fact that the local population was predominantly ethnically Chinese that the general public would be likely to be upset by such a reference to sexual intercourse. The Commissioner had failed to show a "cogent and objective basis" for his view, and there was no information or material before the Commissioner to indicate how well known or otherwise was the product.[36]

Second, the Commissioner had consulted three bodies in the course of making his decision on Zestra's application, and claimed in his explanation for the decision that it was supported by the comments of those bodies. However, none of the comments submitted by those bodies substantially supported the Commissioner's decision. The Police has been consulted, but had made no comment on the proposed PVRM: this could clearly not support the contention that the proposed PVRM would be likely to be received as offensive or have a connotation offensive to good taste or decency. The Home Affairs Bureau had been consulted, yet its view that Zestra was a "medical product for arousal" would not naturally correspond with its view that Zestra would, as a word, be "sexually offensive". This somewhat incoherent statement did not provide substantial support for the Commissioner's conclusion. Finally, the Official Languages Division had been consulted, but had (ironically) described the product as a "tropical oil for female sexual response", rather

---

[35] Road Traffic (Registration and Licensing of Vehicles) Regulations (cap. 374E), reg.12F(2)(a).
[36] *Zestra Asia Ltd* v *Commissioner for Transport* [2007] 4 HKLRD 722, para.45.

than a "topical" oil.[37] In any event, this was merely descriptive and did not express any value judgment on whether the word would be regarded as offensive. In short, none of the views submitted by the consulted bodies provided the requisite support for the Commissioner's decision.

Chu J stated that:

> in judicial review applications, the severity of the decision is not a ground for disturbing it so long as the decision falls within the permitted range of discretion open to the decision maker. However, the critical issue in this application is not whether the standard or approach adopted by the Commissioner is too high or strict. What the applicant's complaint boils down to is: [w]hat objective basis was there for the view that the proposed PVRM is sexually offensive or for the conclusion that it is likely to be offensive to a reasonable man in Hong Kong and/or is offensive to good taste or decency? The Court is therefore not asked to give a view on the moral standard of the community. Neither is it substituting its value or moral judgment for that of the Commissioner.[38]

However, an "objective and rational justification for the Commissioner's conclusion on the proposed PVRM and the decision to refuse the applicant's application ha[d] not been shown", and therefore the decision was *Wednesbury* unreasonable.[39]

Clearly the substantive decision was not one which could lightly be regarded as so unreasonable that no reasonable decision maker would have made it: it was open to the Commissioner to reach the substantive conclusion that he did. First, the vitiating factors related to the process leading to the decision, rather than the decision itself. Second, the decision maker had substantively remained within the four corners of his statutory powers.[40] Third, even if there were deficiencies in the decision-making process which called into question the extent to which the Commissioner's decision was satisfactory, were those deficiencies so egregious that they should be regarded as impairing the legality of the decision? Were these really deficiencies that would not be committed by a reasonable decision maker and which were "overwhelming", to adopt the language of Lord Greene MR? Were they, to use the language of Lord Diplock, "so outrageous in [their] defiance of logic or of accepted moral

---

[37] Counsel for the Commissioner averred that the Official Languages Division had in fact described Zestra as a "topical" oil, but that there was a clerical error when this was communicated to the Commissioner as a "tropical" oil. However, the court found that there was no evidence to support this averment.
[38] *Zestra Asia Ltd* v *Commissioner for Transport* [2007] 4 HKLRD 722, para.48.
[39] *Id.*, para.49.
[40] Though Lord Greene did state that *Wednesbury* unreasonableness could apply even though the body had kept within the four corners of the matters which it ought to consider – *Associated Provincial Picture Houses Ltd* v *Wednesbury Corporation* [1948] 1 KB 223, p.234.

standards that no sensible person who had applied his mind to the question to be decided"[41] could have committed them?

It rather appears that the court applied a lower threshold than the earlier conceptions of *Wednesbury* unreasonableness, and was taking a closer look at how, as a matter of process, discretion had been exercised. This was by no means the only way to impugn the legality of the decision. It could have been argued that the Commissioner had taken into account insufficiently relevant considerations by invoking conceptions of social conservatism which appeared to have no empirical basis. It could have been argued that he failed to take into account relevant considerations by apparently disregarding the views of the consulted bodies which did not factually support the Commissioner's findings, or that he had fettered his discretion by taking a decision which was unsupported by the views of the consulted bodies, suggesting that he had already made up his mind that the proposed PVRM should be rejected. It could have been argued that there was a material error of fact on the basis that the evidence on which the decision was based was non-existent, not reasonably capable of supporting the decision or was wrong or misunderstood. Despite these less extreme options being open to the court, it instead contrasted the decision with the process by which it was made, and held the lack of substantive correlation between them to be *Wednesbury* unreasonable. Rather than holding that no reasonable decision maker would have made this decision (substantive review),[42] it was held that no reasonable decision maker would have made his decision *in this way* (procedural review). This effectively lowers the standard of review, as the way in which the Commissioner exercised his discretion could not easily be described as "outrageous", "arbitrary and capricious" or any of the other adjectives that originally characterised *Wednesbury* unreasonableness as a standard of review. The lack of cogent, objective and rational justification for a decision is a lower standard than that encapsulated in the traditional *Wednesbury* standard.

A similar phenomenon can be seen in the Court of Appeal in *Ng Koon Fat* v *Li Wai Chi*.[43] The case related to the electoral arrangements for an Indigenous Inhabitant Representative (IIR) for Shek Lung Tsai village in the New Territories. A number of persons with the surname Fung registered as electors in the village and were included on the provisional register of electors. The applicant in the case, the incumbent IIR for the village, appealed against the inclusion of the Fungs. The decision to include them on the register was ultimately confirmed by the Revising Officer (RO) under the Village Representative Election Ordinance (cap. 576). The RO had essentially considered two questions in the exercise of his discretion: (i) whether there were any

---

[41] *Council of Civil Service Unions* v *Minister for the Civil Service* [1985] AC 374, p.410.
[42] The court could hardly have done this, as the substantive decision was permitted by the Regulations.
[43] *Ng Koon Fat* v *Li Wai Chi* [2013] 2 HKLRD 109 (CA).

persons surnamed Fung living in the village in 1898, and (ii) if yes, whether the electors in question were descendants of such persons. This would determine the eligibility or otherwise of the Fungs to participate as electors.

The applicant sought judicial review of the RO's decision, including on the ground of *Wednesbury* unreasonableness. This was unsuccessful at first instance,[44] but was revisited by the Court of Appeal. The court was concerned not so much with the substantive decision, as with the reasoning underlying the decision. As Barma JA explained, "it is proper for the Court to have regard to the reasoning of the RO, since it is against the background of that reasoning that the reasonableness or otherwise of the RO's findings and determination should be assessed".[45] He added that the court "should not interfere with a finding or decision of the RO unless it is satisfied that it is clearly or obviously wrong".[46]

The court assessed the way in which the RO had evaluated the evidence before him. It appeared from the evidence that there were two possible versions of fact before the RO, but the court was not persuaded that the RO was entitled to choose whichever of the two versions seemed to him more probable. Where there was nothing to show which version of fact was the more probable of the two, the RO could not "make a guess as to which of the two possibilities represented the true position".[47] Accordingly:

> The conclusion that the material put before the RO could not support the finding that he made ... means, in my view, that the finding was not one which was reasonably open to him, and that it was one which was beyond the range of reasonable findings which he could make. It was, therefore, unreasonable in the *Wednesbury* sense.[48]

The court allowed the appeal and quashed the decisions of the RO. This is again a form of procedural review, where the substantive decision reached by the RO was permitted by the statutory framework and was not in itself *Wednesbury* unreasonable, but the way in which he arrived at the decision was deemed to be. This again shows a lower threshold of review than that traditionally encapsulated in the *Wednesbury* threshold. The decision maker may simply have been acting in a difficult situation, where competing and equally persuasive versions of fact were before him, and he felt compelled to make a decision on the basis of that evidence. This could have been attacked as procedurally unsound, or a material error of fact whereby the evidence on which the decision was based was not reasonably capable of supporting the decision. Resort to *Wednesbury* unreasonableness was unnecessary, and neither the decisions nor the process by which it was made could feasibly be regarded as so unreasonable, illogical or immoral that "no sensible person"

---

[44] *Ng Koon Fat v Li Wai Chi* [2012] HKEC 156.
[45] *Ng Koon Fat v Li Wai Chi* [2013] 2 HKLRD 109 (CA), para.16   [46] *Id.*   [47] *Id.*, para.25.
[48] *Id.*, para.26.

could have exercised his discretion in this way. This stretches *Wednesbury* unreasonableness to breaking point. The court hardly had particularly constructive suggestions on how the relevant officers should have acted.[49]

It will be instructive, as the case law develops, to see whether the courts increasingly adopt this lower standard when applying the ground of unreasonableness to procedure rather than substance. If the trend continues, it is possible that two *Wednesbury* standards might emerge: a higher threshold for review of substantive decisions, and a lower threshold of review for decision-making processes. However, it would probably be regrettable if such a low (procedural) standard of *Wednesbury* review continued. In the first place, the recent cases where this lower standard has been applied suggest that the conduct complained of could be sufficiently captured by other grounds of review. This renders the lowering of the threshold unnecessary and duplicative. Perhaps more fundamentally, it undermines the serious contribution that *Wednesbury* unreasonableness – an already more controversial ground of review – has to make to impugning egregious decisions. The ground should be preserved for marginal cases where outstandingly bad decisions are made, and given that it has its own internal content and logic, it should not be used as a casual label for other defects in the exercise of discretion, nor should the content and logic of other grounds be indiscriminately allowed to bleed into this most exceptional of grounds.

Intensity of Review

Wednesbury unreasonableness is typified by a high threshold (or low intensity) of review.[50] It appears, however, that a lower or higher intensity of *Wednesbury* review might be applied by the courts in particular cases.[51] What the courts search for when reviewing for unreasonableness varies.[52]

Lower Intensity of Review

The courts have expressed reluctance to review particular kinds of decisions out of concern for adherence to the separation of powers. This is typically seen in relation to decisions which are said to be informed by policy considerations to a greater extent than is normally the case. As stated by Sir Thomas Bingham MR in the Court of Appeal of England and Wales:

---

[49] See *id.*, paras.28–30.
[50] *Council of Civil Service Unions* v *Minister for the Civil Service* [1985] AC 374 (HL), p.410; *Lau Kong Yung* v *Director of Immigration* (1999) 2 HKCFAR 300, p.334; *Chiang Lily* v *Secretary for Justice* [2009] HKEC 1562, para.30. This is subject to a potentially lower threshold being applied in cases of procedural review on so-called *Wednesbury* grounds.
[51] This is also related to more general considerations on the variable intensity of judicial review.
[52] See generally Paul Daly, "Wednesbury's Reason and Structure" [2011] Public Law 238.

The greater the policy content of a decision, and the more remote the subject matter of a decision from ordinary judicial experience, the more hesitant the court must necessarily be in holding a decision to be irrational. That is good law and, like most good law, common sense. Where decisions of a policy-laden, esoteric or security-based nature are in issue even greater caution than normal must be shown in applying the test, but the test itself is sufficiently flexible to cover all situations.[53]

The difficulty is identifying what decisions are covered by this lower intensity of review.[54] It must be too broad to refer to decisions informed by policy considerations, as most, if not all, decisions will have some policy content. An area in Hong Kong in which the claim is frequently made is in relation to immigration decisions. Whilst immigration decisions may be reviewed on the basis of *Wednesbury* unreasonableness, the threshold of review has been said to be "necessarily very high".[55] This is said to be due to the particular policy pressures faced by the Director of Immigration in administering a system of immigration in such a densely populated jurisdiction with regionally attractive economic and social standards.[56] Few would deny that proper immigration controls are necessary in Hong Kong given these issues, and that difficult policy issues will be involved.

However, there is a risk of overstatement. First, it is not necessarily the case that any special regime of discretionary control applies to the Director of Immigration,[57] and the view that immigration decisions were entirely a matter for the Director to decide the manner in which his discretion should be exercised and that the courts would not supervise that discretion on *Wednesbury* principles[58] was specifically deemed an erroneous approach.[59] The statement that it "must be always borne in mind that it is for the Director [of Immigration] and not for the courts to administer the scheme of immigration control under the Ordinance"[60] does not indicate a particular limitation on the power of the court in judicial review of the Director's decisions.[61] This is no more than a truism of the separation of powers: it is for any given decision maker to

---

[53] *R v Ministry of Defence, ex parte Smith* [1996] QB 517, p. 556.
[54] Some decisions will be non-justiciable, a distinct matter from intensity of review (which is relevant only to decisions that are justiciable).
[55] *Durga Maya Gurung v Director of Immigration* [2002] HKEC 477 (CA), para.60.
[56] *Id.*, paras.51–57; *Bhupendra Pun v Director of Immigration* [2002] HKLRD (Yrbk) 460, para.9; *Re Singh Sukhmander* [2008] HKEC 1570, para.7; *Gurung Deu Kumari v Director of Immigration* [2010] 5 HKLRD 219, paras.19–22; *Pollard v Permanent Secretary for Security* [2011] 3 HKLRD H1, paras.57 and 62. It was said that immigration control involves decisions of high political and socio-economic content which should be accorded a "broad margin of discretion" – *BI v Director of Immigration* [2016] 2 HKLRD 520, para.107.
[57] *Aguilar Joenalyn Elmedorial v Director of Immigration* [2014] HKEC 225 (CFA), paras. 5–12.
[58] *Krishna Rai v Director of Immigration*, HCAL 145/1999, p.5.
[59] *Aguilar Joenalyn Elmedorial v Director of Immigration* [2014] HKEC 225 (CFA), para.8.
[60] *R v Director of Immigration, ex parte Chan Heung Mui* [1993] 3 HKPLR 533, p.547.
[61] *Durga Maya Gurung v Director of Immigration* [2002] HKEC 477 (CA), para.58.

administer a legislative scheme as appointed by the Legislative Council, and the court is confined to review of legality.[62] Indeed, a high threshold of *Wednesbury* review attached not only to the Director of Immigration, but to other "departmental head[s] of government ... entrusted by the Legislature with administrative responsibilities".[63]

This feeds into a related point which is that, taking the issue of high population density, the Director of Immigration will not be the only official facing difficult policy challenges in this regard. Urban and infrastructure planning will be particularly difficult in a city with high population density. Noise control policy must be challenging where a large number of people live in high density housing in close proximity not only to each other, but to commercial premises and busy roads, railways, waterways and airways. Pollution control must bring policy challenges when there is such a high concentration of commercial and industrial activity as in Hong Kong, exacerbated by its status as an international shipping and aviation hub.[64] Waste disposal policy is increasingly challenging, with existing landfill sites in Hong Kong facing serious capacity issues; whilst health officials must also be faced with difficult policy issues in the population density context, given that diseases can spread more easily and containment is made particularly difficult. This only feeds on the population density issue, before one accounts for the many other, considerable policy challenges facing Hong Kong, such as economic and social inequality, mental health and environmental sustainability. Executive decision makers across the board are faced with difficult decisions as an inherent feature of policy work.

It is also sometimes said that courts exercise deference when "polycentric" decisions are under review, namely decisions which involve a "large number of interlocking and interacting interests and considerations".[65] Thus decisions of the Director of Public Prosecutions were said to be amenable to judicial review but "should only be disturbed in highly exceptional cases" in a case in which *Wednesbury* unreasonableness was alleged.[66] This was due to factors which included:

> the polycentric character of official decision-making in such matters including policy and public interest considerations which are not susceptible of

---

[62] The legality/merits distinction in the immigration context was acknowledged in *Aita Bahadur Limbu v Director of Immigration* [1999] HKEC 788.
[63] *Lau Kong Yung v Director of Immigration* (1999) 2 HKCFAR 300, p.334.
[64] Article 128 of the Basic Law requires the Government to provide conditions and take measures for the maintenance of Hong Kong's status as a centre of international and regional aviation.
[65] Peter Cane, *Administrative Law* (5th edn) (Oxford University Press, 2011), p.274; earlier edition cited with approval in *Pushpanathan v Canada* [1998] 1 SCR 982 (Supreme Court of Canada), para.36.
[66] *Ng Chi Keung v Secretary for Justice* [2016] HKEC 909, para. 121.

judicial review because it is within neither the constitutional function nor the practical competence of the courts to assess their merits.[67]

However, this is again a reflection of the separation of powers and many policy-informed decisions must be of a "polycentric" character. The court must account for what is likely to be the superior knowledge, experience and broader policy view of the decision maker over that of the court in the subject matter to which the impugned decision relates, and the court must accordingly exercise caution in judicial review. The more complex or policy-laden the subject matter, the more difficult it may be to identify the legality/merits distinction. To ensure that the court confines its assessment to that of legality, the intensity of review may be lowered to avoid encroachment on the merits. Deference does not (or should not) imply judicial servility or capitulation,[68] as egregious decisions may be struck down as *Wednesbury* unreasonable even where they are of a complex or policy-laden nature.[69]

It is unclear, however, whether and to what extent decisions are subject to a lower intensity of review unless they are *Wednesbury* unreasonable, or whether they are subject to a lower intensity of *Wednesbury* review. A number of illustrations would suggest that the former approach prevails. It was stated that the court should not second-guess the professional judgment of a disciplinary committee except where it had plainly misread the evidence and come to a conclusion that was contrary to the evidence or plainly wrong.[70] The court would not interfere with disciplinary decisions unless something had gone seriously wrong and an irrational decision was made,[71] or a decision made which was plainly or manifestly wrong or *Wednesbury* unreasonable.[72] It was said often to be a matter of professional judgment as to what information was required to be contained in an Environmental Impact Assessment Report, and that the court was not entitled to interfere unless the exercise of that judgment had been *Wednesbury* unreasonable.[73] The Director of Immigration's determination of facts in exercise of his discretion to grant permission to reside in Hong Kong should be left to the Director unless he

---

[67] *Matalulu v Director of Public Prosecutions* [2003] 4 LRC 712, endorsed in *R (Corner House Research) v Director of the Serious Fraud Office* [2009] 1 AC 756, para. 31. However, a generally lower intensity of review applies to prosecutorial decisions – see pp.104–108.

[68] See *R (on the application of ProLife Alliance) v BBC* [2004] 1 AC 185, p.240; and *R (on the application of Carson) v Secretary of State for Work and Pensions* [2003] EWCA Civ 797, para.73.

[69] If a decision maker misdirects himself or herself in law, or misconstrues the scope of his or her legal powers, or violates his or her discretion such as by fettering or exercising it for an improper purpose, there is generally no reason why the courts should exercise deference to the decision maker, whether or not the case involves policy considerations.

[70] *Tong Pon Wah v Hong Kong Society of Accountants* [1998] 2 HKLRD 427 (CA), p.440.

[71] *Tsang Hing Shing v Commissioner of Police* [2004] HKEC 1540, para.32(3).

[72] *Dr To Chun Fang Albert v Medical Council of Hong Kong* [2011] HKEC 279, paras.14 and 19.

[73] *Chu Yee Wah v Director of Environmental Protection* [2011] 5 HKLRD 469 (CA), para.84.

acted perversely.[74] Even when the court acknowledged the particular policy challenges faced in the immigration context, the standard *Wednesbury* threshold was applied.[75] The wide discretion on the part of police in relation to operational decisions and those concerning the allocation of scarce resources could still be struck down as *Wednesbury* unreasonable,[76] even if care would be taken by the courts in review of such decisions. On the other hand, Sir Thomas Bingham MR's statement in the Court of Appeal of England and Wales appeared to suggest a lower intensity of *Wednesbury* review.[77]

An area in which caution should be urged in the Hong Kong context is where it is said that the courts should exercise deference in relation to decisions subject to political control; for example, where a decision is subject to legislative approval. Lord Scarman stated in *R v Secretary of State for the Environment, ex parte Nottinghamshire County Council* that the court was:

> in the field of public financial administration and we are being asked to review the exercise by the Secretary of State of an administrative discretion which inevitably requires a political judgment on his part and which cannot lead to action by him against a local authority unless that action is first approved by the House of Commons.[78]

He added that judicial review was a "great weapon in the hands of the judges: but the judges must observe the constitutional limits set by our parliamentary system upon their exercise of this beneficent power".[79] First, however, the court would still intervene if the Secretary of State had acted in bad faith, for an improper motive or if the "consequences of his guidance were so absurd that he must have taken leave of his senses".[80] Second, Hong Kong does not have a "parliamentary system" of this nature and its legislature is rather more restricted in its powers than the UK Parliament. Even if the principle is accepted that the courts should exercise deference where a decision is subject to political control, the constitutional context in Hong Kong (including the strongly executive-led nature of the system and the existence of functional constituencies in the Legislative Council) must inform whether and to what

---

[74] *Aita Bahadur Limbu v Director of Immigration* [1999] HKEC 788.
[75] *Pollard v Permanent Secretary for Security* [2011] 3 HKLRD H1.
[76] *R v Chief Constable of Sussex, ex parte International Trader's Ferry Ltd* [1999] 2 AC 418 (HL). (The relevant decision was not struck down in this case). A decision will not be immune from review simply because public finances are a consideration for the decision maker – *R v North and East Devon Health Authority, ex parte Coughlan* [2001] QB 213.
[77] *R v Ministry of Defence, ex parte Smith* [1996] QB 517, p.556.
[78] *R v Secretary of State for the Environment, ex parte Nottinghamshire County Council* [1986] AC 240, p.247; and see *R v Secretary of State for the Environment, ex parte Hammersmith and Fulham London Borough Council* [1991] 1 AC 521 (HL), p.597.
[79] *R v Secretary of State for the Environment, ex parte Nottinghamshire County Council* [1986] AC 240, pp.250–251.
[80] *Id.*, p.247.

extent the courts defer in relation to such decisions.[81] Just as there are questions over the extent to which a parallel application of the *Carltona* principle would be constitutionally appropriate in Hong Kong,[82] so are there questions over the extent to which courts should defer to decision makers on the basis of so-called political control. Crucially, however, the matter is fundamentally informed by the separation of powers.

Higher Intensity of Review

The courts may adopt a more intensive standard of review than *Wednesbury* unreasonableness where human or fundamental rights are involved. As explained by Au J:

> In common law, the court in reviewing in public law a public authority's decision would adopt a standard of review which would correspond with the degree or gravity of the impact of that decision on the affected applicant. At the one end is the standard of conventional *Wednesbury* test ... where no human rights are engaged. At the other end (where human and fundamental rights are engaged and said to be violated), the court would adopt what we now generally describe as the proportionality (or justification) test. In between, the court would review with increasing vigilance a subject decision which has increasingly grave and adverse impact on the affected person's interests (but short of referable human rights) to see if that decision should be quashed, but still and only in my view in the *Wednesbury* sense. What it means however is that, the graver the decision has an impact on the affected person, the more vigilant and closely the court would look at the reasons of and all matters taken into account by the decision maker to see if there is *Wednesbury* unreasonableness in that decision, including for example, whether certain matters or factors should or should not be taken into account as a matter of relevance, and whether there is procedural impropriety.[83]

The principle was developed in a number of English cases. Notable among the relevant pronouncements were Lord Bridge of Harwich's statement that where an individual's right to life was at risk from an administrative decision, the basis of the decision called for "the most anxious scrutiny";[84] his statement in a separate case that a restriction on the freedom of expression required to be justified and that "nothing less than an important competing public interest will be sufficient to justify it";[85] and the Court of Appeal of England and

---

[81] See further Benny Tai, "The Chief Executive" in Johannes Chan and C. L. Lim (eds), *Law of the Hong Kong Constitution* (2nd edn) (Sweet and Maxwell, 2015), pp.206–209.
[82] See pp.165–168.
[83] *Pagtama Victorina Alegre v Director of Immigration* [2016] HKEC 85, para.200.
[84] *R v Secretary of State for the Home Department, ex parte Bugdaycay* [1987] AC 514 (HL), p.531.
[85] *R v Secretary of State for the Home Department, ex parte Brind* [1991] 1 AC 696 (HL), pp.748–749. He added that the "primary judgment as to whether the particular competing

Wales' endorsement of the proposition that the "more substantial the interference with human rights, the more the court will require by way of justification before it is satisfied that the decision is reasonable".[86] The jurisprudential landscape changed significantly, however, with the incorporation of the European Convention on Human Rights into domestic law by the Human Rights Act 1998, after which human rights review has principally been conducted on a statutory basis.

Similarly, human rights review is principally conducted in Hong Kong under the Basic Law and the Bill of Rights. Accordingly, human and fundamental rights issues are less likely to be challenged by way of the conventional grounds of judicial review than if such instruments were not in place. Nevertheless, some have sought a reformulation and adaptation of the *Wednesbury* standard in the human rights context.[87] There might also be justifications for using different standards of review in human rights and non-human rights cases.[88] A heightened intensity of scrutiny can of course be provided for in statute. Thus there is a statutory presumption against reclamation in the harbour to which all public officers and public bodies shall have regard in the exercise of any powers vested in them,[89] which Hartmann J described as follows:

> something more rigorous than the standard *Wednesbury* test is required although, in my judgment, the level of anxious scrutiny that must be applied when there is a substantial interference with a fundamental human right would be to set the test too high.[90]

It should be noted that a higher intensity of scrutiny may apply not only to unreasonableness, but to other grounds. For example, the courts may scrutinise decisions relating to claimants under the Convention Against Torture for conformity with high standards of procedural fairness.[91]

Intensity of Review and the Wider Political Context

It is clear that the way in which unreasonableness is framed and applied as a ground of review has implications for the separation of powers. Judicial

---

public interest justifies the particular restriction imposed falls to be made by the Secretary of State to whom Parliament has entrusted the discretion" but that the court was "entitled to exercise a secondary judgment by asking whether a reasonable Secretary of State, on the material before him, could reasonably make that primary judgment".

[86] *R v Ministry of Defence, ex parte Smith* [1996] QB 517, pp.554 and 564–565.
[87] *Ng Siu Tung v Director of Immigration* (2002) 5 HKCFAR 1, para. 370, per Bokhary PJ.
[88] See James Goodwin, "The Last Defence of Wednesbury" [2012] Public Law 445; and see also Mark Elliott, "The Human Rights Act 1998 and the Standard of Substantive Review" (2001) *Cambridge Law Journal* 301, especially at p.322.
[89] Protection of the Harbour Ordinance (cap.531), s.3.
[90] *Society for the Protection of the Harbour Ltd v Chief Executive-in-Council (No 2)* [2004] 2 HKLRD 902, para.79; and see *Town Planning Board v Society for the Protection of the Harbour Ltd* (2004) 7 HKCFAR 1, paras.65–68.
[91] See p.179.

self-restraint would tend to indicate greater respect for the separation of powers, while a more liberal willingness to review might strain the separation of powers. However, the intensity of review is also potentially affected by the wider political context in Hong Kong, and in particular its strongly executive-led system and the so-called democratic deficit manifesting in constraints on the powers of the Legislative Council and the existence of functional constituencies. There might be an argument for claiming that this political context justifies the courts in scrutinising decisions more closely, with an overall higher intensity of review. If accountability cannot be appropriately secured through political channels, then this may to some extent be compensated by qualitative accountability through judicial review (providing, of course, that the focus remains on legality and not merits). Judicial self-restraint is, after all, fundamentally informed by the broader political and constitutional context in which it operates.[92]

However, it is questionable whether a lack of electoral accountability in the executive (and to a lesser extent the legislature) is appropriately counterbalanced by less restraint on the part of an unelected judiciary. Furthermore, the majority of executive decision makers – even in jurisdictions with a more conventional political system than Hong Kong – are unelected, namely civil servants, administrative tribunal members and so on. Whilst these decision makers may (but will not always) be accountable to an elected head of a government department, the reality is that the bulk of decisions formally taken by a government department or public body are in fact taken by unelected officials, and whilst the head of the department or body will be expected to have overall control and management of his or her staff,[93] judicial review very often involves unelected judges reviewing the decisions of unelected members of the executive. Increased intensity of review, and increased scrutiny for substantive and procedural unreasonableness, is therefore not uncontentiously justified by the wider political context in Hong Kong. There are certainly factors justifying a strong law of judicial review policed by an independent judiciary, but also risks associated with increasing the intensity of scrutiny beyond what is acceptable in the context of the separation of powers.

Unreasonableness vs. Irrationality

Historically, reference seems to have been made to unreasonableness rather than irrationality, but there is now a tendency for the terms to be used interchangeably.[94] Sir William Wade and Christopher Forsyth have questioned whether "irrationality" is a better term, as:

---

[92] See Lord Irvine of Lairg, "Judges and Decision Makers: The Theory and Practice of Wednesbury Review" [1996] Public Law 59, pp.75–78.
[93] Consider the *Carltona* principle and to what extent it is apposite in Hong Kong; see pp.165–168.
[94] See, for example, *Yook Tong Electric Co Ltd* v *Commissioner for Transport* [2003] HKEC 170, para.78.

Virtually all administrative decisions are rational in the sense that they are made for intelligible reasons, but the question then is whether they measure up to the legal standard of reasonableness. 'Irrational' most naturally means 'devoid of reasons', whereas 'unreasonable' means 'devoid of satisfactory reasons'.[95]

A conceptual and practical distinction can be made between unreasonableness and irrationality. Unreasonableness would appear to be a more substantive, evaluative, qualitative assessment, asking whether the decision or the process by which it is made is "bad", and if yes, whether it is so egregiously bad that it should not be recognised as a lawful decision. It is, fundamentally, a qualitative standard, and involves a value judgment on whether the decision or decision-making process is outrageous, absurd, perverse, unfair, frivolous, vexatious and so on. Irrationality could, by contrast, have a more mechanical methodology, and a more objective tenor of assessment. Etymologically, an irrational decision is one that is not reasoned. If this approach was adopted, the nature of the investigation could change to assessing how the decision was made, according to which standards and criteria, whether the decision-making process was conducted in a reasoned and cogent manner, whether it had internal logical consistency and coherence, and so on.

To appreciate how the distinction might operate in practice, consider a variation on the facts of *Zestra*, discussed earlier.[96] It will be recalled that the principal defect was in the process by which the Commissioner for Transport reached a decision, not in the substantive decision itself. There is, however, no fixed correlation between procedural and substantive defects. Assume that the proposed PVRM had not been "ZESTRA", but had instead been "COFFEE". Assume also that the Commissioner had consulted the same three bodies on whether the term "COFFEE" was likely to be offensive to a reasonable person or had a connotation offensive to good taste or decency, in deciding whether to approve the proposed PVRM. Finally, assume (as almost everyone would agree) that "COFFEE" could not reasonably be considered likely to be offensive to a reasonable person or have a connotation offensive to good taste or decency. There are four possible outcomes under the rationality/reasonableness matrix:

1. Rational process and reasonable decision
   The Commissioner follows a rational and reasoned process, consults bodies in the opinion of which "COFFEE" would *not* be likely to be offensive, and adduces evidence that the term would be unlikely to be construed in an offensive way. The Commissioner therefore decides that "COFFEE" is not

---

[95] Wade and Forsyth, *Administrative Law* (11th edn), p.295. The authors stated in an earlier edition that unreasonableness and irrationality "are two different things, and for legal purposes they are best differentiated by the established terminology. For the sake of clarity as well as consistency it seems best to employ 'unreasonableness' as the key word, as the courts in fact often prefer to do".

[96] See pp.230–233.

likely to be offensive and approves the application. He follows a rational process which results in a substantively reasonable decision.

2. Rational process and unreasonable decision
The Commissioner follows a rational and reasoned process, consults bodies in the opinion of which "COFFEE" *would* be likely to be offensive, and adduces evidence that the term could be construed in an offensive way. The Commissioner therefore decides that "COFFEE" is likely to be offensive and rejects the application. He follows a rational process which results in a substantively unreasonable decision (i.e. the decision is so egregious that the court is likely to decide that it is *Wednesbury* unreasonable for a decision maker in the Commissioner's position to decide that "COFFEE" is likely to be offensive and to reject the application on that basis, even though the decision-making process was rational).

3. Irrational process and reasonable decision
The Commissioner consults bodies in the opinion of which "COFFEE" *would* be likely to be offensive, and adduces evidence that the term could be construed in an offensive way. However, the Commissioner decides that "COFFEE" would *not* be likely to be offensive and approves the application; even though the consultation and evidence adduced did not support the decision eventually made. The process followed by the decision maker is irrational given the lack of a coherent, reasoned relationship between the substantive decision and the process by which it was made, but he still arrives at a substantively reasonable decision.

4. Irrational process and unreasonable decision
The decision maker consults bodies in the opinion of which "COFFEE" would *not* be likely to be offensive, and fails to adduce evidence that the term could be construed in an offensive way. The decision maker nevertheless decides that "COFFEE" is likely to be offensive and rejects the application. The process followed by the decision maker is irrational given the lack of a coherent, reasoned relationship between the substantive decision and the process by which it was made, and he arrives at a substantively unreasonable decision.

These scenarios may be represented in tabular form:

Table 18.1 Rationality/reasonableness matrix

	Rational process?	Reasonable decision?
Scenario 1	✓	✓
Scenario 2	✓	✗
Scenario 3	✗	✓
Scenario 4	✗	✗

This matrix demonstrates some important points. First, there is increased analytical clarity in distinguishing between unreasonableness and irrationality, and between qualitative review which is more substantive or more procedural in emphasis. Rational processes will not always result in reasonable decisions, nor will irrational processes always result in unreasonable decisions. Second, irrationality might be used in relation to more procedural aspects of the decision-making process, and unreasonableness in relation to the substantive decision. The difference in terminology might help to separate the two aspects, and may allow variable *Wednesbury* thresholds to be applied in procedural as distinct from substantive review if that is thought desirable. When dealing with cases characterised by more procedural than substantive defects, however, other existing grounds of review would be likely to capture the alleged defects. Irrationality might therefore be used in conjunction with other grounds in a way that unreasonableness should not be.

Of course, the substantive reasonableness of a decision will probably be at least partly informed by the extent to which a rational process was followed in arriving at the decision. The decision-making process and the resulting decision are distinct, but not unrelated. However, there are advantages to being clear about what exactly calls the reasonableness (or rationality) of a decision into question: whether it is the decision-making process, the substantive decision, or both. This helps to focus the analysis on whether a more procedural complaint is being made, or whether the court is being invited to qualitatively assess the substance of the decision. This may also inform the standard and intensity of review that is used, as it seems that a higher standard of review is used when determining substantive unreasonableness than procedural irrationality.

Role of Reasons

Though there is no general common law duty to give reasons,[97] there can be incentives to give reasons even where these might not strictly be legally required, particularly as they might assist the decision maker to defend or preempt a challenge in judicial review. Reasons can point to the underlying reasonableness and rationality of a decision and the decision-making process. This relates both to substantive and procedural considerations. Reasons can support the reasonableness of a substantive decision by explaining why the decision was taken, what was the rationale underlying its being taken, what were its objectives or why it is fair or appropriate. Reasons can also support the rationality of a decision-making process by showing how it was reasoned or arrived at, what considerations were taken into account, what weight was attached to various considerations, how competing considerations were

---

[97] See pp.257–264.

balanced and so on. This can point to consistency, coherence and cogency in procedural logic, which can support both the rationality of the decision-making process and the reasonableness of the substantive decision. Reasons can, in both cases, show that what at first glance appears to be an aberrant or unusual decision is one which, in the circumstances, is properly reasoned and substantively justified. Persuasive reasons could be the difference between a decision being held reasonable or unreasonable. Nevertheless, the voluntary giving of reasons carries its own risks, in particular the possibility that the reasons expose rational deficiency or substantive unreasonableness. However, this should not lead decision makers to the conclusion that the voluntary giving of reasons is the assumption of an unnecessary risk, as the courts may assume that a decision is unlawfully taken in the absence of reasons which indicate otherwise.[98]

---

[98] See p.262.

19

Procedural Fairness, Procedural Impropriety and Natural Justice

There is a long history in the common law tradition of the courts protecting procedural fairness.[1] The courts have developed a framework of common law rules for the upholding of procedural protections and natural justice, in addition to such statutory protections as there may be. These provide an important baseline of procedural protections in individuals' dealings with public bodies, as well as promoting the integrity of a just system of public administration. Though public bodies will often have significant, sometimes overwhelming, power over the individual, the individual is still entitled to fair treatment and procedural propriety.

Lord Bridge of Harwich articulated the theme of this aspect of law:

> the so-called rules of natural justice are not engraved on tablets of stone. To use the phrase which better expresses the underlying concept, what the requirements of fairness demand when any body, domestic, administrative or judicial, has to make a decision which will affect the rights of individuals depends on the character of the decision-making body, the kind of decision it has to make and the statutory or other framework in which it operates. In particular, it is well-established that when a statute has conferred on any body the power to make decisions affecting individuals, the courts will not only require the procedure prescribed by the statute to be followed, but will readily imply so much and no more to be introduced by way of additional procedural safeguards as will ensure the attainment of fairness.[2]

It is not for the courts to take an abstract view of fairness or to consider whether another procedure might have been better or fairer.[3] The courts are concerned with instances of actual unfairness,[4] and they have not admitted

---

[1] Typically this was seen in a judicial or quasi-judicial context, but was extended to a wider range of decision makers – *Ridge* v *Baldwin* [1964] AC 40 (HL).
[2] *Lloyd* v *McMahon* [1987] AC 625, pp.702–703, per Lord Bridge of Harwich.
[3] *R* v *Secretary of State for the Home Department, ex parte Doody* [1994] 1 AC 351, pp.560–561, cited with approval in *Liu Pik Han* v *Hong Kong Federation of Insurers Appeals Tribunal* [2005] HKEC 1046.
[4] It was proposed by Megarry V-C that there is a "substantial distinction between the forfeiture cases and the application cases", namely, between those in which there is a decision to take

such a thing as "technical breach of natural justice".[5] Where the impugned procedure does not cause substantial prejudice to the applicant, the courts retain the discretion to refuse relief.[6]

Right to a Fair Hearing

A person who stands to be directly affected by a decision may be entitled to present his own case or version of the facts to the decision maker. This applies both in the context of an individual over which a decision maker has jurisdiction (for example, an applicant for a licence), and in the context of adjudication, where the adjudicator should hear both sides equally and afford to them an equal opportunity to present their respective case or version of the facts.[7] The principle *audi alteram partem*, literally "hear the other side", is particularly relevant in the latter case, part of which is that "the judge or whoever has to adjudicate must not hear evidence or receive representations from one side behind the back of the other".[8]

---

something away (such as membership of an organisation or a licence), and those in which there is a decision merely to refuse to grant the applicant what he seeks (such as membership of an organisation or a licence). He proposed that a higher standard of procedural fairness attached to forfeiture than to application cases, and that in normal application cases there is no requirement of an opportunity to be heard – *McInnes* v *Onslow-Fane* [1978] 1 WLR 1520 (HL), p.1529. Wade and Forsyth disputed both the notion that such a distinction applies to the exercise of statutory powers, and the claim that there is no requirement of an opportunity to be heard in normal application cases (Wade and Forsyth, *Administrative Law* (11th edn), p.464, fn.459). It is indeed doubtful whether any real distinction exists between forfeiture cases and application cases. In both cases, fairness requirements will be determined in the context of the extent to which the applicant is substantively affected by the decision in question. If Applicant A will be more greatly prejudiced by the decision in an application case (for example, for recognition as a torture claimant) than Applicant B will be prejudiced by the decision in a forfeiture case (for example, failing to have a trading licence renewed), then Applicant A's case will likely attract more stringent requirements of procedural fairness regardless of the forfeiture/application distinction. The distinction seems to be in the vein of the technical approach to natural justice that the courts have claimed to reject. Nevertheless, the courts have sometimes applied the forfeiture/application distinction in Hong Kong: *Pearl Securities Ltd* v *Stock Exchange of Hong Kong Ltd* [1999] 2 HKLRD 243, pp.255–256 (application case; albeit that this was simply borne in mind as one of the factors in determining what fairness required in that case); and *Chan Mei Yee* v *Director of Immigration* [2000] HKEC 788 (forfeiture case).

[5] *George* v *Secretary of State for the Environment* [1979] 77 LGR 689, p.617, per Lord Denning MR. He noted that Kerr J said in *Lake District Special Planning Board* v *Secretary of State for the Environment* [1975] JPL 220 that he "accept[ed] the submission that there can be no such thing as a "technical" breach of the rules of natural justice, since the concept of natural justice is not concerned with the observance of technicalities but with matters of substance". See also *Malloch* v *Aberdeen Corporation (No 1)*, 1971 SC (HL) 85, p.118.

[6] *Leung Fuk Wah Oil* v *Commissioner of Police* [2002] 3 HKLRD 653 (CA), para.40, per Cheung JA; see also *Siu Chi Wan* v *Secretary for Civil Service* [2008] HKEC 1134, paras.52–56.

[7] For an example of this principle violated in court proceedings, see *Yu Cho Lam* v *Commissioner of Police* [2016] 1 HKLRD 257. See also *Kanda* v *Malaya* [1962] AC 322 (PC) (Malaya), p.337.

[8] *Kanda* v *Malaya* [1962] AC 322 (PC) (Malaya), p.337, per Lord Denning. It was said that it is trite that the rule is to safeguard procedural fairness – *Hysan Development Co Ltd* v *Town Planning Board* [2014] HKEC 1869 (CA), para.166.

There may be a statutory duty to hear a party;[9] statute might instead purport to divest an individual of such a right, though this would be subject to Basic Law and Bill of Rights protections. When the statute makes no express provision on the matter, it is to the common law that one must turn to establish whether the applicant can claim a right to be heard. There is no automatic common law right to be heard. The courts have instead applied a fairness test to determine whether the right exists at common law in a given case. As Lord Mustill explained:

> Fairness will very often require that a person who may be adversely affected by the decision will have an opportunity to make representations on his own behalf either before the decision is taken with a view to producing a favourable result; or after it is taken, with a view to procuring its modification; or both.[10]

Moreover, a right to be heard does not translate in every case to a right to be orally heard[11]; fairness will dictate whether a right to be orally heard can be established in the individual circumstances of the case. Nor is a party automatically entitled to an oral hearing under Article 10 of the Bill of Rights,[12] which does not, in any event, require that every element of the protections it confers be present at every stage of a given procedure.[13]

The establishment of a common law right to be heard inevitably depends on context. Nevertheless, certain factors, if sufficiently demonstrated, are likely to weigh in favour of the right to an oral hearing being recognised by the court. They include a situation in which a dispute of fact or law exists which is difficult to examine on paper. In these circumstances, the applicant's interests in fairness would tend to be appropriately served by convening an oral hearing in order to allow the factual or legal dispute to be fairly ventilated.[14] It may also weigh in favour of an oral hearing that the possibility of cross-examination should be afforded to a person subject to particular proceedings.[15]

Where a negative decision could detrimentally affect an existing right or interest, fairness may require there to be an oral hearing so that the applicant is given the best opportunity to present his case. This might include, for example,

---

[9] An example of a statutory right to be orally heard can be found in the Town Planning Ordinance (cap.131), s.6B(3).
[10] *R v Secretary of State for the Home Department, ex parte Doody* [1994] 1 AC 531, per Lord Mustill.
[11] *Ng Nga Wo v Director of Health* [2006] HKEC 843, para.34, per Chu J; *Spruce v The University of Hong Kong* [1993] 2 HKLR 65 (PC), p.72.
[12] *Liu Pik Han v Hong Kong Federation of Insurers Appeals Tribunal* [2005] HKEC 1046, para.33.
[13] *Lam Tat Ming v Chief Executive of the HKSAR* [2012] 1 HKLRD 801, paras.19–20. On the curing of procedural defects, see p.253.
[14] Though complexity alone will not automatically warrant an oral hearing as a matter of fairness – *Ch'ng Poh v Chief Executive of HKSAR* [2003] HKEC 1441, para.110.
[15] *Lam Tat Ming v Chief Executive of the HKSAR* [2012] 1 HKLRD 801, paras.52–55.

a decision to revoke a licence, remove a person from public housing or rescind a permanent residence entitlement.[16] Similarly, if substantial prejudice would be caused to the applicant by not affording the opportunity of an oral hearing, fairness may require that one is offered. This might include, for example, disciplinary proceedings in which the person subject to the proceedings may stand to have pay withheld or be dismissed from employment.[17] Fairness may require there to be an oral hearing where constitutional or fundamental rights, or other important interests, are at stake, so that suitably high procedural safeguards are afforded to best protect such rights. These factors are non-exhaustive and they do not automatically lead to the establishment of the right to an oral hearing. They instead weigh in favour of such a right being established at common law, and as these factors accumulate in a single case, so should the strength of the argument that such a right be established.

There are, by contrast, factors which, if sufficiently established, would tend to weigh against the finding that there should be an oral hearing. If the individual did not request a hearing, this can weigh against his subsequent complaint that no hearing was offered; though he will not be automatically entitled to a hearing if he requests one.[18] If the individual made written representations instead of requesting an oral hearing, he runs the risk of being held to have waived his right to an oral hearing. If the court considers that an oral hearing would serve no useful purpose, or that there is nothing of factual or legal complexity requiring an oral hearing, then the court is less likely to find that fairness requires there to be a hearing.[19]

Where factors weighing in favour of a common law right to an oral hearing are coexistent with factors weighing against it, the court will conduct a balancing exercise to decide whether, overall, fairness requires or does not require that an oral hearing be given. The contextual nature of this exercise is illustrated by contrasting two near-contemporaneous decisions, the first of which is *Ng Nga Wo* v *Director of Health*.[20] An applicant medical practitioner had been convicted in 2001 of an offence under the Dangerous Drugs Regulations (cap.134A) and fined accordingly. In 2005, he was convicted under the Dangerous Drugs Ordinance (cap.134) and again fined. There was correspondence between the Director of Health (in his capacity as Registrar of Clinics) and the clinic at which the applicant was employed with regard to his fitness to be registered as a medical practitioner. The applicant then wrote a particular letter to the Registrar, after which the Registrar decided that he was

---

[16] This is due not to the forfeiture/application distinction as such, but the requirements of fairness in the context of individual cases.
[17] *Id.*
[18] *R (on the application of West)* v *Parole Board for England and Wales* [2002] EWCA Civ 1641, para.44.
[19] In the context of court hearings, see *Chow Shun Yung* v *Wei Pih* (2003) 6 HKCFAR 299, para.37.
[20] *Ng Nga Wo* v *Director of Health* [2006] HKEC 843.

no longer suitable to be employed by any clinic registered under the Medical Clinics Ordinance (cap.343). A request made for review of the decision was declined. No oral hearing was given to the applicant.

It was averred that the Registrar's decision affected the applicant's livelihood. That would be a serious matter for the applicant, and its gravity on his career prospects, professional reputation and income might weigh strongly in favour of an oral hearing. However, there were factors weighing against such a finding. First, there was a period of almost three months during which the applicant made no representations to the Registrar. Second, the form which the applicant's letter took was of importance: it was a "long" letter which constituted a "lengthy and substantial representation". This would impact on any argument that fairness required there to be an oral hearing, for:

> The applicant has not indicated in these proceedings what further representations he would wish to make in addition to what was already stated in this letter. Therefore, it cannot be said that he had no opportunity to put forward his case and advance arguments favourable to him before the Registrar made his decision.[21]

The applicant failed to demonstrate that unfairness had resulted, that any special circumstances or considerations existed which recommended an oral hearing, that he was unaware of the adverse factors against him or that he did not appreciate or had difficulty comprehending the case against him. He also failed to show what prejudice had been suffered by not having had the opportunity of an oral hearing. Furthermore, "[t]he right to be heard does not entail a right to make oral submissions".[22] The submission of full written representations by a putative applicant can (but will not necessarily) discharge the right to be heard.[23] When these factors were balanced against the gravity of the Registrar's decision on the applicant's circumstances, it would not point to the conclusion that fairness required that an oral hearing be given.

This may be contrasted with the decision in *Liu Pik Han v Hong Kong Federation of Insurers Appeals Tribunal*.[24] The applicant was an insurance agent whose registration was suspended by the Insurance Agents Registration Board due to its decision that she was no longer a fit and proper person to act as an insurance agent due to false declarations made to the Board. The applicant exercised a statutory right of appeal to the Hong Kong Federation of Insurers Appeals Tribunal, but the appeal was dismissed. Neither the Board nor the Appeals Tribunal gave the opportunity of an oral hearing.

The applicant faced a charge of serious misconduct which carried with it an imputation of fraud. It would be a serious blemish on her record and have an

---

[21] *Id.*, para.33, per Chu J.
[22] *Id.*, para.34, per Chu J; *Spruce v The University of Hong Kong* [1993] 2 HKLR 65 (PC), p.72.
[23] *Lloyd v McMahon* [1987] AC 625.
[24] *Liu Pik Han v Hong Kong Federation of Insurers Appeals Tribunal* [2005] HKEC 1046.

adverse impact on her career development as an insurance agent. She had already been dismissed from her employment and barred from registration for a substantial period of time; the consequences were not only financial. Furthermore, whilst it was true that the applicant did not request a hearing, she was not told that she could request one. She could therefore not be held to have waived her right to an oral hearing. The real question was whether the issues could be "fairly and properly disposed of without any oral hearing".[25] By contrast with the applicant in *Ng Nga Wo* who had set out lengthy and detailed representations in his letter to the decision maker, the applicant in the present case had only made written representations of a "sketchy nature".[26] There was also a live dispute about the applicant's intent when making the false declarations and her credibility. Though there were inconsistencies in her case, fairness required that the applicant be given an opportunity to explain them at an oral hearing. There were also other ambiguities in relation to which the Board ought to have sought clarification from the applicant. This was a case in which the Board should, as a matter of fairness, have invited the applicant to "attend an oral hearing on its own volition".[27]

The Appeals Tribunal had, meanwhile, dismissed the appeal without offering an oral hearing, providing only uninformative reasons. This was notwithstanding the fact that the applicant had added further materials to support her case, in view of which the "matter cried out for an oral hearing".[28] The Tribunal had therefore also acted unfairly, though it is important to note the court's view that, had the Tribunal afforded the applicant an oral hearing, this might have remedied the absence of an oral hearing by the Board.[29] The court therefore quashed the decisions and granted mandamus for the matter to be brought before a differently constituted Board for consideration.

If a hearing does take place, and if persons other than those expressly authorised to participate in its deliberation contribute thereto or participate therein, this should not result in the decision maker unlawfully divesting or relinquishing its discretion, and any such contribution or participation should be as open, public and fair as practicable.[30] The fairness of a hearing may be influenced by a number of factors, such as the length of the hearing, the scope of the hearing, the complexity of the issues in question, a lack of time for members on the decision-making panel to read and digest the written materials placed before them, and the partial absence of some members who participated in the decision-making process but were not present throughout the hearing.[31]

---

[25] *Id.*, para.38, per Lam J.　　[26] *Id.*, para.40, per Lam J.　　[27] *Id.*, para.43, per Lam J.
[28] *Id.*, para.45, per Lam J.　　[29] *Id.*, para.45.
[30] *Dato Tan Leong Min* v *Insider Dealing Tribunal* [1998] 1 HKLRD 630; *Lam Kwok Pun* v *Dental Council of Hong Kong* [2000] 4 HKC 181.
[31] *Hysan Development Co Ltd* v *Town Planning Board* [2014] HKEC 1869 (CA). If members of a decision-making panel have been wholly or partially absent from a hearing at which representations have been made by the affected person, adequate arrangements should be in

The availability of redress in judicial review for the absence of a fair hearing is subject to the curative principle. If a subsequent procedural step such as an appeal or rehearing occurs which "cures" the deficiency of fairness in the original hearing, the applicant is not necessarily entitled to relief in judicial review on the basis of that deficiency.[32] It was doubted in the Privy Council on appeal from Australia that there was a general rule that appellate proceedings could not cure a failure of natural justice in the original proceedings.[33] This position was followed in Hong Kong in relation to an appeal to a committee of the Urban Council[34] and to the Commissioner of Police.[35] In deciding whether to award relief in judicial review, the court will look to see whether, taking the procedure as a whole – both original and appellate – the applicant has still not been treated fairly.[36] The availability of judicial review does not necessarily cure a procedural defect.[37]

Right to Be Legally Represented

There is sometimes expressly provided in statute a right to be legally represented or a prohibition on legal representation. For example, there is a statutory right of representation before the Appeal Board on Closure Orders (Immediate Health Hazard),[38] whereas counsel or a solicitor are not entitled to be heard by the Appeal Board under the Accreditation of Academic and

---

place to ensure that those members are properly apprised of the relevant representations – *id.*, paras.172–179. Subba Rao J stated in *Rao* v *Andhra Pradesh State Road Transport Corporation* [1959] AIR 308, p.327 that "[i]f one person hears and another decides, then personal hearing becomes an empty formality". See also *R* v *Chester City Council, ex parte Quietlynn Ltd* (1985) 83 LGR 308; and *The Queen* v *Town Planning Board, ex parte REDA* [1996] 2 HKLR 267, p.284.

[32] The curative principle applies not only in relation to hearings, but also to other aspects of procedure such as the giving of reasons (*Akram* v *Secretary for Security* [2000] 1 HKLRD 164); and apparent bias (*Wong Tak Wai* v *Commissioner of Correctional Services* [2010] 4 HKLRD 409 (CA)). An example of a defect which can be cured is where an error of law has been made which can be corrected on appeal – *R* v *Director of Immigration, ex parte Do Giau* [1992] 1 HKLR 287, p.316 (though it was not cured in this case).

[33] *Calvin* v *Carr* [1980] AC 574 (PC) (Australia). The "general rule" had been proposed by Megarry J in *Leary* v *National Union of Vehicle Builders* [1971] Ch 34, p.49. See also *Lloyd* v *McMahon* [1987] AC 625 (HL).

[34] *Sea Dragon Billiard and Snooker Association* v *Urban Council* [1991] 2 HKLR 114 (CA).

[35] *Lee Sze Chung* v *Commissioner of Police* [2003] 3 HKLRD L1 (CA). See also *Liu Pik Han* v *Hong Kong Federation of Insurers Appeals Tribunal* [2005] HKEC 1046, para.45.

[36] *Stock Exchange of Hong Kong Ltd* v *Onshine Securities Ltd* [1994] 1 HKC 319 (CA); *Lee Sze Chung* v *Commissioner of Police* [2003] 3 HKLRD L1 (CA), paras.23–24. Article 10 of the Bill of Rights did "not require every element of the protections conferred to be present at every stage of the determination of a person's rights and obligations, but only that such protections should be effective when the determination is viewed as an entire process" – *Lam Siu Po* v *Commissioner of Police* [2009] 4 HKLRD 575 (CFA), para.109, per Ribeiro PJ.

[37] See *Wong Tak Wai* v *Commissioner of Police* [2010] 4 HKLRD 409 (CA), paras.71–78 (in the context of Article 10 of the Hong Kong Bill of Rights).

[38] Public Health and Municipal Services Ordinance (cap. 132), s.128D(7)(b).

Vocational Qualifications Ordinance[39] – though such a restriction will have to be constitutionally compliant to be valid.

When the statute makes no express provision either way, the court will apply a fairness test to establish whether a party is entitled to have a legal representative address a tribunal or question witnesses.[40] The tribunal will, unless prohibited by statute, have discretion on whether to permit legal representatives to address them, and the function of the court in such cases is to assess whether fairness would have required that the tribunal exercise its discretion to permit legal representatives to address them. In order to enable a tribunal to exercise that discretion, the court may declare as unconstitutional legislative provisions that constitute a blanket restriction on legal representation in certain proceedings, as on the basis that they violate Article 10 of the Bill of Rights.[41] As Bokhary PJ stated in the Court of Final Appeal "our constitution does not permit" legislation that brings about unfairness in disciplinary proceedings, but that does not enable the individual to insist on representation; it merely gives the tribunal the necessary discretion to consider whether legal representatives should be permitted to address the tribunal.[42]

In deciding whether fairness requires that legal representatives be permitted to address the tribunal, various factors will tend to weigh in favour of such a finding. The more serious the charge and potential penalty resulting from tribunal proceedings, the more likely it is that fairness would require representation. If points of law are at issue, or there are procedural difficulties such as the conduct of cross-examination of witnesses, this might also support the contention that fairness requires that legal representatives be permitted to address the tribunal. The lesser the capacity of the individual to present his own case, the greater the argument that fairness requires that he be given an opportunity to have a legal representative address the tribunal on his behalf. This may include the extent to which the individual is uneducated, inarticulate or mentally incapable. Pronounced inequality between the individual and the decision maker may also tip the balance in favour of the individual having a legal representative address the tribunal.[43] For example, there may be pronounced power or informational inequalities between the parties, or a lack of equality of arms.[44] Significant public interest in disciplinary or similar

---

[39] Accreditation of Academic and Vocational Qualifications Ordinance (cap. 592), s.13(4).
[40] *R v Board of Visitors of HM Prison, the Maze, ex parte Hone* [1988] AC 379; *Stock Exchange of Hong Kong Ltd v New World Development Co Ltd* (2006) 9 HKCFAR 234, para.98.
[41] *Lam Siu Po v Commissioner of Police* [2009] 4 HKLRD 575, paras.135–142 and 168–169.
[42] *Id.*, paras.24–26.
[43] These factors are taken from, *inter alia*, discussion in *R v Secretary of State for the Home Department, ex parte Tarrant* [1985] QB 251, pp.285–286; and *Stock Exchange of Hong Kong Ltd v New World Development Co Ltd* (2006) 9 HKCFAR 234, para.101.
[44] *Stock Exchange of Hong Kong Ltd v New World Development Co Ltd* (2006) 9 HKCFAR 234, para.129.

proceedings to which the individual is subject might also recommend that, as a matter of fairness, legal representation is permitted to maximise procedural robustness.[45] This is not an exhaustive list of factors, as fairness criteria are open-ended.

Other factors may tend to weigh against the finding that a legal representative be permitted to address the tribunal, or will at least qualify as "legitimate concerns".[46] For example, if proceedings are of such a nature that speed is required, and if the making of legal representations would obstruct that requirement, this may weigh against the making of those representations. If "over-lawyering" might substantially lengthen and complicate proceedings, so as either to conflict with the objectives of a swift, lay tribunal mechanism, or which would make it difficult for appropriately qualified individuals to accept unremunerated appointment to the tribunal panel, this may also be a relevant factor.[47] The nature of proceedings can be relevant, such as their inherent informality and absence of standard procedures.[48] However, these concerns could only be considered with proper regard for the needs of procedural fairness and for proportionality in any procedural restrictions imposed.[49] They would not override the individual's interests in fairness. In any event, the tribunal, when deciding whether to permit legal representation, must approach the question with a sufficiently open mind, and should not apply a policy (actual or apparent) of not permitting legal representation unless compelling circumstances are demonstrated, in which case the tribunal may be fettering its discretion.[50]

Where the denial of legal representation may have resulted in material prejudice to the affected individual,[51] the court may strike down the decision resulting from the unfair process. It could also order the tribunal to permit legal representation at a rerun of proceedings, though this would in theory involve the court substituting its own decision for the tribunal's discretion on whether or not to permit representation. The court could therefore leave the tribunal to exercise that discretion, and if proceedings are again found to violate the individual's interests in fairness, the matter could again come for judicial review to be struck down a second time; this would be somewhat circuitous but would technically leave intact the tribunal's capacity to exercise

---

[45] *Rowse v Secretary for Civil Service* [2008] 5 HKLRD 217, paras.139–142.
[46] *Stock Exchange of Hong Kong Ltd v New World Development Co Ltd* (2006) 9 HKCFAR 234, para.109, per Ribeiro PJ.
[47] *Id.*, paras.101 and 109. See also *R v Secretary of State for the Home Department, ex parte Tarrant* [1985] QB 251, p.286.
[48] *Rowse v Secretary for Civil Service* [2008] 5 HKLRD 217, para.131.
[49] *Stock Exchange of Hong Kong Ltd v New World Development Co Ltd* (2006) 9 HKCFAR 234, para.109. These factors were reiterated in *Lam Siu Po v Commissioner of Police* [2009] 4 HKLRD 575, para.139; and *Dr Q v Health Committee of the Medical Council of Hong Kong* [2012] 3 HKLRD 206, para.73.
[50] *Rowse v Secretary for Civil Service* [2008] 5 HKLRD 217, para.129.   [51] *Id*, paras.127–141.

its own discretion. Nevertheless, if there is in the court's view a right and wrong answer as to whether an individual should be permitted to have legal representation in particular proceedings, and the court strikes down the wrong decision, leaving the tribunal to exercise its discretion afresh, a certain artificiality attaches to the claim that the tribunal has discretion in this regard.

It is worth noting that Article 35 of the Basic Law is not engaged in relation to representation before bodies other than courts. Article 35 provides, *inter alia*, that "Hong Kong residents shall have the right to confidential legal advice, access to the courts, choice of lawyers for timely protection of their lawful rights and interests or for representation in the courts, and to judicial remedies". If tribunals were regarded as "courts" under this provision, there would follow a constitutional right to representation in tribunals. However, the Court of Final Appeal has held that the reference in Article 35 to "courts" is only to "courts of law", namely those institutions "charged with exercising the independent judicial power" in Hong Kong.[52] In doing so, it expressly overruled two cases which had held otherwise.[53] It is important to recognise, however, that the distinction between courts and tribunals is not always clear cut, as illustrated where "tribunals" are administered by the Judiciary.[54]

Duty of Disclosure

Another aspect of procedural fairness is a potential duty on the decision maker to provide adequate disclosure of such materials as are relevant to the decision-making process:[55]

> The principle that a decision-making body should not see relevant material without giving those affected a chance to comment on it and, if they wish, to controvert it, is fundamental to the principle of law (which governs public administration as much as it does adjudication) that to act in good faith and listen fairly to both sides is 'a duty lying upon everyone who decides anything'.[56]

The Privy Council declined, in an appeal from the Court of Appeal of the Supreme Court of Malaya, to investigate whether the evidence or representations

---

[52] *Stock Exchange of Hong Kong Ltd v New World Development Co Ltd* (2006) 9 HKCFAR 234, para.50.
[53] *Id.*, paras.69 and 134. The overruled cases were *Dr Ip Kay Lo v Medical Council of Hong Kong* [2003] 3 HKLRD 851; and *A Solicitor v Law Society of Hong Kong* [2004] HKEC 219.
[54] See pp.304–305.
[55] *Chan Tak Shing v Chief Executive of the HKSAR* [1999] 2 HKLRD 389; *Leung Fuk Wah v Commissioner of Police* [2002] 3 HKLRD 653; *Chu Ping Tak v Commissioner of Police* [2002] 3 HKLRD 679.
[56] *R v London Borough of Camden, ex parte Paddock* (transcript 8 September 1994), p.8, per Sedley J, quoting from *Board of Education v Rice* [1911] AC 179 (HL), p.182, per Lord Loreburn LC. See also *University of Ceylon v Fernando* [1960] 1 WLR 223 (PC) (Ceylon).

withheld from disclosure worked to the prejudice of the applicant – the risk of prejudice was sufficient.[57] This was followed in Hong Kong, where the view was taken that the fact the document withheld from disclosure contained no new ground of complaint or new facts made no difference in this regard.[58]

This approach was modified in *Leung Fuk Wah* v *Commissioner of Police*, where the Court of Appeal proceeded to investigate the material withheld from disclosure. It was "abundantly clear" that disclosure of new documents would "not have made the slightest difference" to the applicant's petition to the Commissioner of Police. The court exercised its discretion against granting relief on the basis that, as the applicant had not suffered prejudice, failure to observe the principle of fairness should not be a ground for quashing the decision.[59] This accords with the principle that there is no such thing as a technical breach of the rules of natural justice; the breach must produce actual unfairness.[60]

A distinction was later attempted between a total absence of substantive prejudice, and the presence of a risk of prejudice, in an apparent attempt to conciliate the two positions. However, though the court found that there was a risk of substantial prejudice, it only reached that conclusion after examining the material that had been withheld from disclosure.[61] Subsequent cases have also seen the court assess whether and to what extent there has been substantial prejudice resulting from non-disclosure.[62]

Full disclosure is not an automatic right, and there can be legitimate competing interests including maintaining confidentiality in an investigatory process and the public interest.[63] The court must also ensure that the level of disclosure required to meet the requisite standard of fairness would not impede or frustrate the purpose of enabling legislation.[64]

Duty to Give Adequate Reasons

The giving of reasons can increase transparency in public decision-making and improve the accountability of decision makers in both legal and political

---

[57] *Kanda* v *Malaya* [1962] AC 322 (PC) (Malaya), p.337.
[58] *Chan Tak Shing* v *Chief Executive of the HKSAR* [1999] 2 HKLRD 389.
[59] *Leung Fuk Wah* v *Commissioner of Police* [2002] 3 HKLRD 653, paras.75–76.
[60] *George* v *Secretary of State for the Environment* (1979) 38 P & CR 609, p.617, per Lord Denning MR; *The Queen* v *Director of Immigration, ex parte Do Giau* [1992] 1 HKLR 287, p.314; *Yim Shik Shi* v *Secretary for the Civil Service* [2004] HKEC 640; *Cheung Koon Kit* v *Commissioner of Correctional Services* [2004] HKEC 948, para.12, per Hartmann J; *Rowse* v *Secretary for Civil Service* [2008] 5 HKLRD 217, paras.135–141.
[61] *Chu Ping Tak* v *Commissioner of Police* [2002] 3 HKLRD 679.
[62] *Lam Ping Cheung* v *Law Society of Hong Kong* [2006] HKEC 2366; *Siu Chi Wan* v *Secretary for Civil Service* [2008] HKEC 1134, paras.37–39; *Ng Man Yin* v *Registration of Persons Tribunal* [2014] 1 HKLRD 1188, paras.61–67.
[63] *Asia Television Ltd* v *Communications Authority (No 2)* [2013] 3 HKLRD 618.
[64] *Id.*

terms. Legally, if the subject of a decision-making process knows why a particular decision was made, in accordance with which criteria and so on, he or she is in principle better able to identify deficiencies and errors made in the course of the decision-making process. This may better enable the subject to decide whether to appeal or apply for judicial review, but may also give him or her confidence that, even if an unfavourable decision was made, the case was considered fairly, properly and regularly.

The benefits are not all stacked in favour of the aspiring applicant: the giving of reasons can also assist the decision maker. If the decision maker is required to give a statement of reasons for the decision, his or her mind may be more focussed on the questions to be addressed in the course of making the decision, the criteria adopted, considerations that should and considerations that should not be taken into account, consistency among decisions made, and so on.[65] Reasons can also protect a decision maker from allegations that grounds of judicial review have been violated, as the statement of reasons may be used as evidence of what criteria were applied, that certain considerations were or were not taken into account, that exceptional circumstances were properly considered, that the process followed was reasonable and rational etc.[66] In sum, the giving of reasons by public decision makers can evidence and enhance the legal basis on which decisions are made, as well as protecting against broader charges of opacity or unfairness.

A requirement to give reasons can often be found in legislation. It is provided that "[i]f he refuses to grant a licence the [Director of Environmental Protection] shall notify the applicant in writing of his refusal and shall inform him of his reasons therefor",[67] and elsewhere that a "tribunal hearing an appeal under this Part may confirm, vary or reverse the decision under appeal and every decision of a tribunal shall contain a statement of reasons for the decision".[68] Where the "[Surveyors Registration] Board rejects an application for registration or renewal of registration, it shall give reasons for the rejection",[69] and if the Director of Electrical and Mechanical Services is not satisfied that parts of an aerial ropeway are in safe working order, he "shall refuse to permit the use and operation of the ropeway to be resumed and shall provide reasons for his refusal".[70] Failure to provide reasons in such situations will constitute failure to perform an express statutory duty, though a duty to give

---

[65] See *Capital Rich Development Ltd v Town Planning Board* [2007] 2 HKLRD 155, paras.97–98, per Stock JA.
[66] See also *Oriental Daily Publisher Ltd v Commissioner for Television and Entertainment Licensing Authority* (1997–1998) 1 HKCFAR 279, p.290.
[67] Air Pollution Control Ordinance (cap.311), s.15(2).
[68] Securities and Futures Commission Ordinance (cap.24), s.21(7).
[69] Surveyors Registration Ordinance (cap.417), s.14(3).
[70] Aerial Ropeways (Safety) Ordinance (cap.211), s.22(2).

reasons may also be implied from a statutory provision.[71] Legislation may provide that reasons are not required to be given for a decision.[72]

Where the relevant legislation neither requires nor expressly does not require reasons to be given, the question arises as to whether there is a common law duty to give reasons. The courts have considered that there is no general duty at common law to give reasons[73] and, concomitantly, there is no automatic common law right on the part of individuals to receive reasons for decisions to which they are subject. Instead, the courts apply a fairness test[74] to ascertain whether reasons must be given at common law.

As with other applications of a test of procedural fairness, context will swing the pendulum in favour of or against the applicant. Where a decision seems aberrant – that is to say markedly out of line with other, analogous decisions; or markedly out of line with reasonable expectations on the basis of, for example, a statutory duty or prevailing evidence,[75] fairness may require that reasons are given in explanation of the aberrance.[76] Thus if a planning authority received five applications for planning permission for similar external structures to be constructed behind houses in a particular village, and approved four of those applications whilst rejecting one, fairness may require that the sole disappointed applicant is provided with reasons as to why his application has attracted a different, negative outcome. Where the Council of the Stock Exchange refused to approve an application for corporate membership of the stock exchange, reasons should have been given on the basis that corporate membership is rarely refused, the refusal had come after the Securities and Futures Commission had deemed the applicant a fit and proper person to be regarded as a dealer in securities, the refusal had occurred after the membership committee concluded that the applicant was able to comply with the eligibility requirements for membership, and no material adverse to the applicant was produced by the membership committee to members of the Council on the issue of whether the applicant was of good financial standing and integrity.[77]

Where constitutional, fundamental or other important rights are at stake, fairness may require that reasons are provided. It has been said that reasons

---

[71] See, for example, *Eastern Express Publisher Ltd* v *Obscene Articles Tribunal* [1995] 2 HKLR 290, p.294.
[72] See, for example, Control of Obscene and Indecent Articles Ordinance (cap.390), s.14(3)(a). Though see, again, *Eastern Express Publisher Ltd* v *Obscene Articles Tribunal* [1995] 2 HKLR 290, p.294.
[73] See Liu JA's overview in *Tong Pon Wah* v *Hong Kong Society of Accountants* [1998] 2 HKLRD 427, pp.440–443. See also *R* v *Civil Service Appeal Board, ex parte Cunningham* [1992] ICR 816, p.834; and *Ho Ming Sai* v *Director of Immigration* [1994] 1 HKLR 21 (CA), p.29.
[74] This has also been expressed as a test of material prejudice to the putative applicant – *Tong Pon Wah* v *Hong Kong Society of Accountants* [1998] 2 HKLRD 427, p.444, per Liu JA.
[75] See *Padfield* v *Minister of Agriculture, Fisheries and Food* [1968] AC 997, pp.1053–1054; and *Tong Pon Wah* v *Hong Kong Society of Accountants* [1998] 2 HKLRD 427, p.444.
[76] *Pearl Securities Ltd* v *Stock Exchange of Hong Kong Ltd* [1999] 2 HKLRD 243, pp.259–261.
[77] *Id.*, pp.260–261.

must be given when officials conclude that a refugee claimant's fear of persecution is not well-founded – nothing short of this would be compatible with the rule of law[78] – and the Secretary for Security is required to give reasons for his decisions relating to torture claims due to the requirement for him to act according to a high standard of fairness.[79] Fairness may require that reasons are given in disciplinary proceedings, particularly as a negative decision can adversely impact, often to a significant extent, the interests of the applicant: he might be given a written warning, censured, demoted or no longer be considered for promotion, or in some cases have pay withheld or be dismissed from employment. There can also be significant negative implications for the reputation and career prospects of the applicant. The principal objective is to ensure that the applicant is given fair opportunity to understand and properly engage with the proceedings to which he is subject, and to be given the opportunity to identify any deficiencies or irregularities in proceedings. Nevertheless, the common law requirement to provide reasons in disciplinary proceedings still hinges on a test of fairness; there is no automatic requirement to provide reasons for disciplinary decisions.[80]

Fairness may require that reasons are provided when the applicant has a right of appeal from the decision in question.[81] As Lord Mustill explained in *R v Secretary of State for the Home Department, ex parte Doody*: "[s]ince the person affected usually cannot make worthwhile representations without knowing what factors may weigh against his interests, fairness will very often require that he is informed of the gist of the case which he has to answer".[82] Indeed, the applicant is unlikely to have a fair attempt at the use of an appeal mechanism if he or she does not know why an adverse decision was taken, thus facing obvious difficulties in knowing how to better explain or reframe his or her case to the appellate body. The applicant is not necessarily entitled to a favourable decision either before the original decision maker or the appellate body, but he or she is entitled to procedural fairness.

Other factors may also call for the giving of reasons, such as when the decision maker is exercising a judicial function.[83] Judges are required to give reasons for their decisions: the duty of a professional judge to give adequate reasons was described by Chan CJHC as "a principle of paramount importance

---

[78] *C v Director of Immigration* (2013) 16 HKCFAR 280, paras.64–65, per Bokhary NPJ. It was added that those reasons "must be sufficient to meet the reasonable needs for judicial review purposes of that person's legal advisers and of the court" (para.64).

[79] *Re Lau Hei Wing* [2016] 3 HKLRD 652, para.24.

[80] *Tong Pon Wah v Hong Kong Society of Accountants* [1998] 2 HKLRD 427.

[81] Though the lack of a further right of appeal has also been interpreted as a factor supporting that body's giving of reasons: *R v Civil Service Appeal Board, ex parte Cunningham* [1992] ICR 816, p.831, per McCowan LJ.

[82] *R v Secretary of State for the Home Department, ex parte Doody* [1994] 1 AC 531. See also *Eastern Express Publisher Ltd v Obscene Articles Tribunal* [1995] 2 HKLR 290, p.294; and *Leung Sze Ho Albert v Bar Council of Hong Kong Bar Association* [2015] 5 HKLRD 791, para.108.

[83] *R v Civil Service Appeal Board, ex parte Cunningham* [1992] ICR 816, p.831.

in the common law system".[84] However, reasons might not be required of decision makers where this would be harmful to the public interest.[85] The "oracular" nature of a decision can militate against the requirement to give reasons,[86] as can particular categories of decision, such as prosecutorial decisions.[87]

Where the court does find that fairness requires reasons to be given at common law, or where reasons have already been provided (even where they were not legally required to be provided),[88] the court can assess the quality of those reasons. As Li CJ explained in *Oriental Daily Publisher Ltd* v *Commissioner for Television and Entertainment Licensing Authority*[89] – still considered the leading authority on the duty to give reasons[90] – "[w]here there is a duty to give reasons, it must be discharged by giving adequate reasons".[91] This would be a matter of context, though reasons should show that the decision maker has addressed the substantial issues before it and why it has come to its decision. As Li CJ explained, it may not be necessary to address every single issue in the reasons, but they should disclose that the issues arising for serious consideration have been considered.[92]

Reasons may be brief: it is the quality, not quantity, of reasons that matters, and this may mean that the reasons do not require great elaboration.[93]

---

[84] *Zhuo Cui Hao* v *Ting Fung Yee* [1999] 3 HKC 634, p.639. See also *Welltus Ltd* v *Fornton Knitting Co Ltd* [2013] HKEC 369.

[85] *R* v *Civil Service Appeal Board, ex parte Cunningham* [1992] ICR 816, p.831.

[86] *R* v *Higher Education Funding Council, ex parte Institute of Dental Surgery* [1994] 1 WLR 242, pp.260–261.

[87] See *Re Lau Hei Wing* [2016] 3 HKLRD 652, paras.22–32.

[88] *Smart Gain Investment Ltd* v *Town Planning Board* [2007] HKEC 1964, para.84; *Hong Kong Aircrew Officers Association* v *Director-General of Civil Aviation* [2009] HKEC 1086, para.61; *Anderson Asphalt Ltd* v *Secretary for Justice* [2009] 3 HKLRD 215, para.102. This may be subject to limited exceptions, see *Re Lau Hei Wing* [2016] 3 HKLRD 652, paras.22–32.

[89] *Oriental Daily Publisher Ltd* v *Commissioner for Television and Entertainment Licensing Authority* (1997–1998) 1 HKCFAR 279. The requirements set out in this case were an elaboration of those in *Eastern Express Publisher Ltd* v *Obscene Articles Tribunal* [1995] 2 HKLR 290, p.294.

[90] Described by Cheung CJHC in the Court of Appeal as "no doubt" the "leading authority" on the duty to give reasons – *Zhang Rui Hua* v *Wang Lan* [2016] HKEC 291 (CA), para.37.

[91] *Oriental Daily Publisher Ltd* v *Commissioner for Television and Entertainment Licensing Authority* (1997–1998) 1 HKCFAR 279, p.290; echoing *Eastern Express Publisher Ltd* v *Obscene Articles Tribunal* [1995] 2 HKLR 290, p.294, per Findlay J. Lord Brown of Eaton-under-Heywood stated that a reasons challenge would only succeed where the party aggrieved could demonstrate substantial prejudice by the failure to provide an adequately reasoned decision – *South Buckinghamshire District Council* v *Porter (No 2)* [2004] 1 WLR 1953 (HL), p.1964. See also *Capital Rich Development Ltd* v *Town Planning Board* [2007] 2 HKLRD 155 (CA), paras.97–98; *Smart Gain Investment Ltd* v *Town Planning Board* [2007] HKEC 1964, para.87, per Cheung J; and *Leung Sze Ho Albert* v *Bar Council of Hong Kong Bar Association* [2015] 5 HKLRD 791, para.108.

[92] *Oriental Daily Publisher Ltd* v *Commissioner for Television and Entertainment Licensing Authority* (1997–1998) 1 HKCFAR 279, p.291.

[93] *Id.* See also *Capital Rich Development Ltd* v *Town Planning Board* [2007] 2 HKLRD 155, paras.97–98, where Stock JA said, *inter alia*, that reasons should be clear and sufficient, but that

The degree of particularity required would depend entirely on the nature of the issues falling for decision.[94] Mere recitation of a statutory formula would not be sufficient.[95] Reproduction or repetition of the same reasons, either of those produced by another party or those produced by the same party across multiple decisions, might indicate that the matter has not been properly considered or a decision not properly made.[96] If a point of law is relevant to the decision-making process, the reasons should "usually set out the findings of fact, the point of law at issue and the process of reasoning leading to the conclusion".[97] The adequacy of reasons can also require that they are sufficient to meet the reasonable needs of the aggrieved person's legal advisers and the court to deal with an application for judicial review of the underlying decision.[98]

Where no reasons[99] or insufficient reasons have been given by a decision maker, the court may assume that the decision maker had no such reasons.[100] The courts should not have to resort to guesswork to divine the decision maker's position on key issues.[101] The absence of reasons will not automatically undermine the purported rationality of a decision, but the provision of reasons may preempt its rationality being undermined.[102] It has also been stated that "not only is justice not seen to have been done but there is no way, in the absence of reasons from the [decision maker], in which it can be judged

---

sometimes a brief statement of reasons will suffice, depending on the context; *HKSAR* v *Okafor* [2012] 1 HKLRD 1041; *Li Wai Hung Cesario* v *Administrative Appeals Board* [2015] 5 HKLRD 575, para.46; and *Leung Sze Ho Albert* v *Bar Council of Hong Kong Bar Association* [2015] 5 HKLRD 791, para.108.

[94] *South Buckinghamshire District Council* v *Porter (No 2)* [2004] 1 WLR 1953 (HL), p.1964.

[95] *Eastern Express Publisher Ltd* v *Obscene Articles Tribunal* [1995] 2 HKLR 290, p.294.

[96] *Smart Gain Investment Ltd* v *Town Planning Board* [2007] HKEC 1964, paras.100–105; *Hysan Development Co Ltd* v *Town Planning Board* [2014] HKEC 1869 (CA), paras.198–204. If this is committed by a judge, it may indicate that he has abdicated his judicial function or that justice has not been seen to be done by an independent judicial tribunal – *Nina Kung* v *Wong Din Shin* (2005) 8 HKCFAR 387, para.446.

[97] *Oriental Daily Publisher Ltd* v *Commissioner for Television and Entertainment Licensing Authority* (1997–1998) 1 HKCFAR 279, p.291.

[98] *C* v *Director of Immigration* (2013) 16 HKCFAR 280, para.64.

[99] *Padfield* v *Minister of Agriculture, Fisheries and Food* [1968] AC 997, pp.1006–1007 and 1061–1062.

[100] *Eastern Express Publisher Ltd* v *Obscene Articles Tribunal* [1995] 2 HKLR 290, p.294. Though it was said that adverse inference will not readily be drawn, nevertheless, reasons must not give rise to substantial doubt about whether the decision maker erred in law, such as by misunderstanding policy or failing to reach a rational decision on relevant grounds – *South Buckinghamshire District Council* v *Porter (No 2)* [2004] 1 WLR 1953 (HL), p.1964.

[101] *Capital Rich Development Ltd* v *Town Planning Board* [2007] 2 HKLRD 155, paras.97–99.

[102] See *R* v *Secretary of State for Trade and Industry, ex parte Lonhro* [1989] 1 WLR 525, pp.539–540. In *Capital Rich Development Ltd* v *Town Planning Board* [2007] 2 HKLRD 155, para.97, Stock JA said that "clarity and sufficiency of reasons enable a supervisory court in judicial review better to assess the legality of a decision under challenge" and (at para.106) "[t]he fact of the matter is that one cannot know what the Board made of this issue, for they have not said, either in the reasons provided or in the evidence filed in the judicial review, and the court, as well as the objectors, have been left to divine the answer".

whether in fact it has been done".[103] In addition, the court may investigate why reasons have not been given, in other words to scrutinise and evaluate the reasons why reasons have not been given.[104] Whilst evidence might be admitted to elucidate or, exceptionally, correct or add to reasons, evidence could not be admitted to fundamentally alter or contradict the reasons given.[105] If adequate reasons have not been given, the appropriate relief might not be to quash the underlying decision in order for the duty to give adequate reasons to be discharged.[106] For example, an order of mandamus requiring (fresh) reasons to be given may result in the duty being discharged. In some cases, however, such as those in which reasons are so inadequate that they virtually amount to no reasons at all, the court may quash the decision itself.[107]

There may be reluctance on the part of decision makers to provide reasons. As Lord Mansfield CJ is said to have advised a colonial governor in 1790: "Consider what you think justice requires, and decide accordingly. But never give your reasons; for your judgment will probably be right, but your reason will certainly be wrong".[108] The reluctance may be particularly acute in the absence of a statutory duty to give reasons, for any reasons volunteered will be scrutinised for adequacy. Indeed, if reasons are volunteered, it is not necessary for the court to decide whether there was a duty to give reasons: the question becomes one of the adequacy of the reasons given, as though the giving of reasons was obligatory.[109] In addition, the provision of reasons might expose the body providing them to potential violations of grounds of review, as the reasons might provide evidence that, for example, a material error of fact has been committed, or that irrelevant considerations have been taken into account.

However, failure to provide reasons may itself be a sufficient trigger for the launch of an application for judicial review, so public bodies will need to balance these considerations in deciding whether to provide reasons in the absence of a statutory duty to do so. It is nevertheless generally considered "good" administrative practice to provide reasons, and though there is no general common law duty to do so, there has been a judicial expectation that

---

[103] *R v Civil Service Appeal Board, ex parte Cunningham* [1992] ICR 816, p.831, per McCowan LJ.
[104] See *id.*, pp.832–833.
[105] *Smart Gain Investment Ltd* v *Town Planning Board* [2007] HKEC 1964, para.72; *R v Westminster City Council, ex parte Ermakov* [1996] 2 All ER 302, p.315, per Hutchison LJ. It was desirable that the Secretary for Security gave reasons at the time of making a deportation order to avoid the impression or complaint of any "tailoring" of reasons (though not fatal that he did not) – *Akram* v *Secretary for Security* [2000] 1 HKLRD 164, p.171.
[106] *Re SJM Holdings Ltd* [2009] 1 HKLRD 321 (CA), pp.332–333.
[107] *Oriental Daily Publisher Ltd* v *Commissioner for Television and Entertainment Licensing Authority* (1997–98) 1 HKCFAR 279.
[108] Cited in *Tong Pon Wah* v *Hong Kong Society of Accountants* [1998] 2 HKLRD 427, p.442.
[109] *Smart Gain Investment Ltd* v *Town Planning Board* [2007] HKEC 1964, para.84; *R v Criminal Injuries Compensation Board, ex parte Moore* [1999] 2 All ER 90, p.95, per Sedley J.

government departments will in general provide reasons for their decisions.[110] There remains the risk of a public body providing reasons which either wholly or partly misrepresent or conceal the true rationale for the decision, though as a matter of both law and policy, public bodies would of course be advised against active (or inadvertent) pursuit of this course of action.

Bias and Insufficient Impartiality

It is a fundamental requirement of procedural fairness that proceedings be impartially conducted. First, the decision maker should have no personal or direct interest in the outcome of the decision, encapsulated in the maxim *nemo iudex in sua causa* – literally "no one [should be] a judge in his own cause". In addition, the decision maker's mind should not be contaminated by any other factor which may negatively affect his or her impartiality in the course of making a decision. These principles apply both in adjudicative decisions, such as court or tribunal proceedings, and in administrative or non-adjudicative decisions, such as when a licensing panel is deciding whether or not to approve an application for a licence.

One of the most manifest violations of the rules against bias is when the decision maker has a pecuniary or proprietary stake in the outcome.[111] This would involve a conflict of interests which undermines procedural fairness for one or more parties subject to the decision. However, the rules against bias also encapsulate broader prohibitions, such as where the decision maker has an attitude of affinity or hostility to a party, or where the decision maker has or previously had an affiliation with a party, or where the decision maker has previously expressed an opinion on one or more parties or the subject matter to which the decision relates. Rules have been developed on circumstances in which a decision maker would be disqualified from deciding.

The courts in England and Wales liberalised their position in *R v Bow Street Metropolitan Stipendiary Magistrate, ex parte Pinochet Ugarte (No 2)*, by extending automatic disqualification where a judge had a pecuniary or proprietary interest in the outcome of the decision to one in which his interest was neither pecuniary nor proprietary.[112] The case related to litigation involving

---

[110] See *Tong Pon Wah v Hong Kong Society of Accountants* [1998] 2 HKLRD 427, p.443. See also *Capital Rich Development Ltd v Town Planning Board* [2007] 2 HKLRD 155, paras.97–98. The Franks Committee recommended that written reasons be given for tribunal decisions (*Report of the Committee on Administrative Tribunals and Enquiries* (1957) Cmnd 218, para.98), a recommendation subsequently implemented in the UK – the Tribunals and Inquiries Act 1958, s.12, provided for reasons to be given in written or oral form.

[111] See *Dimes v Proprietors of the Grand Junction Canal* (1852) 3 HL Cas. 759.

[112] *R v Bow Street Metropolitan Stipendiary Magistrate, ex parte Pinochet Ugarte (No 2)* [2000] 1 AC 119, pp.134–135. Though see *Meerabux v Attorney General of Belize* [2005] 2 AC 513 (PC) (Belize), paras.21–22.

Augusto Pinochet, the former President of Chile, who had been arrested in London and claimed immunity as a former head of state. His legal entitlement to immunity was decided by a bench including Lord Hoffmann, who had links with Amnesty International which had campaigned against Pinochet. The question before the House of Lords was whether Lord Hoffmann's links with Amnesty International were such as to give the appearance that he might have been biased against Pinochet. The allegation was not one of actual bias on the part of Lord Hoffmann, and the House of Lords was clear that it did not impute any form of bias to him. The issue was rather if, given his links with Amnesty International, justice would have been seen to be done. The court held that the links with Amnesty disqualified Lord Hoffmann, and the decision in which he participated was set aside. As explained by Lord Hutton, "the links ... were so strong that public confidence in the integrity of the administration of justice would be shaken if his decision were allowed to stand".[113]

Appearances matter under this head of review. It would in most cases be difficult to prove actual bias on the part of a decision maker. This would be a question of evidence, and often the evidence would not be sufficient to demonstrate that the decision maker was actually biased;[114] though, of course, if sufficient evidence could be mustered to demonstrate actual bias, the applicant's hand would be strengthened. The objective is rather usually to show that the decision-making process *appears* to be compromised by a real possibility of bias, or that the circumstances are such that there is an appearance of insufficient impartiality in proceedings. In that vein, Lord Hewart CJ's much-quoted statement that it is "of fundamental importance that justice should not only be done, but should manifestly and undoubtedly be seen to be done"[115] continues to inform the judicial approach in this area.

The challenge for the courts is how to assess the appearance of a real possibility of bias. In the courts of England and Wales, various formulations have been used such as a real likelihood of bias, a reasonable suspicion of bias, a real danger of bias and so on.[116] The test laid down by Lord Hope of Craighead in *Porter v Magill* was "whether the fair-minded and informed observer, having considered the facts, would conclude that there was a real possibility that the tribunal was biased".[117] The characteristics of a "fair-

---

[113] *R v Bow Street Metropolitan Stipendiary Magistrate, ex parte Pinochet Ugarte (No 2)* [2000] 1 AC 119, p.146.
[114] See *Locabail (UK) Ltd v Bayfield Properties Ltd* [2000] 2 WLR 870, para.3.
[115] *R v Sussex Justices, ex parte McCarthy* [1924] 1 KB 256, p.259, per Lord Hewart CJ.
[116] See Wade and Forsyth, *Administrative Law* (11th edn), pp.386–387.
[117] *Porter v Magill* [2001] UKHL 67, para.103, representing a modification on the test expressed in *Re Medicaments and Related Classes of Goods (No 2)* [2001] 1 WLR 700, para.85, per Lord Phillips. The modification in *Porter* was accepted in *Lawal v Northern Spirit Ltd* [2003] UKHL 35, para.14, per Lord Bingham.

minded and informed observer" were colourfully set out in a Scottish appeal to the House of Lords,[118] and in Hong Kong it has been added that said observer would be a "realistic and pragmatic person", not "idealistic or rigid in his approach".[119]

The courts in Hong Kong have broadly followed the UK approach,[120] and adopted a very similar formulation to that of Lord Hope of Craighead in *Porter* v *Magill*.[121] Several of the cases involve challenges to the impartiality of judges, but analogous challenges can be made against any reviewable decision maker, even if the issues are not identical. The Court of Appeal of England and Wales stated, as to what might constitute factors that may give rise to apparent bias, that it could not:

> conceive of circumstances in which an objection could be soundly based on the religion, ethnic or national origin, gender, age, class, means or sexual orientation of the judge. Nor, at any rate ordinarily, could an objection be soundly based on the judge's social or educational or service or employment background or history, nor that of any member of the judge's family; or previous political associations; or membership of social or sporting or charitable bodies; or Masonic associations; or previous judicial decisions; or extra-curricular utterances (whether in textbooks, lectures, speeches, articles, interviews, reports or responses to consultation papers); or previous receipt of instructions to act for or against any party, solicitor or advocate engaged in a case before him; or membership of the same Inn, circuit, local Law Society or chambers ...[122]

However, factors which may give rise to bias included personal friendship or animosity between a judge and a member of the public involved in the case, close personal acquaintance with that person, or in a case where the credibility of a person was in issue, the judge had in a previous case rejected that person's evidence in such outspoken terms as to make doubtful his ability to treat his evidence in a subsequent case with an open mind, or where the judge had expressed views on a subject at issue in the case in "such extreme and unbalanced terms as to throw doubt on his ability to try the issue with an objective judicial mind".[123]

---

[118] *Helow v Secretary of State for the Home Department* [2008] UKHL 62, paras.1–3, per Lord Hope of Craighead. See also *Johnson v Johnson* [2000] HCA 48, paras.52–54.

[119] *Wong Tak Wai v Commissioner of Correctional Services* [2010] 4 HKLRD 409, para.138, per Cheung J.

[120] *Deacons v White & Case LLP* (2003) 6 HKCFAR 322; *Falcon Private Bank Ltd v Borry Bernard Edouard Charles Ltd* (2014) 17 HKCFAR 281; *HKSAR v Md Emran Hossain* (2016) 19 HKCFAR 679.

[121] *Chau Siu Woon v Cheung Shek Kong* [2010] 3 HKLRD 49, para.12; *Re Choy Bing Wing, ex parte Director of Housing Department* [2014] HKEC 451, para.36.

[122] *Locabail (UK) Ltd v Bayfield Properties Ltd* [2000] 2 WLR 870, para.25.

[123] *Id.* On acquaintance, see, for example, *Komal Patel v Chris Au* [2016] 1 HKLRD 328. In *Deacons v White and Case LLP* [2003] 2 HKLRD 840 (CA), a judge recused himself on the

The real possibility of bias must be apparent and will not be easily implied – particularly where the impartiality of a judge is disputed, as the fair-minded and informed observer is deemed to be aware of the significance of the judicial oath.[124] For example, a judge's previous refusal to accept an interlocutory application would be unlikely to generate a meritorious argument that, where the judge refused such an application in another action, this would demonstrate actual or apparent bias.[125] Where there had been an outburst of temper from a master to a plaintiff, the Court of Appeal concluded that the master's behaviour "had more to do with being exasperated for not getting proper assistance from the first plaintiff than harbouring any ill will or prejudice against her", and that "there was absolutely no improper motive, bad faith or malice involved", thus failing to prove apparent bias.[126]

In another case, a District Court judge refused to recuse himself notwithstanding an application for recusal by the prosecution and defence. The judge had allegedly doubted the efficacy of an offence over drinks at the end of a criminal law conference a few days before a trial in which the offence was a possible verdict. The judge had stated that he was dealing with a bus accident case in the New Territories involving a charge of this offence; the instant case involved a bus accident in the New Territories. Hartmann J, hearing an application for judicial review of the District Court judge's refusal to recuse himself, stated that a fair-minded and informed observer would not conclude that the remarks of the judge, read in context, could possibly give rise to any real perception of bias.[127]

A judge refused to recuse himself from hearing an application for judicial review involving an issue of human trafficking because of the stance he took in combating the problem when serving as Director of Public Prosecutions. The situation fell, in the judge's view, short of the circumstances which led to the House of Lords' decision that Lord Hardie's purporting to judicially rule on the effect of legislation he promoted as Lord Advocate in Scotland constituted a real possibility of bias in the view of the fair-minded and

---

basis that he and an equity partner of the plaintiff firm (who was therefore effectively a party with a personal interest in the outcome of the proceedings) had been close friends whilst at university together, but had only infrequently been in contact since the judge joined the Bench some ten years before the instant case. The test adopted by the judge was whether an objective onlooker might have a reasonable apprehension of bias. The appeal (*Deacons* v *White and Case LLP* (2003) 6 HKCFAR 322) was dismissed.

[124] *Davidson* v *Scottish Ministers (No 2)* [2004] UKHL 34, para.18; *HKSAR* v *Md Emran Hossain* (2016) 19 HKCFAR 679, paras.41–42.
[125] *Re Choy Bing Wing, ex parte Director of Housing Department* [2014] HKEC 451, paras.35–41.
[126] *Chau Siu Woon* v *Cheung Shek Kong* [2010] 3 HKLRD 49, paras.40–44 and 48, relying on *Johnson* v *Johnson* [2000] HCA 48, para.53.
[127] *Secretary for Justice* v *Li Chau Wing* [2004] HKEC 1417. This was not the first case in which the prosecution had sought recusal; see *ZN* v *Secretary for Justice* [2016] 1 HKLRD 174, para.62.

informed observer.[128] There would be no lack of structural impartiality where a judge who had previously refused leave to appeal participated in the full Court of Appeal's consideration of a renewed application for leave to appeal. This would not automatically give the appearance that the judge had predetermined the application, and it would still have to be demonstrated that the fair-minded and informed observer would conclude that there was a real possibility of bias.[129] Structural impartiality might be lacking, however, if a judge who had previously sat as part of a court refusing legal aid on the merits of a prospective appeal, sat on the substantive appeal itself.[130] A judge was apparently biased where he asked a plaintiff acting in person to leave the courtroom and then, in the plaintiff's absence, continued the hearing for four minutes during which he said to the respondent's counsel that, *inter alia*, the plaintiff did not understand and was not answering the questions put to him, and proposing that counsel for the respondent end the cross-examination to save time.[131]

The Court of Final Appeal recently set out the law on judges criticising counsel or solicitors appearing in a case:

> 29. ... There is no question of a judge somehow having automatically to recuse himself just because he has seriously criticised counsel or solicitors appearing in a case. The test is that involving the objective standard of the fair-minded and informed observer ...
>
> 34. ... We have already rejected the proposition that the fact that the criticisms are justified means that there must be no recusal. There will certainly be cases where justified criticisms may be expressed by the judge in terms and in contexts which will not require recusal. But equally, in some cases, applying the standard of the fair-minded and informed observer, the context and nature of the criticism may be such that recusal ought to follow even though the criticism was justified. Everything depends on the circumstances ...
>
> 36. Of course, if a judge makes criticisms without any discernible rhyme or reason or which are obviously unfair and unreasonable, this might be factored into what the fair-minded and informed observer might apprehend in terms of apparent bias. Conversely, if the criticisms appear capable of being justified, any appellate court would be slow to conclude from the mere fact of such criticisms, that the fair-minded and informed observer would apprehend a risk of bias. But even if the criticisms are or may be justified, if they are

---

[128] *ZN v Secretary for Justice* [2016] 1 HKLRD 174, paras.88–98 and 114–116; in reference to *Davidson v Scottish Ministers (No 2)* [2004] UKHL 34.
[129] *HKSAR v Md Emran Hossain* (2016) 19 HKCFAR 679, paras.35–54; and see *Sengupta v Holmes* [2002] EWCA Civ 1104.
[130] *R v Taito* [2003] 3 NZLR 577 (PC) (New Zealand), discussed in *Md Emran Hossain* (2016) 19 HKCFAR 679, paras.47–48.
[131] *Yu Cho Lam v Commissioner of Police* [2016] 1 HKLRD 257 (CA).

couched in terms or made in a context which raise doubts as to whether the judge can continue to adjudicate with the detachment and impartiality essential to the judicial process, his recusal may be properly required.[132]

It has been said that judges should not recuse themselves too readily in a way that might encourage parties to use this is a channel for having a potentially more favourable judge decide their case.[133] Nevertheless, it has also been said that, where there is real doubt whether, viewed objectively, acquaintance could or would lead to unconscious bias, the prudent course may be to favour recusal.[134] If a judge did not know of a matter relied on as appearing to undermine his impartiality, the appearance of possible bias would be defeated.[135] Where a judge had recused himself or was held to be apparently biased, this may result in all decisions and orders made by that judge being invalidated,[136] but this will not always be the case.[137]

The same instance of conduct, when committed by different decision makers in different settings, will not always lead to the same result in terms of whether the fair-minded and informed observer would perceive a real possibility of bias.[138] The court is entitled to attach some weight to an *ex post facto* declaration by the decision maker that it decided with an open mind where this is consistent with other evidence, such as the decision maker's prior conduct, though a bare *ex post facto* declaration on its own may be viewed as self-serving.[139] It is also important to note that a lack of structural independence in a non-judicial body could be cured by the affected individual having access to a court in judicial review proceedings.[140] Senior government officials would not be lacking in independence merely because they took an adjudicative decision related to public resources, which they would

---

[132] *Falcon Private Bank Ltd v Borry Bernard Edouard Charles Ltd* (2014) 17 HKCFAR 281, paras. 29, 34 and 36, per Ribeiro PJ.
[133] *Re JRL, ex parte CJL* [1986] HCA 39, para.5, per Mason J.
[134] *Locabail (UK) Ltd v Bayfield Properties Ltd* [2000] 2 WLR 870, para.25; *Superb Quo Ltd v Lee Yuen Cheung Co Ltd* [2011] 3 HKLRD G3 (CA), paras.1, 42.
[135] *Auckland Casino Ltd v Casino Control Authority* [1995] 1 NZLR 142, p.148; *Locabail (UK) Ltd v Bayfield Properties Ltd* [2000] 2 WLR 870, para.18; *Ng Chi Keung v Secretary for Justice* [2016] HKLRD 1330, paras.186–192.
[136] *R v Curragh Inc* [1997] 1 SCR 537 (Supreme Court of Canada), pp.542–545.
[137] *Deacons v White and Case LLP* [2003] 2 HKLRD 840 (CA), paras.12–19.
[138] See *HLB Hodgson Impey Cheng v Hong Kong Institute of Certified Public Accountants* (2013) 16 HKCFAR 460, para.68, per Gleeson NPJ. See also *Clark v Kelly*, 2003 SC (PC) 77, para.29. It was stated in *PCCW-HKT Telephone Ltd v Telecommunications Authority* [2007] 2 HKLRD 536, paras.60–63, that the pronouncements of the Telecommunications Authority should not be assessed with the same rigour that one might apply to a court or tribunal, that the court should be slow to condemn the Authority for apparent bias in view of the nature of the Authority's functions, and that the Authority should *prima facie* be trusted and to know of its obligation to carry out a transparent and even-handed consultation.
[139] *PCCW-HKT Telephone Ltd v Telecommunications Authority* [2007] 2 HKLRD 536, paras.66–72.
[140] *Wong Tak Wai v Commissioner of Correctional Services* [2010] 4 HKLRD 409, paras.66 *et seq* and 117–121.

presumably have an interest in protecting.[141] Nor would a public authority be apparently biased where it was legitimately predisposed to a particular outcome, provided this did not constitute illegitimate predetermination of the outcome.[142] However, a disciplinary decision was quashed on the basis that, *inter alia*, a Law Officer in the Department of Justice had played an integral role in the prosecution of the disciplined official for breach of discipline, the giving of advice concerning the official's request for legal representation (which was refused), and thereafter in advising the Secretary for the Civil Service on whether to find the official guilty of such a breach and on the appropriate penalty to be imposed. The fair-minded and informed observer would have concluded that there was a real possibility of bias on the part of the Law Officer.[143] If the Department of Justice had to play multiple roles in the disciplinary process, the danger may be avoided or mitigated by erecting firewalls between different divisions of the Department,[144] though this would not always defeat concerns of bias.[145]

Where a party waives his or her entitlement to object on the ground of bias,[146] this can effectively act as estoppel for the party seeking review on the basis of bias. In order to be valid, the waiver must be given on a voluntarily basis in full knowledge of the facts.[147] The courts may imply there to have been waiver where a party failed to object on grounds of bias at an early opportunity,[148] such as at the impugned hearing:[149] "appellate and reviewing courts tend not to look favourably on complaints of vitiating bias made only after the complainant has taken his chance on the outcome and found it unwelcome".[150] However, this must be balanced against courts discouraging premature applications for review, such as on the ground that a decision maker for whom there appears to be a real possibility of bias might not actually make a

---

[141] *Lam Tat Ming* v *Chief Executive of the HKSAR* [2012] 1 HKLRD 801.
[142] *PCCW-HKT Telephone Ltd* v *Telecommunications Authority* [2007] 2 HKLRD 536, paras.49–53; and see *National Assembly for Wales* v *Condron* [2006] EWCA Civ 1573, para.43.
[143] *Rowse* v *Secretary for Civil Service* [2008] 5 HKLRD 217, paras.144–169.
[144] *Id.*, paras.147–148, referencing also *Cheng Chui Ping* v *Chief Executive of HKSAR* [2002] HKEC 26.
[145] *Rowse* v *Secretary for Civil Service* [2008] 5 HKLRD 217, para.149; *Ch'ng Poh* v *Chief Executive of HKSAR* [2003] HKEC 1441, para.87. It was said that impartiality and independence are distinguishable, though interlinked – *Wong Tak Wai* v *Commissioner of Correctional Services* [2010] 4 HKLRD 409 (CA), para.117, per Cheung J.
[146] *Financial Secretary* v *Wong* (2003) 6 HKCFAR 476, paras.50–51 and 118.
[147] *R* v *Bow Street Metropolitan Stipendiary Magistrate, ex parte Pinochet Ugarte (No 2)* [2000] 1 AC 119, p.137; *Millar* v *Dickson* [2002] 1 WLR 1615, para.31; *Smith* v *Kvaerner Cementation Foundations Ltd* [2007] 1 WLR 370, para.29; *Komal Patel* v *Chris Au* [2016] 1 HKLRD 328, paras.22–27.
[148] *Komal Patel* v *Chris Au* [2016] 1 HKLRD 328.
[149] *Amoy Properties Ltd* v *Committee for Takeovers and Mergers* [1989] HKCU 367.
[150] *Steadman-Byrne* v *Amjad* [2007] EWCA Civ 625, para.17, per Sedley LJ. Though in the majority of situations a person would be unlikely to apply for judicial review where he or she is satisfied with the decision on the merits.

decision unfavourable to the applicant.[151] For example, a licensing adjudicator who is known to be a vegan on ethical grounds would not automatically make a decision unfavourable to an applicant seeking to operate a barbecue pork (*char siu*) restaurant. Where it is legally or factually impossible for a decision maker other than one who is personally interested in a decision to be the entity to make the decision, an objection of bias may not be effective – the so-called necessity principle.[152]

---

[151] An allegation of bias was described as "absurd" before an adverse decision had been made – *Benbecula Ltd v Attorney General* [1994] 3 HKC 238, p.242, per Kaplan J.

[152] See *Dimes v Proprietors of the Grand Junction Canal* (1852) 3 HL Cas. 759; *Phillips v Eyre* (1868–69) LR 4 QB 225; and *X v Education and Accreditation Committee, Medical Council of Hong Kong* [2013] 1 HKLRD 167, paras.63–71.

Part IV
Judicial Remedies, Non-Judicial Remedies and Subsidiary Legislation

Part IV

20

Remedies in Judicial Review

The principal remedies which can be obtained in relation to reviewable acts and decisions can be divided in terms of the applicable procedure.[1] Three of these remedies are available only under judicial review procedure, namely certiorari, prohibition and mandamus.[2] The other three remedies – declaration, injunction[3] and damages – can be sought using either judicial review or ordinary procedure; and one of them (damages) can be sought only in relation to private law liability. The remedies should be used in conformity with the separation of powers, namely to enforce or uphold legality, whilst refraining from encroachment on the merits.

Hong Kong, like England and Wales, has a remedy-driven system of judicial review inasmuch as the choice of remedy bears on the form of action. The relevant provisions are set out in section 21K of the High Court Ordinance:

(1) An application to the Court of First Instance for one or more of the following forms of relief –
  (a) an order of mandamus, prohibition or certiorari;
  (b) an injunction under section 21J restraining a person not entitled to do so from acting in an office to which that section applies,
  shall be made in accordance with rules of court by a procedure to be known as an application for judicial review.
(2) An application for a declaration or an injunction (not being an injunction mentioned in subsection (1)) may be made in accordance with rules of court by way of an application for judicial review, and on such an application the Court of First Instance may grant the declaration or injunction claimed if it considers that, having regard to –

---

[1] There are, in addition, a range of statutory appeals and remedies.
[2] These are based on their counterparts in England and Wales which, since the introduction of Part 54 of the Civil Procedure Rules, have been called quashing orders, prohibiting orders and mandatory orders, respectively. The remedies of certiorari, prohibition and mandamus have a statutory footing in the High Court Ordinance (cap.4), s.21I, however their form and content substantially lies in the common law.
[3] Except an injunction under section 21J of the High Court Ordinance restraining a person not entitled to do so from acting in an office to which that section applies, which must be sought using judicial review procedure.

(a) the nature of the matters in respect of which relief may be granted by orders of mandamus, prohibition or certiorari;
(b) the nature of the persons and bodies against whom relief may be granted by such orders; and
(c) all the circumstances of the case,
it would be just and convenient for the declaration to be made or the injunction to be granted, as the case may be.[4]

One of the limitations on the scope of remedies in judicial review is that they will in general only be available against an actual decision or a decision-making process which has led to an actual decision.[5] Litton NPJ pointed out that it is "not every decision by a decision maker which is susceptible to review: were it otherwise the functioning of the executive arm of government and of statutory bodies and tribunals would be ensnared in multiple applications in the court".[6] Wade and Forsyth stated quashing and prohibiting orders (equivalent to certiorari and prohibition) to be remedies granted in relation to a decisive exercise of discretion.[7] The supervisory jurisdiction does not generally have the "purpose of micro-managing the activities of subordinate tribunals or administrative decision-makers" and "should hardly ever be exercised to review decisions that go only to procedure rather than to the end result".[8] Instead:

> Intermediate steps should normally only be reviewed as part of the entire process *after* the determinative and ultimate action or decision is taken. For example, where a challenge is based on an allegation of an unfair consultation process, it has been said that, unless the preliminary "decision" has a *permanent* judicial effect on the person affected, the court should not entertain such a challenge, in particular, as it is usually difficult to judge whether the process is so materially unfair before the process has ended.[9]

---

[4] A similar provision appears in O.53, r.1, where it is also stated at r.1(3) that "[a]n application for judicial review may include an application for an award of damages, restitution or the recovery of a sum due but may not seek such a remedy alone".

[5] An exception is where there is failure or refusal to exercise discretion.

[6] *Financial Secretary v Wong* (2003) 6 HKCFAR 476, para.93, per Litton NPJ.

[7] Wade and Forsyth, *Administrative Law* (11th edn), p.517, citing *R v St Lawrence's Hospital Statutory Visitors, ex parte Pritchard* [1953] 1 WLR 1158 as evidence of a report not being quashed because it was only an intermediate step towards a decision. The case was cited in this context in *Financial Secretary v Wong* (2003) 6 HKCFAR 476, para.94, where it was said that there was no reason to think that it would then have been decided any differently (per Litton NPJ).

[8] *Financial Secretary v Wong* (2003) 6 HKCFAR 476, para.14, per Bokhary PJ.

[9] *Television Broadcasts Ltd v Communications Authority* [2013] HKEC 729, para.25. Emphasis in the original. Ribeiro PJ stated in the Court of Final Appeal that Article 10 of the Hong Kong Bill of Rights (which provides that a person shall be entitled to a fair and public hearing in the determination of his rights and obligations in a suit at law) "does not require every element of the protections conferred to be present at every stage of the determination of a person's rights and obligations, but only that such protections should be effective when the determination is viewed as an entire process, including as part of that process such appeals or judicial review as may be available" – *Lam Siu Po v Commissioner of Police* (2009) 12 HKCFAR 237, para.109.

The general principle could be seen in the case of *Television Broadcasts Ltd* v *Communications Authority*.[10] The Chief Executive-in-Council had a statutory power to grant domestic free television licences. An application for a licence was first to be made to the Communications Authority, which was under a statutory duty to consider the application and make recommendations thereon to the Chief Executive-in-Council. The applicant in the case was a commercial television broadcaster which sought judicial review of the Authority's recommendations and the way in which it had arrived at those recommendations. The Chief Executive-in-Council had not yet made a decision, and the challenge was directed at what Au J described as "interlocutory and preparatory procedures". Indeed, the recommendations were only advisory and the Chief Executive-in-Council was not bound to follow them. The application was therefore premature; no substantive legal consequences resulted from the alleged wrongs committed by the Authority.[11] Prematurity of this nature is sufficient to result in the dismissal of the application.[12]

There are several policy reasons for preferring potential applicants for judicial review to wait until a decision-making process has come to a conclusion before launching their challenge. First, if intermediate stages were open to judicial review, there could be multiple challenges in the course of a single decision-making process. This would spell an increase in litigation and the consumption of the parties' and the courts' resources. Second, and crucially, the procedural defect complained of might not necessarily result in the making of an adverse decision. For example, an apparently biased decision maker will not necessarily arrive at a decision adverse to the applicant's interests.[13] If a civil servant is subject to disciplinary proceedings chaired by a person with whom he has a history of personal animosity, but the civil servant is exonerated by the chair, why would the civil servant seek to challenge the legality of the proceedings?[14] The premature launch of judicial review proceedings can therefore result in litigation which would not have been pursued had the procedure under challenge been allowed to run its course. It is therefore potentially a waste of the parties' and court's resources.[15] Simultaneous use of

---

[10] *Television Broadcasts Ltd* v *Communications Authority* [2013] HKEC 729.   [11] *Id.*, para.32.

[12] *Tang Keung Hong* v *Poon Kit Sang* [2005] 4 HKLRD 274; *PCCW-HKT Telephone Ltd* v *Telecommunications Authority* [2007] 2 HKLRD 536, para.191.

[13] Though this must be balanced against the risk of the applicant being held to have waived his right to challenge the participation of the decision maker in question should he fail to promptly object to his participation – see pp.270–271 and 297.

[14] This raises the difficult issue of judicial review proceedings only being likely to arise when the aspiring applicant is dissatisfied with the substantive outcome of the relevant decision. Though judicial review is a challenge to the legality of a decision or decision-making process, a person is unlikely to challenge the legality of a decision or decision-making process unless he is dissatisfied with the substantive decision, which is a question of merits. In other words, *ultra vires* decisions will tend to stand as *de facto* effective when they deliver a substantive result agreeable to the affected persons.

[15] Though it might be argued to be in the public interest that unlawful acts and decisions are "righted" even if the applicant is not substantively dissatisfied with the outcome.

judicial review and a statutory objection or appeal process in relation to the same issue is not only likely to be a premature resort to judicial review, but may be considered an abuse of process.[16]

The example of apparent bias is particularly interesting and arose in *PCCW-HKT Telephone Ltd v Telecommunications Authority*.[17] The applicant challenged the Telecommunications Authority's approach to an intermediate stage of a consultation process, alleging that the Authority had predetermined the outcome of the consultation. The applicant therefore sought an order for the Authority to recuse itself from participating in any decisions relating to the issues under consultation. The court held that what was being contested was an interlocutory direction to proceed with the consultation, which was procedural rather than substantive in nature. Even with an averment of apparent bias, this would not automatically lead to the Authority deciding against the applicant.[18] Again, the application would have been refused on the basis of prematurity alone.[19] The court rejected the argument that the timing of the application for judicial review was appropriate because the Authority's apparent bias, if substantiated, would have vitiated the entire consultation, and time and money would needlessly have been spent on the consultation process unless it was declared void at the earliest opportunity.[20] The situation could possibly be different if actual bias was demonstrated,[21] or if automatic disqualification of the decision maker was established, though even an actually biased decision maker will not necessarily decide against the applicant.

The relevance of the ongoing nature of proceedings is that they remain fluid and without a predetermined outcome. Where the Director of Lands issued two separate letters containing "ultimatums" for the payment of a premium, and the applicant sought judicial review on the basis that the ultimatums constituted abuse of power, the court held that there was not the necessary finality in the form of a substantive decision to be subject to review. Contrary to the "ultimatums" given, there was no unambiguous evidence that either party had brought to a close what appeared to be negotiations. Prior to seeking judicial review, the applicant had even replied to the Director with a counter-offer which still appeared to be open.[22] Where the Investigation Committee of the Hong Kong Institute of Certified Public Accountants adopted a draft report stating a *prima facie* case against a firm of accountants, it was

---

[16] *Benbecula Ltd v Attorney General* [1994] 3 HKC 238.
[17] *PCCW-HKT Telephone Ltd v Telecommunications Authority* [2007] 2 HKLRD 536.
[18] See *Financial Secretary v Wong* (2003) 6 HKCFAR 476, para.14; and *PCCW-HKT Telephone Ltd v Telecommunications Authority* [2007] 2 HKLRD 536, paras.187–188.
[19] *PCCW-HKT Telephone Ltd v Telecommunications Authority* [2007] 2 HKLRD 536, paras.177–191.
[20] *Id.*, para.185.
[21] The applicant in the present case had, in its notice of motion, suggested actual bias on the Authority's part, but abandoned that contention at the hearing – *id.*, para.40.
[22] *Rank Profit Industries Ltd v Director of Lands* [2007] HKEC 390, paras.86–99.

premature to apply for judicial review as the Council of the Institute had not yet reached the point of considering whether to exercise its power to refer the matters to Disciplinary Panels, and it was unclear what, if any, action would be taken by the Council in that regard.[23]

This is not an absolute position, however, as the courts have stated that an application would be accepted prior to the making of a decision with substantive legal consequences where irretrievable prejudice could be shown.[24] For example, irretrievable prejudice would result from the decision of a health authority to withdraw life support provision from a patient in a "persistent vegetative state" in accordance with the wishes of the patient's family even though it was uncertain whether such a decision would be lawful. The health authority may seek a declaration of the court as to whether the withdrawal of the life support provision would be lawful, as it could hardly (i) risk withdrawing life support and potentially committing an unlawful act, perhaps even a criminal offence with penalties including imprisonment for the individuals concerned, or (ii) perpetually refrain from withdrawing life support for fear that it may be unlawful to do so.[25]

Remedies may be claimed cumulatively or alternatively.[26] It is generally preferable to seek additional remedies when the applicant is unsure which remedy may be appropriate than to seek to amend the application at a later stage (subject to the qualification that one should of course not pursue remedies that are categorically inappropriate). The court is particularly keen for the grounds not to be amended following the granting of leave.[27] There is a right of appeal against an order granting any relief at the hearing of an application for judicial review.[28]

---

[23] *HLB Hodgson Impey Cheng* v *Hong Kong Institute of Certified Public Accountants* (2013) 16 HKCFAR 460, para.82.

[24] *Television Broadcasts Ltd* v *Communications Authority* [2013] HKEC 729, paras.25, 32, 36 and 39. Au J stated (paras.25–26) that an error of fact in a procedural "decision" would not in itself amount to an exceptional circumstance justifying judicial review prior to the substantive determination being made. See also *Bahamas District of the Methodist Church in the Caribbean and the Americas* v *Symonette* [2000] ULPC 31 (PC) (Bahamas), Privy Council Appeal No. 70 of 1998, para.14; and 張德榮對政制及內地事務局局長 (unrep, HCAL 45/2011, 11 July 2011), paras.13–14.

[25] These facts are taken from *Airedale NHS Trust* v *Bland* [1993] AC 789 (HL). Lord Goff of Chieveley said that it would be "a deplorable state of affairs if no authoritative guidance could be given to the medical profession in a case such as the present, so that a doctor would be compelled either to act contrary to the principles of medical ethics established by his professional body or to risk a prosecution for murder" (pp.862–863).

[26] O.53, r.2.

[27] Litton PJ stated that "[o]nce leave to apply for judicial review is granted, amendment of the grounds should rarely occur. All too often applications are made for amendment after leave to issue proceedings has been granted, as if O.53 r.3 were simply the portals to a playground of infinite possibilities where the administrators could then be made to leap through more and more hoops of fire. It is up to the Judges of the High Court to stop this kind of extravaganza" – *Lau Kong Yung* v *Director of Immigration* (1999) 2 HKCFAR 300, p.340, per Litton PJ.

[28] High Court Ordinance (cap.4), ss.13(2) and 14A; O.59, r.21(1)(f).

Certiorari

Certiorari is one of the most important remedies in judicial review, removing the legal effect of an act or decision. It is available against inferior courts and tribunals in addition to other bodies subject to review. When an *ultra vires* act or decision is quashed by order of certiorari, the act or decision is regarded as a nullity: as far as the law is concerned, the act was never validly performed or the decision never validly made. This is consistent with the *ultra vires* principle whereby a body has no legal power to do any thing that is not within its power to do. The act or decision is void *ab initio*. Yet this is a paradox, as the act was in fact performed or the decision in fact made. If no act was performed or no decision made, there would be nothing to quash.

As certiorari removes the legal effect of an act or decision, there must be an act or decision capable of having its legal effect reduced. A report might not constitute an act or decision the legal effect of which is capable of being removed,[29] nor might the initiation of a multi-stage procedure.[30] If a decision is made pursuant to or in reliance upon a defective report, and the defectiveness of the report taints the legality of the decision, then the decision may be subject to review. It is also possible that a body might be restrained from deciding in reliance on such a report, for example by way of prohibition, but this is subject to the principle that a decision will usually be required to have been made, or a decision-making process to have come to a conclusion, before judicial review will lie.

It is provided by the High Court Ordinance that:

> If, on an application for judicial review seeking an order of certiorari, the Court of First Instance quashes the decision to which the application relates, the Court of First Instance may remit the matter to the court, tribunal or authority concerned, with a direction to reconsider it and reach a decision in accordance with the findings of the Court of First Instance.[31]

This allows the court not only to annul the *ultra vires* decision, but to order that the decision maker retake the decision with or without instructions on how that discretion should be exercised. Any such instructions will usually not instruct the decision maker which decision to make – that being a likely infringement of the separation of powers – but will tend to be confined to directions necessary to ensure that the decision is lawfully retaken.

The court may direct that, where leave is granted, and where an order of certiorari or prohibition is sought by the applicant, the grant of leave shall operate as a stay of the proceedings to which the application relates, either

---

[29] *R v St. Lawrence's Hospital, ex parte Pritchard* [1953] 1 WLR 1158.
[30] *Benbecula Ltd v Attorney General* [1994] 3 HKC 238; and see *Council of Civil Service Unions v Minister for the Civil Service* [1985] AC 374 (HL), pp.408–409, which describes how a decision must affect a person to qualify as subject matter for judicial review.
[31] High Court Ordinance (cap.4), s.21K(5).

until the determination of the application or until the court otherwise orders.[32] If the court exercises its discretion to stay proceedings in this way, it effectively amounts to the grant of a prohibitory injunction.[33] The proceedings stayed include not only the process by which a decision is made, but also the process by which the decision would be implemented.[34]

Prohibition

An order of prohibition, as its name suggests, prohibits a body from doing something, for example prohibiting the implementation of a decision, the cancellation of a licence, the imposition of disciplinary measures, the demolition of a building, the deportation of a person, the participation of an insufficiently impartial adjudicator and so on.

It may be that an applicant seeks one remedy, but a different remedy is thought by the court to be more appropriate.[35] An application for certiorari to quash a removal order was considered in a case before the Court of Appeal to be more appropriately remedied by order of prohibition. The vitiating factor was not the removal order in itself, but the procedural unfairness resulting from the lack of an opportunity for the applicant to be heard. Accordingly, prohibition was issued to prevent the removal order being executed if and until the applicant had been given the opportunity to be heard. That procedural right being satisfied, the removal order might stand as capable of being lawfully executed.[36] For similar reasons, an application for certiorari, prohibition and mandamus was considered more appropriately remedied by order of prohibition alone, as the procedural defect could be cured by affording the affected persons a fair hearing. Prohibition was therefore issued to prevent certain resolutions from being implemented, and further licences from being granted, if and until the affected persons had been given the opportunity to be heard.[37] Where a decision maker had inordinately delayed in determining tax objections, but had not otherwise done anything unlawful as such, it would be more appropriate to issue an order of mandamus requiring the decision maker

---

[32] O.53, r.3(10)(a). If any other relief is sought, the court may at any time grant in the proceedings such interim relief as could be granted in an action begun by writ – O.53, r.3(10)(b).
[33] *Super Lion Enterprises Ltd v Commissioner of Rating and Valuation* [2006] 1 HKLRD 239.
[34] *Anglo Starlite Insurance Co Ltd v Insurance Authority* [1992] 2 HKLR 31; *McGettigan Brian Kevin v Municipal Services Appeals Board* [2013] HKEC 1926; *Sabinano II Marcel R v Municipal Services Appeals Board* [2014] 1 HKLRD 676. *Anglo Starlite* followed the decisions in *R v Licensing Authority, ex parte Smith Kline & French Laboratories Ltd (No 2)* [1990] 1 QB 574, p.604; and *R v Secretary of State for Education and Science, ex parte Avon County Council* [1991] 1 QB 558.
[35] Costs implications may follow from this; see p.62.
[36] *Ng Yuen-shiu v Attorney General* [1981] HKLR 352.
[37] *R v Liverpool Corporation, ex parte Liverpool Taxi Fleet Operators' Association* [1972] 2 WLR 1262.

to determine the objection than to quash the underlying tax assessments by way of certiorari.[38]

If a court is called upon to issue prohibition against proceedings that might not necessarily take place, it will have to conduct a balancing exercise to weigh the benefits of issuing prohibition (such as time and cost savings, preventing putatively unlawful proceedings from going ahead, preventing proceedings from going ahead which might cause substantial prejudice to a party) against the disadvantages of doing so (the putatively unlawful proceedings might never take place, potentially rendering pointless the review application).[39] This goes to the discretionary nature of the remedies in judicial review, and circumstances which may lead the court to refuse to award a remedy.

Mandamus

Mandamus is a remedy which orders a body to do something, for example to direct that a decision or determination be made, a decision be retaken, reasons be provided for a decision, a case be stated or an oral hearing be held. The purpose of mandamus is to enforce a public law duty,[40] but that will not ordinarily extend to compelling a body to make a particular decision. This would typically cause the court to trespass on executive discretion, threatening the separation of powers. Instead, mandamus should in principle be confined to the enforcement of a legal obligation, which will usually be a matter of how to act or decide – such as which considerations may or must lawfully be taken into account, or to compel reasons to be given – rather than what substantively to decide. Thus where the lawfulness of a decision of a licensing authority was tainted, the proper course would not be for the court to order that the licence be granted.[41] The proper course may vary with the circumstances, but could involve one or more of certiorari, mandamus or declaration.[42] Certiorari could issue to quash the unlawful decision of the licensing authority; this could either stand alone, meaning that no (lawful) decision has been taken,[43]

---

[38] *Yue Yuen Marketing Co Ltd* v *Commissioner of Inland Revenue* [2012] 4 HKLRD 761.

[39] See *R* v *Wimbledon Justices, ex parte Derwent* [1953] 1 All ER 390; *Commissioner for Labour* v *Jetex HVAC Equipments Ltd* [1995] 2 HKLR 24; and *Tsoi Kei Lung* v *Secretary for Justice* [2000] HKEC 742.

[40] The remedy can (if appropriate) be used to order the performance of a public law duty even if the time prescribed by statute for its performance has passed – *R* v *Revising Barrister for the Borough of Hanley* [1912] 3 KB 518; *Heland Investment Ltd* v *Attorney General* [1994] 2 HKC 550, p.555. See also *Yue Yuen Marketing Co Ltd* v *Commissioner of Inland Revenue* [2012] 4 HKLRD 761.

[41] *Cheung Kwok-hung* v *Liquor Licensing Board* [1995] 2 HKLR 456. See also *Desmond Keane* v *Director of Legal Aid*, CACV 49/2000, in which an order of mandamus was sought for a substituted decision of the Director of Legal Aid and, alternatively, an order of mandamus to compel reconsideration by the Director of Legal Aid (the application was dismissed).

[42] On the choice between declaration and mandamus, see *Ho Choi Wan* v *Hong Kong Housing Authority (No 2)* [2003] 3 HKLRD J1.

[43] Sometimes declaration will be more appropriate than certiorari – see pp.283–284.

or be combined with an order of mandamus to compel the authority to rehear and determine the licence application[44] – preserving, of course, the authority's lawful discretion in making that determination. It is also possible to solely order mandamus, as this could have the effect of quashing the previous decision,[45] though technically it would not have been quashed. It would rather be an *ultra vires* decision, and therefore not a valid decision in law, with the order of mandamus aiming to result in an *intra vires* decision. It is provided in Order 53 that no action or proceedings shall be begun or prosecuted against any person in respect of anything done in obedience to an order of mandamus.[46]

Declaration

A declaration is an order of the court which declares legal rights, duties or status. A principal difference between an order of certiorari and a declaration is that, whilst certiorari quashes an act, omission or decision, rendering it a legal nullity, declaration does not necessarily have this effect.[47] The remedies of certiorari and declaration have nevertheless not been regarded as mutually exclusive.[48]

Suppose, for example, that the Director of Immigration purports to impose an additional immigration restriction on all residents in Hong Kong, but the restriction could only lawfully be imposed on temporary residents. In other words, the restriction cannot lawfully be imposed on permanent residents. If an order of certiorari was issued by the court, the restriction would be quashed and would have to be remade. However, that may be more disruptive and consuming of resources than is necessary, as the restriction is not unlawful in its entirety, but only as it relates to permanent residents. In this situation, a declaration would likely be more appropriate, as the court can instead declare that the restriction is unlawful and of no legal effect inasmuch as it relates to permanent residents. This achieves two objectives: (i) it establishes that the restriction has no legal effect as it relates to permanent residents, but, crucially, (ii) it retains its legal effect as it relates to temporary residents. The restriction has not been quashed; it has merely been brought within its proper legal limits.

---

[44] See *Cocks* v *Thanet District Council* [1983] 2 AC 286 (HL), p.295.
[45] *Cheung Kwok-hung* v *Liquor Licensing Board* [1995] 2 HKLR 456, p.459, per Godfrey JA.
[46] O.53, r.10.
[47] Certiorari was described as the "primary and most appropriate remedy" for securing nullification of a public law decision, over declaration – *Cocks* v *Thanet District Council* [1983] 2 AC 286 (HL), p.295.
[48] Lord Goddard stated that he knew of "no authority for saying that if an order or decision can be attacked by certiorari the court is debarred from granting a declaration in an appropriate case. The remedies are not mutually exclusive, though no doubt there are some orders, notably convictions before justices, where the only appropriate remedy is certiorari" – *Pyx Granite Co Ltd* v *Ministry of Housing and Local Government* [1959] 3 WLR 346, p.290.

Another situation in which declaration can be useful is where it is unclear which party made a decision, in which case declaratory relief can be granted to the applicant if all the parties were brought before the court.[49] Declaration also tends to be the appropriate remedy when legislation is being tested for constitutionality.[50] If, for example, a section of a particular Ordinance is established to be in violation of the Basic Law, it would make little sense for the court to attempt to "quash" the section by order of certiorari: the section remains on the statute book and is not a standalone act or decision that can readily be invalidated in this way. Instead, the appropriate course would be for the court to issue a declaration that the section is of no legal effect as contrary to the Basic Law.

An order of declaration cannot usually be sought on a so-called hypothetical or academic question. There are a number of policy reasons for this. First, the hypothetical question might never become a real question, in which case the resources of the parties and the court are consumed to no avail. Second, when the hypothetical scenario materialises, there may be new facts or variations on existing facts which were not available or known at the time of the litigation. Hypothetical litigation is therefore litigation on the basis of incomplete facts.[51] Third, not all of the parties relevant to the case may be capable of identification at the hypothetical stage. Furthermore, the general rule against hypothetical challenge is a means of discouraging speculative, frivolous or trivial litigation.[52]

This is, however, a general rule, and the courts have made exceptions. The remedies of review being discretionary, "absent good reason, [the] court does not pronounce on abstract questions of law when there is no dispute before it to be resolved".[53] *Leung v Secretary for Justice* provides a fine example of when there are strong policy reasons favouring the court's ruling on a so-called hypothetical question.[54] The applicant was a twenty-year-old homosexual man who sought to challenge the constitutionality of section 118C of the Crimes Ordinance (cap.200), which purported to criminalise homosexual buggery with or by a man under the age of twenty-one years.[55] However,

---

[49] *Chan Wah v Hang Hau Rural Committee* [2000] 1 HKLRD 411.

[50] Ma CJHC described a challenge to the constitutionality of legislation as a "quintessential situation" for judicial review to be utilised – *Leung v Secretary for Justice* [2006] 4 HKLRD 211, para.21.

[51] See *Cheung Man Wai v Director of Social Welfare* [2000] 3 HKLRD 255 (CA), pp.259–260.

[52] Other protections against litigation of this nature include the rules on standing and arguability at the leave stage, and the rules on costs.

[53] *Rank Profit Industries Ltd v Director of Lands* [2007] HKEC 390, para.102, per Hartmann J. He added that the circumstances in which it may be appropriate, for the sake of the general law, for a court to take on an application that has become "academic" were "rare" (para.116). See also *R (Pretty) v Director of Public Prosecutions* [2002] 1 AC 800, p.851.

[54] *Leung v Secretary for Justice* [2006] 4 HKLRD 211 (CA).

[55] The challenge established that section 118C infringed constitutional rights of privacy and equality enshrined in the Basic Law and the Bill of Rights.

the applicant had not yet performed the act of homosexual buggery, but would nevertheless have to demonstrate sufficient interest in his application for judicial review. The issue was in that sense hypothetical, as he had not been, for example, convicted under section 118C.

Ma CJHC, sitting in the Court of Appeal, stated that the question of whether to permit judicial review in this case was one of discretion, not jurisdiction.[56] Indeed, flexibility was apparently conferred by section 21K(2)(c) of the High Court Ordinance (cap.4), providing that the court may grant a declaration if, having regard to all the circumstances of the case, it would be just and convenient for the declaration to be made; and equivalent wording in (now deleted) rule 1(2)(c) of Order 53 (cap.4A).[57] Clearly it would be deeply unsatisfactory to require the applicant to perform homosexual buggery and obtain a conviction under section 118C before recognising that he had standing to challenge the constitutionality of that section. It would also be unreasonable to expect the applicant to perpetually abstain from homosexual buggery in case section 118C was constitutionally compliant and therefore a criminal offence, even though there was a question as to its constitutionality.

The court gave a number of reasons why it would be proper to allow a declaration to issue in this case, notwithstanding that the question to be addressed was hypothetical. The applicant and many others in his situation were directly affected by section 118C. The question was one of significant public interest, and a whole class of persons (homosexual men) had a direct interest in the outcome of the case. In addition, contrary to one of the reasons for the general rule against issuing a declaration in a hypothetical case that not all the facts may be available at the litigation stage, in the present case there were no further findings of fact necessary – what was at issue was a pure point of law. Moreover, where the constitutionality of a law was involved, especially a criminal law, the sooner the constitutionality or otherwise of that law was established, the better. Finally, there was no question of this decision opening the floodgates, as the applicant had sufficient interest in the matter to which the application related,[58] and his circumstances were exceptional.

There are other situations which might justify a so-called hypothetical or academic question being determined by the court. It has been said that if the real dispute that drove the parties to litigation is no longer in existence at the

---

[56] *Leung v Secretary for Justice* [2006] 4 HKLRD 211, para.28(8); modifying his own contrary expression in *Chit Fai Motors Co Ltd v Commissioner for Transport* [2004] 1 HKC 465 (CA), para.20(1).

[57] *Leung v Secretary for Justice* [2006] 4 HKLRD 211, para.27. This wording is retained by section 21K(2)(c) of the High Court Ordinance (cap.4), but not retained by rule 1 of O.53. It was later unsuccessfully argued that the decision in *Leung v Secretary for Justice* was plainly against the letter or spirit of section 21K – *Right to Inherent Dignity Movement Association v Government of the HKSAR* [2008] HKEC 1835, paras.25–26.

[58] The court also stated that it would more closely assess an applicant's standing in such a case – *Leung v Secretary for Justice* [2006] 4 HKLRD 211, para.27.

time of the hearing, the court has the discretion to determine the issue in question but will closely examine the relevance or utility of any such decision. It was added that this may be easier to demonstrate in the public law sphere:

> because very often in public or administrative law cases, the duties of public bodies fall to be exercised on a continuing basis not only in relation to the parties before the court but also perhaps to others in the future.[59]

The discretion to hear a dispute which is academic between the parties must be exercised with caution and it should not be heard unless there is good reason in the public interest for doing so,[60] but a factor weighing in favour of its being heard is where the same point is likely to or may well arise between the same parties.[61] The example has been given from an English case where the Chancery Division issued a declaration on the legality of retention provisions in the English Football League, even though the player in question (the plaintiff) had by that stage obtained his transfer to another football club.[62] In that case, Wilberforce J stated that:

> In my judgment, the cases, and particularly the leading case of *Guaranty Trust Co. of New York v. Hannay*, establish that even though there is no cause of action apart from the rule under which declaratory judgments may be given ... and even though no consequential relief can be given, the court has ample power to grant a declaratory judgment. Whether such a declaration should be granted is a matter of judicial discretion.[63]

It may be in the public interest to hold a body legally accountable for violations of law even if the applicant in the judicial review application is no longer affected or the issue is settled in relation to him – both the public interest in itself,[64] and in relation to other persons who may already be, or may in the future be, in a similar position as the applicant vis-à-vis the body's violation of law. Lord Denning MR stated in the Court of Appeal of England and Wales that:

> I regard it as a matter of high constitutional principle that if there is good ground for supposing that a government department or a public authority is

---

[59] *Chit Fai Motors Co Ltd v Commissioner for Transport* [2004] 1 HKC 465, para.20(3), per Ma CJHC.
[60] *R v Secretary of State for the Home Department, ex parte Salem* [1999] 1 AC 450, p.457, cited with approval in *Chit Fai Motors Co Ltd v Commissioner for Transport* [2004] 1 HKC 465, para.20(3).
[61] *Chit Fai Motors Co Ltd v Commissioner for Transport* [2004] 1 HKC 465, para.20(3); and see *Wong Yui Hin v Hong Kong Arts Development Council* [2004] HKEC 1102.
[62] *Eastham v Newcastle United Football Club Ltd* [1964] Ch 413.   [63] *Id.*, p.440.
[64] Including public confidence that a body is performing its duties and functions in a lawful and fair manner, and emphasising the importance of proper adherence to its legal obligations – *Wong Yui Hin v Hong Kong Arts Development Council* [2004] HKEC 1102, paras.90–91. Indeed, were the fact that the live issue had passed an automatic bar to the hearing of the dispute, this may create an incentive for a public body to be strategic in the timing of its conduct so that a potentially unlawful act effectively becomes unchallengeable.

transgressing the law, or is about to transgress it, in a way which offends or injures thousands of Her Majesty's subjects, then any one of those offended or injured can draw it to the attention of the courts of law and seek to have the law enforced, and the courts in their discretion can grant whatever remedy is appropriate.[65]

This is a question both of standing and the scope and purpose of judicial review. The courts in Hong Kong have broadly followed this position: for example, where a person applied to challenge a supervision order and related decision, even though the supervision order had by the time of the hearing expired, the court continued to deal with the contested issue. In fact, the issue had not become entirely academic,[66] but in any event if the question was not resolved in the instant case, it would be likely to return and potentially waste resources in the course of doing so:

> In this case there can be no question but that there are many others who are affected by the same point, nor any question in my mind but that this point will soon be brought to the attention of this court for determination by at least one or more other prisoners if I do not decide this case ... [T]he point having now been raised, it will be raised again and it will be raised very soon. What will then happen, were I not now to grant leave, is that legal aid will be granted afresh, counsel instructed afresh and there will be another application for leave to apply for judicial review, perhaps opposed; and that all the public funds now expended will have been wasted unless this court decides to grasp the nettle ... The view I take at this stage is that the court should grant leave despite the fact that the point as between the applicant and the respondents appears academic. This does not preclude the respondents from argument at the substantive stage, and on further evidence if so advised, that relief should not in the exercise of the court's discretion be given.[67]

This essentially boils down to balancing (i) the public interest in not consuming the resources of the court and the public body respondent in transacting a case which deals with a hypothetical or academic issue, against (ii) the public interest in having a question of law resolved sooner rather than later, which may be likely to arise again. Clearly the matter should be one that has a reasonable prospect of arising again in the not too distant future, otherwise every hypothetical or academic issue could in principle be litigated under this pretext.[68] Again, where the constitutionality of legislation is in issue, the

---

[65] *R v Greater London Council, ex parte Blackburn* [1976] 1 WLR 550, p.559. This was described in Hong Kong as the courts shying away from a "technical stance" and tending to "latitude" in such cases – *Lui Tat Hang v Post-Release Supervision Board*, HCAL 154/1999, p.7, per Stock J.
[66] See *id.*, p.8.   [67] *Id.*, pp.8–9, per Stock J.
[68] Consider, in this context, *Right to Inherent Dignity Movement Association v Government of the HKSAR* [2008] HKEC 1835, in which the applicant attempted to raise "tens of "fundamental" "constitutional"/"human rights" issues and grounds, which are all hypothetical or academic in

argument will tend to become particularly strong for resolving the question of law sooner rather than later.[69] It is also worth noting that even though a contested question of public law may appear to have become academic by the time of the hearing in the application for judicial review, there may be other consequences which show that the hearing of the application still serves a useful purpose, for example where obtaining a declaration would assist the applicant in establishing a claim for damages based on breach of contract,[70] which can be permissibly included in an application for judicial review.[71] Finally, the court may also consider the determination of hypothetical or academic issues in a public law context where there are conflicting decisions.[72]

Temporal Limitation of a Declaration

A declaration may be issued so as to become effective only after the expiry of a specified period of time. This can be achieved by suspending the declaration or by declaring temporary validity.[73] The case of *Leung Kwok Hung* v *Chief Executive of HKSAR* provides a useful illustration of circumstances in which it would be undesirable for a declaration to take effect immediately.[74] The case concerned a challenge to the Law Enforcement (Covert Surveillance Procedure) Order and section 33 of the Telecommunications Ordinance (cap.106), which provided a legal basis for law enforcement agencies to conduct covert

---

nature" and which were said to be "very poorly expressed" and "half-baked", and which therefore failed to surpass the arguability threshold and in relation to which the court refused to exercise its discretion to entertain the hypothetical / academic challenges.

[69] See *Re Lee Yee Shing Jacky* [2009] HKEC 605, para.25, in the context of the constitutionality of section 69 of the Inland Revenue Ordinance (cap.112). See also *Pang Yiu Hung Robert* v *Commissioner of Police* [2003] 2 HKLRD 125.

[70] *Wong Yui Hin* v *Hong Kong Arts Development Council* [2004] HKEC 1102.

[71] O.53, Rule 7.

[72] *Chit Fai Motors Co Ltd* v *Commissioner for Transport* [2004] 1 HKC 465 para.20(4).

[73] The following distinction has been made between an order of temporary validity and suspension of a declaration: "[w]here temporary validity is accorded, the result would appear to be twofold. First, the executive is permitted, during such temporary validity period, to function pursuant to what has been declared unconstitutional. Secondly, the executive is shielded from legal liability for so functioning. Looking at the decided cases involving scenarios such as a virtual legal vacuum or a virtually blank statute book, it may be that the courts there thought that, absent such a shield, there would be, even after corrective legislation, chaos between persons and the state and also between persons and persons. The scenario in the present case is nothing like a virtual legal vacuum or a virtually blank statute book. It is by no means as serious as that. I see nothing to justify temporary validity in the present case. This leaves the question of suspension, which would not involve the shield to which I have been referring. The judicial power to suspend the operation of a declaration is a concomitant of the power to make the declaration in the first place. It is within the inherent jurisdiction. There is no need to resort to the doctrine of necessity for the power. Necessity comes into the picture only in its ordinary sense: not to create the power but only for its relevance to the question of whether the power should be exercised in any given case" – *Koo Sze Yiu* v *Chief Executive of the HKSAR* (2006) 9 HKCFAR 441, paras.33–35, per Bokhary PJ.

[74] *Leung Kwok Hung* v *Chief Executive of HKSAR* [2006] HKEC 239.

surveillance operations, such as the secret interception of telecommunications messages. The provisions were challenged as unconstitutional. The Court of First Instance was minded to grant a declaration to that effect,[75] but the consequence of this would have been that Hong Kong was left without an operative body of law regulating covert surveillance by law enforcement agencies. It would also have made it unlawful for those agencies to conduct many forms of covert surveillance. This would have significant implications for public safety and security. As a solution, if the court was required to declare provisions to be unconstitutional and therefore invalid, it may "assume the power to postpone the operation of the declaration of invalidity to allow the Administration and the Legislative Council time to enact corrective legislation".[76] In other words, the "unconstitutional" provisions would continue to be legally effective until the passage of a specified period of time, namely that sufficient to enable the relevant organs to produce replacement provisions – six months in the instant case. This was said to be the first time since the Handover that the courts in Hong Kong had issued an order of temporary validity.[77]

This is more controversial than may at first appear, particularly at the level of principle. Legislation which is unconstitutional is unlawful and therefore of no legal effect. It is invalid *ab initio*. Yet the court, itself an organ of state bound by the constitution (notably the Basic Law) unilaterally declares that unconstitutional legislation – provisions that are legally invalid and therefore not legislation at all – shall continue to be treated as legally valid until the expiry of the specified period of time. That may appear tantamount to the court unilaterally overriding the constitution.[78] However, the Court of First Instance drew on a consideration of similar controversies in Canada.[79] The proposed justification was that the rule of law is also part of the constitution, and the constitutional guarantee of the rule of law "will not tolerate ... chaos and anarchy ... [or] the Province of Manitoba being without a valid and effectual legal system for the present and future".[80] The rule of law would also be threatened in Hong Kong, the court reasoned, by causing such deprivation of safety and security to the residents of Hong Kong as leaving it without a legal framework for conducting covert surveillance, even on a temporary basis. The rule of law lay at the heart of the Basic Law and had "constitutional status" in Hong Kong.[81] As Hartmann J stated:

---

[75] *Id.*, para.152.   [76] *Id.*, para.161, per Hartmann J.
[77] *Id.*, para.160, per Hartmann J. See also *Koo Sze Yiu v Chief Executive of the HKSAR* (2006) 9 HKCFAR 441.
[78] See *Ng Ka Ling v Director of Immigration* (1999) 2 HKCFAR 4, p.25.
[79] The court also noted that the European Court of Human Rights had recognised the remedy of suspending a declaration of invalidity in *Walden v Liechtenstein*, App No.33916/96 (16 March 2000, unreported).
[80] *Manitoba Language Rights* [1985] 1 SCR 721 (Canada), paras.83–84.
[81] *Leung Kwok Hung v Chief Executive of HKSAR* [2006] HKEC 239, para.167, per Hartmann J.

In the result, it seems to me that the remedy of temporary validity, whether it is incorporated into the direct language of a constitution or is employed by a court as a constitutional remedy, is today a recognised means by which, in admittedly exceptional circumstances only, the provisions of a constitution may be protected by the striking down of invalid subsidiary laws without that process itself pulling down the pillars of the constitution upon itself.[82]

In doing so, he referenced Lord Nicholls of Birkenhead's comment in another context that "[r]igidity in the operation of a legal system is a sign of weakness, not strength. It deprives a legal system of necessary elasticity".[83] The court therefore suspended the taking effect of the declarations of invalidity for a period of six months to enable corrective legislation to be put in place. It is important to emphasise that the temporal limitation of a declaration using either an order of temporary validity or suspension would only be apposite in exceptional circumstances.[84]

Injunction

An applicant may seek an injunction by way of judicial review.[85] Injunction can be prohibitory (restraining a future or continuing act) or mandatory. Its grant is discretionary, having regard to the nature of the matters in respect of which relief may be granted by orders of certiorari, prohibition or mandamus, the nature of the persons and bodies against whom relief may be granted by such orders and all the circumstances of the case. In view of those factors, injunction may be granted by way of judicial review if the court considers that it would be "just and convenient for the ... injunction to be granted".[86]

An applicant can seek an interim injunction of either a prohibitory or mandatory nature.[87] In deciding whether to award an interim injunction, the courts approach the matter as one on the balance of convenience rather than strict legal entitlement. This is because the interim order is not a substitute for a perpetual order. The application for a perpetual order is made on the basis of law and legal entitlement, whereas the interim order is sought on an urgent basis or because there is good reason why the applicant cannot reasonably be expected to wait until a perpetual order is made. It is therefore more concerned with whether interim intervention is required to prevent irreparable harm being caused to a party pending decision on a perpetual order. The award of an interim injunction does not guarantee the award of a perpetual injunction at a later stage.

---

[82] *Id.*, para.174, per Hartmann J.
[83] *Re Spectrum Plus Ltd (In Liquidation)* [2005] 2 AC 680, p.699.
[84] See also *Koo Sze Yiu v Chief Executive of the HKSAR* (2006) 9 HKCFAR 441, paras.28–31.
[85] O.53, r.1(2)(b).   [86] High Court Ordinance (cap.4), s.21K(2).
[87] A stay of proceedings can be granted under O.53, r.3(10).

It was explained that whilst the court should be satisfied that the claim is not frivolous or vexatious, and that there is a serious question to be tried, the award of interim relief does not require a probable or prima facie case to be made out. Attempts to resolve conflicts of evidence on affidavit as to the facts, or difficult questions of law, were matters to be dealt with at the trial. The court should instead consider whether the balance of convenience lies in favour of granting or refusing interim relief. The governing principle was to consider whether, if the plaintiff was to succeed at trial in establishing his right to a permanent injunction, he would be adequately compensated by damages for the loss he would have sustained as a result of the defendant having continued to do that which the plaintiff sought to have enjoined. If both parties would stand to be disadvantaged by the decision either to award or not award interim relief, the extent to which one party would be disadvantaged relative to that of the other would be a significant factor in determining where the balance of convenience lies. Various factors would weigh on the balance of convenience, but where they appear to be evenly balanced, it would be prudent to take measures towards the preservation of the status quo.[88]

If irreparable harm or irretrievable prejudice would be caused to the applicant by not awarding interim relief, this would strongly favour the applicant. For example, if a person is liable to be deported to a country where he may face torture, prior to the determination of the legality of his deportation, he will likely suffer irreparable harm or irretrievable prejudice if he is already deported and the court later establishes that his deportation was unlawful. If a building is liable to be demolished, prior to the determination of the legality of the demolition, its owner or operator may suffer irreparable harm or irretrievable prejudice if the building is demolished and the court later establishes that the demolition was unlawful. Damages may not be an adequate remedy in either case. Furthermore, it is not only the adequacy of damages that is important, but broader issues of the public interest.[89]

It is provided that an application for judicial review must be made if the applicant seeks an injunction under section 21J of the High Court Ordinance restraining a person from acting in any office in which he is not entitled to act.[90] The court may thereunder grant an injunction restraining that person from so acting, and if the case requires, declare the office to be vacant.[91]

---

[88] *American Cyanamid* v *Ethicon Ltd* [1975] AC 396.
[89] *Super Lion Enterprises Ltd* v *Commissioner of Rating & Valuation* [2006] 1 HKLRD 239.
[90] High Court Ordinance (cap.4), s.21K(1)(b); O.53, r.1(1)(b).
[91] High Court Ordinance (cap.4), s.21J(1).

Damages, Restitution and Recovery of a Sum Due

It is competent for an award of damages, restitution or recovery of a sum due to be sought in an application for judicial review, subject to a number of conditions. First, the remedy must not be sought alone in the application for review,[92] but must instead be sought alongside any other remedy that is competently sought by way of review. Second, the claim for damages should be included in the statement in support of the application for leave.[93] Third, the claim for damages should arise from a matter to which the application for review relates.[94] Fourth, the court must be satisfied that, if the claim had been made in an action begun by the applicant at the time of making the application, it could have been awarded damages.[95] The award of damages in an application for judicial review is discretionary.[96]

An important limitation on seeking damages in an application for judicial review is that they can only be sought in relation to private law liability. They generally cannot be sought for public law liability (unless statute provides otherwise), but may be brought alongside a claim for breach of a public law duty to save time and resources where the matters are related, by not insisting that a separate action for damages be commenced. Thus an application which sought certiorari to quash a decision resulting from procedural impropriety could not competently seek damages for expenses incurred by the applicant participating in a flawed procedure, as liability for procedural impropriety sounds in public law.[97] A prominent policy reason for disallowing damages to be sought for public law liability is concern for the impact this would have on public resources, such as the possibility of a "compensation culture" developing for public law liability, encouraging persons to bring judicial review applications with financial motives in mind.

If the body whose procedure was tainted with impropriety was also negligent in its improper conduct, the applicant may be able to claim damages in tort on the same application for judicial review.[98] It is important to note that the competency of seeking damages is determined not by the identity of the party defending an action or application (for example, whether it is a public body or a private body), but by the nature of its liability in law. Damages can only be claimed in relation to private law liability, regardless of the public or otherwise nature of the party against which damages are being claimed.[99] Where the application for public law remedies

---

[92] O.53, r.1(3).   [93] *Id.*, r.7(1)(a).
[94] High Court Ordinance (cap.4), s.21K(4)(a); O.53, r.7(1)(a).
[95] High Court Ordinance (cap.4), s.21K(4)(b); O.53, r.7(1)(b).
[96] It is provided in the High Court Ordinance (cap.4), s.21K(4) and O.53, r.7(1) that the judge "may" award damages.
[97] *Financial Secretary v Wong* (2003) 6 HKCFAR 476.
[98] See, however, *Yuen Kun-yeu v Attorney-General* [1987] HKLR 1154 (PC), pp.1176–1177.
[99] Again, statute may provide for exceptions to this rule.

is refused, but the claim for damages remains alive, the court can order proceedings to continue as though begun by writ.

Discretionary Nature of Remedies

It is said that the remedies in judicial review are discretionary. The award of relief is not automatic; even if an applicant successfully establishes violation of one or more grounds of review, he will not necessarily be granted a remedy should the court, in its discretion, regard there as being good reason for refusing it. This does not mean that the award of remedies is arbitrary; it also does not mean that, in the majority of cases, an applicant who successfully establishes violation of one or more grounds of review is not awarded at least one of the remedies he seeks. However, the court retains underlying discretion to withhold relief, and this section explores some of the bases on which the court may do so. As that discretion is general in scope, this is not an exhaustive list.

Availability of Alternative Remedies and Appeals Mechanisms

Judicial review is often described as a process of last resort. This alludes to the fact that the courts generally expect an applicant to have exhausted other remedies and appeals mechanisms prior to attempting judicial review. If an applicant has a statutory right of appeal, perhaps to a senior decision maker or administrative tribunal, he may be expected to use it instead of (or before attempting) judicial review, the reasoning being that the intention of the legislature is that the applicant uses that right of appeal in vindication of his rights.[100] The court must be careful not to adjudicate on matters which would more properly be decided in a statutory appeals procedure.[101] However, the expectation also extends to other remedies, such that an applicant with a remedy available in private law may be expected to have used it to assert his rights, rather than seeking the same by way of judicial review.[102]

This is a general, not universal, expectation. The courts do not insist on it in every case,[103] and there can be valid reasons why an applicant has not exhausted, and cannot reasonably be expected to exhaust, all available

---

[100] See, in the criminal context, p.108.
[101] *Yue Yuen Marketing Co Ltd* v *Commissioner of Inland Revenue* [2012] 4 HKLRD 761, paras.18–19.
[102] As, for example, in *Tsang Kin Chiu* v *Commissioner of Police* [2015] 4 HKLRD 71; and see *Ho Pak Wa* v *Council of the Law Society of Hong Kong* [2016] HKEC 1825, paras.95–97. If there is a contractual or tortious relationship and the allegedly *ultra vires* action is interrelated, the requirement to use judicial review or ordinary procedure will primarily be determined by the rules on procedural exclusivity and the remedies sought.
[103] The court exercised its discretion to quash a decision, despite the applicant having failed to exhaust all available avenues of relief, in *Chan Chi Shing* v *Symon Wong* [2011] HKEC 591, para.79.

remedies. These circumstances have nevertheless been regarded as exceptional,[104] and Lord Scarman has described it as a "proposition of great importance" that a "remedy by way of judicial review is not to be made available where an alternative remedy exists".[105] Where an applicant has failed to exhaust alternative remedies, he or she may be expected to explain the reasons therefore if the court is to be persuaded to exercise its discretion to grant relief notwithstanding that failure.[106]

In particular, the alternative remedy should be suitable and adequate before the applicant would be expected to have used it.[107] This has a number of aspects. First, the alternative remedy should be capable of giving comparable or analogous redress to judicial review. An applicant would not be expected to use the Ombudsman prior to seeking judicial review, for example, because the Ombudsman is incapable of awarding any of the remedies available in judicial process. However, an administrative tribunal might be capable of awarding a comparable remedy to one available in judicial review, so this might be viewed as a suitable alternative remedy. If, however, the case requires the determination of a question of law and the relevant administrative tribunal does not have the power or the means to determine a question of law (such as by way of case stated), then the tribunal is unlikely to be regarded as offering a suitable alternative to judicial review, rendering its attempted utilisation unnecessary. If an applicant seeks damages in judicial review – noting that damages can competently be obtained on an application for judicial review – he or she may be regarded as having failed to exhaust an effective alternative remedy where he or she had not sought the damages in a private law action.[108]

Another aspect of suitability and adequacy is that the process for obtaining the alternative remedy should not be tainted by the same or comparable legal defect as the process under challenge.[109] Suppose that an applicant for a licence to operate a seafood restaurant has his application rejected. He discovers that the chairman of the licensing authority is a militant vegan, a factor likely to vitiate the authority's purported refusal on grounds of bias or insufficient impartiality. The applicant has a statutory right of appeal to an administrative tribunal, but the chairman of the tribunal is a strict vegetarian. The appeals mechanism is tainted by a comparable legal defect to the process under challenge – namely bias or insufficient impartiality – thus a court will be less

---

[104] *R v Chief Constable of the Merseyside Police, ex parte Calveley* [1986] QB 424; *Onshine Securities Ltd v Stock Exchange of Hong Kong Ltd* [1994] 1 HKC 319 (CA); *Stock Exchange of Hong Kong Ltd v New World Development Co Ltd* (2006) 9 HKCFAR 234. See also *O'Neill v Scottish Joint Negotiating Committee for Teaching Staff*, 1987 SLT 648.
[105] *R v Inland Revenue Commissioners, ex parte Preston* [1985] AC 835 (HL), p.852.
[106] *James Yan v v Director of Immigration* [2010] HKEC 1331.
[107] *Yeung Chun Pong v Secretary for Justice (No 4)* [2008] 2 HKC 46, pp.74–75.
[108] *Tsang Kin Chiu v Commissioner of Police* [2015] 4 HKLRD 71, paras.14–22.
[109] This is related to the curative principle in procedural fairness – see p.253.

likely to regard the appeals mechanism as offering a suitable form of redress. In this situation, the applicant would be less likely to be barred from seeking judicial review as a result of the appeals mechanism not being attempted.[110]

There are other factors which might persuade the court that the alternative remedy was not suitable for attempted use. It may be that the alternative remedy would have taken too long to obtain – perhaps the applicant had a statutory right of appeal to a decision maker who was given sixty days to reply. If the application is sufficiently urgent, the court may determine that the time required to use the appeals mechanism would jeopardise the rights or interests of the applicant to such an extent that he is not required to attempt it before seeking judicial review. Likewise, it may be that the alternative remedy is too costly, though the court is likely to approach this justification cautiously. For example, there may be a statutory right to refer the dispute to arbitration following a particular decision, but the costs of arbitration may be too high for the applicant to bear, or disproportionately high compared to the importance of the issue in question. In circumstances of this nature, the court retains discretion to dispense with the general requirement that an applicant is required to resort to an alternative remedy before attempting judicial review, and to permit the applicant to seek judicial review instead of attempting the alternative remedy. Courts must nevertheless be disciplined in the granting of such exceptions whereby they are effectively permitting an application to bypass an appeals or similar mechanism provided for by statute as the proper way of challenging the impugned decision.

Application Is Premature

The court may refuse relief where an application for judicial review is considered premature. Where, for example, reasons have yet to be made available for the decision, it will be premature to apply for review to determine the legality of the decision to which the reasons will relate.[111] The Court of Final Appeal held that unfairness did not automatically follow from a failure to allow legal representatives to address the Disciplinary Committee of the Stock Exchange of Hong Kong's Listing Committee, and that such unfairness could not yet be established. If there was an occurrence during the Committee

---

[110] However, depending on the circumstances, the court might still want the applicant to attempt to use the appeals mechanism. Indeed, the fact that the chairman of an administrative tribunal is a strict vegetarian may objectively give the appearance that he may take a less sympathetic view of the applicant's appeal, but it does not automatically mean that the chairman will reject the appeal. It is quite possible that the chairman takes a sufficiently impartial view of the appeal and may even decide the appeal in the applicant's favour, in which case the matter need never come to court for judicial review. Consider *Secretary of Justice* v *Li Chau Wing* [2004] HKEC 1417, in which a judge's previously expressed (negative) opinion on a particular offence did not necessarily translate into the judge being less inclined to opt for that offence over another.

[111] *Ma Zhujiang* v *Secretary for Justice* [2005] HKEC 1716.

hearing, which had yet to take place, and which did give rise to unfairness, then grounds would lie for judicial review. The instant application for review was "plainly premature".[112] It may also be held premature where a decision-making process has yet to come to a conclusion, such that the prejudicial effect of a decision is yet to be determined. As the final decision might not produce a prejudicial effect, it is too early to say whether there would later arise sufficient grounds for judicial review.[113]

There is nevertheless a risk to not bringing proceedings at the earliest feasible opportunity: if the applicant waits until the decision-making process concludes before applying for judicial review, he or she may be held to have acquiesced in the defect later complained of and thus to have waived his or her right to object.[114] This may be encountered in failing to object to the participation of a biased adjudicator in a decision-making process,[115] even though the participation of a biased adjudicator will not automatically produce an outcome prejudicial or unfavourable to the applicant. Prematurity may result in leave being refused on the basis that it is not reasonably arguable that the court will grant relief under the application for judicial review.[116]

Delay

The issue of delay has primarily been dealt with in Chapter 5. When there is an issue of delay, it usually arises at the leave stage and can prove fatal to an application for leave. However, it can also or alternatively arise as an issue at the substantive hearing, and the court retains discretion to refuse to grant relief sought on the application on the basis of delay.[117] This is clearly provided for in the High Court Ordinance:

> Where the Court of First Instance considers that there has been undue delay in making an application for judicial review, the Court may refuse to grant –
>
> (a) leave for the making of the application; or
> (b) any relief sought on the application,

---

[112] *Stock Exchange of Hong Kong Ltd* v *New World Development Co Ltd* [2006] 9 HKCFAR 234, para.1, per Bokhary PJ.
[113] Nevertheless, for declaration to be granted by way of judicial review, it is not always necessary that a final decision has been reached where a sufficient dispute exists between the parties – *Secretary for Justice* v *Chan Wah* [2000] 3 HKCFAR 459, p.478.
[114] See pp.270–271 and 297.   [115] See pp.270–271.
[116] *Leung Lai Kwok Yvonne* v *Chief Secretary for Administration* [2015] HKEC 1034, paras.38–53. On prematurity, see also *Re Koon Wing Yee* [2008] HKEC 2037; *Chan Chin Yuen* v *Securities and Futures Commission* [2008] HKEC 2196; *HLB Hodgson Impey Cheng* v *Hong Kong Institute of Certified Public Accountants* [2010] 6 HKC 232; and *Chan Chiu Kwok Charles* v *Hong Kong Institute of Surveyors* [2011] HKEC 1279.
[117] As, for example, in *James Yan* v *Director of Immigration* [2010] HKEC 1331, paras.71–72.

if it considers that the granting of relief sought would be likely to cause substantial hardship to, or substantially prejudice the rights of, any person or would be detrimental to good administration.[118]

The issue of delay is most likely to arise at the substantive hearing in one of the following scenarios: (i) the issue of delay arose at the leave stage, but the judge indicated that he or she wished to be addressed about delay at the substantive hearing, perhaps because the application was particularly serious or urgent and the judge did not want to hold up the application at the leave stage merely on the point of delay;[119] (ii) the issue of delay is bound up with the substance of the application making it appropriate for determination at the substantive hearing; (iii) the issue of delay was not raised or identified at the leave stage; or (iv) the applicant delayed after leave was obtained.

Waiver and Acquiescence

If an applicant fails to promptly challenge an impugned decision or conduct, he or she may be held to have acquiesced to the defect complained of, and waived his or her right to object thereto. Waiver has been described as a "voluntary, informed and unequivocal election by a party not to claim a right or raise an objection which it is open to that party to claim or raise", applying in "most litigious situations" including the entitlement to a fair hearing by an independent and impartial tribunal.[120]

It is open to a party to waive any objection as to bias or insufficient impartiality,[121] even though disqualification is said to be automatic.[122] A customs officer subject to disciplinary proceedings could, by failing to make an appropriate application and by attending an investigation interview in person without being accompanied by a lawyer, thereby be taken to have waived his right to be accompanied by a lawyer.[123] However, failure to ask for an oral hearing when one was not told by the authority that one could ask for an oral hearing would not necessarily amount to waiving the right to an oral hearing.[124]

---

[118] High Court Ordinance (cap.4), s.21K(6).
[119] *X v Torture Claims Appeal Board* [2014] HKEC 9.
[120] *Millar v Dickson* [2002] SC (PC) 30 (PC) (Scotland), p.43, per Lord Bingham of Cornhill.
[121] See pp.270–271.
[122] *Locabail (UK) Ltd v Bayfield Properties Ltd* [2000] QB 451, para.15, cited with approval in *Financial Secretary v Wong* [2003] 6 HKCFAR 476, para.50. There was no waiver in *R v Bow Street Metropolitan Stipendiary Magistrates, ex parte Pinochet Ugarte (No 2)* [2000] 1 AC 119 (HL) because Senator Pinochet did not have knowledge of Lord Hoffman's connections with Amnesty International during the case in which Lord Hoffmann was sitting.
[123] *Chan Kar Yiu v Civil Service Bureau* [2004–2005] HKCLRT 24, paras.60–65.
[124] *Liu Pik Han v Hong Kong Federation of Insurers Appeals Tribunal* [2005] HKEC 1046, particularly para.37. On waiver, see *Leung Fuk Wah v Commissioner of Police* [2001] HKEC 951; *Lam Chi Pan v Commissioner of Police* [2009] HKEC 2049; and consider *V v Director of Immigration* [2005] HKEC 1938.

Applicant Undeserving of Remedy

It may be that the applicant has successfully demonstrated that one or more grounds of review have been violated, but the court withholds a remedy because it considers the applicant to be undeserving of relief. The English case of *R v Chief National Insurance Commissioner, ex parte Connor* is a fine, if dramatic, example of this.[125] A woman killed her husband and was initially charged with murder, then convicted of manslaughter. She was placed on probation for a period of two years. The woman qualified for a widow's allowance under social security legislation, though her claim was held to be inadmissible. She appealed to the local tribunal and then to the Chief National Insurance Commissioner, who held her claim inadmissible as a matter of public policy, as the entitlement to the allowance directly resulted from her act of manslaughter. She then sought judicial review of the Commissioner's decision. The Queen's Bench Division held that although the social security legislation did not debar a widow from claiming the allowance where she was responsible for her status of widowhood, as a matter of public policy she was lawfully capable of being determined ineligible for the allowance as she deliberately, consciously and intentionally killed her husband. The fact that the legislation did not specifically debar the widow from claiming the allowance did not mean that broader public policy considerations did not apply. In short, the woman was refused a remedy as she was essentially thought undeserving of relief.

The facts in most cases will fortunately be less extreme than those in *Connor*. In *Cinnamond v British Airports Authority*,[126] a number of taxi drivers had repeatedly breached regulations at London Heathrow Airport by touting passengers around arrival areas and charging them high fares, taking custom away from licensed taxi drivers charging regular fares. The applicant taxi drivers had unpaid fines in relation to convictions under the airport regulations, and the airport operator wrote to the drivers informing them that they were prohibited from entering the airport except as *bona fide* passengers. The taxi drivers argued that the notice and the bylaw under which it was invoked were unlawful. They also complained that they had not been given a fair hearing prior to the prohibition being imposed by the airport operator. It was held that, even if the taxi drivers ordinarily had a legitimate expectation that they would be afforded a fair hearing prior to such a measure being imposed, they could not be said to be put in a position of unfairness as a result of there being no hearing. This was primarily due to their own conduct, namely a history of convictions, unpaid fines and continuing breach of the airport regulations. The taxi drivers' own conduct therefore militated against

---

[125] *R v Chief National Insurance Commissioner, ex parte Connor* [1981] QB 758.
[126] *Cinnamond v British Airports Authority* [1980] 1 WLR 582.

their claim that they suffered unfairness as a result of their procedural legitimate expectation being frustrated.

Futility or No Prejudice

The court may withhold a remedy if it considers its award to be futile or where no prejudice is shown to be suffered by the applicant as a result of putatively unlawful conduct by the public body. For example, suppose there has been procedural impropriety, which ordinarily would affect the legality of the resulting decision. If the resulting decision would be substantively unaffected by the procedural impropriety being put right, should the court award relief? From what is the court awarding relief? Should it take the pragmatic approach and recognise that relief is futile in such a case, as it serves no material purpose? There can, depending on the circumstances of the case, be overlap between futility and inevitability as bases for refusing discretionary relief in judicial review. They also shares similar issues of controversy.

It may be futile to award mandamus ordering reinstatement to the police force where such time has passed that the applicant's training has been interrupted for several years, and the employer–employee relationship may be so damaged that reinstatement would not be an appropriate remedy. This did not necessarily mean that no relief could be awarded, but that mandamus (the order sought by the applicant) was not the appropriate relief.[127] Where it was "abundantly clear" that the disclosure of new documents to a police sergeant would "not have made the slightest difference to his petition" to the Commissioner of Police, this would undermine the claim that unfairness was suffered as a result of those documents not being disclosed to him, leading the court to exercise its discretion against awarding relief.[128] A breach of natural justice by the Council of the Law Society of Hong Kong did not result in any actual prejudice or risk of prejudice to a disciplined solicitor, leading the court to exercise its discretion to refuse relief.[129] Where a university vice chancellor failed to comply with the requirements of natural justice in failing to give a student a fair hearing prior to a decision being made to impose a penalty, the court refused relief as it essentially agreed with the penalty imposed and regarded the procedural omission by the vice chancellor as being insufficient to justify setting aside the decision.[130] Nevertheless, cases in which the court refuses relief even where a breach of the rules of natural justice has been established would be "rare".[131] Relief may be withheld even where the application for judicial review is otherwise successful where it would suffice for the

---

[127] *Chief Constable of the North Wales Police* v *Evans* [1982] 1 WLR 1155 (HL).
[128] *Leung Fuk Wah* v *Commissioner of Police* [2002] 3 HKLRD 653 (CA).
[129] *Lam Ping Cheung* v *Law Society of Hong Kong* [2006] HKEC 2366.
[130] *Glynn* v *Keele University* [1971] 1 WLR 487.
[131] *Chu Ping Tak* v *Commissioner of Police* [2002] 3 HKLRD 679, para.64, per Deputy Judge Cheung.

court to offer guidance or clarification on a point of law, though stopping short of issuing a declaration.[132]

Inevitability

If the court considers that the same decision as has been made, or the same outcome as has occurred, would inevitably follow even if it granted the relief sought, it may exercise its discretion to refuse relief.[133] Where, for example, putative refugees sought review of a decision not to screen them for refugee status, but their application for refugee status would be bound to fail on the merits even if undertaken, relief could be refused as serving no useful purpose. In other words, the substantive outcome was seen to be inevitable.[134] Bokhary PJ advocated this approach in *Ng Siu Tung* v *Director of Immigration*:

> Suppose an administrative decision-maker decides against the holder of a substantive expectation without taking the expectation into account. And suppose the court feels sure that once the expectation is duly taken into account an end result favourable to the holder of the expectation will be reached by the administrative decision-maker or, failing that, by an administrative appeal tribunal of by the courts. If so, the court will of course quash the administrative decision. The court having done that, I do not think that it would be bound to follow the circuitous course of leaving it to the administrative decision-maker to make a fresh decision, knowing that it will undoubtedly intervene again if he or an administrative appeal tribunal were to decide in any way other than favourably to the holder of the expectation. That would cause pointless delay. It would also be to insist that the administrative decision-maker assume the undignified role of a rubber stamp. In my view, the courts would be entitled, in the extreme circumstances postulated, to proceed directly to substantive enforcement: for example by an appropriate declaration.[135]

On the one hand, this is a pragmatic approach with practical advantages. Why, it might be asked, should the time and resources of the decision maker be further consumed by requiring it to go through the decision-making process again only for the same decision or outcome to follow, or where the court "feels sure" that, once the legal defect is rectified by the decision maker, a particular outcome will inevitably result? Why should the applicant have to wait for a new decision to be issued, where that decision will be the

---

[132] See *Secretary for Justice* v *Commission of Inquiry Re Hong Kong Institute of Education* [2009] 4 HKLRD 11, in which the judgment was left to "speak for itself" (para.77).
[133] See *R* v *Tandridge District Council, ex parte al-Fayed* [2000] 80 P & CR 90.
[134] *Nguyen Tuan Cuong* v *Director of Immigration* [1996] HKLY 24 (CA) (Bokhary PJ dissenting on this point). The applicants were successful on appeal to the Privy Council – *Nguyen Tuan Cuong* v *Director of Immigration* [1997] HKLRD 73 (PC).
[135] *Ng Siu Tung* v *Director of Immigration* [2002] 5 HKCFAR 1, para.353.

same as the impugned decision, or where the outcome appears to be one that will inevitably result? Courts are often sympathetic to the consumption of public resources that may result from judicial review, and have a general policy of interfering no more than is necessary to put the contested issue right in law.

However, there are objections to this approach. First, as a practical matter, it requires the court to make an accurate forecast that the same decision will again be made.[136] Second, at the level of principle, it can allow an *ultra vires* decision to stand. This is a doctrinal abomination. An *ultra vires* decision is not a valid decision in law. To refuse relief on the basis that the same decision or outcome will follow should it be ordered to be retaken is to effectively ascribe legality to the *ultra vires* decision. The doctrinally proper approach would be for the court to order that the decision be retaken, this time in accordance with the law. Even if the same substantive decision or outcome follows, it has a wholly different status in law, for it is a decision lawfully made rather than one unlawfully made. The openness of the courts to refusing relief on the basis of inevitability invokes the voidness/voidability distinction and suggests that such a decision is voidable rather than void.[137] This grates with the *ultra vires* principle. Whilst an overly technical or dogmatic approach can lead to undesirable rigidity in the law, the *ultra vires* principle is a central canon of judicial review. The possibility remains that an "inevitable" *ultra vires* decision might be treated as legally valid only if irretrievable prejudice would be caused to the applicant (or perhaps the decision maker) by requiring the decision to be retaken, though the circumstances in which this should be allowed to occur, were the exception to be admitted, must be rare.

There is another aspect to inevitability which borders on (legal) impossibility. Where, for example, a tenderer objects to the manner in which a public body has acted in the course of inviting tenders, the court may refuse relief where a different tender has already been validly accepted by the public body.[138]

Judicial Review Proceedings Continued as though Begun by Writ

The court has the discretion to order judicial review proceedings to continue as though begun by writ. There is no express power to order proceedings begun by writ to continue as though commenced by application for judicial review.[139] The relevant provision is found in Order 53, rule 9(5):

---

[136] Consider, in this regard, *Prem Singh v Director of Immigration* [2003] 6 HKCFAR 26, paras.95–107. See pp.220–221.
[137] See pp.139–140.   [138] *Re an application by Yau Fook Hong Co Ltd* [1985] HKLR 42, p.56.
[139] See *O'Reilly v Mackman* [1983] 2 AC 237, p.284; and *Davy v Spelthorne Borough Council* [1984] AC 262, p.274.

Where the relief sought is a declaration, an injunction or damages and the Court considers that it should not be granted on an application for judicial review but might have been granted if it had been sought in an action begun by writ by the applicant at the time of making his application, the Court may, instead of refusing the application, order the proceedings to continue as if they had been begun by writ; and Order 28, rule 8, shall apply.[140]

It can be seen that this provision applies only where the relief sought is a declaration, injunction or damages. The rule cannot be invoked where the relief sought is otherwise, such as an order of certiorari, prohibition or mandamus.[141] It is possible to siphon off part of the application for judicial review to be continued as though it had been initiated by writ, even where the other part of the application for review is successful and relief awarded. Thus, declarations were granted in an application for judicial review, with the claim for damages being separated and continued as though it had been initiated by writ.[142] Where an application for judicial review is commenced by seeking damages and another remedy competently sought by way of review, but where that other remedy is for some reason no longer pursued – leaving only the claim for damages – it is incompetent for proceedings to continue by way of judicial review. The claim for damages must either be subject to an application under Order 53, rule 9(5), or to an application for leave to withdraw it.[143]

The application under Order 53, rule 9(5) can be made by the applicant or the respondent. Where a public body respondent made such an application, the court refused it on the basis that the subject of the challenge was a "public law matter" and the applicant was entitled to pursue "public law relief".[144] However, even where the application touches on matters of private law, continuation of proceedings as though begun by writ remains at the discretion of the court, and may be refused where, for example, the "private law" issues have not been properly or thoroughly formulated in the application for judicial review. In these circumstances, the court might hold that the claim should be brought afresh by writ and be more appropriately formulated as such.[145] Moreover, though it has been said that a judicial review application may properly be made with the specific intention of underpinning future private law litigation, particularly where a "public law ruling [is] a necessary

---

[140] O.53, r.9(5).
[141] *To Kin Wah* v *Tuen Mun District Officer (No 2)* [2003] 4 HKC 213 (CA), paras.52–56.
[142] *Wong Yui Hin* v *Hong Kong Arts Development Council* [2004] HKEC 1102. See also *Nguyen Tuan Cuong* v *Secretary for Justice* [1999] 1 HKC 242 (CA).
[143] *Matteograssi SpA* v *Airport Authority* [1998] 3 HKC 25. It was observed that, in this case, the application was technically incompetent from the outset: *Matteograssi SpA* v *Airport Authority* [1998] 3 HKC 25, p.35.
[144] *To Kin Wah* v *Tuen Mun District Officer (No 2)* [2003] 4 HKC 213 (CA), paras.52–56.
[145] *R* v *East Berkshire Health Authority, ex parte Walsh* [1985] QB 152, p.166; *Priscilla Sit Ka Yin* v *Equal Opportunities Commission* [1998] HKEC 898; *Fung Yiu Bun* v *Commissioner of Police* [2002] 4 HKC 15, paras.44–50.

pre-condition to a private law claim", this would be distinguishable from using judicial review to establish a matter which can, and can more conveniently, be established in private law proceedings.[146] The application under Order 53, rule 9(5), has been held by the Court of Appeal to be available only after leave has been granted.[147]

Though it may be convenient shorthand to describe proceedings as being converted from judicial review to those begun by writ, the proceedings are technically not converted. They remain judicial review proceedings, but are merely treated as a writ action. There is no hypothetical writ in such a case.[148] The proceedings being continued, it is not competent to join additional parties to the proceedings after Order 53, rule 9(5), has been invoked, which would otherwise allow them to short circuit the procedure.[149]

---

[146] *Rank Profit Industries Ltd* v *Director of Lands* [2007] HKEC 390, paras.110–111. Hartmann J added (para.112), that "if only to guard the integrity of process and to ensure efficient case management, I think that courts exercising judicial review jurisdiction should not, without very good reason, determine matters which can equally, or must, be determined in private civil proceedings already under way". See also *R* v *Secretary of State for the Home Department, ex parte Vafi* (unreported, 2 August 1995).

[147] *Sean Leonard* v *Commissioner of Police* [2008] HKCU 273, paras.15–16. See, on amending Form 86A in this regard, *Ngo Kee Construction Co Ltd* v *Hong Kong Housing Authority* [2001] 1 HKC 493, p.518.

[148] *Nguyen Tuan Cuong* v *Secretary for Justice* [1999] 1 HKC 242 (CA).

[149] *Id*; *Tong Tim Nui* v *Hong Kong Housing Authority* [1999] 4 HKC 466 (CA).

21

Administrative Tribunals and Administrative Complaints

Administrative Tribunals

Administrative tribunals are an important vehicle for the attainment of administrative justice. They vary in form and function but can broadly be divided into three categories. First, a number of appeals boards are administered by the executive and hear appeals against executive decisions. These form the core part of the tribunal system from an administrative law perspective. Second, courts have the power to hear certain administrative appeals.[1] Finally, a number of administrative appeal mechanisms are in place to the Chief Executive and Chief Executive-in-Council, who essentially act in the capacity of administrative tribunals when hearing such appeals.

The classification of a body as a tribunal or otherwise is not always a straightforward exercise. Nomenclature alone is not definitive. First, some bodies designated as tribunals do not function particularly differently from courts. This is especially true of tribunals administered by the Judiciary. Three of these – the Labour Tribunal, the Lands Tribunal and the Small Claims Tribunal – principally adjudicate on horizontal disputes between private parties, such as between employers and employees, or landlords and tenants. The Competition Tribunal hears a mixture of horizontal and vertical disputes, and is essentially a specialisation of a particular aspect of court work. These tribunals are an extended part of the judicial system and are better categorised as such than as administrative tribunals.

The outlier is the Obscene Articles Tribunal which has for some years been performing an administrative function despite being administered by the Judiciary. It has been tasked, in particular, with the function of classifying

---

[1] Sometimes statutes governing appeals boards provide for appeal to the courts on a point of law. Appeal lies either to the Court of First Instance or the Court of Appeal. This is distinct from the power of appeals boards to refer points of law to the courts by way of case stated. Less commonly, statutes provide for appeal to the courts on a point of fact or law. Some statutes provide for appeal to the courts in such general terms that they do not appear strictly to be confined to points of fact or law, potentially leaving open the possibility of appeal on the merits. For further discussion, see Stephen Thomson, 'Clutter and Cobwebs: How Administrative Tribunals in Hong Kong can learn from the UK' (2017) 36(3) *Civil Justice Quarterly* 363, pp.378–381.

articles as obscene, indecent or otherwise; in addition to a judicial determination function on the obscenity or indecency of articles or matter referred by a court or magistrate in the course of proceedings. The possession of this administrative function by a tribunal administered by the Judiciary was strongly condemned by the Judiciary, the Hong Kong Bar Association and the Law Society of Hong Kong,[2] and the Government eventually agreed to remove the Tribunal's administrative functions.[3] There has been no haste in the Government's reform, however, as at the time of writing no legislative proposal had been brought forward, over three years since the Government's statement of intention.

Moreover, a large number of bodies which effectively function as administrative tribunals are not designated as such. Many carry the title of "appeals board", such as the Administrative Appeals Board, the Municipal Services Appeal Board and the Appeal Board (Town Planning). A smaller number of administrative tribunals are known as boards of review, such as the Board of Review (Film Censorship Ordinance) and Board of Review (Inland Revenue Ordinance). The title of a body may indicate its function, but certainly does not define it.

The general function of an administrative tribunal is to adjudicate on vertical disputes between an individual and a public decision maker. This can take many forms, such as appealing against a licensing decision, a tax assessment, or even a decision relating to the approval of a genetically modified organism. Administrative tribunals are structurally and functionally distinguishable from courts in the sense that they generally do not adjudicate on horizontal disputes between private parties. They instead provide a forum in which to appeal against decisions which are essentially unilateral in nature, made by public decision makers.

Appeals Boards

Whereas administrative tribunals in the United Kingdom emerged in the context of a burgeoning welfare state,[4] the appeals boards in Hong Kong have rather arisen in the context of different local priorities such as trade, industry and town planning. Most tribunals are specialised in nature, such as the Board of Review (Inland Revenue Ordinance) which determines appeals against tax

---

[2] *The Role of the Judiciary in the Adjudication System under the Control of Obscene and Indecent Articles Ordinance* (Panel on Administration of Justice and Legal Services, Legislative Council) LC Paper No. CB(2)863/11–12(03), pp.4–5.
[3] HKSAR Government, *Press Release: Review of Control of Obscene and Indecent Articles Ordinance* (13 February 2015). For further discussion of the more judicial type tribunals, see Johannes Chan, "The Judiciary" in Johannes Chan and C. L. Lim (eds), *Law of the Hong Kong Constitution* (2nd edn) (Sweet and Maxwell, Hong Kong, 2015), pp.370–373 in the more general context of Chapter 11.
[4] See Craig, *Administrative Law*, pp.47–50.

assessment decisions of the Commissioner of Inland Revenue, and the Appeal Board (Hotel and Guesthouse Accommodation) which determines appeals against decisions of the Hotel and Guesthouse Accommodation Authority in relation to certification and licensing. A notable exception is the Administrative Appeals Board, established in 1994, which is a more general tribunal hearing appeals on a wide array of topics, from the determination of a person as unsuited to acting as a childminder[5] to the approval of a genetically modified organism.[6]

The appeals boards derive their powers from statute and are subject to judicial review.[7] Individual boards have been established by individual statutes, and there is no overall, unifying framework of organisation or supervision. There is no definitive list of administrative tribunals, and the extent of any such list depends on how "tribunal" is defined. The HKSAR Government's Civil and Miscellaneous Lists are not definitive, as they include many bodies which do not function as tribunals and exclude some which do.[8] Sometimes a more liberal view is taken of tribunals, including bodies which have proceedings resembling those of tribunals. For example, the Air Transport Licensing Authority was considered by one author to be a tribunal, primarily due to its power to hold a public inquiry in the course of its deliberations.[9] However, not all tribunals have public hearings or proceedings resembling a public inquiry, so this is not an appropriate basis on which to frame the definition. Furthermore, the Air Transport Licensing Authority does not function as an administrative tribunal, the core function of such a tribunal being to determine appeals against public decision makers. The Authority is an original decision maker with the power to hold a public hearing in the course of making its decision. Including such a body in the definition of "tribunal" is unduly expansive, and would require that many other bodies be included within the definition that would be more appropriately considered part of the broader system of administrative decision making.

---

[5] Child Care Services Ordinance (cap. 243), s. 15B(2); Administrative Appeals Board Ordinance, sch.1, item 33.

[6] Genetically Modified Organisms (Control of Release) Ordinance (cap. 607), s. 10(1)(a); Administrative Appeals Board Ordinance, sch.1, item 67.

[7] Recent examples of the courts reviewing administrative tribunals include *Cathay Pacific Airways Ltd v Administrative Appeals Board* [2008] 5 HKLRD 539 (error of law); *Sabinano II Marcel R v Municipal Services Appeal Board* [2014] HKEC 370 (failure to take into account all relevant considerations and resulting *Wednesbury* unreasonableness); *B v Torture Claims Appeal Board* [2015] 1 HKLRD 681 (failure to provide reasons); and *Building Authority v Appeal Tribunal (Buildings)* [2016] HKEC 334 (failure to comply with statutory procedure).

[8] The Civil and Miscellaneous Lists tend to refer to "appeal board panels" rather than "appeal boards". However, the board is the decision-making body proper, while the panel is the pool of members all or some of whom are convened to hear appeals, or the members sitting in any given appeal.

[9] Mohan Bharwaney, 'Administrative Tribunals in Hong Kong' (1976) 6 *Hong Kong Law Journal* 189, pp.195, 200 and 215.

The essential nature of tribunal work is adjudicative or quasi-judicial, rather than administrative.[10] First, the powers and processes of tribunals to some extent resemble those in judicial proceedings, and a number of tribunals are expressly invested with analogous powers to those of the Court of First Instance. Second, some tribunals adopt a precedential approach to their own decisions.[11] The Administrative Appeals Board occasionally cites prior decisions as precedents.[12] The Appeal Board (Town Planning) appears to cite prior decisions as precedents more frequently,[13] and sometimes dissenting opinions are published;[14] a standard practice in court judgments. The Board of Review (Inland Revenue Ordinance) routinely cites precedents, and its published decisions even include a section entitled "cases referred to", again resembling law reports. Nevertheless, it is difficult to assess on the evidence currently available just how extensive this practice is across administrative tribunals in Hong Kong, as few tribunals publish all or any of their decisions.

The importance of characterising tribunals as adjudicative or quasi-judicial, rather than administrative, is that it informs some of the characteristics and standards expected of those tribunals. For example, the Court of Appeal recently described the Municipal Services Appeal Board as having a quasi-judicial character,[15] and an expectation followed that it should in most cases adopt a neutral role in any subsequent appeal against its decision.[16] The court explained that as it would be inappropriate for a judicial officer to appear as a party in proceedings challenging his decision,[17] it would likewise be inappropriate for an "appeal board or tribunal discharging a quasi-judicial function in an adversarial setting" to appear in that capacity.[18] In other words, an administrative decision maker whose decision is under challenge may appear as a

---

[10] See also the *Report of the Committee on Administrative Tribunals and Enquiries* (1957) Cmnd 218 ("Franks Report") at para.40. In Australia, the Administrative Appeals Tribunal is regarded as part of the executive rather than the judicial system – Peter Cane, *Administrative Tribunals and Adjudication* (Hart Publishing, 2009), pp.3–4.

[11] See generally Trevor Buck, "Precedent in Tribunals and the Development of Principles" (2006) 25 *Civil Justice Quarterly* 458.

[12] For example, *Tai Kwok Hung* v *Privacy Commissioner for Personal Data*, Administrative Appeal No 4 of 2015 (29 October 2015).

[13] For example, *New Orient Development Ltd* v *Town Planning Board*, Town Planning Appeal No 5 of 2011 (16 July 2013); *Hin Tack Gee Ltd* v *Town Planning Board*, Town Planning Appeal No 15 of 2011 (27 February 2014).

[14] For example, *Lau King Keung and Lau King Tong* v *Town Planning Board*, Town Planning Appeal Nos 1 and 2 of 2010 (24 October 2011); *Man Fung Wing* v *Town Planning Board*, Town Planning Appeal No 11 of 2013 (30 January 2015).

[15] *Orrico Philippe* v *Municipal Services Appeals Board* [2015] 4 HKLRD 111, para.20.

[16] *Dato Tan Leong Min* v *Insider Dealing Tribunal* [1999] 2 HKC 83, pp.99–100; *Orrico Philippe* v *Municipal Services Appeals Board* [2015] 4 HKLRD 111, para.24.

[17] *Nattrass* v *Attorney General* [1996] 1 HKC 480, paras.18–22.

[18] *Orrico Philippe* v *Municipal Services Appeals Board* [2015] 4 HKLRD 111, paras.23–27. The court applied the costs rule set out in *R (Davies)* v *Birmingham Deputy Coroner* [2004] 1 WLR 2739.

party (typically the respondent) in proceedings challenging his decision, but a judicial officer never does.

There may be further implications following from the characterisation of tribunals as administrative (executive) organs or adjudicative, quasi-judicial or even judicial organs. If tribunals are considered to be judicial organs, they may be classed as "courts"[19] under Article 80 of the Basic Law which states that:

> The courts of the Hong Kong Special Administrative Region at all levels shall be the judiciary of the Region, exercising the judicial power of the Region.

This may have implications for the independence and freedom of tribunals from external (including executive) interference,[20] and the appointment[21] and removal[22] of their members. Inclusion of administrative tribunals within this definition would require significant changes to the way in which they are constituted and operated in order for them to be compliant with the Basic Law. There is a need to seriously consider this issue in Hong Kong, where there does not seem to be a proper conceptualisation of tribunals within the separation of powers framework. It is instructive to note, therefore, the controversy surrounding the investment of administrative functions in the Obscene Articles Tribunal, which did not initially seem to have been regarded as problematic.

Administrative tribunals are, notwithstanding their adjudicative or quasi-judicial nature, administered directly by the executive. This typically means that the tribunal is administratively and financially supported by the same department or division of government of which the original decision maker – whose decisions the tribunal reviews – is a member. For example, the Environmental Impact Assessment Appeal Board hears appeals against certain decisions of the Director of Environmental Protection, yet the Board is directly administered by the Environmental Protection Department. Likewise, the Transport Tribunal hears appeals against certain decisions of the Commissioner for Transport, yet the Tribunal is directly administered by the Transport Department. This raises the immediate concern of insufficient distance between the tribunal and the department with which the original decision maker is associated. It was indeed stated by the Franks Committee, which undertook a major review of administrative tribunals in the UK in the 1950s, that "it is important to secure the independence of the personnel of tribunals from the Departments concerned with the subject-matter of their decisions", and that this was "particularly so when a Government department is a frequent party to proceedings before a tribunal".[23]

---

[19] Though see *Lee Yee Shing Jacky* v *Inland Revenue Board* [2011] HKEC 261, para.70 et seq; and *Luk Ya Cheung* v *Market Misconduct Tribunal* [2009] 1 HKLRD 114, p.134. See also *Stock Exchange of Hong Kong Ltd* v *New World Development Co Ltd* (2006) 9 HKCFAR 234 in the context of Art.35 of the Basic Law.

[20] Basic Law, Art.85. [21] *Id.*, Arts.88 and 92. [22] *Id.*, Art.89. [23] *Franks Report*, para.45.

Critically, if tribunals are administered and their membership appointed by the executive, this does not sit comfortably with their characterisation as adjudicative or quasi-judicial bodies. The manner in which courts are administered and judges appointed are fundamentally informed by the judicial role of courts and the concept of judicial independence. Whilst tribunals reside somewhere between the executive and the judiciary in a tripartite conception of the separation of powers,[24] they are located too close to the executive in Hong Kong. This concern is accentuated against the political backdrop in Hong Kong, and can easily undermine public confidence in government and administration. Local political realities may be fostering a more judicialised climate in Hong Kong,[25] where the public have greater confidence in obtaining a fair hearing through judicial or quasi-judicial, rather than political or administrative, channels.[26] If tribunals are perceived to be too close to the administration, there may be a further sense of disenfranchisement and minimal opportunity for securing public accountability and administrative justice.[27]

The current state of administrative tribunals in Hong Kong is in contrast to that of the UK, where the Tribunals, Courts and Enforcement Act 2007 brought most tribunals within a unified hierarchy. There is also general oversight of the UK tribunal system by the Ministry of Justice, a government department,[28] and previously by the Administrative Justice and Tribunals Council.[29] These reforms were made against the backdrop of a number of important reviews of the UK tribunal system, particularly those resulting in the 1957 Franks Report and the 2001 Leggatt Report.[30] These reviews have no parallel in Hong Kong, where there has been no major legislative initiative to reform the administrative tribunal system, nor has the Law Reform Commission published any reports on administrative tribunals or on administrative justice more generally since its establishment in 1980. The result is a scattered

---

[24] Not all have accepted the basis of the categorisation of tribunals between executive and judicial functions: see, for example, J. A. G. Griffith, 'Tribunals and Inquiries' (1959) 22(2) *Modern Law Review* 125, p.129.

[25] Johannes Chan, "Administrative Law, Politics and Governance: The Hong Kong Experience" in Tom Ginsburg and Albert Chen (eds), *Administrative Law and Governance in Asia: Comparative Perspectives* (Routledge, 2009), 156–157. See also Albert H. Y. Chen, "Reflections on Administrative Law and Judicialized Governance in East and Southeast Asia" in the same volume, pp.359–380.

[26] See Ian Scott, *The Public Sector in Hong Kong* (Hong Kong University Press, Hong Kong, 2010), pp.257 and 270.

[27] In addition, independence and impartiality, though distinguishable, are interlinked – *Wong Tak Wai v Commissioner of Correctional Services* [2010] 4 HKLRD 409, para.117.

[28] Public Bodies Act 2011.   [29] Tribunals, Courts and Enforcement Act 2007, ss.44–45.

[30] See also *Report on Non-Departmental Public Bodies* (1980) Cmnd 7797; *Administrative Justice, Some Necessary Reforms: Report of the Committee of the Justice-All Souls Review of Administrative Law in the United Kingdom* (Oxford 1988); and Secretary of State for Constitutional Affairs, *Transforming Public Services: Complaints, Redress and Tribunals* (2004) Cm 6243.

and jumbled array of tribunals which are not unified under any overall framework of standards or supervision. It has also resulted in a tribunal system which lags far behind standards in the UK and elsewhere.[31]

Composition

Administrative tribunals vary significantly in terms of size and form of composition. This is determined by the relevant governing statute, which often provides for an exact number of members to be appointed. Sometimes a minimum or maximum number of members is provided, whilst for some boards there is no stipulation as to the number of members to be appointed. Some have just a handful of members and meet on an infrequent basis. The Banking Review Tribunal, for example, comprises just four members, and the Pharmacy and Poisons Appeal Tribunal has no meetings in some calendar years. Meanwhile, some tribunals have a large pool of members from which a smaller number is convened to determine individual appeals, and sit on a frequent basis due to the high volume of appeals. The tribunal with the largest membership base is the Appeal Tribunal (Buildings) with 466 members, from which is drawn for the determination of individual complaints a panel comprising a chair and not less than two members.[32]

If administrative tribunals are to be effective and transparent mechanisms for securing accountability in public decision making and promoting administrative justice – and if individuals are to be encouraged to make use of them – there must be robust standards of appointment and removal to ensure that members are given the necessary space, freedom and independence to scrutinise public decisions without interference from executive decision makers, conflicts of interest or particular loyalty or patronage to the executive.

Standards and procedures for the appointment and removal of members of administrative tribunals in Hong Kong are seriously inadequate. The Chief Executive appoints most members of administrative tribunals, with some others appointed by government members who are likely to be loyal to the Chief Executive, such as appointments to the Appeal Board (Rabies) by the Secretary for Food and Health,[33] and appointments to the HKSAR Passports Appeal Board by the Secretary for Security:[34] it should be noted that such government members are directly accountable to, and subject to removal by, the Chief Executive.[35] This is substantially a continuation of the colonial practice whereby the Governor was responsible for most tribunal appointments.

---

[31] See further Stephen Thomson, "Clutter and Cobwebs: How Administrative Tribunals in Hong Kong can learn from the UK" (2017) 36(3) *Civil Justice Quarterly* 363.
[32] Buildings Ordinance (cap. 123), s.48(1).   [33] Rabies Ordinance (cap. 421), s.41.
[34] Hong Kong Special Administrative Region Passports (Appeal Board) Regulation (cap. 539A), s.4.
[35] Basic Law, Art.55.

Concerns were raised about this practice in the early 1990s by a Legislative Council ad hoc group which recommended that the Government take steps to minimise the number of persons who were directly or indirectly involved in decision making who sit on these bodies.[36] Nevertheless, the HKSAR Government has continued this tradition of appointment, seemingly content to have the power of appointment concentrated within the senior ranks of the executive.

The concern is, of course, that members who are appointed by the executive may provide less rigorous or independent scrutiny of executive decisions. The appointing authority may be less inclined to appoint persons who have been vocal critics of the government, whereas there may be an incentive to appoint more loyal, pro-establishment individuals who may be relied upon to serve on tribunals in a more passive or conservative manner. Whereas vacancies for tribunals administered by the Judiciary are centrally advertised, vacancies for administrative tribunals are not. Sometimes a representative from a government department associated with the appointing authority will invite nominations from organisations, as is the practice for appointment to the Board of Review (Inland Revenue Ordinance). There is a general invitation for members of the public to express interest in appointment, but this is hidden away in a large block of text on the website of the Home Affairs Bureau.[37] Appointment practices are particularly opaque.

The governing statutes often do not specify clear criteria on which appointments are to be made, nor any qualifications or experience that the potential member is expected to have. A common provision is that the Chief Executive or other appointing authority may appoint "such persons as s/he thinks suitable" without further elaboration on qualifications,[38] conferring wide discretion in the appointment of members. Occasionally, the statute stipulates certain qualifications or experience as prerequisites for appointment. For example, members of the Appeal Board (Buildings Energy Efficiency) are appointed from distinct categories of engineer,[39] whilst appointments to the Appeal Board (Rabies) are made from among medical practitioners and veterinary surgeons.[40]

Nevertheless, even where the statute does not prescribe prerequisite qualifications or experience, departments do in practice have the ability to formulate appointment criteria, and appointment by the Chief Executive may be a mere formality. Whilst the formulation of these criteria can enhance the robustness

---

[36] See Rita Fan, comments at second reading of Municipal Services Appeals Boards Bill 1990 (9 May 1990), pp.50–52. (www.legco.gov.hk/yr89-90/english/lc_sitg/hansard/h900725.pdf).

[37] See Home Affairs Bureau, *'District, Community and Public Relations'* (www.hab.gov.hk/en/policy_responsibilities/District_Community_and_Public_Relations/advisory.htm).

[38] For example, under the Administrative Appeals Board Ordinance, s.6(2); but examples of this are commonplace in the governing statutes of administrative tribunals.

[39] Buildings Energy Efficiency Ordinance (cap. 610), s.34.

[40] Rabies Ordinance (cap. 421), s.41.

of the appointments process, the criteria are often not publicly available. In any event, structural concerns persist as to appointment powers and practices. An alternative basis for appointment could be the UK model, where members are appointed by the independent Judicial Appointments Commission. This can reduce, if not remove, the ability of the executive to fill the ranks of tribunals with loyal, pro-establishment members. However, the question with "independent" commissions is just how independent they really are, and in particular, who appoints its members. In Hong Kong, for example, the Judicial Officers Recommendation Commission could be empowered to oversee administrative tribunal appointments, though the entire membership of the Commission is, in one way or another, appointed by the Chief Executive.[41] Another option would be to appoint members on the advice or recommendation of an external body, which is the method of appointment to a small number of tribunals in Hong Kong. For example, a proportion of members of the Mental Health Review Tribunal are registered medical practitioners appointed by the Chief Executive on the recommendation of the Hospital Authority.[42] There could also be a role for the Legislative Council in the appointment or recommendation for appointment of tribunal members, though the prevalence of pro-establishment functional constituencies might erode the degree of robust scrutiny and critical distance necessary for the Legislative Council to be a truly "independent" appointments or recommendations body. It would nevertheless be more independent than the current arrangement.

It is not just the method of appointment that is important for securing an appropriate degree of independence and impartiality on the part of tribunal members, but the basis for their removal from post. In the UK, the Leggatt Report recommended that tribunal appointments be for a renewable period of five or seven years and that, subject to age, renewal for further such periods should be automatic unless there were grounds for non-renewal such as misbehaviour, incapacity or failure to comply with sitting and training requirements.[43] The underlying principle is to ensure an appropriate degree of security of tenure, whereby tribunal members can scrutinise executive decisions without feeling that they must not scrutinise those decisions too closely or critically, lest they should be removed from post by the executive on a short reappointment cycle. The Leggatt Report's recommendation has not been implemented in Hong Kong, however, where the typical period of appointment is just two or three years, and the statute almost never provides for automatic reappointment. The suggestion is not that the actual practice in Hong Kong is that the appointing or removing authority removes from post or declines to reappoint tribunal members who have been particularly active or

---

[41] See Judicial Officers Recommendation Commission Ordinance (cap. 92), s.3(1).
[42] Mental Health Ordinance (cap. 136), s.59A(2)(b) and (9).   [43] *Leggatt Report*, para.7.7.

close scrutinisers of executive decisions,[44] but the structural conduciveness to this practice is a sufficient concern. It had also been recommended in the UK that government ministers should not have the power to remove tribunal members,[45] but in Hong Kong that is often precisely who commands the power of removal.

In the context of concerns about the number of members serving on tribunals for a long period of time, or serving on a large number of tribunals, the HKSAR Government introduced a "six-year rule" and "six board rule" in the early 2000s. Under the six-year rule, a non-official (non-Government) member should not serve in any one capacity on a board for more than six years "to ensure a healthy turnover of members of advisory and statutory bodies".[46] Nevertheless, at the time of writing, 247 persons have served as non-official members of advisory and statutory bodies for over six years. These include 9 members of the Board of Review (Inland Revenue Ordinance), 8 members of the Municipal Services Appeals Board and 126 members of the Appeal Tribunal (Buildings).[47] Meanwhile, under the six board rule, a non-official member should not serve concurrently on more than six advisory and statutory bodies "to ensure a reasonable distribution of workload".[48] The most recent figures published by the Government, which include other statutory and advisory bodies in addition to tribunals, report that there were 12 appointees in breach of the six board rule, which it should be noted is a significant reduction from the number of members in breach of the rule in the early 2000s.[49]

All tribunals have one or more chairmen. These are typically appointed by the appointing authority from among legally qualified persons, often (but not always) from among persons qualified for appointment as district judges. The rationale for having legally qualified chairmen is that, on most tribunals, they have the power to determine questions of law, whereas ordinary members – rarely required to be legally qualified – do not. It should be noted that most tribunals or their chairmen have an additional power to refer questions of law to the Court of Appeal by way of case stated. In some tribunals the members choose one of their number to act as chairmen.[50]

Tribunal members may be remunerated in accordance with the provisions of the governing statute. The level of remuneration is often determined by the

---

[44] Consider Johannes Chan, "The Judiciary" in Johannes Chan and C.L. Lim (eds), *Law of the Hong Kong Constitution* (2nd edn) (Sweet and Maxwell, Hong Kong, 2015), pp.375–376.
[45] *Franks Report*, para. 51.
[46] Home Affairs Bureau, '*District, Community and Public Relations*' (www.hab.gov.hk/en/policy_responsibilities/District_Community_and_Public_Relations/advisory.htm).
[47] *Id.*   [48] *Id.*
[49] Though an increase on the figures for the immediately preceding year. See Hong Kong Democratic Foundation, *A Study on the Advisory and Statutory Bodies in Hong Kong – A Brief Report* (http://www.hkdf.org/a-study-on-the-advisory-and-statutory-bodies-in-hong-kong-a-brief-report/).
[50] For example, the Amusement Rides (Safety) Ordinance (cap. 449), s.25(3).

appointing authority[51] or the Secretary for Financial Services and the Treasury.[52] As an example of remuneration, the most recently published figures for members of the Administrative Appeals Board were:[53]

Chairman	Annual retainer:	HK$125,710
	Honorarium per full day sitting:	HK$6,460
	Honorarium per written decision:	HK$12,900
Deputy Chairman	Annual retainer:	HK$83,810
	Honorarium per full day sitting:	HK$6,460
	Honorarium per written decision:	HK$12,900

Remuneration for ordinary members of the Administrative Appeals Board was not published. The average annual number of attendances at meetings of the Board was reported as 51 per member.[54]

Powers and Procedure

Whereas courts conducting judicial review are putatively confined to review for legality, not merits, administrative tribunals typically have the power to assess the decision on the facts, law or merits. The extent to which individual tribunals will enter upon the merits will nevertheless vary.[55] Tribunals typically have the power to confirm, vary or reverse the decision appealed against, whilst some also have a specific power to substitute their own decision for that under challenge. A small number have additional substantive powers, such as the power of the Air Pollution Control Appeal Board to award compensation,[56] and the power of the Mental Health Review Tribunal to discharge a patient.[57] Some, but not all, have the power to award costs.

As administrative tribunals are not unified under a single governing framework, procedure varies among individual tribunals. The process usually begins with the appellant lodging a notice of appeal with the secretariat of the relevant tribunal. The secretariat will then convene a panel of members, often from a larger pool of members, to hear the appeal. This will typically comprise a chair and a number of ordinary members.

Almost all tribunals have the power to obtain evidence, order the production of documents and other materials, and summon witnesses for questioning or to give evidence at a hearing. Consistent with their quasi-judicial nature,

---

[51] Administrative Appeals Board Ordinance, s.6(6).
[52] Municipal Services Appeals Board Ordinance (cap. 442), s.6(1).
[53] List of Government Boards and Committees with Remuneration for Non-Official Members (Financial Services and the Treasury Bureau, HKSAR Government, 2018), p.24 (www.fstb.gov.hk/tb/en/docs/epaper6.pdf).
[54] Id.
[55] See Tom Mullen, "A Holistic Approach to Administrative Justice?" in Michael Adler (ed), Administrative Justice in Context (Hart Publishing, 2010), p.390.
[56] Air Pollution Control Ordinance (cap. 311), s.33(6).   [57] Mental Health Ordinance, s.59E.

tribunals usually have the power to administer oaths and receive evidence under oath. There are often penalties specified by the governing statute for failure to comply with the directions of the tribunal, including various levels of fine and terms of imprisonment. Some tribunal chair are invested with the power to certify a person as being in contempt, that certification being made to the Court of First Instance which may impose penalties consistent with a finding of contempt.[58] Meanwhile, some tribunals are directly invested with the same powers to punish for contempt of court as those of the Court of First Instance.[59] Beyond the basic procedural framework which is prescribed in the governing statute, it is often provided that the chair shall have the power to determine the practice and procedure of the tribunal to the extent that it is not provided for, or inconsistent with, that specified in statute.[60]

There is variation across the tribunals in terms of whether and when hearings must be held in public. A number of statutes provide that hearings shall be held in public, unless the tribunal or its chair determines otherwise.[61] The reverse can be provided, such that the tribunal is required to hold its hearings in private unless the board or its chair determines otherwise,[62] though this is a less common provision. Other variations include provision that a tribunal may determine an appeal without a hearing if satisfied that the appeal can be justly determined in its absence,[63] and that the tribunal may determine the appeal on the basis of written submissions where the parties so consent.[64] There is of course a need to balance the advantages of holding hearings in public to promote openness, transparency and accountability, with factors that may justify the full or partial restriction of proceedings to being held in private. These might include security or defence considerations, personal or financial circumstances, sensitive commercial information or professional capacity and reputation. The recommendation of the Franks Committee was that the chair should have discretion in this regard.[65] Whilst this discretion is subject to the usual judicial controls, supervision by a body invested with general oversight of administrative tribunals may give more confidence that this discretion is being exercised appropriately.

A number of governing statutes confer a right to appear and be legally represented at proceedings.[66] Less commonly, the statute specifies that legal representatives are not entitled to be heard by the tribunal.[67] To the extent that a tribunal has discretion on whether to hold a hearing at all, in public or in

---

[58] For example, the Environmental Impact Assessment Ordinance (cap. 499), s.19(9) and (10).
[59] Securities and Futures Ordinance (cap. 571), s.221. There is a general right of appeal to the Court of Appeal against a finding of contempt: High Court Ordinance (cap. 4), s.50.
[60] For example, the Administrative Appeals Board Ordinance, s.21(1).
[61] For example, *id.*, s.17.   [62] Immigration Ordinance (cap. 115), sch. 1A, para.10.
[63] *Id.*, para.12.
[64] Accreditation of Academic and Vocational Qualifications Ordinance (cap. 592), s.13(1).
[65] *Franks Report*, paras.76–81.   [66] For example, the Buildings Ordinance (cap. 123), s.52.
[67] Accreditation of Academic and Vocational Qualifications Ordinance, s.13(4).

private, the usual common law rules on the exercise of discretion will apply, including promoting the objectives and policy of the statute, and the rules against fettering of discretion.

Despite recommendations implemented in the UK that written reasons be given for tribunal decisions,[68] there is no equivalent, blanket provision in Hong Kong. A number of statutes do provide for reasons to be given for the decisions of particular tribunals, though it is not always stated that such reasons must be in writing. Several statutes make no specific provision on the giving of reasons, and there is no automatic common law duty to provide reasons. Sometimes a right of appeal is conferred, though this is usually limited to appeal on a point of law to the Court of Appeal[69] or, less commonly, to the Court of First Instance.[70] It is also possible for appeal to be permitted on a question of fact or law,[71] and even appeal on the merits, whether to another tribunal[72] or to the courts.[73] Most statutes governing administrative tribunals do not confer a right of appeal, and it is sometimes provided that decisions of the tribunal are final[74] and/or not subject to appeal.[75]

Appeals to the Chief Executive and Chief Executive-in-Council

Prior to the Handover, the Governor and Governor-in-Council exercised an appellate function in the context of specific statutory frameworks. The number of statutory avenues for appealing to the Governor and Governor-in-Council was reduced against the background of concerns about procedural standards and transparency. The HKSAR Government indicated, some years ago, that appeals to the Chief Executive-in-Council (CEIC) had been scaled down in order to comply with the Bill of Rights, and to "relieve the Executive Council of minor decision making".[76] Nevertheless, this relic of the colonial era survives in the form of various appeals to the Chief Executive and CEIC.[77] These are clearly distinct legal entities; for example, the Country Parks Ordinance provides that the Chief Executive is to decide an appeal by way of petition, or to direct that the petition be referred to the CEIC.[78] The Ordinance

---

[68] *Franks Report*, para. 98; Tribunals and Inquiries Act 1958, s.12.
[69] Banking Ordinance (cap. 155), s.101H.   [70] Land Drainage Ordinance (cap. 446), s.33.
[71] Securities and Futures Ordinance, s.266.
[72] Public Health and Municipal Services Ordinance, s.125B(4).
[73] Pharmacy and Poisons Ordinance (cap. 138), s.30A; Public Health and Municipal Services Ordinance (cap. 132), s.128D(16).
[74] Town Planning Ordinance (cap. 131), s.17B(9).
[75] Bedspace Apartments Ordinance, s.28(8).
[76] Secretary for Justice, comments to Legislative Council (30 May 2002), 6855 (www.legco.gov.hk/yr01-02/english/counmtg/hansard/cm0530ti-translate-e.pdf).
[77] On the Chief Executive more generally, see Benny Tai, "The Chief Executive" in Johannes Chan and C. L. Lim (eds), *Law of the Hong Kong Constitution* (2nd edn) (Sweet and Maxwell, 2015), pp. 205–243. A statutory right of appeal is sometimes created to other senior members of government.
[78] Country Parks Ordinance (cap. 208), ss.17(9) and (10).

thereafter provides that the "decision of the Chief Executive or the Chief Executive in Council shall be final".[79] Appeals to the Chief Executive and the CEIC are required by statute to be made by way of petition or otherwise than by way of petition. At the time of writing, the following number of statutory appeal mechanisms existed under each classification:[80]

Table 21.1 Number of statutory appeal mechanisms to Chief Executive and Chief Executive-in-Council

	Chief Executive	Chief Executive-in-Council
Appeals by way of petition	14	13
Appeals otherwise than by way of petition	4	10

This classification directly affects the procedural requirements attaching to the appeal. Where an appeal is directed to the CEIC, the Administrative Appeals Rules provide that there shall be a hearing only when the appeal is one otherwise than by way of petition.[81] Where the appeal is to the CEIC by way of petition, the appeal is determined without a hearing unless the CEIC appoints a committee for the purpose of hearing the appeal.[82] As the Administrative Appeals Rules do not govern appeals to the Chief Executive,[83] however, such appeals carry no statutory right to a hearing or legal representation.

The CEIC hears an appeal in an administrative or executive capacity, and not in a judicial or quasi-judicial capacity.[84] In addition, it was judicially confirmed that, in accordance with the separation of powers under the Basic Law, the legislature could not place judicial power in the hands of the executive.[85] The Executive Council is specifically designated by the Basic Law as assisting the Chief Executive in policy-making,[86] and she is not bound by its advice.[87] Whilst there are different procedural requirements attaching to appeals to the Chief Executive and those to the CEIC, it is clear that the decision is essentially capable of being finally determined by the Chief Executive alone, or very significantly directed by her. This is also seen in the composition of the Executive Council, members of which are appointed and removed by the Chief Executive.[88] The CEIC was described by the Court of First Instance as an "inherently political entity",[89] and it is worth noting that,

---

[79] *Id.*, s.17(11).
[80] These exclude appeal mechanisms relating to disciplinary procedures, such as those under the Police (Discipline) Regulations (cap. 232A), reg.26; and Public Finance Ordinance (cap. 2), s.34.
[81] Administrative Appeals Rules (cap. 1A), r.7.   [82] *Id.*, rr.9 and 11.
[83] Interpretation and General Clauses Ordinance (cap. 1), s.64; Administrative Appeals Rules, r.2. Art.48(13) of the Basic Law provides that the Chief Executive shall "handle petitions and complaints".
[84] Interpretation and General Clauses Ordinance, s.64(4).
[85] *Yau Kwong Man v Secretary for Security* [2002] HKEC 1142 at para.38.
[86] Basic Law, Art.54.   [87] *Id.*, Art.56.   [88] *Id.*, Art.55.
[89] *Television Broadcasts Ltd v Communications Authority* [2016] HKEC 238 at para.123.

at the time of writing, a number of Executive Council members served as members of the Chief Executive Election Committee, Hong Kong deputies to the National People's Congress of the PRC and/or members of the National Committee of the Chinese People's Political Consultative Conference of the PRC.

It appears that the brief or memorandum for the CEIC to consider an appeal is prepared by the head of the government department relevant to the appeal, unless that person is him- or herself the decision maker whose decision is under appeal.[90] Where a committee has been appointed to which to refer the appeal,[91] the hearing of the committee is held in private.[92] Though the appellant may be heard in person or through counsel or a solicitor, if the appellant is heard in person he shall not also be heard through counsel or a solicitor without special leave of the CEIC or a committee appointed by her.[93] In addition, the committee merely advises the CEIC, which is not bound to accept the committee's advice.[94] The decisions of the CEIC must be communicated to the appellant and respondent,[95] but there is no statutory duty for reasons to be provided. In the course of determining an appeal otherwise than by way of petition, the CEIC may state a case for the Court of Appeal on a point of law.[96] It was recently held that the CEIC did not "offer the guarantees of a tribunal that possesses the requisite independence and impartiality",[97] and therefore that a statutory appeal to the CEIC did not satisfy the requirements of Article 10 of the Bill of Rights.[98] Though there is an attempted ouster of review in relation to appeals to the CEIC,[99] this cannot be regarded as immunising those appeals from judicial scrutiny in accordance with the usual rules on purported ouster of jurisdiction.

Though appeals to the CEIC are statutorily designated as being heard in an administrative or executive capacity, and not in a judicial or quasi-judicial capacity,[100] the Office of the Chief Executive has stated in correspondence with the author that statutory appeals or objections to the Chief Executive (or her delegated authority) are heard in a quasi-judicial capacity. Though appeals to the Chief Executive carry no statutory right to a hearing or legal representation, the Office has stated that the appellant is entitled to a fair hearing. It was added that the appellant or objector may make representations in writing and that an oral hearing "is not usually necessary". It has also been stated that the appellant or objector would be informed of the decision in writing, sent by registered post.[101] The procedure by which the Chief Executive determines appeals remains subject to judicial review. Though the Office has suggested that the Chief Executive may decide an appeal or objection through a

---

[90] *Id.*, at para.134.   [91] Administrative Appeals Rules, r.9.   [92] *Id.*, r.10.   [93] *Id.*, r.7.
[94] *Id.*, r.10.   [95] *Id.*, r.12.   [96] *Id.*, rr.2 and 13.
[97] *Television Broadcasts Ltd v Communications Authority* [2016] HKEC 238, para.128.
[98] *Id.*, para.137. For further discussion, see Thomson, "Clutter and Cobwebs", pp.383–385.
[99] Interpretation and General Clauses Ordinance, s.64(3).   [100] *Id*, s.64(4).
[101] Correspondence with the Office of the Chief Executive (2016), on file with the author.

delegated authority, there was a fairly high profile instance of the Chief Executive being found to have acted unlawfully in purporting to delegate his decision-making power to determine a disciplinary appeal under the Public Service (Administration) Order 1997.[102] This was the case of *Rowse v Secretary for Civil Service*,[103] in which the Chief Executive purported to delegate that power to the Chief Secretary for Administration, and in which other grounds of review were also violated. The quasi-judicial nature of a decision-making power indeed militates against the legality of such a power being delegated.[104]

Ombudsman

The Ombudsman provides a complaint mechanism for persons aggrieved by the acts or conduct of public bodies. The office was established in 1989 as the Commissioner for Administrative Complaints, becoming known as the Ombudsman from 1996.[105] The office is governed by the Ombudsman Ordinance (cap.397), modelled primarily on the Parliamentary Commissioner (Ombudsman) Act 1962 in New Zealand, and the Parliamentary Commissioner Act 1967 in the United Kingdom.[106] Hong Kong has a unified ombudsman system in the sense that the Ombudsman has jurisdiction over all bodies which are subject to such supervision. In the UK, for example, there are a number of specialised ombudsmen, such as the Parliamentary and Health Service Ombudsman, the Financial Ombudsman Service, and the Local Government Ombudsman. Some of the UK ombudsmen even have jurisdiction over private bodies, whereas this is not the case in Hong Kong, the Ombudsman having previously accepted no jurisdiction over such bodies.[107]

The Ombudsman is assisted by a Deputy Ombudsman and two Assistant Ombudsmen. There were, at the time of writing, around 120 staff working in the Office of the Ombudsman. There are eight investigation teams, divided between the leadership of the Assistant Ombudsmen. In addition to a number of support staff, there is also a Panel of Advisers appointed by the Ombudsman on a statutory basis,[108] and subject to the same obligations of secrecy as Ombudsman staff.[109] This is a provision designed to promote voluntary sharing of information with the Ombudsman without fear of dissemination or reprisal, and the confidentiality of complaints.

---

[102] Public Service (Administration) Order 1997, s.20.
[103] *Rowse v Secretary for Civil Service* [2008] 5 HKLRD 217.   [104] See p.170.
[105] It assumed part of the function of the Office of Members of the Executive and Legislative Councils (OMELCO); see p.330 and Legislative Council, 'A Companion to the History, Rules and Practices of the Legislative Council of the Hong Kong Special Administrative Region', paras.15.4–15.20 (www.legco.gov.hk/general/english/procedur/companion/chapter_15/chapter_15.html).
[106] Office of the Ombudsman, *Report on Review of Jurisdiction: Part 1*, November 2006, para.1.1 – see www.legco.gov.hk/yr08-09/english/panels/ajls/papers/aj0427cb2-1384-9-e.pdf.
[107] *Id.*, para.2.7.   [108] Ombudsman Ordinance, s.6A.   [109] *Id.*, s.15.

The focus of the Ombudsman's work is maladministration. She does not, unlike the ombudsman institutions in Macau and Mainland China, have general anti-corruption jurisdiction, this being vested in the Independent Commission Against Corruption.[110] Maladministration can take two forms: lawful and unlawful. The former gives the Ombudsman jurisdiction over acts that are beyond the reach of judicial review, whereas the latter gives rise to some overlap in the types of acts and decisions that may be supervised by either process. Complaint to the Ombudsman over acts of unlawful maladministration may be useful when, for example, a person is unable or unwilling to make an application for judicial review, or there is some other reason why litigation might not be appropriate or possible, such as where an applicant is out of time, or their application for legal aid is refused.

Maladministration is defined by section 2 of the Ombudsman Ordinance as follows:

> inefficient, bad or improper administration and, without derogation from the generality of the foregoing, includes –
>
> (a) unreasonable conduct, including delay, discourtesy and lack of consideration for a person affected by any action;
> (b) abuse of any power (including any discretionary power) or authority including any action which-
>   (i) is unreasonable, unjust, oppressive or improperly discriminatory or which is in accordance with a practice which is or may be unreasonable, unjust, oppressive or improperly discriminatory; or
>   (ii) was based wholly or partly on a mistake of law or fact; or
> (c) unreasonable, unjust, oppressive or improperly discriminatory procedures.

This is not an exhaustive definition and maladministration is capable of taking many different forms. Some examples of maladministration were given by the then Leader of the House of Commons, Richard Crossman MP, when the Parliamentary Commissioner Bill was being taken through the UK Parliament in 1966. These have become known as the "Crossman Catalogue":[111]

- Bias
- Neglect
- Inattention
- Delay
- Incompetence
- Inaptitude

---

[110] See further Stephen Thomson, "The Public Sector Ombudsman in Greater China: Four 'Chinese' Models of Administrative Supervision" (2017) 39(2) *University of Pennsylvania Journal of International Law* 435.

[111] HC Deb, vol.734, col.51 (18 October 1966).

- Perversity
- Turpitude
- Arbitrariness.

The Annual Report for 1993 issued by the UK Parliamentary Commissioner for Administration gave the following examples of maladministration:[112]

- Rudeness (though this is a matter of degree)
- Unwillingness to treat the complainant as a person with rights
- Refusal to answer reasonable questions
- Neglecting to inform a complainant on request of his or her rights or entitlements
- Knowingly giving advice which is misleading or inadequate
- Ignoring valid advice or overruling considerations which would produce an uncomfortable result for the overruler
- Offering no redress or manifestly disproportionate redress
- Showing bias, whether because of colour, sex, or any other grounds
- Omission to notify those who thereby lose a right of appeal
- Refusal to inform adequately of the right to appeal
- Faulty procedures
- Failure by management to monitor compliance with adequate procedures
- Cavalier disregard of guidance which is intended to be followed in the interest of equitable treatment to those who use a service
- Partiality
- Failure to mitigate the effects of rigid adherence to the letter of the law where that produces manifestly inequitable treatment.

The website of the Office of the Ombudsman in Hong Kong states that maladministration includes:[113]

- Abuse of power
- Delay/inaction
- Disparity in treatment, unfairness
- Error, wrong advice/decision
- Failure to follow procedures
- Faulty procedures
- Ineffective control
- Lack of response/reply to complainant/enquirer
- Negligence, omissions
- Selective enforcement
- Staff attitude.

---

[112] Parliamentary Commissioner for Administration, *Annual Report for 1993* (HC 290 1993–1994, HMSO) (13 March 1994).
[113] Office of the Ombudsman, *'The Ombudsman's Role and Jurisdiction'* (www.ombudsman.hk/en-us/about_this_office/role_and_jurisdiction.html).

Examples not stated in the lists already cited might include:

- Inconsistency
- Dishonesty
- Failure to assign one or more specific members of staff to an enquirer/person subject to decision throughout the life cycle of the enquiry/decision-making process
- Failure to be capable of contact through more than one channel of communication (post, telephone, fax, email, etc.)
- Long waiting times in telephone queues
- Unreasonably expensive cost to contact organisation by telephone
- Burying contact information in difficult-to-access areas of a website
- Failure to comply with published targets, including targets relating to response times and the time within which a decision shall be made
- The use of inappropriately technical or specialist language in communications
- Routinely responding with standard form responses rather than engaging with the substance of enquiries
- Adoption of unreasonable policies (whether or not unreasonable in the *Wednesbury* sense)
- Lack of proportionality
- Inflexibility beyond that required to meet legal obligations
- Obstinacy or unhelpfulness.

The Ombudsman is empowered to investigate allegations of maladministration against any organisation listed in Part 1 of Schedule 1 to the Ordinance in the exercise of its administrative functions (note that this would appear not to include judicial or quasi-judicial functions).[114] The list of organisations is diverse and at the time of writing includes bodies as various as the Competition Commission, the Department of Health, the Equal Opportunities Commission, the Hong Kong Observatory and Radio Television Hong Kong. The Ombudsman identified three criteria for the selection of candidate organisations for inclusion in Schedule 1. First, the organisation exercises executive powers, performs administrative action and is not solely an advisory, adjudicative or appellate body. Second, the organisation has extensive interface with or impact upon the public or a substantial sector thereof. Finally, it is substantially funded (by more than half its revenue) by general revenue or statutory fees or charges, or by donations specifically earmarked for a public service, the administration of which is undertaken or supervised by Government or public officials.[115] The scope of the Ombudsman's work extends over actions taken on behalf of organisations listed in Part 1 of Schedule 1 to the Ordinance, including work

---

[114] Ombudsman Ordinance, s.7(1)(a).
[115] Office of the Ombudsman, *Report on Review of Jurisdiction: Part 1*, November 2006, para.2.6 – see www.legco.gov.hk/yr08-09/english/panels/ajls/papers/aj0427cb2-1384-9-e.pdf.

outsourced by one of those organisations to a contractor. Recommendations are made to the organisation rather than to the contractor. In this way, the scope of the Ombudsman's jurisdiction helps ensure that "Government departments can contract out the work but not the responsibility".[116]

The Ombudsman may investigate any action taken by or on behalf of the ICAC, Hong Kong Auxiliary Police Force, Hong Kong Police Force and the Secretariat of the Public Service Commission in the exercise of their administrative functions only in relation to the Code on Access to Information.[117] These organisations may not be investigated by the Ombudsman except as their actions relate the Code on Access to Information.

The Ombudsman's process of investigation begins in one of two ways. First, a person claiming to have sustained injustice as a result of maladministration may submit a complaint to the Ombudsman.[118] The complainant can be a natural or legal person. Prior to 1994, complaints were referred to the Commissioner for Administrative Complaints by Legislative Council members, but the system was opened up to direct public access. The Ombudsman has discretion on whether to undertake, continue or discontinue an investigation,[119] and the investigation may be undertaken or continued even if the complainant has withdrawn the complaint.[120] Second, the Ombudsman has the power to investigate where she is of the opinion that any person may have sustained injustice in consequence of maladministration, even where no complaint has been received.[121] This is known as a direct investigation and forms an increasingly important part of the Ombudsman's work. In the most recent year for which statistics are available, covering April 2016 to March 2017, reports have been published on direct investigations in diverse areas including tree management, the Marine Department's follow-up mechanism on recommendations made in Marine Incident Investigation Reports, the temporary closure of public swimming pools and beaches due to lifeguard shortages, regulation of kindergarten application fees, and special transport services for persons with mobility difficulties.[122]

Before commencing an investigation, the Ombudsman is required to notify the head of the organisation affected of her intention to conduct an investigation, and may seek the head's comments.[123] In some cases the Ombudsman may instead notify the Chief Secretary for Administration.[124] Procedure is regulated as the Ombudsman thinks fit, with a power to obtain any information, document or thing, or to make such inquiries, as she thinks fit.[125]

---

[116] *Id.*, para.2.47.
[117] Ombudsman Ordinance, s.7(1)(b). The Ombudsman's jurisdiction was extended to investigate alleged breaches of the Code on Access to Information in 1996.
[118] Ombudsman Ordinance, s.7(1).   [119] *Id.*, s.9.   [120] *Id.*, s.11.   [121] *Id.*, s.7(1).
[122] Office of the Ombudsman, *Annual Report 2017*, p.25.
[123] Ombudsman Ordinance, s.12(1).   [124] *Id.*, s.12(2).   [125] *Id.*, s.12(3).

Investigations are conducted in private, and counsel and solicitors have no right of audience before the Ombudsman, though may appear before her as she thinks fit.[126] It is not necessary for the Ombudsman to hold a hearing, though she has the power to do so.[127] In practice, this power is rarely exercised. The Ombudsman may obtain evidence and summon witnesses, and has the power to administer oaths.[128]

The conclusion of the investigation process is marked by the Ombudsman's decision on whether to report to the head of the organisation affected or, if the Ombudsman thinks fit, to the Chief Executive. The decision on whether to report is at the Ombudsman's discretion, and can comprise a report of her opinion and reasons, together with a statement of any remedy which she considers should be provided, a statement of any recommendation she thinks fit to make, and a copy of the comments made by or on behalf of the head of the organisation affected.[129] If a report is provided, the Ombudsman may specify a period of time within which she considers it reasonable in all the circumstances for the report to be acted upon.[130] Failure on the part of the organisation to adequately act upon the report within that period enables the Ombudsman, if she thinks fit, to submit the report and recommendations, together with any further observations, to the Chief Executive. The Ombudsman is likewise enabled where the report did not specify a time period, but such time has elapsed as the Ombudsman thinks was reasonable in which to adequately act in all the circumstances.[131] In addition, where the Ombudsman considers that a serious irregularity or injustice has occurred, she may make a further report to the Chief Executive, which must thereafter be laid before the Legislative Council.[132] Accordingly, whilst there is no strict legal liability for failure to implement or properly follow up on the findings or recommendation of the Ombudsman (including the recommendation that a remedy be provided to the complainant), there is the possibility of political accountability should such failure occur.

The Ombudsman has the power to publish a report on an investigation if she is of the opinion that it is in the public interest to do so. The report must not disclose the identity of any person aggrieved, complainant or officer of the organisation whose action is subject to the investigation or otherwise involved in the investigation. The identity of the organisation may, however, be disclosed.[133] The Ombudsman also has the power to address a complaint by way of mediation if she is of the opinion that there has been minor or no maladministration.[134] Participation in mediation is voluntary on the part of both the complainant and the organisation subject to the complaint.[135] This is an increasingly significant part of the Ombudsman's work, and in the most

---

[126] *Id.*, s.12(4). [127] *Id.*, s.12(5). [128] *Id.*, s.13. [129] *Id.*, s.16(1). [130] *Id.*, s.16(2).
[131] *Id.*, s.16(3). [132] *Id.*, ss.16(5) and (6). [133] *Id.*, s.16A. [134] *Id.*, s.11B(1).
[135] *Id.*, s.11B(4).

recent annual report, mediation was used to settle almost 4.6 per cent of all complaints pursued and concluded.[136]

There are some important restrictions on the investigatory powers of the Ombudsman. This includes a prohibition on investigation where the complainant has had knowledge of the impugned action for more than twenty-four months prior to the complaint being received by the Ombudsman, which means that a person who is out of time for leave to apply for judicial review (the general limit for which is three months from the date on which grounds for review first arose) may still have time within which to make a complaint to the Ombudsman. Anonymous complaints, those not made by the individual aggrieved or his or her personal representative, and actions in relation to contractual or other commercial transactions, excluding tendering procedures, are not subject to investigation. The Ombudsman is also generally prohibited from investigating any action in respect of which the complainant has or had a statutory right of appeal, objection or review on the merits to the Chief Executive, the Chief Executive-in-Council or any statutory tribunal, board or authority; or where the complainant has or had a remedy by way of court or tribunal proceedings, other than by way of judicial review. An important qualification to this general prohibition is that the Ombudsman may investigate if she is satisfied that in the particular circumstances it is not reasonable to expect the complainant to resort to, or to have resorted to, that other right or remedy.[137] The Ombudsman does not generally investigate maladministration as it relates to personnel matters.[138]

Relationship with Judicial Review

The function of the Ombudsman is clearly distinguishable from that of judicial review, not least as she has no power to provide a remedy or to order the provision of redress. However, the work of the Ombudsman provides a complement to judicial review. For example, as noted, the Ombudsman provides an opportunity for grievances to be redressed when a person is out of time for leave to apply for judicial review. This of course applies only to persons who have suffered unlawful maladministration, as lawful maladministration is clearly not liable to be struck down by the courts. Whilst the Ombudsman has no power to award a remedy or to enforce the implementation of a recommendation, there is reported to be a high rate of compliance with Ombudsman recommendations.[139] The service provided by the Ombudsman is also free of charge, making it particularly accessible to complainants.

---

[136] Office of the Ombudsman, *Annual Report (2017)*, p.28.   [137] Ombudsman Ordinance, s.10.
[138] *Id.*, s.8 and Sch.2(5); Office of the Ombudsman, *Report on Review of Jurisdiction: Part 1*, November 2006, paras. 3.2–3.9 – see www.legco.gov.hk/yr08-09/english/panels/ajls/papers/aj0427cb2-1384-9-e.pdf.
[139] Office of the Ombudsman, *Annual Report (2017)*, p.25.

The Ombudsman can also perform acts that courts in judicial review cannot. She can initiate direct investigations into suspected maladministration, giving her a proactive function, whereas courts can act only in response to an application for judicial review. There can be a number of reasons why a dispute never ends up in court, such as failure by an applicant to successfully obtain legal aid, whereas the service provided by the Ombudsman is free of charge for complainants, and the Ombudsman's power of direct investigation does not require there to be a complainant in the first place for issues of concern in public administration to be challenged. Moreover, the standard of evidence required to be presented to the Ombudsman will tend not to be as rigorous as that presented to a court in support of a judicial review application. Perhaps a complainant has evidence of maladministration which would be too weak to support an application for judicial review, whereas that evidence may be sufficient to persuade the Ombudsman to investigate the allegation of maladministration.

Litigation is also a remedy-oriented process. The applicant for judicial review must require a remedy and state what remedy he or she requires. It is not necessary to be seeking a particular remedy when complaining to the Ombudsman. This is particularly useful where the complainant does not know what remedy he or she needs or desires, or where he or she does not require a remedy. For example, the complainant might seek an investigation into staff attitude at a particular organisation, or to see that certain practices are not repeated, or that a process is made more efficient. These objects are generally beyond the scope of judicial review, whereas the Ombudsman can investigate these issues without the need for the investigation process to be geared towards the obtainment of a remedy.

The Ombudsman is also (in contrast to the courts) unconstrained by the separation of powers from making recommendations for the improvement of executive processes and from entering upon the merits. The courts would be seen to trespass on executive discretion if they recommended changes to administrative practices in the name of expediency, efficiency or good administration (in a non-legal sense), whereas the Ombudsman is under no such restrictions. The work of the Ombudsman should therefore not be regarded as inferior to judicial review simply because she has no power to award a remedy or to require an organisation to implement her recommendations. Her work is of a different nature and complements judicial review as part of an array of mechanisms for achieving administrative justice and the promotion of transparency and accountability in public administration.

Finally, it is worth noting that a public body cannot necessarily ignore the findings or recommendations of the Ombudsman with impunity. Not only can there be political consequences for an organisation in respect of which a critical report is published, and perhaps made to the Chief Executive to be laid before the Legislative Council, there could potentially also be legal consequences. For example, if the Ombudsman has made recommendations in a situation of unlawful maladministration which the organisation ignores, and decisions are taken by that organisation in future which continue to be characterised by such unlawful maladministration, it could feasibly be argued that the body, in failing to take into account the recommendations of the Ombudsman, has failed to take into account a relevant consideration.[140]

Effectiveness of the Ombudsman

The Ombudsman is appointed by the Chief Executive for a renewable period of five years.[141] She may resign office at any time or, in the event of inability to discharge the functions of her office, or misbehaviour, be removed from office by the Chief Executive with the approval by resolution of the Legislative Council.[142] Although the Ombudsman is not to be regarded as a servant or agent of the Government nor as enjoying any status, immunity or privilege of the Government,[143] questions will inevitably arise about the extent to which the Ombudsman is an independent control on executive action when she is appointed by the Chief Executive. Moreover, her office is to some extent operationally reliant on the executive.[144] It would be a structural improvement were the Ombudsman to be appointed by a non-executive body, such as the Legislative Council.

A complainant can request that the Ombudsman review her decision by submitting a "request for review". This is conducted internally and there is no time limit within which such a request must be made. Upon receipt of the request for review, the Assistant Ombudsman usually asks the Chief Investigation Officer to consult with the original case officer on whether there are grounds for reviewing the case, such as new evidence, arguments or perspectives. Where any such grounds are identified, a review will be conducted. This results in the Chief Investigation Officer or the original case officer submitting to the Ombudsman for approval their analysis and recommendation on whether to uphold or vary the original decision. The Ombudsman then communicates her decision in writing to the complainant with reasons. Where no such grounds for review are identified, the Chief Investigation Officer or the original case officer will seek approval from the Ombudsman to decline the request for review. If the Ombudsman approves, the decision will be communicated in writing to the complainant with reasons. In the three years preceding a 2013 Legislative Council briefing paper, the percentage of complainants submitting requests for review was 3 per cent, 2 per cent and 1 per cent, respectively, suggesting that "[t]here does not seem to be a prevailing trend of

---

[140] Though consider Jason Varuhas, "Governmental Rejections of Ombudsman Findings: What Role for the Courts?" (2009) 72(1) *Modern Law Review* 102.
[141] Ombudsman Ordinance, ss.3 and 3A. [142] *Id.*, s.4. [143] *Id.*, s.6B(1).
[144] It is provided that the expenses of the Ombudsman and any salary or benefit payable to any persons appointed by her shall be paid out of monies appropriated by the Legislative Council, though the salary or other benefit payable to the person appointed as Ombudsman is charged on the general revenue – Ombudsman Ordinance (cap.397), ss.3(6) and 6(3), and Sch.1A(1).

disagreement with the decisions made by The Ombudsman".[145] The statistics provided in the annex to the briefing paper also disclose that, in the three full years under review, 54 per cent, 28 per cent and 36 per cent of requests for review were declined. For cases in which a review was conducted, only 12 per cent, 12 per cent and 10 per cent, respectively, resulted in the original decision being varied.

The Ombudsman is subject to judicial review,[146] though this of course accounts only for unlawful acts. There is no formal, non-legal supervision of the Ombudsman, either for evaluating the effectiveness of her work or for any (lawful) maladministration committed by her office.[147] The Administration previously considered whether there should be external review of the Ombudsman's decisions, but concluded that judicial review provided a "safeguard" and an "effective check and balance system", and there was no "need to duplicate another independent and impartial set up and have another layer of authority to review the decisions of The Ombudsman".[148] Judicial review can do no more, however, than ensure that the Ombudsman acts lawfully when reviewing cases, and does not provide a form of qualitative review on the work of the Ombudsman.

It has been suggested that the Ombudsman's role should be expanded to include human rights protection. However, it was said that "the essence of the Office's work was to ensure the protection of individual rights by public administration", and the Ombudsman had a role to play in that regard alongside other bodies such as the Equal Opportunities Commission and the Privacy Commissioner for Personal Data. The Administration was of the view that human rights protection was already extensively provided for through

---

[145] Legislative Council briefing paper (LC Paper No CB(4)513/12–13(01)), Brief prepared by the Administration Wing, Chief Secretary for Administration's Office, The Office of the Ombudsman, *Establishing an independent mechanism to review the decisions of The Ombudsman* (26 March 2013), p.4. The low percentage of complainants submitting a request for review could, however, be explained by other factors, such as satisfaction with the original decision, insufficient confidence in the likelihood of successful review, and being unaware that a request for review can be made.

[146] See, for example, *Ong Kin Kee Tony v Commissioner for Administrative Complaints* [1997] HKLRD 1191.

[147] The Ombudsman is, however, under a duty to submit an annual report to the Chief Executive who shall cause it to be tabled in the Legislative Council – Ombudsman Ordinance, sch.1A, para.3(4). There is also an established practice of the Ombudsman meeting regularly with the Legislative Council to discuss her work and development plan – Legislative Council briefing paper (LC Paper No CB(4)513/12–13(01)), Brief prepared by the Administration Wing, Chief Secretary for Administration's Office, The Office of the Ombudsman, *Establishing an independent mechanism to review the decisions of The Ombudsman* (26 March 2013), p.5.

[148] Legislative Council briefing paper (LC Paper No CB(4)513/12–13(01)), Brief prepared by the Administration Wing, Chief Secretary for Administration's Office, The Office of the Ombudsman, *Establishing an independent mechanism to review the decisions of The Ombudsman* (26 March 2013), p.4.

other mechanisms and that there was no obvious need for establishing a further such mechanism.[149]

Though it might be asked whether the Ombudsman would be more effective if she had the power to award remedies, this would raise a number of issues. First, it could lead to competition with the courts in relation to unlawful maladministration, as a complainant might be able to pursue a remedy before the courts or the Ombudsman. This could introduce overlap in the determinations of courts and the Ombudsman, and give rise to procedural and policy complications. The potential for overlap could be minimised by limiting the Ombudsman to the award of remedies in cases of lawful maladministration (which are of course incapable of judicial redress), but this would lead to difficult cases on the boundary between lawful and unlawful maladministration (including the potential for litigation to determine whether an act is lawful or unlawful for these purposes). It would also diminish the scope of the Ombudsman's jurisdiction by removing unlawful maladministration from her oversight or requiring a segregation of lawful and unlawful maladministration in a single complaint, which may be impractical.

The investment in the Ombudsman of the power to award remedies would probably also require a greater degree of formality and transparency in the Ombudsman's investigation procedure. As noted, proceedings are at present conducted in private and this could presumably not be allowed to continue if the Ombudsman had the power to award remedies, when parties would be entitled to demand greater transparency of, and engagement with, the resolution process. The Ombudsman might also be required to hold hearings more regularly than at present, and it might have to be reconsidered whether counsel and solicitors should be afforded a right of audience before the Ombudsman. It would also have to be considered whether it is appropriate for the Ombudsman to have the power to conduct direct investigations, as potential complainants could be prejudiced by the conduct of a direct investigation, noting that a remedy could have resulted had the investigation been initiated by submission of a complaint. Conversely, if potential complainants could rely on a direct investigation to support the award of a remedy, the Ombudsman would have to tread very carefully before launching a direct investigation, as this could open the floodgates and instigate a tide of claims against an organisation.

The dual power of being able to award a remedy and make recommendations would give the Ombudsman immense power over executive bodies. It would redefine the role of the Ombudsman, amalgamating executive and

---

[149] Legislative Council briefing paper (LC Paper No CB(2)1384/08–09(09)), Background brief prepared by the Legislative Council secretariat for meeting on 27 April 2009, *Review of the Jurisdiction of the Office of the Ombudsman* (21 April 2009), p.5. Consider, by way of background, Carole J. Petersen, "The Paris Principles and Human Rights Institutions: Is Hong Kong Slipping Further Away From the Mark?" (2003) 33 *Hong Kong Law Journal* 513, pp.514–515.

judicial functions, and shift her role from one of administrative supervision to a form of "judicial" review. Though it might on the face of it appear that the Ombudsman's role and capacity would be strengthened by giving her the power to award remedies, this would require a major reconceptualisation and reform of the Ombudsman, and carry significant resource implications which, not least, would question whether the service could continue to be available free of charge to the complainant.

Legislative Council Redress System

The Legislative Council Redress System is a framework through which members of the public can complain or make representations to members of the Legislative Council about Government actions or policies, legislation or other issues of public concern. The Redress System finds its roots in the Office of the Unofficial Members of the Executive and Legislative Councils (UMELCO), established in 1963 and renamed in 1986 as the Office of Members of the Executive and Legislative Councils (OMELCO).[150] These offices heard complaints about maladministration in addition to broader policy issues and matters of public concern; when the Office of the Commissioner for Administrative Complaints (COMAC; now the Ombudsman) was established in 1989, cases of maladministration were referred to the COMAC.[151] However, cases of maladministration do not seem to be exclusively within the jurisdiction of the Ombudsman and may still be considered under the Redress System.[152] The Redress System is legally underpinned by Article 73(8) of the Basic Law, which provides that the Legislative Council has the power and function to receive and handle complaints from Hong Kong residents.

Members of the Legislative Council are assigned to a weekly duty roster in groups of seven. The Public Complaints Office of the Legislative Council Secretariat attempts to assign members to the duty roster so as to have at

---

[150] Prior to 1963, the only way to seek redress of grievances of this nature was by petitioning the Governor or the Legislative Council through Unofficial Members at sittings of the Legislative Council, to be done in accordance with the relevant Standing Orders – Legislative Council, 'A Companion to the History, Rules and Practices of the Legislative Council of the Hong Kong Special Administrative Region', para.15.5 (www.legco.gov.hk/general/english/procedur/companion/chapter_15/chapter_15.html). See further Legislative Council, 'A Companion to the History, Rules and Practices of the Legislative Council of the Hong Kong Special Administrative Region', paras.7.48–7.59 (www.legco.gov.hk/general/english/procedur/companion/chapter_7/chapter_7.html).
[151] Legislative Council, 'A Companion to the History, Rules and Practices of the Legislative Council of the Hong Kong Special Administrative Region', para.15.14 (www.legco.gov.hk/general/english/procedur/companion/chapter_15/chapter_15.html).
[152] See the Ombudsman Ordinance (cap.397); and Legislative Council, 'A Companion to the History, Rules and Practices of the Legislative Council of the Hong Kong Special Administrative Region', para.15.16 (www.legco.gov.hk/general/english/procedur/companion/chapter_15/chapter_15.html).

least one member on duty from each main political party or affiliation or group of members without affiliation.[153] Complaints are made to the Public Complaints Office and sifted by a Complaints Officer, who may seek relevant information from the Government. Complaints are not taken forward where they are not justified, relate to a Government policy or decision that is considered appropriate, or which seek a remedy that cannot be supported. Where a complaint is deemed to be justified, the Member dealing with the complaint may request that the Government take remedial action or, if a policy or legal change is considered necessary, refer the issue to a committee of the Legislative Council or raise the matter at a Legislative Council meeting.[154] Where a complainant is not satisfied with the outcome and requests that the case be referred to another Member, such a request would ordinarily not be entertained unless there was a new aspect to the case that justified otherwise. This was considered to "prevent duplication of efforts and deter abuse of the Redress System".[155]

A number of matters are considered to be outside the scope of the Redress System, namely, court decisions, matters that are sub judice or which could involve criminal charges, and matters relating to judicial or quasi-judicial proceedings; matters outside the jurisdiction of the HKSAR; requests for legal advice or legal services; private disputes; labour disputes between individual employers and employees (except those of wider public concern or which relate to discrimination against trade union leaders); complaints against individual members of the Legislative Council and District Councils; and complaints and matters which are handled by independent or statutory bodies, such as the Independent Commission Against Corruption, Independent Police Complaints Council or Administrative Appeals Board. The House Committee excluded these matters from the scope of the Redress System in recognition of the independence of the judicial system, the existence of a statutory or independent channel for dealing with particular kinds of complaint or appeal, the existence of professional and statutory bodies charged with regulating and overseeing the practice of trades and the conduct and performance of their members, and the jurisdiction of the Legislative Council.[156]

---

[153] *Id.*, para.15.21 (www.legco.gov.hk/general/english/procedur/companion/chapter_15/chapter_15.html).

[154] Legislative Council, *'Legislative Council Secretariat (Handling of Complaints)'* (www.legco.gov.hk/yr99-00/english/panels/hg/papers/a586e02.pdf).

[155] Legislative Council, *'A Companion to the History, Rules and Practices of the Legislative Council of the Hong Kong Special Administrative Region'*, para.15.29. (www.legco.gov.hk/general/english/procedur/companion/chapter_15/chapter_15.html).

[156] *Id.*, paras.15.17–15.18 (www.legco.gov.hk/general/english/procedur/companion/chapter_15/chapter_15.html).

22
Other Remedial Mechanisms

Commissions of Inquiry

A Commission of Inquiry may be set up by the Chief Executive-in-Council to "inquire into the conduct or management of any public body, the conduct of any public officer or into any matter whatsoever" which in the opinion of the Chief Executive-in-Council is "of public importance".[1] Commissions of Inquiry have tended to be set up when there has been a calamity, scandal or cause for significant public concern. Since 1966, the following sixteen Commissions of Inquiry have been appointed:[2]

Table 22.1 Commissions of Inquiry appointed since 1966

Appointing Governor/Chief Executive	Commission of Inquiry	Date of Appointment	Commissioners
Sir David C.C. Trench	The Commission of Inquiry into the Kowloon Disturbances, 1966	3 May 1966	1. Michael Joseph Patrick Hogan 2. Kenneth Lo Ching-kan 3. Lindsay Tasman Ride 4. Maurice Wong Ping-kin
Sir David C.C. Trench	The Commission of Inquiry into the Collapse of Spectator Stand at Sek Kong	27 November 1968	1. W.K. Thomson 2. Lam Chik-ho 3. Yuen Tat-cho
Sir Hugh Norman-Walker (Acting Governor)	The Commission of Inquiry into the Fire on the Jumbo Floating Restaurant	6 November 1971	1. Derek Cons, District Judge (Chair) 2. Raymond Y.K. Kan 3. S.C. Johnson
Sir Murray MacLehose	The Commission of Inquiry into the Rainstorm	22 June 1972	1. Yang Ti-liang, District Judge (Chair)

---

[1] Commissions of Inquiry Ordinance (cap.86), s.2(1).
[2] See Legislative Council Secretariat, *Information Note: Commissions of Inquiry* (IN19/02–03) (www.legco.gov.hk/yr02-03/english/sec/library/0203in19e.pdf).

Other Remedial Mechanisms

Table 22.1 (*cont.*)

Appointing Governor/Chief Executive	Commission of Inquiry	Date of Appointment	Commissioners
	Disasters, 1972		2. S. Mackey 3. Eric Cumine
Sir Murray MacLehose	The Commission of Inquiry into the Case of Peter Fitzroy Godber	13 June 1973	1. Justice Alastair Blair-Kerr, Senior Puisne Judge
Sir Murray MacLehose	The Commission of Inquiry into the Ap Lei Chau Oil Spill	13 November 1973	1. Justice W.E. Collier 2. S. Mackey 3. Peter P.K. Ng
Sir Murray MacLehose	The Commission of Inquiry into the Hong Kong Telephone Company Limited	21 February 1975	1. Sir Alastair Blair-Kerr (Chair) 2. G.M. Macwhinnie 3. J.L. Soong 4. Lydia Dunn 5. C.P. Hung 6. L.K. Ding
Sir Murray MacLehose	The Commission of Inquiry into the Leung Wing-sang Case	6 February 1976	1. Justice T.L. Yang, Judge of the Supreme Court
Sir Murray MacLehose	The Commission of Inquiry into the Accident at Sek Kong Air Strip on 1 July 1977	16 September 1977	1. Justice A. Zimmern, Judge of the High Court
Sir Murray MacLehose	The Commission of Inquiry into Inspector MacLennan's Case	8 July 1980	1. Justice T.L. Yang, Judge of the High Court
Chris Patten	The Commission of Inquiry into Witness Protection	12 January 1993	1. Justice Kempster V-P
Chris Patten	The Commission of Inquiry into the Garley Building Fire	17 December 1996	1. Justice Woo Kwok-hing
Tung Chee-hwa	The Commission of Inquiry on the New Airport	21 July 1998	1. Justice Woo Kwok-hing (Chair) 2. Edgar Cheng Wai-kin
Donald Tsang	The Commission of Inquiry on Allegations relating to the Hong Kong Institute of Education	15 February 2007	1. Justice Wally Yeung Chun-kuen (Chair) 2. Lee Jark Pui
Leung Chun-ying	The Commission of Inquiry into the Collision of Vessels near Lamma Island on 1 October 2012	22 October 2012	1. Justice Michael Victor Lunn (Chair) 2. Benjamin Tang Kwok-bun
Leung Chun-ying	The Commission of Inquiry into Excess Lead Found in Drinking Water	13 August 2015	1. Justice Andrew Chan Hing-wai (Chair) 2. Alan Lai Nin

Governors Sir Edward Youde and Sir David Wilson did not appoint any Commissions of Inquiry, nor (yet) has incumbent Chief Executive, Carrie Lam Cheng Yuet-ngor. Mechanisms for inquiry can be established outside the Commissions of Inquiry statutory framework, such as The Committee of Inquiry on the Sai Wan Ho Development on Inland Lot No. 8955,[3] The Independent Panel of Inquiry on the Incidents Relating to the Equal Opportunities Commission,[4] and The Independent Panel of Inquiry on the Harbour Fest.[5]

Commissions of Inquiry are principally fact-finding mechanisms, and proceedings tend accordingly to be inquisitorial. There will often be a process of information gathering, in both documentary and oral form, typically with one or more hearings. The inquiry is led by one or more Commissioners[6] appointed by the Chief Executive-in-Council, with provision for the appointment of secretaries, a legal adviser and other staff.[7] The Chief Executive-in-Council also sets out the terms of reference for the Commission, which can include the substantive terms of investigation and a timeframe within which the Commission is expected to report. For example, The Commission of Inquiry into Excess Lead Found in Drinking Water was expected to report to the Chief Executive within nine months with the following substantive objectives:

(a) ascertain the causes of excess lead found in drinking water in public rental housing developments;
(b) review and evaluate the adequacy of the present regulatory and monitoring system in respect of drinking water in Hong Kong; and
(c) make recommendations with regard to the safety of drinking water in Hong Kong.[8]

The terms of reference can specifically exclude matters from the scope of the Commission's investigation, such as the provision regarding The Commission of Inquiry on the New Airport that the civil liability of any party for any loss or damage and its quantification should be outside its terms of reference.[9]

---

[3] See Barry Mortimer, Cheng Hon-kwan and Anthony Chan Kin-keung, *Report of the Independent Committee of Inquiry on the Sai Wan Ho Development on Inland Lot No. 8955* (18 April 2006).

[4] See Tam Sheung-wai; Lai Ip Po-Ping, Fanny; and Wu Ting-yuk, Anthony, *Report of the Independent Panel of Inquiry on the Incidents Relating to the Equal Opportunities Commission* (2 February 2005).

[5] See Moses Mo-Chi Cheng and T. Brian Stevenson, *Report of the Independent Panel of Inquiry on the Harbour Fest* (15 May 2004).

[6] It is standard practice for a judge to be appointed as sole Commissioner, or as Chair where more than one Commissioner is appointed.

[7] Commissions of Inquiry Ordinance (cap.86), s.2(2).

[8] Andrew Chan Hing Wai and Alan Lai Nin, *Report of the Commission of Inquiry into Excess Lead Found in Drinking Water* (May 2016), p.5.

[9] Woo Kwok-hing and Edgar Cheng Wai-kin, *Report of the Commission of Inquiry on the New Airport* (January 1999), p.6.

Commissions are invested with broad powers of investigation, including the power to receive materials and evidence, summon persons to give evidence, issue warrants of arrest to compel the attendance of persons not complying with their summonses, administer oaths and affirmations, examine persons on oath or affirmation, enter and inspect any premises, and issue warrants for entering premises and seizing articles and documents.[10] They also have the power to regulate their own procedure within the framework of the Ordinance,[11] and where oral evidence is given, to order that such evidence be given by way of cross-examination without any examination-in-chief.[12] Proceedings of the Commission may be held in private.[13] A person subject to or implicated in the inquiry has a statutory right to be legally represented.[14]

Evidence given by any person before a Commission is not admissible against him or her in civil or criminal proceedings unless such proceedings relate to their being charged with perjury, or where he or she acts in contempt of Commission proceedings.[15] It has been held that witness statements of fact which had been taken pursuant to a Commission of Inquiry could be produced in civil proceedings where those statements were not being used against the persons making the statements.[16] A Commission can be empowered by the Chief Executive-in-Council to deal with contempt of its proceedings and to impose the relevant statutory sentences.[17] In such matters, in addition to giving effect to warrants of arrest, the Commission is invested with the powers of a judge.[18] Commission proceedings are deemed to be judicial proceedings,[19] even though not all Commissioners are judges.[20] The cost of Commission proceedings is charged to the general revenue of Hong Kong.[21]

---

[10] Commissions of Inquiry Ordinance (cap.86), s.4.   [11] *Id.*, s.4(1)(m).   [12] *Id.*, s.5(a).
[13] *Id.*, ss.3(e) and 4(1)(i).   [14] *Id.*, s.6.   [15] *Id.*, ss.7–9.
[16] *Chow Sang Sang Jewellery Co Ltd v Ryoden Lift and Escalator Co Ltd* [2001] HKLRD (Yrbk) 57. This concerned The Commission of Inquiry into the Garley Building Fire. Some of the witnesses had expressed a desire that their statements remain confidential; however the Commissioner ordered disclosure of their statements on the basis that justice and fairness so required. Sakhrani J stated in the case that there were two competing public interests: one in the proper administration of justice by making all relevant material available to litigants which is necessary for the fair disposal of proceedings; the other in not harming society as a whole by disclosing statements which would inhibit the free flow of information to public authorities – *Chow Sang Sang Jewellery Co Ltd v Ryoden Lift and Escalator Co Ltd* [2001] HKLRD (Yrbk) 57, para.12.
[17] Commissions of Inquiry Ordinance (cap.86), ss.3(g) and 9. See also *In the Matter of So Sau-Chung* [1966] HKLR 523.
[18] Commissions of Inquiry Ordinance (cap.86), s.10.
[19] *Id.*, s.11. However, it was held in *In The Matter of So Sau-Chung* [1966] HKLR 523 that Commissioners are not a "court of law", but are an "administrative tribunal appointed by the Governor for a particular purpose, and nothing more" (p.535, per Blair-Kerr J). A statutory oath or affirmation can be required of Commissioners by the Chief Executive-in-Council – Commissions of Inquiry Ordinance (cap.86), s.3(f) and the Schedule.
[20] Though this is not necessarily incongruous, as administrative tribunals, the proceedings of which are often quasi-judicial in nature, are primarily staffed by persons other than judges.
[21] Commissions of Inquiry Ordinance (cap.86), s.14.

The recommendations of Commissions of Inquiry can be implemented through legislative or non-legislative channels.[22] A Commission report can expose malpractice and offences committed,[23] and can be used in subsequent judicial proceedings, including criminal proceedings.[24] It was confirmed that Commissions of Inquiry are susceptible to judicial review, being creatures of statute with "manifestly" public functions and able to affect the rights of individuals who have no avenue of redress provided by the Commissions of Inquiry Ordinance.[25] This applies even though the Commission is not making a "decision" *per se*.[26] It is possible to seek judicial review of a Commission's report findings on the basis of, for example, procedural unfairness.[27] There is no attempted ouster of judicial review of Commission proceedings.[28]

Independent Commission Against Corruption

Corruption is a serious blight on any society, a counterweight to the development of clean, honest, transparent government, an affront to the rule of law and subversive of good community ethics. It can occur from the lowest levels of public administration to the highest levels of government: from an administrator in a public hospital accepting a bribe to move a patient up a waiting list for medical treatment, to a government department awarding a commercial tender to a bidder in return for political patronage. Hong Kong fares well by

---

[22] See, for example, Legislative Council Panel on Economic Development, *The 2017 Policy Address and Policy Agenda: Policy Initiatives of the Transport Branch of the Transport and Housing Bureau*, LC Paper No. CB(4)410/16–17(07), para.28; and Legislative Council Panel on Development, *Briefing by the Secretary for Development on the Chief Executive's 2017 Policy Address and the Overall Land Supply Situation: Follow-up Actions Arising from the Discussion at the Meeting on 24 January 2017*, LC Paper No. CB(1)618/16–17(01), paras.28–36. The Places of Public Entertainment (Amendment) Ordinance 1970 was enacted as a result of recommendations made in the Report of The Commission of Inquiry into the Collapse of the Spectator Stand at Sek Kong. It may be lawful for counsel to a Commission of Inquiry to assist in the drafting of the Commission's report; see *Canada (Attorney-General) v Canada (Commissioner of the Inquiry on the Blood System)* (1997) 142 DLR (4th) 237 (Federal Court of Appeal), noted in *Medical Council of Hong Kong v Helen Chan* (2010) 13 HKCFAR 248, para.49.

[23] See, for example, *HKSAR v So Ping Chi* [2016] HKEC 1399, involving the General Manager and Principal Ship Purveyor of the Local Vessel Safety Section of the Local Vessel Safety Branch of the Marine Department having issued an instruction for the non-enforcement of a lifejacket requirement, for which he was convicted of misconduct in public office. The commission of the offence came to light after investigations conducted by the Transport and Housing Bureau and the Marine Police following the Report of The Commission of Inquiry into the Collision of Vessels near Lamma Island on 1 October 2012.

[24] See, for example, *Cunningham v The Queen* [1977] HKLR 302.

[25] *Secretary for Justice v Commission of Inquiry Re Hong Kong Institute of Education* [2009] 4 HKLRD 11.

[26] See pp.276–279.

[27] See *Re Wong Chi Kin* [2014] HKEC 1590 (though see para.26 for concern about who should be the proper respondent).

[28] Commissions of Inquiry Ordinance (cap.86), s.12(1).

Asian standards, ranked as the joint 13th cleanest jurisdiction of the 180 listed worldwide by the Corruption Perceptions Index 2017 published by Transparency International. This compares favourably with other East Asian jurisdictions, such as Japan (20th), Taiwan (joint 29th), South Korea (51st) and Mainland China (joint 77th). Only Singapore (joint 6th) ranks higher than any other Asian jurisdiction.[29] This suggests that, in comparative terms, anti-corruption mechanisms and practices in Hong Kong are fairly effective.

The Independent Commission Against Corruption (ICAC) is the designated anti-corruption institution in Hong Kong.[30] The ICAC was established in 1974 in the wake of the findings of the Commission of Inquiry into the Case of Peter Fitzroy Godber and public outrage over the incident.[31] Prior to the establishment of the ICAC, anti-corruption work was to a great extent in the hands of the police, which was for a significant period itself troubled by corruption. Whilst anti-corruption legislation could be found in Hong Kong as long ago as in 1898,[32] it was with the establishment and development of the ICAC that the fight against corruption entered a new era in the jurisdiction.

The ICAC is a statutory body,[33] but also has a footing in the Basic Law which stipulates that it shall function independently and be accountable to the Chief Executive.[34] The Commissioner Against Corruption is appointed by the Central People's Government on the nomination of the Chief Executive.[35] A person is eligible for appointment as Commissioner only if he is a permanent resident with Chinese citizenship and no right of abode in a foreign country.[36] On point of accountability to the Chief Executive, it is statutorily provided that the Commissioner shall be subject to the orders and control of the Chief Executive, that he shall not be subject to the direction or control of any person other than the Chief Executive, and that he shall hold office on such terms and conditions as the Chief Executive may think fit.[37] The Commissioner has the power to regulate the administration and finances of the Commission by way of Commission standing orders,[38] giving relative financial autonomy, which is an important aspect of structural independence. The ICAC is subject to accounting and audit requirements,[39] and the Commissioner is required to

---

[29] Transparency International, *Corruption Perceptions Index 2017*.
[30] The Competition Commission also performs a role in this regard, for example in relation to bid-rigging and other anti-competitive conduct under the Competition Ordinance (cap.619).
[31] Peter Godber was a Police Chief Superintendent who absconded from Hong Kong whilst under criminal investigation, apparently taking advantage of his position when absconding.
[32] Misdemeanours Punishment Ordinance 1898.
[33] Independent Commission Against Corruption Ordinance (cap.204). [34] Basic Law, Art.57.
[35] *Id.*, Art.48(5). The Commissioner has the power to appoint such other officers as the Chief Executive thinks necessary to assist the Commissioner in the performance of his functions under the Ordinance – Independent Commission Against Corruption Ordinance (cap.204), s.8.
[36] Basic Law, Art.101.
[37] Independent Commission Against Corruption Ordinance (cap.204), s.5. It is provided in s.12 that the Commissioner exercises a number of duties "on behalf of the Chief Executive".
[38] *Id.*, s.11. [39] *Id.*, ss.15–16.

submit an annual report to the Chief Executive which shall be laid before the Legislative Council.[40]

The ICAC had, at the time of writing, around thirteen hundred staff. Under the leadership of the Commissioner Against Corruption is an Operations Department, a Corruption Prevention Department and a Community Relations Department, described as a three-pronged approach. The Operations Department is the law enforcement arm of the ICAC, receiving complaints about alleged corruption and conducting investigations into alleged or suspected offences such as those under the Independent Commission Against Corruption Ordinance (cap.204), the Prevention of Bribery Ordinance (cap.201) and the Elections (Corrupt and Illegal Conduct) Ordinance (cap.554).[41] The Operations Department is split between four Investigation Branches (with a further for internal investigations), two under the leadership of the Director of Investigation (Government Sector) and two under the leadership of the Director of Investigation (Private Sector). An officer authorised by the Commissioner may without warrant arrest a person if he reasonably suspects one or more of certain offences to have been committed, including bribery, electoral offences or blackmail.[42] The officer has the power of search and seizure,[43] and to take fingerprints, photographs and samples.[44] It is a criminal offence to resist or obstruct an officer,[45] make a false report to an officer,[46] or falsely pretend to be an officer.[47] Decisions on whether to prosecute are made by the Secretary for Justice.

To take the example of specific investigatory powers conferred under the Prevention of Bribery Ordinance (cap.201), the Commissioner has the power to authorise an officer to investigate a suspected offence and can, with leave of the Court of First Instance, require a person to, for example, produce accounts, books, documents, articles and so on.[48] The Inland Revenue Department can in certain circumstances, on an application by the Commissioner or an investigating officer with the approval of the Commissioner or the Deputy Commissioner, be ordered by the Court of First Instance to produce or give access to materials relevant to a suspected offence under the Ordinance.[49] The Commissioner or an investigating officer may apply *ex parte* to the Court of First Instance in chambers for an order requiring the provision of information by a person suspected of having committed an offence under the Ordinance and/or other relevant persons, including a statement enumerating property, its means of acquisition, expenditure and liabilities. Public bodies can also be required to provide documents, and banks to provide copies of accounts,

---

[40] *Id.*, s.17.   [41] *Id.*, s.12.
[42] *Id.*, s.10. The procedure after arrest is detailed in s.10A, including the arrested person being taken to a police station or to the Commission offices, where the person may be detained.
[43] *Id.*, s.10C; see also *id.*, s.10B.   [44] *Id.*, ss.10D–10G.   [45] *Id.*, s.13A.   [46] *Id.*, s.13B.
[47] *Id.*, s.13C.
[48] Prevention of Bribery Ordinance (cap.201), s.13. See also Independent Commission Against Corruption Ordinance (cap.204), s.13.
[49] Prevention of Bribery Ordinance (cap.201), s.13A.

relevant to the case.[50] The most high-profile investigation undertaken by the ICAC to date has been that into former Chief Executive Donald Tsang, who was in 2017 convicted of misconduct in public office.[51]

The Corruption Prevention Department examines the practices and procedures of government departments and public bodies and secures revision of any that may be conducive to corruption. It also advises private organisations and individuals on anti-corruption measures, on request. The Community Relations Department performs corruption education and information work and raises public awareness of the relevant issues.

The most recent ICAC Annual Report discloses that 2,891 corruption complaints were received for the year under review, in addition to 858 election-related complaints.[52] 1,906 new non-election cases and 808 new election cases were handled.[53] 199 persons were prosecuted and 31 formally cautioned, of which 10 were government servants (of which three were from the Hong Kong Police Force), four were from public bodies, and 163 were from the private sector.[54] Of the 199 prosecutions, 139 were made under the Independent Commission Against Corruption Ordinance (cap.204), 58 were made under the Prevention of Bribery Ordinance (cap.201), and two were made in relation to election offences. Reports were made on the recommendation of the Operations Review Committee to the Secretary for Civil Service on alleged misconduct committed by 55 government servants, compared to 90 in the preceding year.[55]

Equal Opportunities Commission

The Equal Opportunities Commission is a statutory body charged with the task of tackling discrimination on the basis of sex, disability, family status and race. It was established in 1996 by the Sex Discrimination Ordinance (cap.480),[56] but its powers are rooted in four principal statutory regimes.[57] The Commission comprises a chairperson and between four and sixteen members, each appointed by the Chief Executive.[58] The Commission is not

---

[50] Id., s.14.   [51] Though proceedings continue at the time of writing.
[52] Independent Commission Against Corruption, *Annual Report 2016*, p.36.   [53] Id., p.38.
[54] Id., pp.39 and 99.   [55] Id., p.41.
[56] Sex Discrimination Ordinance (cap.480), s.63. There are various exemptions from the scope of the Ordinance, perhaps most notably any discrimination between males and females arising from the Government's Small House Policy, pursuant to which benefits relating to land in the New Territories are granted to male indigenous villagers – id., s.62 and Sch.5, Part 2. For background, see Carole J. Petersen, '*Equal Opportunities: A New Field of Law for Hong Kong*' in Raymond Wacks (ed), *The New Legal Order in Hong Kong* (Hong Kong University Press, 1999), pp.595–599.
[57] Namely the Sex Discrimination Ordinance (cap.480) (SDO), Disability Discrimination Ordinance (cap.487) (DDO), Family Status Discrimination Ordinance (cap.527) (FSDO), and Race Discrimination Ordinance (cap.602) (RDO).
[58] SDO, s.63(3).

to be regarded as a servant or agent of the Government or as enjoying any status, immunity or privilege of the Government.[59]

The Commission may issue codes of practice for the elimination of discrimination, the promotion of equality of opportunity, and the elimination of harassment and vilification.[60] This must be published in the Gazette and tabled in the Legislative Council (except in relation to family status discrimination),[61] which may amend one of the codes of practice.[62] The codes of practice are not primary or subsidiary legislation, yet they may be amended by the legislature. It is stated that failure by a person to observe any provision in a code of practice (except in relation to family status discrimination) shall not in itself render him liable to any proceedings, but the code may be used in evidence in proceedings under the Ordinance, and the court "shall" take a provision of the code into account in determining any question to which the provision appears to be relevant.[63]

The Commission has the power to conduct a formal investigation, either on its own motion or when so required by the Chief Secretary for Administration.[64] The terms of reference of such an investigation must be drawn up by the Commission, or the Chief Secretary for Administration after consulting the Commission (where he requires an investigation by the Commission).[65] Where an investigation is confined to the activities of a specific person and the Commission proposes to investigate any act of that person which is unlawful under the Ordinance, the Commission must inform that person and offer him or her an opportunity to make oral and/or written representations.[66] If the person makes oral representations, he or she has a right to be represented by counsel, a solicitor or another person of his choice (the latter subject to the Commission objecting on the ground of unsuitability).[67] The Commission has the power to obtain information, require the production of documents, and require a person to provide oral information at a specified time and place.[68] Failure to comply with a notice requiring such information can result in an order of compliance or direction from the District Court.[69] Alteration of a document of which production has been required, or knowingly or recklessly

---

[59] Id., s.63(7).
[60] Id., s.69(1); DDO, s.65(1); FSDO, s.47(1); RDO, s.63(1).
[61] SDO, s.69(4); DDO, s.65(4); RDO, s.63(4).
[62] SDO, s.69(5); DDO, s.65(5); RDO, s.63(5).
[63] SDO, s.69(14); DDO, s.65(13); RDO, s.63(14).
[64] SDO, s.70; DDO, s.66; FSDO, s.48; RDO, s.64.
[65] SDO, s.71(2); DDO, s.67(2); FSDO, s.49(2); RDO, s.65(2).
[66] SDO, s.71(4); DDO, s.67(4); FSDO, s.49(4); RDO, s.65(4).
[67] SDO, s.71(4); DDO, s.67(4); FSDO, s.49(4); RDO, s.65(5).
[68] SDO, s.72(1); Sex Discrimination (Formal Investigations) Rules (cap.480A), s.5 and Sch.1; DDO, s.68(1); Disability Discrimination (Formal Investigations) Rules (cap.487A), s.5 and Sch.1; FSDO, s.50(1); Family Status Discrimination (Formal Investigations) Rules (cap.527B), s.5 and Sch.1; RDO, s.66(1); Race Discrimination (Formal Investigations) Rules (cap.602A), s.5 and Sch.1.
[69] SDO, s.72(4); DDO, s.68(4); FSDO, s.50(4); RDO, s.66(5).

making a statement which is materially false or misleading, is an offence carrying a fine at level 4.[70]

At the conclusion of an investigation, the Commission must produce a report.[71] It may recommend that a person changes their policies or procedures, or make recommendations to the Chief Secretary for Administration such as proposed changes in the law.[72] The report is published or made available for inspection,[73] unless the investigation was one required by the Chief Secretary for Administration in which case the Commission shall deliver the report to him.[74] It is then for the Chief Secretary for Administration to decide in what manner the report shall be published, and whether the Commission shall publish the report.[75] Confidentiality restrictions apply.[76]

In addition to its powers of investigation, the Commission has the power to issue enforcement notices. A notice can be served in the course of an investigation ordering a person not to commit certain acts, namely unlawful discriminatory acts, unlawful acts of harassment, or a contravention of sections of the Ordinance prohibiting various other discriminatory acts and practices.[77] This can include an order to discontinue or change a practice or arrangement.[78] A person on whom an enforcement notice is served may appeal against the notice to the District Court.[79] The Commission is required to keep a register of enforcement notices which are open to public inspection.[80] It also has the power to apply in certain circumstances (essentially situations of persistent discrimination, harassment or vilification) for an injunction restraining a person from committing the acts which may be the subject of an enforcement notice.[81]

The Commission can also provide assistance to persons claiming to have suffered discrimination or harassment, including assistance in the formulation and presentation of their case in proceedings, the provision of advice and

---

[70] SDO, s.72(5); DDO, s.68(5); FSDO, s.50(5); RDO, s.66(6) and (7).
[71] SDO, s.73(2); DDO, s.69(2); FSDO, s.51(2); RDO, s.67(2).
[72] SDO, s.73(1); DDO, s.69(1); FSDO, s.51(1); RDO, s.67(1).
[73] SDO, s.73(5); DDO, s.69(5); FSDO, s.51(5); RDO, s.67(5).
[74] SDO, s.73(3); DDO, s.69(3); FSDO, s.51(3); RDO, s.67(3).
[75] SDO, s.73(3); DDO, s.69(3); FSDO, s.51(3); RDO, s.67(3).
[76] SDO, s.74; DDO, s.70; FSDO, s.52; RDO, s.68.
[77] SDO, ss.42–45; DDO, ss.41–47; FSDO, ss.30–33; RDO, ss.41–45.
[78] SDO, s.77(2); Sex Discrimination (Formal Investigations) Rules (cap.480A), s.6 and Sch.2; DDO, s.73(2); Disability Discrimination (Formal Investigations) Rules (cap.487A), s.6 and Sch.2; FSDO, s.55(2); Family Status Discrimination (Formal Investigations) Rules (cap.527B), s.6 and Sch.2; RDO, s.71(2); Race Discrimination (Formal Investigations) Rules (cap.602A), s.6 and Sch.2.
[79] SDO, s.78; DDO, s.74; FSDO, s.56; RDO, s.72.
[80] SDO, s.80; DDO, s.76; FSDO, s.58; RDO, s.74.
[81] SDO, ss.81–82; DDO, ss.77–78; FSDO, ss.59–60; RDO, ss.75–76. The Commission can also apply in certain circumstances for the imposition of a financial penalty not exceeding HK$10,000 for the first occasion on which a penalty is imposed, and HK$30,000 for the second and any subsequent occasion on which a penalty is imposed in respect of the same person (SDO, s.82(5) and (6); DDO, s.78(5) and (6); FSDO, s.60(5) and (6); RDO, s.76(5) and (6)).

arranging for legal representation.[82] It can also, on receipt of a complaint, attempt to effect a settlement by means of conciliation between the parties.[83] Conciliation is free of charge and is aimed at securing a mutually acceptable conciliation agreement signed by both parties and treated as binding.[84] The Commission may, in the context of conciliation, set up a conference to be held in private. The legislation allows for considerable procedural flexibility in this regard. A person is not generally entitled to be represented by another at the conference unless the person presiding at the conference so consents. A person who has been directed to attend the conference and fails to attend, without reasonable excuse, commits an offence and is liable on conviction to a fine at level 4. If the person presiding at the conference determines that the matter cannot be settled by conciliation, that the attempt to settle the matter by conciliation has been unsuccessful, or that the matter is such that it should be referred to the Commission, then he is required to refer the matter to the Commission with a report relating to the investigation.[85]

It is provided that the Commission may decide not to conduct an investigation, or to discontinue an investigation, if satisfied that the act complained of is not unlawful under the Ordinance, the person aggrieved by the act does not desire for the investigation to be conducted or to continue, a period exceeding twelve months has elapsed since the act occurred, a representative complaint should not be classed as such, or it is of the opinion that the complaint is frivolous, vexatious, misconceived or lacking in substance.[86] In any of these circumstances, the complainant has a statutory right to be notified of the decision and to receive reasons for it.[87] The Commission states that respondents are "given every opportunity to provide information to refute the allegations and/or to claim an exception if applicable".[88] Complainants also

---

[82] SDO, ss.83 and 85; DDO, ss.79 and 81; FSDO, ss.61 and 63; RDO, ss.77 and 79.
[83] SDO, s.84(3)(b); DDO, s.80(3)(b); FSDO, s.62(3)(b); RDO, s.78(3)(b).
[84] Equal Opportunities Commission, *Complaint Handling Procedures: Information for Complainant* (July 2016), p.4.
[85] Sex Discrimination (Investigation and Conciliation) Rules (cap.480B), ss.7–8; Disability Discrimination (Investigation and Conciliation) Rules (cap.487B), ss.7–8; Family Status Discrimination (Investigation and Conciliation) Rules (cap.527A), ss.7–8; Race Discrimination (Investigation and Conciliation) Rules (cap.602B), ss.7–8.
[86] SDO, s.84(4); DDO, s.80(4); FSDO, s.62(4); RDO, s.78(4). On representative complaints, see the Sex Discrimination (Investigation and Conciliation) Rules (cap.480B), ss.3–4; Disability Discrimination (Investigation and Conciliation) Rules (cap.487B), ss.3–4; Family Status Discrimination (Investigation and Conciliation) Rules (cap.527A), ss.3–4; and the Race Discrimination (Investigation and Conciliation) Rules (cap.602B), ss.3–4.
[87] SDO, s.84(5); DDO, s.80(5); FSDO, s.62(5); RDO, s.78(5).
[88] Equal Opportunities Commission, *Complaint Handling Procedures: Information for Respondent* (December 2013), p.1. It is stated (p.2) that the type of information which a respondent may offer to the Commission in relation to an allegation arising out of employment may, for example, include performance appraisal reports, counselling notes, evidence of warnings, interview summaries and reports, interview questions, a copy of the job advertisement, duty statement, list of job criteria, equal opportunity policy, sexual harassment policy and grievance procedures.

have the right, within twenty-four months of the occurrence of the act subject to the complaint (or later if the District Court considers that in the circumstances of the case it is just and equitable to admit the complaint[89]), to institute civil proceedings in the District Court.[90]

The most recently published figures covering a full reporting year (2016–2017) disclose that a total of 607 complaints were received in that year. Thirty-five per cent were made under the Disability Discrimination Ordinance (mostly employment-related), 33 per cent under the Race Discrimination Ordinance (overwhelmingly non-employment-related), 30 per cent under the Sex Discrimination Ordinance (mostly employment-related), and 2 per cent under the Family Status Discrimination Ordinance (all employment-related).

Conciliation was attempted in just over 38 per cent of cases, with a success rate of 71 per cent compared to 67 per cent in the previous year. Two per cent of cases were resolved early. Forty-eight per cent of cases were discontinued due to a lack of substance, whilst 10 per cent were withdrawn by the complainant and 2 per cent were discontinued for other reasons. The Commission initiated thirty-five investigations into incidents involving unlawful acts, the majority under the Disability Discrimination Ordinance, mainly on accessibility and service provision. The Commission handled twenty-three applications for legal assistance under the Sex Discrimination Ordinance (of which just over 38 per cent were successful), twenty-five under the Disability Discrimination Ordinance (of which 40 per cent were successful), one under the Family Status Discrimination Ordinance (which was unsuccessful), and two under the Race Discrimination Ordinance (of which 50 per cent were successful).[91]

Privacy Commissioner for Personal Data

The Privacy Commissioner for Personal Data is a statutory corporation sole, established in 1996. He plays an important role in the supervision of personal data handling, including personal data handled by public bodies. His functions and powers are to:

(a) monitor and supervise compliance with the provisions of [the] Ordinance;
(b) promote and assist bodies representing data users to prepare ... codes of practice for guidance in complying with the provisions of [the] Ordinance, in particular the data protection principles;
(c) promote awareness and understanding of, and compliance with, the provisions of [the] Ordinance, in particular the data protection principles;

---

[89] SDO, s.86(3); DDO, s.82(3); FSDO, s.64(4); RDO, s.80(4).
[90] SDO, ss.76 and 86; DDO, ss.72 and 82; FSDO, ss.54 and 64; RDO, ss.70 and 80.
[91] Equal Opportunities Commission, *Moving Forward: A Renewed Commitment to Equality, 2016/17 Annual Report*.

(d) examine any proposed legislation (including subsidiary legislation) that the Commissioner considers may affect the privacy of individuals in relation to personal data and report the results of the examination to the person proposing the legislation;
(e) carry out inspections, including inspections of any personal data systems used by data users which are departments of the Government or statutory corporations;
(f) for the better performance of his other functions, undertake research into, and monitor developments in, the processing of data and information technology in order to take account of any likely adverse effects such developments may have on the privacy of individuals in relation to personal data;
(g) liaise and co-operate with any person in any place outside Hong Kong –
   (i) performing in that place any functions which, in the opinion of the Commissioner, are similar (whether in whole or in part) to any of the Commissioner's functions under this Ordinance; and
   (ii) in respect of matters of mutual interest concerning the privacy of individuals in relation to personal data; and
(h) perform such other functions as are imposed on him under this Ordinance or any other enactment.[92]

The Commissioner is appointed by the Chief Executive for a period of five years and is eligible for reappointment for not more than one further period of five years.[93] The pay and terms and conditions of the Commissioner's appointment are determined by the Chief Executive.[94] Nevertheless, the Commissioner is not to be regarded as a servant or agent of the Government or as enjoying any status, immunity or privilege of the Government.[95] He may be removed from office by the Chief Executive only with the approval by resolution of the Legislative Council in the event of the Commissioner's inability to perform the functions of his office or misbehaviour.[96] He may employ staff and determine their employment, remuneration, pension and welfare arrangements,[97] and is supported by a Personal Data (Privacy) Advisory Committee of (in addition to the Commissioner) four to eight persons appointed by the Secretary for Constitutional and Mainland Affairs of whom at least one shall have five or more years of experience in data processing.[98]

---

[92] Personal Data (Privacy) Ordinance (cap.486), s.8(1). The six data protection principles are: (i) purpose and manner of collection of personal data, (ii) accuracy and duration of retention of personal data, (iii) use of personal data, (iv) security of personal data, (v) general availability of information, and (vi) access to personal data – *id.*, Sch.1.
[93] *Id.*, s.5(3) and (4).   [94] *Id.*, s.5(6).   [95] *Id.*, s.5(8).   [96] *Id.*, s.5(5)(b).   [97] *Id.*, s.9.
[98] *Id.*, s.11.

The Commissioner may issue codes of practice, notice of which is recorded in the Gazette.[99] Failure to comply with a provision in a code of practice does not in itself give rise to liability, but any provision in a code of practice which appears to a specified body[100] to be relevant to a requirement in the Ordinance which has allegedly been breached shall be admissible in evidence.[101] The Commissioner also keeps and maintains a register of data users.[102] He operates a system of inspections, complaints and investigations, and may inspect any personal data system used by a data user to assist him in making recommendations to the data user.[103]

A person may submit a complaint to the Commissioner in relation to data use.[104] The Commissioner shall carry out an investigation where he receives a complaint, and may carry out an investigation where has reasonable grounds to believe that an act or practice may contravene a requirement of the Ordinance in relation to personal data.[105] The Commissioner has discretion to refuse to carry out an investigation, or terminate an existing investigation, initiated by complaint in various circumstances including where the complainant had actual knowledge of the act or practice complained of for more than two years between the act or practice concerned and the Commissioner receiving the complaint, where the complaint is made anonymously, the complainant cannot be identified or traced, or the Commissioner is satisfied that the relevant data user has not been a data user for at least two years immediately preceding the date on which the Commissioner received the complaint.[106] He also has discretion to refuse to carry out an investigation, or terminate an existing investigation, initiated by complaint where the complaint (or a complaint substantially similar in nature) has previously been determined not to have contravened a requirement of the Ordinance, the act or practice complained of is trivial, the complaint is frivolous or vexatious or not made in good faith, the primary subject matter of the complaint is not related to personal data privacy, or investigation is for any other reason unnecessary.[107] In any of these circumstances, the Commissioner must notify the complainant of the refusal together with reasons therefor.[108] The complainant has a statutory right of appeal to the Administrative Appeals Board against such a decision.[109]

The Commissioner may, where he deems it to be in the public interest, carry out or continue an investigation even if the complainant has withdrawn the complaint.[110] The Commissioner may convene a hearing to take place in public unless he determines that it should be held in private or the

---

[99] *Id.*, s.12. There is a consultation requirement imposed on the Commissioner under s.12(9) in relation to the approval or revision of a code of practice.
[100] Namely a magistrate, court, the Administrative Appeals Board or the chair of the Administrative Appeals Board.
[101] Personal Data (Privacy) Ordinance (cap.486), s.13. [102] *Id.*, s.15. [103] *Id.*, s.36.
[104] *Id.*, s.37. [105] *Id.*, s.38. [106] *Id.*, s.39(1). [107] *Id.*, s.39(2).
[108] *Id.*, s.39(3) and (3A). [109] *Id.*, s.39(4). [110] *Id.*, s.40.

complainant (if any) requests in writing that the investigation be conducted in private.[111] There is no statutory right to a hearing before the Commissioner,[112] and no general right to have legal representatives address any such hearing.[113] Nevertheless, a person who may be criticised or adversely affected by a report or recommendation of the Commissioner must be given an opportunity to be heard.[114] The Commissioner may obtain information and other evidence and summon witnesses,[115] and may enter premises for the purposes of inspection or investigation.[116] He also has the power to administer oaths.[117] There is a statutory duty of secrecy on the Commissioner and other prescribed officers which it is an offence to violate without lawful excuse.[118] It is also an offence, liable on conviction to a fine at level 3 and imprisonment for six months, for a person to without lawful excuse obstruct, hinder or resist the Commissioner or a prescribed officer in the performance of their functions or powers, or to fail to comply with their lawful requirements, or to make a false or misleading statement to them.[119]

At the conclusion of an inspection or investigation, the Commissioner may make recommendations to the relevant data user.[120] The complainant is also informed of the recommendations where the investigation is initiated by complaint,[121] unless the complaint has been withdrawn.[122] The Commissioner may serve an enforcement notice on a data user where the data user has failed to comply with a requirement of the Ordinance.[123] The complainant may appeal to the Administrative Appeals Board against the Commissioner's decision, including the decision not to serve an enforcement notice on the data user.[124] Appeal can also be made to the Administrative Appeals Board against an enforcement notice.[125] The Commissioner may publish a report following an inspection setting out his recommendations,[126] and may publish a report following an investigation setting out the result of the investigation, any recommendations and other relevant comments.[127] Reports must not reveal the identity of individuals except that of the Commissioner, a prescribed officer and the data user.[128] Failure to comply with an enforcement notice attracts substantial penalties. On a first conviction there is a fine at level 5 and imprisonment for two years and, if the offence continues post-conviction, a daily penalty of HK$1,000. On a second or subsequent conviction, there is

---

[111] *Id.*, s.43(2).   [112] *Id.*, s.43(4).   [113] *Id.*, s.43(3).   [114] *Id.*, s.43(5).
[115] *Id.*, ss.43(1)(a) and 44–45.   [116] *Id.*, s.42.   [117] *Id.*, s.44(7).   [118] *Id.*, s.46.
[119] *Id.*, s.50B.   [120] *Id.*, s.47.   [121] *Id.*, s.47(3).   [122] *Id.*, s.47(3A).   [123] *Id.*, s.50.
[124] *Id.*, s.47(4). 28 cases appealed to the Administrative Appeals Board were concluded during the reporting year 2016–2017, of which 11 per cent were partly successful, 61 per cent were unsuccessful and 28 per cent were withdrawn – Annual Report of the Commissioner (2016–2017), p.83.
[125] Personal Data (Privacy) Ordinance (cap.486), s.50(7).   [126] *Id.*, s.48(1).   [127] *Id.*, s.48(2).
[128] *Id.*, s.48(3) and (4). The provisions of sections 47 and 48 do not apply in some cases – see *id.*, s.49.

a fine at level 6 and imprisonment for two years, and a daily penalty of HK$2,000 if the offence continues post-conviction.[129]

There are important exemptions from requirements in the Ordinance. These include exemptions for personal data held by or on behalf of the Government for the purposes of safeguarding security, defence or international relations,[130] personal data held for the purposes of crime prevention or detection and tax assessment or collection,[131] in certain circumstances personal data relating to physical or mental health,[132] certain personal data relating to the care and guardianship of minors,[133] personal data covered by legal professional privilege,[134] circumstances potentially leading to self-incrimination (except under the Ordinance),[135] where data is to be used exclusively for preparing statistics or carrying out research,[136] certain due diligence exercises,[137] and for certain purposes where records are transferred to the Government Records Service and the records are used.[138]

The volume of complaints made each year to the Commissioner has significantly increased. The most recently published annual report for the Commissioner states that 1,741 complaints were received for the year, representing a 14 per cent decrease on the immediately preceding year; and that 256 compliance checks were carried out, representing a 10.5 per cent decrease from the immediately preceding year.[139] Of the 1,741 complaints received, 72 per cent were complaints against private sector organisations, 17 per cent were against individuals, and 11 per cent were against public sector organisations.[140] The three areas in which complaints were most commonly made against public sector organisations were electioneering, the police, and hospital and health services.[141] 26 per cent of complaints against public sector organisations involved the lack of security measures to protect personal data; 25 per cent involved the use or disclosure of personal data beyond the scope of the collection purpose and without the consent of the individual; and 20 per cent involved the excessive or unfair collection of personal data.[142] 78 per cent of compliance checks were conducted on private sector organisations, whilst 22 per cent were conducted on government departments, statutory bodies, non-government organisations and government-funded educational institutions.[143]

The outcome of complaints against private sector organisations, individuals and public sector organisations appear to have been aggregated in the annual report. 41 per cent were completed after preliminary enquiries (e.g. through conciliation or mediation, or by expressing the complainants' concerns to the

---

[129] *Id.*, s.50A. [130] *Id.*, s.57. See also *id.*, s.58A. [131] *Id.*, s.58. [132] *Id.*, s.59.
[133] *Id.*, s.59A. [134] *Id.*, s.60. [135] *Id.*, s.60A. [136] *Id.*, s.62. [137] *Id.*, s.63B.
[138] *Id.*, s.63D.
[139] Annual Report of the Commissioner (2016–2017), p.7. The annual number of complaint cases for the immediately preceding three years were 2,022 (2015–2016), 1,690 (2014–2015) and 1,888 (2013–2014); see Annual report of the Commissioner (2016–2017), p.54.
[140] *Id.*, p.49. [141] *Id.*, p.51. [142] *Id.*
[143] Annual Report of the Commissioner (2016–2017), p.33.

parties complained against); 25 per cent were closed because the complaints were anonymous, the parties complained against were not traceable or the complainants did not respond to the Commissioner's enquiries after being invited to elaborate on their allegations; 12 per cent were withdrawn by the complainants; 9 per cent were outside the jurisdiction of the Ordinance; 7 per cent were completed after the carrying out of formal investigations; and 6 per cent were transferred to the police for criminal investigation.[144] Of the 133 formal investigations completed during the reporting period, 3 per cent were found to have contravened provisions of the Ordinance with the issuance of enforcement notices; 1 per cent was found to have contravened data protection principles with the issuance of an enforcement notice; 1 per cent was found not to have contravened provisions of the Ordinance; 2 per cent were transferred to the police for criminal investigation; and 93 per cent were discontinued for various reasons.[145] Parties complained against were directed to take remedial actions including the revision of operational practices to prevent similar data breach in the future; proper guidance to be given to staff to ensure compliance with the Ordinance; the supply or correction of personal data or the reduction of the fee for complying with data access requests; the deletion of personal data unnecessarily collected or disclosed to third parties; remedial actions which met the complainants' privacy expectations; and undertakings to cease malpractice leading to complaints.[146]

A finding of interest in the annual report for the immediately preceding year relates to ten commonly used sets of public registers maintained by the Government and public bodies, namely the Bankruptcy Register, Births Register, Business Register, Companies Register, Land Registers, Marriage Register, Register of Notice of Intended Marriage, Securities and Futures Commission Register of Licensed Persons, Register of Vehicles, and Registers of Electors. The Government created guidelines on 30 December 2000 on the protection of personal data in relation to public registers. The Commissioner conducted research to establish the extent to which the registers complied with the Government's own guidelines, including an examination of 82 register-related instances of legislation enacted or amended during the period 1 January 2001 to 31 March 2014.

The Commissioner's research produced some illuminating findings. Only 39 per cent of register-related legislative enactments detailed the purposes of the publication of data and/or the permissible secondary use of such data, and only 6 per cent contained explicit provisions introducing measures to safeguard against possible misuse of personal data. Furthermore, only four of the ten sets of registers aforementioned had the purposes of the register specified in the relevant legislation; only one of the registers had legislative safeguards against misuse of data, and only one of the remaining nine registers provided

---

[144] Annual Report of the Commissioner (2016–2017), p.55.   [145] *Id.*, p.56.   [146] *Id.*, p.57.

for administrative safeguards against misuse of data. The Commissioner described this as "particularly worrying as most of the operators of the registers have no discretion to reject a request for data access".[147] In addition, for two out of the three registers in relation to which the operators had discretion to decide on the provision of specific kinds of personal data upon request, there were no policies set out governing the exercise of that discretion.

The Commissioner concluded that although the registers were generally administered in accordance with the law, there was "room for improvement" and the "lack of a purpose specified in the establishing legislation for the public registers posed an enforcement hurdle for the Commissioner". The Commissioner recommended that the Government establish a dedicated organisational structure and mechanism to oversee and monitor compliance by Government bureaux and departments with its own guidelines. He also recommended that a personal data clearance clause be introduced to the law drafting process (in line with the human rights clearance clause and Basic Law clearance clause), and that the Department of Justice be given a gatekeeper role to ensure that serious consideration would be given in future legislative enactment or amendment processes to the incorporation of specific purposes of public registers.[148]

Audit Commission

The Audit Commission is a statutory body charged with the function of auditing public sector finances. The present institution builds on a long tradition of public audit in Hong Kong, the first Auditor-General having been appointed in 1844. The current statutory framework was enacted in 1971, and in 1978 the Public Accounts Committee (PAC) of the Legislative Council was established to receive reports of the Director of Audit on the accounts of Government and other bodies. The PAC has the status of a standing committee of the Legislative Council.[149] It consists of a chair, deputy chair and five members who are each members of the Legislative Council appointed by the President in accordance with an election procedure determined by the House Committee.[150] PAC meetings are generally open to the public,[151] and matters are decided by majority vote.[152] The PAC or its chair have the power to invite any public officer or other relevant person to produce information or an explanation in relation to the matters within its remit.[153]

The Director of Audit is appointed by the Central People's Government on the nomination of the Chief Executive.[154] A person must, in order to be eligible for appointment as Director of Audit, be a Chinese citizen who is a permanent resident of the HKSAR with no right of abode in any foreign

---

[147] Annual Report of the Commissioner (2015–2016), p.81.   [148] *Id.*, pp.81–82.
[149] Rules of Procedure of the Legislative Council, r.72(1).   [150] *Id.*, r.72(3).   [151] *Id.*, r.72(5).
[152] *Id.*, r.72(3C).   [153] *Id.*, r.72(8).   [154] Basic Law, Art.48(5).

country and having ordinarily resided in Hong Kong for a continuous period of not less than fifteen years.[155] There is no fixed term of appointment for the Director, who can be dismissed or required to retire from office, in which case a full statement of the circumstances surrounding his or her dismissal or retirement must be made at the first opportunity to the Legislative Council.[156] The salary of the Director is determined by the Chief Executive.[157]

The principal duties of the Director are to:

(a) examine, inquire into and audit the accounts of all accounting officers in respect of public moneys, stamps, securities, stores and any other Government property; and
(b) examine, inquire into and audit the accounts, statements and records kept in respect of the accounts or funds specified in column 2 of Schedule 1 by the public officers specified opposite such accounts or funds.[158]

The Director's powers include requiring public officers to provide information or explanations, and searching and taking extracts from Government books, documents and records.[159] In addition to the Basic Law's provision for the Audit Commission's independence of function,[160] it is statutorily provided that the Director shall not be subject to the direction or control of any other person or authority.[161] The Director is supported by other staff,[162] at present numbering 193 from directorate rank to clerical grades.[163]

The Director of Accounting Services is required, within five months or such longer period as the Chief Executive may determine, to transmit to the Director of Audit a statement of the assets and liabilities of the Government, an annual statement of the receipts and payments by the Government, a statement of the assets and liabilities of certain other funds, a statement of the receipts and payments of certain other funds, and such other statements as the Chief Executive may determine.[164] Following the Director's examination and audit of the statements, he must, within seven months or such longer period as the Chief Executive may determine, prepare and submit to the President of the Legislative Council a report on those statements.[165] Within one month of the President receiving the report and statements, or such longer period as the President may determine, copies thereof are laid before the Legislative Council and submitted to the Government.[166] Within three months of the copies of the report and statements being laid before the Legislative

---

[155] *Id.*, Arts.61 and 101. [156] Audit Ordinance (cap.122), s.4. [157] *Id.*, s.4A.
[158] *Id.*, s.8(1). [159] *Id.*, s.9.
[160] Basic Law, Art.58 states: "A Commission of Audit shall be established in the Hong Kong Special Administrative Region. It shall function independently and be accountable to the Chief Executive".
[161] Audit Ordinance (cap.122), s.9(3). [162] See *id.*, s.10.
[163] Audit Commission, 'About Us' (revised 22 November 2017) (www.aud.gov.hk/eng/aboutus/about_org.htm).
[164] Audit Ordinance (cap.122), s.11. [165] *Id.*, s.12(1). [166] *Id.*, s.12(2).

Council, or such longer period as the President may determine, a copy of the PAC's report is laid before the Legislative Council and submitted to the Government.[167] There is a statutory duty on the Director to report to the President any matter which in his opinion constitutes a serious irregularity in relation to the accounts and audit issues within his remit.[168] Though the Director's principal jurisdiction is over Government and other public bodies, he has the statutory power to audit the records and accounts of other persons and bodies if he is authorised to do so in writing by the Chief Executive in the public interest.[169]

The current practice is for the Director of Audit to submit three reports annually to the President. In October, a report is submitted on HKSAR Government accounts, whilst in both April and October, reports are submitted on the results of Value For Money (VFM) audits. The regularity audit aims to "provide [the Legislative Council] with an overall assurance that the Government's financial and accounting transactions and those of funds of a public or quasi-public nature are proper and that they conform to accepted accounting standards".[170] VFM audits aim to "provide independent information, advice and assurance about the economy, efficiency and effectiveness with which the audited body... has discharged its functions".[171] Whereas all bodies and funds subject to audit by the Commission undergo a regularity audit,[172] a smaller number of bodies are selected for each VFM audit.

In the most recent financial year, the number of accounts certified by the Commission was 82, and the number of VFM Reports issued to audited bodies was 18, in line with that of immediately preceding years.[173] The most recently available figures show that, over the past five years, between 0.022 per cent and 0.025 per cent of total government expenditure was spent on VFM audits, namely, between HK$93.5 million and HK$106.9 million.[174] It is a general policy of the Commission that VFM audits are not conducted on the basis of individual complaints, though between 490 and 797 complaints (including requests for conducting audit reviews) were received annually in the most recent five years for which statistics are available.[175]

---

[167] *Id.*, s.12(2A); Rules of Procedure of the Legislative Council, rr.72(9) and (10).
[168] Audit Ordinance (cap.122), s.13.
[169] *Id.*, s.15. A fee can be charged of the audited person or body for this – Audit Ordinance (cap.122), ss.15 and 17.
[170] Audit Commission, *Annual Report 2016-2017*, p.4.   [171] *Id.*, p.6.
[172] See Audit Commission, *Annual Report 2016-2017*, pp.10–14.
[173] Audit Commission, 'Examination of Estimates of Expenditure 2016–17: Controlling Officer's Reply (Question Serial No 5051)' (www.aud.gov.hk/pdf_e/aud1603e.pdf).
[174] Audit Commission, 'Examination of Estimates of Expenditure 2016–17: Controlling Officer's Reply (Question Serial No 6588)' (www.aud.gov.hk/pdf_e/aud1604e.pdf).
[175] Audit Commission, 'Examination of Estimates of Expenditure 2016–17: Controlling Officer's Reply (Question Serial No 6589)' (www.aud.gov.hk/pdf_e/aud1605e.pdf). The basis on which audit subjects are selected was also detailed therein, and it was stated that the Commission generally plans and schedules its VFM audits about one year in advance.

23

Subsidiary Legislation

The Legislative Council may be the primary legislature in Hong Kong, but it is not the only legislator. The Legislative Council may confer legislative power on secondary legislators: secondary, because the entity upon which that power is conferred has no legislative power but for, and to that extent that, it is conferred upon it by the Legislative Council. The legislation made by a secondary legislator is in Hong Kong called subsidiary legislation,[1] though is also referred to as delegated legislation, secondary legislation or subordinate legislation. Subsidiary legislation and subordinate legislation are each defined as "any proclamation, rule, regulation, order, resolution, notice, rule of court, bylaw or other instrument made under or by virtue of any Ordinance and having legislative effect".[2]

There are a number of reasons why the Legislative Council may "delegate" legislative power to another entity. Often the reasons reflect practical constraints. The Legislative Council may not have the physical capacity to itself enact all legislation, noting that much legislation may often be technical or procedural in nature. It will sometimes lack the knowledge, information or expertise necessary to formulate all detailed and technical parts of the legislation. There may be a need or desire to introduce a broad legislative framework on a given date, but for the detail to be worked out or fine-tuning to be done at some point in the future, perhaps when further information is available or after certain events have occurred. There may need to be transitional provisions which are not appropriately dealt with by the Legislative Council, and there may be little to be gained (and time and resources to be lost) by having provisions which frequently require to be changed from having to come before the primary legislature on each occasion.

A common recipient of delegated legislative power is the Chief Executive-in-Council. Sometimes powers are conferred on the Chief Executive alone; at other times on designated members of Government, public officials or public bodies. It is not always an executive body that is the recipient of such

---

[1] Interpretation and General Clauses Ordinance (cap.1), Part V; *Lau Kong Yung* v *Director of Immigration* [1999] 2 HKLRD 516 (CA), p.537.
[2] Interpretation and General Clauses Ordinance (cap.1), s.3.

powers; for example, it is provided that the Rules Committee of the High Court has the power to make rules of court regulating and prescribing the procedure and practice to be followed in the High Court (such rules being a form of subsidiary legislation).[3] Typically, the recipient of delegated legislative powers will be an executive body, however, and this raises separation of powers difficulties. On the one hand, it seems uncontroversial for the legislature to entrust such powers to the executive, as the executive enjoys those powers at the sole behest of, and only to the extent prescribed by, the legislature. The powers can be modified or revoked by the legislature at any time. There is in principle no relinquishment of control by the legislature and thus no strain placed on the separation of powers. Moreover, if the secondary legislator violates the scope or terms of its powers, it will be subject to judicial control.

However, the legislature must have the resources, capacity, competence and diligence to properly supervise and scrutinise the legislative activities of the secondary legislator. If the volume of subsidiary legislation is too great, or the priorities of the Legislative Council otherwise dictate, or it is insufficiently diligent, or its oversight is tainted by partisanship, then subsidiary legislation might not be properly scrutinised. This may allow errors and excesses to go undetected or activities not otherwise meeting with the approval of the Legislative Council to go unchallenged. At worst, the secondary legislator could abuse or misuse its legislative power. In any of these situations, the separation of powers is affected because the executive is able to generate subsidiary legislation without the processes and safeguards of the primary legislature being observed. A substantial part of the legislative exercise is carried outside the legislature proper, and potentially beyond its regular oversight. Checks between legislature and executive might not operate in the manner envisaged, and the balance may tip in favour of the executive – the more potently in a system already dominated by the executive. The extent to which the integrity of the separation of powers is maintained under subsidiary legislation depends on effective supervision and scrutiny by the Legislative Council, and such a prized principle should arguably not be hostage to such fragile contingencies as those described.

It is for the Legislative Council to decide what matters to entrust to a body for future determination by way of subsidiary legislation, but it is thought that matters of principle should generally be decided by the primary legislature, whereas matters of detail may be entrusted to a secondary legislator. The UK Cabinet Office stated in a paper that matters may be more appropriately dealt with by way of delegated legislation where they may need adjusting more frequently than that for which Parliament can be expected to legislate by primary legislation, where there are rules which may be better made after

---

[3] High Court Ordinance (cap.4), ss.54–57.

some experience is gained in administering the new statute and which it is not essential to have as soon as the statute begins to operate, where the use of delegated powers in a particular area has strong precedent and is uncontroversial, and where there are transitional and technical matters which would be appropriately dealt with by way of delegated legislation.[4]

Subsidiary legislation must be published in the Gazette.[5] If provision is made in the parent Ordinance for the subsidiary legislation to become effective on a date other than the date of publication in the Gazette, the beginning of that other date will be the time at which the subsidiary legislation becomes effective.[6] Otherwise it becomes effective at the beginning of the date of publication,[7] though in practice the Government generally sets the commencement date of subsidiary legislation subject to negative vetting to a date after expiry of the scrutiny period.[8] The commencement date can be provided by the parent Ordinance to be capable of being fixed by notice by a specified person,[9] and different provisions in subsidiary legislation can become effective, or be repealed, on different dates.[10] Subsidiary legislation which is still in force, made under an Ordinance which is wholly or partly repealed and replaced, continues to be in force as if made under the repealing Ordinance to the extent that it is not inconsistent with the repealing Ordinance.[11] It is provided that subsidiary legislation may amend any forms contained in the Ordinance under which such subsidiary legislation was made and may prescribe new forms.[12]

In addition to the powers conferred upon the secondary legislator by the parent Ordinance, the subsidiary legislation may provide that contravention or breach of the subsidiary legislation is an offence punishable on summary conviction to a fine not exceeding HK$5,000 and/or to a term of imprisonment not exceeding six months.[13] It may also impose fees and charges,[14] unless the parent Ordinance specifies otherwise. The power to create subsidiary legislation therefore brings with it the power to create criminal offences, where and to the extent that this is not inconsistent with the parent Ordinance. This is particularly significant considering that the secondary legislator is typically an executive body.

---

[4] UK Cabinet Office, *Guide to Making Legislation* (July 2017), p.139.
[5] Interpretation and General Clauses Ordinance (cap.1), s.28(2).   [6] *Id.*, s.28(3)(b).
[7] *Id.*, s.28(3)(a).
[8] Legislative Council Secretariat, *Report of the Subcommittee to Study Issues Relating to the Power of the Legislative Council to Amend Subsidiary Legislation* (LC Paper No. CB(2)975/11–12) (9 February 2012), appendix VI. This is also sometimes provided for by statute – as, for example, by the Accreditation of Academic and Vocational Qualifications Ordinance (cap.592), s.17(4); Construction Workers Registration Ordinance (cap.583), s.23(5)(a); Legislation Publication Ordinance (cap.614), s.18; and Road Traffic Ordinance (cap.374), ss.39G(2), 39H(2) and 39I(2).
[9] Interpretation and General Clauses Ordinance (cap.1), s.28(4).   [10] *Id.*, s.28(5).
[11] *Id.*, s.36.   [12] *Id.*, s.28(1)(f).   [13] *Id.*, s.28(1)(e).
[14] *Id.*, s.29. See also *id.*, s.29A, on the variation of fees and charges.

Scrutiny of Subsidiary Legislation by the Legislative Council

There are two main processes by which the Legislative Council may scrutinise subsidiary legislation made by a secondary legislator. These are known as negative vetting and positive vetting.

Negative vetting refers to the process prescribed in section 34 of the Interpretation and General Clauses Ordinance (cap.1). It is a statutory requirement that subsidiary legislation is laid on the table of the Legislative Council at its next sitting after publication of the subsidiary legislation in the Gazette.[15] The Legislative Council then has 28 days from the date of the sitting at which the subsidiary legislation was laid on the table to pass a resolution to amend the subsidiary legislation, which resolution will be backdated to the date of publication in the Gazette, but "without prejudice to anything done thereunder".[16] The resolution is to be published in the Gazette not later than fourteen days after its being passed or within such extended period as the Chief Executive may permit.[17]

Positive vetting refers to the process prescribed in section 35 of the Interpretation and General Clauses Ordinance (cap.35). An Ordinance may provide that subsidiary legislation is subject to the approval of the Legislative Council or some other entity which may amend it in whole or in part.[18] For example, it is provided that no exemption or modification shall be made by the Chief Executive in relation to the applicability of provisions of the Pension Benefits Ordinance (cap.99) unless a draft of such exemption or modification has been laid before and approved by resolution of the Legislative Council.[19]

There are some situations in which neither negative nor positive vetting applies. A notable example is found in the United Nations Sanctions Ordinance (cap.537), which requires the Chief Executive to make regulations to give effect to an instruction of the Ministry of Foreign Affairs of the PRC to implement, cease implementing, modify or replace sanctions decided by the Security Council of the United Nations. However, it is provided that sections 34 and 35 of the Interpretation and General Clauses Ordinance (cap.1) shall not apply to such regulations made by the Chief Executive.[20] In other words, neither the negative nor positive vetting procedure applies, and the Legislative Council is therefore unable to amend or reject the regulations. This provision has been subject to criticism. The Subcommittee to Examine the Implementation in Hong Kong of Resolutions of the United Nations Security Council in relation to Sanctions was "gravely concerned" that the exclusion of sections 34 and 35 "may have deprived LegCo of its constitutional role in scrutinizing

---

[15] *Id.*, s.34(1).
[16] *Id.*, s.34(2). This is subject to provisions in ss.34(3) and (4). Where subsidiary legislation is amended by an Ordinance, this does not prevent an entity on whom power was conferred by an Ordinance to make that subsidiary legislation from amending the subsidiary legislation (s.37A).
[17] *Id.*, s.34(5). [18] *Id.*, s.35. [19] Pension Benefits Ordinance (cap.99), s.33(2).
[20] United Nations Sanctions Ordinance (cap.537), s.3(5).

and, where necessary, amending subsidiary legislation, thereby placing the legislative powers in the hands of the executive government".[21] Yash Ghai argued that an "Ordinance that takes away from the LegCo the ultimate control over the enactment of subsidiary legislation" would be "unconstitutional", in view of the Basic Law's investment of the legislative function in the Legislative Council.[22] For this reason, he concluded that the United Nations Sanctions Ordinance's exclusion of sections 34 and 35 was "unconstitutional".[23]

The Ordinance does not, however, remove the ultimate control over the enactment of subsidiary legislation from the Legislative Council, for the Council retains the capacity to amend the Ordinance by removing the exclusion of negative and positive vetting procedures, or even to repeal the Ordinance. What may be true, however, is that this practical lack of oversight by the Legislative Council is undesirable from the perspective of ensuring robust observance of the separation of powers. Exacerbating in effect are two particular features of the regulations which the Chief Executive may make under the Ordinance. First, the substantive scope of such regulations is, as far as the plain text of the Ordinance is concerned, virtually limitless. The regulations can also exclude "any person, property, goods, technical data, services, transaction, ship, train or aircraft or any class thereof" from application of the regulations.[24] Second, the regulations may provide that any contravention thereof is a criminal offence punishable on summary conviction to a fine not exceeding HK$500,000 and imprisonment for a term not exceeding two years, or on conviction on indictment to an unlimited fine and imprisonment for a term not exceeding seven years.[25] This is a considerable power of criminalisation which can be created outside the primary legislative process – though it can again be argued that the Legislative Council established such powers and can amend or remove them, and is thus reflective of legislative intention. It is, however, questionable whether such provisions are appropriate from the perspective of the protection of individual rights, the separation of powers and the rule of law.[26]

---

[21] Legislative Council Secretariat, *Phase 1 Report of the Subcommittee to Examine the Implementation in Hong Kong of Resolutions of the United Nations Security Council in Relation to Sanctions* (27 June 2008) (LC Paper No. CB(1)2051/07–08), p.6, para.21. The Subcommittee was set up on the recommendation of the House Committee of the Legislative Council to provide scrutiny of regulations made by the Chief Executive under the Ordinance.

[22] Yash Ghai, "Memorandum to the Subcommittee on UN Sanctions on The United Nations Sanctions Ordinance: The Legislative Process" (CB(1)1665/04–05(01)), pp.4–5, published in Legislative Council Secretariat, *Phase 1 Report of the Subcommittee to Examine the Implementation in Hong Kong of Resolutions of the United Nations Security Council in Relation to Sanctions* (LC Paper No. CB(1)2051/07–08), appendix III.

[23] *Id.*, p.6.   [24] United Nations Sanctions Ordinance (cap.537), s.3(4).

[25] *Id.*, ss.3(3) and (4).

[26] This is not the only example of separation of powers controversies in relation to subsidiary legislation. The Chief Executive purported to make the Country Park (Designation) (Consolidation) (Amendment) Order 2010, which was subject to negative vetting. The Legislative Council resolved to repeal the Order, but the Administration argued that the Council's purported repeal was unlawful. The impasse only came to an end with the

This is not the only example of the disapplication of vetting procedures. It is provided that a notice of the Commissioner of Transport to vary a toll for using the Western Harbour Crossing,[27] or for using the Tai Lam Tunnel and Yuen Long Approach Road,[28] is not subject to negative vetting. The Council of the Hong Kong Academy of Medicine may make bylaws in relation to membership of the Hong Kong Academy of Medicine, such bylaws not subject to negative vetting.[29] A notice of the Director-General of Civil Aviation published in the Gazette of a revision to limits of liability under the Montreal Convention[30] is not subject to negative vetting,[31] nor are rules made by the Council of the Hong Kong Institute of Certified Public Accountants.[32] Negative vetting does not apply to a scheme made by the Airport Authority for determining airport charges,[33] nor to a notice of the Secretary for Commerce and Economic Development published in the Gazette in relation to a change of company or franchise for the Tung Chung Cable Car,[34] or an order of the Chief Executive-in-Council revoking the Tung Chung Cable Car franchise.[35] Sometimes negative vetting is specified not to apply, but positive vetting or an alternative vetting procedure applies.[36] It is sometimes specifically provided in an Ordinance that a notice, document or instrument is subsidiary legislation,[37] or is not subsidiary legislation,[38] for the purposes of the negative vetting procedure.

Administration deciding "not to take out [a] judicial review application on the grounds that it attaches great importance to maintaining a good relationship between the Executive Authorities and the Legislature", and the Administration changed their proposals in relation to the country park – Legislative Council, *Report of the Subcommittee to Study Issues Relating to the Power of the Legislative Council to Amend Subsidiary Legislation* (Appendix I to LC Paper No CB(2)975/11–12), appendix I, para.15. See the full Report for further discussion.

[27] Western Harbour Crossing Ordinance (cap.436), s.52(3).
[28] Tai Lam Tunnel and Yuen Long Approach Road Ordinance (cap.474), s.45(3).
[29] Hong Kong Academy of Medicine Ordinance (cap.419), s.13(5).
[30] Convention for the Unification of Certain Rules for International Carriage by Air (28 May 1999).
[31] Carriage by Air Ordinance (cap.500), s.21(3).
[32] Professional Accountants Ordinance (cap.50), s.51(4).
[33] Airport Authority Ordinance (cap.483), s.34(9)(b).
[34] Tung Chung Cable Car Ordinance (cap.577), s.16(3). [35] *Id.*, s.27(6).
[36] For example, under the Criminal Jurisdiction Ordinance (cap.461), s.2(5); Pension Benefits Ordinance (cap.99), s.33(2); Pension Benefits (Judicial Officers) Ordinance (cap.401), ss.37(2) and 38(3); and Pensions Ordinance (cap.89), s.20A(2).
[37] For example, under the Payment Systems and Stored Value Facilities Ordinance (cap.584), s.58 (1); and Road Traffic Ordinance (cap.374), s.109(6).
[38] For example, a notice of the Commissioner of Customs and Excise to approve an area as part of the cargo transhipment area of Hong Kong International Airport, under the Import and Export Ordinance (cap.60), s.2AA(2); a code of practice on land boundary surveys and related matters approved and issued by the Land Survey Authority, under the Land Survey Ordinance (cap.473), s.29(8); certain notices or guidelines issued under the Payment Systems and Stored Value Facilities Ordinance (cap.584) (s.58(2)); rules made by the Vocational Training Council, under the Vocational Training Council Ordinance (cap.1130), s.20(3); an order of the Secretary for Labour and Welfare on pension and gratuity rates, under the Volunteer and Naval Volunteer Pensions Ordinance (cap.202), s.35(5); rules made by the Council of The Education

The Legislative Council enjoys the power to amend subsidiary legislation, whereas this power is generally not enjoyed by the UK Parliament. This can be traced to the 1937 Amendment Ordinance which amended section 40 of the Interpretation Ordinance 1911, requiring that all regulations shall be laid on the table of the Legislative Council which may thereafter rescind or amend the regulations.[39] Positive vetting was introduced for the first time by the Interpretation Ordinance 1950.[40] However, the current provision on negative vetting (unlike previously) is that subsidiary legislation may be amended but not entirely rejected.[41] This again contrasts with the position in the UK, where delegated legislation is annulled or passed into law, but generally incapable of amendment.[42]

Judicial Review of Subsidiary Legislation

There is a clear statutory basis for invalidating subsidiary legislation that is inconsistent with the provisions of any Ordinance.[43] An exception is where a so-called Henry VIII clause is enacted, by which primary legislation provides for a secondary legislator to amend primary legislation. An example of this can be found in section 28(1) and (2)(s) of the Legal Aid Ordinance (cap.91), which provides that the Chief Executive-in-Council may "make regulations prescribing any matter which by this Ordinance is to be or may be prescribed

---

University of Hong Kong for the better carrying out of the objects of The Education University of Hong Kong and its parent Ordinance, under The Education University of Hong Kong Ordinance (cap.444), s.22(3); a notice published in the Gazette by the Registrar of Patents specifying a publication to be the official journal of record under the Patents Ordinance (cap.514) (s.150A(6)); a notice published in the Gazette by the Registrar of Patents requiring the use of such forms as he may specify in connection with the granting of a patent or related proceeding, under the Patents Ordinance (cap.514), s.150(3); a notice published in the Gazette by the Registrar of Trade Marks specifying a publication to be the official journal of record under the Trade Marks Ordinance (cap.559) (s.73(6)); a notice published in the Gazette by the Registrar of Trade Marks requiring the use of such forms as he may specify in connection with the registration of a trade mark or related proceeding, under the Trade Marks Ordinance (cap.559), s.74(3); a notice published in the Gazette by the Registrar of Designs requiring the use of such forms as he may specify in connection with the registration of a design or related proceeding, under the Registered Designs Ordinance (cap.522), s.84(3); a notice published in the Gazette by the Registrar of Designs specifying a publication to be the official journal of record under the Registered Designs Ordinance (cap.522) (s.84A(6)).

[39] Administration Wing, Chief Secretary for Administration's Office/Department of Justice, *Power of Legislature to Amend Subsidiary Legislation – Differences between the Parliament of the United Kingdom and the Hong Kong Legislature* (LC Paper No. CB(2)1974/10–11(02)) (June 2011), paras.2–3.

[40] *Id.*, paras.4–5. [41] See Interpretation and General Clauses Ordinance (cap.1), s.34(2).

[42] See Royal Commission on the Reform of the House of Lords, *A House for the Future* (January 2000), CM 4534, p.70.

[43] Interpretation and General Clauses Ordinance (cap.1), s.28(1)(b); *Cheung Yick Hung* v *Law Society of Hong Kong* [2017] 1 HKC 97 (CA), para.31. See, for example, *Mohan* v *McElney* [1983] 1 HKC 243 (CA); *Attorney General* v *Chan Foo* [1990] HKCU 393; and *The Dragon No 1* [1998] 3 HKC 684.

and generally for the better carrying out of this Ordinance", including regulations which "modify any provision of this Ordinance so far as it appears to be necessary to meet the circumstances where a person seeking or receiving legal aid" falls into particular categories.[44] It is provided in section 273 of the Companies Ordinance that the Chief Executive-in-Council may "make regulations modifying any of the provisions of this Division [of the Ordinance] with respect to" particular authorisations and information relating to share redemptions and buy-backs.[45] A far-reaching Henry VIII clause appears in the Emergency Regulations Ordinance (cap.241), providing that the Chief Executive-in-Council may make "any regulations whatsoever which he may consider desirable in the public interest" in what he considers to be an occasion of emergency or public danger, and:

> A regulation or any order or rule made in pursuance of such a regulation shall have effect notwithstanding anything inconsistent therewith contained in any enactment; and any provision of an enactment which may be inconsistent with any regulation or any such order or rule shall, whether that provision shall or shall not have been amended, suspended or modified in its operation under subsection (2), to the extent of such inconsistency have no effect so long as such regulation, order or rule shall remain in force.[46]

Each purported instance of subsidiary legislative power must find a basis in primary legislation, for it is the Legislative Council that is designated as the legislature of the SAR.[47] Moreover, subsidiary legislation is susceptible to being declared unconstitutional as in violation of one or more provisions of the Basic Law or the Bill of Rights.[48] Thus a standing order issued by the Commissioner of Correctional Services requiring all male prisoners to have their hair cut, whilst not requiring the same of female prisoners, was initially held to be unlawful as in violation of both the Sex Discrimination Ordinance (cap.480) and Article 25 of the Basic Law.[49]

It was said that unreasonableness is not, in itself, a ground for holding subsidiary legislation to be *ultra vires*, but is instead a factor to be taken into consideration in determining whether the subsidiary legislation falls within or beyond the powers conferred by the enabling Ordinance.[50] Moreover, there is a presumption against legislation (or subsidiary legislation) providing for the inconvenient or unreasonable.[51] However, where subsidiary legislation would violate the rules of natural justice without express power being given to that

---

[44] Legal Aid Ordinance (cap.91), s.28(1) and (2)(s).
[45] Companies Ordinance (cap.622), s.273.
[46] Emergency Regulations Ordinance (cap.241), s.2(1) and (4).
[47] Basic Law, Art.66.
[48] *Lam Siu Po* v *Commissioner of Police* (2009) 12 HKCFAR 237.
[49] *Leung Kwok Hung* v *Commissioner of Correctional Services* [2017] HKCU 136. Though the appeal was allowed in *Leung Kwok Hung* v *Commissioner of Correctional Services* [2018] HKCA 225.
[50] *Attorney General* v *Tsang Kwok-kuen* [1971] HKLR 266, p.276.
[51] *Chu Kwok-fai* v *The Queen* [1973] HKLR 107, p.113.

effect by the parent legislation, the relevant subsidiary legislative provision can be held to be *ultra vires* of the enabling Ordinance.[52] A purported exercise of discretion under subsidiary legislation may be struck down as in breach of the rules of natural justice.[53] Subsidiary legislation can be declared unlawful on the basis that it is so uncertain in its terms as to be meaningless.[54] Otherwise, uncertainty or unreasonableness in application, or inconsistency with the general law, are relevant to validity only insofar as they assist in answering the question of whether the subsidiary legislation falls within or without the power to make it.[55]

The remedy typically sought against *ultra vires* subsidiary legislation would be a declaration that the subsidiary legislation is unlawful (and/or unconstitutional), perhaps also with an order of prohibition or an injunction to restrain a body from implementing or relying upon it. A person might decide to treat the subsidiary legislation as of no legal effect and thereby ignore it, pleading its unlawfulness in their defence in civil or criminal proceedings should they materialise. Depending on the circumstances, however, this may be a risky strategy.[56] A decision made on the basis of *ultra vires* subsidiary legislation will itself be liable to be struck down as *ultra vires*.

Administrative Rules

Administrative rules have an ambiguous legal status. They are not legislation and tend to be regarded as having no strict legal effect, though they can shape the behaviour of decision makers and have a material bearing on the position of persons affected by rules or decisions made in relation to them.[57]

An example of a set of administrative rules is CAD371, issued by the Civil Aviation Department,[58] containing 74 pages of provisions on the avoidance of aircrew fatigue. Aircraft operators are required to present to the Director-General of Civil Aviation, for approval, a scheme for the regulation of their crew flight times; and they are not permitted to fly their aircraft without such approval.[59] Hartmann J stated the following:

> While it can sometimes be difficult to ascertain where delegated legislation begins and ends, I am satisfied that CAD371 is not, nor can it be deemed to be, legislation of any kind. It may be said that CAD371 contains administrative

---

[52] *Lau Ping v The Queen* [1970] HKCU 31.
[53] *R v English Schools Foundation* [2004] 3 HKC 343.
[54] *Kruse v Johnson* [1898] 2 QB 91; *Noise Control Authority v Step In Ltd* (2005) 8 HKCFAR 113, para.40.
[55] *Noise Control Authority v Step In Ltd* (2005) 8 HKCFAR 113, para.40.   [56] See pp.69–72.
[57] See *Re Leung Mo Chu (t/a Alliance Trading Co)* [1980] HKC 621.
[58] Civil Aviation Department, *The Avoidance of Fatigue in Aircrews* (CAD 371) (2nd edn) (May 2010, reissued April 2013).
[59] Air Navigation (Hong Kong) Order 1995 (cap.448C), art.54; Civil Aviation Department, *The Avoidance of Fatigue in Aircrews* (CAD371) (2nd edn) (May 2010, reissued April 2013), para.1.3.

rules but, if so, they are not rules of law. The fact that actions of the Director-General in respect of CAD371 may, for the reasons given earlier in this judgment, be subject to judicial review goes no way to elevating CAD371 into a document of legal effect. CAD371 may be ignored entirely by an operator without subjecting the operator to any legal liability. All it means is that the operator is almost bound to be unsuccessful in seeking the Director-General's approval for any scheme proposed by him pursuant to art.54(1) of the Air Navigation Order.[60]

As unlawful policies can be struck down as unlawful, so can administrative rules be struck down. They can also be tested for constitutionality.[61] In addition, as a decision maker may be expected generally to comply with or adequately take into account a policy as a relevant consideration, but not to adhere to the policy too rigidly, the same applies in principle to administrative rules.[62]

Another example of a set of administrative rules is the Code of Conduct for Persons Licensed by or Registered with the Securities and Futures Commission.[63] This is one of the codes of conduct and sets of guidelines published by the Commission under the Securities and Futures Ordinance (cap.571), though it is specifically provided that such codes and guidelines are not subsidiary legislation.[64] It is also provided that failure on the part of a person to comply with the provisions set out in a code or guideline published under the Ordinance shall not in itself render him liable to any judicial or other

---

[60] *Cathay Pacific Airways Flight Attendants Union* v *Director-General of Civil Aviation* [2005] HKEC 1337, para.36. See also *Hong Kong Aircrew Officers Association* v *Director-General of Civil Aviation* [2009] HKEC 1086. The language used in the instrument may indicate (but will not necessarily be conclusive of) whether it is to be regarded as subsidiary legislation, a set of administrative rules or some other form of guidance (*Shiu Wing Steel Ltd* v *Director of Environmental Protection* [2003] HKCU 1101, paras.60–76).

[61] *Kong Yunming* v *Director of Social Welfare* (2013) 16 HKCFAR 950; *Leung Sze Ho Albert* v *Bar Council of Hong Kong Bar Association* [2015] 5 HKLRD 791; *Choi King Fung* v *Hong Kong Housing Authority* [2017] HKEC 549. Cf *Hong Kong Bar Association* v *Anthony Chua* (1994) 4 HKPLR 637.

[62] This will also turn on how the legal power by which the administrative rules are created is framed. For example, art.54(1)(b) of the Air Navigation (Hong Kong) Order 1995 (cap.448C) refers to a scheme being approved by the Chief Executive (or his or her delegated authority) "subject to such conditions as he thinks fit". If such conditions take the form of a specific and detailed set of provisions, as in the case of CAD371, then these could generate legitimate expectations for aircraft operators and would be expected to substantially guide the conduct of the decision maker (see *Yim Shik Shi* v *Secretary for the Civil Service* [2004] HKEC 1813, paras.11 and 21). However, the decision maker will still be expected not to fetter his or her discretion.

[63] Securities and Futures Commission, "Code of Conduct for Persons Licensed by or Registered with the Securities and Futures Commission" (18th edn) (June 2017). Other codes of conduct issued by the Commission include Securities and Futures Commission, "Code of Conduct for Persons Providing Credit Rating Services" (June 2011); and Securities and Futures Commission, "Code of Conduct for Share Registrars" (2003).

[64] Securities and Futures Ordinance (cap.571), s.169(6) and 399(8).

proceedings. However, in any proceedings under the Ordinance before any court, the code or guideline shall be admissible in evidence, and if any provision set out in the code or guideline appears to the court to be relevant to any question arising in the proceedings, it shall be taken into account in determining that question.[65] The Explanatory Notes to the Code of Conduct state that the Commission will be guided by the Code in considering whether a licensed or registered person satisfies the requirement that it is a fit and proper person to remain licensed or registered, and in that context, will have regard to the general principles, as well as the letter, of the Code. However, it is added that:

> [t]o reflect the realities of today's markets, the Commission recognizes that conduct of business principles should be flexible enough to differentiate between professional and non-professional investors and some provisions of the Code need not be observed in the case of professionals.[66]

This would appear, in principle, to militate (at least to some extent) against fettering of discretion. It is also provided that the Code "does not have the force of law and should not be interpreted in a way that would override the provision of any law".[67]

There is a wide array of administrative rules in place, other examples of which include the eligibility rules for Comprehensive Social Security Assistance (CSSA),[68] the allocation rules for Public Rental Housing (PRH),[69] the Code of Practice for Fire Safety in Buildings,[70] the Code of Practice for Owners of Boilers and Pressure Vessels,[71] the Code of Practice for the Lighting, Signing

---

[65] *Id.*, s.399(6). A slightly different provision appears in s.169(4).

[66] Securities and Futures Commission, "Code of Conduct for Persons Licensed by or Registered with the Securities and Futures Commission'" (18th edn) (June 2017), p.vii.

[67] *Id.*, p.viii. See *Ever-long Securities Co Ltd v Wong Sio Po* [2004] 2 HKLRD 143; and *DBS Bank (Hong Kong) Ltd v San-Hot HK Industrial Co Ltd* [2013] 4 HKC 1, para.217.

[68] See *Kong Yunming v Director of Social Welfare* (2013) 16 HKCFAR 950.

[69] See Hong Kong Housing Authority, "Application Guide for Public Rental Housing" (revised February 2015).

[70] Buildings Department, "Code of Practice for Fire Safety in Buildings 2011" (revised October 2015). It is stated (p.ii) that the Code was issued to "provide *guidance* on compliance with the requirements laid down in" the relevant building regulations (emphasis added).

[71] Labour Department, "Code of Practice for Owners of Boilers and Pressure Vessels" (May 2016), issued under section 18A of the Boilers and Pressure Vessels Ordinance (cap.56). It is provided in section 18A(2) that "[f]ailure on the part of any person to observe the provisions of any [Code issued under section 18A] or to accept any such particular advice shall not of itself render that person liable to criminal proceedings of any kind, but any such failure may, in any proceedings whether civil or criminal and including proceedings for an offence under this Ordinance, be relied upon by any party to the proceedings as tending to establish or negative any liability which is in question in those proceedings".

and Guarding of Road Works,[72] the School Administration Guide,[73] and the Code of Conduct of the Hong Kong Bar Association.[74]

The Chief Executive has the power to issue executive orders.[75] These appear to be a particular kind of administrative rule made under the authority of the Basic Law. Executive orders have been described as follows:

> These are directions of an administrative kind which are made by the Chief Executive for the purpose of implementing laws and carrying out government policies ... [A]ny restrictions on the fundamental rights must be prescribed by law. The Executive Order is not law.[76]

The executive order in that case, the Law Enforcement (Covert Surveillance Procedure) Order, gazetted in August 2005, was held not to comprise "legal procedures" for the purposes of Article 30 of the Basic Law.[77] In an earlier case, the procedures laid down by an executive order in relation to the appointment and removal of public officeholders under Article 48(7) of the Basic Law were deemed to fall within the scope of "legal procedures".[78] Further acts and decisions, including the making of regulations, may purportedly be made under the authority of an executive order, as was the case for the Public Service (Disciplinary) Regulation, which was made under the authority of the Public Service (Administration) Order 1997.[79]

Departmental Circulars and Memoranda

Departmental circulars and memoranda can take a number of different forms, but often provide information or instructions, and may be addressed to an

---

[72] Highways Department, "Code of Practice for the Lighting, Signing and Guarding of Road Works" (5th edn) (2017).
[73] Education Bureau, "School Administration Guide (2017/18 School Year)" (2017).
[74] Hong Kong Bar Association, "Code of Conduct" (revised September 2017). The Code was "not subsidiary legislation", though it enjoyed statutory recognition and underpinning, and was susceptible to judicial review – *Leung Sze Ho Albert v Bar Council of Hong Kong Bar Association* [2015] 5 HKLRD 791, paras.56–58. Cf *Hong Kong Bar Association v Anthony Chua* (1994) 4 HKPLR 637.
[75] Basic Law, Art.48(4).
[76] *Leung Kwok Hung v Chief Executive of the HKSAR* [2006] HKCU 731, paras.29 and 38.
[77] Article 30 provides that: "The freedom and privacy of communication of Hong Kong residents shall be protected by law. No department or individual may, on any grounds, infringe upon the freedom and privacy of communication of residents except that the relevant authorities may inspect communication *in accordance with legal procedures* to meet the needs of public security or of investigation into criminal offences" (emphasis added). See also *Koo Sze Yiu v Chief Executive of the HKSAR* (2006) 9 HKCFAR 441; and pp.288–290.
[78] *Association of Expatriate Civil Servants of Hong Kong v Chief Executive of HKSAR* [1998] 1 HKLRD 615. The executive order in this case was the Public Service (Administration) Order 1997. See also *Wong Kei Kwong v Principal Assistant Secretary for Civil Service* [2008] HKEC 261. The provisions of this Order were also considered in, for example, *Rowse v Secretary for Civil Service* [2008] 5 HKLRD 217.
[79] See *Association of Expatriate Civil Servants of Hong Kong v Chief Executive of HKSAR* [1998] 1 HKLRD 615.

internal or external audience.[80] They can purport to regulate the employment terms and conditions of employees of the public body concerned,[81] or affect the way in which the body performs its contractual obligations.[82] It has been said that circulars have "no legal force, but they may be challenged in judicial review".[83] They are not subsidiary legislation, but they can still affect and shape the conduct, including legal conduct, of the body issuing the circular or memorandum and persons subject to or affected by it. Accordingly, "[d]eclarations may be granted to settle arguments about the legality of action recommended in circulars".[84] Declarations were sought on the meaning of provisions in the Animal and Plants (Protection of Endangered Species) Ordinance (cap.187) in response to a departmental circular issued to all ivory traders in Hong Kong which signalled stricter enforcement of the Ordinance.[85] In another case it was held that a departmental circular directing that a school converting from the Bought Place Scheme to the Direct Subsidy Scheme would not be permitted to charge additional fees for a certain period from the Bought Place Scheme pupils was not unlawful and that there was nothing in it that was irrational or unreasonable.[86] A challenge to the legality of decisions expressed in a departmental circular issued by the Civil Service Bureau on the service terms of civil servants was unsuccessful.[87] As circulars and memoranda may contain representations, they are capable of founding legitimate expectations. They can also serve as evidence of departmental policy or acts or decisions taken.

---

[80] For example, the Securities and Futures Commission issued a 'Circular to intermediaries and other persons engaging in activities concerning over-the-counter (OTC) derivative products or transactions' (22 October 2015) to "update the market on the implementation of the OTC derivatives regulatory regime, and to highlight the transitional arrangements for market participants who intend to continue with their existing OTC derivatives activities in Hong Kong". This was clearly an informational circular directed at an audience external to the Securities and Futures Commission. By contrast, the Civil Service Bureau issued a circular headed 'Arrangements for Reimbursement / Direct Payment of Medical Expenses' (CSB Circular No. 2/2013, 21 March 2013), setting out new administrative arrangements on the reimbursement and direct payment of medical expenses for civil servants. This was a circular containing both information and instructions, directed at an "internal" audience, in other words civil service employees.

[81] See *Lau Hon Cheong* v *Attorney-General* [1987] 3 HKC 1 (CA); and *Cheng Ho Kee* v *Secretary for Justice* [2004] HKCFI 114, which went on appeal as *Cheng Ho Kee* v *Secretary for Justice* (2006) 9 HKCFAR 705.

[82] See, for example, Civil Service Bureau, "Guidelines on the Management of Time-off Granted under CSR 904" (CSB Circular No. 2/2007, 11 January 2007).

[83] *Dr Wang Tze Sam* v *Attorney General* [1996] HKCFI 243, para.15, per Sears J.

[84] *Id.*, per Sears J. Examples of such cases are *Royal College of Nursing of the United Kingdom* v *Department of Health and Social Security* [1981] AC 800 (HL); and *Gillick* v *West Norfolk and Wisbech Area Health Authority* [1986] AC 112 (HL).

[85] *Attorney General* v *Yau Kwok-lam, Johnny* [1988] 2 HKLR 394 (CA). The case was brought by way of originating summons.

[86] *Dr Wang Tze Sam* v *Attorney General* [1996] HKCFI 243.

[87] *Association of Expatriate Civil Servants of Hong Kong* v *Secretary for the Civil Service* [1998] HKCFI 316.

Index

abuse of power, 1–2
   administrative law and, 2
   bad faith, 150
   defined, 151
   good faith, 150
   improper purposes or motives and, 150–153
   legitimate expectations as, 151, 207
   types of, 151
   Wednesbury unreasonableness and, 152
acquiescence, 138–139
   remedies and, 297
   ultra vires decisions and, 140
administrative law
   abuse of power and, 2
   constitutional law and, 32–34
   elements of, 3
   human rights and, 32–34
   misuse of power and, 2
administrative rules, 360–363
   Basic Law and, 363
   by Chief Executive, 363
   framing of, 361
   status of, 360
   types of, 361–363
   unconstitutionality of, 361
administrative tribunals, 3, 304–319
   appeals boards, 304–310
      composition of, 310–314
      establishment of, 306
      functions of, 306–308
      impartiality concerns about, 308–309
      independence of, 308
      powers of, 314–316
      procedures of, 314–316
   Chief Executive and, appeals to, 316–319
   Chief Executive-in-Council and, appeals to, 316–319
   classification of, 304–305

   functions of, 305
   in UK, 308–310
ADR. *See* alternative dispute resolution
agency, 125–129, 171
   duty of care and, 128
   legitimate expectations and, 127–128
   in public law, 126–127
   statutory corporation and, 125
   statutory discretion and, 126
   ultra vires decision and, 125, 128–129
alternative dispute resolution (ADR), 48
alternative remedies, 140, 293–295
   suitability of, 294–295
ambiguity, as ground of judicial review, 141–143
amendment of grounds, 279
ancillary powers, 129–133. *See also* implied powers
   public interest and, 131
   public policy and, 131
   ultra vires decisions and, 130
appeals. *See also* statutory appeals
   administrative tribunals and, 304–310
   alternative remedy as, 293–295
   delay due to, 48–49
appeals boards, 194–197, 304–310. *See also* administrative tribunals
arbitrariness, 1
arguability, 40, 109–117
   flexibility of, 114
   potential, 110, 112, 114–117
   qualitative filters and, 110
   reasonable, 112–114
   standing and, 53–54, 110
   thresholds of, 110–117
      authoritative guidance on, 112–113
      leave stage and, 114–116
Audit Commission, 3, 349–351

Audit Commission (cont.)
  duties and powers of, 350
  Legislative Council and, 350–351
  VFM audits, 351
Australia, 134, 145–146, 148, 183–184, 307
authoritarianism, 1–2
authority, 125–129
  duty of care and, 128
  legitimate expectations and, 127–128
  statutory corporation and, 125
  statutory discretion and, 126
  ultra vires decision and, 125, 128–129

Bahamas, 307
Basic Law
  amendment of, 28
  Chief Executive under, 7–9
  common law influence on, 29
  human rights and, 33
  interpretation of, 27–28
  non-justiciability under, 97–99, 106–108
  ouster clauses and, 89
  PLA and, 16–17
  PRC Constitution and, 26–27
  proportionality and, 32–33
  right to legal representation and, 256
Belize, 264
bias, 33, 139–141, 264–271
  appearance of, 265
  fair-minded and informed observer, 265–266
  necessity principle, 271
  recusal of judges and, 268–269
  remedies and, 278
Bill of Rights Ordinance
  human rights and, 33
  ouster clauses and, 95
  principle of legal certainty, 142
  proportionality and, 32–33
  right to legal representation and, 253
British Virgin Islands 134

Canada, 125, 134, 158, 193–194
Cao Erbao, 15–16
Carltona principle, 163–168
  constitutional context and, 165–168
  Legislative Council and, 167–168
cause of action estoppel, 140–141
central government, 7–12
  Chief Executive, 7–9
    appointment of, 8–9
    under Basic Law, 7–9
    Executive Council in relationship with, 10
    NPC and, 8–9
  Chief Executive-in-Council, 9–11
  civil service, 11–12
    Civil Service Code, 12
  Executive Council, 9–11
    Chief Executive-in-Council, relationship with, 10
Central Tender Board, 22–23
certainty. *See* legal certainty; uncertainty
certifications, 18–21. *See also* licensing
certiorari, 65–66, 280–281
  declaration as distinct from, 283
  ultra vires decisions and, 280
Chief Executive, 7–9
  acts of state and, 101
  administrative tribunals and, appeals to, 316–319
  appointment of, 8–9
  under Basic Law, 7–9
  Carltona principle and, 168
  deference, 102–104
  NPC and, 8–9
  power of pardon and commuting of sentence, 102–104
  public interest standing, 61
Chief Executive-in-Council, 9–11
  administrative tribunals and, appeals to, 316–319
  subsidiary legislation and, 352–353
China, Mainland. *See also* People's Republic of China
  governmental presences of, in Hong Kong, 15–17
    Liaison Office, 15–16
    Office of the Commissioner of the Ministry of Foreign Affairs, 16
    PLA, 16–17
    Xinhua News Agency, 15
  HKSAR government offices in, 17–18
civil service, 11–12
  Civil Service Code and, 12
  Civil Service Bureau, 11–12
  Civil Service Code, 12
collateral attack, 72–74
  judicial review of, 73
  private law rights, 73
  procedural exclusivity and, 74
collateral challenge, 68–74
  collateral attack, 72–74

judicial review of, 73
private law rights, 73
procedural exclusivity and, 74
collateral defence, 68–72
  as abuse of process, 68
  in criminal contexts, 71–72
  defined, 68
  judicial review, 71–72
  loan guarantees and, 70–71
  ultra vires decision, 68–70
collateral defence, 68–72
  as abuse of process, 68, 68n29
  in criminal context, 71–72
  defined, 68
  judicial review, 71–72
  loan guarantees and, 70–71
  ultra vires decision, 68–70
Commissioner for Administrative Complaints (COMAC), 330
Commissions of Inquiry, 3, 332–336
  appointments of, timeline for, 332–333
  functions of, 334–335
  recommendations of, 336
common law
  Basic Law influenced by, 29
  as constitutional basis of judicial review, 28–31
  in HKSAR, 25, 28–31
  rule of law and, 29–31
compliance. *See* non-compliance
consent. *See also* waiver and consent
  of parties, and procedural exclusivity, 74–75
considerations
  irrelevant, 154–158
    reasons and, 155
    threshold for, 156–157
  relevant, 154–155, 158–162
    failure to take into account, 158–161
    intensity of review, 161–162
    Wednesbury reasonableness and, 161–162
constitutional law
  human rights and, 32–34
  proportionality and, 32–33
contracts, fettering discretion through, 183–189
  ultra vires decisions and, 187
  as unlawful, 184–188
  validity of contract and, 188
Convention of Peking, 24–25
corruption, 1, 336–339
councils. *See specific councils*

Crédit Suisse, 70–71, 70n32, 71n33
criminal context, collateral defence in, 71–72
curative principle, in procedural fairness, 253

damages, 291–293
danger of bias, 265–266
declaration, 283–290
  certiorari as distinct from, 283
  hypothetical questions and, 284–288
  order of temporary validity, 288
  suspension of, 288
  temporal limitation of, 288–290
deference, in intensity of review, 102–108
  for *Wednesbury* unreasonableness, 237–240
delay, in applications for leave or judicial review. *See also* time limits
  ADR and, 48
  appeals and, 48–49
  detriment arising from, 50–51
  leave and, 43–44
  prejudice arising from, 50–51
  promptness of, 45
  reasons justifying, 45–51
  remedies and, 296–297
  substantial hardship arising from, 50–51
  ultra vires principle and, 140
delegated legislation. *See* subsidiary legislation
delegation of power, 163–171
  agency and, 171
  Carltona principle, 163–168
    constitutional context and 165–168
    Legislative Council and, 167–168
  nature of, 169–170
  status of delegator, 168–169
  subsidiary legislation and, 163
Deng Xiaoping, 27
departmental circulars and memoranda, 363–364
Departmental Tender Committees, 23
Dicey, A. V., 29
disclosure, duty of, 256–257
  competing interests and, 257
discretion, 125–143. *See also* individual grounds
  agency and, 126
  authority and, 126
  costs of, 62
  delay and, 43
  divestiture of, 171–174
  insufficient retention of, 172

discretion (cont.)
    at leave stage, 38, 40
    relinquishment of, 171–174
    remedies, discretionary nature of, 68, 216–217, 285–288, 290–292
    statutory, 126
District Councils, 12–13
divestiture of discretion, 171–174
duty of care, 128
duty to give reasons, 245–246, 257–264
    adequacy of reasons, 261–264

election petition, 13–14, 87, 95–97, 200
Equal Opportunities Commission, 3, 58–59, 68, 339–343
error of fact, 190–197, 279
    error of law as distinct from, 202–203
    jurisdictional, 191–194
    non-jurisdictional, 193–197
error of law, 33–34, 190–191, 198–203
    error of fact as distinct from, 202–203
estoppel, 128, 137–141
    res judicata, 140–141
        cause of action estoppel, 140–141
        issue estoppel, 140
ex parte applications and hearings, 45, 339
Executive Council, 9–11. *See also* Chief Executive-in-Council

fair hearing, right to, 248–253
fairness. *See* procedural fairness
fettering of discretion, 34, 175–184
    contracts and, 183–189
    lawful policies, unlawful application of, 179–183
    obligation to decide, 175–178
        with open mind, 176–178
    unlawful policies, 178–179, 182
Fiji, 105
futility, remedies and, 299–300

government. *See* central government; local government
Government Logistics Department Tender Board, 23
grounds of judicial review. *See also* individual grounds
    amendment of, 279

Handover, of Hong Kong to PRC
    Chief Executive's power after, 103
    continuity during, 25

delegation of power and, 168
international treaties after, 100–101
Hang Wah Chong principle, 78–79
hardship, as result of delay, 50–51
Heung Yee Kuk, 14–15
human rights
    administrative review and, 32–34
    Basic Law and, 33
    Bill of Rights and, 33
    constitutional review and, 32–34
    Ombudsman and, 328–329
    Wednesbury unreasonableness and, 240–241

ICAC. *See* Independent Commission Against Corruption
ICCPR. *See* International Covenant on Civil and Political Rights
illegality, 123
immigration, *Wednesbury* unreasonableness and, 236–237
impartiality. *See also* bias; insufficient impartiality
    of administrative tribunals, 308–309
    of decision-makers, 269–270
    of judges, 266–267
    structural, 268
implicit representations, 208–209
implied powers, 129–133
improper purposes or motives, 144–153
    abuse of power, 150–153
    misuse of power, 150–153
Independent Commission Against Corruption (ICAC)
    administrative structure, 338
India, 92, 99–100
injunction, 290–291
    damages and, 291
    interim, 290–291
insufficient impartiality, 139–140, 264–271
intensity of review
    deference, 102–108
    non-justiciability, 97–101
    power of pardon and commuting of sentence, 102–104
    prosecutorial discretion and, 104–108
    relevant considerations and, 161–162
    Wednesbury unreasonableness and, 235–242
inter partes hearings, 45
interim injunctions, 290

Index

International Covenant on Civil and Political Rights (ICCPR), 33
irrationality, 242–245
  unreasonableness as distinct from, 242–245
irrelevant considerations, 154–158
  reasons and, 155
  threshold for, 156–157
issue estoppel, 140

judges. *See also* judicial review
  impartiality of, 266–267
  recusal of, bias and, 268–269
judicial independence, judicial review and, 3
judicial review. *See also* leave; remedies; statutory exclusion of review; statutory limitation of review; individual grounds
  administrative law distinguished from, 3
  of collateral attack, 73
  of collateral defence, 71–72
  constitutional foundation of, 24–34
  development of, 122–123
  judicial independence and, 3
  Ombudsman and, relationship with, 325–327
  overview of grounds, 121–124
  publicness and, 64, 75–86
    determination of, 80–82
    Hang Wah Chong principle, 78–79
    source of power and, 76–77
    public/private distinction with, 83–86
  purpose and function of, 2, 121–122
  scope of, 64
  of subsidiary legislation, 358–360
  ultra vires theory, 32
jurisdiction. *See also* non-justiciability
  ouster clauses and, 91–92

Lam Cheng Yuet-ngor, Carrie, 334
leave stage, 37–41. *See also* delay
  arguability and, 109–117
  delay and, 37–41
  discretion in, 38, 40
  exclusion of review, 87–93
  as legal filter, 37
  limitation of review, 93–97
  non-justiciability, 97–101
  public/private divide, 64–86
  standing and, 52–63
legal aid
  delay of court applications and, 47
  personal standing and, 57

legal certainty, principle of, 142
legal representation, right to, 253–256
legality, merits compared to, 2
Legislative Council
  Audit Commission and, 350–351
  Carltona principle and, 167–168
  legislative supremacy and, 32
  Ombudsman and, 327–328
  Provisional, 55
  public interest standing and, 59
  statutory exclusion of review and, 88
  subsidiary legislation and, 352–354
    amendment powers of, 358
    disapplication of vetting procedures, 355–357
    negative vetting by, 355
    positive vetting by, 355
    scrutiny of, 355–358
Legislative Council Redress System, 3, 330–331
legislative supremacy, 31–32
legitimate expectations, 127–128, 204–224
  abuse of power and, 207
  assessment of legitimacy, 212–214
    reasonableness of expectation in, 212–213
  establishment of, 204, 206–207
  estoppel and, 138–139
  judicial control and, 204
  judicial protection of, 217–221
    procedural expectations, 217–221
    substantive expectations, 217–221
  policy considerations, overriding, 215–216
  procedural, 205
    judicial protection of, 217–221
  as relevant consideration, 207, 214–216
    policy considerations, 215–216, 219
  reliance, 209–211
  representations
    by decision-makers, 208
    implicit, 208–209
    knowledge of, 209–211
    by public bodies, 207–211, 213–214
  separation of powers and, 204–205, 214, 220–221
  substantive, 205
    enforcement of, 218
    judicial protection of, 217–221
  ultra vires representations and, 221–223
Leung Chung Hang, Sixtus, 28, 61
licensing, 18–21
  for communications, 20
  environmental regulation through, 19

Index

licensing (cont.)
  for exports, 18–19
  for imports, 18–19
  operation of establishments, 20–21
  transportation, 19–20
local government, 12–15
  District Councils, 12–13
  Heung Yee Kuk, 14–15
  Rural Committees, 14

Macau, 27, 320
Mainland China. *See* China
maladministration, 320–325
Malaysia, 90–91, 148, 190, 199–200, 256–257
mandamus, 65–66, 282–283
Mauritius, 105
merit of acts, legality compared to, 2
misuse of power, 1–2. *See also* abuse of power
  administrative law and, 2
  improper purposes or motives and, 150–153
    bad faith and, 150
    doctrine of legitimate expectation and, 151
    good faith and, 150
motives. *See* improper purposes or motives

National People's Congress (NPC), 8–9, 26
natural justice. *See also* procedural fairness
  rules of, 247
  technical breach of, 247–248
necessity principle, 271
negative vetting, 355
New Zealand, 22, 80, 186–187, 319
non-compliance, with statutory requirements, 133–137
non-justiciability, 40, 97–101, 105. *See also* intensity of review
  under Basic Law, 97–99, 106–108
  Chief Executive and, 101–104
  intensity of review, 101–108
  international treaties and, 99–101
  jurisdiction and, 99–100
NPC. *See* National People's Congress (NPC)

obligation to decide, 175–178
  with open mind, 176–178
Office of Members of the Executive and Legislative Councils (OMELCO), 330
Office of the Commissioner of the Ministry of Foreign Affairs, 16

Ombudsman, 3, 319–330
  effectiveness of, 327–330
  human rights and, 328–329
  judicial review and, relationship with, 325–327
  Legislative Council and, 327–328
  maladministration, 320–325
  remedies and, 329–330
OMELCO. *See* Office of Members of the Executive and Legislative Councils
"one country, two systems," 8–9, 27–28
Opium Wars, 24
ouster clauses, 87–88, 92
  Basic Law and, 89
  jurisdiction and, 91–92
  rule of law and, 89–90
  ultra vires decisions and, 92–93

People's Liberation Army (PLA), 16–17
People's Republic of China (PRC). *See also* Handover; Mainland China; National People's Congress; People's Liberation Army
  Convention of Peking and, 24–25
  "one country, two systems," 8–9, 27–28
  PRC Constitution, 26–27
  Treaty of Nanking, 24–25
  Xinhua News Agency, 15
permits, 18–21. *See also* licensing
personal, 56–59
  inconsistent approach to, 56–58
PLA. *See* People's Liberation Army
Political Appointment System, 12
polycentric decision-making, 237–238
positive vetting, 355
potential arguability, 110, 112, 114–117
PPPs. *See* Public Private Partnerships
PRC. *See* People's Republic of China
prejudice
  from delay, 50–51
  duty of disclosure and, 257
Principal Officials Accountability System, 10–11
Private Commissioner for Personal Data, 3, 343–349
private law
  collateral attack, 73
  damages under, 292–293
  estoppel in, 128, 138
  judicial review and, 83–86
  public/private divide, 64, 79, 83–86
procedural exclusivity, 66–68, 85–86

procedural fairness, 32, 247–271. *See also* bias; procedural impropriety
  bias, 264–271
  curative principle, 253
  duty of disclosure, 256–257
  duty to give reasons, 257–264
  right to fair hearing, 248–253
  right to legal representation, 253–256
procedural impropriety, 123. *See also* procedural fairness
procurement. *See* public procurement
prohibition, 65–66, 281–282
proportionality
  Basic Law and, 32–33
  Bill of Rights and, 32–33
  constitutional law and, 32–33
  procedural fairness and, 32
  separation of powers and, 225
  Wednesbury unreasonableness and, 32, 225
Provisional Legislative Council, 55
public authority, *ultra vires* and, 69
public element, 64–68, 76–77, 80–82. *See also* remedies
  Datafin principle, 75–78
  Hang Wah Chong principle, 78–79
public interest, 58–60
  Chief Executive and, 61
  costs and, 61–63
  discretion of the court, 62
  judicial review, 62
  justifications for, 59–60
  Legislative Council, 59
  limitations of, 60–61
  limits to, 60
  rule of law and, 60
Public Private Partnerships (PPPs), 85
public procurement, 22–23
  regulation of, 22–23
  scope of, 23
  WTO GPA, 22
public registers, 348–349
Public Works Tender Board, 23
public/private divide, 64, 79, 83–86

qualitative filters, arguability and, 109–111

rationality. *See* irrationality
reasonableness. *See* unreasonableness
reasons, 245–246, 257–264
  adequacy of reasons, 262–264

relevant considerations, 158–162, 190
  failure to take into account, 158–161
  improper purposes or motives and, 144–145
  intensity of review and, 161–162
  legitimate expectations and, 214–216
  unsuccessful arguments for, 160–161
  Wednesbury unreasonableness and, 161–162, 226
relinquishment of discretion, 171–174
remedies, 65–66
  acquiescence and, 297
  alternative, 293–295
  alternative claims for, 279
  appeals and, 293–295
  bias and, 278
  certiorari, 65–66, 280–281
    declaration as distinct from, 283
    ultra vires decisions and, 280
  cumulative claims for, 279
  damages and, 291–293
  declaration, 283–290
    certiorari as distinct from, 283
    hypothetical questions and, 284–288
    order of temporal validity, 288
    suspension of, 288
    temporal limitation of, 288–290
  delay and, 296–297
  discretionary nature of, 293–301
  futility, 299–300
  inevitability and, 300–301
  injunction, 290–291
    damages and, 291
    interim, 290–291
  mandamus, 65–66, 282–283
  Ombudsman and, 329–330
  prematurity, 295–296
  prohibition, 65–66, 281–282
  recovery of sum, 292–293
  restitution, 292–293
  scope of, 275–276
    limitations of, 276
  undeserving applicants, 298–299
  waiver and, 297
  writ, judicial review proceedings continued as though begun by, 301–303
representative standing, 58–63
  limits to, 60
  organisational standing, 58, 60
  proxy standing, 58

representative standing (cont.)
  public interest, 58–60
    Chief Executive and, 61
    costs and, 61–63
    justifications for, 59–60
    limitations of, 60–61
    limits to, 60
    rule of law and, 60
res judicata, 140–141
  cause of action estoppel, 140–141
  issue estoppel, 140
restitution, 292–293
review. *See* intensity of review; judicial review; procedural review; substantive review
rolled-up hearing, 284–288
rule of law, 2–3, 29–31, 60, 89–90
Rural Committees, 14

Scotland, 64, 134–136, 184–185, 266–268
selective enforcement, of rules, 1, 321
separation of powers
  legitimate expectations and, 204–205, 214, 220–221
  rule of law and, 2–3
  subsidiary legislation and, 356–357
  unreasonableness and, 225
South Africa, 100, 151–152
standing
  arguability and, 53–54
  challenge merits as factor in, 54
  defined, 52
  leave stage and, 54
  as legal filter, 52–53
  personal, 56–59
    inconsistent approach to, 56–58
  public interest, 58–60
    Chief Executive, 61
    costs and, 61–63
    discretion of the court, 62
    justifications for, 59–60
    limitations of, 60–61
    limits to, 60
    rule of law and, 60
  qualitative filtering and, 53–54
  representative, 58–63
    limits to, 60
    organisational standing, 58, 60
    proxy standing as, 58
  statutory test of sufficient interest, 53
statutory appeals, 48

statutory corporation, 125
statutory exclusion of review, 87–93
  Legislative Council and, 88
  ouster clauses, 87–88, 92
    Basic Law and, 89
    jurisdiction and, 91–92
    rule of law and, 89–90
    ultra vires decisions and, 92–93
statutory limitation of review, 93–97
  ouster clauses, 93–97
    partial, 95–97
    time-limited, 93–95
structural impartiality, 268
subsidiary legislation
  Chief-Executive-in-Council and, 352–353
  delegation of power to make, 163
  judicial review of, 358–360
  Legislative Council and, 352–354
    amendment powers of, 358
    disapplication of vetting procedures, 355–357
    negative vetting by, 355
    positive vetting by, 355
    scrutiny by, 355–358
  process of, 353–358
  separation of powers and, 356–357
  ultra vires, 359–360
substantive expectations, 205
  enforcement of, 218
  judicial protection of, 217–221
substantive invalidity, in judicial review, 122
substantive review, of unreasonableness, 229–230
sufficient interest. *See also* standing
  arguability and, 110

Taiwan, 15, 18, 148–149
tendering, 22–23
  evaluation of, 22–23
    Central Tender Board, 22–23
    Departmental Tender Committees, 23
    Government Logistics Department Tender Board, 23
    Public Works Tender Board, 23
  scope of, 23
thresholds
  of arguability, 115–117
  for irrelevant considerations, 156–157
  for *Wednesbury* unreasonableness, 233, 235
time limits, application for leave, 44–45

Index

time-limited ouster clauses, 93–95
  establishment of, 94
  length of, 94–95
treaties. *See also specific treaties*
  non-justiciability and, 99–101
Treaty of Nanking, 24–25, 100
Tribunals, Courts and Enforcement Act (2007), UK, 309
Trinidad and Tobago, 105, 136
Tsang, Donald, 11, 339
Tung Chee Hwa, 10–11

UK. *See* United Kingdom
ultra vires, 137–138
  agency and, 125, 128–129
  authority and, 125, 128–129
  collateral defence, 68–70
  constitutional basis, 31–32
  fettering of discretion and, through contracts, 187
  legality of rent increases, 69–70
  legitimate expectations and, 221–223
  litigation by public authority, 69
  ouster clauses and, 92–93
  sanctity compromised, 140
  subsidiary legislation and, 359–360
  voidness and, 280, 301
UMELCO. *See* Unofficial Members of the Executive and Legislative Councils
uncertainty, as ground of judicial review, 141–143
UNHCR. *See* United Nations High Commissioner for Refugees
United Kingdom (UK). *See also* Handover
  administrative tribunals in, 308–310
  Hong Kong under sovereignty of, 24–25
  legislative supremacy in, 31–32
United Nations High Commissioner for Refugees (UNHCR), 158–159
unlawful delegation of power. *See* delegation of power
unlawful policies, 178–179, 182
  failure to apply policy, 182–183
  inflexibility of, 179
  rigid adoption of policy, 182
  Wednesbury unreasonableness and, 183
Unofficial Members of the Executive and Legislative Councils (UMELCO), 330

unreasonableness. *See Wednesbury* unreasonableness

Value for Money (VFM) audits, 351
voidness, voidability and, 139–140, 301

waiver, remedies and, 297
waiver and consent, 139–140
Wednesbury unreasonableness, 225–246
  Carltona principle and, 240
  error of fact and, 192–193, 197
  fettering of discretion and
    in obligation to decide, 176–177
    unlawful policies and, 183
  formulation of, 225–230
  in human rights review, 240–241
  intensity of review for, 235–242
    for decision-makers, 238
    deference and, 235–240
    higher, 240–241
    immigration decisions and, 236–237
    lower, 235–240
    political context and, 241–242
    polycentric decisions, 237–238
  irrationality and, 227, 242–246
    as distinct from, 242–245
    matrix for, 244–245
  lower threshold of, 233, 235
  procedural review, 230–231
  proportionality and, 32, 225
  relevant considerations and, 161–162, 226
  rule of law and, 31
  separation of powers and, 225
  standard of review for, 227–229
  substantive review, 229–230
World Trade Organisation Government Procurement Agreement (WTO GPA), 22
writ, judicial review proceedings continued as though begun by, 301–303
WTO GPA. *See* World Trade Organisation Government Procurement Agreement

Xinhua News Agency, 15

Yau Wai Ching, 28, 61